A Reader in

International
Corporate
Finance

Volume One

A Reader in

International Corporate Finance

Edited by
Stijn Claessens and Luc Laeven

Volume One

 **THE WORLD BANK**

ISBN-10:   0-8213-6698-X
ISBN-13:   978-0-8213-6698-1
eISBN: 0-8213-6699-8
eISBN-13:   978-0-8213-6699-8
DOI: 10.1596/978-0-8213-6698-1

Library of Congress Cataloging-in-Publication data has been applied for.

Contents

Foreword

This two-volume set reprints more than twenty of what we think are the most influential articles on international corporate finance published over the course of the past six years. The book covers a range of topics covering the following six areas: law and finance, corporate governance, banking, capital markets, capital structure and financing constraints, and political economy of finance. All papers have appeared in top academic journals and have been widely cited in other work.

The purpose of the book is to make available to researchers and students, in an easy way and at an affordable price, a collection of articles offering a review of the present thinking on topics in international corporate finance. The book is ideally suited as an accompaniment to existing textbooks for courses on corporate finance and emerging market finance at the graduate economics, law, and MBA levels.

The articles selected reflect two major trends in the corporate finance literature that are significant departures from prior work: One is the increased interest in international aspects of corporate finance, particularly topics specific to emerging markets. The other is the increased awareness of the importance of institutions in explaining differences in corporate finance patterns—at the country and firm levels—around the world. The latter has culminated in a new literature known as the "law and finance literature," which focuses on the legal underpinnings of finance. It has also been accompanied by a greater understanding of the importance of political economy factors in countries' economic development and has led to the increased application of a political economy framework to the study of corporate finance.

This collection offers an overview of the present thinking on topics in international corporate finance. We hope that the papers in this book will serve the role of gathering in one place the background reading most often used for an advanced course in corporate finance. We also think that researchers will appreciate the benefit of having all these articles in one place, and we hope that the book will stimulate new research and thinking in this exciting new field. We trust the students and their instructors will deepen their understanding of international corporate finance by reading the papers. Of course, any of the remaining errors in the papers included in this book are entirely those of the authors and not of the editors.

Acknowledgments

The editors wish to thank the following authors and publishers who have kindly given permission for the use of copyright material.

Blackwell Publishing for the following articles:
Stijn Claessens and Luc Laeven (2003), "Financial Development, Property Rights, and Growth," *Journal of Finance*, Vol. 58 (6), pp. 2401–36; Stijn Claessens, Simeon Djankov, Joseph Fan, and Larry Lang (2002), "Disentangling the Incentive and Entrenchment Effects of Large Shareholdings," *Journal of Finance*, Vol. 57 (6), pp. 2741–71; Alexander Dyck and Luigi Zingales (2004), "Private Benefits of Control: An International Comparison," *Journal of Finance*, Vol. 59 (2), pp. 537–600; Maria Soledad Martinez Peria and Sergio L. Schmukler (2001), "Do Depositors Punish Banks for Bad Behavior? Market Discipline, Deposit Insurance, and Banking Crises," *Journal of Finance*, Vol. 56 (3), pp. 1029–51; Peter Blair Henry (2000), "Stock Market Liberalization, Economic Reform, and Emerging Market Equity Prices," *Journal of Finance*, Vol. 55 (2), pp. 529–64; Utpal Bhattacharya and Hazem Daouk (2002), "The World Price of Insider Trading," *Journal of Finance*, Vol. 57 (1), pp. 75–108; Rafael La Porta, Florencio Lopez-de-Silanes, and Andrei Shleifer (2006), "What Works in Securities Laws?" *Journal of Finance*, Vol. 61 (1), pp. 1–32; Art Durnev, Randall Morck, and Bernard Yeung (2004), "Value-Enhancing Capital Budgeting and Firm-Specific Stock Return Variation," *Journal of Finance*, Vol. 59 (1), pp. 65–105; Laurence Booth, Varouj Aivazian, Asli Demirgüç-Kunt, and Vojislav Maksimovic (2001), "Capital Structures in Developing Countries," *Journal of Finance*, Vol. 56 (1), pp. 87–130; Mihir Desai, Fritz Foley, and James Hines (2004), "A Multinational Perspective on Capital Structure Choice and Internal Capital Markets," *Journal of Finance*, Vol. 59 (6), pp. 2451–87; Thorsten Beck, Asli Demirgüç-Kunt, and Vojislav Maksimovic (2005), "Financial and Legal Constraints to Growth: Does Firm Size Matter?" *Journal of Finance*, Vol. 60 (1), pp. 137–77.

Elsevier for the following articles:
Thorsten Beck, Asli Demirgüç-Kunt, and Ross Levine (2003), "Law, Endowments, and Finance," *Journal of Financial Economics*, Vol. 70 (2), pp. 137–81; Stefano Rossi and Paolo F. Volpin (2004), "Cross-Country Determinants of Mergers and Acquisitions," *Journal of Financial Economics*, Vol. 74 (2), pp. 277–304; Paola Sapienza (2004), "The Effects of Government Ownership on Bank Lending," *Journal of Financial Economics*, Vol. 72 (2), pp. 357–84; Kee-Hong Bae, Jun-Koo Kang, and Chan-Woo Lim (2002), "The Value of Durable Bank Relationships: Evidence from Korean Banking Shocks," *Journal of Financial Economics*, Vol. 64 (2), pp.

147–80; Geert Bekaert, Campbell R. Harvey, and Christian Lundblad (2005), "Does Financial Liberalization Spur Growth?" *Journal of Financial Economics*, Vol. 77 (1), pp. 3–55; Raghuram G. Rajan and Luigi Zingales (2003), "The Great Reversals: The Politics of Financial Development in the 20th Century," *Journal of Financial Economics*, Vol. 69 (1), pp. 5–50; Simon Johnson and Todd Mitton (2003), "Cronyism and Capital Controls: Evidence from Malaysia," *Journal of Financial Economics*, Vol. 67 (2), pp. 351–82.

Oxford University Press for the following article:
Inessa Love (2003), "Financial Development and Financing Constraints: International Evidence from the Structural Investment Model," *Review of Financial Studies*, Vol. 16 (3), pp. 765–91.

American Economic Association for the following article:
Raymond Fisman (2001), "Estimating the Value of Political Connections," *American Economic Review*, Vol. 91 (4), pp. 1095–1102.

MIT Press for the following articles:
Josh Lerner and Antoinette Schoar (2005), "Does Legal Enforcement Affect Financial Transactions? The Contractual Channel in Private Equity," *Quarterly Journal of Economics*, Vol. 120 (1), pp. 223–46; Marianne Bertrand, Paras Mehta, and Sendhil Mullainathan (2002), "Ferreting Out Tunneling: An Application to Indian Business Groups," *Quarterly Journal of Economics*, Vol. 117 (1), pp. 121–48; Rafael La Porta, Florencio Lopez-de-Silanes, and Guillermo Zamarripa (2003), "Related Lending," *Quarterly Journal of Economics*, Vol. 118 (1), pp. 231–68.

We would like to thank Rose Vo for her assistance in obtaining the copyrights of the articles from the authors and publishers, Joaquin Lopez for his technical assistance in reproducing the papers, Stephen McGroarty of the Office of the Publisher of the World Bank for his assistance and guidance in publishing the book, and the World Bank for financial support.

The views presented in these published papers are those of the authors and should not be attributed to, or reported as reflecting, the position of the World Bank, the International Monetary Fund, the executive directors of both organizations, or any other organization mentioned therein. The book was largely completed when the second editor was at the World Bank.

Book Title:

Introduction

Volume I. Part I. Law and Finance

Volume I begins with an examination of the legal and financial aspects of international capital markets. In recent years, there has been an increased interest in international aspects of corporate finance. There are stark differences in financial structures and financing patterns of corporations around the world, particularly as they relate to emerging markets. Recent work has suggested that most of these differences can be explained by differences in laws and institutions of countries and in countries' economic and other endowments. These relationships have been the focus of a new literature on law and finance. La Porta et al. (1997, 1998) were the first to show that the legal traditions of a country determine to a large extent the financial development of a country. They started a large literature investigating the determinants and effects of legal systems across countries.

In chapter 1, "Law, Endowments, and Finance," Thorsten Beck, Asli Demirguc-Kunt, and Ross Levine contribute to this literature by assessing the importance of both legal traditions and property rights institutions. The law and finance theory suggests that legal traditions brought by colonizers differ in protecting the rights of private investors in relation to the state, with important implications for financial markets. The endowments theory argues that initial conditions as proxied by natural endowments, including the disease environment—influence the formation of long-lasting property rights institutions that shape financial development, even decades or centuries later. Using information on the origin of the law and on the disease environment encountered by colonizers centuries ago, the authors extract the independent effects of both law and endowments on financial development. They find evidence supporting both theories, although the initial endowments theory explains more of the cross-country variation in financial development than the legal traditions theory does. This suggests that there are economic and other forces at play that make certain initial conditions translate into the institutional environments of today.

In chapter 2, "Financial Development, Property Rights, and Growth," Stijn Claessens and Luc Laeven add to this literature by showing that better legal and property rights institutions affect economic growth through two equally important channels: one is improved access to finance resulting from greater financial development, the channel already highlighted in the law and finance literature; the other is improved investment allocation resulting from more secure property rights, as firms and other investors allocate resources raised in a more efficient manner. Quantitatively, the effects of these two channels on economic growth are similar. This suggests that the legal system is important not only for financial sector development but also for an efficient operation of the real sectors. Better property rights, for example, can stimulate investment in sectors that are more intangibles-intensive or that heavily depend on intellectual property rights, such as the services, software, and telecommunications industries. As these industries have become drivers of growth in many countries, the second channel has become more important.

In chapter 3, "Does Legal Enforcement Affect Financial Transactions? The Contractual Channel in Private Equity," Josh Lerner and Antoinette Schoar show that legal tradition and law enforcement have direct implications for how financial contracts are shaped. Taking a much more micro approach and using data on private equity investments in developing countries, they show that investments in high-enforcement and common law nations often use convertible preferred stock with covenants, while investments in low-enforcement and civil law nations tend to use common stock and debt and rely on equity and board control. While relying on ownership rather than contractual provisions may help to alleviate legal enforcement problems, there appears to be a real cost to operating in a low-enforcement environment because transactions in low-enforcement countries have lower valuations and returns. In other words, the low-enforcement environments force investors to use less-than-optimal contracts to assure their ownership and control rights, which in turn makes the operations of the businesses less efficient.

Volume I. Part II. Corporate Governance

Corporate governance is another field that has gained increased interest from academics and policy makers around the world in the past decade, spurred by major corporate scandals and governance problems in a host of countries, including the corporate scandals of Enron in the United States and Parmalat in Italy and the expropriation of minority shareholders in the East Asian crisis countries and other emerging countries. Governance problems are particularly pronounced in many emerging countries where family control is the predominant form of corporate ownership and where minority shareholder rights are often not enforced.

In chapter 4, "Disentangling the Incentive and Entrenchment Effects of Large Shareholdings," Stijn Claessens, Simeon Djankov, Joseph Fan, and Larry Lang show that ownership of firms in East Asian countries is highly concentrated and that there is often a large difference between the control rights and the cash-flow rights of the principal shareholder of the firm. They argue that the larger the cash-flow rights of the shareholder, the more his or her incentives are aligned with those of the minority shareholder because the investor has his or her own money at stake. On the other hand, control rights give the principal owner the ability to direct the firm's resources. The larger the difference between control and cash-flow rights, the more likely that the principal shareholder is entrenched and that the minority shareholders are expropriated as the controlling owner directs resources to his or her own advantages. Using data on a large number of listed companies in eight East Asian countries, the authors find that firm value increases with the cash-flow rights of the largest shareholder, consistent with a positive incentive effect; however, firm value falls when the control rights of the largest shareholder exceed its cash-flow ownership, consistent with an entrenchment effect. This suggests expropriation, which may have further economic costs as resources are poorly invested.

The private benefits of control for the controlling shareholder are often substantial, particularly in environments where shareholder rights are low. This explains why concentrated ownership is the predominant form of ownership around the world, particularly in developing economies, but also in continental Europe, where property rights are weaker and often poorly enforced. In chapter 5, "Private Benefits of Control: An International Comparison," Alexander Dyck and Luigi Zingales propose a method that estimates the private benefits of control. For a sample of 39 countries and using individual transactions, they find that private benefits of control vary widely across countries, from a low of –4 percent to a high of +65 percent. Across countries, higher private benefits of control are associated with less developed capital markets, more concentrated ownership, and more privately negotiated privatizations. Legal institutions plus enforcement and pressure by the media appear to be important factors in curbing private benefits of control. Because private benefits are associated with inefficient investment, their findings confirm the importance of establishing strong property rights and enforcing these to increase growth.

Controlling shareholders often devise complex ownership structures of firms (for example, through pyramidal structures) to create a gap between voting rights and cash-flow rights and to be able to direct resources through internal markets to affiliated firms. This is particularly the case for business groups in emerging markets. Owners of such business groups are often accused of expropriating minority shareholders by tunneling resources from firms where they have low cash-flow rights—with little costs of taking away money—to firms where they have high cash-flow rights—with large gains of bringing in money. In chapter 6, "Ferreting Out Tunneling: An Application to Indian Business Groups," Marianne Bertrand, Paras Mehta, and Sendhil Mullainathan propose a methodology to measure the extent of tunneling activities in business groups. This methodology rests on isolating and then testing the distinctive implications of the tunneling hypothesis for the propagation of earnings shocks across firms within a group. Using data on Indian business groups, the authors find a significant amount of tunneling, much of it occurring via nonoperating components of profit. This suggests a cost-of-business group that may have to be mitigated by some other measures, such as better property rights, increased disclosure, and specific restrictions (such as preventing or limiting intragroup ownership structures).

The threat of takeover can play a potentially important disciplining role for poorly governed firms because management risks being removed; however, in practice, the market for corporate control is generally inactive in countries where it is most needed: where shareholder protection is weak. The rules limiting takeovers are often more restricted in these environments, making domestic takeovers more difficult. Still, there is evidence that foreign takeovers can have important positive implications for the governance of local target firms, particularly in countries with poor investor protection. This is the theme of chapter 7, "Cross-Country Determinants of Mergers and Acquisitions," by Stefano Rossi and Paolo Volpin. They study the determinants of mergers and acquisitions (M&As) around the world by focusing on differences in laws and regulations across countries. They find that M&A activity is significantly larger in countries with better accounting standards and stronger shareholder protection. In cross-border deals, targets are typically from countries with poorer investor protection than their acquirers' countries, suggesting that cross-border transactions play a governance role by improving the degree of investor protection within target firms. As such, globalization and internationalization of financial services can help countries improve their corporate governance arrangements.

Volume I. Part III. Banking

Another common feature of developing countries is the predominance of state banks. State banks also played an important role in many industrial countries, at least until recently, but many governments have privatized in the past decade. In 1995, government ownership of banks around the world averaged around 42 percent (La Porta et al. 2002). In chapter 8, "The Effects of Government Ownership on Bank Lending," Paola Sapienza uses information on individual loan contracts in Italy, where lending by state-owned banks represents more than half of total lending, to study the effects of government ownership on bank lending behavior. She finds that lending by state banks is inefficient. State-owned banks charge lower interest rates than do privately owned banks to similar or identical firms, even if firms are able to borrow more from privately owned banks. State-owned banks also favor large firms and firms located in depressed areas, again in contrast to the choices of private banks. Finally, the lending behavior of state-owned banks is affected by the electoral results of the party affiliated with the bank: the stronger the political party in the area where the firm is borrowing, the lower the interest rates charged. This suggests that the political forces affect the lending behavior of state-owned banks in an adverse manner and offers an argument for the privatization of state-owned banks.

Private banks can, however, also have problems when not properly governed and monitored. When banks are privately owned in emerging economies, they are often part of business groups. This can create incentive problems that result in lending on preferential terms. More generally, banks in many countries lend to firms controlled by the bank's owners. This type of lending is known as "insider lending" or "related lending." In chapter 9, "Related Lending," Rafael La Porta, Florencio Lopez-de-Silanes, and Guillermo Zamarripa examine the benefits of related lending, using data on bank-borrower relationships in Mexico. The authors show that related lending in Mexico is prevalent and takes place on better terms than arm's-length lending. This could still be consistent with an efficient allocation of resources, but the authors show that related loans are significantly more likely to default and that when they default, they have lower recovery rates than unrelated loans. Their evidence for Mexico supports the view that related lending is often a manifestation of looting, particularly in weak institutional environments. The costs of this are often incurred by the government and taxpayers, as happened in Mexico when many of the private banks experienced financial distress and had to be rescued by the government, which provided fiscal resources for their recapitalization.

However, close ties between banks and industrial groups need not be inefficient; they can create valuable relationships, particularly in environments where hard information on borrowers is sparse. As such, relationships can substitute for a weaker institutional environment. In chapter 10, "The Value of Durable Bank Relationships: Evidence from Korean Banking Shocks," Kee-Hong Bae, Jun-Koo Kang, and Chan-Woo Lim examine the value of durable bank relationships in the Republic of Korea, using a sample of exogenous events that negatively affected Korean banks during the financial crisis of 1997–98. The authors show that adverse shocks to banks have a negative effect not only on the value of the banks themselves but also on the value of their client firms. They also show that this adverse effect on firm value is a decreasing function of the financial health of both the banks and their client firms. These results indicate that bank relationships were valuable to this group of firms; however, whether the relationship supported an efficient allocation of resources is not clear.

Given the importance of banks in developing countries' financial intermediation, it is essential that banks be properly supervised and monitored, a task most often assigned to the bank supervisory agency. When bank supervisors fail to discipline banks, however, it is up to the depositors to monitor banks and punish banks for bad behavior by withdrawing deposits. In chapter 11, "Do Depositors Punish Banks for Bad Behavior? Market Discipline, Deposit Insurance, and Banking Crises," Maria Soledad Martinez Peria and Sergio Schmukler study whether this form of market discipline is effective and whether it is affected by the presence of deposit insurance. They focus on the experiences of Argentina, Chile, and Mexico during the 1980s and 1990s. They find that depositors discipline banks by withdrawing deposits and by requiring higher interest rates, and their responsiveness to bank risk taking increases in the aftermath of crises. Deposit insurance does not appear to diminish the extent of market discipline. This suggests that in a weak institutional environment, where bank supervision fails to mitigate excessive risks taking by banks, depositors and other bank claimholders can play an important role in the monitoring of financial institutions.

Volume II. Part I. Capital Markets

Volume II opens with a selection of articles on capital markets. Equity and bond finance raised in capital markets (as an alternative to bank finance) has become increasingly important for corporations around the world. The increase in the use of markets for raising capital are in part resulting from rising equity prices that have triggered new issuance. Lower interest rates have also caused many firms to opt for corporate bonds. Also important, especially in developing countries, as institutional fundamentals are improving substantially, there has been an improved willingness on the part of international investors to invest and provide funds. As emerging stock markets have been liberalized, global investors have been increasingly seeking to diversify assets in these markets. The effects of these measures have been researched in a number of papers.

Stock market liberalization (that is, the decision by a country's government to allow foreigners to purchase shares in that country's stock market) has been found to have real effects on the economic performance of a country. In chapter 1, "Stock Market Liberalization, Economic Reform, and Emerging Market Equity Prices," Peter Blair Henry shows that a country's aggregate equity price index experiences substantial abnormal returns during the period leading up to the implementation of its initial stock market liberalization. This result is consistent with the prediction of standard international asset-pricing models that stock market liberalization reduces a country's cost of equity capital by allowing for risk sharing between domestic and foreign agents. This reduced cost of capital in turn can be expected to lead to greater investment and growth.

Stock market liberalization has indeed been found to have positive ramifications for overall investment and economic growth. In chapter 2, "Does Financial Liberalization Spur Growth?" Geert Bekaert, Campbell Harvey, and Christian Lundblad show that equity market liberalizations, on average, lead to a 1 percent increase in annual real economic growth. This effect appears to have been most pronounced in countries with a strong institutional environment, suggesting that liberalization must be accompanied by a strengthening of the institutional environment to reap all of the benefits.

Other evidence confirms the need for additional policy measures besides liberalization. Not all stock markets work as efficiently as they should. In particular, insider trading is a common feature of many stock markets. Although most stock markets have established laws to prevent insider trading, enforcement is poor in many countries, and investors get worse prices and rates of return. In chapter 3, "The World Price of Insider Trading," Utpal Bhattacharya and Hazem Daouk analyze the quality of enforcement of insider trading laws. They show that while insider trading laws exist in the majority of countries with stock markets, enforcement—as evidenced by actual prosecutions of people engaging in insider trading—has taken place in only about one-third of these countries. Their empirical analysis shows that the cost of equity in a country does not change after the introduction of insider trading laws, but only decreases significantly after the first prosecution, suggesting that enforcement of the law is critical, rather than just the adoption of the insider trading law.

The question remains, however, whether stock markets should be regulated by relying mostly on the government using public enforcement by securities commissions and the like or whether the emphasis should be on self-regulation, relying on private enforcement by giving individuals the legal tools to litigate in case of abuses. In chapter 4, "What Works in Securities Laws?" Rafael La Porta, Florencio Lopez-De-Silanes, and Andrei Shleifer tackle this complex matter by examining the effect of different designs of securities laws on stock market development in 49 countries. The authors find little evidence that public enforcement benefits stock markets, but strong evidence that laws mandating disclosure and facilitating private enforcement through liability rules benefit stock markets' development—with regard to the size of the market, the number of firms listed, and the new issuance. Their results echo those analyzing the banking system, where it has been found that supervision by government authorities often does not deliver the results desired, but that private sector oversight can be effective, especially in weak institutional environments.

A well-functioning stock market should allow firms not only to raise financing but also to produce more informative stock prices. Where stock prices are more informative, this induces better governance and more efficient capital investment decisions. However, in many developing countries, the cost of collecting information on firms is high, resulting in less trading by investors with private information, leading to less informative stock prices. In chapter 5, "Value-Enhancing Capital Budgeting and Firm-Specific Stock Return Variation," Art Durnev, Randall Morck, and Bernard Yeung introduce a method to gauge the informativeness of a company's stock price. They base their measure of informativeness on the magnitude of firm-specific return variation. The idea is that a more informative stock displays a higher stock variation because stock variation occurs because of trading by investors with private information. The authors document this measure of stock price informativeness for a large number of countries. They then go on to show that the economic efficiency of corporate investment, as measured by Tobin's Q (the ratio of the market value of a firm's assets to the replacement value of its assets—a measure of firm efficiency and growth prospects), is positively related to the magnitude of firm-specific variation in stock returns, suggesting that more informative stock prices facilitate more efficient corporate investment.

Volume II. Part II. Capital Structure and Financial Constraints

Because of large institutional differences and differences in the relative importance of the banking system and the equity and bond markets, it will come as no surprise that capital structures of firms vary widely across countries. In chapter 6, "Capital Structures in Developing Countries," Laurence Booth, Varouj Aivazian, Asli Demirguc-Kunt, and Vojislav Maksimovic document capital structure choices of firms in 10 developing countries and then analyze the determinants of these structures. They find that although some of the factors that are important in explaining capital structure in developed countries (such as profitability and asset tangibility of the firm) carry over to developing countries, there are persistent differences across countries, indicating that specific country factors are at work. The authors explore obvious candidates such as the institutional framework governing bankruptcy, accounting standards, and the availability of alternative forms of financing, but their smaller set of countries does not allow them to explain in a definite way which of these may be more important.

More generally, it is difficult to disentangle the impact of different institutional features on capital structure choices in a cross-country setting because there are so many country-specific factors to control for. In chapter 7, "A Multinational Perspective on Capital Structure Choice and Internal Capital Markets," Mihir Desai, Fritz Foley, and James Hines therefore take advantage of a unique dataset on the capital structure of foreign affiliates of U.S. multinationals to further our understanding of the institutional determinants of capital structure. The authors find that capital structure choice is significantly affected by three institutional factors: tax environment, capital market development, and creditor rights. They show that financial leverage of subsidiaries is positively affected by local tax rates. They also find that multinational affiliates are financed with less external debt in countries with underdeveloped capital markets or weak creditor rights, likely reflecting the disadvantages of higher local borrowing costs. Instrumental variable analysis—to control for other factors driving these results—indicates that greater borrowing from parent companies substitutes for three-quarters of reduced external borrowing induced by weak local capital market conditions. Multinational firms therefore appear to employ internal capital markets opportunistically to overcome imperfections in external capital markets. As such, globalization and internationalization of financial services can offer some benefits for countries with weak institutional environments.

Besides a limited way to control for cross-country differences, another complication of studying the determinants of capital structure is that not all firms demand external finance. Many successful firms finance their investments internally and do not need to access outside finance. For these firms, financial sector development thus matters less. The important question is whether those firms that are financially constrained are better able to obtain external finance in more developed financial systems, with positive ramifications for firm growth. Here the difficulty arises in how to measure which firms are financially constrained. In chapter 8, "Financial Development and Financing Constraints: International Evidence from the Structural Investment Model," Inessa Love addresses this question by using an investment Euler equation to infer the degree of financing constraints of individual firms. She provides evidence that financial development affects growth by reducing the financing constraints of firms and in that way improving the efficient allocation of investment. The magnitude of the changes, which run through changes in the cost of capital, is large: in a country with a low level of financial development, the cost of capital is twice as large as in a country with an average level of financial development.

In chapter 9, "Financial and Legal Constraints to Growth: Does Firm Size Matter?" Thorsten Beck, Asli Demirguc-Kunt, and Vojislav Maksimovic expand on the analysis of what financial sector development means for the growth prospects of individual firms. They use firm-level survey data covering 54 countries to construct a self-reported measure of financing constraints to address the question of how much faster firms might grow if they had more access to financing. The authors find that financial and institutional development weakens the constraining effects of financing constraints on firm growth in an economically and statistically significant way and that it is the smallest firms that benefit most from greater financial sector development.

Volume II. Part III. Political Economy of Finance

Politics plays an important role in finance. Financial development and financial reform are often driven by political economy considerations, and where finance is a scarce commodity, political connections are often especially valuable for firms in need of external finance. Whether these connections are good, in the sense that they support an efficient allocation of resources, is one question that has been more closely analyzed recently. Also, a number of papers have also researched from various angles how political economy factors affect the institutions necessary for financial sector development.

In chapter 10, "The Great Reversals: The Politics of Financial Development in the 20th Century," Raghuram Rajan and Luigi Zingales show that financial development does not change monotonically over time. By most measures, countries were more financially developed in 1913 than in 1980 and only recently have many countries surpassed their 1913 levels. To explain these changes, they propose an interest group theory of financial development wherein incumbents oppose financial development because it fosters greater competition through lowering entry barriers for newcomers. The theory predicts that incumbents' opposition will be weaker when an economy allows both cross-border trade and capital flows because then their hold on the allocation of rents is less. Consistent with this theory, they find that trade and capital flows can explain some of the cross-country and time-series variations in financial development. This in turn suggests that liberalization of trade and capital flows can be an important means of fostering greater financial sector development because they weaken the political economy factors holding back an economy.

The last two chapters in Volume II provide further empirical evidence of the value of political connections in developing countries, but now using firm-level data for particular countries. In chapter 11, "Estimating the Value of Political Connections," Raymond Fisman shows that the market value of politically connected firms in Indonesia under President Suharto declined more when adverse rumors circulated about the health of the president. Because the same firms did not perform better than other firms, this suggests that these connected firms obtained favors, yet allocated resources less efficiently. In chapter 12, "Cronyism and Capital Controls: Evidence from Malaysia," Simon Johnson and Todd Mitton provide empirical evidence for Malaysia that the imposition of capital controls during the Asian financial crises benefited primarily firms with strong connections to Prime Minister Mahathir, again without an improved performance when compared with other firms. These chapters indicate that the operation of corporations in developing countries, including their financing and financial structure, importantly depends on their relationships with politicians. As such, financial sector reform cannot avoid considering how to address political economy issues.

Available online at www.sciencedirect.com

SCIENCE @ DIRECT®

Journal of Financial Economics 70 (2003) 137–181

JOURNAL OF
Financial
ECONOMICS

www.elsevier.com/locate/econbase

Law, endowments, and finance ☆

Thorsten Beck[a], Asli Demirgüç-Kunt[a], Ross Levine[b,c],*

[a] *The World Bank, Washington, DC 20433, USA*
[b] *Department of Finance, Carlson School of Management, University of Minnesota, Minneapolis, MN 55455, USA*
[c] *National Bureau of Economic Research, Inc., Cambridge, MA 02138-5398, USA*

Received 5 October 2001; accepted 4 September 2002

Abstract

Using a sample of 70 former colonies, this paper assesses two theories regarding the historical determinants of financial development. The law and finance theory holds that legal traditions, brought by colonizers, differ in terms of protecting the rights of private investors vis-à-vis the state, with important implications for financial markets. The endowment theory argues that the disease environment encountered by colonizers influences the formation of long-lasting institutions that shape financial development. The empirical results provide evidence for both theories. However, initial endowments explain more of the cross-country variation in financial intermediary and stock market development.
© 2003 Elsevier B.V. All rights reserved.

JEL classification: G2; K2; O11; P51

☆ We thank David Arseneau, Pam Gill, and Tolga Sobaci for excellent research assistance, and Agnes Yaptenco and Kari Labrie for assistance with the manuscript. We thank without implicating Daron Acemoglu, John Boyd, Maria Carkovic, Tim Guinnane, Patrick Honohan, Phil Keefer, Paul Mahoney, Alexander Pivovarsky, Andrei Shleifer, Oren Sussman, an anonymous referee, seminar participants at the Banco Central de Chile, the University of Minnesota, Harvard University, the World Bank, the University of Maryland, and UCLA, and conference participants at the Fedesarrollo conference on Financial Crisis and Policy Responses in Cartagena, the Crenos conference on Finance, Institutions, Technology, and Growth in Alghero, and the CEPR Summer Finance Conference in Gerzensee. We give special thanks to Simon Johnson. His guidance led us to focus and thereby improve the paper. Parts of this paper were originally part of a working paper titled "Law, Politics, and Finance," which was a background paper for the 2002 World Development Report. This paper's findings, interpretations, and conclusions are entirely those of the authors and do not necessarily represent the views of the World Bank, its Executive Directors, or the countries they represent.

*Corresponding author. Department of Finance, Carlson School of Management, University of Minnesota, Minneapolis, MN 55455, USA. Tel.: +1-612-624-9551; fax: +1-612-626-1335.

E-mail address: rlevine@csom.umn.edu (R. Levine).

Keywords: Law; Endowments; Financial development; Economic development; Property rights

1. Introduction

A substantial body of work suggests that well-functioning financial intermediaries and markets promote economic growth (see, e.g., Levine, 1997). The view that financial systems exert a first-order impact on economic growth raises critical questions: How have some countries developed well-functioning financial systems, while others have not? Why do some countries have strong laws and property rights protection that support private contracting and financial systems, while others do not? While considerable research examines the finance-growth relationship, much less work examines the fundamental sources of differences among nations in financial development.

This paper empirically evaluates two theories concerning the historical determinants of financial systems. First, the *law and finance* theory holds that: (a) legal traditions differ in terms of the priority they attach to protecting the rights of private investors vis-à-vis the state; (b) private property rights protection forms the basis of financial contracting and overall financial development; and, (c) the major legal traditions were formed in Europe centuries ago and were then spread through conquest, colonization, and imitation (see La Porta et al., 1998, henceforth LLSV). Thus, the law and finance theory predicts that historically determined differences in legal traditions help explain international differences in financial systems today.

The law and finance theory focuses on the differences between the two most influential legal traditions, the British Common law and the French Civil law (see, e.g., Hayek, 1960; LLSV, 1998). According to this theory, the British Common law evolved to protect private property owners against the crown (Merryman, 1985).[1] This facilitated the ability of private property owners to transact confidently, with positive repercussions on financial development (North and Weingast, 1989). In contrast, the French Civil law was constructed to eliminate the role of a corrupt judiciary, solidify state power, and restrain the courts from interfering with state policy.[2] Over time, state dominance produced a legal tradition that focuses more on

---

[1] While landholding rights in England were originally based on King William I's feudal system, the courts developed legal rules that treated large estate holders as private property owners and not as tenants of the king. Indeed, the common law at the dawn of the 17th century was principally a law of private property (e.g., Littleton, 1481; Coke, 1628). During the great conflict between Parliament and the English kings in the 16th and 17th centuries, the crown attempted to reassert feudal prerogatives and sell monopoly rights to cope with budgetary shortfalls. Parliament (composed mostly of landowners and wealthy merchants) along with the courts took the side of the property owners against the crown. While King James I argued that royal prerogative superseded the common law, the courts asserted that the law is king, *Lex, Rex*. The Stuarts were thrown out in 1688.

[2] By the 18th century, there was a notable deterioration in the integrity and prestige of the judiciary. The crown sold judgeships to rich families and the judges unabashedly promoted the interests of the elite. [Refer to Dawson, 1968, p. 373]. Unsurprisingly, the French Revolution strove to eliminate the role of the

T. Beck et al. / Journal of Financial Economics 70 (2003) 137–181   139

the rights of the state and less on the rights of individual investors than the British Common law (Hayek, 1960; Mahoney, 2001). According to the law and finance theory, a powerful state with a responsive legal system will have the incentives and capabilities to divert the flow of society's resources from optimal toward favored ends, and therefore this power will hinder the development of free, competitive financial systems. Thus, the law and finance theory predicts that countries that have adopted a French Civil law tradition will tend to place less emphasis on private property rights protection and will enjoy correspondingly lower levels of financial development than countries with a British Common law tradition.

The law and finance theory focuses on the origin of a country's legal tradition. The French imposed the Napoleonic Code in all conquered lands and colonies. Furthermore, the Code shaped the Spanish and Portuguese legal systems, which further spread the French Civil law to Spanish and Portuguese colonies. Similarly, the British instituted the Common law in its colonies. According to the law and finance theory, the spread of legal traditions had enduring influences on national approaches to private property rights and financial development—British colonizers advanced a legal tradition that stresses private property rights and fosters financial development, whereas in contrast colonizers that spread the French Civil law implanted a legal tradition that is less conducive to financial development.

The endowment theory, on the other hand, emphasizes the roles of geography and the disease environment in shaping institutional development; we apply this theory to the development of private property rights and financial institutions. Acemoglu et al. (2001, henceforth AJR) base their theory on three premises. First, AJR note that Europeans adopted different types of colonization strategies. At one end of the spectrum, the Europeans settled and created institutions to support private property and check the power of the state. These settler colonies include the United States, Australia, and New Zealand. At the other end of the spectrum, Europeans did not aim to settle but rather to extract as much from the colony as possible. In these "extractive states," Europeans did not create institutions to support private property rights; instead, they established institutions that empowered the elite to extract gold, silver, etc. (e.g., Congo, Ivory Coast, and much of Latin America).

The second component of AJR's theory holds that the type of colonization strategy was heavily influenced by the feasibility of settlement. Mortality rates were startlingly high in some places. In the first year of the Sierra Leone Company, 72 percent of the Europeans died. In the 1805 Mungo park expedition in Gambia and Niger, all of the Europeans died before completing the trip. In these inhospitable environments, Europeans tended to create extractive states (AJR, 2001). In areas where endowments favored settlement, Europeans tended to form settler colonies.

(footnote continued)
judiciary in making and interpreting the law. Robespierre even argued that, "the word jurisprudence... must be effaced from our language." [Quoted from Dawson, 1968, p. 426] Glaeser and Shleifer (2002) explain how antagonism toward jurisprudence and the exaltation of the role of the state encouraged the development of easily verifiable "bright-line-rules" that do not rely on the discretion of judges. Thus, codification supported the strengthening of the government and relegated judges to a relatively minor, bureaucratic role.

For instance, AJR note that the Pilgrims decided to settle in the American colonies instead of Guyana partially because of the high mortality rates in Guyana. Moreover, Curtin (1964, 1998) documents that European newspapers published colonial mortality rates widely, so that potential settlers would have information about colonial endowments. Thus, according to the endowment theory, the disease environment shaped colonization strategy and the types of institutions established by European colonizers.

The final piece of the AJR theory of institutional development stresses that the institutions created by European colonizers endured after independence. Settler colonies tended to produce post-colonial governments that were more democratic and more devoted to defending private property rights than extractive colonies. In contrast, since extractive colonies had institutions for effectively extracting resources, the post-colonial elite frequently assumed power and readily exploited the pre-existing extractive institutions. Young (1994) presents historical evidence that once authoritarian institutions are efficiently extracting resources from the bulk of society, post-independence rulers tend to use these institutions to their own advantage and profit. This was the case in Sierra Leone, Senegal, and Congo. Latin America was similar. For instance, while Mexicans gained independence from European colonialists, the elite that assumed power took advantage of the existing institutions to extract resources rather than create institutions to protect private property contracts, and foster broad-based economic development. Furthermore, Engerman et al. (1998) demonstrate the long-lasting impact of initial institutions on voting rights: once regimes restrict voting rights to protect the elite from the masses, the government tends to resist changes in suffrage policies for long periods.

While AJR (2001) focus on institutional development in general, their theory is applicable to the financial sector. In an extractive environment, colonizers will not construct institutions that favor the development of free, competitive financial markets because competitive markets may threaten the position of the extractors. In settler colonies, however, colonizers will be much more likely to construct institutions that protect private property rights and hence foster financial development. Thus, according to the endowment theory, differences in endowments shaped initial institutions and these initial institutions have had long-lasting repercussions on private property rights protection and financial development.[3]

Although the law and endowment theories both stress the importance of initial institutions in shaping the financial systems we observe today, they highlight very different causal mechanisms. The law and finance theory focuses on the legal

---

[3] Engerman and Sokoloff (1997) note another channel through which geographical endowments shape initial institutions with enduring effects on economic development. Namely, they show that agriculture in southern North America and much of South America is conducive to large plantations. Thus, colonists developed long-lasting institutions to protect the few landowners against the many peasants. In contrast, northern North America's agriculture is conducive to small farms, so more egalitarian institutions emerged. Thus, again, endowments influence the formation of institutions associated with openness and competition. Our primary reason for focusing on the AJR (2001) measure of settler mortality and not also examining agricultural endowments is that AJR (2001) have assembled data for a broad cross-section of countries.

T. Beck et al. / Journal of Financial Economics 70 (2003) 137–181 141

tradition brought by the colonizer. The endowment theory focuses on the disease and geography endowments encountered by the colonizer and how these endowments shaped both colonization strategy and the construction of long-lasting institutions. In the law and finance theory, the identity of the colonizer is crucial, but the identity of the colonizer is irrelevant according to the endowment theory. Similarly, in the endowment theory, the endowments of the lands where Europeans arrived are crucial, but the law and finance theory gives no weight to the mortality rates of European colonizers in explaining the development of today's private property rights and financial systems. This is admittedly overstated. Proponents of the law and finance theory do not argue that endowments are irrelevant. Similarly, proponents of the endowment theory do not contend that legal origin is irrelevant. Rather, each theory articulates very distinct mechanisms about how the colonization period shaped national views toward private property rights and financial development. We stress—and empirically evaluate—these distinct predictions. While these two explanations of financial development offer very different causal mechanisms, they are not necessarily mutually exclusive.

To evaluate empirically the law and endowment theories of financial development, we use cross-country regressions on a sample of 70 former colonies, for reasons described below. We examine whether cross-country differences in financial institutions are accounted for by cross-country differences in legal tradition and/or initial endowments, while controlling for other possible determinants. To measure financial development, we use measures of: (i) financial intermediary development; (ii) equity market development; and, (iii) private property rights protection. For simplicity, we use the term "financial development" to refer to each of these three measures. We measure financial development over the period 1990–1995. To measure legal tradition, we use the LLSV (1999) indicators specifying whether the country has a British or French legal tradition, as determined by the origin of each country's Company/Commercial law. To measure initial endowments, we primarily use the AJR measure of settler mortality rates as European settlers arrived in various parts of the globe. For robustness, we also use the absolute value of the latitude of each country as an alternative, albeit less precise, indicator of initial endowments, since many authors argue that tropical climates are not conducive to institutional and economic development. In conducting the cross-country comparisons, we control for other potential determinants of financial development. Specifically, we include measures of ethnic diversity, religious composition, years of independence since 1776, and continent dummy variables. Further, we also assess whether the political structure of a country is the only mechanism through which the legal tradition and initial endowments influence current financial development.

We focus on a sample of 70 former colonies for two reasons. First, we have the AJR (2001) data on settler mortality, which is a key building block of AJR's (2001) empirical assessment of the endowment theory. Second, some observers stress that European colonization offers a unique break, i.e., a natural identifying condition (AJR, 2001, 2002; Engerman and Sokoloff, 1997). As European conquerors and colonizers landed, they brought different legal traditions. Colonization represents a period during which legal traditions were exogenously established around the globe and thus provides a natural starting point for examining the law and endowment theories of financial development. For these reasons, we use a sample of 70 former colonies with data on settler mortality. This sample only includes countries with British and French legal origins.

This paper makes four contributions.[4] First, this paper applies AJR's (2001) endowment theory of institutions directly to the study of financial development. Although AJR (2001) carefully document the connections running from endowments to institutions to the level of economic development today, we examine whether initial colonial endowments explain a wide array of current measures of financial development. Since financial development helps explain technological innovation, the efficiency of capital allocation across industries and firms, output volatility, the likelihood of a systemic banking crisis, and economic growth, even when controlling for the levels of economic and institutional development, it is important to assess whether endowments influence financial development.[5] Second, this is the first paper to consider simultaneously the legal and endowment views of financial development. This is crucial to assessing two very different visions of how the institutions founded by Europeans continue to shape national approaches to private property and financial systems in former colonies. Third, although others have shown that legal tradition shapes financial development (LLSV, 1997, 1998, 2000), this paper goes much further in evaluating the robustness of the law and finance view by controlling for endowments, religion, ethnic diversity, length of independence, etc. This assessment is critical if we are to have much confidence in legal theories of financial development. Fourth, while some analysts argue that the structure and competitiveness of the political system shapes institutions and policies, this is the first paper to examine whether legal origin and both disease and geographical endowments explain cross-country differences in financial development beyond their ability to account for differences in national political systems.

The paper is organized as follows. Section 2 describes the data and presents figures that motivate the analysis. Section 3 discusses the regression results, and a series of robustness tests are presented in Section 4. Section 5 concludes.

2. Data and initial assessments

This section describes the data and presents figures that document: (1) British Common law countries tend to have higher levels of financial development than

---

[4] Pivovarsky (2001) also examines the relationship between institutions and financial development. He analyzes the impact of current institutions, instrumented by settler mortality and legal origin, on financial development and finds a strong effect of the exogenous component of institutions on financial development. Our contribution is distinct, however, in that we compare the direct effects of endowments and legal origin on financial system development.

[5] In particular, see Beck et al. (2000) on the finance and productivity growth relationship, Wurgler (2000) on the finance and industry allocation of capital relationship, Demirgüç-Kunt and Maksimovic (1998) on the finance and firm growth link, Demirgüç-Kunt and Detragiache (2002) on the finance and crisis relationship, Easterly et al. (2000) on the finance and output volatility link, and Levine and Zervos (1998), Rajan and Zingales (1998), and Beck and Levine (2002, 2003) on the finance–growth relationship.

T. Beck et al. / Journal of Financial Economics 70 (2003) 137–181   143

French Civil law countries; and, (2) countries with high levels of European mortality during the initial stages of colonization tend to have lower levels of financial development than those countries with initially low settler-mortality rates.

2.1. Financial development

To measure financial development, we use indicators of financial intermediary development, stock market development, and property rights protection. The goal is to proxy for the degree to which national financial systems facilitate the acquisition of firm information, ease corporate governance, help agents manage risk, and mobilize savings effectively. Unfortunately, we do not have direct and comparable measures of the ability of national financial systems to provide these benefits for a broad cross-section of countries. Thus, we use a variety of indicators of financial development to assess the connections between law, endowments, and finance.

PRIVATE CREDIT equals financial intermediary credits to the private sector divided by gross domestic product (GDP) and is measured over 1990–1995. PRIVATE CREDIT excludes credit to the public sector and cross-claims between financial intermediaries, and thus measures the amount of savings that is channeled through debt-issuing financial intermediaries to private borrowers. For most countries, PRIVATE CREDIT is obtained from data available from the International Monetary Fund (IMF). To maximize the size of the sample, however, we also use World Bank data sources for a few countries that lack IMF data; the countries and sources are specified in the data appendix. Past work shows a strong connection between PRIVATE CREDIT and economic growth (see Levine et al., 2000). PRIVATE CREDIT ranges from values above 0.9 in the United States, Hong Kong, Singapore, South Africa, and Malaysia, to values less than 0.03 in Sierra Leone, Uganda, Angola, and Zaire.

STOCK MARKET DEVELOPMENT equals the total value of outstanding equity shares as a fraction of GDP and is averaged over the period 1990–1995.[6] This measures the overall size of the equity market relative to the size of the economy.[7] The data are primarily collected from the World Bank's International Finance Corporation. However, we use additional data sources to complete the dataset, as specified in the appendix. There are large cross-country differences as shown in

---

[6] For both STOCK MARKET DEVELOPMENT and PRIVATE CREDIT, we have conducted the analyses using data averaged over the 1975–1995 period instead of the 1990–1995 period. We get the same results. Since there are fewer countries with data over the 1975–1995 period, we present the results with the 1990–1995 averages.

[7] Since there are differences in ownership concentration across countries, LLSV (1998) suggest using an adjustment whereby STOCK MARKET DEVELOPMENT is multiplied by one minus the median ownership share of the three largest shareholders in the ten largest non-financial, privately-owned domestic firms in the country. This paper obtains the same conclusions using this adjusted measure. Since we only have these ownership share figures for a sub-sample of countries, however, making this adjustment substantially reduces our dataset. Thus, we report the results using the standard STOCK MARKET DEVELOPMENT indicator for market size.

Table 1, Panel A. STOCK MARKET DEVELOPMENT is greater than 0.65 in the United States, Chile, Singapore, South Africa, Hong Kong, and Malaysia, and is indistinguishable from zero in 29 countries.

PROPERTY RIGHTS is an index of the degree to which the government enforces laws that protect private property. The data are for 1997 and were obtained from LLSV (1999) and the Index of Economic Freedom. While PRIVATE CREDIT and STOCK MARKET DEVELOPMENT are direct measures of the size of financial intermediaries and equity markets respectively, PROPERTY RIGHTS does not directly measure the size of a component of the financial sector. Rather, PROPERTY RIGHTS measures a key input into the efficient operation of financial contracts and the development of formal financial institutions: the degree of protection of private property rights. The law and endowment theories stress the degree to which national institutions emphasize private property rights versus the rights of the state. This difference in emphasis may influence a variety of indicators of financial development. While PROPERTY RIGHTS as defined is one attempt to measure this difference, there may be measurement problems or other differences in emphasis on state versus private rights that affect financial contracting beyond narrow indicators of property rights protection. Hence, we examine a variety of financial development indicators. The maximum value of PROPERTY RIGHTS is five, while a value of one indicates the weakest property rights protection. Nine former colonies have the maximum value of five. Only Haiti and Rwanda have the minimum value of one, while 15 countries have a value of two for PROPERTY RIGHTS. We do not have data on PROPERTY RIGHTS for the Central African Republic, so there are only 69 countries in the PROPERTY RIGHTS regressions.

2.2. Legal origin

LLSV (1998, 1999) identify the legal origin of each country's company or commercial law as French, British, German, Scandinavian, or Socialist.[8] Given we are examining former colonies with data on settler mortality from AJR (2001), we

---

[8] One may further refine the categorization of legal traditions, as described by the following examples. First, Franks and Sussman (1999) and Coffee (2000) describe differences in two Common law countries: the United Kingdom and the United States. While in the U.K. there is freedom of contracting (Glendon et al., 1982), in the U.S. the judiciary has a more important role to play in developing law. In both systems, however, the legislature does not have a monopoly on creating law, as in the original French legal system, as designed by Napoleon. In both the U.K. and the U.S., case law is a source of law, while not in France. Second, different colonization strategies may have intensified differences across legal traditions. England did not try to replace Islamic, Hindu, or African law. English courts in the colonies, therefore, used local laws and customs in deciding cases. This quickly produced an Indian Common law distinct from English Common law. While perhaps chaotic, this allowed for the integration of common law with local circumstances. In contrast, the French imposed the Code although serious conflicts frequently existed with local customs. Also, legal scholars study differences across the French Civil law countries of Latin America. While recognizing that each country's legal system is special, the comparative law literature clearly emphasizes that there are key differences across the major legal families

T. Beck et al. / Journal of Financial Economics 70 (2003) 137–181   145

have data for only French and British legal-origin countries.[9] Thus, we do not include many of the most developed countries in the LLSV (1998, 1999) sample. The FRENCH LEGAL ORIGIN dummy variable equals one if the country adopted its company/commercial law from the French Civil law and zero otherwise. In the regressions, British legal origin is captured in the constant.

Fig. 1 clearly shows that financial development is substantially higher in countries with a British Common law tradition than in countries with a French Civil law tradition. French Civil law countries have, on average, lower levels of PRIVATE CREDIT, STOCK MARKET DEVELOPMENT, and PROPERTY RIGHTS than British Common law countries. There are 45 French Civil law countries and 25 British Common law countries. Table 1, Panel B correlations confirm Fig. 1: the FRENCH LEGAL ORIGIN dummy variable is significantly, negatively correlated with each of the three financial development indicators. Furthermore, Fig. 2 illustrates that in Common law countries, eight countries have PRIVATE CREDIT greater than 0.6 (Australia, Canada, New Zealand, Malaysia, Singapore, South Africa, Hong Kong, and the United States), while among French Civil law countries, only Malta has PRIVATE CREDIT greater than 0.6.

Fig. 2 also demonstrates clearly that legal origin does not completely explain the cross-country variation observed in financial systems today. Fig. 2 documents that there are many Common law countries with poorly developed financial inter- mediaries, and a few French legal origin countries that have well-developed financial intermediaries. For instance, many Common law countries have PRIVATE CREDIT less than 0.3, with countries such as Uganda, Sierra Leone, Ghana, Sudan, and Tanzania registering extremely low PRIVATE CREDIT levels. Thus, we need to know more than legal origin to account for cross-country differences in financial systems.

2.3. Endowments

As Europeans arrived around the world, they encountered very different environments. In some lands, Europeans found hospitable environments. In others, conditions were less hospitable and Europeans died in large numbers. According to AJR (2001), these location specific endowments fundamentally influenced the types of long-lasting institutions created by European colonists.

To measure endowments, we use the AJR (2001) measure of SETTLER MORTALITY. AJR (2001) compile data on the death rates faced by settlers. Curtin (1989) constructs data on the mortality and disease rates of European soldiers in colonies during the early nineteenth century. The raw data come from the British,

---

[9] Although we have data on settler mortality for Vietnam and Myanmar (which are classified as socialist legal origin countries by LLSV, 1999), we do not include these two countries because we do not have comparable information on financial development for these economies. Also, there are 70 countries in our sample of former colonies with settler mortality data. We also constructed a larger sample of 95 non-European countries. This 95-country sample, however, does not have settler mortality data. For the 95-country sample, we conducted the analyses using latitude instead of settler mortality and obtained the same results reported below.

Table 1
Summary statistics and correlations

Summary statistics are presented in Panel A and correlations are presented in Panel B, respectively. Private Credit is the value of credits by financial intermediaries to the private sector as a share of GDP. Stock Market Development measures the value of shares listed on the stock exchange as a share of GDP. Property Rights reflects the degree to which government enforces laws that protect private property, with higher numbers indicating better enforcement. French Legal Origin is a dummy variable that takes on the value one for countries with French Civil law tradition, and zero otherwise. Settler Mortality is the log of the annualized deaths per thousand European soldiers in European colonies in the early 19th century. Latin America and Africa are dummy variables that take the value one if the country is located in Latin America or Sub-Saharan Africa, respectively. Catholic, Muslim, and Other Religion indicate the percentage of the population that follows a particular religion (Catholic, Muslim, or religions other than Catholic, Muslim, or Protestant, respectively). Independence is the percentage of years since 1776 that a country has been independent. Ethnic Fractionalization is the probability that two randomly selected individuals in a country will not speak the same language. Legislative Competition is an indicator of competition in the last legislative election. Checks measures the number of veto-players in the political decision making process. These last two measures are averaged over 1990–1995. Detailed variable definitions and sources are given in the data appendix.

Panel A: Summary statistics:

	N	Mean	Std. dev	Min	Max
Private Credit	70	0.32	0.30	0.01	1.48
Stock Market Development	70	0.19	0.40	0.00	1.89
Property Rights	69	3.12	0.99	1.00	5.00
French Legal Origin	70	0.64	0.48	0.00	1.00
Settler Mortality	70	4.67	1.24	2.15	7.99
Africa	70	0.40	0.49	0.00	1.00
Latin America	70	0.36	0.48	0.00	1.00
Catholic	70	39.44	36.89	0.10	97.3
Muslim	70	23.90	33.87	0.00	99.4
Other Religion	70	25.79	23.58	0.30	86.0
Independence	70	0.32	0.32	0.00	1.00
Ethnic Fractionalization	70	0.42	0.31	0.00	0.89
Legislative Competition	68	5.81	1.62	1.00	7.00
Checks	68	2.68	1.40	1.00	6.00

T. Beck et al. / Journal of Financial Economics 70 (2003) 137–181   147

Panel B: Correlation matrix of variables

	Private Credit	Stock Market Development	Property Rights	French Legal Origin	Settler Mortality	Africa	Latin America	Catholic	Muslim	Other Religion	Independence	Ethnic Fractionalization	Legislative Competition
Stock Market Development													
Property Rights	0.618***	0.487***											
French Legal Origin	-0.370***	-0.430***	-0.461***										
Settler Mortality	-0.669***	-0.528***	-0.438***	0.238**									
Africa	-0.408***	-0.228*	-0.426***	0.061	0.651***								
Latin America	-0.105	-0.140	0.064	0.244**	-0.178	-0.509***							
Catholic	-0.133	-0.194	-0.114	0.479***	-0.118	-0.356***	0.706***						
Muslim	-0.157	-0.141	-0.103	0.006	0.271**	0.240**	-0.500***	-0.652***					
Other Religion	0.283**	0.421***	0.187	-0.552***	-0.137	0.166	-0.379***	-0.548***	-0.175				
Independence	0.057	-0.016	0.041	0.330***	-0.323***	-0.475***	0.630***	0.700***	-0.421***	-0.384***			
Ethnic Fractionalization	-0.269**	-0.062	-0.213*	-0.076	0.433***	0.718***	-0.551***	-0.370***	0.229*	0.229*	-0.437***		
Legislative Competition	0.408***	0.271**	0.401***	-0.032	-0.601***	-0.699***	0.513***	0.425***	-0.387***	-0.143	0.392***	-0.506***	
Checks	0.378***	0.323***	0.373***	-0.202*	-0.497***	-0.543***	0.383***	0.248**	-0.285**	-0.010	0.317***	-0.306**	0.664***

*, **, *** indicate significance levels of 10%, 5%, and 1%, respectively.

148 *T. Beck et al. / Journal of Financial Economics 70 (2003) 137–181*

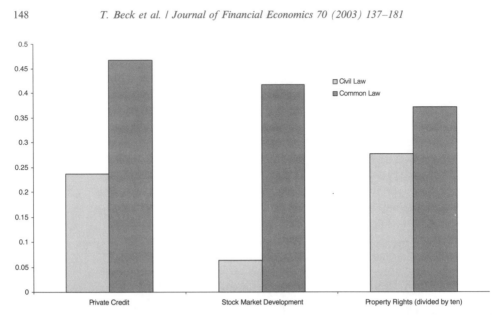

Fig. 1. Financial development across Common and Civil law countries. Private Credit is the value of credits by financial intermediaries to the private sector as a share of GDP. Stock Market Development measures the value of shares listed on the stock exchange as a share of GDP. Property Rights reflects the degree to which government enforces laws that protect private property, with higher numbers indicating better enforcement. Civil law countries are countries whose legal system is of French Civil law origin, whereas Common law countries are countries whose legal system is of British Common law origin.

French, and United States governments during the period 1817–1848. The standard measure is annualized deaths per thousand soldiers, with each death replaced by a new soldier. Curtin (1998) adds similar data on soldier mortality during the second half of the nineteenth century. Finally, Gutierrez (1986) uses Vatican records to construct estimates of the mortality rates of bishops in Latin America from 1604 to 1876. Since some of these data overlap with Curtin's separate estimates, AJR confirm the compatibility of the two data series before constructing an overall measure of the logarithm of annualized deaths per thousand Europeans, SETTLER MORTALITY, for a large group of former colonies. As in AJR (2001), we use the logarithm to diminish the impact of outliers. The AJR (2001) measure forms the core of our analysis of the relation between endowments and finance. This measure ranges from 2.15 (Australia and New Zealand) to 7.99 (Mali).

Fig. 3 shows a generally negative, though certainly not linear, relation between SETTLER MORTALITY and financial development.[10] The absence of a linear relationship is especially pronounced for STOCK MARKET DEVELOPMENT since many countries have stock market capitalization ratios of zero. Consequently, we use a Tobit estimator to check our results. Table 1, Panel B shows that there is a

---

[10] When we experimented with a non-linear transformation (e.g., the inverse of the log settler mortality rate), we obtain the same conclusions discussed below. Furthermore, we re-ran the analyses using the logarithm of PRIVATE CREDIT. Again, we confirm the conclusions discussed below.

T. Beck et al. / Journal of Financial Economics 70 (2003) 137–181

149

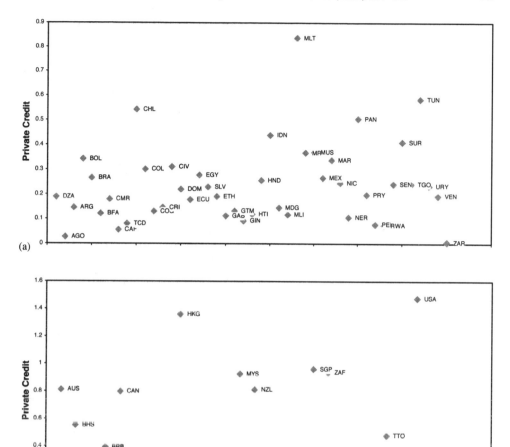
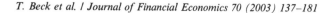

Fig. 2. (a) Private credit in Civil law countries: Private Credit is the value of credits by financial intermediaries to the private sector as a share of GDP. Civil law countries are countries whose legal system is of French Civil law origin, whereas Common law countries are countries whose legal system is of British Common law origin. There are 45 Civil law and 25 Common law countries in the sample. (b) Private Credit in Common law countries: Private Credit is the value of credits by financial intermediaries to the private sector as a share of GDP. Civil law countries are countries whose legal system is of French Civil law origin, whereas Common law countries are countries whose legal system is of British Common law origin. There are 45 Civil law and 25 Common law countries in the sample.

significant, negative correlation between SETTLER MORTALITY and each of the three financial development indicators at the one-percent significance level. The data indicate that in colonies where early settlers found very inhospitable environments, we do not observe well-developed financial systems today.

14 A Reader in International Corporate Finance

150 T. Beck et al. / Journal of Financial Economics 70 (2003) 137–181

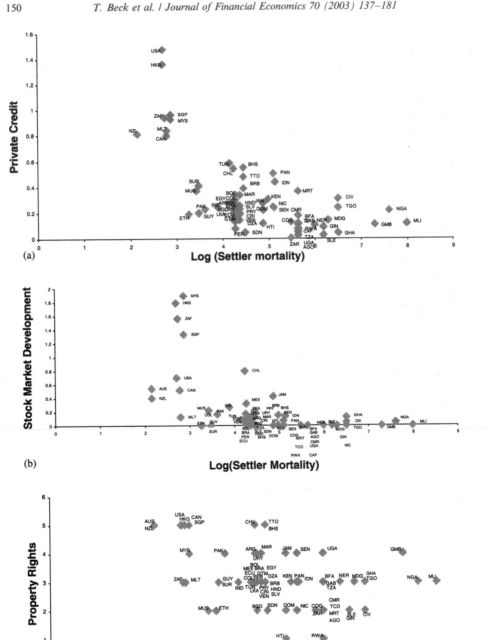

T. Beck et al. / Journal of Financial Economics 70 (2003) 137–181 151

2.4. Other possible determinants of financial development

To assess the robustness of our results, we include several other potential determinants of financial development in our empirical analysis. ETHNIC FRACTIONALIZATION measures the probability that two randomly selected individuals from a country are from different ethnolinguistic groups. LSSV (1999, p. 231) argue, "...political theories predict that, as ethnic heterogeneity increases, governments become more interventionist." Recent studies show that in highly ethnically diverse economies, the group that comes to power tends to implement policies that: (a) expropriate as many resources as possible from the ethnic losers; (b) restrict the rights of other groups; and, (c) prohibit the growth of industries or sectors that threaten the ruling group (see, e.g., Alesina et al., 1999; Easterly and Levine, 1997). When this view is applied to the financial sector, the implication is clear: greater ethnic diversity implies the adoption of policies and institutions that are focused on maintaining power and control, rather than on creating an open and competitive financial system. Table 1, Panel B indicates that there is a significant, negative correlation between ETHNIC FRACTIONALIZATION and PRIVATE CREDIT. Thus we include ETHNIC FRACTIONALIZATION to examine the independent impacts of law and endowments on financial development.

INDEPENDENCE equals the fraction of years since 1776 that a country has been independent. We include this measure because a longer period of independence may provide greater opportunities for countries to develop institutions, policies, and regulations independent of their colonial heritage. In the simple correlations, however, we do not find a significant link between INDEPENDENCE and financial development.

We also examine religious composition. Many scholars argue that religion shapes national views regarding property rights, competition, and the role of the state (LLSV, 1999; Stulz and Williamson, 2003). Putnam (1993, p. 107), for instance, contends that the Catholic Church fosters "vertical bonds of authority" rather than "horizontal bonds of fellowship." Similarly, Landes (1998) argues that Catholic and Muslim countries tend to develop xenophobic cultures and powerful bonds between church and state to maintain control, bonds which limit competition and private property rights protection.

Fig. 3. (a) Settler Mortality and Private Credit: Private Credit is the value of credits by financial intermediaries to the private sector as a share of GDP. Settler Mortality is the log of the annualized deaths per thousand European soldiers in European colonies in the early 19th century. The sample comprises 70 countries of Common law and French Civil law origin. (b) Settler Mortality and Stock Market Development: Stock Market Development measures the value of shares listed on the stock exchange as a share of GDP Settler Mortality is the log of the annualized deaths per thousand European soldiers in European colonies in the early 19th century. The sample comprises 70 countries of Common law and French Civil law origin. (c) Settler Mortality and Property Rights: Property rights reflects the degree to which government enforces laws that protect private property, with higher numbers indicating better enforcement. Settler Mortality is the log of the annualized deaths per thousand European soldiers in European colonies in the early 19th century. The sample comprises 70 countries of Common law and French Civil law origin.

CATHOLIC, MUSLIM, and OTHER RELIGION equal the fraction of the population that is Catholic, Muslim, or of another (non-Protestant) religion. The Protestant share of the population is omitted (and therefore captured in the regression constant). The data are from LLSV (1999).

Table 1, Panel B shows that countries with a higher population proportion that is neither Catholic, nor Muslim, nor Protestant, have higher levels of financial development than countries where a higher fraction of the country is either Catholic or Muslim. Thus, we control for religious composition in examining the independent relations between financial development and both legal origin and endowments.

We note there is a very large, positive, and significant correlation between CATHOLIC and FRENCH LEGAL ORIGIN (0.48). Thus, it may be particularly difficult to distinguish fully between CATHOLIC and the Civil law tradition.

Finally, we include one dummy variable for countries in LATIN AMERICA and another for countries in Sub-Saharan AFRICA. A large number of studies find that countries in Sub-Saharan Africa and Latin America perform more poorly than countries in other regions of the world even after controlling for economic policies, institutional development, and other factors. Easterly and Levine (1997) provide related analyses and citations.

There are important problems with including continent dummies. First, continent dummies do not proxy for a clear explanation of why countries in these regions have worse institutions or perform more poorly. Second, Latin America is primarily a French legal-origin continent; the correlation between Catholic and Latin America is 0.71 and is significant at the one-percent level. Thus, including continent dummies may weaken our ability to identify linkages between financial development and legal origin without offering a clear, alternative explanation. Third, many Sub-Saharan African countries have high settler mortality rates. The correlation between AFRICA and SETTLER MORTALITY is 0.65 and is significant at the one-percent level. Thus, including the AFRICA dummy may decrease the ability to find a link between financial development and endowments without offering an alternative theory. Including these continent dummies, however, may control for region-specific characteristics that are not captured by any of the other explanatory variables. Therefore, while recognizing the problems associated with interpreting continent dummies, we include them in assessing the relations between law, endowments, and finance.[11]

3. Regression results

This section presents regressions on the relationship between financial development and both law and endowments while controlling for other possible

---

[11] In a previous version, we also included GDP per capita as a control variable. However, institutional development also influences economic development (as shown by AJR, 2001), so including GDP per capita together with initial endowments may bias the coefficient on legal origin and settler mortality/latitude toward zero. Further, unlike the other regressors, GDP per capita is endogenous, which causes estimation problems as shown by AJR (2001).

T. Beck et al. / Journal of Financial Economics 70 (2003) 137–181 153

determinants of financial development. The dependent variable is one of the three measures of financial development, PRIVATE CREDIT, STOCK MARKET DEVELOPMENT, or PROPERTY RIGHTS. We use the dummy variable FRENCH LEGAL ORIGIN to assess the links between law and finance. We use SETTLER MORTALITY to assess the relationship between endowments and finance. As control variables, we use continent dummy variables (for Latin American and Africa), measures of religious composition, the percentage of years the country has been independent since 1776, and ethnic diversity. We also include a regression where we control concurrently for continent dummies, time since independence, and ethnic fractionalization. We do not include religious composition dummies in this regression since they never enter significantly at the five-percent significance level. The reasons for including these particular controls were discussed above.

3.1. Law and finance

Table 2 presents regressions of financial development on French legal origin and various combinations of the control variables. Table 2 does not include measures of endowments.

The results indicate a strong, negative relation between French legal origin and financial development. When controlling for continent, religious composition, ethnic diversity, and independence, French legal origin enters negatively and significantly at the five-percent level in all of the financial development regressions. The results suggest an economically large impact. For instance, the smallest coefficient (in absolute value) on FRENCH LEGAL ORIGIN in the STOCK MARKET DEVELOPMENT regressions is −0.27, and the mean and standard deviation values of STOCK MARKET DEVELOPMENT are 0.19 and 0.40, respectively. For illustrative purposes, the coefficient suggests that if Argentina had a British Common law tradition, its low level of stock market capitalization (0.10) would be substantially larger and closer to that of New Zealand (0.37).

In sum, French Civil law countries tend to have lower levels of financial development than British Common law countries after controlling for many national characteristics. This result is consistent with the LLSV (1998) view that the identity of the colonizer matters because of the legal traditions the colonizers brought.

3.2. Endowments and finance

Table 3 indicates a robust, negative association between SETTLER MORTAL-ITY and financial development. SETTLER MORTALITY enters with a negative coefficient and is significant at the five percent level in all of the PRIVATE CREDIT and STOCK MARKET DEVELOPMENT regressions. The coefficient sizes are economically large. According to the smallest coefficient (in the absolute sense) in the PRIVATE CREDIT regression in Table 3 (−0.14), a one standard deviation reduction in the logarithm of mortality rates (1.24) would increase PRIVATE CREDIT by 0.17, and the mean and standard deviation of PRIVATE CREDIT are 0.32 and 0.30, respectively. Thus, the estimates in Table 3 can account for why

154   T. Beck et al. / Journal of Financial Economics 70 (2003) 137–181

Table 2
Law and finance

The regression estimated is: Financial Sector Development $= \alpha + \beta_1$ French Legal Origin $+ \beta_2 X$, where Financial Sector Development is either Private Credit, Stock Market Development, or Property Rights. Private Credit is the value of credits by financial intermediaries to the private sector as a share of GDP. Stock Market Development measures the value of shares listed on the stock exchange as a share of GDP. Property Rights reflects the degree to which government enforces laws that protect private property, with higher numbers indicating better enforcement. French Legal Origin is a dummy variable that takes on the value one for countries with French Civil law tradition, and zero otherwise. The regressions also include a vector of control variables, X. Latin America and Africa are dummy variables that take the value one if the country is located in Latin America or Sub-Saharan Africa, respectively. Catholic, Muslim, and Other Religion indicate the percentage of the population that follows a particular religion (Catholic, Muslim, or religions other than Catholic, Muslim, or Protestant, respectively). Independence is the percentage of years since 1776 that a country has been independent. Ethnic Fractionalization is the probability that two randomly selected individuals in a country will not speak the same language. Regressions are estimated using Ordinary Least Squares. Robust standard errors are given in parentheses. *, **, *** indicate significance at the 10% 5%, and 1% levels, respectively. Detailed variable definitions and sources are given in the data appendix.

	French Legal Origin	Latin America	Africa	Catholic	Muslim	Other Religion	Independence	Ethnic Fractionalization	Adjusted-R^2	Obs.
Private Credit	-0.233*** (0.088)								0.124	70
	-0.136** (0.067)	-0.292*** (0.092)	-0.417*** (0.100)						0.378	70
	-0.181** (0.086)			-0.002 (0.003)	-0.003 (0.003)	-0.001 (0.005)			0.121	70
	-0.275*** (0.097)						0.191 (0.136)		0.148	70
	-0.247*** (0.084)							-0.289*** (0.095)	0.203	70
	-0.168** (0.080)	-0.352*** (0.112)	-0.348*** (0.107)				0.170 (0.179)	-0.109 (0.133)	0.384	70
Stock Market Development	-0.356*** (0.118)								0.173	70
	-0.278*** (0.101)	-0.242* (0.128)	-0.312** (0.143)						0.240	70

T. Beck et al. / Journal of Financial Economics 70 (2003) 137–181

155

	(1)	(2)	(3)	(4)	(5)	(6)	(7)	(8)	(9)	(10)
Property Rights	−0.265** (0.107)	−0.395*** (0.111)	−0.362*** (0.117)	−0.308*** (0.102)	−0.947*** (0.241)	−0.836*** (0.206)	−1.065*** (0.291)	−1.103*** (0.235)	−0.995*** (0.232)	−0.856*** (0.203)
				−0.299*** (0.104)		−0.250 (0.265)				−0.286 (0.297)
				−0.315* (0.177)		−0.969*** (0.243)				−1.014*** (0.293)
	0.002 (0.004)						−0.002 (0.005)			
		0.002 (0.004)					−0.005 (0.009)			
			0.006 (0.005)				−0.007 (0.011)			
			0.176** (0.082)	0.224 (0.150)				0.692** (0.346)		0.182 (0.393)
			−0.121 (0.122)	0.087 (0.176)					−0.813** (0.339)	0.178 (0.477)
R^2	0.199	0.179	0.170	0.237	0.198	0.351	0.182	0.232	0.253	0.334
Obs.	70	70	70	70	69	69	69	69	69	69

Table 3

Endowments and finance

The regression estimated is: Financial Sector Development $= \alpha + \beta_1$ Settler Mortality $+ \beta_2 X$, where Financial Sector Development is either Private Credit, Stock Market Development, or Property Rights. Private Credit is the value of credits by financial intermediaries to the private sector as a share of GDP. Stock Market Development measures the value of shares listed on the stock exchange as a share of GDP. Property rights reflects the degree to which government enforces laws that protect private property, with higher numbers indicating better enforcement. Settler Mortality is the log of the annualized deaths per thousand European soldiers in European colonies in the early 19th century. The regressions also include a vector of control variables, X. Latin America and Africa are dummy variables that take the value one if the country is located in Latin America or Sub-Saharan Africa, respectively. Catholic, Muslim, and Other Religion indicate the percentage of the population that follows a particular religion (Catholic, Muslim, or religions other than Catholic, Muslim, or Protestant, respectively). Independence is the percentage of years since 1776 that a country has been independent. Ethnic Fractionalization is the probability that two randomly selected individuals in a country will not speak the same language. Regressions are estimated using Ordinary Least Squares. Robust standard errors are given in parentheses. The symbols *, **, *** indicate significance at the 10%, 5%, and 1% levels, respectively. Detailed variable definitions and sources are given in the data appendix.

	Settler Mortality	Latin America	Africa	Catholic	Muslim	Other Religion	Independence	Ethnic Fractionalization	Adjusted-R^2	Obs.
Private Credit	-0.164***								0.440	70
	(0.030)									
	-0.137***	-0.230***	-0.163						0.500	70
	(0.038)	(0.086)	(0.113)							
	-0.161***			-0.004	-0.003	-0.002			0.490	70
	(0.028)			(0.003)	(0.210)	(0.004)				
	-0.178***						-0.168		0.460	70
	(0.031)						(0.138)			
	-0.166***							0.025	0.432	70
	(0.033)							(0.076)		
	-0.140***	-0.224*	-0.131				-0.038	-0.080	0.489	70
	(0.038)	(0.128)	(0.121)				(0.176)	(0.103)		

	(1)	(2)	(3)	(4)	(5)	(6)	(7)	(8)	R^2	Obs.
Stock Market Development	−0.170*** (0.047)								0.267	70
	−0.182** (0.071)	−0.204 (0.132)							0.305	70
	−0.159*** (0.042)		−0.008 (0.199)						0.372	70
	−0.191*** (0.056)			−0.001 (0.003)	−0.001 (0.003)	0.004 (0.005)			0.297	70
	−0.198*** (0.059)						−0.260 (0.158)	0.261 (0.167)	0.292	70
	−0.189** (0.073)	−0.145 (0.127)	−0.057 (0.198)				−0.099 (0.180)	0.141 (0.183)	0.294	70
Property Rights	−0.349*** (0.099)								0.177	69
	−0.151 (0.117)	−0.489* (0.290)							0.220	69
	−0.339*** (0.092)		−0.993** (0.352)						0.194	69
	−0.377*** (0.104)			−0.015* (0.009)	−0.012 (0.008)	−0.010 (0.011)			0.175	69
	−0.338*** (0.113)						−0.336 (0.387)	−0.102 (0.415)	0.166	69
	−0.180 (0.125)	−0.271 (0.407)	−1.010** (0.332)				−0.418 (0.550)	0.345 (0.514)	0.214	69

countries such as Nicaragua and Jamaica with bad endowments (log settler mortality rates of 5.1 and 4.9, respectively) have lower levels of financial intermediary development (0.25 and 0.27, respectively) than Chile (0.54), which had a log settler mortality rate of 4.2. Furthermore, SETTLER MORTALITY enters all of the PROPERTY RIGHTS regressions negatively and significantly, except those including continent dummies. As noted, there is an extremely high correlation between AFRICA and SETTLER MORTALITY. Also, as we report below, when we use an alternative measure of property rights protection, settler mortality continues to enter significantly even when controlling for AFRICA.

These results support the view that high settler mortality rates are negatively associated with the level of financial development today, and are robust to an assortment of control variables. Such findings are fully consistent with the AJR (2001, 2002) assertion that a colony's environmental endowments influenced how it was colonized—whether it was an extractive colony or a settler colony—with long-lasting implications for institutional development.

3.3. Law, endowments, and finance

Table 4 presents regression results on the relation between financial development and both law and endowments while controlling for other exogenous determinants of financial development.

Table 4 regressions provide strong support for the endowment view of financial development. SETTLER MORTALITY enters all of the PRIVATE CREDIT and STOCK MARKET DEVELOPMENT regressions significantly at the five-percent level even when controlling for legal origin, continent, religious composition, the length of time the country has been independent, and ethnic diversity. The sizes of the coefficients on SETTLER MORTALITY in the PRIVATE CREDIT and STOCK MARKET DEVELOPMENT regressions are very similar to those in Table 3, in which the regressions do not also control for legal origin. Also similar to Table 3, the Table 4 regressions indicate that SETTLER MORTALITY exerts a statistically significant impact on PROPERTY RIGHTS except when controlling for the AFRICA dummy variable (because of the very high correlation between the rate of settler mortality and countries in Sub-Saharan Africa). As discussed below, however, when we use an alternative measure of property rights protection, settler mortality enters significantly even when controlling for the AFRICA dummy variable.

In sum, poor endowments—as measured by settler mortality—are negatively associated with financial development today. Even when controlling for the legal tradition of the colonizers and other possible determinants of financial development, initial endowments of the colonies help explain cross-country variation in financial development today, which is strongly supportive of the AJR (2001, 2002) endowment view.

Table 4 regressions also provide support for the law and finance view, though some qualifications are necessary. When controlling for SETTLER MORTALITY, the relationship between financial intermediary development (PRIVATE CREDIT)

T. Beck et al. / Journal of Financial Economics 70 (2003) 137–181   159

and legal origin is not robust to the inclusion of various control variables. However, FRENCH LEGAL ORIGIN is negatively and significantly associated with PROPERTY RIGHTS in all of the regressions when controlling for SETTLER MORTALITY. Putting aside regressions that include CATHOLIC (which is extremely positively correlated with French Civil law), FRENCH LEGAL ORIGIN is also negatively and significantly linked with STOCK MARKET DEVELOPMENT. To the extent that equity markets rely more than banking institutions on well-functioning legal systems to defend the rights of individual investors, these findings are consistent with the thrust of the law and finance view.

Subject to the qualifications discussed above, we interpret the results as generally consistent with the LLSV (1998) theory that the French Civil law tends to place greater emphasis on the rights of the state versus the rights of individuals, with negative repercussions on financial contracting. In contrast, the British Common law tends to place greater emphasis on the contractual rights of individual investors, with positive implications for financial development. While LLSV (1998) document the link between financial development and legal origin, this paper goes much further in controlling for alternative explanations. Our results demonstrate a strong connection between legal origin and both stock market development and private property rights protection, but we also show that the link between legal origin and financial intermediary development is not robust to the inclusion of numerous control variables.

In comparing the independent explanatory power between law and endowments, Tables 2–4 indicate that endowments explain a greater amount of the cross-country variation in financial intermediary and stock market development than legal origin. Consider, for instance, the regressions in Tables 2–4 that do not include any regressors beyond FRENCH LEGAL ORIGIN and SETTLER MORTALITY. The adjusted R-square in the PRIVATE CREDIT–FRENCH LEGAL ORIGIN regression is 0.12 (Table 2), while it is 0.44 in the PRIVATE CREDIT–SETTLER MORTALITY regression (Table 3). Furthermore, when adding FRENCH LEGAL ORIGIN to the SETTLER MORTALITY regression, the adjusted R-square only rises from 0.44 to 0.48 (Table 4). As also indicated above, legal origin does not enter the PRIVATE CREDIT regression robustly when including various control variables, but endowments remain negatively and significantly linked with financial intermediary development across various control variables. Turning to private property rights protection, the explanatory power of law and endowments in the PROPERTY RIGHTS regressions is very similar. However, the STOCK MARKET DEVELOPMENT regressions again illustrate the greater explanatory power of endowments. The adjusted R-square in the STOCK MARKET DEVELOPMENT–FRENCH LEGAL ORIGIN regression is 0.17 (Table 2), and is 0.27 in the SETTLER MORTALITY regression (Table 3). Furthermore, when adding FRENCH LEGAL ORIGIN to the SETTLER MORTALITY regression, the adjusted R-square only rises from 0.27 to 0.36 (Table 4). Thus, while legal origin significantly enters all of the stock market development regressions that do not control for religious composition (Table 4), endowments explain a greater

Table 4
Law, endowments, and finance.

The regression estimated is: Financial Sector Development $= \alpha + \beta_1$ French Legal Origin $+ \beta_2$ Settler Mortality $+ \beta_3 X$, where Financial Sector Development is either Private Credit, Stock Market Development, or Property Rights. Private Credit is the value of credits by financial intermediaries to the private sector as a share of GDP. Stock Market Development measures the value of shares listed on the stock exchange as a share of GDP. Property rights reflects the degree to which government enforces laws that protect private property, with higher numbers indicating better enforcement. French Legal Origin is a dummy variable that takes on the value one for countries with French Civil law tradition, and zero otherwise. Settler Mortality is the log of the annualized deaths per thousand European soldiers in European colonies in the early 19th century. The regressions also include a vector of control variables, X. Latin America and Africa are dummy variables that take the value one if the country is located in Latin America or Sub-Saharan Africa, respectively. Catholic, Muslim, and Other Religion indicate the percentage of the population that follows a particular religion (Catholic, Muslim, or religions other than Catholic, Muslim, or Protestant, respectively). Independence is the percentage of years since 1776 that a country has been independent. Ethnic Fractionalization is the probability that two randomly selected individuals in a country will not speak the same language. Regressions are estimated using Ordinary Least Squares. Robust standard errors are given in parentheses. The symbols *, **, *** indicate significance at the 10%, 5%, and 1% levels, respectively. Detailed variable definitions and sources are given in the data appendix.

	Settler Mortality	French Legal Origin	Latin America	Africa	Catholic	Muslim	Other Religion	Independence	Ethnic Fractionalization	Adjusted-R^2	Obs.
Private Credit	-0.151***	-0.141**								0.480	70
	(0.026)	(0.059)									
	-0.130***	-0.097*	-0.194*	-0.148						0.514	70
	(0.034)	(0.055)	(0.082)	(0.108)							
	-0.157***	-0.054			-0.004	-0.003	-0.002			0.486	70
	(0.028)	(0.074)			(0.003)	(0.002)	(0.003)				
	-0.160***	-0.115						-0.090		0.478	70
	(0.028)	(0.077)						(0.134)			
	-0.148***	-0.144**							-0.024	0.472	70
	(0.028)	(0.059)							(0.073)		
	-0.127***	-0.108	-0.0214*	-0.110				0.029	-0.100	0.505	70
	(0.035)	(0.069)	(0.117)	(0.121)				(0.185)	(0.110)		
Stock Market Development	-0.145***	-0.268***								0.358	70
	(0.038)	(0.085)									
	-0.164***	-0.229***	-0.118	0.028						0.363	70
	(0.061)	(0.079)	(0.123)	(0.181)							

T. Beck et al. / Journal of Financial Economics 70 (2003) 137–181

Property Rights									R²	N
−0.147*** (0.040)	−0.146 (0.090)			0.000 (0.003)					0.380	70
−0.156*** (0.049)	−0.240*** (0.072)				0.001 (0.003)		−0.095 (0.135)		0.353	70
−0.167*** (0.049)	−0.246*** (0.080)					0.005 (0.005)		0.178 (0.150)	0.364	70
−0.161** (0.063)	−0.232*** (0.071)	−0.123 (0.115)	−0.012 (0.190)				0.044 (0.163)	0.098 (0.171)	0.346	70
−0.279*** (0.080)	−0.781*** (0.223)								0.304	69
−0.088 (0.101)	−0.810*** (0.216)	−0.183 (0.274)	−0.786** (0.334)						0.348	69
−0.277*** (0.082)	−0.853*** (0.310)			−0.004 (0.008)	−0.003 (0.008)	−0.008 (0.010)			0.281	69
−0.251*** (0.087)	−0.856*** (0.227)						0.256 (0.371)		0.299	69
−0.232** (0.095)	−0.833*** (0.231)							−0.398 (0.401)	0.307	69
−0.082 (0.110)	−0.816*** (0.216)	−0.197 (0.328)	−0.860** (0.371)				0.091 (0.434)	0.184 (0.480)	0.328	69

proportion of the cross-country variation in stock market development than legal origin. It is difficult to compare the sizes of the coefficients on SETTLER MORTALITY and FRENCH LEGAL ORIGIN because a change in legal origin is obviously large and discrete. Nevertheless, we compare a change in legal origin with a change in SETTLER MORTALITY from the second quintile to the fourth quintile (i.e., a change of 2.1), which is less than a two standard deviation change in SETTLER MORTALITY (2.5). Using, for instance, the coefficients in the last row of the stock market development indicators in Table 4, this implies a change in STOCK MARKET DEVELOPMENT of 0.23 from a legal origin change and 0.34 from the endowment change. The effect of the endowment change is approximately 50% larger.

Turning to the control variables, the regression analyses do not indicate a robust, consistent relationship between the continent dummy variables, the religious composition measures, the length of national independence, nor the level of ethnic diversity, on the one hand, and financial development, on the other hand, when controlling for legal origin and national endowments. The Table 4 regressions—as well those in Tables 2 and 3 —do not demonstrate a significant, robust relation between any of these control variables and any of the measures of financial development when controlling for legal origin and endowments. As emphasized above, French Civil law countries also tend to be predominantly Catholic, much of Latin America adopted the French Civil law tradition, and Sub-Saharan Africa had very high rates of settler mortality. Nevertheless, while a consistent pattern of results emerges for law and endowments, we do not observe a robust set of results on the continent dummies, religious composition variables, independence indicator, or ethnic diversity measure.

4. Robustness test

4.1. Political structure

As a robustness check, we control for political structure. North (1990) argues that once groups gain power, they shape policies and institutions to their own advantages. The work of Finer (1997) and Damaska (1986) further suggests that centralized or otherwise powerful states will be more responsive to and efficient at implementing the interests of the elite than a decentralized or more competitive political system endowed with checks and balances. LLSV (1998) do not control for political structure in their examination of the law and finance view. In a different approach, Rajan and Zingales (2003) argue that financial systems do not develop monotonically over time. This observation is not fully consistent with the law and endowment theories, which are based on time invariant factors. Rajan and Zingales (2003) instead propose a theory of financial development based on controlling interest groups. In our sensitivity analyses, we focus on the political structure view because we encounter data limitations concerning interest groups for our broad cross-section of countries.

T. Beck et al. / Journal of Financial Economics 70 (2003) 137–181   163

To assess whether law and endowments continue to explain cross-country differences in financial development after controlling for the structure of the political environment, we use two measures of political openness. LEGISLATIVE COMPETITION is an index of the degree of competitiveness of the last legislative election, ranging from 1 (non-competitive) to 7 (most competitive). CHECKS measures the number of influential veto players in legislative and executive initiatives. These data are from Beck et al. (2001a). The politics and finance view predicts that greater competition and more checks and balances will limit the ability of the elite to dictate policy and institutional development.

To control for the endogenous determination of political structures, we use instrumental variables.[12] As instruments, we include the religious composition variables, independence, and ethnic diversity. We include the religious variables since Landes (1998) and others argue that the Catholic and Muslim religions tend to produce hierarchical political systems. We include independence since more years of independence may permit greater latitude to shape domestic political institutions. We include ethnic diversity since some theories suggest that ethnic diversity will tend to create political systems that stymie competition and permit greater discretion on the part of the controlling party (see, e.g., Alesina et al., 1999). The instrumental variables significantly explain cross-country variation in the political structure indexes at the one-percent significance level. Nevertheless, given the valid skepticism associated with obtaining fully acceptable instrumental variables for political structure, we note that: (i) we present these exploratory results as a robustness check on the endowment and law theories and not as a strong test of the political channel; and, (ii) we are particularly circumspect in interpreting these instrumental variable regressions.

Table 5 instrumental variable results are consistent with the law and endowment theories while controlling for the structure of the political system, and suggest that the politics mechanism is not the only channel through which legal origin and endowments influence financial development. As shown, legal origin and endowments continue to enter the financial development regressions significantly even when controlling for the exogenous component of political structure except for SETTLER MORTALITY in the PROPERTY RIGHTS regressions. The political structure variables do not enter any of the financial development regressions significantly. Thus, there is no evidence in Table 5 that political structure explains cross-country variation in financial development beyond the explanatory power of legal origin and environmental endowments. Furthermore, the results do not suggest that political structure is the only channel through which legal origin and initial endowments influence financial development. If political structure were the only channel through which law and initial endowments influence financial development, we would have found significant coefficients on the political structure indicators and insignificant coefficients on the legal origin and endowment indicators. We find the opposite. Moreover, we run two-stage least squares regressions with financial

---

[12] We find the same results hold when using ordinary least squares and not instrumenting for political structure.

Table 5

Law, endowments, politics, and finance

The regression estimated in is: Financial Sector Development $= \alpha + \beta_1$ French Legal Origin $+ \beta_2$ Settler Mortality $+ \beta_3$. Political Structure, where Financial Sector Development is either Private Credit, Stock Market Development, or Property Rights and Political Structure is either Legislative Competition or Checks. Private Credit is the value of credits by financial intermediaries to the private sector as a share of GDP. Stock Market Development measures the value of shares listed on the stock exchange as a share of GDP. Property Rights reflects the degree to which government enforces laws that protect private property, with higher numbers indicating better enforcement. French Legal Origin is a dummy variable that takes on the value one for countries with French Civil law tradition, and zero otherwise. Settler Mortality is the log of the annualized deaths per thousand European soldiers in European colonies in the early 19th century. Legislative Competition is an indicator of competition in the last legislative election. Checks measures the number of veto-players in the political decision process. These last two measures are averaged over 1990–1995. Detailed variable definitions and sources are given in the data appendix. All regressions are estimated using Instrumental Variables, two-stage least squares. In the first-stage regressions the Political Structure indicators are regressed on Legal Origin, Settler Mortality, Catholic, Muslim, Other Religion, Independence and Ethnic Fractionalization. Robust standard errors are given in parentheses. The symbols *, **, *** indicate significance at the 10%, 5%, and 1% levels, respectively. P-Values are given in parentheses for the test of the over-identifying restrictions (OIR).

	OIR χ^2-test (p-value)	Settler Mortality	French Legal Origin	Legislative Competition	Checks	Adjusted-R^2	Obs.
Private Credit	3.693 (0.449)	−0.169*** (0.051)	−0.123** (0.059)	−0.037 (0.048)		0.429	68
	2.405 (0.662)	−0.184*** (0.044)	−0.160** (0.064)		−0.083 (0.060)	0.317	68
Stock Market Development	1.232 (0.873)	−0.199** (0.090)	−0.215** (0.083)	−0.090 (0.079)		0.224	68
	2.445 (0.655)	−0.177** (0.074)	−0.274** (0.105)		−0.095 (0.086)	0.192	68
Property Rights	3.214 (0.523)	−0.186 (0.154)	−0.858*** (0.223)	0.093 (0.154)		0.348	67
	3.055 (0.549)	−0.177 (0.159)	−0.780*** (0.225)		0.160 (0.243)	0.323	67

development as the dependent variable and political structure as the only explanatory variable in the second stage. The instruments are legal origin and settler mortality. While political structure enters the financial development regression significantly and with the predicted sign, the instruments do not pass the test of over-identifying restrictions. These results do not reject the importance of political factors in shaping finance. Rather, the evidence in this paper suggests that legal origin and endowments influence financial development beyond the structure of the political system.[13]

---

[13] Beck et al. (2003) examine the different channels through which legal origin affects financial development.

T. Beck et al. / Journal of Financial Economics 70 (2003) 137–181 165

4.2. Alternative samples

To assess the robustness of the results, we examine different subsamples of countries. In these robustness checks, we only include two regressions to keep the table to a manageable length. We include one regression with only the legal origin and endowment variables as regressors and a second regression that also includes continent dummy variables, years of independence, and ethnic diversity. We do not include the religious indicators because they do not enter any of the Tables 2–4 regressions significantly at the five percent level.

Table 6 presents regression results on five different sub-samples of countries. Panel A excludes Australia, Canada, New Zealand, and the United States from the regression. After omitting these countries, the data continue to support both the law and endowment views of financial development. The results are fully consistent with the full-sample results in Table 4. FRENCH LEGAL ORIGIN enters all of the STOCK MARKET DEVELOPMENT and PROPERTY RIGHTS regressions significantly, but does not enter the PRIVATE CREDIT regression significantly when controlling for other determinants. SETTLER MORTALITY enters all of the PRIVATE CREDIT and STOCK MARKET DEVELOPMENT regressions significantly, but does not enter significantly in the PROPERTY RIGHTS regression when controlling for AFRICA. In Panels B and C, we examine French legal origin and British legal origin countries separately to test whether settler mortality accounts for cross-country variation in financial development within each group. Again, the results support the view that the disease environment encountered by European settlers shaped the formation of long-lasting financial institutions. The results do suggest, however, that the SETTLER MORTALITY-finance relationship is stronger for the British legal origin sample of countries than for the French legal origin sample. SETTLER MORTALITY enters negatively and significantly in all the regressions in Panel C (British-only legal origin countries), except for the PROPERTY RIGHTS regression in which we include the African dummy variable (which we discuss above). SETTLER MORTALITY is not as robustly related to equity market development and property rights in the French legal origin subsample—it does not enter significantly once we control for AFRICA. Further, SETTLER MORTALITY explains less than half of the cross-country variation in financial development among French Civil law countries than among British Common law countries, as can be seen from comparing the adjusted R^2 statistics in Panels B and C. Finally, we also examine high and low settler mortality countries. Here, we assess whether legal origin explains financial development within the high (above the median) settler mortality countries and within the low (below the median) settler mortality countries. Note there are more countries in Panel E than Panel D because Algeria and Morocco have exactly the median level of SETTLER MORTALITY and are allocated to the below-median group. When we allocate them to the above-median group, or split them between the two groups, we obtain the same results. The results are broadly consistent with earlier findings. FRENCH LEGAL ORIGIN is not strongly associated with financial intermediary development (PRIVATE CREDIT) in the high-mortality countries. Nevertheless, legal

Table 6

Law, endowments, and finance: alternative samples.

The regressions estimated in Panel A are: Financial Sector Development $= \alpha + \beta_1$ French Legal Origin $+ \beta_2$ Settler Mortality $+ \beta_3 X$, where Financial Sector Development is either Private Credit, Stock Market Development, or Property Rights. Private Credit is the value of credits by financial intermediaries to the private sector as a share of GDP. Stock Market Development measures the value of shares listed on the stock exchange as a share of GDP. Property rights reflects the degree to which government enforces laws that protect private property, with higher numbers indicating better enforcement. French Legal Origin is a dummy variable that takes on the value one for countries with French Civil law tradition, and zero otherwise. Settler Mortality is the log of the annualized deaths per thousand European soldiers in European colonies in the early 19th century. The regressions also include a vector of control variables, X. Latin America and Africa are dummy variables that take the value one if the country is located in Latin America or Sub-Saharan Africa, respectively. Independence is the percentage of years since 1776 that a country has been independent. Ethnic Fractionalization is the probability that two randomly selected individuals in a country will not speak the same language. The regressions in Panel A exclude Australia, Canada, New Zealand and the U.S., the regressions in Panels B–C are: Financial Sector Development $= \alpha + \beta_1$ Settler Mortality $+ \beta_2 X$. The regressions in Panel B include only French Legal Origin and in Panel C only British Legal Origin countries. The regressions estimated in Panels D–E are: Financial Sector Development $= \alpha + \beta_1$ French Legal Origin $+ \beta_2 X$. The regressions in Panel D include countries with Settler Mortality above the median and the regressions in Panel E countries with Settler Mortality below the median. There are more countries in Panel E than in Panel D because Algeria and Morocco have exactly the median level of Settler Mortality and are allocated to the below-median group. Regressions are estimated using Ordinary Least Squares. Robust standard errors are given in parentheses. The symbols *, **, *** indicate significance at the 10%, 5%, and 1% levels, respectively. Detailed variable definitions and sources are given in the data appendix.

Panel A: Excluding Australia, Canada, New Zealand, and the United States

	Settler Mortality	French Legal Origin	Latin America	Africa	Independence	Ethnic Fractionalization	Adjusted-R^2	Obs.
Private Credit	−0.129***	−0.102*					0.379	66
	(0.030)	(0.061)						
	−0.127***	−0.031	−0.072	−0.088	−0.216**	−0.063	0.419	66
	(0.041)	(0.064)	(0.095)	(0.114)	(0.100)	(0.100)		
Stock Market Development	−0.161***	−0.291***					0.342	66
	(0.051)	(0.106)						
	−0.180**	−0.281***	−0.212	−0.009	0.147	0.046	0.342	66
	(0.069)	(0.100)	(0.158)	(0.192)	(0.212)	(0.166)		
Property Rights	−0.200**	−0.654***					0.173	65
	(0.084)	(0.233)						
	−0.025	−0.571**	0.243	−0.832**	−0.517	0.380	0.238	65
	(0.101)	(0.230)	(0.369)	(0.323)	(0.484)	(0.478)		

T. Beck et al. / Journal of Financial Economics 70 (2003) 137–181   167

Panel B: French Legal Origin countries

	Settler Mortality	Latin America	Africa	Independence	Ethnic Fractionalization	Adjusted-R^2	Obs.
Private Credit	-0.080*** (0.029)					0.217	45
	-0.066** (0.029)	-0.044 (0.088)	-0.161* (0.086)	-0.243** (0.095)	-0.082 (0.086)	0.390	45
Stock Market Development	-0.037** (0.016)					0.057	45
	-0.018 (0.024)	0.023 (0.059)	0.001 (0.065)	0.034 (0.077)	-0.054 (0.065)	0.018	45
Property Rights	-0.204* (0.112)					0.047	44
	0.015 (0.120)	-0.073 (0.269)	-0.957** (0.392)	-0.141 (0.389)	0.352 (0.509)	0.087	44

Panel C: British legal origin countries

	Settler Mortality	Latin America	Africa	Independence	Ethnic Fractionalization	Adjusted-R^2	Obs.
Private Credit	-0.204*** (0.042)					0.532	25
	-0.158** (0.066)	-0.074 (0.217)	0.017 (0.261)	0.561 (0.444)	-0.136 (0.387)	0.526	25
Stock Market Development	-0.227*** (0.064)					0.330	25
	-0.313** (0.113)	-0.176 (0.313)	0.007 (0.478)	-0.547 (0.573)	0.477 (0.687)	0.329	25
Property Rights	-0.335*** (0.108)					0.205	25
	-0.086 (0.193)	0.226 (0.909)	-0.816 (0.750)	1.339 (0.870)	0.131 (1.471)	0.184	25

Table 6 (continued)

Panel D: Countries above median for settler mortality

	French Legal Origin	Latin America	Africa	Independence	Ethnic Fractionalization	Adjusted-R^2	Obs.
Private Credit	-0.039 (0.060)					-0.014	34
	0.025 (0.040)	-0.055 (0.046)	0.331*** (0.024)	-0.356*** (0.082)	-0.040 (0.083)	0.538	34
Stock Market Development	-0.082** (0.037)					0.178	34
	-0.062** (0.027)	-0.078 (0.047)	-0.152*** (0.013)	-0.136 (0.097)	-0.050 (0.057)	0.342	34
Property Rights	-1.036*** (0.327)					0.249	33
	-0.654** (0.309)	0.374 (0.535)	-0.783*** (0.181)	-2.458*** (0.740)	0.346 (0.723)	0.400	33

Panel E: Countries below median for settler mortality

	French Legal Origin	Latin America	Africa	Independence	Ethnic Fractionalization	Adjusted-R^2	Obs.
Private Credit	-0.414*** (0.128)					0.297	36
	-0.303** (0.142)	-0.305* (0.170)	-0.012 (0.235)	0.197 (0.285)	-0.150 (0.294)	0.314	36
Stock Market Development	-0.611*** (0.190)					0.313	36
	-0.613*** (0.217)	-0.001 (0.255)	0.290 (0.399)	0.011 (0.290)	0.037 (0.429)	0.255	36
Property Rights	-0.870** (0.324)					0.194	36
	-0.824** (0.318)	-0.569* (0.284)	-1.424*** (0.473)	0.968** (0.420)	-0.120 (0.775)	0.358	36

T. Beck et al. / Journal of Financial Economics 70 (2003) 137–181 169

origin is strongly and negatively associated with STOCK MARKET DEVELOP-
MENT and PROPERTY RIGHTS in both subsamples and PRIVATE CREDIT in
the low-mortality sample. While one notes some differences when looking across
different subsamples, the same basic pattern emerges as in the full sample: law and
endowments explain financial development, though the endowment-intermediary
(PRIVATE CREDIT) relationship is more robust than the law-intermediary
(PRIVATE CREDIT) relationship.

4.3. Alternative indicators of financial development

Next, we examine alternative measures of financial development. Specifically,
instead of examining financial intermediary credit to the private sector (PRIVATE
CREDIT), we use the demand and interest-bearing liabilities of financial
intermediaries (LIQUID LIABILITIES). Also, instead of using market capitalization to measure stock market development, we examine the total value of stock
transactions in the economy as a share of GDP (TOTAL VALUE TRADED).
Finally, instead of utilizing the private property rights protection index as used by
LLSV (1999), we examine: (a) the International Country Risk Guide (ICRG)
measure of the degree to which a country adheres to the rule of law (RULE OF
LAW); and, (b) the Kaufmann et al. (1999) AGGREGATE RULE OF LAW index.
However, the RULE OF LAW and AGGREGATE RULE OF LAW indicators are
available for fewer countries, 63 and 68, respectively, than the PROPERTY
RIGHTS measure used throughout the paper thus far.

Table 7 indicates that these alternative indicators produce results that are
consistent with those discussed above. Settler mortality is significantly, negatively
associated with the new measures of financial intermediary development, stock
market development, and property rights protection. Although the RULE OF
LAW–SETTLER MORTALITY relationship weakens when including continent
dummy variables, years of independence, and ethnic diversity, the AGGREGATE
RULE OF LAW–SETTLER MORTALITY relationship remains significant when
controlling for these country traits. Since SETTLER MORTALITY loses its
significant relationship with two of our three measures of private property rights
protection, only when including a dummy variable for AFRICA (where settler
mortality rates were very high), we interpret these findings as broadly consistent with
the view that the initial endowments in the various colonies helped shape
institutional approaches to the protection of private property rights.

FRENCH LEGAL ORIGIN is negatively associated with all the alternative
financial development indicators except financial intermediary development. As
noted above, the relationship between law and financial intermediary development is
more fragile than the endowment–intermediary relationship. Unlike in the
PROPERTY RIGHTS regressions of Tables 2–4, SETTLER MORTALITY
explains a larger share of the variation in the RULE OF LAW and AGGREGATE
RULE OF LAW regressions than FRENCH LEGAL ORIGIN. As discussed in
Section 3.3, we draw this conclusion by comparing adjusted-R^2 statistics across
regressions with only legal origin, with only SETTLER MORTALITY, and then

Table 7

Law, endowments, and finance alternative finance indicators.

The regression estimated is: Financial Sector Development $= \alpha + \beta_1$ French Legal Origin $+ \beta_2$ Settler Mortality $+ \beta_3 X$, where Financial Sector Development is either Liquid Liabilities, Total Value Traded, Rule of Law, or Aggregate Rule of Law. Liquid Liabilities is currency plus demand and interest-bearing liabilities of banks and nonbank financial intermediaries, divided by GDP. Total value traded is the total value of shares traded as a share of GDP. Rule of law (ICRG) accounts for the degree to which a country adheres to the rule of law. Aggregate Rule of Law is an aggregate indicator estimated with an unobserved-components model using a large number of individual indicators from different sources (Kaufmann et al., 1999). French Legal Origin is a dummy variable that takes on the value one for countries with French Civil law tradition, and zero otherwise. Settler Mortality is the log of the annualized deaths per thousand European soldiers in European colonies in the early 19th century. The regressions also include a vector of control variables, X. Latin America and Africa are dummy variables that take the value one if the country is located in Latin America or Sub-Saharan Africa, respectively. Independence is the percentage of years since 1776 that a country has been independent. Ethnic Fractionalization is the probability that two randomly selected individuals in a country will not speak the same language. Regressions are estimated using Ordinary Least Squares. Robust standard errors are given in parentheses. The symbols *, **, *** indicate significance at the 10%, 5%, and 1% levels, respectively. Detailed variable definitions and sources are given in the data appendix.

	Settler Mortality	French Legal Origin	Latin America	Africa	Independence	Ethnic Fractionalization	Adjusted-R^2	Obs.
Liquid Liabilities	-0.150*** (0.02958)	-0.073 (0.05731)					0.433	70
	-0.148*** (0.034)	0.054 (0.058)	-0.085 (0.079)	-0.210** (0.083)	-0.439*** (0.117)	-0.015 (0.107)	0.604	70
Total Value Traded	-0.058*** (0.018)	-0.105** (0.041)					0.274	70
	-0.043** (0.020)	-0.081*** (0.030)	-0.129** (0.050)	-0.109 (0.074)	0.035 (0.070)	0.049 (0.087)	0.292	70
Rule of Law	-0.285** (0.133)	-0.553* (0.314)					0.141	63
	0.041 (0.180)	-0.668** (0.334)	-1.246*** (0.448)	-0.764 (0.592)	0.881 (0.555)	-1.109* (0.625)	0.238	63
Aggregate Rule of Law	-0.362*** (0.076)	-0.395* (0.190)					0.349	68
	-0.292** (0.129)	-0.373* (0.216)	-0.494* (0.262)	-0.169 (0.407)	0.187 (0.303)	-0.441 (0.355)	0.348	68

T. Beck et al. / Journal of Financial Economics 70 (2003) 137–181 171

with SETTLER MORTALITY and legal origin dummies included simultaneously. The regressions with only SETTLER MORTALITY and only the legal origin dummy variable for this sample of countries are not reported.

4.4. Alternative endowment indicator

Next, we use an alternative measure of endowments, LATITUDE, which equals the absolute value of the latitude of each country normalized to lie between zero and one. We take the data from LLSV (1999). Countries that are closer to the equator will tend to have a more tropical climate that is inhospitable to European settlers and therefore will more likely foster extractive institutions.[14] However, LATITUDE is not as precise an indicator of the conditions facing European settlers as SETTLER MORTALITY and thus LATITUDE is not as precise an empirical proxy for the AJR (2001) endowment theory as SETTLER MORTALITY. LATITUDE directly measures geographic location, not climatic conditions. Accordingly, we have focused our analyses on SETTLER MORTALITY, and only include LATITUDE in our robustness checks.

Table 8 regressions with LATITUDE indicate, albeit less robustly than those with SETTLER MORTALITY, that countries closer to the equator have lower levels of financial development than countries in more temperate climates. LATITUDE is positively associated with PROPERTY RIGHTS after using the array of control variables discussed above. LATITUDE is also significantly and positively linked with PRIVATE CREDIT in all of the regressions that do not include AFRICA, which is very highly correlated with LATITUDE. There is not a strong link between LATITUDE and stock market development. Using LATITUDE, we do find a strong link between legal origin and financial development. FRENCH LEGAL ORIGIN enters significantly in all regressions and its inclusion substantially increases the adjusted R^2 over those regressions that only include LATITUDE. Especially given the imprecise nature of LATITUDE as proxy for the AJR (2001) endowment theory, we view Table 8 as confirmation of our earlier findings.

4.5. Tobit estimation

Finally, we estimate the stock market development equations using a Tobit estimator. Both STOCK MARKET DEVELOPMENT (market capitalization divided by GDP) and TOTAL VALUE TRADED (stock market trading divided by GDP) have many countries with zero values. Thus, we re-estimate the equation using a Tobit estimator. As shown in Table 9, we find that both legal origin and endowments enter significantly in all of the regressions when using the Tobit estimator, confirming earlier results.

---

[14] While some authors stress the direct impact of tropical environments on production (Kamarck, 1976; Crosby, 1989; and Gallup et al., 1998), AJR (2002) and Easterly and Levine (2003) show that the environment tends to influence economic development primarily through its impact on institutions.

172   T. Beck et al. / Journal of Financial Economics 70 (2003) 137–181

Table 8
Law, endowments, and finance: alternative endowment indicator

The regression estimated in Panel A is: Financial Sector Development $= \alpha + \beta_1$ Latitude $+ \beta_3 X$, where Financial Sector Development is either Private Credit, Stock Market Development, or Property Rights. Private Credit is the value of credits by financial intermediaries to the private sector as a share of GDP. Stock Market Development measures the value of shares listed on the stock exchange as a share of GDP. Property Rights reflects the degree to which government enforces laws that protect private property, with higher numbers indicating better enforcement. Latitude is the absolute value of the latitude of a country, scaled between zero and one. The regressions also include a vector of control variables, X. Latin America and Africa are dummy variables that take the value one if the country is located in Latin America or Sub-Saharan Africa, respectively. Independence is the percentage of years since 1776 that a country has been independent. Ethnic Fractionalization is the probability that two randomly selected individuals in a country will not speak the same language. The regression estimated in Panel B is: Financial Sector Development $= \alpha + \beta_1$ French Legal Origin $+ \beta_2$ Latitude $+ \beta_3 X$. French Legal Origin is a dummy variable that takes on the value one for countries with French Civil law tradition, and zero otherwise. Regressions are estimated using Ordinary Least Squares. Robust standard errors are given in parentheses. The symbols *, **, *** indicate significance at the 10%, 5%, and 1% levels, respectively. Detailed variable definitions and sources are given in the data appendix.

Panel A: Latitude and finance

	Latitude	Latin America	Africa	Independence	Ethnic Fractionalization	Adjusted-R^2	Obs.
Private Credit	1.048***					0.189	70
	(0.300)						
	0.423	-0.319**	-0.380***	0.034	-0.018	0.346	70
	(0.327)	(0.147)	(0.125)	(0.168)	(0.135)		
Stock Market Development	0.491					0.012	70
	(0.386)						
	-0.171	-0.402**	-0.470*	0.085	0.121	0.120	70
	(0.680)	(0.198)	(0.244)	(0.126)	(0.198)		
Property Rights	3.232***					0.165	69
	(0.784)						
	2.600***	-0.040	-1.122***	-0.569	0.708	0.267	69
	(0.952)	(0.429)	(0.339)	(0.474)	(0.462)		

T. Beck et al. / Journal of Financial Economics 70 (2003) 137–181   173

Panel B: Latitude, law and finance

	Latitude	French Legal Origin	Latin America	Africa	Independence	Ethnic Fractionalization	Adjusted-R^2	Obs.
Private Credit	0.970***	−0.206***					0.286	70
	(0.276)	(0.079)						
	0.381	−0.162**	−0.288**	−0.312**	0.122	−0.055	0.392	70
	(0.301)	(0.078)	(0.127)	(0.122)	(0.171)	(0.141)		
Stock Market Development	0.360	−0.346***					0.175	70
	(0.355)	(0.122)						
	−0.251	−0.312***	−0.341=	−0.339	0.256**	0.051	0.229	70
	(0.613)	(0.104)	(0.179)	(0.134)	(0.127)	(0.173)		
Property Rights	2.924***	−0.873***					0.335	69
	(0.659)	(0.224)						
	2.398***	−0.821***	0.120	−0.783**	−0.120	0.517	0.392	69
	(0.843)	(0.201)	(0.341)	(0.308)	(0.353)	(0.453)		

Table 9
Law, endowments, and stock market development: Tobit regressions

The regression estimated is: Financial Sector Development $= \alpha + \beta_1$ French Legal Origin $+ \beta_2$ Settler Mortality $+ \beta_3 X$, where Financial Sector Development is either Stock Market Development or Total Value Traded. Stock Market Development measures the value of shares listed on the stock exchange as a share of GDP. Total value traded is the total value of shares traded as a share of GDP. French Legal Origin is a dummy variable mat takes on the value one for countries with French Civil law tradition, and zero otherwise. Settler Mortality is the log of the annualized deaths per thousand European soldiers in European colonies in the early 19th century. The regressions also include a vector of control variables, X. Latin America and Africa are dummy variables that take the value one if the country is located in Latin America or Sub-Saharan Africa, respectively. Independence is the percentage of years since 1776 that a country has been independent. Ethnic Fractionalization is the probability that two randomly selected individuals in a country will not speak the same language. Regressions are estimated using Tobit, censored-normal. Standard errors are given in parentheses. The symbols *, **, *** indicate significance at the 10%, 5%, and 1% levels, respectively. Detailed variable definitions and sources are given in the data appendix.

	Settler Mortality	French Legal Origin	Latin America	Africa	Independence	Ethnic Fractionalization	Adjusted-R^2	Obs.
Stock Market Development	-0.269*** (0.051)	-0.353*** (0.116)					0.337	70
	-0.207*** (0.069)	-0.413*** (0.140)	-0.087 (0.177)	-0.347 (0.234)	0.246 (0.244)	0.342 (0.291)	0.329	70
Total Value Traded	-0.117*** (0.024)	-0.144*** (0.055)					0.792	70
	-0.059* (0.031)	-0.170*** (0.064)	-0.121 (0.080)	-0.301*** (0.108)	0.142 (0.111)	0.176 (0.134)	1.014	70

T. Beck et al. / Journal of Financial Economics 70 (2003) 137–181 175

5. Conclusions

This paper assesses two theories regarding the historical determinants of financial development. The *law and finance theory* predicts that historically determined differences in legal origin can explain cross-country differences in financial development observed today. Specifically, the law and finance theory predicts that countries that inherited the British Common law tradition obtained a legal tradition that tends to both emphasize private property rights and support financial development to a much greater degree than countries that obtained the French Civil law tradition. The *endowment theory*, on the other hand, predicts that the initial environmental endowments encountered by European colonizers shaped the types of long-lasting institutions created by those colonizers. Specifically, hospitable endowments favored the construction of settler colonies, where Europeans established secure property rights. In contrast, colonies with high settler mortality rates fostered the construction of extractive colonies, where Europeans established institutions that facilitated state control and resource extraction. According to the endowment theory, the long-lasting institutions created by colonizers continue to influence financial development today.

Although both the law and endowment theories stress the importance of how initial conditions influence institutions today, there are crucial differences. The law and finance theory focuses on the legal tradition spread by the colonizer. Thus, the identity of the colonizer is key. The endowment theory focuses on how the colony's endowments shaped the construction of long-lasting institutions. Thus, the endowment theory focuses on the conditions of the colony, not the identity of the colonizer.

The paper provides qualified support for the law and finance theory (Hayek, 1960; LLSV, 1998). One important qualification is that the connection between legal origin and financial intermediary development is not robust to controlling for endowments and other country characteristics. Legal origin, however, explains cross-country differences in private property rights protection even after controlling for initial endowment indicators, religious composition, ethnic diversity, and the fraction of years the country has been independent since 1776. Furthermore, except when controlling for religious composition (there is a strong correlation between French legal heritage and the Catholic religion), there is a robust link between legal origin and stock market development—French Civil law countries have significantly lower levels of stock market development than British Common law countries after controlling for other country characteristics.

The data provide strong support for the endowment view. Countries with poor geographical endowments, as measured by the log of settler mortality, tend to have less developed financial intermediaries, less developed stock markets, and weaker property rights protection. These results hold after controlling for legal origin, the percentage of years since 1776 the country has been independent, the religious composition of the country, and the degree of ethnic diversity. In terms of comparing the law and endowment theories, the empirical results indicate that both the legal systems brought by colonizers and the initial endowments in the colonies are important determinants of stock market development and private property rights protection. However, initial endowments are more robustly associated with financial intermediary development than legal origin. Moreover, initial endowments explain more of the cross-country variation in financial intermediary and stock market development than legal origin. In sum, and consistent with AJR's (2001) endowment theory, we find a robust link between initial endowments and current levels of financial development.

Appendix A

Table 10
The financial development and institutions across countries are presented in Table 10. In Table 11 a description of the variables is presented. Financial development and institutions across countries

Country name	Country code	Private credit	Stock market development	Property rights	Legal origin	Settler mortality	Legislative competition	Checks
Algeria	DZA	0.19	0.00	3	F	78.2	3.50	1.00
Angola	AGO	0.03	0.00	2	F	280	4.83	2.00
Argentina	ARG	0.15	0.10	4	F	68.9	7.00	4.00
Australia	AUS	0.81	0.54	5	B	8.55	7.00	4.33
Bahamas	BHS	0.55	0.00	5	B	85	7.00	4.00
Bangladesh	BGD	0.21	0.02	2	B	71.41	6.67	3.17
Barbados	BRB	0.39	0.21	3	B	85	6.67	3.67
Bolivia	BOL	0.34	0.01	3	F	71	7.00	5.33
Brazil	BRA	0.27	0.16	3	F	71	7.00	4.17
Burkina Faso	BFA	0.12	0.00	3	F	280	4.00	1.00
Cameroon	CMR	0.18	0.00	2	F	280	5.75	2.00
Canada	CAN	0.80	0.51	5	B	16.1	7.00	4.00
Central African Republic	CAF	0.06	0.00		F	280	5.17	1.67
Chad	TCD	0.08	0.00	2	F	280	2.50	1.00
Chile	CHL	0.54	0.79	5	F	68.9	7.00	4.00
Colombia	COL	0.30	0.12	3	F	71	7.00	2.00
Congo	COG	0.13	0.00	2	F	240	5.00	2.00
Costa Rica	CRI	0.15	0.06	3	F	78.1	7.00	2.33
Cote d'Ivoire	CIV	0.31	0.05	2	F	668	5.67	1.83
Dominican Republic	DOM	0.22	0.00	2	F	130	7.00	5.00
Ecuador	ECU	0.18	0.10	3	F	71	7.00	3.67
Egypt	EGY	0.28	0.07	3	F	67.8	6.00	2.00
El Salvador	SLV	0.23	0.06	3	F	78.1	7.00	3.33
Ethiopia	ETH	0.19	0.00	2	F	26	2.67	1.00
Gabon	GAB	0.11	0.00	3	F	280	6.50	1.67
Gambia	GMB	0.11	0.00	4	B	1470	5.50	2.67
Ghana	GHA	0.05	0.12	3	B	668	3.00	2.00
Guatemala	GTM	0.13	0.01	3	F	71	7.00	3.17
Guinea	GIN	0.09	0.00	2	F	483	1.00	1.00
Guyana	GUY	0.20	0.00	3	B	32.18	6.50	1.50

T. Beck et al. / Journal of Financial Economics 70 (2003) 137–181   177

Table 10 (*continued*)

Country name	Country code	Private credit	Stock market development	Property rights	Legal origin	Settler mortality	Legislative competition	Checks
Haiti	HTI	0.12	0.00	1	F	130	6.00	1.83
Honduras	HND	0.26	0.05	3	F	78.1	7.00	2.00
Hong Kong	HKG	1.36	1.79	5	B	14.9	N/A	N/A
India	IND	0.24	0.27	3	B	48.63	7.00	5.83
Indonesia	IDN	0.44	0.14	3	F	170	6.00	1.00
Jamaica	JAM	0.21	0.42	4	B	130	6.67	3.67
Kenya	KEN	0.31	0.15	3	B	145	5.50	2.00
Madagascar	MDG	0.14	0.00	3	F	536.04	6.33	2.83
Malaysia	MYS	0.93	1.89	4	B	17.7	7.00	6.00
Mali	MLI	0.12	0.00	3	F	2940	5.00	2.00
Malta	MLT	0.84	0.12	3	F	16.3	7.00	3.00
Mauritania	MRT	0.37	0.00	2	F	280	3.50	2.50
Mauritius	MUS	0.37	0.22	2	F	30.5	7.00	5.00
Mexico	MEX	0.27	0.32	3	F	71	6.83	2.00
Morocco	MAR	0.34	0.08	4	F	78.2	7.00	1.00
New Zealand	NZL	0.81	0.40	5	B	8.55	7.00	2.83
Nicaragua	NIC	0.25	0.00	2	F	163.3	7.00	2.25
Niger	NER	0.11	0.00	3	F	400	3.67	1.67
Nigeria	NGA	0.22	0.05	3	B	2004	1.00	1.00
Pakistan	PAK	0.23	0.16	4	B	36.99	7.00	5.50
Panama	PAN	0.50	0.07	3	F	163.3	7.00	3.17
Paraguay	PRY	0.20	0.01	3	F	78.1	7.00	3.00
Peru	PER	0.08	0.08	3	F	71	7.00	3.67
Rwanda	RWA	0.07	0.00	1	F	280	4.17	1.00
Senegal	SEN	0.24	0.00	4	F	164.66	6.50	2.00
Sierra Leone	SLE	0.03	0.00	2	B	483	2.67	1.00
Singapore	SGP	0.96	1.33	5	B	17.7	6.00	2.00
South Africa	ZAF	0.94	1.56	3	B	15.5	7.00	2.00
Sri Lanka	LKA	0.20	0.17	3	B	69.8	7.00	3.17
Sudan	SDN	0.05	0.00	2	B	88.2	N/A	N/A
Surinam	SUR	0.41	0.00	3	F	32.18	7.00	4.33
Tanzania	TZA	0.05	0.00	3	B	145	4.50	1.00
Togo	TGO	0.24	0.00	3	F	668	4.33	1.50
Trinidad and Tobago	TTO	0.48	0.12	5	B	85	6.67	3.67
Tunisia	TUN	0.58	0.08	3	F	63	5.17	1.00
Uganda	UGA	0.03	0.00	4	B	280	4.00	1.00
Uruguay	URY	0.23	0.01	4	F	71	7.00	4.00
USA	USA	1.48	0.69	5	B	15	7.00	4.67
Venezuela	VEN	0.19	0.12	3	F	78.1	7.00	4.67
Zaire	ZAR	0.00	0.00	2	F	240	2.83	1.00

178 *T. Beck et al. / Journal of Financial Economics 70 (2003) 137–181*

Table 11
Variable descriptions and sources

Variable	Description	Sources
Private Credit	$\{(0.5)^*[F(t)/P\ e(t) + F(t-1)/P\ e(t-1)]\}/[GDP(t)/P\ a(t)]$, where F is credit by deposit money banks and other financial institutions to the private sector (lines 22d and 42d in International Financial Statistics, IFS), GDP is line 99b, $P\ e$ is end-of-period CPI (line 64), and $P\ a$ is the average CPI for the year. Average for 1990–1995. Data for Angola, Guinea, and Tanzania are calculated using data from IFS and World Development Indicators (WDI); for Angola, IFS data for 1996–1998 are used and GDP data are from WDI; for Guinea, GDP data from WDI are used and given the lack of CPI indicators, the ratio of line 22d plus 42d divided by GDP is calculated.	Beck et al. (2001b), IFS, IFC, and own calculations
Stock Market Development	$\{(0.5)^*[F(t)/P\ e(t) + F(t-1)/P\ e(t-1)]\}/[GDP(t)/P\ a(t)]$, where F is the total value of outstanding shares, GDP is line 99b (IFS), $P\ e$ is end-of, period CPI (line 64, IFS) and $P\ a$ is the average CPI for the year. Average for 1990–1995. For Guatemala and El Salvador, IFC data from 1996 and 1997 are used to calculate the variables. For Malta, data for 1994 and 1995 are taken from the stock exchange's web-page. For all countries that do not have stock markets or that introduced stock markets after 1995, a zero was entered. Also, for Nicaragua, a zero was entered since no data is found, the exchange was founded in 1993, and it is reported to be very small.	Beck et al. (2001b), IFC, IFS, WDI and own calculations
Property Rights	An index of the degree to which government protects and enforces laws that protect private property. Measured in 1997 and ranges from 1 to 5.	La Porta et al. (1999), Heritage Foundation
Liquid Liabilities	$\{(0.5)^*[F(t)/P\ e(t) + F(t-1)/P\ e(t-1)]\}/[GDP(t)/P\ a(t)]$, where F is currency plus demand and interest-bearing liabilities of banks and nonbank financial intermediaries (line 55l in IFS), GDP is line 99b, $P\ e$ is end-of period CPI (line 64) and $P\ a$ is the average CPI for the year. Average for 1990–1995. Data for Angola, Guinea, and Tanzania are calculated using data from IFS and World Development Indicators (WDI); for Angola, IFS data for 1996–1998 are used and GDP data are from WDI; for Guinea, GDP data from WDI are used and given the lack of CPI indicators, the ratio of line 55l divided by GDP is calculated	
Total Value Traded	The total value of shares traded as a ratio of GDP. Average for 1990–1995. For Guatemala and El Salvador IFC data from 1996 and 1997 are used to calculate the variable. For Malta, data for 1994 and 1995 are taken from the stock exchange's web-page. For all countries that do not have stock markets or that introduced stock markets after 1995, a	Beck et al. (2001b), IFC, IFS and own calculations

T. Beck et al. / Journal of Financial Economics 70 (2003) 137–181 179

Table 11 (*continued*)

Variable	Description	Sources
	zero was entered. Also, for Nicaragua, a zero is entered, since no data is found, the exchange was founded in 1993, and it is reported to be very small.	
Rule of Law	An indicator of the degree to which the country adheres to the rule of law (ranging from 0 to 6). Average for 1990–1995.	International Country Risk Guide (ICRG)
Aggregate Rule of Law	An indicator of the strength and impartiality of the legal system. An aggregate indicator that is estimated with an unobserved-component model from individual indicators of the efficiency of the legal system from 11 sources. Measured in 1998.	Kaufmann et al. (1999)
French Legal Origin	Dummy variable that takes on value one if a country legal system is of French Civil law origin.	La Porta et al. (1999)
Settler Mortality	Log of the annualized deaths per thousand European soldiers in European colonies in the early 19th century.	Acemoglu et al. (2001)
Latitude	Absolute value of the latitude of a country, scaled between zero and one.	La Porta et al. (1999)
Africa	Dummy variable that takes on value one if country is in Sub-Saharan Africa.	Easterly and Levine (1997)
Latin America	Dummy variable that takes on value one if country is in Latin America.	Easterly and Levine (1997)
Catholic	Percentage of population that follows Catholic religion, in 1980. Ranges from 0 to 100.	La Porta et al. (1999)
Muslim	Percentage of population that follows Muslim religion, in 1980. Ranges from 0 to 100.	La Porta et al. (1999)
Other Religion	Percentage of population that follows religion other than Catholic, Muslim, or Protestant, in 1980. Ranges from 0 to 100.	La Porta et al. (1999)
Independence	Percentage of years since 1776 that a country has been independent.	Easterly and Levine (1997)
Ethnic Fractionalization	Probability that two randomly selected individuals in a country will not speak the same language.	Easterly and Levine (1997)
Legislative Competition	Index of the number of parties competing in the last legislative election, ranging from 1 (non-competitive) to 7 (competitive). Average for 1990–1995.	Beck et al. (2001b)
Checks	Measure of the number of veto-players in the political decision-making process, both in the executive and the legislature. Average for 1990–1995.	Beck et al. (2001b)

180   *T. Beck et al. / Journal of Financial Economics 70 (2003) 137–181*

References

Acemoglu, D., Johnson, S., Robinson, J.A., 2001. The colonial origins of comparative development: an empirical investigation. American Economic Review 91, 1369–1401.

Acemoglu, D., Johnson, S., Robinson, J.A., 2002. Reversal of fortunes: geography and institutions in the making of the modern world income distribution. Quarterly Journal of Economics 117, 1231–1294.

Alesina, A., Baqir, R., Easterly, W., 1999. Public goods and ethic divisions. Quarterly Journal of Economics 114, 1243–1284.

Beck, T., Levine, R., 2002. Industry growth and capital allocation: does having a market- or bank-based system matter? Journal of Financial Economics 64, 147–180.

Beck, T., Levine, R., 2003. Stockmarkets, banks, and growth: panel evidence. Journal of Banking and Finance, forthcoming.

Beck, T., Levine, R., Loayza, N., 2000. Finance and the sources of growth. Journal of Financial Economics 58, 261–300.

Beck, T., Clarke, G., Groff, A., Keefer, P., Walsh, P., 2001a. New tools and new tests in comparative political economy: the database of political institutions. World Bank Economic Review 15, 165–176.

Beck, T., Demirgüç-Kunt, A., Levine, R., 2001b. The financial structure database. In: Demirguc-Kunt, A., Levine, R. (Eds.), Financial Structure and Economic Growth: A Cross-Country Comparison of Banks, Markets, and Development. MIT Press, Cambridge, MA, pp. 17–80.

Beck, T., Demirgüç-Kunt, A., Levine, R., 2003. Law and finance. Why does legal origin matter? Journal of Comparative Economics, forthcoming.

Coke, E., 1628. [1979 version]. The First Part of the Institutes of the Laws of England. Garland Publishing, Inc., New York, NY.

Coffee, J., 2000. Privatization and corporate governance: the lessons from the securities market failure. Unpublished working paper 158, Columbia Law School, New York.

Crosby, A.W., 1989. Ecological Imperialism: The Biological Expansion of Europe, 900–1900. Cambridge University Press, Cambridge.

Curtin, P.D., 1964. The Image of Africa. University of Wisconsin Press, Madison, WI.

Curtin, P.D., 1989. Death by Migration: Europe's Encounter with the Tropical World in the Nineteenth Century. Cambridge University Press, New York, NY.

Curtin, P.D., 1998. Disease and Empire: The Health of European Troops in the Conquest of Africa. Cambridge University Press, New York, NY.

Damaska, M.R., 1986. The Faces of Justice and State Authority: A Comparative Approach to the Legal Process. Yale University Press, New Haven, CT.

Dawson, J.P., 1968. The Oracles of the Law. University of Michigan Law School, Ann Arbor, MI (Reprinted in 1986 by William S. Hein & Co., Inc., Buffalo, New York).

Demirgüç-Kunt, A., Detragiache, E., 2002. Does deposit insurance increase banking system stability? An empirical investigation. Journal of Monetary Economics 49, 1373–1406.

Demirgüç-Kunt, A., Maksimovic, V., 1998. Law, finance, and firm growth. Journal of Finance 53, 2107–2137.

Easterly, W., Levine, R., 1997. Africa's growth tragedy: policies and ethnic divisions. Quarterly Journal of Economics 112, 1203–1250.

Easterly, W., Levine, R., 2003. Tropics, germs, and crops: how endowments influence economic development. Journal of Monetary Economics 50, 3–40.

Easterly, W., Islam, R., Stiglitz, J., 2000. Shaken and stirred: explaining growth volatility. World Bank Conference on Development Economics.

Engerman, S., Sokoloff, K., 1997. Factor endowments, institutions, and differential paths of growth among new world economies. In: Haber, S.H. (Ed.), How Latin America Fell Behind. Stanford University Press, Stanford, CA, pp. 260–304.

Engerman, S., Mariscal, E., Sokoloff, K., 1998. Schooling, suffrage, and the persistence of inequality in the Americas, 1800–1945. Unpublished working paper, Department of Economics, UCLA.

Finer, S., 1997. The History of Government, Vols. I–III. Cambridge University Press, Cambridge, UK.

Franks, J., Sussman, O., 1999. Financial innovations and corporate insolvency. Unpublished working paper, London Business School.

Gallup, J.L., Sachs, J.D., Mellinger, A.D., 1998. Geography and economic development. National Bureau of Economic Research Working Paper No. 6849.

Glaeser, E., Shleifer, A., 2002. Legal origins. Quarterly Journal of Economics 117, 1193–1230.

Glendon, M.A., Gordon, M.W., Osakwe, C., 1982. Comparative Legal Tradition in a Nutshell. Wes Publishing Co., St. Paul, MN.

Gutierrez, H., 1986. La mortalite des eveques latino-americains aux XVIIe et XVII siecles. Annales de Demographie Historique 29–39.

Hayek, F., 1960. The Constitution of Liberty. The University of Chicago Press, Chicago, IL.

Kamarck, A., 1976. The Tropics and Economic Development: A Provocative Inquiry into the Poverty of Nations. The Johns Hopkins University Press, Baltimore, MD.

Kaufmann, D., Kraay, A., Zoido-Lobatón, P., 1999. Aggregating Governance Indicators. World Bank Research Working Paper 2195.

La Porta, R., Lopez-de-Silanes, F., Shleifer, A., Vishny, R.W., 1997. Legal determinants of external finance. Journal of Finance 52, 1131–1150.

La Porta, R., Lopez-de-Silanes, F., Shleifer, A., Vishny, R.W., 1998. Law and finance. Journal of Political Economy 106, 1113–1155.

La Porta, R., Lopez-de-Silanes, F., Shleifer, A., Vishny, R.W., 1999. The quality of government. Journal of Law, Economics, and Organization 15, 222–279.

La Porta, R., Lopez-de-Silanes, F., Shleifer, A., Vishny, R.W., 2000. Investor protection and corporate governance. Journal of Financial Economics 58, 3–27.

Landes, D., 1998. The Wealth and Poverty of Nations. W.W. Norton, New York, NY.

Levine, R., 1997. Financial development and economic growth: views and agenda. Journal of Economic Literature 35, 688–726.

Levine, R., Zervos, S., 1998. Stock markets, banks, and economic growth. American Economic Review 88, 537–538.

Levine, R., Loayza, N., Beck, T., 2000. Financial intermediation and growth: causality and causes. Journal of Monetary Economics 46, 31–77.

Littleton, T., 1481. [1903 version] In: Wambaugh, E. (Ed.), Littleton's Tenures in English. John Bryne & Co., Washington, D.C.

Mahoney, P., 2001. The common law and economic growth: Hayek might be right. Journal of Legal Studies 30, 503–525.

Merryman, J.H., 1985. The Civil Law Tradition: An Introduction to the Legal Systems of Western Europe and Latin America. Stanford University Press, Stanford, CA.

North, D., 1990. Institutions, Institutional Change, and Economic Performance. Cambridge University Press, Cambridge, UK.

North, D., Weingast, B.R., 1989. Constitutions and commitment: the evolution of institutions governing public choice in seventeenth-century England. Journal of Economic History 49, 803–832.

Pivovarsky, A., 2001. Essays on institutions and finance. Ph.D. Dissertation, John F. Kennedy School, Harvard University.

Putnam, R., 1993. Making Democracy Work: Civic Traditions in Modern Italy. Princeton University Press, Princeton, NJ.

Rajan, R.G., Zingales, L., 1998. Financial dependence and growth. American Economic Review 88, 559–586.

Rajan, R.G., Zingales, L., 2003. The great reversals: the politics of financial development in the 20th century. Journal of Financial Economics 69, 5–50.

Stulz, R., Williamson, R., 2003. Culture, openness, and finance. Journal of Financial Economics, forthcoming.

Wurgler, J., 2000. Financial markets and the allocation of capital. Journal of Financial Economics 58, 187–214.

Young, C., 1994. The African Colonial State in Comparative Perspective. Yale University Press, New Haven, CT.

THE JOURNAL OF FINANCE • VOL. LVIII, NO. 6 • DECEMBER 2003

Financial Development, Property Rights, and Growth

STIJN CLAESSENS and LUC LAEVEN*

ABSTRACT

In countries with more secure property rights, firms might allocate resources better and consequentially grow faster as the returns on different types of assets are more protected against competitors' actions. Using data on sectoral value added for a large number of countries, we find evidence consistent with better property rights leading to higher growth through improved asset allocation. Quantitatively, the growth effect is as large as that of improved access to financing due to greater financial development. Our results are robust using various samples and specifications, including controlling for growth opportunities.

RECENTLY, NUMEROUS PAPERS HAVE ESTABLISHED that financial development fosters growth and that a country's financial development is related to its institutional characteristics, including its legal framework. The financial development and growth literature has established that finance matters for growth both at the macroeconomic and microeconomic level (King and Levine (1993), Levine (1997)). The law and finance literature has found that financial markets are better developed in countries with strong legal frameworks (La Porta et al. (1998), Beck, Demirgüç-Kunt, and Levine (2003)). These well-developed financial markets make it easier for firms to attract financing for their investment needs (Demirgüç-Kunt and Maksimovic (1998), Rajan and Zingales (1998)). Related work has established that debt structures of firms differ across institutional frameworks (Rajan and Zingales (1995), Demirgüç-Kunt and Maksimovic (1999), and Booth et al. (2000)).[1]

*Claessens is from the University of Amsterdam and CEPR and Laeven is from the World Bank. We are grateful to Richard Green (the editor) and an anonymous referee who helped us to substantially improve the paper. We thank Thorsten Beck, Sudipto Dasgupta, Charles Goodhart, Simon Johnson, Ross Levine, Inessa Love, Enrico Perotti, Sheridan Titman, and Chris Woodruff for helpful suggestions, and Ying Lin for excellent research assistance. We received helpful comments from seminar participants at Korea University, Universidad Argentina de la Empresa, London School of Economics, Stockholm School of Economics, University of Amsterdam, the 17th Annual Congress of the European Economic Association in Venice, and the Third Annual Conference on Financial Market Development in Emerging and Transition Economies at Hong Kong University of Science and Technology. We thank Raghu Rajan and Luigi Zingales for the use of their data, Ray Fisman and Inessa Love for providing their data on U.S. sectoral sales growth, and Walter Park for providing his index data on patent rights. The views expressed in this paper are those of the authors and do not necessarily represent those of the World Bank.

[1] In particular, it has been established that firms in developing countries have a smaller fraction of their total debt in the form of long-term debt.

Thus far the literature has not paid much attention to differences across countries in terms of firms' asset structure, that is, to differences in the allocation of investable funds by firms across various types of assets. However, these differences are large as well. Demirgüç-Kunt and Maksimovic (1999) find that firms in developing countries have higher proportions of fixed assets to total assets and less intangible assets than firms in developed countries. This is surprising since the literature on firms' optimal capital structure (Harris and Raviv (1991)) suggests that a lack of long-term financing—typical in a developing country—would make it more difficult to finance fixed assets. Why is it that firms in developing countries have more fixed assets? Is it that they need more fixed collateral to attract external financing? Or does the preference for fixed assets and a corresponding lower share of intangible assets arise in countries with worse property rights because the returns on fixed assets are easier to secure from the firm's point of view than the returns on intangible assets? More generally, what is the role of property rights in terms of affecting investment patterns of firms?

In this paper, we empirically explore the role of property rights in influencing the allocation of investable resources. We start from the well-established proposition that greater financial sector development increases the availability of external resources and thereby enhances firm investment. We also acknowledge the literature demonstrating the importance of a good legal framework and well-established property rights for overall economic growth. In terms of channels through which property rights affect firm growth, we focus on the allocation of investable resources by a firm. At the firm level, our idea of property rights is the degree of protection of the return on assets against powerful competitors. This notion of property rights is different from what is common in the literature where it is typically regarded as the protection of assets against actions by government. By focusing on the asset side of a firm's balance sheet, we instead use the term property rights as referring to the protection of entrepreneurial and other investment in firm assets against actions of other firms. We argue that a firm operating in a market with weaker property rights may be led to invest more in fixed assets relative to intangible assets because it finds it relatively more difficult to secure returns from intangible assets than from fixed assets.

The argument goes as follows. A firm is always at risk of not getting the returns from its assets (tangible or intangible) due to actions by the government, its own employees, or other firms. Since our notion of property rights is protection against powerful competitors, rather than against the government, we assume no risk of expropriation by the government (or equivalently, we assume the risk to be identical for tangible and intangible assets). For the firm's employees and other firms, in particular powerful competitors, it is relatively easy to steal the intangible assets of a firm if property rights are not secure. In a narrow sense, this is because the value of many intangible assets—patents (property rights to inventions and other technical improvements), copyrights (property rights to authors, artists, and composers), and trademarks (property rights for distinctive commercial marks or symbols)—purely derive from the existence of (intellectual) property rights. Without property rights protection, employees can simply walk away with many of a firm's intangible assets and competitors can easily copy them. As such, property rights in a narrow sense are very important for securing returns on intangible assets. In contrast, stealing physical property such as buildings and machinery is more difficult, particularly for competing firms, even when general property rights are not secure. In a broader sense therefore, property rights matter more for securing returns from intangible assets than from tangible assets. It follows that property rights matter more for intangible assets than for tangible assets. More generally, we argue that the degree to which firms allocate resources in an optimal way will depend on the strength of a country's property rights, with the allocation effect being important for consequent firm growth.

As noted, the literature has already shown that across countries, firm growth is affected by the development of financial markets. As such, there are two effects to consider in a cross-country study, a finance effect and an asset allocation effect. The finance effect determines the available resources for investment and thus affects firm growth. The asset allocation effect determines the efficiency of firm investment and thus also affects growth. We empirically investigate the importance of the finance and asset allocation effects for different industries in a large number of countries. We find less growth in countries with a lower level of financial development, consistent with the hypothesis that firms lack access to finance and thus underinvest. And in countries with less secure property rights, there is less growth, consistent with the hypothesis that the allocation of firms' investment is inefficient as firms underinvest in intangible assets. Our results are robust to using different country samples and estimation techniques, including instrumental variables and variations in country controls. Empirically, the two effects appear to be equally important drivers of growth in sectoral value added. Our estimates predict that the difference in growth rates between the 75th and 25th percentile intangible-intensive industry will be 1.4% per year higher in a country with a property rights index of five, the 75th percentile country, compared to an index of three, the 25th percentile country. For comparison, the average growth rate in our sample is 3.4% per year. Therefore, a differential rate of 1.4% due to an improvement in the property rights index from three to five represents a large increase.

Although we do an array of robustness tests, our results do come with provisos. Apart from the usual caveats related to possible weaknesses in the data and the choice of a particular time period and country sample, there are methodological issues. Most important may be the fact that to test fully for the role of the asset allocation mechanism, we need both an instrument for the mechanism and an instrument for property rights. While instruments for the property rights have been developed, instruments for the actual asset allocation do not (yet) exist. When and if appropriate instruments are found, the asset allocation mechanism needs to be tested further.

The paper is structured as follows. Section I reviews the related literature, develops the finance and asset allocation effects, and presents our methodology to separate the two effects empirically. Section II presents the data used in our empirical application. Section III presents the empirical results concerning the relationships between growth in value added and the finance and asset allocation effects. Section IV presents a number of robustness tests, and Section V concludes.

I. Related Literature and Hypothesis

Our work is related to several strands of literature. The starting point is the work by King and Levine (1993), Levine and Zervos (1998), Beck, Levine, and Loayza (2000), and others that has established an empirical link between financial development and economic growth. Also related is the law and finance literature initiated by La Porta et al. (1997). This literature focuses on the relationship between the institutional framework of a country and its financial development (see also La Porta et al. (1998), Rajan and Zingales (1998), and Demirgüç-Kunt and Maksimovic (1998)). The literature has established that financial sector development is higher in countries with better legal systems and stronger creditor rights since such environments increase the ability of lenders to collateralize their loans and finance firms. In an extension, Beck et al. (2003) show that both legal systems and a country's initial endowments are important determinants of financial development and private property rights protection, with initial endowments explaining relatively more of the cross-country variation in financial development than legal origin.

The second strand we draw on is the capital structure literature (Myers (1977), Titman and Wessels (1988), and Harris and Raviv (1991)). This literature relates firms' liability structure to firm asset choices, among others. It has established that real, tangible assets, such as plant and equipment, can support more debt than intangible assets. In particular, fixed assets can support more long-term debt because they have greater liquidation and collateralizable value. Holding other factors constant, debt ratios will be lower the larger the proportion of firm values represented by intangible assets (Myers (1977)). Bradley, Jarrell, and Kim (1984) provide empirical support for the argument that a larger amount of intangible assets reduces the borrowing capacity of a firm.[2]

The third strand of literature relates to the role of property rights in affecting overall investment and investment patterns. Besley (1995) shows the role of property rights for investment incentives and provides evidence for the importance of property rights in the context of land ownership by farmers in Ghana. Johnson, McMillan, and Woodruff (2002) show for a sample of firms in post-communist countries that weaker property rights discourage the reinvestment of firm earnings, even when bank loans are available, suggesting that secure property rights are both a necessary and sufficient condition for entrepreneurial investment. The role of property rights in affecting investment patterns has also been acknowledged, although less explicitly studied. Mansfield (1995) hints that there may be a relationship between the protection of property rights and the allocation of investable resources between fixed and intangible assets. Using a survey of firm

---

[2] Work by Rajan and Zingales (1995) and Demirgüç-Kunt and Maksimovic (1999) confirms that debt maturity and asset structures for cross sections of countries are related in this way, with firms with more fixed assets being able to support a greater amount of long-term debt.

Financial Development, Property Rights, and Growth 2405

managers, he states that "most of the firms we contacted seemed to regard intellectual property rights protection to be an important factor . . . [influencing] investment decisions" (p. 24). Stern, Porter, and Furman (2000) show that the strength of a country's intellectual property rights affects its innovative capacity, as measured by the degree of international patenting. In developing countries, the lower degree of investment in intangible assets may relate to the weaker protection of property rights. More generally, the institutional economics literature (North (1990)) suggests that investment in particular types of assets will be higher the more protected the property rights of the assets are.

These three strands have not yet merged in investigating empirically the effects of institutions on both firm financing and asset allocation, and consequently on growth. Here we want to test two hypotheses: whether firms in countries with better developed financial systems have more access to finance and are therefore able to invest more overall, and whether firms in countries with better property rights invest more efficiently across types of assets. In turn, both aspects will be reflected in higher growth rates. The law and finance literature has already established that firms in a country with a better legal framework and more developed financial markets find it easier to attract external financing. Empirical investigation of how a country's property rights protection affects firms' asset allocation has not yet occurred.

For our empirical tests, we use the setup of Rajan and Zingales (1998, RZ hereafter) to assess the relationship between financial development, property rights, and growth.[3] The RZ model relates the growth in real value added in a sector in a particular country to a number of country and industry-specific variables. In the case of RZ, the specific test focuses on financial development and the argument of RZ is that financially dependent firms can be expected to grow more in countries with a higher level of financial development. In addition to including country indicators and industry indicators, they overcome some of the identification problems encountered in standard cross-country growth regressions by interacting a country characteristic (financial development of a particular country) with an industry characteristic (external financial dependence of a particular industry). This approach is less subject to criticism regarding an omitted variable bias or model specification than traditional approaches and allows them to isolate the impact of financial development on growth. In the regression results explaining sectoral growth, RZ find a positive sign for the interaction between the external financial dependence ratio and the level of financial development. They also find a similar effect when including an interaction term between the typical external dependence variable for the particular sector and the quality of a country's legal framework.

Their results provide support for the finance effect. We expand the RZ model to test for the asset allocation effect. We add to the basic model in RZ a variable that is the interaction of the typical ratio for each industrial sector of intangible-to-

---

[3] Other papers that use this approach include Cetorelli and Gambera (2001), which investigates the effects of bank concentration on sectoral growth, and Fisman and Love (2003), which investigates the effects of trade credit usage on sectoral growth.

fixed assets and an index of the strength of countries' property rights. We then test whether industrial sectors that typically use many intangible assets grow faster (slower) in countries with more (less) secure property rights. If intangible-intensive sectors grow faster in countries with better property rights, then we have indirect evidence that property rights affect firms' asset choices and consequently (through that channel) growth. We also perform a number of robustness tests on the importance of controlling for country-specific factors and using instrumental variables to control for the possible (residual) endogeneity of some variables.

In line with RZ, we use U.S. firm data to construct proxies at the industry level for the typical external financial dependence for a particular industrial sector and the typical ratio of intangible to fixed assets for a particular industry. The presumption here is that the well-developed financial markets and the well-protected property rights in the United States should allow U.S. firms to achieve the desired financial and asset structures for their respective industrial sector. This approach offers a way to identify the desired extent of external financial dependence and the optimal asset mix of an industry anywhere in the world.[4] It assumes that there are technological and economic reasons why some industries depend more on external finance and intangible assets than others do, and that these differences, to a large degree, prevail across countries. This does not mean that we assume a sector in two countries with the same degree of property protection to have exactly the same optimal mix of intangibles and tangible assets. Local conditions such as growth opportunities are allowed to differ between countries. We only assume the rank order of optimal asset mixes across industries to be similar across countries. Furthermore, we explicitly conduct tests for the importance of this assumption.

Following RZ, the regressions include the industry's market share in total manufacturing in the specific country to control for differences in growth potential across industries. Industries with large market shares may have less growth potential than industries with small initial market shares when there is an industry-specific convergence. The initial share may also help to control for other variations between countries, such as in their initial comparative advantage among certain industries based on factors other than financial development and property rights protection. Finally, in line with RZ, we use country and industry dummies to control for country-specific and industry-specific factors.

II. Data

We use industry-specific and country-specific data from a variety of sources. Table I presents an overview of the variables used in our empirical analysis and their sources. Most of the variables are self-explanatory and have been used in other cross-country studies of firm financing structures and firm growth.

---

[4] The advantage of this approach is that we do not need information on the actual asset mix for industries in different countries. The comparability of such data would be limited because accounting practices, particularly with respect to intangible assets, differ greatly around the world.

Financial Development, Property Rights, and Growth   2407

In line with RZ, we use the ratio of private credit to GDP as a proxy for financial development. As proxies for the level of protection of property rights, we use three broad indexes of property rights and two indexes of intellectual property rights, as well as a specific index of patent rights. These indexes of property rights come from different sources, each having some advantages and disadvantages. Our main property rights index is the rating of protection of property rights from the Index of Economic Freedom constructed by the Heritage Foundation. This relatively broad index of property rights is available for a large set of countries and has been used by other researchers (e.g., Johnson, Kaufmann, and Zoido-Lobaton (1998) and La Porta et al. (1999, 2002)). A second index of property rights rates the protection of intellectual property rights in particular by using data from the "Special 301" placements of the Office of the U.S. Trade Representative (USTR). "Special 301" requires the USTR to identify those countries that deny adequate and effective protection for intellectual property rights or deny fair and equitable market access for persons that rely on intellectual property protection. Countries can be placed on different lists depending on their relative protection of intellectual property. For example, countries which have the most onerous or egregious acts, policies, or practices and which have the greatest adverse impact on relevant U.S. products are designated "priority foreign countries." As such, the index weights the degree of property rights protection with the economic impact that protection deficiencies have on U.S. trade. We use these qualifications to construct an index of intellectual property rights protection. The third index is the patent rights index constructed by Ginarte and Park (1997). This index focuses more specifically on the protection of patents. A fourth index is the property rights index of the World Economic Forum (2002), which measures the general legal protection of private property in a country. The fifth index is the intellectual property rights index of the World Economic Forum, which measures the protection of intellectual property in a country. The two World Economic Forum indexes are available only for the year 2001. The sixth index is the property rights index constructed by Knack and Keefer (1995) using data from the International Country Risk Guide (ICRG). This index measures property rights in a broad sense and includes five measures: quality of the bureaucracy, corruption in government, rule of law, expropriation risk, and repudiation of contracts by the government. Table I presents more details on these six indexes of property protection.

Our main index of protection of property rights covers the period 1995 to 1999; the Special 301 index of protection of intellectual property rights covers the period 1990 to 1999; the World Economic Forum indexes refer to 2001; and the Knack and Keefer index covers the period 1982 to 1995. The growth regressions, however, include data for the period 1980 to 1989, as in RZ. Ideally, one would want to use property rights indexes for the period 1980 to 1989 as well; however, this is not possible for the property rights indexes available to us due to data limitations. The one exception is the Ginarte and Park patent rights index, for which we do have data for the period 1980 to 1989. Therefore, this index does not suffer from the nonoverlapping time period problem and we can use the patent rights index for the year 1980—the beginning of the period 1980 to 1989—in the regressions.

Table I

Definition and Source of the Variables

This table describes the variables collected for our study. The first column gives the names of the variable as we use it. The second column describes the variable and provides the source from which it was collected.

Variable	Description
Property (Freedom)	A rating of property rights in each country (on a scale from 1 to 5). The more protection private property receives, the higher the score. The score is based, broadly, on the degree of legal protection of private property, the probability that the government will expropriate private property, and the country's legal protection of private property. The index equals the median rating for the period 1995 to 1999. Source: The Index of Economic Freedom from the Heritage Foundation. We reversed the original order of the index.
Intellectual Property (301)	An index of intellectual property rights (on a scale from 1 to 5). The more protection private property receives, the higher the score. The index is calculated using the "Special 301" placements of the Office of the U.S. Trade Representative (USTR). Special 301 requires the USTR to identify those countries that deny adequate and effective protection for intellectual property rights or deny fair and equitable market access for persons that rely on intellectual property protection. Countries that have the most onerous or egregious acts, policies, or practices and that have the greatest adverse impact on relevant U.S. products are designated "Priority foreign countries." Countries can also be placed on other lists. We assign the following ratings: 1 = Priority foreign countries; 2 = 306 Monitoring; 3 = Priority watch list; 4 = Watch list; 5 = Not listed. The index equals the median rating for the period 1990 to 1999. Source: International Intellectual Property Alliance. Original source: USTR.
Patent rights (GP)	An index of patent rights (on a scale from 0 to 5) in 1980. The more protection patents receive, the higher the score. The index criteria are: coverage, membership, duration, enforcement, and loss of rights. Source: Ginarte and Park (1997).
Property (WEF)	An index of property rights (on a scale from 1 to 7) in 2001. The more protection private property receives, the higher the score. A 1 indicates that assets are poorly delineated and not protected by law, while 7 indicates that assets are clearly delineated and protected by law. Source: Global Competitiveness Report, World Economic Forum (2002).
Intellectual property (WEF)	An index of intellectual property rights (on a scale from 1 to 7) in 2001. The more protection intellectual property receives, the higher the score. A 1 indicates that intellectual property protection is weak or nonexistent, while 7 indicates that intellectual property protection is equal to the world's most stringent. Source: Global Competitiveness Report, World Economic Forum (2002).
Property (ICRG)	A measure of property rights in each country (on a scale from 0 to 10). The index equals the average rating between 1982 and 1995. The more protection private property receives, the higher the score. The score is based on the average of five measures: quality of the bureaucracy, corruption in government, rule of law, expropriation risk, and repudiation of contracts by the government. Source: International Country Risk Guide and Knack and Keefer (1995).
Private credit	Private credit divided by GDP in 1980. Source: Rajan and Zingales (1998) and the International Financial Statistics of the International Monetary Fund.

Financial Development, Property Rights, and Growth 2409

Variable	Description
Market cap	Stock market capitalization divided by GDP in 1980. Source: Rajan and Zingales (1998).
Accounting	Accounting standards in 1983 (on a scale from 0 to 90). Higher scores indicate more disclosure. Source: Center for International Financial Analysis and Research and Rajan and Zingales (1998).
Human capital	Human capital is the average for 1980 of the years of schooling attained by the population over 25 years of age. Source: Barro and Lee (1993).
Rule of Law	Assessment of the law and order tradition in the country (on a scale from 0 to 10). Average of the months of April and October of the monthly index between 1982 and 1995. Lower scores indicate less tradition for law and order. Source: International Country Risk Guide and La Porta et al. (1997).
Legal origin	Identifies the legal origin of the Company Law or Commercial Code of each country. There are four possible origins: (1) English Common law, (2) French Commercial Code, (3) German Commercial Code, and (4) Scandinavian Commercial Code. Source: La Porta et al. (1999).
European settler mortality	European settler mortality rate, measured in terms of deaths per annum per 1000 "mean strength." Source: Acemoglu et al. (2001).
GDP per capita	The logarithm of GDP per capita in 1980. Source: World Development Indicators of the World Bank.
Growth in value added	Average annual real growth rate of value added in a particular sector in a particular country over the period 1980 to 1989. The sectors are classified on the basis of ISIC. Source: United Nations Database on Industrial Statistics and Rajan and Zingales (1998).
Growth in average size	Average growth in average size by ISIC sector over the period 1980 to 1989. Source: United Nations Database on Industrial Statistics and Rajan and Zingales (1998).
Growth in number	Average growth in number of establishments by ISIC sector over the period 1980 to 1989. Source: United Nations Database on Industrial Statistics and Rajan and Zingales (1998).
Fraction of sector in value added	Fraction of ISIC sector in value added of total manufacturing sector in 1980. Source: Rajan and Zingales (1998).
Financial dependence	External financial dependence of U.S. firms by ISIC sector averaged over the period 1980 to 1989. Source: Rajan and Zingales (1998).
Sales growth	Real annual growth in sales of U.S. firms by ISIC sector averaged over the period 1980 to 1989. Source: Fisman and Love (2002).
Tobin's Q	Tobin's Q of U.S. firms by ISIC sector averaged over the period 1980 to 1989. Tobin's Q is defined as the sum of the market value of equity plus the book value of liabilities over the book value of total assets. Source: COMPUSTAT.
Intangible intensity	Ratio of intangible assets-to-net fixed assets of U.S. firms by ISIC sector over the period 1980 to 1989. Source: COMPUSTAT. Intangibles is COMPUSTAT item 33 and represents the net value of intangible assets. Intangibles are assets that have no physical existence in themselves, but represent rights to enjoy some privilege. In COMPUSTAT, this item includes blueprints or building designs, patents, copyrights, trademarks, franchises, organizational costs, client lists, computer software patent costs, licenses, and goodwill (except on unconsolidated subsidiaries). Intangibles excludes goodwill on unconsolidated subsidiaries, which are included in Investments and Advances under the Equity Method (COMPUSTAT item 31). Net fixed assets is COMPUSTAT item 8 and represents net property, plant and equipment, which equals gross property, plant and equipment (COMPUSTAT item 7) less accumulated depreciation, depletion and amortization (COMPUSTAT item 196).

For the other property rights indexes, we use index values as of their first available date.

Although the indexes of property protection are from different sources and for different time periods, they appear quite related and are highly positively correlated. The correlation between our main property rights index and the other five indexes of protection of (intellectual) property rights ranges, for example, from 0.49 to 0.78. The fact that the property rights indexes relate to different time periods could nevertheless raise concerns in our specification, in part because property rights may have evolved in response to economic performance. We believe these concerns to be small, mostly because measures of institutional frameworks have been found to be stable over long periods of time (Acemoglu, Johnson, and Robinson (2001, 2002)). Also, RZ show that the sample means of the accounting standards variable they use do not differ significantly between 1983 and 1990.

This stability also applies to our property rights indexes, which do not change much over the time for which they are available. Table II shows that the mean property rights index for countries sampled in the first and last available year is not statistically significantly different for any of the three indexes. Note that the sample mean of the Ginarte and Park patents rights index—the only index for which we have data for the period 1980 to 1989—for countries sampled in 1980 does not significantly differ statistically from the sample mean in 1990 for the same set of countries. In addition, we find that the relative ordering of the different property rights indexes does not change much over time, as the Spearman rank order correlations of the respective indexes are high. A t-test of differences further confirms that the property rights indexes in the first and last available year are not statistically different. As a further robustness check, we also perform our regressions instrumenting the property rights indexes with variables that predate the period 1980 to 1989, using the methodology used by Beck et al. (2000) and by Acemoglu et al. (2001).

Table III presents the summary statistics of the country-specific variables grouped by developing and developed countries (Table AI in the Appendix presents the same summary statistics, but by individual country). We only use the classification developing versus developed countries to illustrate the differences in the various variables by institutional settings. The country summary statistics show that, as a group, developing countries have less developed financial systems, weaker law and order systems, worse protection of (intellectual) property rights, and fewer patents per capita. All variables except for the stock market capitalization-to-GDP ratio and the accounting standards show a statistically significant difference between the two groups of countries. Other work has documented extensively the differences in the degree of law and order between developed and developing countries. This difference in legal frameworks partly relates to the difference in the private credit-to-GDP ratio between these two groups of countries, where low contract enforcement environments have hindered the development of financial systems in developing countries.

The degree of financial development and the protection of property rights tend to go together and are both related to the overall level of development of a country. As such, it could be difficult to analyze the differential effects of financial

Table II
Stability of Property Rights Measures over Time

This table reports for each of the three property rights indexes the sample mean and standard deviation for the first year and the last year of the sample period across all sampled countries, the *t*-statistic for a test of difference in the sample means assuming unequal variances, the rank order correlation coefficient, and a test of independence of the property rights indexes in the first year and the last year of the sample period. The null hypothesis of the test of independence is that the property rights indexes are independent. The sources and definitions of the data are reported in Table I. Significance level [a] corresponds to 1%.

| Property rights index | Year | Statistics across Countries | | Number of Observations | Test of Difference in Means t-statistic | Rank Order Correlation Spearman's ρ | Test of Independence p-value |
		Mean	St.d. Dev.				
Property (Freedom)	1995	3.93	0.96	44			
Property (Freedom)	2000	3.89	0.97	44	− 0.22	0.90	0.000[a]
Intellectual property (301)	1990	4.29	0.60	28			
Intellectual property (301)	2000	4.03	0.81	28	− 1.36	0.76	0.000[a]
Patents (GP)	1980	2.69	0.91	44			
Patents (GP)	1990	2.74	1.00	44	0.29	0.97	0.000[a]

Table III

Descriptive Statistics of Institutional Variables

This table reports summary statistics of the variables used in our study. For each variable, we report the mean across all sampled countries, across developing countries, and across developed countries. To classify countries as developing or developed, we use the World Bank classification of countries. For comparison purposes, we also present t-statistics of tests of differences in the means of the variables across developing and across developed countries. The sources and definitions of the data are reported in Table I. Significance level [a] corresponds to 1%.

	Means across Countries			t-Tests of Difference in Means
	Developed Countries	Developing Countries	All Countries	Developed vs. Developing Countries
Property (Freedom)	4.68	3.42	3.96	7.10[a]
Intellectual property (301)	4.47	3.74	4.12	3.97[a]
Patents (GP)	3.33	2.20	2.67	5.44[a]
Property (WEF)	6.11	4.69	5.33	7.66[a]
Intellectual property (WEF)	5.74	3.47	4.51	10.64[a]
Property (ICRG)	9.14	5.42	7.03	11.82[a]
Private credit to GDP	0.49	0.26	0.36	4.37[a]
Market capitalization to GDP	0.24	0.17	0.20	0.64
Law and order	9.23	4.40	6.67	11.74[a]
Accounting standards	0.65	0.66	0.65	−0.12
Settler mortality rate	2.49	4.36	4.03	−6.25[a]
Human capital	7.92	4.07	5.84	5.72[a]
GDP per capita	9.04	6.84	7.79	10.28[a]
Number of countries	19	25	44	

development and property rights on the level of external financing available and the allocation of investment across different assets. However, the correlation between the two concepts is not perfect. That is, there exist countries with good property rights and underdeveloped financial systems. Chile, for example, scores high on the protection of property rights (with a property rights index of five) but its level of financial development is only average (reflected by a level of private credit to GDP of 36%). France, on the other hand, has a relatively well-developed financial system (reflected by a level of private credit to GDP of 54%) but the protection of its property rights is only average (with a property rights index of four). Calculating the simple correlation between the property rights index and the level of financial development, 0.59, confirms that the relationship between the two concepts is high but not perfect. The correlations of the interaction variables are even less perfect, less than 0.20.

Our data set includes 45 countries.[5] For the growth regressions, as in RZ, we need to drop the benchmark country, the United States, and we are therefore left

[5] The countries include Australia, Austria, Bangladesh, Belgium, Brazil, Canada, Chile, Colombia, Costa Rica, Denmark, Egypt, Finland, France, Germany, Greece, India, Indonesia, Israel, Italy, Jamaica, Japan, Jordan, Kenya, Korea, Malaysia, Mexico, Morocco, the Netherlands, New Zealand, Nigeria, Norway, Pakistan, Peru, the Philippines, Portugal, Singapore, South Africa, Spain, Sri Lanka, Sweden, Turkey, the United Kingdom, the United States, Venezuela, and Zimbabwe.

Financial Development, Property Rights, and Growth   2413

with 44 countries. As we collected additional data, the number of countries included in our data set somewhat exceeds that in RZ, who use data on 41 countries.

Like RZ, we construct benchmark data on an industry basis. We use the benchmark data from RZ for all of our industry variables, but construct our own intangible-to-fixed assets variable. We assume that the intangible-to-fixed assets ratio for each industry in the United States forms a good benchmark (like RZ, who use the U.S. external financial dependence ratio as a benchmark). We refer to the ratio of intangible to fixed assets as the intangible intensity. In the same way RZ calculate the external financial dependence ratios by industry, we calculate the benchmark of intangible intensity using COMPUSTAT data on U.S. firms for the years 1980 to 1989. We measure intangibles by the net value of intangible assets, that is, using COMPUSTAT item 33. Generally, intangibles are assets that have no physical existence in themselves but represent rights to enjoy some privilege. In COMPUSTAT, this item includes blueprints or building designs, patents, copyrights, trademarks, franchises, organizational costs, client lists, computer software patent costs, licenses, and goodwill (except on unconsolidated subsidiaries). Intangibles in the COMPUSTAT data excludes goodwill on unconsolidated subsidiaries, which are included in investments and advances under the equity method (COMPUSTAT item 31). We measure tangibles by net fixed assets, that is, using COMPUSTAT item 8. This represents net property, plant, and equipment, which equals gross property, plant, and equipment (COMPUSTAT item 7) less accumulated depreciation, depletion, and amortization (COMPUSTAT item 196).

Table IV reports the intangible-intensity benchmarks for U.S. firms in different industrial sectors on a two-digit SIC level. The total number of firms used to calculate these benchmarks is 5,241. The average intangible-intensity ratio during the 1980s for U.S. manufacturing firms is 77%. The variation of intangible intensity across industries is large: It ranges from as low as 2.0% for the petroleum and coal products industry to as high as 454% for the printing and publishing industry. The variation concurs with notions of what constitute relatively capital-intensive versus more knowledge-intensive industries. The stone, clay, glass, and concrete products industry, for example, relies mainly on fixed assets for production, as would be expected since the technology used in this sector is well-established and embodied in the fixed assets. It has an intangible-intensity ratio of 5%. The chemical and allied products industry and the electrical and electronic industry, in contrast, rely heavily on intangible assets as inputs, such as patents and licenses. They have an intangible-intensity ratio of 96% and 77%, respectively. The data show that the various technical and economic reasons that make various types of products require different input mixes can be benchmarked well at the industry level.

III. Empirical Results

In this section, the regression results are presented. In the first set of regressions, the dependent variable is the average annual real growth rate of value added in a particular sector in a particular country over the period 1980 to 1989,

Table IV
Sectoral Measure of Intangible Intensity

The table reports the measure of intangible intensity for each sector based on U.S. firm-level data. Intangible intensity is measured by the ratio of intangible assets to net fixed assets. The data are averages for all U.S. firms in the COMPUSTAT (U.S.) database for the period 1980 to 1989. For external financial dependency benchmarks across sectors, we refer to the original source: Table I in Rajan and Zingales (1998). The table also reports the number of U.S. firms used to construct the benchmark for each industrial sector. As in Rajan and Zingales (1998) we focus on manufacturing firms and use 1980 to 1989 data to construct the benchmarks. The total number of firms is 5,241.

SIC Code	Industrial Sectors	Intangible Intensity	Number of Firms
20	Food and kindred products	0.75	304
21	Tobacco manufactures	0.49	21
22	Textile mill products	0.21	131
23	Apparel and other textile products	0.53	139
24	Lumber and wood products	1.20	97
25	Furniture and fixtures	0.49	87
26	Paper and allied products	0.20	130
27	Printing and publishing	4.54	202
28	Chemicals and allied products	0.96	556
29	Petroleum and coal products	0.02	86
30	Rubber and miscellaneous plastics	0.46	191
31	Leather and leather products	0.33	41
32	Stone, clay, glass, and concrete products	0.05	96
33	Primary metal industries	0.11	191
34	Fabricated metal products	0.31	277
35	Industrial machinery and equipment	0.25	795
36	Electrical and electronic equipment	0.77	815
37	Transportation equipment	0.24	262
38	Instruments and related products	0.90	660
39	Miscellaneous manufacturing industries	2.29	160
	Mean	0.76	
	Median	0.48	
	Standard deviation	1.03	

with one observation per sector in each country. The specification for the first set of regressions is as follows:

$$
\begin{aligned}
Growth_{j,k} = {} & Constant + \Psi_1 \cdot Industry\ dummies_j \\
& + \Psi_2 \cdot Country\ controls_k \\
& + \psi_3 \cdot Industry\ share\ of\ manufacturing\ value\ added_{j,k} \\
& + \psi_4 \cdot External\ dependence_j \cdot Financial\ development_k \\
& + \psi_5 \cdot Intangible\ intensity_j \cdot Property\ rights_k \\
& + \varepsilon_{j,k},
\end{aligned}
\tag{1}
$$

where each industry is indicated by index j and each country by index k. Uppercase Greek letters indicate vectors of coefficients, indexed by industry j or

Financial Development, Property Rights, and Growth 2415

country k. Growth is the average annual real growth rate of value added in industry j in country k. The industry dummies correct for industry-specific effects. The vector of country control variables differs per specification and can include the following variables: private credit to GDP, index of property rights, stock market capitalization to GDP, human capital, rule of law, accounting standards, and the logarithm of per capita GDP. The exact vector of country control variables is described in greater detail in the presentation of the specific empirical results. As a measure of financial development, we use private credit to GDP. As a measure of external financial dependence at the sectoral level, we use the data from RZ. As a measure of intangible intensity, we use the ratio of intangible to fixed assets for U.S. firms on the sectoral level. For the property rights index, we use the Economic Freedom property rights index.

The results are presented in Table V. We first discuss the basic regression specifications, which are estimated using OLS and include country dummies (columns 1 to 3). Industry dummies (not reported) are used in all regressions. The industry's market share in total manufacturing in a specific country has a negative sign in all regressions, in line with RZ, suggesting that there is some industry-specific convergence. In terms of the main hypotheses, we find that industrial sectors that rely relatively more on external finance develop disproportionately faster in countries with better-developed financial markets because the coefficient for the interactive variable private credit to GDP times external financial dependence is positive and statistically significant (at the 1% level, column 1). Hence, consistent with the findings of RZ, we find that financial development facilitates economic growth through greater availability of external financing. As noted by Beck et al. (2000) and others, the quality of the legal system influences financial sector development and overall growth. Interacting the external financial dependence variable with the index of the quality of the legal framework used by La Porta et al. (1998), instead of the financial development variable, also leads to a positive coefficient (not reported). The regression result confirms the law and finance view that increased availability of external financing and better legal systems enhance firm growth.

In terms of the asset allocation effect, we find that industrial sectors using relatively more intangible assets develop faster in countries with better protection of property rights, because the coefficient for the interactive variable property rights times intangible intensity is statistically significant and positive (column 2). Hence, better property rights facilitate economic growth as they favor growth through better asset allocation, that is, in firms that would naturally choose a higher share of investment in intangible assets.[6] The asset allocation effect on growth appears to be in addition to the increase in firm growth due to greater external financing, since in the regressions where both the external financial dependence and the intangible-intensity variables are included (column 3), both interactive variables are statistically significant. Additionally, the coefficients in

---

[6] Exclusion of sectors with a relatively high estimated usage of intangible assets, such as printing and publishing and/or miscellaneous manufacturing industries, does not qualitatively alter the results (not reported).

Table V
The Average Effect of Financial Development and Property Rights on Industrial Growth

The dependent variable is the average annual real growth rate of value added in a particular sector in a particular country over the period 1980 to 1989. Table I describes all variables in detail. As a measure for protection of property rights, we use the property rights index from the Index of Economic Freedom from the Heritage Foundation. All regressions include industry dummies and a constant but these are not reported. Regressions (1) to (3) and regressions (6) to (8) include country dummies but these are not reported. Regressions (4) and (5) include country-specific variables rather than country dummies. Regression (6) uses legal origin as the instrumental variable (IV) for property rights. Regression (7) uses European settler mortality as IV for property rights. Robust standard errors are shown below the coefficients. The United States is dropped as it is the benchmark. Significance levels [a] and [b] correspond to 1% and 5%, respectively.

	(1)	(2)	(3)	(4)	(5)	(6) IV legal origin	(7) IV mortality
Fraction of sector in value added of manufacturing in 1980	−1.041[a] (0.2454)	−0.9721[a] (0.2482)	−1.076[a] (0.2491)	−1.040[a] (0.2210)	−0.4511[a] (0.1028)	−0.9672[a] (0.2480)	−1.463[a] (0.3658)
Sectoral measure of financial dependence * private credit to GDP	0.1401[a] (0.0383)		0.1354[a] (0.0376)	0.1376[a] (0.0380)	0.0509[a] (0.0204)		
Sectoral measure of intangible intensity * property (freedom)		0.0103[a] (0.0029)	0.0092[a] (0.0028)	0.0091[a] (0.0033)	0.0067[a] (0.0024)	0.0090[a] (0.0033)	0.0259[b] (0.0107)
Private credit to GDP				−0.0213 (0.0163)	0.0488[a] (0.0151)		
Property (freedom)				−0.0004 (0.0050)	0.0030 (0.0058)		
Stock market capitalization to GDP					0.0253[a] (0.0068)		
Human capital					−0.0008 (0.0017)		
Rule of law					0.0019 (0.0022)		
Accounting standards					0.0428[b] (0.0180)		
Log of per capita GDP					−0.0205[a] (0.0043)		
R²	0.2711	0.2548	0.2757	0.1028	0.2386	0.2547	0.2391
N	1242	1277	1242	1242	830	1277	635
Number of countries	44	44	44	44	33	44	23

the regressions including both effects are of similar magnitudes as in the two regressions where each of them was included separately (columns 1 and 2), suggesting that the two variables measure complementary effects.[7]

The effects of external financial development and property protection on firm growth are not only both statistically significant but are also equally economically important. We can use the regression coefficient estimates of Table V to infer how much higher the growth rate of an industry at the 75th percentile of intangible intensity would be compared to an industry at the 25th percentile level, when the industries are located in a country at the 75th percentile of property protection, rather than in a country at the 25th percentile. The industry at the 75th percentile, instruments and related products, has an intangible-intensity ratio of 0.90. The industry at the 25th percentile, textile mill products, has an intangible-intensity ratio of 0.21. The country at the 75th percentile of property protection has a value of five for the property rights index and the country at the 25th percentile has a value of three. The estimated coefficient for the interaction term in regression 2 of Table V equals 0.010 and we can set the industry's initial share of manufacturing at its overall mean. The regression coefficient estimates therefore predict the difference in growth rates between the 75th and 25th percentile intangible-intensive industry to be 1.4% per year higher in a country with a property rights index of five compared to one with an index of three. For comparison, the average growth rate is 3.4% per year. Therefore, a differential rate of 1.4% due to an improvement in the property rights index from three to five represents a large increase.

The effect of financial development on differential real firm growth can be calculated in a similar way using the estimated coefficient for the interaction term of regression 1 in Table V of 0.140. The coefficient estimate predicts the difference between the growth rate of the 75th and 25th percentile external financial dependence industry to be 1.4% higher in a country at the 75th percentile of financial development compared to one at the 25th percentile.[8] Thus, the effects of property protection and financial development on differential firm growth are not only both statistically significant, but also of similar economic importance. In other words, the asset allocation effect is economically as important as the finance effect.

The relative importance of the two effects can also be demonstrated by a comparison of two countries, Egypt and Finland. Egypt is a country with a relatively low degree of property protection, having a value of three for the property rights

[7] The two interacted variables, external financial dependence and intangible intensity interacted with financial development and property rights indexes, do appear to measure different concepts as the correlation between these variables is low. The correlation between the external financial dependence variable interacted with the financial development measure and the intangible intensity measure interacted with the property rights index is 0.149. Similar correlations are found when the other four property rights indexes are used (not reported).

[8] RZ used the same approach to compute the effect of financial development on differential real firm growth. Our estimated effect differs somewhat from the differential growth rate effect estimated in RZ, 1.3%, because our sample is slightly larger and because we use private sector credit instead of total capitalization as our measure of financial development.

index (at the 25th percentile of property protection), while Finland is a country with a relatively high degree of property protection, having a value of five for the property rights index (at the 75th percentile of property protection). The regression coefficient estimates predict that if Egypt had had the same property rights as Finland, but its actual financial development, then the growth rate in value added of its industry at the median level of intangible intensity, 0.48, would have been 1.0% per year higher. Egypt is also a country with a relatively low level of financial development, with a level of private credit to GDP of 21% (at the 25th percentile of financial development), while Finland is a country with a relatively high level of financial development, with a level of private credit to GDP of 48% (at the 75th percentile of financial development). If Egypt had had the same financial development as Finland, but its actual degree of property protection, then the growth rate in value added of its industry at the median level of external financial dependence, 0.23, would have been 0.9% per year higher. Again, the two effects are quite large and of comparable magnitude.

These numerical interpretations can be compared to the results found by Hall and Jones (1999) and Acemoglu et al. (2001) for the effects of institutions on output and income level. Hall and Jones (1999) explore the effects of differences in institutions and government policies, which they call social infrastructure, on output per worker in a cross section of countries. Their findings imply that the observed difference in social infrastructure between Niger and the United States is more than enough to explain the 35-fold difference in output per worker. Acemoglu et al.'s (2001) findings imply that improving Nigeria's institutions to the level of Chile could, in the long run, lead to as much as a 7-fold increase in Nigeria's income (in practice Chile is over 11 times as rich as Nigeria). Although these papers study the effects of institutions on the output or income level, rather than the rate of growth, it shows that our results are of comparable orders.

Thus far, our specifications have focused on the differential effect on growth of property rights across industries with different asset mixes (captured by the interaction term of property rights and the intangible-intensity measure). To avoid possible biases caused by any omitted country-specific regressors, we have included country dummies to capture any institutional or other differences affecting growth, such as comparative advantage or general level of development. Since we are less interested in the importance of general country differences, we use this approach rather than a vector of specific country control variables. Still, the use of country dummies could introduce a misspecification to the extent that any omitted institutional differences important for growth are correlated with our two interaction variables. Examples of such country-specific variables that have been used in the general growth literature, besides financial depth and property rights, include the level of per capita GDP, human capital, and other institutional variables (Romer (1990), Barro (1991), and Levine and Zervos (1998), among others). Furthermore, we want to analyze the first-order country effects of property rights to investigate whether property rights affect firm growth mainly through the asset allocation channel or also in other ways. We therefore replace our country dummies with country-specific institutional and

Financial Development, Property Rights, and Growth 2419

other variables and thus perform a robustness check on whether any of our earlier results are affected if we control in other ways for country differences.

We start by documenting the fact that the effects of better property rights on growth work mostly through improved asset allocation as opposed through, for example, an improvement in the overall business environment that increases growth opportunities. We show this by including in our basic regression specification the property rights index (and private credit to GDP) directly in addition to the interacted variables. The results are reported in column 4 of Table V, where we exclude country dummies. We do not find a direct, statistically significant effect of the quality of a country's property rights on industrial sector growth. Most important, including the property rights index directly does not change the magnitude or the significance of the coefficients for the interaction variables in any meaningful way. Both the financial dependence and the asset mix interaction variables remain statistically significant and neither changes much in terms of magnitude. This suggests that the major effect of improved property rights on sectoral growth operates through improvements in asset allocation and that the interaction variable does not capture any general effects, for example, of improvements in the business environment leading to greater growth opportunities.

For other country-specific variables, we use the ratio of private credit to GDP in 1980, stock market capitalization over GDP in 1980, a measure of the level of human capital in 1980, a measure of the quality of the legal system, an accounting standards indicator, and the logarithm of per capita income in 1980. RZ and Cetorelli and Gambera (2001) have also used these variables in the same model. We expect a positive effect on growth of private credit to GDP and stock market capitalization to GDP as proxies for the development of the banking system and stock market respectively, and for financial development more generally. The level of human capital is measured as the average of the number of years of schooling attained by the population over 25 years of age in 1980 (as in Barro and Lee (1993)) and is expected to have a positive effect on growth in value added. The quality of the legal system is measured by the law and order tradition variable of La Porta et al. (1998) and is also expected to have a positive effect on growth. The accounting standards indicator is an index reflecting the quality of accounting standards and is taken from RZ. This variable is also expected to have a positive effect on growth since it proxies for the quality of information investors have regarding firms and that firms have regarding investment prospects. Per capita GDP is included to capture the convergence effects of the economy as a whole to a long-run steady state and is expected to have a negative coefficient (see, among others, Barro (1991)). The model continues to include industry dummies to control for any sector-specific effects and the property rights indexes. Since the country variables included in the two interaction terms—private credit to GDP and an index of property rights—are now also part of the country controls, we can assess both the overall effect of financial development and property protection on value added growth as well as the finance and asset allocation effects captured by the two interaction terms. Note that data on accounting standards is missing for some countries, reducing the sample of countries to 33.

The results of this specification are reported in column 5 of Table V. Except for the human capital variable, the country controls have the expected relationships with growth. The direct effect of the quality of property rights on growth remains insignificant, however, which suggests that better property rights by themselves do not translate into higher growth rates of sectoral value added. The depth of the financial system—measured by private credit to GDP and the size of the stock market as a ratio to GDP—has a positive and statistically significant influence on growth in sectoral value added. The degree of human capital in the country, proxied by the average number of years of schooling attained by the population over 25 years of age and the degree to which the rule of law applies, do not have a statistically significant effect on growth in sectoral value added. The accounting index, however, is statistically significantly positive. The general level of development, proxied by the log of income per capita, has a negative sign, confirming the convergence effect.

The focus of our attention, the interaction between property rights and the allocation of resources, is very robust to these changes in model specification. The coefficient on the interaction term between the property rights indexes and the intangible-intensity measure remains positive and statistically significant in both specifications. The size of the coefficient is also only somewhat smaller than those in the regressions with country dummies, and the coefficient remains statistically significant at the 1% level. The general result about the importance of the asset allocation effect is thus not altered. Also, the interaction term between financial development and external financial dependence remains statistically significant positive. The regression results in columns 4 and 5 thus show that the effect of property rights on growth operates in an important way through asset allocation, and does not have a direct, first-order effect on growth.

Another concern is that the quality of property rights is affected by the investment behavior of firms and the resulting growth patterns. At the macro level, countries that grow faster may demand greater property rights protection, since a larger share of economic output derives from more property-rights-intensive investments. At the more micro level, sectors that are more dependent on property rights may seek a higher degree of protection of property rights relevant to their industry. Due to these and other concerns about potential endogeneity, we instrument the property rights variable with a number of predetermined institutional variables. Following RZ, we use the colonial origin of a country's legal system (indicating whether the legal origin is English, French, German, or Scandinavian) as reported in La Porta et al. (1998) as one instrument. As also shown by La Porta et al. (1998), legal origin tends to have a long-lasting effect on a country's institutional structure, whereas the legal origin of a country is largely determined by the country colonizing it. As such, legal origin is a good instrumental variable and has been used in several other papers. Following Acemoglu et al. (2001), we also use the settler mortality rate of European bishops, soldiers, and sailors stationed in colonies in the 17th, 18th, and 19th centuries as an instrument. As argued by Acemoglu et al. (2001), the willingness of colonizing powers to settle and develop long-lasting institutions depended greatly on the ability of colonizers to survive physically. They show that the settler mortality rate is a good instrumental variable for past institutional characteristics that last into today (in their application, the particular institutional characteristic is the risk of expropriation of private property).

The instrumental variables (IV) results based on the specification of column 2 are presented in columns 6 and 7, using respectively legal origin or mortality rates as instruments for property rights. Since the European countries had the institutions that they were exporting to their colonies, we can not apply settler mortality rates as an instrumental variable for the European countries, that is, the colonizing countries themselves. This reduces the sample to 23 countries when using mortality rates as an instrumental variable. The results are nevertheless very robust to the use of instruments.[9] We again find a statistically significant effect of property rights on growth in sectoral value added through the asset allocation of resources. Interestingly, the magnitude of the coefficients for the interaction variable increases when using mortality rates as an instrumental variable (column 7). Because restricting the sample to former colonies results in a large reduction in the number of observations, we will only use legal origin as an instrument for property rights in what follows.[10]

As an additional investigation into the channels through which financial development and property rights affect firm growth, and following RZ, we analyze whether industries in countries with better financial development and property rights grow faster because new establishments are added to the industry or because existing establishments grow faster. There are two reasons why it is interesting to decompose the effects of access to financing and asset allocation in terms of number and average size of firms. First, as highlighted by RZ, the creation of new establishments is more likely to require external funds, while the expansion of existing establishments may more easily rely on internal funds. Thus, the effect of financial development could be more pronounced for new firms than for the growth of existing firms. Second, new firms are often set up in reaction to and to take advantage of new technological developments, while established firms tend to grow through expansion of scale, perhaps also because they are slower in reacting to new developments.[11] Furthermore, existing firms may be able to preserve the value of their assets in ways other than by resorting to formal property rights (e.g., by using their name recognition, distribution or supply networks, or general economic and political influence). Thus, the importance of property rights that protect the returns to (new) technology and help assure a good allocation of an economy's overall resources might be more pronounced for the emergence of new firms than for the growth of existing firms.

---

[9] The first-stage regressions show strong relationships between the instrumented variables and the potentially endogenous variables, that is, between settler mortality and legal origin and property rights and financial development (not reported).

[10] The results presented in Table V are based on all available data (up to 44 countries). As a further robustness test, we also reestimated the regression models using the subset of 41 countries used in RZ, which implied excluding Indonesia, Jamaica, and Nigeria. The results are very similar to those in Table V (not reported).

[11] In fact, many new firms that take advantage of new technological developments are spun off from existing firms that have developed some elements of these new technologies.

As before, we follow RZ and use data derived from the UN Industrial Statistics Yearbook database for the growth in the number of establishments and the growth in the average size of existing establishments. The growth in the number of establishments is calculated by RZ as the logarithm of the number of end-of-period establishments less the logarithm of the number of beginning-of-period establishments. The average size of establishments in the industry is calculated by dividing the value added in the industry by the number of establishments, with the growth in average size again defined as the difference in logarithms. RZ report that in their sample of countries roughly two-thirds of the growth in value-added results from an increase in the average size of existing establishments, while the remaining one-third is accounted for by an increase in the number of establishments.

We use the same specification as for our basic regression but with the growth in number of establishments or the growth in average size as the dependent variable instead of the growth in total value added by sector. We use again industry dummies and do not use country-specific institutional variables, but country dummies. The time period studied remains 1980 to 1989. The exact specification is as follows:

$$
\begin{aligned}
Growth_{j,k} = {} & Constant + \Phi_1 \cdot Industry\ dummies_j \\
& + \Phi_2 \cdot Country\ dummies_k \\
& + \phi_3 \cdot Industry\ share\ of\ manufacturing\ value\ added_{j,k} \\
& + \phi_4 \cdot External\ dependence_j \cdot Financial\ development_k \\
& + \phi_5 \cdot Intangible\ intensity_j \cdot Property\ rights_k \\
& + \varepsilon_{j,k},
\end{aligned}
\tag{2}
$$

where the dependent variable is either the growth in the average size or the growth in the number of establishments in industry j in country k.

Table VI reports the results, with columns 1 and 2 depicting the OLS results and columns 3 and 4 the instrumental variable results. As Table VI indicates, the external financial dependence interacted with the financial development variable is statistically significant in explaining both the growth in average firm size (column 1) and the growth in the number of establishments (column 2). This contrasts with RZ, who do not find any statistical significance (see their Table VII), perhaps because they use accounting standards as a measure for financial development rather than private credit to GDP and do not include the asset allocation interaction variable.

Interestingly, the asset allocation variable interacted with the property rights variable is not significant when explaining the growth in the average size of firms but is significant when explaining the growth in the number of establishments. This finding is consistent across all of our measures of property rights (not reported). It is also not affected by using legal origin as an instrumental variable for property rights (columns 3 and 4). It suggests, in terms of affecting growth through asset allocation, that the protection of property rights is most important through stimulating the growth of new establishments. Well-protected

Table VI

The Average Effect of Financial Development and Property Rights on Growth in Average Size and Growth in the Number of Establishments

The dependent variable is either the average growth in average size or the average growth in the number of establishments of a particular sector in a particular country over the period 1980 to 1989. Table I describes all variables in detail. All regressions include industry dummies, country dummies, and a constant but these are not reported. Regressions (3) and (4) use legal origin as the instrumental variable (IV) for property rights. Robust standard errors are shown below the coefficients. The United States is dropped as it is the benchmark. For Costa Rica, France, Indonesia, Italy, Jamaica, the Netherlands, South Africa, and Zimbabwe, we do not have data on the growth of the average size and the number of establishments. Significance levels [a], [b], and [c] correspond to 1%, 5%, and 10%, respectively.

	(1) Growth Average Size	(2) Growth Number	(3) Growth Average Size IV Legal Origin	(4) Growth Number IV Legal Origin
Fraction of sector in value added of manufacturing in 1980	-0.8687^a (0.3131)	-0.3399^b (0.1702)	-0.8396^a (0.3143)	-0.3038^c (0.1624)
Sectoral measure of financial dependence * private credit to GDP	0.0856^a (0.0289)	0.0480^b (0.0220)		
Sectoral measure of intangible intensity * property (freedom)	0.0001 (0.0021)	0.0069^a (0.0022)	0.0007 (0.0036)	0.0082^b (0.0034)
R^2	0.4329	0.3656	0.4164	0.3619
N	1071	1104	1100	1133
Number of countries	36	36	36	36

property rights can thus influence growth by allowing new firms to come to market in those industries that typically rely less on tangibles in their optimal production mix. For established firms relying more on intangible inputs, growth seems less affected by the strength of property rights in the country. This may be because such firms have other means of protecting their returns from investments.

IV. Further Robustness Tests

We have already shown that the results are robust to different control variables, to alternative means of controlling for country differences, to the use of instrumental variables, and to changes in the sample of countries. We next present evidence that the results are also robust to the particular measure of protection of property rights chosen, to differences in growth opportunities related to the level of general development, and to inclusion of data from alternative time periods.

First, we use the five alternative measures of the degree to which countries protect property rights: Special 301, the patent rights index of Ginarte and Park (1997), the property rights index and the intellectual property rights index of the

Table VII

The Average Effect of Financial Development and Property Rights on Industrial Growth: Alternative Measures of Property Rights

The dependent variable in all regressions is the average annual real growth rate of value added in a particular sector in a particular country over the period 1980 to 1989. Table I describes all variables in detail. We use five alternative measures for protection of property rights. In regressions (1) and (6), we use a measure for protection of intellectual property rights which is calculated using the Special 301 placements of the Office of the U.S. Trade Representative. We use the median rating during 1990 to 1999. In regressions (2) and (7), we use the patent rights index by Ginarte and Park (1997). We use the rating for the year 1980. A higher rating of the patent rights index indicates more protection of patent rights. In regressions (3) and (8), we use the property rights index of the World Economic Forum. We use the rating for the year 2001. In regressions (4) and (9), we use the intellectual property rights index of the World Economic Forum. We use the rating for the year 2001. In regressions (5) and (10), we use the property rights index of Knack and Keefer (1995). Average over 1982 to 1995. All regressions include industry dummies, country dummies, and a constant, but these are not reported. Robust standard errors are shown below the coefficients. The United States is dropped as it is the benchmark. Significance levels [a] and [b] correspond to 1% and 5%, respectively.

	(1)	(2)	(3)	(4)	(5)	(6)	(7)	(8)	(9)	(10)
Fraction of sector in value added of manufacturing in 1980	-0.5225^a (0.1561)	-0.9592^a (0.2449)	-1.053^a (0.2655)	-1.055^a (0.2659)	-0.9802^a (0.2493)	-0.5708^a (0.1625)	-1.064^a (0.2458)	-1.139^a (0.2652)	-1.141^a (0.2656)	-1.082^a (0.2503)
Sectoral measure of financial dependence * private credit to GDP						0.0740^a (0.0252)	0.1357^a (0.0382)	0.1355^a (0.0389)	0.1360^a (0.0390)	0.1353^a (0.0376)
Sectoral measure of intangible intensity * intellectual property (301)	0.0062^a (0.0023)					0.0052^b (0.0021)				
Sectoral measure of intangible intensity * patents (GP)		0.0074^a (0.0026)					0.0066^a (0.0026)			
Sectoral measure of intangible intensity * property (WEF)			0.0109^a (0.0029)					0.0093^a (0.0027)		
Sectoral measure of intangible intensity * intellectual property (WEF)				0.0072^a (0.0019)					0.0062^a (0.0018)	
Sectoral measure of intangible intensity * property (ICRG)					0.0043^a (0.0012)					0.0037^a (0.0012)
R^2	0.3269	0.2521	0.2581	0.2575	0.2548	0.3592	0.2734	0.2789	0.2786	0.2755
N	1119	1277	1211	1211	1277	1090	1242	1179	1179	1242
Number of countries	36	44	42	42	44	36	44	41	41	44

World Economic Forum, and the property rights index of Knack and Keefer (1995). The regression specification we use is identical to model (1) in Section III, where we include industry and country dummies and the fraction of sector in value added in manufacturing in 1980. We include the interaction term between intangible intensity and the property rights index, varying between the five property rights indexes. We also estimate specifications that include, besides the interaction term between the property rights index and the intangible-to-fixed assets measure, also the interaction term between external financial dependence and private credit to GDP. The estimation technique remains OLS. The dependent variable is the same as in Table V, the real growth rate in sectoral value added of a particular country over the period 1980 to 1989.

The results are presented in Table VII and are very similar to those of column 2 and 3 of Table V. Both without including the interaction term between external dependence and financial development (columns 1 to 5) and with including this interaction term (columns 6 to 10), we find statistically significant coefficients on the interaction term between the intangible-intensity measure and all of the five alternative property rights measures. The results with the alternative measures of the degree of property rights protection are also robust to the use of legal origin and European settler mortality as instruments (not reported). This suggests that the results are not due to the particular property rights index chosen.

Second, we want to investigate whether growth opportunities differ across industries and countries in such a way that they confound the relationships between our interaction variables and growth in sectoral value added. In particular, it is possible that the external financial dependence and asset mix variables are proxies for growth opportunities at the sectoral level. Provided that financial development is high and property rights are protected, it may not be those industries with a particular external financial dependence or intangible intensity that grow fast, but rather those with better growth opportunities. If these growth opportunities happen to be correlated with our financial development and property rights variables, then a bias in the estimations can arise. In particular, countries with similar levels of financial development or property rights may experience the same growth patterns across industries because their firms face similar patterns of growth prospects, not because their levels of financial sector development or quality of property rights protection imply a greater supply of resources for firms or a better allocation of resources by firms. Correspondingly, countries with different levels of financial development or property rights may have different growth opportunities and consequently grow in different ways, not because of differences in the supply of external financing or the protection of property rights.

In a recent paper, Fisman and Love (2002) explore this hypothesis using the RZ model, focusing on financial development. They use the actual U.S. sales growth at the sectoral level as a measure for sectoral growth opportunities at a global level. When they substitute the industry's actual sales growth for the industry's external financial dependence ratio in the interaction term with financial development, they find a positive coefficient for this new interaction variable. Furthermore, when including both the old and new interaction variables, that is, the industries' external financial dependence times countries' financial development as well as the industries' actual sales growth times countries' financial development, they find that the interaction variable with external financial dependence is no longer statistically significant. This suggests, if indeed actual U.S. sales growth rates are a good proxy for (global) growth opportunities, that it is the similarity (or difference) in growth opportunities for countries at similar (or different) levels of financial development that leads to the positive relationship between growth and the interaction variable external financial dependence times countries' financial sector development.

A similar possibility may arise with respect to the asset allocation hypothesis and our asset mix variable. If growth opportunities systematically vary across countries with the degree of property rights protection, then a statistically significant coefficient for our interaction variable could be inaccurately interpreted as support for the asset allocation hypothesis. To investigate this possibility, we use the same approach as Fisman and Love (2000). Specifically, we interact both the external financial development and property rights variables with the U.S. sectoral sales growth rates and include these two new interaction variables as well in the regressions. The estimation technique remains OLS, and the dependent variable remains the average annual real growth rate of value added in a particular sector in a particular country over the period 1980 to 1989. The new specification thus becomes

$$
\begin{aligned}
Growth_{j,k} = {} & Constant + \Gamma_1 \cdot Industry\ dummies_j \\
& + \Gamma_2 \cdot Country\ dummies_k \\
& + \gamma_3 \cdot Industry\ share\ of\ manufacturing\ value\ added_{j,k} \\
& + \gamma_4 \cdot External\ dependence_j \cdot Financial\ development_k \\
& + \gamma_5 \cdot Growth\ opportunities_j \cdot Financial\ development_k \\
& + \gamma_6 \cdot Intangible\ intensity_j \cdot Property\ rights_k \\
& + \gamma_7 \cdot Growth\ opportunities_j \cdot Property\ rights_k \\
& + \varepsilon_{j,k}.
\end{aligned}
\tag{3}
$$

In this extended specification of the model, we include the interaction between the growth opportunities of industry j and financial development in country k, and the interaction between the growth opportunities of industry j and property rights in country k.

Table VIII shows the results where the specifications vary in how many interacted variables they include and which proxy we use for growth opportunities. Columns 2 to 4 in Table VIII show the regression results of adding the interacted U.S. sales growth variable in this way to the model, with column 1 repeating the results of column 3 of Table V. Column 2 confirms the result of Fisman and Love, that is, the interaction term between financial development and U.S. sales growth "dominates" the interaction term between financial development and external financial dependence in terms of sectoral growth, as the coefficient on the interaction term between financial development and external financial dependence is no longer statistically significant. In column 3, we add the interaction term between

Financial Development, Property Rights, and Growth 2427

property rights and U.S. sales growth. Although this new interaction term is also statistically significant, our main result—a positive relationship between sectoral growth and the interaction term property rights and asset mix—is robust to this change in specification, although the statistical significance for our main result decreases somewhat. When we add both new interaction variables, that is, the interaction between U.S. sales growth and financial development and between U.S. sales growth and property rights, to the model (column 4), our main result still holds, but the RZ and Fisman and Love variables are no longer statistically significant. This suggests that the asset allocation effect remains an important explanation of firm growth.

The measure of growth opportunities used in Fisman and Love, that is, the actual sales growth at the sectoral level, is an ex post measure. It is therefore highly correlated with actual growth in value added, our dependent variable, and as such may not be the best measure to use for growth opportunities and could explain the reduced significance of the interaction variables in columns 3 and 4. As an alternative, more forward-looking proxy for growth opportunities, we use Tobin's Q ratio, that is, the ratio of the market value of the firm to the book value of its assets. We use COMPUSTAT data to construct the industry-level median of the time-average Tobin's Q of U.S. firms during the period 1980 to 1989. The results of using this alternative measure of growth opportunities in the interaction variables are presented in columns 5 to 7 of Table VIII. In contrast to the actual sales growth measure, we find that the interaction variables with Tobin's Q do not enter significantly in any of the regressions, showing that the results are dependent on the proxy used for growth opportunities. Our main result is strengthened, however, as the coefficients for the interaction variable property rights and asset mix become more statistically significant. This suggests that growth opportunities, as measured by firms' Tobin's Q, do not vary across countries in such a systematic way with the degree of property rights protection as to affect the relationship between property rights and actual growth that is occurring through improved asset allocation.

As a third robustness test, we investigate whether using U.S. sectoral data biases our results in some way. It could be the case, for example, that investment opportunities in poorer countries are different from those in the United States due to differences in the general level of a country's development rather than differences in property rights. For a poor country with the same property rights as a rich country, for example, the sectoral measure of intangible intensity may not relate in the same way to relative growth rates because growth opportunities differ due to its general lower level of development. Any relationship between growth and our interaction term of intangible intensity times property rights may then be spurious because it reflects differences in growth opportunities, and not the asset allocation effect. We test for this possibility by adding an interaction variable between the U.S. sectoral asset mix and countries' per capita GDP to the regression. We use the level of per capita GDP as a measure of the overall level of a country's economic development and of corresponding country-level investment opportunities. The same robustness test was performed by RZ, but then by using an interaction between external dependence and per capita GDP.

Table VIII
The Average Effect of Financial Development and Property Rights on Industrial Growth: Different Growth Opportunities and Income Levels

The dependent variable in all regressions is the average annual real growth rate of value added in a particular sector in a particular country over the period 1980 to 1989. Table I describes all variables in detail. All regressions include industry dummies, country dummies, and a constant, but these are not reported. Robust standard errors are shown below the coefficients. Regression (9) includes only those observations for which the property rights index takes a low value of three, regression (10) includes only those observations for which the property rights index takes a median value of four, and regression (11) includes only those observations for which the property rights index takes a high value of five. The United States is dropped as it is the benchmark. Significance levels [a], [b], and [c] correspond to 1%, 5%, and 10%, respectively.

	(1)	(2)	(3)	(4)	(5)	(6)	(7)	(8)	(9) Property Index = 3	(10) Property Index = 4	(11) Property Index = 5
Fraction of sector in value added of manufacturing in 1980	-1.076^a (0.2491)	-1.071^a (0.2496)	-1.074^a (0.2471)	-1.072^a (0.2478)	-1.068^a (0.2510)	-1.064^a (0.2522)	-1.066^a (0.2528)	-1.077^a (0.2503)	-1.466^a (0.2255)	-0.9445^a (0.3819)	-0.2194^c (0.1178)
Sectoral measure of financial dependence * private credit to GDP	0.1354^a (0.0376)	0.0649 (0.0458)	0.0896^a (0.0338)	0.0617 (0.0457)	0.1176^a (0.0364)	0.1124^a (0.0324)	0.1183^a (0.0364)	0.1353^a (0.0376)			
Sectoral measure of sales growth * private credit to GDP		1.170^c (0.6806)		0.5671 (0.5426)							
Sectoral measure of Tobin's Q * private credit to GDP			0.3377^b (0.1731)	0.2915^c (0.1612)	0.0318 (0.0430)		-0.0136 (0.0363)				
Sectoral measure of intangible intensity * property (freedom)	0.0092^a (0.0028)	0.0075^a (0.0025)	0.0048^c (0.0026)	0.0046^c (0.0026)	0.0088^a (0.0028)	0.0071^a (0.0028)	0.0071^a (0.0028)	0.0086^b (0.0038)			
Sectoral measure of sales growth * property (freedom)						0.0185 (0.0129)					
Sectoral measure of Tobin's Q * property (freedom)							0.0198 (0.0133)				
Sectoral measure of intangible intensity * per capita GDP 1980								0.0005 (0.0022)	-0.0049 (0.0046)	0.0027 (0.0023)	0.0056 (0.0045)
R^2	0.2757	0.2793	0.2832	0.2839	0.2761	0.2783	0.2784	0.2757	0.3030	0.3781	0.4546
N	1242	1242	1242	1242	1242	1242	1242	1242	387	381	471
Number of countries	44	44	44	44	44	44	44	44	14	13	15

If investment opportunities relate systematically to a country's level of development and affect the ability of sectors with different asset mix to grow, rather than a country's property rights affecting growth through the asset mix chosen, then this new interaction variable should be significant and our old interaction variable should no longer be significant. The specification becomes

$$
\begin{aligned}
Growth_{j,k} = {} & Constant + \Theta_1 \cdot Industry\ dummies_j \\
& + \Theta_2 \cdot Country\ dummies_k \\
& + \theta_3 \cdot Industry\ share\ of\ manufacturing\ value\ added_{j,k} \\
& + \theta_4 \cdot External\ dependence_j \cdot Financial\ development_k \\
& + \theta_5 \cdot Intangible\ intensity_j \cdot Property\ rights_k \\
& + \theta_6 \cdot Intangible\ intensity_j \cdot Per\ capita\ GDP_k \\
& + \varepsilon_{j,k}.
\end{aligned}
\tag{4}
$$

In this extended specification of model (1), we include the interaction between the intangible intensity of industry j and per capita GDP of country k.

Controlling for differences in the level of development in this way does not alter our main result since the new interaction variable is not statistically significant, while our old interaction variable still is significant (column 8 in Table VIII). Thus, variations in property rights across countries that lead to different growth patterns do not seem to be due to simple differences in investment opportunities related to the level of development, but rather to differences in the asset mix chosen in response to variations in property rights.

As an alternative robustness test along the same lines, we test whether for countries with the same level of property rights, investment opportunities differ in a systematic way with income levels such as to confound the relationship between assets mix and growth. If investment opportunities across sectors do not vary in a systematic way with income level, then for the same level of property rights, we should not find an effect across countries of the income level variable interacted with the asset mix variable. Columns 9 to 11 in Table VIII show the results of regressions for three subsamples of countries with each having the same degree of protection of property rights (as measured by our main property rights index), but different levels of per capita GDP. Using this specification, we do not find an income level effect since the coefficients for the interaction term between asset mix and per capita GDP are insignificant in each of the three cases.

Finally, we explore the robustness of our result to the time period chosen. Particularly, we explore the sensitivity of results to the inclusion of data from the 1990s. First, we use as the dependent variable the average annual real growth rate of value added in a particular sector in a particular country over the period 1980 to 1999, rather than only the 1980s. Using growth rates over a longer period has some advantages since we are interested in the long-run relationships between property rights, financial development, and growth. The main drawback of including growth data from the 1990s is that the number of countries drops sharply, from 44 to 19. This is because data on sectoral growth in value added

Table IX
The Average Effect of Financial Development and Property Rights on Industrial Growth: Different Time Periods

The dependent variable in all regressions is the average annual real growth rate of value added in a particular sector in a particular country. In regressions (1) and (3), the average annual real growth rate is calculated over the period 1980 to 1989. In regressions (2) and (4), the average annual growth rate is calculated over the period 1980 to 1999. Regressions (1) and (2) use intangible-intensity values based on data from the 1980s, while regressions (3) and (4) use intangible-intensity values based on data from the 1990s. Table I describes all variables in detail. All regressions include industry dummies, country dummies, and a constant, but these are not reported. Robust standard errors are shown below the coefficients. The United States is dropped from all regressions as it is the benchmark country. Significance levels [a], [b], and [c] correspond to 1%, 5%, and 10%, respectively.

	(1) Growth over 1980–89; Intangibility over 1980s	(2) Growth over 1980–99; Intangibility over 1980s	(3) Growth over 1980–89; Intangibility over 1990s	(4) Growth over 1980–99; Intangibility over 1990s
Fraction of sector in value added of manufacturing in 1980	-1.076^{a} (0.2491)	-0.2256^{b} (0.1012)	-1.047^{a} (0.2470)	-0.1973^{b} (0.0974)
Sectoral measure of financial dependence * private credit to GDP	0.1354^{a} (0.0376)	0.0449^{c} (0.0259)	0.1398^{a} (0.0379)	0.0516^{b} (0.0262)
Sectoral measure of intangible intensity * property (freedom)	0.0092^{a} (0.0028)	0.0074^{a} (0.0018)	0.0078^{c} (0.0047)	0.0056^{b} (0.0026)
R^2	0.2757	0.6133	0.2735	0.6061
N	1242	478	1242	478
Number of countries	44	19	44	19

are not available for many countries, since the United Nations database on Industrial Statistics includes data on sectoral growth in value added with a lag of several years for most countries. The results of using growth rates over the 1980s and the 1990s are reported in column 2 of Table IX, where column 1 reports for ease of comparison the results using the same specification for the 1980s (as already reported in Table V, column 3). We find that our main result is not qualitatively altered, because the coefficients for both the interactive variable external financial dependence times financial development and the interactive variable intangible intensity times property rights remain statistically significant and positive.

As a further robustness test of the time period studied, we also reestimated model (1) using the growth data of the 1980s, but with the sectoral intangible-intensity variable measured over the 1990s rather than the 1980s. This test investigates whether the use of a particular time period for the benchmark, industry level of intangible intensity, affects our findings. Our main result does not change qualitatively either when using this different benchmark (column 3 in Table IX), although the statistical significance is reduced somewhat. This robustness should not be a surprise, since the correlation between the sectoral intangible-intensity variables for the two different time periods is high, 0.90. Our results are also robust to using the average growth rates over the period 1980 to 1999 and the intangible-intensity values for the 1990s (column 4 in Table IX). Overall, our results do not seem to be affected by the particular time period chosen.

V. Conclusions

Countries differ from each other in many ways. Two aspects are the degree of their financial sector development and the quality of their property rights. This paper argues that an environment with poorly developed financial systems and weak property rights has two effects on firms: First, it reduces the access of firms to external financing and, second, it leads firms to allocate resources in a suboptimal way. The importance of the lack of financing effect has already been shown in the law and finance literature. We investigate the importance of property rights for firm growth by studying its impact on firms' allocation of investable resources. We find evidence suggesting that the effect of insecure property rights on the asset mix of firms, the asset allocation effect, is economically as important as the lack of financing effect, because it impedes the growth of firms to the same quantitative magnitude. Furthermore, the evidence suggests that the asset allocation effect is particularly important in hindering the growth of new firms.

While we use the ratio of tangibles and intangible assets as a measure of asset mix, the implications of our results probably go beyond this particular asset choice and may imply that an efficient allocation of firm resources can more generally be impeded by weak property rights. Our results may imply that the degree to which firms allocate resources in an optimal way will depend on the strength of a country's property rights and that firms' asset allocation is an important channel through which property rights affect firm growth. Thus, our results may have the policy implication that, just as it is important to have a good financial system, requiring in turn a functioning legal system, it is also important to assure the protection of returns to different types of assets. To the extent that the emergence of the "new economy" has increased the economic returns to assets on which yields are more difficult to secure, our results could even underestimate the overall costs of weak property rights. If indeed new economy assets and future growth opportunities are more related to intangible assets, then any under-allocation of investable resources towards intangible assets may impede the future growth of firms and economies more generally, and even more so going forward.

Appendix: The Values of the Institutional Variables by Individual Country

Table AI reports the values of the country variables for the countries studied. Property (freedom) is a rating of property rights in each country (on a scale from 1 to 5). The index equals the median rating for the period 1995 to 1999, and the source is the Index of Economic Freedom from the Heritage Foundation. We reversed the original order of the index. Intellectual property (301) is an index of intellectual property rights (on a scale from 1 to 5). The index is calculated using the Special 301 placements of the Office of the U.S. Trade Representative. The index equals the median rating for the period 1990 to 1999. Patent rights (GP) is an index of patent rights (on a scale from 0 to 5) in 1980. The source of the patent rights index is Ginarte and Park (1997). Property (WEF) is an index of property rights for the year 2001 (on a scale from 1 to 7). The source is the World Economic Forum (2002). Intellectual property (WEF) is an index of intellectual property rights for the year 2001 (on a scale from 1 to 7). The source is the World Economic Forum (2002). Property (ICRG) is a measure of property rights in each country (on a scale from 0 to 10). The index equals the average rating for the period 1982 to 1995. The source is Knack and Keefer (1995). Each property rights index is constructed such that the more protection property receives, the higher the score of the index. Private credit is private credit divided by GDP in 1980. The source is RZ and the International Financial Statistics of the International Monetary Fund. Market cap is stock market capitalization divided by GDP in 1980. The source is RZ. Accounting is accounting standards in 1983 on a scale from 0 to 90, with higher scores indicating more disclosure. The source is RZ. Human capital is the average for 1980 of the years of schooling attained by the population over 25 years of age. The source of the human capital variable is Barro and Lee (1993). Rule of law is an assessment of the law and order tradition in the country (on a scale from 0 to 10). The rating is the average of the months of April and October of the monthly index between 1982 and 1995. The source is La Porta et al. (1997). Legal origin identifies the legal origin of the Company Law or Commercial Code of each country. There are four origins: (1) English Common Law, (2) French Commercial Code, (3) German Commercial Code, and (4) Scandinavian Commercial Code. The source is La Porta et al. (1999). European settler mortality is the European settler mortality rate, measured in terms of deaths per annum per 1,000 mean strength. The source is Acemoglu et al. (2001). GDP per capita is the logarithm of GDP per capita in 1980. The source is the World Development Indicators of

Table AI

The Values of the Institutional Variables by Individual Country

Country	Property (Freedom)	Intellectual Property (301)	Patents (GP)	Property (WEF)	Intellectual Property (WEF)	Property (ICRG)	Private Credit	Market Cap	Accounting Standards	Human Capital	Rule of Law	Legal Origin	European Settler Mortality	GDP per Capita
Australia	5.00	4.00	3.23	6.20	6.00	9.30	0.28	0.38	0.70	10.08	10.00	1.00	2.15	9.20
Austria	5.00	5.00	3.81	6.40	6.20	9.45	0.77	0.03	0.48	6.22	10.00	3.00	n.a.	9.16
Bangladesh	2.00	n.a.	1.99	3.70	2.20	2.85	0.07	0.00	n.a.	1.68	n.a.	1.00	4.27	4.79
Belgium	5.00	5.00	3.38	5.90	5.50	9.58	0.29	0.09	0.63	8.79	10.00	2.00	n.a.	9.33
Brazil	3.00	3.00	1.85	5.00	4.10	6.64	0.23	0.05	0.69	2.98	6.32	2.00	4.26	7.41
Canada	5.00	4.00	2.76	6.20	5.80	9.73	0.45	0.46	0.68	10.16	10.00	1.00	2.78	9.26
Chile	5.00	4.00	2.41	5.60	4.20	6.44	0.36	0.34	0.60	5.99	7.02	2.00	4.23	7.84
Colombia	3.00	4.00	1.12	4.30	3.00	5.54	0.14	0.05	0.39	4.23	2.08	2.00	4.26	7.05
Costa Rica	3.00	n.a.	1.94	5.20	3.70	6.47	0.26	0.04	n.a.	4.81	n.a.	2.00	4.36	7.68
Denmark	5.00	5.00	3.62	6.40	6.30	9.80	0.42	0.09	0.62	10.14	10.00	4.00	n.a.	9.41
Egypt	3.00	3.00	1.99	5.60	4.10	4.96	0.21	0.01	n.a.	2.16	4.17	2.00	4.22	6.33
Finland	5.00	5.00	2.95	6.50	6.40	9.76	0.48	0.06	0.71	9.61	10.00	4.00	n.a.	9.23
France	4.00	5.00	3.90	6.40	6.60	9.37	0.54	0.10	0.76	5.97	8.98	2.00	n.a.	9.34
Germany	5.00	5.00	3.86	6.50	6.30	9.55	0.78	0.09	0.68	8.46	9.23	3.00	n.a.	9.42
Greece	4.00	3.00	2.46	5.00	3.90	6.56	0.44	0.08	0.44	6.56	6.18	2.00	n.a.	8.25
India	3.00	3.00	1.62	4.90	3.00	5.80	0.24	0.05	0.71	2.72	4.17	1.00	3.88	5.48
Indonesia	3.00	4.00	0.33	3.80	2.90	4.38	0.20	0.00	n.a.	3.09	3.98	2.00	5.14	6.21
Israel	4.00	4.00	3.57	6.30	4.90	7.22	0.67	0.35	n.a.	9.14	4.82	1.00	n.a.	8.18
Italy	4.00	4.00	3.71	6.20	5.70	8.07	0.42	0.07	0.69	5.83	8.33	2.00	n.a.	8.77
Jamaica	4.00	n.a.	2.86	4.90	3.50	5.05	0.15	0.02	n.a.	3.60	n.a.	1.00	4.87	7.11
Japan	5.00	4.00	3.94	6.10	5.50	9.34	0.86	0.30	0.67	8.17	8.98	3.00	n.a.	9.20
Jordan	4.00	4.50	1.86	5.80	4.60	5.15	0.54	0.50	n.a.	2.93	4.35	2.00	n.a.	7.01
Kenya	3.00	n.a.	2.57	n.a.	n.a.	5.58	0.20	0.00	n.a.	2.44	5.42	1.00	4.98	6.03
Korea, Rep.	5.00	3.00	3.28	4.70	4.00	6.90	0.50	0.08	n.a.	6.85	5.35	3.00	n.a.	7.25
Malaysia	4.00	4.00	2.57	5.20	3.50	7.09	0.48	0.65	0.78	4.49	6.78	1.00	2.87	7.43
Mexico	3.00	4.00	1.40	4.60	3.60	5.76	0.16	0.07	n.a.	3.51	5.35	2.00	4.26	7.88
Morocco	3.50	n.a.	2.38	n.a.	n.a.	5.05	0.16	0.02	n.a.	n.a.	n.a.	1.00	4.36	6.69
Netherlands	5.00	5.00	4.24	6.50	6.50	9.87	0.60	0.19	0.73	8.20	10.00	2.00	n.a.	9.32
New Zealand	5.00	4.00	3.32	5.90	5.30	9.80	0.19	0.33	0.61	12.14	10.00	1.00	2.15	8.92

Table AI
(continued)

Country	Property (Freedom)	Intellectual Property (301)	Patents (GP)	Property (WEF)	Intellectual Property (WEF)	Property (ICRG)	Private Credit	Market Cap	Accounting Standards	Human Capital	Rule of Law	Legal Origin	European Settler Mortality	GDP per Capita
Nigeria	3.00	n.a.	3.05	3.80	2.50	3.85	0.12	n.a.	0.62	n.a.	2.73	1.00	7.60	6.81
Norway	5.00	5.00	3.29	5.90	5.30	9.69	0.34	0.06	0.71	10.32	10.00	4.00	n.a.	9.51
Pakistan	4.00	4.00	1.99	n.a.	n.a.	4.21	0.25	0.03	0.69	1.74	3.03	1.00	3.61	5.67
Peru	3.00	4.00	1.02	4.10	3.00	4.19	0.11	0.06	n.a.	5.44	2.50	2.00	4.26	6.74
Philippines	4.00	4.00	2.67	4.30	2.90	3.62	0.28	0.10	0.63	6.00	2.73	2.00	n.a.	6.59
Portugal	4.00	5.00	1.98	5.30	4.90	7.94	0.52	0.01	0.52	3.23	8.68	2.00	n.a.	7.74
Singapore	5.00	4.00	2.57	6.50	5.60	8.69	0.57	1.62	0.73	3.69	8.57	1.00	2.87	8.45
South Africa	3.00	4.00	3.57	5.30	4.50	7.50	0.26	1.20	0.81	4.61	4.42	1.00	2.74	7.97
Spain	4.00	4.00	3.29	5.90	5.30	7.99	0.76	0.09	0.42	5.15	7.80	2.00	n.a.	8.53
Sri Lanka	3.00	n.a.	2.79	4.20	3.10	4.64	0.21	0.06	n.a.	5.18	1.90	1.00	4.25	5.53
Sweden	4.00	4.00	3.47	5.90	5.80	9.80	0.42	0.11	0.81	9.47	10.00	4.00	n.a.	9.57
Turkey	4.00	3.00	1.80	4.20	3.10	5.76	0.14	0.01	n.a.	2.62	5.18	2.00	n.a.	6.99
UK	5.00	5.00	3.57	6.30	6.10	9.40	0.25	0.38	0.80	8.35	8.57	1.00	n.a.	9.17
Venezuela	3.00	4.00	1.35	3.80	3.00	5.82	0.30	0.05	n.a.	4.93	6.37	2.00	4.36	8.29
Zimbabwe	3.00	n.a.	2.90	3.90	2.90	5.09	0.30	0.45	n.a.	2.40	3.68	1.00	n.a.	6.09
Average	3.96	4.12	2.67	5.33	4.51	7.03	0.36	0.20	0.65	5.84	6.67	1.91	4.03	7.79

Financial Development, Property Rights, and Growth 2435

the World Bank. More detail on the definitions and sources of the variables can be found in Table I. Countries are sorted in ascending alphabetical order. The abbreviation n.a. stands for not available.

REFERENCES

Acemoglu, Daron, Simon Johnson, and James A. Robinson, 2001, The colonial origins of comparative development: An empirical investigation, *American Economic Review* 91, 1369–1401.

Acemoglu, Daron, Simon Johnson, and James A. Robinson, 2002, Reversal of fortune: Geography and institutions in the making of the modern world income, *Quarterly Journal of Economics* 117, 1231–1294.

Barro, Robert J., 1991, Economic growth in a cross section of countries, *Quarterly Journal of Economics* 106, 407–443.

Barro, Robert J., and Jong-Wha Lee, 1993, International comparisons of educational attainment, *Journal of Monetary Economics* 32, 363–394.

Beck, Thorsten, Asli Demirgüç-Kunt, and Ross Levine, 2003, Law, endowments, and finance, *Journal of Financial Economics*, forthcoming.

Beck, Thorsten, Ross Levine, and Norman Loayza, 2000, Finance and the sources of growth, *Journal of Financial Economics* 58, 261–300.

Besley, Timothy, 1995, Property rights and investment incentives: Theory and evidence from Ghana, *Journal of Political Economy* 103, 903–937.

Booth, Laurence, Varouj Aivazian, Asli Demirgüç-Kunt, and Vojislav Maksimovic, 2000, Capital structures in developing countries, *Journal of Finance* 56, 87–130.

Bradley, Michael, Gregg A. Jarrell, and E. Han Kim, 1984, On the existence of an optimal capital structure: Theory and evidence, *Journal of Finance* 39, 857–878.

Ceterolli, Nicola, and Michele Gambera, 2001, Banking market structure, financial dependence and growth: International evidence from industry data, *Journal of Finance* 56, 617–648.

Demirgüç-Kunt, Asli, and Vojislav Maksimovic, 1998, Law, finance, and firm growth, *Journal of Finance* 53, 2107–2137.

Demirgüç-Kunt, Asli, and Vojislav Maksimovic, 1999, Institutions, financial markets, and firm debt maturity, *Journal of Financial Economics* 54, 295–336.

Fisman, Raymond, and Inessa Love, 2002, Patterns of industrial development revisited: The role of finance, Mimeo, Columbia University.

Fisman, Raymond, and Inessa Love, 2003, Trade credit, financial intermediary development, and industry growth, *Journal of Finance* 58, 353–374.

Ginarte, Juan Carlos, and Walter Park, 1997, Determinants of patent rights: A cross-national study, *Research Policy* 26, 283–301.

Hall, Robert E., and Charles I. Jones, 1999, Why do some countries produce so much more output per worker than others? *Quarterly Journal of Economics* 114, 83–116.

Harris, Milton, and Artur Raviv, 1991, The theory of capital structure, *Journal of Finance* 46, 297–355.

Johnson, Simon, Daniel Kaufmann, and Pablo Zoido-Lobaton, 1998, Government in transition: Regulatory discretion and the unofficial economy, *American Economic Review* 88, 387–392.

Johnson, Simon, John McMillan, and Christopher Woodruff, 2002, Property rights and finance, *American Economic Review* 92, 1335–1356.

King, Robert G., and Ross Levine, 1993, Finance and growth: Schumpeter might be right, *Quarterly Journal of Economics* 108, 717–737.

Knack, Steven, and Philip Keefer, 1995, Institutions and economic performance: Cross-country tests using alternative measures, *Economics and Politics* 7, 207–227.

La Porta, Rafael, Florencio Lopez-de-Silanes, Christian Pop-Eleches, and Andrei Shleifer, 2002, The guarantees of freedom, Mimeo, Harvard University.

La Porta, Rafael, Florencio Lopez-de-Silanes, Andrei Shleifer, and Robert W. Vishny, 1997, Legal determinants of external finance, *Journal of Finance* 52, 1131–1150.

La Porta, Rafael, Florencio Lopez-de-Silanes, Andrei Shleifer, and Robert W. Vishny, 1998, Law and finance, *Journal of Political Economy* 106, 1113–1155.

La Porta, Rafael, Florencio Lopez-de-Silanes, Andrei Shleifer, and Robert W. Vishny, 1999, The quality of government, *Journal of Law, Economics and Organization* 15, 222–279.

Levine, Ross, 1997, Financial development and growth, *Journal of Economic Literature* 35, 688–726.

Levine, Ross, and Sara Zervos, 1998, Stock markets, banks, and economic growth, *American Economic Review* 88, 537–558.

Mansfield, Edwin, 1995, Intellectual property protection, direct investment, and technology transfer, Discussion paper 27, International Finance Corporation, Washington, DC.

Myers, Stewart C., 1977, Determinants of corporate borrowing, *Journal of Financial Economics* 5, 146–175.

North, Douglass C., 1990. *Institutions, institutional change, and economic performance* (Cambridge University Press, Cambridge, MA).

Rajan, Raghuram, and Luigi Zingales, 1995, What do we know about capital structure: Some evidence from international data, *Journal of Finance* 50, 661–691.

Rajan, Raghuram, and Luigi Zingales, 1998, Financial dependence and growth, *American Economic Review* 88, 559–586.

Romer, Paul M., 1990, Endogenous technological change, *Journal of Political Economy* 98, S71–S102.

Stern, Scott, Michael E. Porter, and Jeffrey L. Furman, 2000, The determinants of national innovative capacity, NBER Working Paper No. 7876.

Titman, Sheridan, and Roberto Wessels, 1988, The determinants of capital structure choice, *Journal of Finance* 43, 1–19.

World Economic Forum, 2002, *Global Competitiveness Report* (Oxford University Press, Oxford, UK).

DOES LEGAL ENFORCEMENT AFFECT FINANCIAL TRANSACTIONS? THE CONTRACTUAL CHANNEL IN PRIVATE EQUITY*

JOSH LERNER AND ANTOINETTE SCHOAR

Analyzing 210 developing country private equity investments, we find that transactions vary with nations' legal enforcement, whether measured directly or through legal origin. Investments in high enforcement and common law nations often use convertible preferred stock with covenants. In low enforcement and civil law nations, private equity groups tend to use common stock and debt, and rely on equity and board control. Transactions in high enforcement countries have higher valuations and returns. While relying on ownership rather than contractual provisions may help to alleviate legal enforcement problems, these results suggest that private solutions are only a partial remedy.

I. INTRODUCTION

A large literature in economics and finance has documented a systematic relationship between a country's legal system and the development and liquidity of its financial markets. Starting with La Porta et al. [1997, 1998], these works identify legal origin as a crucial determinant of minority shareholder protection against expropriation by corporate insiders, with common law systems providing better protection than civil law ones. Glaeser, Johnson, and Shleifer [2001] and Djankov et al. [2003] suggest that parties in common law countries can more readily enforce commercial contracts. Common law and high enforcement nations have broader and more valuable capital markets, more public offerings, dispersed ownership of public firms, and other indicators of financial development (also see Demirgüc-Kunt and Levine [2001]).

Much less attention, however, has been directed to under-

* We thank many private equity groups for making this study possible by providing the transaction information. Teresa Barger, Richard Frank, Felda Hardymon, Gustavo Herrero, Mario Mahler, Kenneth Morse, Bruce Purdue, Kanako Sekine, and Camille Tang Yeh introduced us to many groups. Zahi Ben-David, Adam Kolasinski, Jiro Kondo, and especially Yok Nam Ng provided excellent research assistance. We also thank our legal research team: Arturo Garcia de Leon, May Fong Yue Lo, Alexander Nadmitov, Rahul Singh, Michiel Vissier, Agata Waclawik, and Feng Wang, as well as Sridhar Gorthi of Trilegal. We thank Erik Bergloff, Nittai Bergman, Peter Henry, Katharina Lewellen, Roberta Romano, Andrei Shleifer, Per Strömberg, Amir Sufi, Yishay Yafeh, and participants at presentations at Harvard University, the London School of Economics, the Stockholm Institute for Financial Research, and the Western Finance Association annual meeting for helpful comments. Harvard Business School's Division of Research provided financial assistance. All errors are our own.

The Quarterly Journal of Economics, February 2005

standing the specific avenues through which the nature of the legal system affects financial development. The current paper highlights the importance of what we term "the contractual channel": the ability of investors to enter into complex, state-dependent contracts. We document that investors in countries with effective legal enforcement rely on specific contracting contingencies and securities that shift control rights depending on the performance of the investment and enable investors to separate cash flow and control rights. A large theory literature points to the benefits of these contracting possibilities for entrepreneurs and investors (as we describe in the following section). By way of contrast, investors in countries with difficult legal enforcement seem to be required to secure control rights through majority ownership. These results suggest that a critical impact of the legal system is the way it constrains the ability of private parties to write contracts that are complex or state contingent. Parties cannot easily undo deficiencies of the law through private transactions if the legal system does not enforce certain types of contracts.

We focus on a specific set of transactions: private equity investments. We concentrate on these transactions since they are better documented than most private financial transactions, and follow a relatively standardized setup. Private equity transactions represent a relatively modest share of the absolute value of investments made in most developing countries. But we think that they are representative of the legal and economic considerations that private parties face in any contract negotiation. We collect data on the actual contractual relationships between investors and entrepreneurs in 210 transactions from a wide variety of private equity groups and countries.

We find that investments in countries with a common law tradition and with better legal enforcement are far less likely to employ common stock or straight debt, and more likely to use convertible preferred stock. Similarly, transactions in these nations are generally associated with greater contractual protections for the private equity groups. These contracts look similar to U. S. contracts, which an extensive theoretical literature suggests are a second-best solution to contracting in private equity. In contrast, investors in countries with civil law or socialist legal background and where legal enforcement is difficult rely more heavily on obtaining majority control of the firms they invest in, use debt more often, and have more board representation. These findings suggest that private equity groups here rely on ownership, which may substitute for the lack of contractual protections. We also verify that our results are not driven by the tendency of common law-based funds to invest in common law countries.

Finally, we investigate the consequences of these differences: can the parties successfully address the absence of the contractual channel by relying on large ownership stakes? We find that firms' valuations are significantly higher in nations with a common law tradition, and superior legal enforcement and private equity funds investing in common law countries enjoy higher returns. We point out, however, that this evidence is only suggestive of any effects of contracting constraints on investment outcomes.

These results suggest that systematic differences in legal enforcement impose constraints on the type of contracts that can be written. This inability to separate cash flow rights from control rights has the potential to seriously distort the contracting process by forcing the parties to rely on large equity stakes. Private equity investors face constraints in diversifying their portfolio, since they have to hold larger stakes of a given firm than they would like for pure control purposes. Entrepreneurs might have reduced incentives since they are forced to give up a substantial amount of cash flow (and control) rights early on. These findings suggest that the lack of contract enforcement may not be easily undone by private contracting arrangements that emphasize ownership.

The plan of this paper is as follows. Section II lays out the theoretical motivation for the analysis. Section III describes the construction of the data set. The analysis is in Section IV. The final section concludes the paper.

II. The Economics of Private Equity

Financial contracts are written to assign cash flow and control rights between contracting parties, e.g., a private equity group and an entrepreneur. An extensive literature on optimal contracting, starting with Holmström [1979], has analyzed the role of contracts in alleviating principal-agent problems through the contingent allocation of cash flow rights. It relies on the assumption that contracts can be enforced costlessly.

The literature on incomplete contracting—see Grossman and Hart [1986] and Hart and Moore [1990]—highlights that if courts are unable to enforce or even verify complicated, state-dependent contracts, the allocation of control rights can allow the parties to reach a second-best agreement. Aghion and Bolton [1992] and Hellmann [1998] show that convertible preferred securities allow control rights to be transferred to the party that makes better use of them. In particular, these securities allocate control to the entrepreneur when things are going well, but allow the investors to assert control if the firm is doing poorly. These securities will give stronger incentives to entrepreneurs than majority control based on common stock contracts, since they prevent the holdup of entrepreneurs by investors if the entrepreneurs are running the firm well.

In the context of private equity, Kaplan and Strömberg [2003] and Gompers [1998] identify a number of benefits to investors and entrepreneurs from being able to separate cash flow and control rights, typically through the use of convertible preferred securities.[1] The ability to maintain control rights without majority cash flow rights allows investors to invest relatively small amounts of capital early on without fearing expropriation, thereby allowing capital diversification. Entrepreneurs benefit since they do not have to give away cash flow rights early on when valuations are still very low.

It might well be, however, that private equity groups in certain nations are unable to enforce contracts involving the separation of ownership and control or more complicated contingencies, since it may be difficult to educate judges and lawyers about these contract features. In these instances, we envision that firms will employ third-best contracts, which entail the use of controlling blocks of common stock or straight debt. We expect this pattern to be most prevalent in nations where the legal system is less well developed. Moreover, we would predict that control through majority ownership of common stock and control through contract contingencies would be substitutes. Obviously, if courts are so inefficient or corrupt that they cannot enforce any

---

1. Unlike in public settings, in private equity preferred stock refers to a security that awards liquidation rights to the investor if the company does not achieve a threshold performance level. In the following, we refer to the group of securities as convertible preferred stock to avoid confusion with preferred that only has preferential voting rights.

contract at all, even majority ownership would not protect investors.

Bergman and Nicolaievsky [2003] develop a formal model that starts from a similar assumption as put forward here: legal regimes differ in their ability to enforce complicated contingencies to prevent investor expropriation. They find supporting evidence in Mexico. The focus of the analysis is complementary to the current paper, since the paper aims to contrast the use of contractual contingencies in private versus public firms, where renegotiation between different groups of investors is more difficult.

In a contemporaneous paper, Kaplan, Martel, and Strömberg [2003] examine venture capital contracts for a set of high-income European countries. They find that most of the contractual variation between common law and civil law countries in their sample is explained by the fact that private equity groups use contracts that are similar to the ones they employ in their home countries. It is possible that the higher sophistication of the judicial system in these countries allows private equity groups to experiment with contracts that are different from those customarily employed in the local market. One might also conjecture, however, that a perceived sense of similarity between the United States and Continental Europe led investors in some cases to make contracting choices that might ultimately be very difficult to enforce in these countries.[2]

Our hypothesis was informally corroborated in our conversations with investment professionals at private equity groups. The groups indicated that they place much greater emphasis on having controlling equity blocks in nations with poor contract enforcement, largely due to their inability to enforce more complex contracts. One group operating in Latin America, for instance, had initially employed convertible preferred securities in all its transactions. Their enthusiasm for this investment strategy waned, however, when they began litigating with one of their portfolio companies in Peru. The private equity investors found

---

2. Similarly, Cumming and MacIntosh [2002] examine the types of transactions funded and exit routes employed in twelve Asian nations. They argue that the legal regimes affect the types of investments selected and the way in which the private equity groups exit their holdings, but not returns. Qian and Strahan [2004] show that bank loans in countries with better legal protection are less likely to be secured and have more covenants.

themselves unable to convince the judge that their preferred stock agreement gave them the right to replace a third-generation founder of the company, even if the group's shares were only convertible into 20 percent of the firm's equity. After this experience, the private equity group structured its subsequent investments as common stock deals in which they held the majority of the equity. In many nations, our interviewees asserted, not only were the entrepreneurs unfamiliar with equity investments that used securities other than common stock, but key actors in the legal system—lawyers and judges—were suspicious and indeed hostile to such transactions. As a result, they chose to employ common stock there. These conversations did not yield a consistent answer to the question of whether the efforts to address the ineffectiveness of the contractual channel through a reliance on ownership would be successful.[3]

III. The Data

We constructed the sample by asking private equity groups that invest in developing nations[4] to give us a representative array of their transactions in terms of the type of deal, the location and industry of the firm, and the success of the transaction. For each transaction we obtained the investment memorandum, the associated stock purchase agreements, and any other documents associated with the structuring of the transaction. We deliberately attempted to recruit as diverse an array of private equity funds as possible. In a study along these lines, selection biases are an almost inevitable consequence. We tried to ameliorate this concern by obtaining transactions from groups with

3. While there are a few examples, we did not discover many instances where contracting parties in countries with poor legal enforcement relied on private arbitrators instead. See, for example, Johnson, McMillan, and Woodruff [2002] for an analysis of private contract enforcement mechanisms.

4. According to the World Bank, developing nations are those countries that have either low- or middle-level per capita incomes, have underdeveloped capital markets, and/or are not industrialized. It should be noted, however, that the application of these criteria is somewhat subjective. For instance, Kuwait appears on many lists of developing nations despite its high per capita gross domestic product. The reason for its inclusion lies in the income distribution inequality that exists there, which has not allowed it to reach the general living standards of developed countries. For the purposes of this paper, we take an expansive view of what constitutes a developing nation, and simply eliminate any transactions taking place in the 24 nations that were original members of the Organisation for Cooperation and Development or joined within fifteen years of its creation (i.e., through the addition of New Zealand in 1973).

LEGAL ENFORCEMENT AND FINANCIAL TRANSACTIONS   **229**

TABLE I

CONSTRUCTION OF SAMPLE

This table summarizes the key features associated with the construction of the sample of 210 private equity transactions.

Private equity group		Year of deal		Industry of firm		Deal type		Country of firm	
Group 1	8	1987	2	Distribution/Retail	14	Buyout	28	Argentina	18
Group 2	6	1988	2	Finance	16	Corp. acquisition	10	Bolivia	2
Group 3	6	1992	3	Food	29	Distress	4	Brazil	18
Group 4	5	1993	4	Health care	9	Expansion	97	Bulgaria	8
Group 5	3	1994	2	Information tech	24	IPO	12	Chile	7
Group 6	3	1995	5	Internet	9	Privatization	10	China	13
Group 7	10	1996	10	Manufacturing	32	Venture capital	49	Estonia	8
Group 8	8	1997	17	Media	8			Ghana	3
Group 9	6	1998	35	Natural resources	11			Hong Kong	13
Group 10	6	1999	31	Real estate	4			India	28
Group 11	11	2000	34	Services	17			Korea	10
Group 12	3	2001	40	Software	10			Indonesia	2
Group 13	2	2002	22	Telecom	14			Latvia	4
Group 14	4	2003	3	Other	13			Malaysia	2
Group 15	10							Mexico	14
Group 16	8							Peru	2
Group 17	6							Poland	13
Group 18	5							Romania	18
Group 19	10							Singapore	6
Group 20	13							South Africa	2
Group 21	14							Taiwan	4
Group 22	8							Tanzania	2
Group 23	5							Thailand	3
Group 24	7							Uruguay	2
Group 25	21							Yugoslavia	6
Group 26	13							Other	5
Group 27	7								
Group 28	2								

diverse backgrounds. But it is likely that the private equity groups that participated in this study are more Western-oriented and sophisticated than their peers. The presence of this bias should, in fact, reduce the observed variation between legal regimes and thus makes the substantial differences that we see even more striking.

Table I summarizes the sample. The 210 transactions are from 28 private equity groups, who contributed between 2 and 21 deals for our sample. The transactions occurred between 1987 and 2003, with the bulk of investments between 1996 and 2002. Thirty distinct countries are represented with no single nation or region dominating the sample. The industries include a broad array, from food to information technology. We classified the transactions by type using the definitions in European Venture Capital Association [2002]. The investments are dominated by expansion transactions, as well as venture capital and buyout transactions.

Panel A of Table II shows that the average GNP per capita for the countries in our sample is $2142 per year. Moreover, 27 percent of the investments are based in countries that have British legal origin, 30 percent have French legal origins, and 42 percent are in former socialist countries. In comparison, 56 percent of the investments included in this study are funded by private equity partnerships that are based either in the United States or United Kingdom. While U. K.- and U. S.-based partnerships in our sample are more likely to invest in countries with British legal origin, we find that they also invest in a large fraction of deals that are not based in common law countries. This heterogeneity is important, since it will allow us to analyze whether a given partnership adjusts the contract terms in response to the environment of the country where the deal takes place.

Panel B of Table II provides an initial overview of the transactions. The differences between this sample and U. S. transactions are striking. In the United States nearly 80 percent of private equity transactions are dominated by convertible preferred stock (see Kaplan and Strömberg [2003]).[5] Common stock is quite rare, found in only a little more than 10 percent of the U. S. deals. In contrast, in our sample 54 percent of the transactions employ common stock, while convertible preferred stock is only encountered in 21 percent of the deals.[6] Similarly, many of the protections commonly employed by venture capitalists in the United States are rarely found here. Kaplan and Strömberg

---

5. It should be noted that Kaplan and Strömberg's sample includes only venture capital transactions, which would encompass transactions described as "venture capital" and "expansion" transactions in the developing world. (The category of "expansion" deals is not frequently employed in the United States.) Legal texts (e.g., Bartlett [1995]), however, suggest that we would observe similar patterns if we examined all U. S. private equity transactions.

6. We tried as best as possible to avoid any bias in our coding of contractual terms that are purely based on differences in contractual language. For example, any security structure that has payoff streams equivalent to a convertible preferred would be classified as such, even if the contract did not explicitly use that term.

LEGAL ENFORCEMENT AND FINANCIAL TRANSACTIONS   **231**

TABLE II

CHARACTERISTICS OF DEVELOPING COUNTRY PRIVATE EQUITY TRANSACTIONS

The sample consists of 210 investments in developing countries by private equity groups (PEGs). The first panel describes the features of the transactions; the second panel, the features of the nation and the private equity group involved in the transaction. We do not record the medians and standard deviations of the dummy variables.

Panel A: Setting of transactions

	Mean	Median	Standard dev	Minimum	Maximum
Per capita gross national product	2142	1743	2561	181	12368
Logarithm of rule of law index	0.22	0.28	0.59	−1.25	1.85
English legal family nation	0.27			0	1
French legal family nation	0.30			0	1
Socialist legal family country	0.42			0	1
U. K.- or U. S.-based private equity group	0.56			0	1

Panel B: Nature of transactions

	Mean	Median	Standard dev	Minimum	Maximum
Size of financing (1997 $MMs)	4.31	3.29	5.12	0.17	18.53
Implied valuation (1997 $MMs)	5.12	4.18	4.92	0.45	61.38[a]
Straight debt	0.11			0	1
Common stock	0.55			0	1
Straight preferred stock	0.09			0	1
Participating preferred stock	0.05			0	1
Convertible preferred stock	0.21			0	1
Warrants	0.06			0	1
Contingent equity	0.34			0	1
PEG's maximum equity stake	0.47	0.40	0.37	0	1
PEG's minimum equity stake	0.33			0	1
Difference in PEG ownership	0.15	0.01	0.26	0	1
PEG has control when maximum stake	0.37			0	1
PEG has control when minimum stake	0.29			0	1
Antidilution provisions	0.27			0	1
Automatic conversion provisions	0.26			0	1
Maximum board size	6.50	6	2.03	3	12
Minimum board size	5.40	5	1.95	3	11
Maximum PEG board seats	2.66	2	1.89	0	9
Minimum PEG board seats	1.35	1	1.24	0	6
Maximum founder/manager board seats	3.22	3	1.87	0	7
Minimum founder/manager board seats	2.47	2	1.72	0	6
Supermajority sum	18.47	15	12.98	0	57

a. The size of the financing is greater than the valuation in the largest transaction (a leveraged buyout which entailed the purchase of all of the firm's equity) because part of the financing proceeds were used to cover fees to investment bankers, lawyers, and others.

[2003] find that venture capitalists obtain redemption rights in 84 percent of the transactions, antidilution protection in 95 percent of deals, and founder vesting requirements in 42 percent of transactions. The corresponding shares in our sample are much lower: 31 percent, 27 percent, and 5 percent.

Finally, the structure of the boards differs little from that seen in the United States. The mean U. S. transaction has a board with 6.2 members, of which two seats were allocated to the founders and managers and two-and-a-half to venture capitalists [Kaplan and Strömberg 2003]. The patterns here are similar, though we see a slightly greater representation of founders and managers on the boards.

IV. ANALYSIS

We now analyze how contractual choices vary across countries with different legal structure and enforcement. The econometric analyses throughout the paper employ a similar structure. We use the existence of different contract provisions as dependent variables: we create a dummy variable equal to one if the deal contains, for example, an antidilution right and zero otherwise. The main explanatory variables we are interested in are the countries' legal origin and, alternatively, the enforcement of contracts, measured as the "time-to-contract-dispute-resolution" (see Djankov et al. [2003]). We control for industry, deal type, and year fixed effects.[7] We also include per capita gross national product (in current dollars) averaged over the 1990s as a control for the national economic development. We also replicate our results employing logit specifications without industry dummy variables and the results are generally very similar.

IV.A. Security Structure

In Table III we begin by examining the security structure employed in countries with different legal origins. The economet-

---

7. We use dummy variables for the observations in three time periods in the reported regressions: the years 1993 to 1997, 1998 to 2000, and 2001 to 2003. These periods correspond, respectively, to the years when many institutions made initial investments into private equity funds focusing on leveraged buyouts in developing nations, the growth of venture capital funding in these nations, and the recent sharp falloff in venture capital and private equity activity there. The results are robust to the use of dummy variables for each year, as well as to the use of controls measuring the annual level of private equity fundraising worldwide and of foreign direct investment into developing nations.

LEGAL ENFORCEMENT AND FINANCIAL TRANSACTIONS   233

TABLE III
SECURITY STRUCTURE AND LEGAL REGIME

The sample consists of 210 investments in developing countries made by private equity groups (PEGs). The dependent variables are dummies denoting whether common stock, straight debt, or convertible preferred stock was employed in the transaction. Independent variables include dummy variables denoting nations with British or socialist legal origin (French legal origin is the omitted category) and the time to resolve commercial disputes in that nation. U. K./U. S.-based PEG is a dummy if the private equity fund is based in the United Kingdom or United States. GNP per capita is the per capita gross national product of the country averaged over the 1990s. All regressions employ ordinary least squares specifications. Standard errors are clustered at the private equity group.

	Common stock		Debt		Convertible preferred stock	
British legal origin	-0.19 ***[0.09]	-0.17 **[0.09]	-0.13 ***[0.06]	-0.11 **[0.06]	0.17 **[0.09]	0.17 **[0.09]
Socialist legal origin	0.09 [0.09]	0.07 [0.09]	-0.05 [0.06]	-0.08 [0.06]	-0.05 [0.08]	-0.01 [0.08]
Dispute time		0.07 [0.05]		0.10 **[0.05]		-0.09 *[0.05]
U. K./U. S.-based PEG		-0.03 *[0.02]		-0.18 ***[0.05]		0.11 **[0.06]
GNP per capita	-0.06 [0.07]	-0.05 [0.06]	0.05 [0.06]	0.08 **[0.04]	0.01 [0.03]	0.03 [0.05]
Industry dummies	Y	Y	Y	Y	Y	Y
Deal type dummies	Y	Y	Y	Y	Y	Y
Year dummies	Y	Y	Y	Y	Y	Y
N of observations	210	210	210	210	210	210
Adjusted R^2	0.11	0.09	0.07	0.11	0.09	0.07

* = Significant at the 10 percent level; ** = significant at the 5 percent level; *** = significant at the 1 percent level.

ric specification follows the description above, with French legal origin as the omitted category. Columns (1), (4), and (7) of Table III show that private equity transactions in common law countries less frequently use common stock or debt in their transaction and much more often employ convertible preferred stock compared with those in French or socialist legal origin nations.

One concern is that the observed contract structure could be biased due to selection problems. Private equity groups based in common law countries, such as the United States and the United Kingdom, may be disproportionately investing in common law nations, and vice versa for civil law countries. In this case, the structure of the deal might not be driven by the contracting constraints in the country of the transaction, but rather by the familiarity of the private equity group with the contracts in its domestic market. To alleviate this concern, we include a dummy variable equal to one if the private equity group is based in a common law country and zero otherwise. The results in columns (2), (5), and (8) suggest that this potential selection bias does not explain our results. While indeed deals done by private equity groups based in common law countries look more similar to U. S.-style private equity contracts (i.e., they are less likely to rely on common stock or debt and are more likely to use preferred stock), this control does not eliminate the effect on the British legal origin dummy. In fact, the coefficient on the dummy is almost completely unchanged in all specifications. We also repeat the analysis including group fixed effects (not reported). Again, the results on the legal origin of countries are very similar in direction and magnitude.

Finally, we use time-to-resolve-contract-dispute as an alternative proxy for the quality of enforcement of the legal system. We focus on this variable, since it captures more precisely the quality of the enforcement of laws through the court system. We do not include the legal origin indicators in these regressions, since Djankov et al. [2003] show that dispute resolution time is strongly correlated with a country's legal origin. The results in columns (3), (6), and (9) show that countries that take a longer time to resolve contract disputes are less likely to rely on preferred stock and are more likely to use debt.

In unreported regressions we repeat this and subsequent analysis excluding any countries that have legal restrictions on private equity transactions. We want to prevent our results from being "hard wired" by legal rules in different countries (see the Appendix for a summary). For example, in the case of the People's Republic of China, firms can only get permission to use security structures other than common stock in very exceptional cases. We find that the results presented above are qualitatively unchanged when excluding nations restricting security types from the sample. This suggests that our findings reflect the investors' contracting *choices* and not just the constraints imposed by different legal regimes.

IV.B. Allocation of Equity and Board Control

In Table IV we first examine whether the private equity group controls the company's equity. The dependent variable in columns (1) and (2) is a dummy that takes on the value one if the private equity investors own at least 50 percent of the equity when at their minimum stake. The size of the stake can vary, due to contingent clauses in the main contract that call for supplemental equity grants to founders and managers in case of good performance and side-agreements regarding vesting. We find that in countries with British legal origins, as well as those with quick dispute resolution, private equity groups are much less likely to have equity control of a firm in the minimum stake scenario.

Similarly, in columns (3) and (4) of Table IV, we see that the difference between the maximum and minimum equity stake a private equity group can hold in a given firm is significantly larger in common law countries. In countries with poor enforcement, firms avoid contingent equity stakes. The difference in ownership stakes is predominantly driven by the fact that investors in countries with better legal enforcement are willing to invest without a controlling equity stake, since they can achieve minority shareholder protection through other contractual provisions.

The last four columns of Table IV investigate the structure of the board as specified in the stock purchase agreements, examining the overall board size as well as the seats assigned to the private equity group. We see that common law nations tend to have larger boards with fewer private equity group representatives on the board. Similarly, nations where the time to resolve disputes is shorter have larger boards. (In unreported regressions we show that countries with quick dispute resolution have more

TABLE IV
EQUITY OWNERSHIP, BOARD COMPOSITION, AND LEGAL REGIME IN DEVELOPING COUNTRY PRIVATE EQUITY TRANSACTIONS

The sample consists of 210 investments in developing countries by private equity groups (PEGs). The dependent variables in the first four columns are a dummy denoting whether the PEG has control of the firm's equity when it has its minimum contractually specified share of the equity and the difference in the equity ownership stake in the minimum and maximum scenarios. The dependent variables in the last four columns are the logarithms of the number of seats on the board, as well as the seats assigned to the PEG. Independent variables include dummy variables denoting nations with British or socialist legal origin (French legal origin is the omitted category) and the time to resolve commercial disputes in that nation. GNP per capita is the per capita gross national product of the country averaged over the 1990s. All regressions employ ordinary least squares specifications. Standard errors are clustered at the private equity group.

	Does PEG have control when min. ownership stake?	Difference between min. and max. stake	Number of board seats	Number of PEG board seats
British legal origins	-0.20 ***[0.07]	-0.20 ***[0.07]	0.17 ***[0.08]	-0.06 **[0.03]
Socialist legal origins	-0.10 *[0.06]	-0.10 *[0.06]	0.05 [0.08]	0.04 [0.03]
Dispute time	0.11 ***[0.05]	0.11 ***[0.05]	-0.16 ***[0.07]	0.09 [0.07]
GNP per capita	0.09 ***[0.04]	0.02 [0.04]	0.01 [0.04]	0.03 [0.04]
Industry dummies	Y	Y	Y	Y
Deal type dummies	Y	Y	Y	Y
Year dummies	Y	Y	Y	Y
Number of observations	194	194	197	197
Adjusted R^2	0.08	0.09	0.06	0.07

* = Significant at the 10 percent level; ** = significant at the 5 percent level; *** = significant at the 1 percent level.

LEGAL ENFORCEMENT AND FINANCIAL TRANSACTIONS 237

TABLE V

CONTROL RIGHTS AND LEGAL REGIME IN DEVELOPING COUNTRY
PRIVATE EQUITY TRANSACTIONS

The sample consists of 210 investments in developing countries by private equity groups (PEGs). The dependent variables are dummies denoting whether the PEG group has antidilution protection and automatic conversion and the sum of the score of supermajority provisions. (A higher score implies greater use of supermajority provisions.) Independent variables include dummy variables denoting nations with British or socialist legal origin (French legal origin is the omitted category) and the time to resolve commercial disputes in that nation. GNP per capita is the per capita gross national product of the country averaged over the 1990s. All regressions employ ordinary least squares specifications. Standard errors are clustered at the private equity group.

	Antidilution rights		Automatic conversion		Supermajority	
British legal origins	0.20 ***[0.09]		0.17 ***[0.07]		1.76 ***[0.61]	
Socialist legal origins	−0.08 [0.09]		−0.07 [0.08]		1.06 **[0.56]	
Dispute time		−0.09 [0.06]		−0.04 [0.03]		−1.01 **[0.53]
GNP per capita	0.05 |0.04|	0.01 |0.04|	0.12 ***|0.05|	0.10 **|0.05|	−0.22 |0.35|	−0.72 *|0.40|
Industry dummies	Y	Y	Y	Y	Y	Y
Deal type dummies	Y	Y	Y	Y	Y	Y
Year dummies	Y	Y	Y	Y	Y	Y
Number of observations	210	210	194	194	210	210
Adjusted R^2	0.09	0.05	0.05	0.02	0.18	0.17

* = Significant at the 10 percent level; ** = significant at the 5 percent level; *** = significant at the 1 percent level.

managers on the board.) Table IV suggests that investors use board and equity control to protect their investments in countries with poor legal enforcement. If other methods of enforcing investor rights are effective, equity and board control are less critical.

IV.C. Control Rights

Table V analyzes control rights that affect the prerogatives of the private equity investors without the need for obtaining a controlling ownership stake. We focus on a number of the most important provisions. The first two columns analyze the existence of antidilution provisions, i.e., the right to have some compensation if subsequent financings are done at a lower valuation. This protects investors against losing their equity through dilutive financing rounds. The next two columns focus on the existence of automatic-conversion provisions. Lawyers typically interpret the latter as protecting the lead private equity investor against individual or smaller private equity investors, who may seek to hold up an IPO or acquisition by refusing to convert their shares. In the last two columns we look at supermajority provisions. These provisions require that a fraction greater than one-half of the investors approves a decision specified in the contract. Typical supermajority provisions include voting on major acquisitions, changes in the business plan that change the nature of the firm, change in top management, etc. These provisions protect minority shareholders from mismanagement or outright fraud by the management of the company.[8]

A common theme emerges from the analysis in Table V: transactions in common law countries are much more likely to include contractual protections for the private equity investors than those with French or socialist legal origin. This pattern holds whether we examine antidilution, automatic conversion, and supermajority protections. We again replicate these findings using the time-to-resolve-contract-dispute variable as an alternative proxy for the quality of contractual enforcement. We see that dispute resolution time is most strongly related to the use of supermajority provisions.

IV.D. Correlation of Different Contract Parts

So far, we have analyzed each of the contractual features in isolation. We now want to understand whether the different contract features (security structure, ownership stakes, and other control provisions) are used as complements or substitutes in financial contracting. To undertake this analysis, we regress each of the contract provisions of interest on each other, as well as controls for the logarithm of gross national product and dummy variables for the year, industry, and deal type.

We find in Table VI a strong negative correlation between common stock and convertible preferred stock. Moreover, pre-

---

8. We identify nineteen different types of provisions in these agreements. We score each of these clauses from zero to three, with a higher score representing a more stringent supermajority clause. Instead of using a simple sum of the scores, we also conducted a principal component analysis. Our results are very similar.

TABLE VI

CORRELATION IN THE USE OF CONTRACTING TOOLS OF PRIVATE EQUITY CONTRACTS

The sample consists of 210 investments in developing countries by private equity groups (PEGs). We regress the contract provision at the top of the column on the provisions at the beginning of each row. Each cell contains the coefficients from separate regressions of the contract provisions on the right-hand-side variables (standard errors are reported in brackets). We control for log of gross national product and year, industry, deal type dummies. All variables are defined as before.

	Debt	Common stock	Preferred stock	Antidilution	Automatic conversion	PEG equity stake
Common stock	0.08 [0.04]***					
Preferred stock	−0.02 [0.04]	−0.21 [0.07]***				
Antidilution	−0.01 [0.04]	−0.25 [0.07]***	0.16 [0.07]***			
Automatic conversion	−0.09 [0.05]**	−0.50 [0.07]***	0.34 [0.08]***	0.43 [0.07]***		
PEG maximum equity stake	0.22 [0.09]***	−0.02 [0.14]	0.20 [0.16]	0.18 [0.16]	−0.07 [0.17]	
Board size	−0.03 [0.08]	0.04 [0.15]	0.38 [0.15]***	0.16 [0.17]	0.06 [0.14]	0.10 [0.12]

ferred stock offerings are more likely to employ other protections such as antidilution and automatic conversion terms, while these provisions are negatively associated with common stock. We also find a strong positive correlation between the maximum ownership stakes that the private equity group obtains and the use of debt. The correlations between the minimum ownership stake and the use of debt and between board size and preferred stock are significantly positive.

Overall, these results suggest that contracts differ systematically in the way they aim to provide investors with control rights. Preferred security structures and control provisions such as antidilution clauses are generally used as complements. Deals with common shares and debtlike securities rely more heavily on controlling ownership stakes rather than other control provisions. Taken together, these results suggest that private equity groups rely on either (a) protection of minority shareholders through detailed specification of behavior that is ruled out or (b) control through ownership of a majority of the common stock and board dominance.

IV.E. Consequences

A natural question, suggested by La Porta et al. [2002], relates to the consequences of these investment choices. We would like to examine this question by looking at the relationship between transaction structures and investment outcomes. Given the relative recentness of most of the investments, and the difficulties that investors have recently had in exiting developing country investments, such an analysis would be premature. We focus instead on two proxies: valuations and fund returns.

When we look at the valuations of the financings in Table VII, we see that investments in common law countries and those with quick dispute resolution have higher valuations. These results hold even after controlling for the size of the firm, measured by sales in the year of the investment. These findings suggest that the differences in legal regime affect not just the structure of transactions, but also have real effects on firms' valuations.[9]

---

9. Similarly, we observe that the amount of capital invested is larger in common law countries than civil law countries holding constant firm size. Our

LEGAL ENFORCEMENT AND FINANCIAL TRANSACTIONS 241

TABLE VII
FINANCING VALUATION IN DEVELOPING COUNTRY PRIVATE EQUITY TRANSACTIONS

The sample consists of 210 investments in developing countries by private equity groups (PEGs). The dependent variable is the logarithm of the implied "postmoney" valuation of the transaction. Independent variables include dummy variables denoting nations with British or socialist legal origin (French legal origin is the omitted category) and the time to resolve commercial disputes in that nation. GNP per capita is the per capita gross national product of the country averaged over the 1990s. Sales is a control for the size of the firm: the annual sales in the year the investment was made (in 1997 dollars). All regressions employ ordinary least squares specifications. Standard errors are clustered at the private equity group.

	Implied valuation	
British legal origins	0.75	
	*[0.42]	
Socialist legal origins	−1.62	
	***[0.43]	
Dispute time		−0.49
		*[0.30]
GNP per capita	0.27	0.43
	[0.25]	[0.28]
Sales	0.15	0.19
	***[0.06]	***[0.07]
Industry dummies	Y	Y
Deal type dummies	Y	Y
Year dummies	Y	Y
Number of observations	193	193
Adjusted R^2	0.26	0.18

* = Significant at the 10 percent level; ** = significant at the 5 percent level; *** = significant at the 1 percent level.

We also examine the overall returns of funds that are active in developing countries. We use Private Equity Intelligence's *2004 Private Equity Performance Monitor,* which has data on over 1700 private equity funds (for more details see Lerner, Schoar, and Wong [2004]). We examine all listed funds active primarily in developing countries of a certain type, e.g., excluding funds active in both common and civil law developing countries. Private equity funds that were active in common law developing nations had an average return multiple 19 percent

---

interpretation of these results must be cautious since we only observe realized transactions. Investments that are completed in noncommon law countries, despite the many difficulties there, might be particularly promising. Thus, there may not be as many differences in the intensive margin, i.e., the observed amount of financing, as along the extensive margin (the number and types of deals that are done). Since we cannot construct an exhaustive sample of transactions, it is very difficult to draw any conclusions about the extensive margin.

better than the typical fund established in that subclass and that year, while those in socialist and civil law countries had a multiple 49 percent worse than the benchmark (significantly different at the 1 percent confidence level).[10] It must be acknowledged that we can analyze only the investors' (private) returns, not the returns to society as a whole. We anticipate, however, that the two measures should be correlated: for example, there are unlikely to be many social returns from a liquidated company. We hope to explore this question in future work.

V. Conclusions

This paper seeks to understand how differences in the enforcement of commercial laws, measured directly as well as through legal origin, affect financial contracting. We focus on a well-documented and reasonably systematized set of transactions, private equity investments. We find that investments in nations with effective legal enforcement are more likely to employ preferred stock and to have more contractual protections for the private equity group, such as supermajority voting rights and antidilution provisions. By way of contrast, contracts in low enforcement countries tend to rely more heavily on common stock (or even debt) and control the firm via majority ownership and board dominance. Relying on ownership as opposed to contractual protections seems to be only a partial remedy: these investments have lower valuations and returns.

The results suggest the importance of a contractual channel between legal enforcement and financial transactions. The legal system appears to profoundly shape the transactions into which private equity groups enter, and efforts to address this problem by relying on ownership rather than contractual protections are only partially successful. Exploring this channel outside of private equity would be a natural next step.

---

10. The return multiple is the ratio of the value of distributed investments and undistributed holdings to their cost. These results are also robust to using internal rates of return: the adjusted IRRs are -2.6 percent and -22.6 percent, respectively (significantly different at the 5 percent confidence level).

LEGAL ENFORCEMENT AND FINANCIAL TRANSACTIONS   243

APPENDIX: KEY LEGAL PROVISIONS AFFECTING PRIVATE EQUITY INVESTORS IN NINE
NATIONS MOST FREQUENTLY REPRESENTED IN THE SAMPLE

Class of limitation	Argentina	Brazil	Hong Kong
Security Type	No restrictions, but preferred stock can only have same vote as common stock. Also possible to have common stock with enhanced voting rights (up to 5 votes).	No restrictions.	No restrictions.
Super-Majority Provisions	No restrictions.	No restrictions.	No restrictions. Many corporate events require approval of 75% of shareholders.
Management Equity Holdings	No restrictions. Ambiguities surround tax treatment of options.	Limitations on types of firms who can issue stock options. Special disclosure requirements for option-issuing firms. Disadvantageous tax treatment of options.	No restrictions, except that shareholders in private firms must first offer shares to other investors.
Reinvestment and Antidilution Provisions	Equity holders can maintain pro rata share. Provision can be waived with shareholder vote.	Equity holders can maintain pro rata share. Restrictions on unreasonably dilutive financings.	Equity holders can maintain pro rata share.
Domiciling Entity	Could be domiciled overseas until recently. Now substantial difficulties to do so.	Can be domiciled overseas, but may be more difficult to enforce corporate rights locally.	Can be domiciled overseas.

(continued on next page)

APPENDIX
(CONTINUED)

India	Mexico	People's Republic of China
Preferred stocks cannot have any voting rights, except in special circumstances. Limits on extent of returns preferred shareholders can enjoy.	No restrictions, but some limitations on voting rights of preferred shareholders.	Most domestic and foreign private equity investments must employ common stock-like structure. Some large investments may use other securities, but must receive authorities' permission first.
No restrictions. Some corporate events require approval of 75% of shareholders.	No restrictions. Some legal protections for minority shareholders (e.g., right to name at least one director).	No restrictions. Some corporate events must have 2/3rds approval by investors. For foreign investments, decisions must be approved by 2/3rds of directors in many cases.
No restrictions on private firms.	No restrictions.	For most investments, not possible to issue equity to management. May be allowed in certain very large investments, but permission of authorities may be required.
Equity holders can maintain pro rata share. Provision can be waived with shareholder vote.	Equity holders can maintain pro rata share. Provision can be waived with shareholder vote.	Equity holders have preemptive right to purchase shares, except for certain very large investments.
Can be domiciled overseas.	Can be domiciled overseas.	Cannot be domiciled overseas.

LEGAL ENFORCEMENT AND FINANCIAL TRANSACTIONS   **245**

Poland	Republic of Korea	Romania
No restrictions, but limitations on voting (no more than 2–3× common stock), dividend, and liquidation preference rights of preferred shareholders.	No restrictions, but only common stock had voting rights until late 1990s. Now, no restrictions.	No restrictions, but investors cannot require that classes of shareholders vote as a block.
No restrictions. Some corporate events must have 75% approval by investors.	No restrictions.	No restrictions.
No restrictions.	No restrictions.	No restrictions.
Equity holders can maintain pro rata share. Provision can be waived with 80% shareholder vote.	Equity holders have preemptive right to purchase shares, with limited exceptions.	Equity holders have preemptive right to purchase shares, except for some private firms.
Can be domiciled overseas.	Can be domiciled overseas. May entail loss of attractive tax incentives for startups.	These restrictions cannot be avoided by domiciling company in another country.

246   *QUARTERLY JOURNAL OF ECONOMICS*

Harvard University and National Bureau of Economic Research
Massachusetts Institute of Technology and National Bureau of Economic
Research

References

Aghion, Philippe, and Patrick Bolton, "An Incomplete Contracts Approach to Financial Contracting," *Review of Economic Studies,* LIX (1992), 473–494.

Bartlett, Joseph W., *Equity Finance: Venture Capital, Buyouts, Restructurings, and Reorganizations,* 2nd edition (New York, NY: John Wiley, 1995).

Bergman, Nittai, and Daniel Nicolaievsky, "Investor Protection and the Coasian View," unpublished working paper, Harvard University, 2003.

Cumming, Douglas J., and Jeffrey G. MacIntosh, "A Law and Finance Analysis of Venture Capital Exits in Emerging Markets," unpublished working paper, University of Alberta, 2002.

Demirgüç-Kunt, Asli, and Ross Levine, *Financial Structure and Economic Growth: A Cross-Country Comparison of Banks, Markets, and Development* (Cambridge, MA: MIT Press, 2001).

Djankov, Simeon, Rafael La Porta, Florencio Lopez-de-Silanes, and Andrei Shleifer, "Courts," *Quarterly Journal of Economics,* CXVIII (2003), 453–517.

European Venture Capital Association, *EVCA Yearbook* (Zaventum, Belgium: EVCA and KPMG, 2002).

Glaeser, Edward L., Simon Johnson, and Andrei Shleifer, "Coase versus the Coasians," *Quarterly Journal of Economics,* CXVI (2001), 853–899.

Gompers, Paul A., "An Examination of Convertible Securities in Venture Capital Investments," unpublished working paper, Harvard University, 1998.

Grossman, Sanford J., and Oliver D. Hart, "The Costs and Benefits of Ownership: A Theory of Vertical and Lateral Integration," *Journal of Political Economy,* XCIV (1986), 691–719.

Hart, Oliver, and John Moore, "Property Rights and the Nature of the Firm," *Journal of Political Economy,* XCVIII (1990), 1119–1158.

Hellmann, Thomas, "The Allocation of Control Rights in Venture Capital Contracts," *Rand Journal of Economics,* XXIX (1998), 57–76.

Holmström, Bengt, "Moral Hazard and Observability," *Bell Journal of Economics,* X (1979), 74–91.

Johnson, Simon, John McMillan, and Christopher Woodruff, "Courts and Relational Contracts," *Journal of Law, Economics and Organization,* XVIII (2002), 221–277.

Kaplan, Steven N., Frederic Martel, and Per Strömberg, "How Do Legal Differences and Learning Affect Financial Contracts?" Working Paper No. 10097, National Bureau of Economic Research, 2003.

Kaplan, Steven N., and Per Strömberg, "Financial Contracting Meets the Real World: An Empirical Analysis of Venture Capital Contracts," *Review of Economic Studies,* LXX (2003), 281–316.

La Porta, Rafael, Florencio Lopez-de-Silanes, Andrei Shleifer, and Robert Vishny, "Legal Determinants of External Finance," *Journal of Finance,* LII (1997), 1131–1150.

La Porta, Rafael, Florencio Lopez-de-Silanes, Andrei Shleifer, and Robert Vishny, "Law and Finance," *Journal of Political Economy,* CVI (1998), 1133–1155.

La Porta, Rafael, Florencio Lopez-de-Silanes, Andrei Shleifer, and Robert Vishny, "Investor Protection and Corporate Valuation," *Journal of Finance,* LVII (2002), 1147–1170.

Lerner, Josh, Antoinette Schoar, and Wan Wong, "Smart Institutions, Foolish Choices?: The Limited Partner Performance Puzzle," unpublished working paper, Harvard University and MIT, 2004.

Qian, Jun, and Philip Strahan, "How Law and Institutions Shape Financial Contracts: The Case of Bank Loans," unpublished working paper, Boston College, 2004.

THE JOURNAL OF FINANCE • VOL. LVII, NO. 6 • DECEMBER 2002

Disentangling the Incentive and Entrenchment Effects of Large Shareholdings

STIJN CLAESSENS, SIMEON DJANKOV,
JOSEPH P. H. FAN, and LARRY H. P. LANG*

ABSTRACT

This article disentangles the incentive and entrenchment effects of large owner-ship. Using data for 1,301 publicly traded corporations in eight East Asian econ-omies, we find that firm value increases with the cash-flow ownership of the largest shareholder, consistent with a positive incentive effect. But firm value falls when the control rights of the largest shareholder exceed its cash-flow ownership, con-sistent with an entrenchment effect. Given that concentrated corporate ownership is predominant in most countries, these findings have relevance for corporate gov-ernance across the world.

THE EFFECTS OF OWNERSHIP STRUCTURES on the value of firms have been re-searched extensively, with the role of large investors receiving special atten-tion. Investors with large ownership stakes have strong incentives to maximize their firms' value and are able to collect information and oversee managers, and so can help overcome one of the principal–agent problems in the modern corporation—that of conflicts of interest between shareholders and man-agers (Jensen and Meckling (1976)). Large shareholders also have strong incentives to put pressure on managers or even to oust them through a proxy fight or a takeover. For example, Shleifer and Vishny (1997, p. 754) point

* University of Amsterdam and Centre for Economic Policy Research; World Bank and Centre for Economic Policy Research; Hong Kong University of Science and Technology; and Chinese University of Hong Kong, respectively. Joseph P. H. Fan gratefully acknowledges the Hong Kong Government's Earmarked Grant for research support. Larry H. P. Lang gratefully ac-knowledges the financial support of the Hong Kong Government's Earmarked Grant and Direct Grant. The authors are grateful for the helpful comments of Lucian Bebchuk, Erik Berglof, Alexander Dyck, Caroline Freund, Ed Glaeser, Simon Johnson, Tarun Khanna, Florencio Lopez-de-Silanes, Randall Morck, Tatiana Nenova, Raghuram Rajan, Henri Servaes, Daniel Wolfen-zon, and Luigi Zingales, the article's two anonymous referees, seminar participants at the World Bank, International Monetary Fund, Federation of Thai Industries, Georgetown Univer-sity, George Washington University, Hong Kong University of Science and Technology, Korean Development Institute, Korea Institute of Finance, Vanderbilt University, University of Illinois, University of Michigan, University of Amsterdam, 1999 National Bureau for Economic Re-search summer conference on corporate finance, 2000 American Economic Association annual meetings, and especially of Rafael La Porta, Andrei Shleifer, and René Stulz. An earlier version of this article was called "Expropriation of Minority Shareholders: Evidence from East Asia." The opinions expressed here do not necessarily reflect those of the World Bank.

out, "Large shareholders thus address the agency problem in that they have both a general interest in profit maximization, and enough control over the assets of the firm to have their interest respected."

Less work has been done on the costs—in terms of lower firm valuation—associated with the presence of large investors. Again, according to Shleifer and Vishny (1997, p. 758), "Large investors may represent their own interests, which need not coincide with the interests of other investors in the firm, or with the interests of employees and managers." Empirically, Morck, Shleifer, and Vishny (1988) find an inverse U-shaped relationship between managerial equity ownership and firm valuation for a sample of U.S. firms. One interpretation is that firms' performance improves with higher managerial ownership, but that, after a point, managers become entrenched and pursue private benefits at the expense of outside investors.

The costs of large shareholdings and entrenchment are formalized in the model of Stulz (1988), which predicts a concave relationship between managerial ownership and firm value. In the model, as managerial ownership and control increase, the negative effect on firm value associated with the entrenchment of manager-owners starts to exceed the incentive benefits of managerial ownership. In that model, the entrenchment costs of manager ownership relate to managers' ability to block value-enhancing takeovers. McConnell and Servaes (1990) provide empirical support for this relationship for U.S. firms.

But ownership structures exhibit relatively little concentration in the United States. Elsewhere, most firms are predominantly controlled by a single large shareholder (La Porta, Lopez-de-Silanes, and Shleifer (1999)). Thus, studying non-U.S. firms can provide evidence about the effects of large shareholders that is difficult to detect in U.S. data. Moreover, the literature indicates that the positive incentive effect relates to the share of cash-flow rights held by large shareholders and that the negative entrenchment effect relates to the share of control rights held by large shareholders. Non-U.S. firms exhibit far more divergence between cash-flow rights and control rights than do U.S. firms, because in most countries, the largest shareholder often establishes control over a firm despite little cash-flow rights. Using a sample of corporations outside the United States, we are thus better able to disentangle the incentive and entrenchment effects of large ownership that are so difficult to tell apart in U.S. data.

To do so, we investigate the valuation of publicly traded East Asian corporations relative to their ownership structures. In previous work, we found that more than two-thirds of East Asian firms are controlled by a single shareholder (Claessens, Djankov, and Lang (2000)). East Asian firms also show a sharp divergence between cash-flow rights and control rights—that is, the largest shareholder is often able to control a firm's operations with a relatively small direct stake in its cash-flow rights. Control is often enhanced beyond ownership stakes through pyramid structures and cross-holdings among firms, and sometimes through dual-class shares, with the divergence between cash-flow rights and control rights most pronounced in

Incentive and Entrenchment Effects of Large Shareholdings 2743

family-controlled firms.[1] Finally, managers of East Asian corporations are usually related to the family of the controlling shareholder. Thus, it is possible to analyze the relative importance of incentive and entrenchment effects in East Asian corporations, because ownership is highly concentrated and the divergence between cash-flow rights and control rights is large, while manager-owner conflicts are generally limited.

Our analysis uses data for 1,301 publicly traded corporations from eight East Asian economies: Hong Kong, Indonesia, South Korea, Malaysia, the Philippines, Singapore, Taiwan, and Thailand. Using regression techniques, we find that relative firm value—as measured by the market-to-book ratio of assets—increases with the share of cash-flow rights in the hands of the largest shareholder. This result is consistent with previous studies on the positive incentive effects associated with increased cash-flow rights in the hands of one or a few shareholders. But we find that the entrenchment effect of control rights has a negative effect on firm value. This finding complements that of Morck, Stangeland, and Yeung (2000). Using data for Canadian public corporations, they show that concentrated corporate control impedes growth, because entrenched controlling shareholders have a vested interest in preserving the value of existing capital. Our work also complements that of La Porta et al. (2002), who document lower valuations for firms in countries with worse protection of minority shareholders. Such countries tend to have more concentrated ownership structures.

Our results also support the predictions of theoretical studies that investigate the effects on firm value of the separation of cash-flow rights and control rights. Grossman and Hart (1988) and Harris and Raviv (1988) show that separating ownership and control can lower shareholders' value and may not be socially optimal. Shleifer and Vishny (1997, p. 759) argue that "as ownership gets beyond a certain point, large owners gain nearly full control of the company and are wealthy enough to prefer to use firms to generate private benefits of control that are not shared by minority shareholders." Bebchuk, Kraakman, and Triantis (2000) argue that separating control rights from cash-flow rights can create agency costs an order of magnitude larger than the costs associated with a controlling shareholder who also has a majority of the cash-flow rights in his or her corporation.

In this article, we show that, for the largest shareholders, the difference between control rights and cash-flow rights is associated with a value discount and that the discount generally increases with the size of the wedge between control rights and cash-flow rights. We do not have strong evidence on which mechanism separating ownership and control is associated with the value discounts. Pyramid schemes, cross-holdings among firms, and the

---

[1] Pyramiding is defined as the ultimate ownership of a firm running through a chain of ownership of intermediate corporations. Cross-holdings refer to horizontal and vertical ownership links among corporations that can enhance the control of a large, ultimate shareholder. Dual-class shares refer to shares with different voting rights.

issuance of dual-class shares are all associated with lower corporate valuation, but none of the associations is individually statistically significant.

Finally, we investigate whether a certain type of owner—families, the state, or widely held corporations and widely held financial institutions—drives our results. We find that concentrated ownership in the hands of all types of owners is associated with a higher market-to-book ratio. We also find that the wedge between control and ownership is associated with value discounts for family-controlled firms and somewhat for state-controlled corporations, but not significantly when the principal owner is a widely held corporation or financial institution. The differences in valuation effects by type of owner could arise from the fact that managers at firms owned by widely held corporations and financial institutions have fewer ways to divert benefits to themselves compared with managers at firms owned by families and the state.

The rest of the paper is structured as follows. Section I describes the selection criteria for the data sample and the construction of the industry origin, ownership, control, and corporate valuation variables. Section II investigates the evidence on the incentive and entrenchment effects of large shareholdings and conducts some robustness tests. Section III studies the effects of various mechanisms used for the separation of ownership and control, and the relation between the type of ownership and corporate valuation. Section IV concludes.

I. Sample Selection and Data

This section describes the selection criteria used and the resulting sample of corporations. It also provides details on the construction of the data on ownership and control structures and provides statistics on key variables for the sample. Finally, it describes the valuation measure used for the empirical tests that follow.

A. Sample Selection

Our starting point for the data is Claessens et al. (2000), who collected 1996 data on ownership for corporations in Hong Kong, Indonesia, Japan, Korea, Malaysia, the Philippines, Singapore, Taiwan, and Thailand. Their main source was Worldscope, supplemented by other sources that provide ownership structures as of December 1996 or the end of fiscal 1996. From a complete sample of 5,284 publicly listed corporations in the nine East Asian economies, ownership data were collected for 2,980 firms.

For this analysis, we take a subset of these firms. First, we exclude from the sample all Japanese corporations. We do so for several reasons. Worldscope provides data on 1,740 publicly listed Japanese corporations, and Japanese corporations also dominate the sample for which we have ownership data (1,240 of 2,980 corporations). Thus, Japanese firms could influence the results too much. An unbalanced outcome is even more likely given the fea-

Incentive and Entrenchment Effects of Large Shareholdings   2745

tures of Japanese firms—most have dispersed ownership structures, and ownership and management are separated far more often than in other East Asian economies. The most important shareholders in Japan are widely held financial institutions, again unlike many economies in the region. But these financial institutions and their affiliated firms often work together to influence the governance of the owned corporations, a phenomenon that cannot be captured by formal ownership data. Thus, including Japan in our set of East Asian economies would be less useful for disentangling the incentive and entrenchment effects of concentrated ownership and control.

Second, we exclude firms that operate in certain industrial sectors—specifically, financial corporations and regulated utilities. For financial firms, profitability and valuation data are difficult to calculate and to compare with firms in other sectors. For regulated utilities, profitability and valuation can be strongly influenced by government regulations. To determine the primary industry in which each firm operates, we rely on historical segment sales data from Worldscope. If such information is not provided, we rely on information from the *Asian Company Handbook* (1998).[2] We next determine the sector to which each firm belongs according to the two-digit Standard Industrial Classification (SIC) system, using the largest share of sales revenue among the firm's activity in each sector. We then use Campbell (1996) to classify firms into 11 industries.[3] We exclude all financial corporations (SIC 6000–6999) and regulated utilities (SIC 4900–4999), making for 304 corporations excluded using those criteria.

Third, we need to know whether a firm consolidates its financial statements and, if so, the method used, because our valuation measure can be distorted by accounting rules on consolidation.[4] Specifically, excessive consolidation of sales and balance sheet items can result when partly owned subsidiaries are treated like fully owned subsidiaries—the full method of consolidation. This method tends to understate the true market-to-book ratio of the consolidated corporation because the book value includes 100 percent of the assets of the subsidiaries, while the market value includes only the actual stakes owned. The market-to-book ratio of the consolidated corporation is not distorted when the corporation uses cost, proportional, or equity consolidation methods. Under these methods, the parent corporation includes its prorated share of subsidiaries in its balance sheet (as well as any dividends received from subsidiaries in its income statement). Accordingly,

---

[2] We still had to exclude 53 firms that do not report their segment sales to Worldscope or the *Asian Company Handbook*.

[3] The industries are petroleum (SIC 13, 29), consumer durables (SIC 25, 30, 36, 37, 50, 55, 57), basic industry (SIC 10, 12, 14, 24, 26, 28, 33), food and tobacco (SIC 1, 2, 9, 20, 21, 54), construction (SIC 15, 16, 17, 32, 52), capital goods (SIC 34, 35, 38), transportation (SIC 40, 41, 42, 44, 45, 47), unregulated utilities (SIC 46, 48), textiles and trade (SIC 22, 23, 31, 51, 53, 56, 59), services (SIC 72, 73, 75, 76, 80, 82, 87, 89), and leisure (SIC 27, 58, 70, 78, 79).

[4] La Porta et al. (2000) further discuss the biases resulting from different consolidation methods.

these methods do not distort balance sheet items and so do not understate the market-to-book ratio.

Worldscope almost always says whether a firm consolidates its financial statements. When Worldscope does not report that information, we exclude the corporation—making for 82 dropped corporations. More than two-thirds of the remaining corporations have consolidated financial statements.[5] Worldscope also indicates whether the consolidation covers all significant subsidiaries and whether the annual report is on a cost basis (unconsolidated). But Worldscope does not indicate at what level the corporation has done the consolidation, and in particular, whether partly owned subsidiaries are treated as fully owned subsidiaries. Lacking that information, we cannot investigate whether the consolidation method used affects the firm valuation. We can only investigate whether the fact that the corporation consolidates or not affects our results.

These sample selection criteria leave us with 1,301 corporations in eight East Asian economies—about 37 percent of the sample of 3,544 publicly traded corporations in these economies.

B. Ownership and Control Definitions

Following La Porta et al. (1999), we analyze ultimate ownership and control patterns. In most cases, the immediate shareholders of a corporation are corporate entities, nonprofit foundations, or financial institutions. We then identify their owners, the owners of those owners, and so on. We do not consider ownership by individual family members to be separate, and we use total ownership by each family group—defined as a group of people related by blood or marriage—as the unit of analysis.

Studying the separation of ownership and control requires data on both cash-flow rights and control rights, which we calculate using the complete chain of ownership. Suppose that a family owns 11 percent of the stock of publicly traded firm A, which in turn has 21 percent of the stock of firm B. We then say that the family controls 11 percent of firm B—the weakest link in the chain of control rights. In contrast, we say that the family owns about 2 percent of the cash-flow rights of firm B, the product of the two ownership stakes along the chain. We make the distinction between cash-flow rights and control rights by using for each firm information on pyramid structures, cross-holdings among firms, and dual-class shares. To determine effective control at any intermediate levels as well as the ultimate level, we need to use a cutoff point above which we assume that the largest shareholder has effective control over the intermediate and final corporations. We use 10 percent as the cutoff point in our empirical analysis because that level is com-

---

[5] That number is highest for Hong Kong, Malaysia, and Singapore, where 76, 75, and 75 percent of corporations use consolidated accounts, respectively. In contrast, only 34 percent of Korean corporations have consolidated accounts, 51 percent of Indonesian corporations, and 57 percent of Taiwanese corporations.

Incentive and Entrenchment Effects of Large Shareholdings   2747

monly used by other studies. But we also provide information using the 20 percent and 40 percent levels, to show the distributions of large ownership across economies and types of owners.

Information on pyramid structures and cross-holdings among firms is limited because our data cover only listed corporations. Many East Asian corporations affiliated with business groups, and hence with pyramid structures and cross-holdings, are unlisted. At the end of 1996, for example, the three biggest business groups in Korea—Hyundai, Samsung, and LuckyGoldstar—had 46, 55, and 48 affiliated firms, respectively. Of those, only 16, 14, and 11 were publicly listed. Covering only listed corporations may create a bias in terms of ownership structures and firm valuation. Unlisted corporations could have direct and indirect ownership links with listed corporations, resulting in a possible underreporting of our measures for ultimate control and ownership, since we assume that someone other than a related shareholder controls the unlisted corporations. Anecdotal evidence suggests that such underreporting can lead to considerable underestimates.[6] In addition, complex ownership structures and group-affiliated corporations presumably increase opportunities for the entrenchment of large shareholders—even where ownership structures are similar to those of independent corporations.

Because we likely underestimate the ultimate ownership and influence of large shareholders for group-affiliated firms, we may underestimate the effect of ownership structures on firm valuation. But group affiliation may also affect firm valuation, because there may be intragroup financial transfers that are not market based. The direction of the effect on firm value is unclear. Firm valuations for group-affiliated firms could be lower or higher than for comparable independent firms, depending on the net costs they incur or the net benefits they receive from group affiliation. We control for some firm-specific factors, such as age and size, that may be correlated with the possible net costs or benefits from group affiliation. But these factors likely do not fully control for the influence on firm value of affiliation with specific groups. Thus, we account for the possibility that the valuations of group-affiliated firms are not independent of each other by running regressions in which all firms in a business group are considered jointly.[7]

In terms of dual-class shares, the financial information service Datastream provides data on all classes of listed shares. For the firms under investigation, 88 cases of dual-class shares are found. Of those, some preferred shares are more like debt instruments because they are redeemable

[6] Some Korean firms are illustrative. Samsung Corporation, part of the Samsung *chaebol*, is partly owned by Samsung Life Insurance, which is not listed. But Samsung Life Insurance is controlled by the same family that has a large direct stake in Samsung Corporation, increasing the family's overall control stake in Samsung Corporation. Similarly, control for Samsung Electromagnetic is underestimated because it is also partly owned by Samsung Life Insurance (as well as other Samsung corporations).

[7] Still, not being able to cover unlisted firms in a group does not allow us to fully investigate the effect on firm value of variables like the size of business groups.

or callable at the option of the corporation at a preset price, are convertible into common shares, or receive a fixed cumulative dividend unrelated to the profits of the corporation. We consider such preferred shares to be debt-like instruments and do not include them as shares that further separate ownership and control. Following this methodology, we end up with 43 corporations with dual-class shares—5 in Hong Kong, 37 in Korea, and 1 in the Philippines. Dual-class shares are now legally forbidden in Hong Kong and Singapore, but the corporations in the Hong Kong sample are protected by a grandfather clause. In Indonesia, Malaysia, Taiwan, and Thailand, dual-class shares could exist in principle, but Datastream covers none.

C. Sample Characteristics

The number of corporations for each economy is shown in Table I. Korea has the largest share of corporations in the sample, 21.6 percent, followed by Hong Kong with 17.3 percent. The Philippine sample is the smallest, accounting for 5.9 percent of the corporations. About 20 percent of the corporations in our sample are in the consumer durables industry. Corporations in basic industry, construction, and textiles and trade each account for about 13 percent of the sample. Petroleum companies and unregulated utilities make up the smallest number of corporations in our sample.

In terms of ownership structure, we define corporations as being widely held or having large ultimate owners. We apply the commonly used definition of a widely held corporation as one that does not have any owner with 10 percent or more of control rights. Ultimate owners are split into three groups: families, including all related individuals with large stakes; the state or municipality; and the combined group of widely held corporations and widely held financial institutions, such as banks and insurance companies. Ownership types are used in some of the regressions below to investigate whether any of the effects differ by type of owner.

We start by reporting aggregate data on the distribution of ultimate control by ownership type (Table II). Only four percent of corporations do not have a single controlling shareholder at the 10 percent cutoff level of control rights. Table II also shows ultimate ownership structures at the 20 and 40 percent cutoff levels for the share of control rights in the hands of the largest shareholder (though these higher cutoff levels are not used in our empirical analysis). These higher cutoff levels show how concentrated ownership structures are. At the 20 percent cutoff level, 18 percent of corporations are widely held. In contrast, 77 percent are widely held at the 40 percent cutoff level—indicating that in many corporations, the largest shareholder has a control stake of less than 40 percent. At lower control levels, families are the largest shareholders, covering more than two-thirds of corporations at the 10 percent cutoff level and three-fifths at the 20 percent level.

At the 10 percent cutoff, corporate sectors do not differ much in terms of ownership patterns across the eight economies. (The exception is Korea, which has a larger share—13 percent—of widely held corporations.) More

Incentive and Entrenchment Effects of Large Shareholdings 2749

Table I
The Sample of Publicly Traded East Asian Corporations by Economy and Industry

This table shows the distribution of sample corporations across industries and economies. The source of the data is Claessens et al. (2000), Worldscope, and *Asian Company Handbook* (1998). The industrial classification is based on Campbell (1996). Industries are defined as follows: petroleum (SIC 13, 29), consumer durables (SIC 25, 30, 36, 37, 50, 55, 57), basic industry (SIC 10, 12, 14, 24, 26, 28, 33), food and tobacco (SIC 1, 2, 9, 20, 21, 54), construction (SIC 15, 16, 17, 32, 52), capital goods (SIC 34, 35, 38), transportation (SIC 40, 41, 42, 44, 45, 47), unregulated utilities (SIC 46, 48), textiles and trade (SIC 22, 23, 31, 51, 53, 56, 59), services (SIC 72, 73, 75, 76, 80, 82, 87, 89), and leisure (SIC 27, 58, 70, 78, 79). The sample excludes financial companies (SIC 60–69) and regulated utilities (SIC 49).

Industry	Hong Kong	Indonesia	Korea, Rep. of	Malaysia	Philippines	Singapore	Taiwan	Thailand	Total Number	Total Percentage of Total
Petroleum	1	1	12	4	6	3	1	1	29	2.2
Consumer durables	57	17	59	17	7	44	29	29	259	19.9
Basic industry	10	24	55	22	14	16	24	12	177	13.6
Food and tobacco	13	21	20	17	18	18	15	11	133	10.2
Construction	22	4	44	49	11	14	14	16	174	13.4
Capital goods	22	12	35	8	3	21	16	6	123	9.5
Transportation	19	4	6	10	1	12	6	5	63	4.8
Unregulated utilities	5	5	3	3	6	4	1	5	32	2.5
Textiles and trade	43	33	35	15	6	9	17	10	168	12.9
Services	7	7	4	15	3	15	4	7	62	4.8
Leisure	26	4	8	11	2	20	2	8	81	6.2
Total	225	132	281	171	77	176	129	110	1,301	100.0
Percentage of total	17.3	10.1	21.6	13.1	5.9	13.5	9.9	8.5	100.0	

The Journal of Finance

Table II

**Control of East Asian Corporations by Owner Type
and Economy, 1996 (Percentage of Corporations in the Sample)**

Data for 1,301 publicly traded corporations (excluding financial institutions, SIC 60–69, and regulated utilities, SIC 49), based on Worldscope, supplemented by information from the *Asian Company Handbook* (1998). All data are as of December 1996 or the end of fiscal 1996. To determine effective control at any intermediate as well as ultimate level, a cutoff level of 10 percent was used in all empirical analyses. Above that level, the largest shareholder is assumed to have effective control over the intermediate or final corporation. The 20 percent and 40 percent cutoff levels are also used here to show the distribution of large ownership across economies and owner types. The percentages in the last four columns sum to 100, subject to rounding.

			Percentage of Firms with Ultimate Control		
Economy	Number of Firms in Sample	Percentage of Firms with Dispersed Control	Family-owned	State-owned	Owned by a Widely Held Corporation or Financial Institution
10 percent cutoff for effective control of the largest shareholder					
Hong Kong	225	0	72	3	24
Indonesia	132	1	73	9	17
Korea, Rep. of	281	13	73	2	12
Malaysia	171	1	75	12	12
Philippines	77	4	51	3	43
Singapore	176	1	55	29	15
Taiwan	129	5	59	2	35
Thailand	110	1	72	5	21
Total	1,301	4	68	8	20
20 percent cutoff for effective control of the largest shareholder					
Hong Kong	225	8	69	1	23
Indonesia	132	6	70	8	16
Korea, Rep. of	281	41	52	0	7
Malaysia	171	11	70	11	9
Philippines	77	19	45	1	34
Singapore	176	9	53	24	14
Taiwan	129	29	47	1	24
Thailand	110	6	68	5	20
Total	1,301	18	60	6	16
40 percent cutoff for effective control of the largest shareholder					
Hong Kong	225	72	20	0	8
Indonesia	132	50	35	5	10
Korea, Rep. of	281	94	5	0	1
Malaysia	171	80	13	2	5
Philippines	77	83	8	1	8
Singapore	176	71	17	5	8
Taiwan	129	93	5	1	1
Thailand	110	53	35	4	8
Total	1,301	77	16	2	5

pronounced differences emerge at the 20 percent cutoff. In Korea, 41 percent of corporations are widely held, while in Indonesia and Thailand only 6 percent of corporations fall into that category, indicating that ownership structures are much more concentrated in Indonesia and Thailand. State control is high in Singapore, at 24 percent, while control by widely held corporations and financial institutions is important in the Philippines, at 34 percent. At the 40 percent cutoff, differences become smaller across economies in terms of type of controlling shareholder (except in Indonesia and Thailand, where families still control more than one-third of the sample corporations).

D. The Valuation Measure

As noted, we use the market-to-book ratio of assets to measure firm valuation. Researchers have used the market-to-book ratio as well as Tobin's Q to measure variations in market values resulting from different ownership structures. Market value is defined here as the sum of the market value of common stock and the book value of debt and preferred stock. To calculate the value of equity, we use end-1996 shares of common stock and stock prices, both from Worldscope. We do not try to calculate the replacement cost of assets in the denominator, as we would need to do if we were using Tobin's Q, for two reasons. Most important, the data required to calculate replacement values are generally not available, and the eight economies have different ways of accounting for depreciation of physical assets. In addition, we did not want to impose a fixed depreciation formula, given that the age of assets varies by economy. Instead, we use the book value of assets as reported in firms' balance sheets when calculating the market-to-book ratio.

Mean and median market-to-book ratios of the sample corporations are shown in Table III. This table provides insights into the relative value of firms by their main industrial sector and economy of origin. Unregulated utilities have the highest firm valuation, with a mean market-to-book ratio of 1.79 and a median of 1.42. Service and leisure corporations also have high valuations. Firm values are lowest in textiles and trade, with a mean market-to-book ratio of 1.27 and a median of 1.07.

The range of median firm valuations across economies is similar in magnitude to that across sectors. Malaysian corporations have the highest relative valuations, with a mean of 1.70 and a median of 1.43. They are followed by Singaporean corporations, with a mean of 1.63 and a median of 1.38, and Taiwanese corporations, with a mean of 1.59 and a median of 1.35. Korean and Philippine corporations have the lowest valuations. The valuation data reported here for Hong Kong, Korea, and Singapore are lower than those in La Porta et al. (2002). Our median values are 1.12, 1.00, and 1.38, respectively, compared with their 1.15, 1.06, and 1.52. This difference is likely accounted for by the different year of data coverage—1996 compared with 1995—because East Asian stock markets experienced a decline over this pe-

Table III
Valuations of East Asian Corporations by Economy and Industry, 1996 (Market-to-Book Ratio)

The market-to-book ratio is the ratio of the market value of assets to the book value of assets at the end of 1996. Market value is defined as the sum of the market value of common stock and the book value of debt and preferred stock. The book value of assets comes from firms' balance sheets. All corporations, including those without an ultimate controlling owner, are included. Industries are defined as follows: petroleum (SIC 13, 29), consumer durables (SIC 25, 30, 36, 37, 50, 55, 57), basic industry (SIC 10, 12, 14, 24, 26, 28, 33), food and tobacco (SIC 1, 2, 9, 20, 21, 54), construction (SIC 15, 16, 17, 32, 52), capital goods (SIC 34, 35, 38), transportation (SIC 40, 41, 42, 44, 45, 47), unregulated utilities (SIC 46, 48), textiles and trade (SIC 22, 23, 31, 51, 53, 56, 59), services (SIC 72, 73, 75, 76, 80, 82, 87, 89), and leisure (SIC 27, 58, 70, 78, 79). The sample excludes financial companies (SIC 60–69) and regulated utilities (SIC 49).

Industry	Hong Kong	Indonesia	Korea, Rep. of	Malaysia	Philippines	Singapore	Taiwan	Thailand	Total
Petroleum									
Mean	0.77	0.37	1.76	1.31	1.19	2.29	1.15	1.20	1.51
Median	0.77	0.37	1.50	1.59	1.01	1.40	1.15	1.20	1.20
Consumer durables									
Mean	1.31	0.92	1.30	1.94	1.48	1.59	1.67	1.20	1.40
Median	1.08	0.79	0.99	2.00	1.24	1.29	1.64	1.23	1.18
Basic industry									
Mean	1.63	1.62	1.10	2.00	1.21	1.67	1.69	1.57	1.48
Median	1.47	1.24	0.99	1.78	1.06	1.47	1.34	1.31	1.17
Food and tobacco									
Mean	1.85	1.65	1.10	1.72	1.13	2.16	1.42	1.40	1.55
Median	1.51	1.45	1.01	1.35	0.92	1.88	1.22	1.31	1.24

Incentive and Entrenchment Effects of Large Shareholdings   2753

Construction								
Mean	1.12	1.35	1.13	1.52	1.53	1.19	1.53	1.24	1.32
Median	1.11	1.38	0.89	1.25	1.18	1.18	1.40	1.02	1.14
Capital goods								
Mean	1.35	1.37	1.27	2.13	0.76	1.61	1.44	1.16	1.41
Median	1.17	1.41	0.91	1.74	0.57	1.58	1.20	1.07	1.17
Transportation								
Mean	1.10	1.38	1.46	1.41	1.56	1.56	1.79	1.23	1.37
Median	1.12	1.26	0.94	1.30	1.56	1.43	1.53	1.22	1.24
Unregulated utilities								
Mean	0.94	1.88	1.93	1.89	1.12	1.76	1.94	3.18	1.79
Median	0.89	1.88	2.08	1.51	1.06	1.51	1.94	1.88	1.42
Textiles and trade								
Mean	1.38	1.15	1.11	1.47	1.16	1.40	1.50	1.04	1.27
Median	1.08	1.02	1.00	1.43	0.97	1.29	1.18	0.85	1.07
Services								
Mean	1.07	1.30	2.43	1.94	1.51	1.66	1.50	1.91	1.68
Median	0.99	1.53	2.34	1.18	1.87	1.58	1.60	1.11	1.36
Leisure								
Mean	1.24	1.65	1.68	1.50	1.32	1.53	2.22	1.13	1.43
Median	1.25	1.58	1.80	1.32	1.32	1.31	2.22	1.21	1.32
Total								
Mean	1.31	1.36	1.25	1.70	1.25	1.63	1.59	1.38	1.43
Median	1.12	1.13	1.00	1.43	1.06	1.38	1.35	1.22	1.19

riod. Another reason for the difference could be that La Porta et al. (2002) use only the 20 to 30 largest publicly traded corporations in each economy, while our samples are much larger.[8]

II. Ownership and Control Concentration and Their Effect on Firm Value

As noted, we seek evidence about the effects of ownership and control concentration on firm value when there is a controlling shareholder. We want to test two hypotheses. The first is that the more concentrated cash-flow rights in the hands of the largest shareholder are, the stronger is that shareholder's incentive to have the firm run properly, because having the firm running properly would raise his wealth; likewise, his incentive to reduce the value of the firm by extracting private benefits is weaker, because doing so would lower his wealth. Both effects should result in a positive relationship between firm values and the largest shareholder's cash-flow rights.

In contrast, the second hypothesis holds that the more concentrated control is in the hands of the largest shareholder, the more entrenched the shareholder is and the better able he is to extract value—to the detriment of the firm's value to minority shareholders. This hypothesis suggests a negative relationship between firm values and the largest shareholder's control rights. The agency problem of entrenchment and value extraction will be especially pronounced when there is a big divergence between control rights and cash-flow rights, because the willingness to extract value is less restrained by the controlling shareholder's cash-flow stake.

A. *Graphical Evidence*

To investigate these two hypotheses, we first present figures showing the association between market-to-book ratios and the cash-flow and control stakes of the largest shareholder. We then conduct a series of regressions.

---

[8] In a previous version of this article (Claessens et al. (1999a)), we used an industry-adjusted valuation measure as our dependent variable. Each firm's valuation was adjusted relative to the economy-wide average for the industries in which the firm operated, taking into account the shares each industry represented in the firm's overall sales. The idea was to take out both economy and industry effects, since the economies in the sample are at different stages of development and since firm valuation can vary widely across industries. The adjustment was burdensome, however, because many publicly listed corporations in East Asia operate in multiple segments. For example, if firms are classified as multisegment if they derive less than 90 percent of their sales from one two-digit SIC code, then more than two-thirds of corporations from Hong Kong, Malaysia, and Singapore have multiple segments. In contrast, less than 20 percent of U.S. corporations operate in multiple segments (Claessens et al. (1999b)). Adjusting for multisegment firms thus adds an extra layer of complexity in computing industry-adjusted valuation measures. Still, we ran regressions using these industry adjustments and found similar, even slightly stronger, results as when using the market-to-book ratio; see Claessens et al. (1999a).

Incentive and Entrenchment Effects of Large Shareholdings 2755

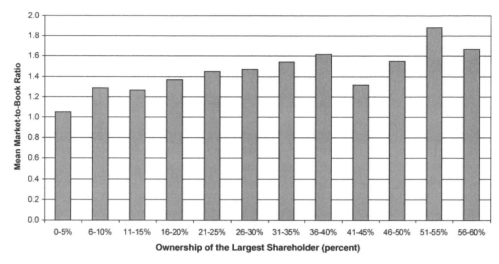

Figure 1. Company valuation and ownership of the largest shareholder in East Asian corporations, 1996.

We start by plotting the association between market-to-book ratios and the cash-flow stake of the largest shareholder (Figure 1). Firm value, as measured by the market-to-book ratio, generally increases with the share of cash-flow rights in the hands of the largest owner. This pattern is consistent with the positive incentive effect of larger cash-flow ownership on firm value. But the relationship is not monotone. Ownership by the largest shareholders of 41 to 50 percent, for example, is associated with lower mean market valuation than ownership of 36 to 40 percent, and the difference is statistically significant. Ownership of 51 to 55 percent is associated with the highest mean market-to-book ratios, with valuation falling again for ownership concentration above 55 percent.

The association between firm valuation and the separation of control and ownership rights is shown in Figure 2. The figure suggests that the larger the wedge is between control and ownership rights, the lower a firm's valuation is. Corporations with no separation of control and ownership rights have the highest value. Corporations with a separation of more than 35 percentage points—that is, when the control rights of the largest shareholder exceed his ownership rights by 35 percentage points or more—have the lowest value. Again, the relationship is not monotone. Corporations with moderate levels of separation, such as 11 to 15 percentage points, are valued higher than corporations with separation levels of 1 to 10 percentage points. Once the separation of ownership and control reaches 15 percentage points, however, there is a monotone decrease in firm value.

These two figures provide suggestive evidence on our two hypotheses. Figure 1 provides evidence in favor of the incentive effects associated with increased cash-flow rights in the hands of the largest shareholder. Figure 2 is

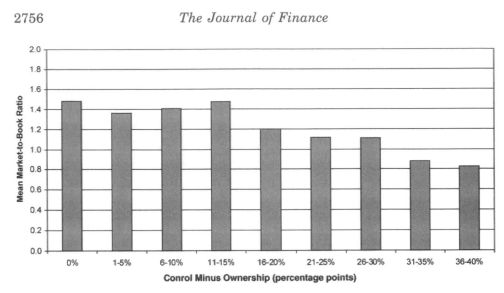

Figure 2. Company valuation and the difference between control and ownership of the largest shareholder in East Asian corporations, 1996.

generally consistent with the entrenchment effect. As the control rights of the largest shareholder increase relative to his ownership rights, firm valuation appears to fall. But in both figures, the association with market-to-book ratios is not monotone, and here we did not control for other factors influencing firm valuation. Thus, multivariate analysis allowing for nonlinear relationships is needed to investigate more precisely the incentive and entrenchment hypotheses.

B. Regression Results

We start by including as control variables several firm-specific variables commonly used in studies of firm valuation. Specifically, we include sales growth in the previous year and capital spending relative to sales in the previous year. We expect both variables to have a positive relationship with firm value, because they proxy for a firm's growth prospects and investment.

We also include firm age (measured in years since establishment) and firm size (measured by the log of total assets in the previous year). On the one hand, we expect age and size to be positively related to firm value for the same reasons often mentioned in studies of firms in developed economies: older and larger firms have better disclosure, more liquid trading, more attention from analysts, and more diversified activities leading to lower risk of financial distress. On the other hand, younger and smaller firms may have more growth opportunities. Furthermore, in East Asia, smaller firms may be less diversified, leading to smaller value discounts. (Claessens et al. (1999b) show that diversification is associated with a value discount for East Asian corporations.)

Incentive and Entrenchment Effects of Large Shareholdings   2757

We do not expect to introduce significant colinearities in the regressions by using this set of variables, because the correlations between the variables are very low. For example, the correlation between sales growth and capital spending over sales is just 0.0263, and the correlation between firm age and firm size is only 0.1272. We also include industry dummy variables in all the regressions to correct for possible valuation differences among industries. The leisure sector is used as the numeraire.

We next want to control for possible within-economy correlations that could bias our analysis. The Breusch and Pagan (1980) Lagrange multiplier test rejects the null hypothesis that errors are independent within country samples, suggesting that a fixed-effects specification cannot be used. To correct for within-economy correlations, we use a random-effects specification that assumes each sample has a common explanatory variable component, which may differ across economies. In other words, we do not treat corporations in a given economy as independent observations. This specification takes explicit account of the correlated errors among our observations within an economy and produces consistent standard errors. Moreover, a random-effects specification is preferable to fixed effects when a subsample of the population is used, as we have done here (Greene (1997, p. 623)).

Table IV presents regression results that link firm valuation to the ownership and control of the largest shareholder, with ownership and control as continuous variables. The table presents three specifications, with the first the basic regression, the second the basic regression with a dummy added for whether the firm consolidates its financial statements (using either the full or cost method), and the third a specification that investigates possible nonmonotonicity in the relationship. As noted, consolidation tends to understate the market-to-book ratio with the full consolidation method but not with the cost method. Because we do not know the method of consolidation for each firm, the consolidation dummy will pick up the combined effects of no bias of the market-to-book ratio with the cost method and the understatement of the market-to-book ratio with the full method. Thus, we should expect a negative sign for the consolidation dummy.

For all three regression specifications, we find that ownership concentration is positive and associated with increased firm valuation at a statistically significant (one percent) level. The three coefficients for the ownership variable are similar and are economically significant. A one standard deviation increase in the ownership stake of the largest shareholder induces a 0.091 increase in the market-to-book ratio, or an increase of more than 6.4 percent of the average (under regression specification 1). Increases in control rights over ownership rights are associated with lower firm values for all three specifications. The coefficients on the control minus ownership variable are also highly economically significant. A one standard deviation increase in the concentration of control over ownership rights in the hands of the largest shareholder lowers relative values by 0.076—more than a 5.3 percent drop (again under specification 1). The incentive and entrenchment effects of large shareholdings are thus large and economically significant.

Table IV
Regression Results on the Relationship between Firm Value and the Largest Shareholder's Ownership and Control

The regressions are performed using a random-effects (economy-level) specification. Numbers in parentheses are standard errors. The dependent variable is the ratio of the market value of assets to the book value of assets at the end of 1996. Market value is defined as the sum of the market value of common stock and the book value of debt and preferred stock. The book value of assets comes from firms' balance sheets. The main independent variables are the share of cash-flow rights held by the largest shareholder (ownership) and the share of voting rights held by the largest shareholder (control). Control minus ownership is a continuous variable measuring the simple difference between the share of control rights and the share of cash-flow rights in the hands of the largest shareholder. Control exceeds ownership is a dummy equal to one if control rights are higher than cash-flow rights; otherwise, it is zero. Control exceeds ownership, high is a dummy equal to one if control rights are higher than cash-flow rights and if this separation is higher than the median separation in corporations where control and ownership differ; otherwise, it is zero. Sales growth, capital spending over sales, firm age, firm size, and industry dummies (the leisure sector is the numeraire) are included as control variables. The consolidation dummy equals one if the corporation consolidates its financial statements; otherwise, it is zero.

Independent variable	Specification 1		Specification 2		Specification 3	
Ownership	0.0073^a	(0.0020)	0.0073^a	(0.0020)	0.0080^a	(0.0020)
Control minus ownership	-0.0103^a	(0.0033)	-0.0103^a	(0.0033)		
Control exceeds ownership					-0.0234	(0.0621)
Control exceeds ownership, high					-0.1260^a	(0.0552)
Sales growth	0.5568^a	(0.1145)	0.5603^a	(0.1147)	0.5574^a	(0.1148)
Capital spending over sales	-0.1105	(0.1156)	-0.1100	(0.1157)	-0.1106	(0.1162)
Firm age (years)	0.0005	(0.0012)	0.0005	(0.0012)	0.0007	(0.0012)
Firm size (log of assets)	-0.0476^a	(0.0135)	-0.0476^a	(0.0135)	-0.0463^a	(0.0135)
Consolidation dummy			-0.0260	(0.0467)		
Petroleum	0.1126	(0.1763)	0.1101	(0.1764)	0.1169	(0.1766)
Consumer durables	-0.0601	(0.1042)	-0.0624	(0.1043)	-0.0560	(0.1044)
Basic industry	0.0485	(0.1098)	0.0440	(0.1102)	0.0557	(0.1100)
Food and tobacco	0.0625	(0.1153)	0.0591	(0.1155)	0.0687	(0.1155)
Construction	-0.1313	(0.1100)	-0.1324	(0.1100)	-0.1242	(0.1102)
Capital goods	-0.0498	(0.1172)	-0.0528	(0.1174)	-0.0438	(0.1175)
Transportation	-0.0501	(0.1370)	-0.0491	(0.1371)	-0.0456	(0.1373)
Unregulated utilities	0.3752^b	(0.1708)	0.3792^b	(0.1710)	0.3655^b	(0.1712)
Textiles and trade	-0.2803^c	(0.1637)	-0.2794^c	(0.1638)	-0.2806^c	(0.1641)
Services	0.0873	(0.1835)	0.0861	(0.1836)	0.0834	(0.1839)
Constant	0.8532	(2.4950)	0.8932	(2.4967)	0.4968	(2.4947)
R^2	0.0716		0.0718		0.0685	
Number of observations	1,301		1,301		1,301	

[a] Significant at the 1 percent level; [b] significant at the 5 percent level; [c] significant at the 10 percent level.

The regression results do not appear to be influenced by whether firms consolidate their financial statements. When the dummy is included for whether a firm consolidates (Table IV, specification 2), the dummy has a

Incentive and Entrenchment Effects of Large Shareholdings 2759

negative sign but is not statistically significant. More importantly, the co-efficients for the ownership, control minus ownership, and other variables barely change, if at all. If firms were more likely to have subsidiaries and consolidate their financial statements when ownership is concentrated, our results would be biased against finding a positive effect on firm value of ownership structures. That the coefficients do not change when we include a dummy for whether firms consolidate suggests that consolidation and the methods used to consolidate do not bias our results.

Figure 2 suggests that the degree of entrenchment of the largest share-holder to the detriment of firm value (and other shareholders) might be higher when there is more than a 15 percentage point gap between control rights and cash-flow rights. The importance for this sample of a high level of separation between control rights and cash-flow rights is confirmed in the regression result that includes two dummies (specification 3). The first dummy—control exceeds ownership—equals one when control rights exceed cash-flow rights. The second dummy—control exceeds ownership, high—equals one when the separation between control rights and cash-flow rights exceeds the median separation for all firms with separation. This median separation is 15.1 percentage points.

The first dummy has a negative coefficient but is not statistically signif-icant. The second dummy is statistically significant at the one percent level and has a large economic effect, because it indicates a 12.6 percentage point reduction in the market-to-book ratio. This outcome suggests that, for this sample of firms, a large wedge between control and ownership stakes leads to value losses.

This critical wedge of about 15 percentage points contrasts with the find-ings in Morck et al. (1988), who show that the entrenchment effect for U.S. manager-owners becomes apparent at a low concentration of control, start-ing at just over five percent. This difference may be due to the fact that in Morck et al. and Stulz (1988), entrenchment arises from managers' ability to prevent takeovers. In the United States, it is possible to prevent takeovers with low ownership concentration. But, in East Asia, takeovers are rare to begin with. Presumably, the valuation discount brought about by entrenched owners in East Asia arises from actions other than blocking value-enhancing takeovers. Such other actions may include private benefits and direct ex-propriation through transfer of financial wealth to affiliated firms, and would require large control stakes. Reducing such behavior by large stakeholders would require strong action by minority shareholders—a difficult task in these economies given their weak corporate governance and poor enforce-ment (Johnson et al. (2000)).

Among the other explanatory variables, sales growth in the previous year and firm size have significant explanatory power, with sales growth show-ing a positive coefficient and size a negative coefficient. The first finding is common, because higher growth reflects better future growth opportunities and so higher firm valuation. The second suggests that for this sample, be-ing smaller leads to higher relative valuation, suggesting that small firms have better growth prospects. Given the East Asian context, lower values for large firms may also derive from their more extensive diversification (Claessens et al. (1999b)).

The other firm-specific variables are statistically insignificant for all three specifications. This is perhaps not surprising given that their simple correlation coefficients with the market-to-book ratio are low. For example, the correlation coefficient between firm age and the market-to-book ratio is only 0.0413. The industry dummies are jointly statistically significant in explaining firm valuation. Individually, however, the only statistically significant industry dummies are for unregulated utilities, with a coefficient of 0.3752, and textiles and trade, with a coefficient of -0.2803 (under specification 1).

C. Tests of Robustness

C.1. Accounting for Group Effects

Observations within business groups may not be independent due to the common ownership and the sometimes common management of members of such groups, which can lead to intragroup financial transfers that are not necessarily market based. Such transfers could lead to interdependent valuation measures among firms that are members of the same group. To address this concern, we treat all observations within each business group as a single observation and rerun the regressions of Table IV. Because definitions of business groups vary across East Asia, we identify group membership broadly by including all firms in the same group if they are part of a set of firms linked through pyramiding or if they have cross-holdings with other firms. This definition leads to a larger set of affiliated corporations than does the conventional use of ownership links above a certain threshold. As such, this definition should provide a conservative bound on any group effect.

We use two alternative regression specifications when collapsing all observations within each business group into a single observation. The first regresses the median market-to-book ratio within a business group on the medians of the explanatory variables of all corporations belonging to that group. Stand-alone firms, that is, firms not belonging to any group, are treated as separate observations in this regression. In the second specification, we weigh within-group observations with weights equal to the assets contributed by each firm to the group as a share of total group assets, in effect giving more importance to large members of the group. This adjustment accounts for the possibility that within-group ownership structures and net financial transfers lead to a size-related bias in the relationship between ownership structures and firm valuation.

Claessens et al. (2000) show that smaller firms are more likely to be controlled by a single shareholder. If smaller firms also gain more value from group affiliation relative to large firms, as might be expected, then weighing by size would bias our analysis against finding a relationship between ownership structures and firm valuation. Again, stand-alone firms are treated as separate observations in the weighted regression. The resulting sample for both specifications has 872 observations.

Table V shows the regression results using both the basic specification of Table IV and the specification that investigates large differences between ownership rights and control rights. We do not use industry dummies in either specification. Industry dummies would not be meaningful, because we collapse all within-group firm observations to one observation per group and because within each group these firms typically engage in many industries. The main results on ownership and control rights are maintained. The ownership stake of the largest shareholder in specifications 1 and 3 continues to have a positive and statistically significant relationship with firm value, with coefficients similar to those in Table IV. The coefficients on the control minus ownership variable are again negative and statistically significant and of the same order as in Table IV.

In the specifications with the dummy variables, 2 and 4, the coefficients are not statistically significant for the first dummy, control exceeds ownership. But they have the same magnitude as the coefficients of the same variable in Table IV. The coefficients are statistically significant for the second dummy, control exceeds ownership, high, and of somewhat larger magnitude than the coefficients of the same variable in Table IV. Comparing the median specifications (1 and 2) and the value-weighted least squares specifications (3 and 4) shows that the coefficients of the ownership variables are similar, suggesting that the distribution of firm size within each business group does not bias the results.

Sales growth is the only statistically significant control variable in these specifications. The magnitude of its coefficient is slightly different from those in Table IV, possibly because of the smaller weight given to firms in business groups. A general comparison of Tables IV and V suggests that entrenchment effects are equally severe in group-affiliated firms, because the coefficients are similar regardless of whether all firms affiliated with a single group are reduced to one observation. Together, the regression results show that the dependence among firms in business groups does not alter our main results for valuation or ownership and control structures.

C.2. Results by Economy

We also study the relationship between firm valuation and ownership and control in the hands of the largest shareholder at the economy level, using the basic specification of Table IV. We include but do not report the four control variables: sales growth, capital spending over sales, firm age, and firm size. Higher ownership rights in the hands of the largest owner are associated with higher valuations in six economies, and this relationship is statistically significant in all six except the Philippines (Table VI). That outcome may be due to the fact that the Philippine sample is the smallest of the eight economies, with just 77 observations. Singapore and Taiwan show

Table V

Regression Results on the Relationship between Firm Value and the Largest Shareholder's Ownership and Control, by Business Group

The regressions are performed using a random-effects specification in which all observations within a business group are collapsed into one observation. Stand-alone corporations are treated as separate observations, that is, each is viewed as its own business group. Specifications 1 and 2 are run on the median value within each business group for both the dependent and independent variables. In specifications 3 and 4, the business group observations are reached by weighing each group affiliate observation by its assets as a share of the group's total assets. Numbers in parentheses are standard errors. The dependent variable is the ratio of the market value of assets to the book value of assets at the end of 1996. Market value is defined as the sum of the market value of common stock and the book value of debt and preferred stock. The book value of assets comes from firms' balance sheets. The main independent variables are the share of cash-flow rights held by the largest shareholder (ownership) and the share of voting rights held by the largest shareholder (control). Control minus ownership is a continuous variable measuring the simple difference between the share of control rights and the share of cash-flow rights in the hands of the largest shareholder. Control exceeds ownership is a dummy equal to one if control rights are higher than cash-flow rights; otherwise, it is zero. Control exceeds ownership, high is a dummy equal to one if control rights are higher than cash-flow rights and if this separation is higher than the median separation in corporations where control and ownership differ; otherwise, it is zero. Sales growth, capital spending over sales, firm age, firm size, and industry dummies (the leisure sector is the numeraire) are included as control variables.

Independent Variable	Specification 1		Specification 2		Specification 3		Specification 4	
Ownership	0.0077[a]	(0.0024)	0.0079[a]	(0.0023)	0.0070[a]	(0.0024)	0.0072[a]	(0.0025)
Control minus ownership	−0.0109[b]	(0.0045)			−0.0095[b]	(0.0046)		
Control exceeds ownership			−0.0211	(0.0542)			−0.0178	(0.0517)
Control exceeds ownership, high			−0.1416[a]	(0.0627)			−0.1387[a]	(0.0583)
Sales growth	0.6494[a]	(0.1452)	0.6502[a]	(0.1453)	0.6404[a]	(0.1453)	0.6411[a]	(0.1462)
Capital spending over sales	−0.1297	(0.1307)	−0.1292	(0.1303)	−0.1418	(0.1315)	−0.1422	(0.1318)
Firm age (years)	0.0006	(0.0016)	0.0006	(0.0016)	0.0005	(0.0016)	0.0005	(0.0016)
Firm size (log of assets)	−0.0277[c]	(0.0160)	−0.0275[c]	(0.0159)	−0.0260[c]	(0.0160)	−0.0265[c]	(0.0161)
Constant	0.4410	(3.2895)	0.4457	(3.2901)	0.5200	(3.2242)	0.5215	(3.3245)
R^2	0.0392		0.0398		0.0396		0.0408	
Number of observations	872		872		872		872	

[a] Significant at the 1 percent level; [b] significant at the 5 percent level; [c] significant at the 10 percent level.

Incentive and Entrenchment Effects of Large Shareholdings 2763

Table VI

Regression Results on the Relationship between Firm Value and the Largest Shareholder's Ownership and Control, by Economy

The regressions are performed on each economy sample using an ordinary least squares specification. Numbers in parentheses are standard errors. The dependent variable is the ratio of the market value of assets to the book value of assets at the end of 1996. Market value is defined as the sum of the market value of common stock and the book value of debt and preferred stock. The book value of assets comes from firms' balance sheets. The main independent variables are the share of cash-flow rights held by the largest shareholder (ownership) and the share of voting rights held by the largest shareholder (control). Control minus ownership is a continuous variable measuring the simple difference between the share of control rights and the share of cash-flow rights in the hands of the largest shareholder. Sales growth, capital spending over sales, firm age, and firm size are included as control variables but are not reported. Industry dummies are not included, given the smaller sample size at the economy level.

Economy	Constant	Ownership	Control Minus Ownership	R^2	Number of Observations
Hong Kong	1.4429[a] (0.1877)	0.0088[a] (0.0037)	−0.0181[b] (0.0083)	0.0502	225
Indonesia	0.9852[a] (0.2827)	0.0252[a] (0.0072)	−0.0133[a] (0.0059)	0.1583	132
Korea, Rep. of	1.1871[a] (0.1429)	0.0268[a] (0.0063)	−0.0038 (0.0107)	0.0675	281
Malaysia	2.0198[a] (0.2743)	0.0084[b] (0.0043)	−0.0201[c] (0.0109)	0.0364	171
Philippines	1.5051[a] (0.2694)	0.0051 (0.0091)	−0.0019 (0.0204)	0.0056	77
Singapore	2.3004[a] (0.2237)	−0.0111[c] (0.0068)	−0.0090 (0.0115)	0.0153	176
Taiwan	2.1297[a] (0.2113)	−0.0070 (0.0086)	−0.0118 (0.0152)	0.0084	129
Thailand	1.2455[a] (0.3839)	0.0130[a] (0.0057)	−0.0190[c] (0.0105)	0.0389	110

[a] Significant at the 1 percent level; [b] significant at the 5 percent level; [c] significant at the 10 percent level.

a negative relationship between ownership rights and firm valuation, but the relationship is statistically significant only in Singapore.[9]

Most of the coefficients on ownership rights for the economy-specific samples are larger than those for the overall sample. This is especially the case in economies with weaker corporate governance, such as Indonesia and Korea, suggesting that the incentive effects of concentrated ownership are more important in these settings, consistent with the findings of La Porta et al. (2002).

---

[9] The result for Singapore disappears when state firms are excluded, and the coefficient on ownership rights then becomes marginally significantly positive (at the 10 percent level). This outcome suggests that state-controlled firms are driving the negative coefficient for the sample of Singaporean firms.

The wedge between ownership and control rights is associated with lower valuations in all eight economies, and this relationship is statistically significant in Hong Kong, Indonesia, Malaysia, and Thailand. Again, the statistically significant coefficients are somewhat larger than those for the whole sample. These four economies also display a positive, statistically significant coefficient for ownership stakes, suggesting that incentive and entrenchment effects can go together. That the coefficients are larger suggests that while the incentive effects of concentrated ownership can be more important in settings with weak corporate governance, so can the entrenchment effects, leading to unclear net effects of ownership concentration on firm value.

C.3. Reverse Causality

Another issue that might arise is the possibility of reverse causality in terms of the impact on firm valuation of deviations between ownership and control rights. Suppose that the largest shareholder considers his firm overvalued and wants to invest his money elsewhere. He might then want to lower his ownership rights but maintain his control rights. Firm values would then adjust with a lag to their equilibrium levels. We could then find that as deviations become large, firm valuation becomes lower, but that would tell us little about the possible entrenchment effect of the separation of control and ownership. This possibility would imply changes in ownership and control patterns that are followed (with some lag) by lower valuations.

It seems unlikely, however, that firms can change their ownership structures quickly and frequently in light of temporary overvaluations or undervaluations. (La Porta et al. (1999) report that ownership structures for the top 20 to 30 East Asian firms are relatively stable over time.) More generally, our regression results are based on cross-sectional relationships. The possibility of reverse causality would thus lead to a bias only if insiders changed their cash-flow rights quickly and frequently in light of temporary overvaluations or undervaluations, while maintaining their control rights, and did so systematically across many corporations. Such behavior seems unlikely.

III. Owner Types and Mechanisms for Separating Ownership and Control

Previous research has documented that a large shareholding in general and the separation of ownership and control in particular is usually associated with family ownership (La Porta et al. (1999) and Claessens et al. (2000)). Thus, we investigate whether a particular type of owner is largely responsible for our results. We study separately the effects on firm value of ownership by families, the state, or widely held corporations and financial institutions. The control stakes of the largest shareholder are used to classify firms into one of these ownership categories. The family is the largest blockholder in 908 firms, or nearly 70 percent of the sample. Few corpora-

Incentive and Entrenchment Effects of Large Shareholdings 2765

tions are controlled by the state—111 in total—and most are from Singapore (see Table II). Finally, 282 observations have widely held controlling owners, either corporations or financial institutions.

We also study the relationship between corporate valuation and divergencies in cash-flow rights and control rights for these three types of owners. We use the same specifications as for regressions 1 and 3 in Table IV, with the same firm-specific control variables and industry dummies (the latter are not reported). When we consider the effects on corporate value of ownership and control rights for each type of controlling shareholder, we find that the ownership variable has a similar coefficient for all three types of controlling shareholders (Table VII). Only with the state as controlling owner is the coefficient not statistically significant, and then only for the first specification. Still, significance levels are generally lower than in Table IV. The coefficient for the difference between control and ownership stakes is statistically significant at the 5 percent level for family control and at the 10 percent level for state control.

Some results are less robust, however. In particular, for specifications using the dummy for high divergence between control and ownership as well as the dummy for any difference between control and ownership (specifications 2, 4, and 6), only the coefficient for the first dummy in the case of state ownership is statistically significant. The other coefficients lose their statistical significance. These weaker results could be due to the smaller set of firms for each regression. Nevertheless, the results suggest that family control, and to some extent state ownership, are driving the main results. This could be because managers at widely held corporations and financial institutions are less able than families and the state to efficiently divert benefits to themselves.

So far the results do not yet shed light on which mechanisms separating control rights from ownership rights may be driving the results. As noted, in East Asian corporations, deviations between control and ownership rights come about through different means, including pyramiding, cross-holdings, and dual-class shares. Bebchuk (1999) and Wolfenzon (1999) suggest that pyramiding is associated with value discounts. Cross-holdings could also be associated with value losses because they facilitate nonmarket-based financial transfers among corporations within a group, either horizontally or vertically. Besides pyramid structures and cross-holdings, dual-class shares, while not common in East Asia, can separate control from ownership rights and be associated with value loss. For a larger sample of countries, Nenova (2001) highlights the role of dual shares in environments with poor corporate governance as a mechanism for value transfers.

To measure the importance of each of these mechanisms, we construct dummy variables to explain the relative variations in firm valuation (Table VIII). Pyramid is a dummy equal to one if the firm is part of a pyramid structure (including if it is the apex firm at the top of a pyramid), and zero otherwise. Crosshold is a dummy equal to one if the firm is controlled (at least partly) by a cross-holding, and zero otherwise. Dualclass is a dummy

Table VII
Regression Results on the Relationship between Firm Value and the Largest Shareholder's Ownership and Control, by Owner Type

The regressions are performed using a random-effects specification. Numbers in parentheses are standard errors. A corporation is family owned if the largest ultimate shareholder is a family group, state owned if the largest shareholder is the state, and company owned if the largest shareholder is a widely held corporation or financial institution. The dependent variable is the ratio of the market value of assets to the book value of assets at the end of 1996. Market value is defined as the sum of the market value of common stock and the book value of debt and preferred stock. The book value of assets comes from firms' balance sheets. The main independent variables are the share of cash-flow rights held by the largest shareholder (ownership) and the share of voting rights held by the largest shareholder (control). Control minus ownership is a continuous variable measuring the simple difference between the share of control rights and the share of cash-flow rights in the hands of the largest shareholder. Control exceeds ownership is a dummy equal to one if control rights are higher than cash-flow rights; otherwise, it is zero. Control exceeds ownership, high is a dummy equal to one if control rights are higher than cash-flow rights and if this separation is higher than the median separation in corporations where control and ownership differ; otherwise, it is zero. Sales growth, capital spending over sales, firm age, firm size, and industry dummies are included as control variables but are not reported.

Independent Variable	Family		The State		Widely Held Corporation or Financial Institution	
	Specification 1	Specification 2	Specification 3	Specification 4	Specification 5	Specification 6
Ownership	0.0086[b]	0.0084[a]	0.0073	0.0121[c]	0.0086[c]	0.0075[c]
	(0.0026)	(0.0025)	(0.0070)	(0.0062)	(0.0045)	(0.0041)
Control minus ownership	−0.0090[b]		−0.0247[c]		−0.0189	
	(0.0037)		(0.0130)		(0.0154)	

Incentive and Entrenchment Effects of Large Shareholdings 2767

Control exceeds ownership		−0.0494 (0.0722)		0.1218 (0.1845)		0.1086 (0.1816)
Control exceeds ownership, high		−0.0342 (0.0828)		−0.4806[b] (0.2264)		−0.3685 (0.3331)
Sales growth	0.6621[b] (0.1341)	0.6323[a] (0.1358)	0.1833 (0.1241)	0.1847 (0.1346)	0.5105[b] (0.2491)	0.4833[c] (0.2557)
Capital spending over sales	−0.1370 (0.1334)	−0.0814 (0.1332)	−0.0043 (0.4329)	0.0229 (0.4341)	−0.0353 (0.2729)	−0.1959 (0.2726)
Firm age (years)	0.0011 (0.0014)	0.0014 (0.0014)	0.0061 (0.0047)	0.0043 (0.0050)	−0.0020 (0.0030)	−0.0030 (0.0031)
Firm size (log of assets)	−0.0358[b] (0.0169)	−0.0373[b] (0.0165)	0.0512 (0.0482)	0.0023 (0.0461)	−0.0714[b] (0.0284)	−0.0889[a] (0.0278)
Constant	−0.6068 (2.8349)	−1.1551 (2.8243)	−11.4143 (9.4312)	−7.1866 (10.0226)	6.0540 (6.0331)	8.2864 (6.0979)
R^2	0.0523	0.0496	0.0450	0.0855	0.0714	0.0811
Number of observations	908	908	111	111	282	282

[a] Significant at the 1 percent level; [b] significant at the 5 percent level; [c] significant at the 10 percent level.

Table VIII
Regression Results on the Relationship between Firm Value and Pyramiding, Cross-Holdings, and Dual-Class Shares

The regressions are performed using a random-effects specification. Numbers in parentheses are standard errors. Pyramid is a dummy equal to one if the firm is part of a pyramid structure; otherwise, it is zero. Crosshold is a dummy equal to one if the firm is controlled (at least partly) by a cross-holding; otherwise, it is zero. Dualclass is a dummy equal to one if the firm has issued dual-class shares; otherwise, it is zero. The dependent variable is the ratio of the market value of assets to the book value of assets at the end of 1996. Market value is defined as the sum of the market value of common stock and the book value of debt and preferred stock. The book value of assets comes from firms' balance sheets. The main independent variables are the share of cash-flow rights held by the largest shareholder (ownership) and the share of voting rights held by the largest shareholder (control). Sales growth, capital spending over sales, firm age, firm size, and industry dummies are included as control variables but are not reported.

Independent Variable	Specification 1		Specification 2		Specification 3		Specification 4	
Ownership	0.0119^a	(0.0020)	0.0095^a	(0.0020)	0.0118^a	(0.0020)	0.0091^a	(0.0020)
Pyramid dummy	−0.0571	(0.1365)					−0.0136	(0.0524)
Crosshold dummy			−0.0332	(0.0507)			−0.0077	(0.0732)
Dualclass dummy					−0.0468	(0.0703)	−0.1595	(0.1360)
Sales growth	0.5754^a	(0.1138)	0.5683^a	(0.1146)	0.5778^a	(0.1137)	0.5622^a	(0.1149)
Capital spending over sales	−0.1149	(0.1157)	−0.0897	(0.1151)	−0.1152	(0.1157)	−0.0862	(0.1153)
Firm age (years)	0.0012	(0.0012)	0.0009	(0.0012)	0.0011	(0.0012)	0.0008	(0.0012)
Firm size (log of assets)	-0.0312^a	(0.0136)	-0.0400^a	(0.0134)	-0.0314^b	(0.0136)	-0.0420^a	(0.0134)
Constant	−0.7902	(2.4572)	−0.0173	(2.4722)	−0.7560	(2.4576)	0.1212	(2.4780)
R^2	0.0474		0.0480		0.0467		0.0491	
Number of observations	1,301		1,301		1,301		1,301	

[a] Significant at the 1 percent level; [b] significant at the 5 percent level.

equal to one if the firm has issued dual-class shares, and zero otherwise. We run four specifications, using a dummy for each mechanism separately and then combining all three dummies in the final regression. This final regression does not create any collinearity problems, because the three variables are not highly correlated. (The simple correlation between Pyramid and Crosshold is 0.2876, between Pyramid and Dualclass 0.1457, and between Crosshold and Dualclass 0.0174.)

All three dummy variables have a negative coefficient, a sign that these mechanisms reduce value, correcting for ownership structures and other factors. But none of the three is statistically significant. The ownership variable remains positive and statistically significant, with coefficients similar to those in Tables IV and V. While the entrenchment of the largest shareholders in East Asian corporations may thus be supported by combinations of pyramiding, cross-holdings, and dual-class shares, the evidence suggests that the separation of ownership and control is what leads to value discounts, not any mechanism in particular.[10]

An alternative hypothesis to the two we have explored here could be that value discounts are due to bad management, and the likelihood of bad management is related to the ownership structure. Multiple layers of pyramidal ownership and numerous cross-holdings could mean that the controlling owner-manager at the apex of the pyramid does not have the capacity to monitor the managers of all its affiliated firms. The result could be bad performance and value discounts. But Claessens et al. (2000) show that for more than two-thirds of firms with concentrated ownership, managers come from the controlling families. Controlling owners that are managers are thus not limited to apex firms, but are widespread throughout business groups. As such, managers would have few incentives to mismanage firms for which they are also controlling owner. So, although appealing, this alternative hypothesis does not hold for the average corporation in our sample. Nevertheless, we did split the sample into firms managed by people who belong to the controlling shareholder's family and firms with unrelated managers, and we found similar results (not reported).

IV. Conclusion

This article documents the relationships between ownership and control stakes held by the largest shareholder on the one hand, and market valuation on the other hand, for a large sample of publicly traded corporations in East Asia. Its main contribution is disentangling the incentive and entrenchment effects of large ownership that are so difficult to tell apart in U.S. data. We show that firm valuation increases with cash-flow ownership in the hands of the largest shareholder. This result is consistent with a large

---

[10] Including in the regression only firms with families as the largest controlling shareholder, however, we find that, for these firms, pyramid structures are negatively related to firm value at a statistically significant (10 percent) level.

literature on the positive incentive effects associated with increased cash-flow rights in the hands of a single or few shareholders. We also find a negative entrenchment effect with large controlling shareholders: Increases in control rights by the largest shareholder are accompanied by declines in firm values. This negative effect is particularly severe for large deviations between control and ownership rights.

When investigating individual ownership types, we find that our results appear to be driven by family control. We also provide support for the predictions of theoretical studies that separating control rights and cash-flow rights can create agency costs larger than the costs associated with a controlling shareholder who also has a majority of cash-flow rights. Because concentrated corporate ownership is predominant in most countries outside the United States, these findings may have relevance worldwide. The results suggest that the risk of expropriation of minority shareholders by large, controlling shareholders is an important principal–agent problem in most countries.

The degree to which certain ownership and control structures are associated with entrenchment discounts likely depends on economy-specific circumstances. These may include the quality of banking systems, the legal and judicial protection of individual shareholders, and the degree of financial disclosure required. This is especially the case for a number of the economies in this study, because they have been identified as having deficient corporate governance and weak institutional development. The exact magnitude to which institutional differences across economies affect the valuation discount is an important issue for future research.

REFERENCES

Asian Company Handbook, 1998, winter edition (Toyo Keizai Shinposha, Tokyo).

Bebchuk, Lucian, 1999, A rent-protection theory of corporate control and ownership, NBER working paper 7203.

Bebchuk, Lucian, Reinier Kraakman, and George Triantis, 2000, Stock pyramids, cross-ownership, and dual class equity: The creation and agency costs of separating control from cash flow rights, in Randall K. Morck, ed.: *Concentrated Corporate Ownership* (University of Chicago Press, Chicago, IL).

Breusch, Trevor, and Adrian Pagan, 1980, The Lagrange multiplier test and its applications to model specifications in econometrics, *The Review of Economic Studies* 47, 239–253.

Campbell, John, 1996, Understanding risk and return, *Journal of Political Economy* 104, 298–345.

Claessens, Stijn, Simeon Djankov, Joseph Fan, and Larry Lang, 1999a, The expropriation of minority shareholders: Evidence from East Asia, World Bank, Washington, DC.

Claessens, Stijn, Simeon Djankov, Joseph Fan, and Larry Lang, 1999b, The patterns and valuation effects of corporate diversification: A comparison of the United States, Japan, and other East Asian economies, World Bank, Washington, DC.

Claessens, Stijn, Simeon Djankov, and Larry Lang, 2000, The separation of ownership and control in East Asian corporations, *Journal of Financial Economics* 58, 81–112.

Greene, William, 1997, *Econometric Analysis* (MacMillan, New York).

Grossman, Sanford, and Oliver Hart, 1988, One-share, one-vote, and the market for corporate control, *Journal of Financial Economics* 20, 175–202.

Harris, Milton, and Artur Raviv, 1988, Corporate governance: Voting rights and majority rules, *Journal of Financial Economics* 20, 203–235.

Incentive and Entrenchment Effects of Large Shareholdings   2771

Jensen, Michael, and William Meckling, 1976, Theory of the firm: Managerial behavior, agency costs, and ownership structure, *Journal of Financial Economics* 3, 305–360.

Johnson, Simon, Peter Boone, Alasdair Breach, and Eric Friedman, 2000, Corporate governance in the Asian financial crisis, 1997–1998, *Journal of Financial Economics* 58, 141–186.

La Porta, Rafael, Florencio Lopez-de-Silanes, and Andrei Shleifer, 1999, Corporate ownership around the world, *Journal of Finance* 54, 471–518.

La Porta, Rafael, Florencio Lopez-de-Silanes, Andrei Shleifer, and Robert W. Vishny, 2002, Investor protection and corporate valuation, *Journal of Finance* 57, 1147–1170.

McConnell, John, and Henri Servaes, 1990, Additional evidence on equity ownership and corporate value, *Journal of Financial Economics* 27, 595–612.

Morck, Randall, Andrei Shleifer, and Robert Vishny, 1988, Management ownership and market valuation: An empirical analysis, *Journal of Financial Economics* 20, 293–315.

Morck, Randall, David Stangeland, and Bernard Yeung, 2000, Inherited wealth, corporate control and economic growth: The Canadian disease, in Randall K. Morck, ed.: *Concentrated Corporate Ownership* (University of Chicago Press, Chicago, IL).

Nenova, Tatiana, 2001, The value of a corporate vote and private benefits: Cross-country analysis, Manuscript, Harvard University.

Shleifer, Andrei, and Robert W. Vishny, 1997, A survey of corporate governance, *Journal of Finance* 52, 737–783.

Stulz, René, 1988, Managerial control of voting rights: Financing policies and the market for corporate control, *Journal of Financial Economics* 20, 25–54.

Wolfenzon, Daniel, 1999, A theory of pyramidal structures, Manuscript, Harvard University.

THE JOURNAL OF FINANCE • VOL. LIX, NO. 2 • APRIL 2004

Private Benefits of Control: An International Comparison

ALEXANDER DYCK and LUIGI ZINGALES*

ABSTRACT

We estimate private benefits of control in 39 countries using 393 controlling blocks sales. On average the value of control is 14 percent, but in some countries can be as low as −4 percent, in others as high a +65 percent. As predicted by theory, higher private benefits of control are associated with less developed capital markets, more concentrated ownership, and more privately negotiated privatizations. We also analyze what institutions are most important in curbing private benefits. We find evidence for both legal and extra-legal mechanisms. In a multivariate analysis, however, media pressure and tax enforcement seem to be the dominating factors.

THE BENEFITS OF CONTROL OVER corporate resources play a central role in modern thinking about finance and corporate governance. From a modeling device (Grossman and Hart (1980)) the idea of private benefits of control has become a centerpiece of the recent literature in corporate finance, both theoretical and empirical. In fact, the main focus of the literature on investor protection and its role in the development of financial markets (La Porta, Lopez-de-Salines, and Shleifer (2000)) is on the amount of private benefits that controlling shareholders extract from companies they run.

In spite of the importance of this concept, there are remarkably few estimates of how big these private benefits are, even fewer attempts to document empirically what determines their size, and no *direct* evidence of their impact on financial development. All of the evidence on this latter point is *indirect*, based on the (reasonable) assumption that better protection of minority shareholders is correlated with higher financial development via its curbing of private benefits of control (La Porta et al. (1997)).

The lack of evidence is no accident. By their very nature, private benefits of control are difficult to observe and even more difficult to quantify in a reliable

*Dyck is from the Harvard Business School and Zingales is from the University of Chicago. Chris Allen, Mehmet Beceren, and Omar Choudhry provided invaluable research assistance in preparing the data. We thank Andrew Karolyi, John Matsusaka, David Moss, Tatiana Nenova, Krishna Palepu, Mark Roe, Julio Rotemberg, Abbie Smith, Debora Spar, Per Stromberg, Rene Stulz, an anonymous referee, Richard Green (the editor), and seminar participants from Georgetown University, Harvard Business School, the NBER corporate finance program, University of Chicago, the University of Pennsylvania (Wharton), and the University of Southern California, and the University of Toronto for helpful comments. We also gratefully acknowledge financial support from the Division of Research, Harvard Business School, the Center for Research on Security Prices, and the George Stigler Center at the University of Chicago. Any errors are our own.

way. A controlling party can appropriate value for himself only when this value is not verifiable (i.e., provable in court). If it were, it would be relatively easy for noncontrolling shareholders to stop him from appropriating it. Thus, private benefits of control are intrinsically difficult to measure.

Two methods have been used in attempting to quantify them. The first one, pioneered by Barclay and Holderness (1989), focuses on privately negotiated transfers of controlling blocks in publicly traded companies. The price per share an acquirer pays for the controlling block reflects the cash flow benefits from his fractional ownership and the private benefits stemming from his controlling position in the firm. By contrast, the market price of a share after the change in control is announced reflects only the cash flow benefits noncontrolling share-holders expect to receive under the new management. Hence, as Barclay and Holderness have argued, the difference between the price per share paid by the acquiring party and the price per share prevailing on the market reflects the differential payoff accruing to the controlling shareholder. In fact, after an adjustment, this difference can be used as a measure of the private benefits of control accruing to the controlling shareholder.

The second method relies on the existence of companies with multiple classes of stock with differential voting rights. In this case, one can easily compute the market value of a vote (Lease, McConnell, and Mikkelson (1983, 1984), DeAngelo and DeAngelo (1985), Rydqvist (1987)). On a normal trading day market transactions take place between noncontrolling parties who will never have direct access to the private benefits of control. Hence, the market value of a vote reflects the expected price a generic shareholder will receive in case of a control contest. This in turn is related to the magnitude of the private benefits of control. Thus, if one is willing to make some assumptions on the probability a control contest will arise, the price of a voting right can be used to estimate the magnitude of the private benefits of control (Zingales (1994, 1995a)).

In this paper we use the Barclay and Holderness (1989) method to infer the value of private benefits of control in a large (39) cross section of countries. Based on 393 control transactions between 1990 and 2000 we find that on average corporate control is worth 14 percent of the equity value of a firm, ranging from a −4 percent in Japan to a +65 percent in Brazil. Interestingly, the premium paid for control is higher when the buyer comes from a country that protects investors less (and thus is more willing or able to extract private benefits). This and other evidence suggest that our estimates capture the effect the institutional environment has on private benefits of control.

Given the large number of transactions from countries with different levels of financial development in our data set, we are able to provide a direct test of several theoretical propositions on the effects private benefits of control have on the development of financial markets. Theory predicts that where private benefits of control are larger, entrepreneurs should be more reluctant to go public (Zingales (1995b)) and more likely to retain control when they do go public (Zingales (1995b) and Bebchuk (1999)). In addition, where private benefits of control are larger a revenue maximizing Government should be more likely to sell a firm through a private sale than through a share offering (Zingales (1995b) and Dyck (2001)).

We find strong evidence in support of all these predictions. A one standard deviation increase in the size of the private benefits is associated with a 67 percent reduction in the ratio of external market capitalization of equity to GNP, an 11 percent reduction in the percentage of equity held by noncontrolling shareholders, and a 36 percent increase in the number of privatized companies sold in private negotiations rather than through public listings. This evidence gives support to the prominent role private benefits have come to play in corporate finance.

While the existence of private benefits is not necessarily bad, their negative effect on the development of security markets raises the question of what affects their average size across countries. Thus far, the literature has emphasized the law as the primary mechanism to curb private benefits by giving investors leverage over controlling shareholders. The right to sue management, for instance, limits the discretionary power of management and, with it, the ability to extract private benefits (Zingales (1995a)) and so does any right attributed to minority shareholders (La Porta et al. (1997)). A common law legal origin is similarly argued to constrain management by lowering the standard of proof in legal suits and increasing the scope of management decisions subject to judicial review (Johnson et al. (2000)). Consistent with this literature, we analyze the effect the law has on the size of private benefits.

Besides the law, we also consider extra-legal institutions, which have been mentioned in the literature as possible curbs for private benefits: competition, labor pressures, and moral norms. To these well-known mechanisms we add two: public opinion pressure and corporate tax enforcement. Reputation is a powerful source of discipline, and being ashamed in the press might be a powerful deterrent (Zingales (2000)), especially where the press is more diffused. Similarly, effective tax enforcement can prevent some transactions (such below market transfer prices) that expropriate minority shareholders. We find that a high level of diffusion of the press, a high rate of tax compliance, and a high degree of product market competition are associated with lower private benefits of control.

Given the noisiness of the proxies used and the paucity of degrees of freedom, it is impossible to establish reliably which factor is more important. That in a multivariate analysis newspapers' circulation and tax compliance are most important suggests these extra legal mechanisms deserve further study.

Our paper complements and expands the existing work in this area that focuses on the voting premia such as Zingales (1998), who assembles estimates of the voting premium across seven countries, and Nenova (2001a), who uses the price of differential voting shares in 18 countries. We complement the existing work by providing an alternative estimate of the private benefits of control, available for a broader cross section of countries. While in a few cases our estimates differ from Nenova's (she finds that both Brazil and Australia have a ratio of value of control to value of equity equal to 0.23, while we find only 0.02 for Australia and 0.65 for Brazil), overall our estimates are remarkably similar. Moreover, we are able to understand the differences between the two sets of estimates in terms of a sample selection bias present in estimates based on differential voting shares. These findings give confidence that the extraction of private benefits is a real phenomenon, which can be consistently estimated.

Our paper also expands the existing work. The estimates for 39 countries allow us to test several theoretical propositions on the effects private benefits of control have on the development of financial markets. Our large sample of countries and their institutional variation enable us to test alternative theories of the major factors driving the magnitude of private benefits of control and to identify some new ones.

The rest of the paper proceeds as follows. Section I discusses how the measure developed by Barclay and Holderness (1989) relates to the magnitude of the private benefits of control. Section II describes the data used and presents our estimates. Section III uses these estimates to test several theoretical predictions regarding the effects private benefits of control have on the development of markets. Section IV analyzes the correlation between the magnitude of the private benefits of control and the various institutional characteristics. Section V discusses our findings and concludes.

I. Theoretical Framework

A. *What Are Private Benefits of Control?*

The theoretical literature often identifies private benefits of control as the "psychic" value some shareholders attribute simply to being in control (e.g., Harris and Raviv (1988) and Aghion and Bolton (1992)). Although this is certainly a factor in some cases, it is hard to justify multimillion dollar premia with the pure pleasure of command. Another traditional source of private benefits of control is the perquisites enjoyed by top executives (Jensen and Meckling (1976)).

The use of a company's money to pay for perquisites is the most visible but not the most important way in which corporate resources can be used to the sole (or main) advantage of the controlling party. If the law does not effectively prevent it, corporate resources can be appropriated by the large shareholder through outright theft. Fortunately such activities, while documented in a few cases, are generally rare.

Nevertheless, there are several reasons why more moderate versions of these strategies might be more pervasive. Educated economists can legitimately disagree on what is the "fair" transfer price of a certain asset or product. As a result, small deviations from the "fair" transfer price might be difficult or impossible to prove in court. If these small deviations are applied to large volume trade, however, they can easily generate sizeable private benefits. Similarly, it is easy to disagree over who is the best provider of an asset or product when the relationship might involve considerations of quality and price.

Or consider the value of the information a corporate executive acquires thanks to his or her role in the company. Some of this information pertains directly to the company's business while some reflects potential opportunities in other more or less related areas. It is fairly easy for a controlling shareholder to choose to exploit these opportunities through another company he or she owns or is associated with, with no advantage for the remaining shareholders. The net present value of these opportunities represents a private benefit of control.

The common feature of all the above examples is that some value, whatever the source, is not shared among all the shareholders in proportion of the shares owned, but it is enjoyed exclusively by the party in control. Hence, the name private benefits of control.

Control does not only confer benefits: sometimes it involves costs as well. Maintaining a controlling block, for instance, forces the largest shareholder to be not well diversified. As a result, it might value the controlling block less. At the same time, a fledging company might inflict a loss in reputation to the controlling party and, in some extreme cases, even some legal liabilities. For this reason we do not necessarily expect all our estimates to be always positive. In particular, we expect a higher frequency of negative value of control for financially distressed companies (see also Barclay and Holderness (1989)).

Note that the existence of private benefits of control is not necessarily inefficient. First of all, private benefits might be the most efficient way for the company to capture some of the value created. Imagine, for instance, that a corporate executive acquires valuable information about investment opportunities in other lines of businesses, which the company cannot or does not want to pursue. The executive could sell this information in the interest of shareholders. But the price she will be able to fetch is probably very low. Thus, it might be efficient that the executive exploits this opportunity on her own. Second, even if the *extraction* of private benefits generates some inefficiency, their *existence* might be socially beneficial, because their presence makes value-enhancing takeovers possible (Grossman and Hart (1980)).

Given the difficulties in distinguishing whether private benefits are socially costly, consistently in this analysis we shy away from any welfare consideration. Even the implications of the effects of private benefits on the development of security markets should be interpreted as a positive statement, not a normative one. In fact, in at least one of the models from where these implications are derived (Zingales (1995b)), the level of private benefits has no efficiency consequences, but only distributional ones.[1]

B. How to Measure Private Benefits?

Unfortunately, it is very difficult to measure the private benefits directly. Psychic values are intrinsically difficult to quantify, as is the amount of resources captured by the controlling shareholder to her own benefit. As argued above, a controlling party will find it possible to extract corporate resources to his or her benefit only when it is difficult or impossible to prove that this is the case. In

---

[1] Bebchuk and Jolls (1999) discuss additional issues associated with a welfare evaluation of private benefits.

other words, if private benefits of control were easily quantifiable, then those benefits would not be private (accruing only to the control group) any longer because outside shareholders would claim them in court.

Nevertheless, there are two methods to try to assess empirically the magnitude of these private benefits of control. The first one, pioneered by Barclay and Holderness (1989), is simple. Whenever a control block changes hands, they measure the difference between the price per share paid by the acquirer and the price quoted in the market the day after the sale's announcement. As we will show momentarily, this difference (which we shall call the control premium) represents an estimate of private benefits of control enjoyed by the controlling party.

The second method of estimating the value of private benefits of control uses the price difference between two classes of stock, with similar or identical dividend rights, but different voting rights. If control is valuable, then corporate votes, which allocate control, should be valuable as well. How valuable? It depends on how decisive some votes are in allocating control and how valuable control is. If one can find a reasonable proxy for the strategic value of votes in winning control—for example in forming a winning coalition block—then one can infer the value of control from the relationship between the market price of the votes and their strategic role. This is the strategy followed by Rydqvist (1987), Zingales (1994, 1995a), and Nenova (2001a).

Both methods suffer from a common bias: They capture only the common value component of private benefits. If an incumbent enjoys a psychic benefit from running the family company, this value is unlikely to be shared by any other potential buyer and hence is unlikely to be reflected into the value of a controlling block when this changes hands (and hence in the value of a voting right). If, as it is likely, psychic benefits are more idiosyncratic to the controlling shareholder, then companies with large nonmonetary private benefits are less likely to change hands (it is more difficult to find somebody that values control more than the incumbent) and when they do, they are likely to exhibit lower control premia.[2] Hence, both methods tend to underestimate the value of control, and more so in countries where the major source of private benefits is nonpecuniary. [3]

Besides this bias, both methods have pluses and minuses. The estimates obtained using the control premia method are relatively model free (albeit, see Section II.C. below). If we are careful in isolating only the transactions that transfer control, we do not have to worry about the proper model of how private benefits will be shared among different parties and what is the probability of a takeover (e.g., Nicodano and Sembenelli (2001)). On the other hand, sales of controlling blocks are relatively rare and might not occur randomly over time. Furthermore, any systematic overpayment or any delay in incorporating

---

[2] The reason why a superior voting share trades at a premium is that its holder expects to receive a differential premium (see Zingales (1995b)). Hence, if a potential buyer is not willing to pay any more for control, the premium disappears.

[3] We thank the referee for pointing out this bias.

public information can bias the estimates (a problem we will deal with in Section III.E.).

Estimates obtained using dual class shares are often based on many firms and therefore are less likely to be driven by outliers. On the other hand, dual class shares are not allowed in every country. Hence, the second method limits the number of countries that can be included in the study. More importantly, the proportion of dual class companies differs widely across countries. Hence, the estimates obtained using the second method represent a differently selected universe of companies in each country. In any case, given the importance of private benefits in our understanding of corporate finance, it makes sense to explore both approaches. Nenova (2001a) has followed the voting rights approach while we use control premia.

C. Theoretical Relation between Control Premium and Size of the Private Benefits of Control

An implicit assumption in the Barclay and Holderness (1989) approach for estimating private benefits is that the sale price reflects the buyers' willingness to pay. However, as Nicodano and Sembenelli (2001) point out, if there is imperfect competition in the market for controlling blocks, the Barclay and Holderness approach can misestimate private benefits. We illustrate this point with a simple bargaining model.

Let λ, on the interval [0, 1], be the bargaining power of the controlling shareholder selling out, $B_{s,b}$ the level of private benefits extracted by the seller (buyer), and $Y_{s,b}$ the level of security benefits generated by the seller (buyer), then the price P paid for a controlling block of shares with α cash flow rights, on the interval [0, 1], is

$$P = \lambda(B_b + \alpha Y_b) + (1 - \lambda)(B_s + \alpha Y_s) \tag{1}$$

and the per share price of the controlling block equals

$$\frac{P}{\alpha} = \frac{\lambda B_b + (1 - \lambda)B_s}{\alpha} + \lambda Y_b + (1 - \lambda)Y_s. \tag{2}$$

To compute the control premium, Barclay and Holderness (1989) subtract from equation (2) the price prevailing in the market after the announcement that control has changed hands, which should equal to Y_b. Thus, they obtain

$$\frac{\lambda B_b + (1 - \lambda)B_s}{\alpha} - (1 - \lambda)(Y_b - Y_s). \tag{3}$$

They then multiply this price difference by the size of the controlling block α. Hence, their estimate of private benefits of control $\hat{B}$ is

$$\hat{B} = \lambda B_b + (1 - \lambda)B_s - \alpha(1 - \lambda)(Y_b - Y_s). \tag{4}$$

In a perfectly competitive market ($\lambda = 1$), $\hat{B}$ collapses to B_b and thus the control premium is a legitimate estimate of the private benefits of control the buyer expects to enjoy. When the market is not perfectly competitive, but the security value is the same for the buyer and the seller ($Y_b = Y_s$), $\hat{B}$ is still a legitimate estimate of the private benefits of control, albeit this time it represents a weighted average of the private benefits of the seller and those of the buyer.

The problem arises when the security values are different ($Y_b \neq Y_s$). By subtracting the price after the announcement from the per share price paid for the controlling block (the step from equation (2) to equation (3) above), Barclay and Holderness implicitly assume that the seller is able to capture the full value of the security benefits produced by the buyer. When this is not true, $\hat{B}$ misestimates the average value of private benefits, where the extent of this bias is represented by the term $\alpha(1 - \lambda)(Y_b - Y_s)$.

To understand this bias, consider the other extreme case, where the buyer has all the bargaining power, ($\lambda = 0$). In this case, $\hat{B}$ collapses to $B_s - \alpha(Y_b - Y_s)$. Intuitively, the sale price of the controlling block does not reflect the differential ability of the new buyer to create security benefits, while the price on the exchange does reflect this ability. Hence, $\hat{B}$ misestimates the value of private benefits by the difference in security value times the amount of security value contained in the controlling block (α). Since the magnitude of this bias is zero if $\lambda = 1$ and $B - \alpha(Y_b - Y_s)$ when $\lambda = 0$, in general it is $\alpha(1 - \lambda)(Y_b - Y_s)$. All the terms in this bias, except for the bargaining power of the seller, are observable. Hence, if we can estimate λ, we can adjust our estimates.

II. Data and Descriptive Statistics

An example motivates our sample selection strategy and definition of our dependent variable. In January 1999 Ofer Brothers Investment Limited, an investment vehicle for Sami and Yuli Ofer of Israel, bought 53 percent of the shares and control of Israel Corporation Limited from the Eisenberg family. The price per share for the control block was reported to be 508 shekels per share while the exchange price after announcement of the transfer was 363 shekels per share. The price premium paid per share for the controlling block over the postannouncement price in this case is 40 percent. A better measure of the value of the private benefits of control is the total premium paid divided by the equity value of the firm. In this example, the Ofer brothers paid a 40 percent premium relative to the postannouncement price for 53 percent of the firms' equity, which produces an estimate of private benefits as a percentage of equity of 21 percent. This example turns out to be fairly typical of Israeli deals where we calculate a mean private benefit as a percentage of equity of 27 percent and a median value of 21 percent.

As suggested by this example, to construct a measure of private benefits, we need to identify transactions that meet at least three criteria. First, the transaction must involve a transfer of a block of shares that convey control rights. Second, we need to observe the price per share for the control block. Third, we have to observe the exchange price after the market has incorporated the

Private Benefits of Control 545

identity of the new acquirer in its expectation of future cash flow. We also add a fourth criterion, implicit in this choice of an Israeli deal—both the control and the postannouncement market prices should not be restricted by regulation. Many countries do not follow the Israeli (and U.S.) approach of allowing buyers and sellers to determine their own prices but impose some link between the exchange and the control price. As we will explain, we will eliminate all these cases from our sample.

A. Identifying Transactions

To identify transactions that convey control rights we use the SDC international mergers and acquisitions database. SDC describes its sources as: "Over 200 English and foreign language news sources, SEC filings and their international counterparts, trade publications, wires and proprietary surveys of investment banks, law firms, and other advisors." The database provides extensive information on transactions that involve transfers of blocks of shares that may convey control, including details of the parties to the transaction, the value of the transaction, and the date of announcement and conclusion of the transaction. SDC provides extensive international coverage with 7,144 transactions in 1990 (including 396 transactions from non-OECD countries) and steadily increasing numbers over the decade, including 21,881 transactions in 1999 (including 3,300 from non-OECD countries).

To identify candidates for control sales, we began with the complete set of control transactions in publicly traded companies during the period 1990 to 2000. We then restricted our attention to completed purchases of blocks larger than or equal to 10 percent of the stock.[4] Since we wanted transactions that conveyed control, we further restricted our attention to transactions that result in the acquirers moving from a position where they hold less than 20 percent of the shares to a position where they have assembled more than 20 percent of the shares. We exclude all transactions that were conducted through open market purchases and were identified by SDC as tender offers, spinoffs, recapitalizations, self-tenders, exchange offers, repurchases, and acquisitions of remaining interest. We further restricted ourselves to transactions where there was a reported transaction value or price per share in the control block.

We refined our sample by exploiting additional available qualitative data to screen out transactions that do not involve control transfers (e.g., transfer of shares among subsidiaries of common parent, where acquirer is not the largest shareholder) or were problematic for other reasons (e.g., involved related parties, reported price per share based on securities that could not be valued objectively, transfer involved the exercise of options). This step involved reading multiple news stories for every transaction resulting from searches of Lexis-Nexis and Dow-Jones Interactive to confirm the details of the transaction

---

[4] We have also explored the robustness of our results if we were to further restrict this criterion and exclude deals where block is less than 15 percent. The results are unchanged although we lose some countries as a result of a lack of observations.

collected by SDC and collecting ownership information through use of company annual reports and other sources. This process significantly increased our confidence in the observations included in the data set, but inevitably involved greater use of discretion in determining whether an observation was included in our data set.

To ensure the availability of exchange prices, we restricted ourselves to transactions involving companies available in the Datastream International database. To implement the criterion that the difference between the control price and the exchange price not be driven by legal requirements, we excluded observations driven by legal requirements. We first excluded all instances where the controlling block was purchased as part of a public offer, as in this circumstance there are usually laws that require all shareholders be treated equally. We researched rules regarding mandatory tender offers across different countries and only include transactions where there is no forced linkage between prices for the control block and prices on the exchange. For example, in Britain where the city code on takeovers requires that those who purchase a stake greater than or equal to 30 percent of the shares make an equal offer to all remaining shareholders on the same terms as the block sale, we restrict our attention to block sales less than 30 percent. As an illustration of the importance of this legal threshold, more than one quarter of our observations in Britain are between 29 and 30 percent, with a median block size of 25 percent.

Finally, we eliminated all transactions where there are ex ante or ex post indications (in SDC synopsis, news stories, or Datastream) of a tender offer for the remaining stock in the six months following the announcement. This criterion, also used by Barclay and Holderness (1989), is meant to eliminate events where the expectation of a tender offer distorts the value of minority shares.

Table I summarizes our variable definitions and sources. The data appendix provides a more complete description of the construction of our sample. Appendix Table AI lists countries and rules regarding control transactions. Appendix Table AII lists the number of equities available for Datastream in each sample year from each of our countries.

B. Descriptive Statistics of the Raw Control Premium

Table II presents descriptive statistics of the block premia from our sample by country in which the acquired firm is located. After imposing our criteria, we have an unbalanced panel of 393 observations from 39 countries for the time period 1990 to 2000.[5] The sample includes more than 40 observations from active equity markets such as the United Kingdom and the United States. For

[5] We only include countries in our analysis if there were two or more transactions over our sample period. The final sample is based on all of the data available over the 10-year sample period for every country aside from the U.S. For the U.S., there were many more potential observations and we limited ourselves to an initial sample based on the first 20 transactions for each calendar year over our 10-year sample period that met our sample selection criteria.

Private Benefits of Control 547

Table I
Description of Variables

Variable	Description
Block premia as a percentage of the value of equity	The block premia are computed as the difference between the price per share paid for the control block and the price on the Exchange two days after the announcement of the control transaction, divided by the price on the Exchange after the announcement and multiplied by the proportion of cash flow rights represented in the controlling block. Securities Data Corporation, Datastream International, 20-Fs, Company annual reports, Lexis-Nexis, Dow-Jones interactive, various country sources including ISI Emerging markets and country company yearbooks.
The change in security value	The difference between the security value of the buyer (market price at $t + 2$) and of the seller (market price at $t - 30$) normalized by the market price at $t + 2$. We subtract from this amount the percentage difference in the level of the market index over the same time period (between date $t + 2$ and $t - 30$ normalized by the level of the index at date $t + 2$). Datastream International.
Majority block	A dummy variable that takes the value one if the control block includes 50 percent of all shares or 50 percent of all voting shares. Securities Data Corporation, 20-Fs, Company annual reports, Lexis-Nexis, Dow-Jones interactive, various country sources including ISI Emerging markets and country company yearbooks.
Another large shareholder	A dummy variable that takes the value one if there is another shareholder with a stake in excess of 20 percent after the block sale. Securities Data Corporation, Company annual reports, Lexis-Nexis, Dow-Jones interactive, various country sources including ISI Emerging markets and country company yearbooks.
Financial distress	A dummy variable that takes the value one if earnings per share in the target are zero or negative in the year of the block trade or the year preceding the block trade. Datastream International.
Seller identity	Dummy variables to identify seller identity. Includes dummies for individual seller, the company itself (through new share issues), a corporate entity, or unknown. A corporate entity is the most prevalent category and is the excluded category. Securities Data Corporation, Company annual reports, Lexis-Nexis, Dow-Jones interactive, various country sources including ISI Emerging markets and country company yearbooks.
Foreign acquirer	A dummy variable that takes the value one if the acquirer is from a different country than the target. Where acquirer is unknown, assume acquirer is from same country as target. Securities Data Corporation.
Acquirer identity	Dummy variables to identify if the acquirer is a public company, subsidiary, the government, or a private company. A public company is the most prevalent group and is the excluded category. Securities Data Corporation.
Cross listed	Dummy variable that takes the value one if the company's stock is listed in the United States either on an exchange, on Portal under rule 144A, or as an over-the-counter listing. Data provided by Andrew Karolyi based on Citibank Universal Issuance Guide.

Table I—*Continued*

Variable	Description
Industry type	Dummy variables that indicate the acquired companies industrial type (two digit SIC). Manufacturing is the most prevalent group and is the excluded category. Securities Data Corporation, Global Access.

	Agriculture, forestry, & fishing	(01–09)
	Mining	(10–14)
	Construction	(15–17)
	Manufacturing	(20–39)
	Transportation & pub. utilities	(40–49)
	Wholesale trade	(50–51)
	Retail trade	(52–59)
	Finance, insurance, & real estate	(60–67)
	Services	(70–89)

Variable	Description
Tangibility of assets	The median value of the percentage of total assets that are fixed for U.S. firms in the same three digit SIC code as the acquired firm. Securities Data Corporation, Standard and Poor's Research Insight (COMPUSTAT)
Stock market synchronicity	As a measure of valuation uncertainty we use the average R^2 of firm-level regressions of bi-weekly stock returns on local and U.S. market indexes in each country in 1995. Returns include dividends and are trimmed at 25 percent. Higher levels indicate that stocks are more likely to move together. Morck et al. (2000).
Control premia based on voting/ nonvoting shares	"Control benefits based on a sample of 661 dual-class firms in 18 countries using data for 1997. Control benefits are extracted from the total value of the votes in the control block, based on a baseline control contest model in the case of a dual class firm," Nenova (2001a). Nenova (2001a).
Log GDP per capita	Average log GDP per capita 1970 to 1995. World Bank.
Ownership concentration	"The average percentage of common shares owned by the three largest shareholders in the 10 largest nonfinancial, privately owned domestic firms in a given country. A firm is considered privately owned if the state is not a known shareholder in it." La Porta et al. (1998). La Porta et al. (1998), derived from: Moodys International, CIFAR, EXTEL, Worldscope, 20-F's, Price-Waterhouse, and various country sources.
Initial public offerings/ population	"Ratio of the number of initial public offerings of equity in a given country to its population (in millions) for the period 1995:7–1996:6." La Porta et al. (1997). La Porta et al. (1997), derived from: Securities Data Corporation, AsiaMoney, LatinFinance, GT Guide to World Equity Markets, and World Development Report, 1996.
Number of listed firms/ population	"Ratio of the number of domestic firms listed in a given country to its population (in millions) in 1994." La Porta et al. (1997). La Porta et al. (1997) derived from: Emerging Market Factbook and World Development Report, 1996.
External market capitalization/ GNP	"The ratio of the stock market capitalization held by minorities to gross national product for 1994. The stock market capitalization held by minorities is computed as the product of the aggregate stock market capitalization and the average percentage of common shares not owned by the top three shareholders in the ten largest nonfinancial, privately owned domestic firms in a given country. A firm is considered privately owned if the State is not a known shareholder in it." La Porta et al. (1997). La Porta et al. (1997), derived from Moodys International, CIFAR, EXTEL, Worldscope, 20-F's, Price-Waterhouse, and various country sources

Table I—*Continued*

Variable	Description
Takeover laws	A dummy variable that takes the value one if the transaction takes place in the presence of a legal requirement to make a mandatory offer if the shareholding after acquisition exceeds a threshold, yet the transaction lies below the threshold. Data presented in Appendix Table I. ISSA Handbook, 6th and 7th editions, EIU country commerce guides, exchange web sites, country company handbooks.
Accounting standards	"Index created by examining and rating companies' 1990 annual reports on their inclusion or omission of 90 items. These items fall into seven categories (general information, income statements, balance sheets, funds flow statement, accounting standards, stock data, and special items). A minimum of three companies in each country were studied. The companies represent a cross section of various industry groups; industrial companies represented 70 percent, and financial companies represented the remaining 30 percent." La Porta et al. (1998). La Porta et al. (1998) derived from: International accounting and auditing trends, Center for International Financial Analysis and Research.
Antidirector rights	"An index aggregating shareholder rights formed by adding one when (1) the country allows shareholders to mail their proxy vote to the firm, (2) shareholders are not required to deposit their shares prior to the general shareholder's meeting, (3) cumulative voting or proportional representation of minorities in the board of directors is allowed, (4) an oppressed minorities mechanism is in place, (5) the minimum percentage of share capital that entitles a shareholder to call for an extraordinary shareholder's meeting is less than or equal to 10 percent (the sample median), or (6) shareholders have preemptive rights that can be waived only by a shareholders' vote. The index ranges from zero to six." La Porta et al. (1998). La Porta et al. (1998) based on company law or commercial code. Pistor et al. (2000) for Czech Republic and Poland.
Rule of law	"Assessment of the law and order tradition in the country produced by the country risk rating agency International Country Risk (ICR). Average of the months of April and October of the monthly index between 1982 and 1995. Scale from zero to 10, with lower scores for less tradition for law and order (we changed the scale from its original range going from zero to six)." La Porta et al. (1998). La Porta et al. (1998), derived from: International Country Risk guide. Pistor et al. (2000) for Czech Republic and Poland.
Competition laws	Response to survey question, "competition laws prevent unfair competition in your country?" Higher scores suggest agreement that competition laws are effective. World Competitiveness Yearbook, 1996.
Newspaper circulation/ population	Circulation of daily newspapers/population. UNESCO Statistical yearbook 1996, as reported in World Competitiveness Report, for Taiwan based on Editors and Publishers' Association Year Book and AC Nielsen, Hong Kong, as reported in "Asian Top Media—Taiwan" www.business.vu.edu
Violent crime	This is a proxy for moral norms suggested by Coffee (2001). It is the reported number of murders, violent crimes, or armed robberies per 100,000 population. Interpol and country data for 1993 as reported in World Competitiveness Yearbook, 1995.

Table I—*Continued*

Variable	Description
Catholic	This is another proxy for moral norms suggested by Stulz and Williamson (2001). The indicator variable takes the value one if the country's primary religion is Catholic. 2000 CIA World Factbook as reported in Stulz and Williamson (2001).
Labor power	We use as an index of labor power the extent of statutory employee protections based on the average of indicators on regular contracts (procedural inconveniences, notice and severance pay for no-fault-dismissals, difficulty of dismissal) and short-term contract (fixed-term and temporary) as derived in Pagano and Volpin (2000). An alternate index is the weighted average of indicators on regular contracts, short-term contract and collective dismissals as derived by Pagano and Volpin (2000). The index is from Pagano and Volpin (2000) based on data from OECD 1999.
Tax compliance	"Assessment of the level of tax compliance. Scale from 0 to 6 where higher scores indicate higher compliance. Data is for 1995." La Porta et al. (1999). The Global Competitiveness Report 1996 as reported in La Porta et al. (1999).
Cheating on taxes	Response to survey question "cheating on taxes if you have a chance is justified?" Scaled from one to 10 where one is never justified and 10 is always justified. World Values Survey, 1996.
Legal origin	Identifies the legal origin of the company law or commercial code of each country. Categories include English common law, French commercial code, German commercial code, Scandinavian civil law, and former Soviet bloc country. La Porta et al. (1998), derived from Reynolds and Flores (1989).

some countries despite looking at the full population of control transactions available in SDC, we have relatively few observations as a result of the combination of weak coverage by Datastream, few reported prices for control sales, and limited observability of control premia as a result of laws regarding tender offers in case of control sales. The rank ordering of countries by control premia is very similar using mean and median values suggesting that our results are not driven by a few outliers.

The first column of Table III presents the average control premium by country, computed as the coefficient of fixed country effects in a regression where the dependent variable is $\hat{B}$ (calculated as in (4)) normalized by Y_b. Overall, the average control premium is 14 percent if each country has an equal weight and 10 percent if each observation receives equal weight. In 10 of our 39 sample countries, we find that the control premia exceeds 25 percent of equity value. These high private benefit countries include Argentina, Austria, Colombia, Czech Republic, Israel, Italy, Mexico, Turkey, and Venezuela (of these Brazil has the highest estimated value of 65 percent. At the other extreme, we have 14 countries where private benefits are 3 percent of the value of equity or less.) These low private benefit countries include Australia, Canada, Finland, France, Hong Kong, Japan, Netherlands, New Zealand, Norway, Singapore, South Africa, Taiwan, United Kingdom, and United States.

Private Benefits of Control   551

Table II
Block Premium as Percent of Firm Equity

This table presents descriptive statistics by country on the block premia in the 393 control block transactions we study. The block premia are computed as the difference between the price per share paid for the control block and the price on the Exchange two days after the announcement of the control transaction, divided by the price on the Exchange after the announcement and multiplied by the proportion of cash flow rights represented in the controlling block. Securities Data Corporation, Datastream International, 20-Fs, Company annual reports, Lexis-Nexis, Dow-Jones interactive, various country sources including ISI Emerging markets and country company yearbooks.

Country	Mean	Median	Standard Deviation	Minimum	Maximum	Number of Observations	Number of Positive Observations
Argentina	0.27	0.12	0.26	0.05	0.66	5	5
Australia	0.02	0.01	0.04	−0.03	0.11	12	8
Austria	0.38	0.38	0.19	0.25	0.52	2	2
Brazil	0.65	0.49	0.83	0.06	2.99	11	11
Canada	0.01	0.01	0.04	−0.02	0.06	4	2
Chile	0.18	0.15	0.19	−0.08	0.51	7	6
Colombia	0.27	0.15	0.34	0.06	0.87	5	5
Czech Republic	0.58	0.35	0.80	0.01	2.17	6	6
Denmark	0.08	0.04	0.11	−0.01	0.26	5	3
Egypt	0.04	0.04	0.05	0.01	0.07	2	2
Finland	0.02	0.01	0.06	−0.07	0.13	14	9
France	0.02	0.01	0.11	−0.10	0.17	4	2
Germany	0.10	0.11	0.14	−0.24	0.32	17	14
Hong Kong	0.00	0.02	0.05	−0.12	0.05	8	6
Indonesia	0.07	0.07	0.03	0.05	0.09	3	3
Israel	0.27	0.21	0.32	−0.01	0.89	9	8
Italy	0.37	0.16	0.57	−0.09	1.64	8	7
Japan	−0.04	−0.01	0.09	−0.34	0.09	21	5
Malaysia	0.07	0.05	0.10	−0.08	0.39	40	30
Mexico	0.34	0.47	0.35	−0.04	0.77	5	4
Netherlands	0.02	0.03	0.05	−0.07	0.06	5	4
New Zealand	0.03	0.04	0.09	−0.17	0.18	16	12
Norway	0.01	0.01	0.05	−0.05	0.13	12	8
Peru	0.14	0.17	0.11	0.03	0.23	3	3
Philippines	0.13	0.08	0.32	−0.40	0.82	15	11
Poland	0.13	0.12	0.11	0.02	0.28	4	4
Portugal	0.20	0.20	0.14	0.11	0.30	2	2
Singapore	0.03	0.03	0.03	−0.01	0.06	4	3
South Africa	0.02	0.00	0.03	0.00	0.07	4	2
South Korea	0.16	0.17	0.07	0.04	0.22	6	6
Spain	0.04	0.02	0.06	−0.03	0.13	5	4
Sweden	0.07	0.03	0.09	−0.01	0.22	11	10
Switzerland	0.06	0.07	0.04	0.01	0.15	8	8
Taiwan	0.00	0.00	0.01	−0.01	0.00	3	2
Thailand	0.12	0.07	0.19	−0.08	0.64	12	11
Turkey	0.37	0.11	0.58	0.05	1.41	5	5
United Kingdom	0.01	0.00	0.04	−0.06	0.17	41	21
United States	0.01	0.02	0.09	−0.20	0.25	46	27
Venezuela	0.27	0.28	0.21	0.04	0.47	4	4
Average/Number	0.14	0.11	0.18	−0.04	0.48	393	284

These estimates assume the seller has all the bargaining power. If this assumption is not valid, these estimates would be downward biased on average, since the bias is proportional to $-(Y_b - Y_s)$, which on average is negative six percentage points.[6] More importantly, the bias can differ across deals and countries, since both the improvement in security value, $(Y_b - Y_s)$, and the percentage of voting rights contained in the controlling block, α, differ across deals (and thus a fortiori across countries). All the terms of this bias, $\alpha(1 - \lambda)(Y_b - Y_s)$, are observable, except for the seller's bargaining power (λ). Unfortunately, we do not have enough degrees of freedom to estimate reliably a country-specific λ. Therefore, we initially restrict it to be equal across all transactions, and we estimate $(1 - \lambda)$ as a coefficient of the term $\alpha(Y_b - Y_s)$ inserted in our previous regression (column 1 of Table III), where the dependent variable is $\frac{B}{Y_B}$ and the other explanatory variables are the country fixed effects. The estimate of λ so obtained equals 0.655 and is statistically different from zero at the 10 percent level. Not only does this estimate lie in the [0, 1] interval, as predicted by the model, but it is also very reasonable. It suggests that on average the seller captures two-thirds of the gains from trade.

Table III (column 2) presents the estimates of the country fixed effects obtained in this way. A few countries see the estimated private benefits of control increase after this adjustment. For example, the estimate for the United States goes from 1.0 to 2.7 percent. The overall ranking, however, remains substantially unchanged.[7]

Of course, the seller's bargaining power is unlikely to be constant across all deals. The question is how potential differences in bargaining power can affect our estimates. If differences in the bargaining power have large effects on our private benefits estimates, then our estimates should be correlated with proxies for the buyer's bargaining power. A proxy for the buyer's bargaining power is the announcement return experienced by the buyer of the controlling block. In our sample, we have 203 observations where the acquirer is a publicly traded company and the stock price is reported in Datastream for 115 of those. As we show later (in Table IV, panel B), we regress the acquirers' cumulative abnormal returns around the transaction on our estimates of private benefits. We find no significant correlation between the two, thus potential biases do not seem to be of the first order. Nevertheless, to address this problem in the next section, we introduce additional control variables, which will proxy for deal-specific differences in the relative bargaining power of the parties involved.

Our major concern, however, is not variability across deals, but systematic variability across countries, which might bias our cross-country comparison. In particular, if competition for control is stronger in some countries than others, imposing an equal λ will artificially inflate the estimates of private benefits in countries with strong competition and reduce them in others. To exclude this

---

[6] With an average controlling block size of 37 percent, the maximum downward bias, on average, in our sample of 2.2 percent if the seller has no bargaining power and there is no bias if sellers have all the bargaining power.

[7] While λ is constrained to be fixed across countries, the term $\alpha(Y_b - Y_s)$ does differ across deals (and a fortiori across countries). Thus, the adjustment introduced in column 2 could alter the relative ranking across countries.

possibility, we divide countries in quartiles according to our estimates of private benefits and we re-estimate λ, imposing it to be equal only within each quartile. We find that countries with higher levels of private benefits have lower estimated lambdas than countries with lower levels of private benefits. These results suggest that our assumption of equal λ across countries tends, if anything, to dampen the cross-country differences in the level of private benefits.

C. Differences in Deal and Firm Characteristics

Cross-country differences in the level of private benefits could be driven by systematic differences in deal characteristics and firm characteristics, which affect the amount of control transferred, the size of the private benefits, and the relative bargaining power of the parties involved. To increase confidence that our estimates of block premia reflect country differences rather than other characteristics, we generate revised estimates based on a regression of our raw data against firm and deal characteristics.[8]

C.1. Differences in the Extent the Block Carries Control

First of all, we assume that all transactions transfer absolute control. This is probably incorrect. The transfer of a 20 percent block does not carry the same amount of control as the transfer of a 51 percent block. Similarly, the transfer of a 30 percent block when there is another shareholder controlling 20 percent carries less control than the transfer of the same block when the rest of the shares are dispersed. Thus, per given size of private benefits control blocks above 50 percent are likely to fetch a higher price. Similarly, the presence of another large shareholder (a stake in excess of 20 percent) should reduce the premium.[9]

In our sample, 27 percent of the transactions involve sales that exceed 50 percent of the votes, and in 16 percent of the cases the acquirer has to deal with another large shareholder with more than a 20 percent stake.[10] As shown in Table III, ceteris paribus an absolute majority of votes increases the value of a controlling block by 9.5 percent of the total value of equity, significant at the 5 percent level. Contrary to expectations, the presence of another large shareholder has a positive effect on the premium, but this is not statistically significant.

C.2. Differences in the Extent of the Seller's Bargaining Power

In estimating the private benefits of control, we assumed that the seller's bargaining power is constant across deals. As we just discussed, variations in

[8] Summary statistics for the characteristics of the deals that we use later in our empirical analysis are provided in our earlier working paper, Dyck and Zingales (2002a).

[9] In Canada and Australia we used 15 percent since exceeding 20 percent would trigger a mandatory offer for remaining shares.

[10] An alternative approach to identify the likelihood that a stake brings control is to calculate a Shapley value associated with control. Unfortunately, we were not able to collect information on a consistent basis on the ownership status of other shareholders. For example, some countries might report the presence of all shareholders with stakes that exceed 5 percent while other countries might only report holdings that exceed 10 percent or higher.

Table III
Estimated Block Premia by Country

The dependent variable is the block premia as a percent of firm equity. Each regression includes country fixed effects. In addition, in column (2) we introduce the buyer's proportion of the difference in security value between the buyer and seller. In column (3) we introduce several deal characteristics: whether it is a majority block, whether there is another large shareholder, whether the firm is in financial distress, whether the block was created by issuing new shares, whether the buyer is foreign, and if the firms' shares are cross listed in the United States. In column (4) we introduce several industry and seller/buyer characteristics: identity of the buyer (individual, government, subsidiary, dispersed), identity of the seller (individual, government, subsidiary, dispersed), two-SIC code industry dummies, and the proportion of fixed to total assets. Definitions for each of the variables can be found in Table I. All regressions are estimated by OLS. Robust standard errors are in parentheses.

Independent Variables	Dependent Variable: Block Premium			
	(1)	(2)	(3)	(4)
Buyer's proportion of change in security value		−0.345 (0.214)	−0.323 (0.211)	−0.319 (0.209)
Stake greater than 50%			0.095** (0.039)	0.095** (0.039)
Another large shareholder			0.041 (0.043)	0.018 (0.040)
Financial distress in selling firm			−0.054* (0.028)	−0.043 (0.028)
Sold through new share issue			0.041 (0.057)	0.034 (0.059)
Buyer is foreign			0.069** (0.034)	0.065* (0.036)
Cross-listed in the US			−0.062 (0.040)	−0.067* (0.039)
Buyer individual or private				−0.042 (0.026)
Buyer government				0.008 (0.046)
Buyer subsidiary				−0.001 (0.049)
Buyer dispersed or unknown				−0.039 (0.044)
Seller individual				0.021 (0.029)
Seller government				0.008 (0.100)
Seller unknown				0.028 (0.031)
Fixed assets as percent of total				−0.097 (0.062)
Industry—Agriculture, Forestry, Fishing				−0.03 (0.050)
Industry—Mining				−0.071 (0.071)
Industry—Construction				−0.027 (0.042)
Industry—Transportation & utilities				0.066* (0.031)
Industry—Wholesale Trade				0.046 (0.047)
Industry—Retail Trade				−0.057 (0.055)
Industry—Finance, Insurance, Real Est.				0.055 (0.045)
Industry—Services				−0.024 (0.038)

Private Benefits of Control 555

Argentina	0.268**	(0.111)	0.268**	(0.112)	0.158	(0.131)	0.197	(0.123)
Australia	0.020	(0.013)	0.029	(0.018)	-0.001	(0.034)	0.051	(0.052)
Austria	0.383***	(0.099)	0.364***	(0.082)	0.318***	(0.054)	0.309***	(0.050)
Brazil	0.650***	(0.252)	0.653***	(0.249)	0.606***	(0.229)	0.652***	(0.245)
Canada	0.013	(0.017)	0.016*	(0.009)	-0.06	(0.056)	-0.055	(0.075)
Chile	0.183***	(0.069)	0.213***	(0.070)	0.149**	(0.065)	0.165**	(0.067)
Colombia	0.273*	(0.142)	0.274**	(0.129)	0.197	(0.137)	0.242*	(0.132)
Czech Republic	0.578*	(0.312)	0.600*	(0.320)	0.462	(0.297)	0.555*	(0.325)
Denmark	0.077	(0.048)	0.076*	(0.045)	0.039	(0.050)	0.036	(0.070)
Egypt	0.038	(0.024)	0.035**	(0.015)	-0.050	(0.061)	0.025	(0.082)
Finland	0.025	(0.016)	0.028	(0.018)	-0.016	(0.027)	-0.010	(0.036)
France	0.019	(0.052)	0.035	(0.049)	0.040	(0.059)	0.080	(0.077)
Germany	0.095***	(0.034)	0.090***	(0.033)	-0.020	(0.052)	0.016	(0.059)
Hong Kong	0.003	(0.019)	0.026	(0.021)	0.045	(0.033)	0.040	(0.044)
Indonesia	0.072***	(0.017)	0.032	(0.025)	-0.034	(0.040)	0.043	(0.047)
Israel	0.270**	(0.107)	0.284**	(0.113)	0.238**	(0.108)	0.259**	(0.114)
Italy	0.369*	(0.199)	0.578*	(0.201)	0.323*	(0.191)	0.311	(0.192)
Japan	-0.043**	(0.021)	-0.041**	(0.020)	-0.070	(0.044)	-0.038	(0.054)
Malaysia	0.072***	(0.017)	0.072***	(0.014)	0.063***	(0.018)	0.093***	(0.032)
Mexico	0.345**	(0.146)	0.581**	(0.150)	0.296**	(0.143)	0.322**	(0.144)
Netherlands	0.016	(0.020)	-0.031	(0.047)	-0.054	(0.068)	-0.015	(0.060)
New Zealand	0.027	(0.024)	0.044	(0.027)	-0.028	(0.042)	0.026	(0.046)

Table III—*Continued*

Country Fixed Effects	Dependent Variable: Block Premium			
	(1)	(2)	(3)	(4)
Norway	0.015 (0.014)	0.019 (0.019)	0.007 (0.026)	0.052 (0.041)
Peru	0.142*** (0.053)	0.121 (0.075)	0.067 (0.080)	0.060 (0.082)
Phillipines	0.129 (0.083)	0.169** (0.085)	0.115 (0.081)	0.142* (0.079)
Poland	0.133*** (0.052)	0.134*** (0.041)	0.003 (0.081)	0.041 (0.092)
Portugal	0.203*** (0.073)	0.215*** (0.075)	0.159*** (0.052)	0.197*** (0.059)
Singapore	0.030* (0.016)	0.027 (0.019)	0.024 (0.035)	0.042 (0.069)
South Africa	0.017 (0.015)	0.035* (0.019)	-0.045 (0.061)	0.005 (0.072)
South Korea	0.157*** (0.027)	0.146*** (0.036)	0.086 (0.066)	0.088 (0.086)
Spain	0.041 (0.027)	0.049* (0.026)	0.021 (0.042)	0.047 (0.058)
Sweden	0.074*** (0.027)	0.083*** (0.029)	0.033 (0.047)	0.041 (0.057)
Switzerland	0.063*** (0.015)	0.061*** (0.016)	-0.073 (0.056)	-0.067 (0.074)
Taiwan	-0.004 (0.004)	-0.011** (0.005)	-0.047 (0.039)	-0.040 (0.074)
Thailand	0.125** (0.054)	0.142** (0.057)	0.073 (0.080)	0.121 (0.084)
Turkey	0.371 (0.246)	0.362 (0.226)	0.276 (0.232)	0.346 (0.249)
United Kingdom	0.014* (0.007)	0.016* (0.009)	0.000 (0.019)	0.040 (0.033)
United States	0.01 (0.013)	0.027 (0.016)	0.002 (0.031)	0.044 (0.038)
Venezuela	0.270*** (0.094)	0.305*** (0.103)	0.256** (0.105)	0.221** (0.112)
Number of observations	393	393	393	393
R-squared	0.389	0.399	0.431	0.459

*significant at 10% level; **significant at 5% level; ***significant at 1% level.

the seller's bargaining power can affect our estimates of the private benefits of control: Per given size of private benefits of control, the lower the seller's bargaining power, the lower our estimates. We try to control for these differences with three proxies.

First, if the company is in financial distress, the seller is more likely to be forced to sell. Hence, her bargaining power is smaller. As a proxy for financial distress, we create a dummy variable that takes value one if earnings per share are zero or negative in the year of the block trade or the year preceding the block trade.[11] In our sample, 27 percent of the firms are in financial distress in the year of the block trade and 23 percent in the year preceding the block trade. As expected, firms in financial distress exhibit a control premium that is 5.4 percentage points lower. This effect is statistically significant at the 10 percent level.

Similarly, that the acquisition of a controlling block takes the form of an equity infusion probably indicates that a company needs to raise equity, a sign of a weak bargaining position. We insert a dummy if the block was formed by newly issued equity (16 percent). This method is particularly diffused in Japan where in a majority of cases control is transferred by a financially distressed company via a private placement of newly issued equity. This clustering underscores the importance of controlling for industry firms' and deals' characteristics, to avoid attributing to the Japan institutional framework a feature due to the particular economic phase Japan has been going through during our sample period. Contrary to expectations, the fact a block was created through a new equity offering has a positive effect on the premium, but this is not statistically significant.

Finally, companies that can be acquired by foreigners are likely to face more competition. We attempt to capture this possibility by introducing a dummy variable equal to one if the acquirer is foreign. As a result of the increased competition, the bargaining power of the seller in these transactions is likely to be bigger. We find that foreign buyers pay a premium of 6.9 percent that is statistically significant at the 5 percent level.

C.3. Cross Listing in the United States

Coffee (1999), Reese and Weisbach (2001), and Doidge, Karolyi, and Stulz (2001) argue that foreign companies list in the United States to submit themselves to tougher governance rules and precommit to extract less private benefits of control. Since we want to measure the country-specific value of private benefits, we want to control for companies that might have lower than average private benefits due to their borrowing of foreign institutions. To this purpose we insert a dummy variable equal to one for any company that is cross listed in the United States as well as in its home market.[12] As expected, cross-listed companies enjoy lower private benefits, although given the paucity of cross

---

[11] While other measures of cash flow are preferable, earnings per share is one of the few data items consistently reported in Datastream for the companies in our database.

[12] We obtained the list of cross listing from Doidge, Karolyi, and Stulz (2001). We thank Andrew Karolyi for kindly providing us with the data.

listed companies in our sample (23), the statistical significance of this effect is just below conventional levels (p-value = 12 percent).

C.4. Estimates of Private Benefits Controlling for Differences in Deal and Firm Characteristics

After inserting all these deals' and firms' characteristics into our basic regression, we re-estimate the country fixed effects. The results are reported at the bottom of column 3 in Table III. Since many of the control variables included capture part of the value of control, the country fixed effects cannot any longer be interpreted as the estimates of the average value of private benefits in that country, but only as relative rankings. Including these controls dramatically lowers the ranking for countries characterized by higher than average incidence of foreign acquirers and sales of majority stakes like Germany, Switzerland, Egypt, and Poland.

On the one hand, these estimates represent an improvement over our raw data, for they keep constant deal characteristics. On the other hand, they suffer from an econometric problem. To estimate the impact of these deal and firm characteristics, we had to assume that this impact is constant across countries. In some cases this assumption might be untenable. The difference between acquiring a 51 percent stake rather than a 30 percent one might be huge in a country where private benefits of control are large, but it might be small or even irrelevant in a country where the private benefits of control are very tiny.[13] The regression, however, imposes the same effect on all the countries, underestimating differences across countries.

In the rest of the paper, where we explore the effects and causes of these cross-country differences, we focus on this refined measure that controls for deal (and other) characteristics. But recognizing that this procedure may bias the results because deal characteristics may not be constant across countries, we also test results without controls.

D. Differences in Industry and Buyer/Seller Characteristics

Cross-country differences could also arise because of other differences in industry and deal characteristics. Private benefits might differ across industry. The media industry, for instance, is often mentioned (Demsetz and Lehn (1985)) as an industry where private benefits are larger. Similarly, individuals might value opportunities to consume prerequisites more highly than corporate blockholders (see e.g., Barclay and Holderness (1989)). We want to make sure our cross-country comparison is not affected by any systematic difference in the industry characteristics of the deals or the nature of the seller and the buyer.

---

[13] Since we have enough observations for the U.S. (46), we can assess the realism of our assumption by estimating the same specification restricted to U.S. data. While the other coefficients are very similar to the ones reported in Table IV, the coefficient of the majority block dummy is small and insignificant. "Imposing" to the U.S. the same majority dummy effect as other countries, thus, will distort its average level of private benefits upward.

For this reason, we re-estimate the country averages, controlling for differences in industry characteristics and identity of the controlling party.

To capture industry differences, we introduce an industry dummy based on the two-digit SIC code of the acquired firm. About three quarters of our transactions are accounted for by manufacturing (39 percent); finance, insurance, and real estate (24 percent); and services (10 percent). In a crude way these controls capture differences in private benefits linked to product market competition. Second, we construct a measure of tangibility of assets (percentage of total assets that are fixed) based on the three-digit SIC code the acquired firm belongs to. The argument for this control is that insiders will have more difficulty diverting resources if assets are tied down and easily observable, as is the case with tangible assets. To avoid potential endogeneity problems, we use U.S. averages (see Rajan and Zingales (1998)).[14]

Table III column 4 shows that firms with more tangible assets have lower private benefits, and firms in wholesale trade, finance (financial, insurance, and real estate sector), and transportation and utilities have a higher level of private benefits than firms in manufacturing, although these differences are not statistically significant. We also collected information on the identity of the acquirer and the seller. To identify characteristics of the seller, we focus exclusively on the news stories, identifying whether the seller is an individual, the company itself (through new share issues), a corporate entity, or unknown. Here we find the most common seller to be a corporation, followed next by individuals (18 percent), new share issues (16 percent), unidentified (8 percent) and the government (3 percent). We use SDC data to identify whether the acquirer is a public company, subsidiary, the government, or a private company. The typical transaction in our sample involves a public acquirer (41 percent), although private acquirers are also very common (41 percent). We provide a further classification using news stories and the SDC synopsis field. We identify 13 percent of our transactions involving an individual acquirer, using as our criteria whether the stories mention the name of an individual or if the private company involved is identified with a particular individual. We also identify 4 percent of transactions involving a financial intermediary who purchases the shares and then resells the shares to institutional investors. We interpret these acquisitions as the dispersal of the controlling stake. None of these buyer or seller characteristics turns out to be significant.

At the bottom of column 4 of Table III, we report the estimates of the country average level of private benefits after we control for the above differences in level of private benefits across industries. The relative ranking, however, does not seem to be affected very much by these industry controls.

Finally, the level of private benefits extracted might be endogenous to the size of the controlling block. Large shareholders who retain a larger block of

---

[14] We derive U.S. measures in a two-step procedure. First, we computed the average ratio of fixed assets (property plant and equipment) to total assets for all companies that in each three-digit SIC-code for the period 1990 to 1999. Then we took the median value across all companies. We then impute this value for all of the companies in our sample.

equity have less of an incentive to dilute minority shareholders, because they internalize more the inefficiency they generate (see Burkart, Gromb and Panunzi (1998)). For this reason, in an unreported regression, we also inserted the size of the controlling block α. Since it has no effect on the value of control, we dropped it.

E. Alternative Interpretations

Thus far, we have interpreted block premia as indicative of private benefits. Yet, there are alternative interpretations that we need to consider. The most important alternative interpretation, already considered and rejected by Barclay and Holderness (1989) in their U.S. sample, is that control premia arise from a systematic overpayment, possibly due to a winner's curse problem.

As in Barclay and Holderness (1989), we check for this possibility by looking at the announcement effect on the stock price of the acquiring company. If these premia reflect overpayments, acquiring firms should experience negative returns at the announcement of the transaction. In our sample, we have 203 observations where the acquirer is a publicly traded company and the stock price is reported in Datastream for 115 of those. Table IV presents the results of our analysis. Inconsistent with the overpayment hypothesis, the mean value of the announcement effect is slightly positive (0.5 percent) and not statistically different from zero.

Another implication of the overpayment hypothesis is that the buyer's announcement return should be negatively related to the size of the control premium. In Table IV, panel B, we regress the acquirers' cumulative abnormal returns around the transaction on the raw control premium. We focus on a 16-day event window ($t-8$ to $t+7$) to allow for information about the transaction to be leaked in advance or to be communicated slowly to the market although results are not significantly affected by the choice of window. The coefficient is indeed negative, but is neither economically nor statistically significant (coefficient of −0.018, p-value of 0.64).

The results above reject the hypothesis that on average the control premium is due to overpayment. It is still possible, thus, that this might be true in some countries. In particular, we are concerned that in less developed countries, where there is more uncertainty about the value of a company, the winner's curse is more severe leading to a higher apparent premium and distorting our international comparisons. While such behavior is inconsistent with a rational bidding process (Milgrom and Weber (1982)), we still want to ensure it is not present in the data.[15] As a measure of the degree of company-specific information available we use the synchronicity measure developed by Morck, Yeung, and Yu (2000). This is a measure of how much stock prices move together. The more they move together, the less company-specific information is revealed. If there is more overpayment in less developed markets, we should observe that the control premium is more negatively correlated with the acquirer's return in

---

[15] A rational bidder knows that if he bids his valuation he will overpay, the more so the more uncertainty there is about the fundamental value of the asset. Thus, the more uncertainty there is, the more he will shade his bid.

Table IV

Does the Control Premium Come from Overpayment?

Panel A reports the summary statistics of the cumulative abnormal returns (CAR) of the stock price of the acquiring company around the date the acquisition of the controlling block is announced. We use a window from eight days prior to the announcement to seven days after the announcement. We have 203 transactions involving publicly traded acquirers, of which 115 have stock prices reported in Datastream. Panel B reports the OLS estimates of two regressions, where the dependent variable is the acquirer' CAR from $t - 8$ and $t + 7$ and the independent variables are: (1) the raw block premia (Table III column 1); (2) the raw block premia (Table III column 1) interacted with a measure of how much stock prices move together at the country level (see Morck et al. (2000)). Definitions for each of the variables can be found in Table I. Robust standard errors are in parentheses.

Panel A: Cumulative Abnormal Returns of the Acquirer	
	from $t - 8$ to $t + 7$
Mean	0.005
Median	0.000
Maximum	0.333
Minimum	−0.408
Standard deviation	0.110
Number of observations	115

Panel B: Systematic Differences in Cumulative Abnormal Returns		
	Dependent Variable: Cumulative Abnormal Return of Acquirer (from $t - 8$ to $t + 7$)	
Independent Variables	(1)	(2)
Block premia	0.018 (0.040)	0.106 (0.156)
Block premia × synchronicity in target nation		0.419 (0.835)
Constant	0.007 (0.011)	0.007 (0.012)
Number of observations	115	105
R squared	0.001	0.008

a country with a high level of synchronicity. In fact, the interaction coefficient is positive and not statistically significant.

A second alternative interpretation that could potentially explain a larger premia in underdeveloped markets is that the buyer has superior information and there is a delay in incorporating new information. On average, delays in adjusting will spuriously inflate our estimates of private benefits. To test for this possibility we re-estimated the private benefits using the market price 30 days after the announcement rather than two days after. The results (not reported) are virtually identical. If anything, the average premium in developing countries, like Brazil, goes up rather than down. We also examined the cumulative abnormal returns to shareholders in target firms from two days to 30 days after the announcement and tested whether the initial level of private benefits was related to the subsequent cumulative abnormal returns. We found no such effect with an insignificant relationship between control premia and postannouncement returns (coefficient = 0.009, p-value = 0.80).

Another alternative interpretation focuses on liquidity differences between developed and less developed markets. Differences in liquidity cannot explain our findings either. While a lack of liquidity reduces the willingness to pay for shares on the exchange and this effect is more pervasive in less developed markets, the lack of liquidity also impacts the price that is paid for large blocks. Large noncontrolling blocks generally sell at a discount to the exchange price (Holthausen, Leftwich, and Mayers (1990)) and the more so the more illiquid is the market for the underlying stock. Thus, if the control value were zero there would be a bigger discount in less liquid markets for large blocks. Therefore liquidity differences suggest that, if anything, more underdeveloped countries should have smaller block premia, not larger ones.

We are also concerned about a possible distortion due to selective nondisclosure. In fact, one of the criteria we had to impose to obtain our estimates was the observability of the price paid for the controlling block. A worrisome possibility is that in countries with better protection of investors, controlling parties are more fearful to disclose large premia. In such a case, we would estimate lower private benefits in the United States, not because they are indeed lower, but because large premia are less likely to be disclosed.

To check for this possibility, we compute the percentage of deals we have to drop because the terms are not disclosed. On average, 33 percent of the deals do not disclose the terms, going from 0 percent in Taiwan and other countries to 70 percent in Austria and 82 percent in the Czech Republic. Contrary to the selective nondisclosure argument, we find that countries with higher premium tend to have a higher percentage of deals that are not disclosed (correlation 0.2, not statistically significant). Similarly, if we use as a proxy of shareholders' protection the antidirector rights index constructed by La Porta et al. (1997), we find (not surprisingly) that in countries that protect shareholders a greater percentage of deals are disclosed. In sum, if selective nondisclosure biases our results it biases them in the direction of attenuating the cross-country differences rather than amplifying them.

Finally, if the acquirers of the controlling block, for instance, already owned a large stake in the company beforehand, they might be willing to pay a premium only because they internalize a fraction of the increase in the security value via their toeholds (Grossman and Hart (1980) and Shleifer and Vishny (1986)). Toeholds, however, are unusual in our sample. The average shareholding prior to purchasing the control stake is just 1 percent, in 76 percent of the cases the acquirer has no prior shareholding, and in 86 percent of the cases the prior shareholding is less than 1 percent. Nevertheless, to examine the impact of a toehold we re-estimate the regressions in Table III (not reported) introducing the initial toehold as an additional regressor. The initial toehold has a negative and statistical insignificant impact (p-value of 0.20 to 0.32) on our private benefits' estimates. All of our results are unaffected by the inclusion of this additional regressor.

F. Are We Really Estimating Private Benefits?

Therefore, we can reject all these alternative interpretations, but what evidence do we have that our estimates indeed capture private benefits of control?

At the anecdotal level, we have papers documenting the pervasiveness of self-dealing transactions in countries like Italy (Zingales (1994)) and the Czech Republic (Glaeser, Johnson, and Shleifer (2001)). It is reassuring, thus, that our estimated private benefits for these two countries are very high (respectively, 37 percent and 58 percent). It is particularly interesting to stress the difference between Poland and the Czech Republic. Both are former socialist countries, with a similar level of GDP per capita. Nevertheless, our estimates are very different (11 percent for Poland and 58 percent for the Czech Republic).

At a more systematic level, if our measures reflect the different ability to extract private benefits in different countries, they should be affected in predictable ways by country-specific institutions that restrict the ability to extract private benefits. We will explore these implications in Section IV. One limitation with this approach, however, is that it is difficult to separate specific institutions from a broad institutional context. More subtle tests of whether these estimates really reflect the ability to extract private benefits are whether our estimated private benefits depend not only upon the institutional variables of the country of the company whose control has been acquired, but also on institutions of the country of the acquiring company (when this is different) and on institutions of the country where a company's shares are listed (when a company cross lists in the United States).

An acquirer coming from a country with less investor protection is better able to siphon out corporate resources from a subsidiary than an acquirer coming from a country with very rigid rules. This should result in a higher willingness to pay and, in a nonperfectly competitive market, at a higher price. Thus, we should observe higher estimated private benefits when the foreign acquirer comes from a country with poor protection of investors.

For this reason, in Table V column 1, we re-estimate our basic specification (see Table III) inserting as an additional explanatory variable the interaction between the foreign acquirer's dummy (equal to one if the acquirer comes from a country different from the target) and a measure of the difference in legal protection between the two countries. This measure is the difference between the La Porta et al. (1998) measure of antidirector rights for the country of the acquiring company and the one for the country of the acquired company. As Table V shows, companies coming from more investor friendly countries pay, on average, a control premia that is 2.7 percent less, and this effect is statistically significant. In the bottom of Table V, we present country fixed effects with this control.

The finding is interesting per se within the context of the debate on corporate governance convergence. Coffee (1999) predicts that companies from countries with better protection of investors will end up buying companies from countries with weaker protection. Our result suggests that in the presence of controlling blocks this might not be the case. Companies from countries with better investor protection are more limited in their ability to extract private benefits and thus ceteris paribus are able to bid less for the controlling block. This engenders the risk that controlling blocks may end up in the hands of companies from the countries with the worst rules, not the best ones.

Table V

Does Legal Protection in the Investor's Country of Origin Affect the Acquirer's Willingness to Pay for Control?

The dependent variable is the block premia as a percent of firm equity. The explanatory variables include all of the variables introduced in Table II column (4). In column 1, we include the interaction between the foreign acquirer's dummy (equal to one if the acquirer comes from a country different from the target) and a measure of the difference in legal protection between the two countries. This measure is the difference between the La Porta et al. (1998) measure of antidirector rights for the country of the acquiring company and the one for the country of the acquired company. In column 2, we include the interaction between the dummy for cross listing in the U.S. and a measure of the difference in investor protection between the U.S. and the country where the target firm is located. Robust standard errors are in parentheses.

Independent Variables	Dependent Variable: Block Premium			
	(1)		(2)	
Foreign acquirer dummy	0.063*	(0.035)	0.060*	(0.036)
Cross listed in the US	−0.060	(0.039)	0.113	(0.083)
Interaction of relative strength of antidirector rights (home—target nation) and foreign acquirer	−0.027**	(0.011)	−0.028**	(0.011)
Interaction of relative strength of antidirector rights (home—target nation) and cross listed in the US			−0.070**	(0.034)
Variables Controlled for:				
Buyer's proportion of change in security value	y		y	
Ownership variables	y		y	
Financial distress	y		y	
Buyer identity	y		y	
Seller identity	y		y	
Industry group	y		y	
Tangibility of assets	y		y	
Country fixed effects				
Argentina	0.183	(0.114)	0.183	(0.113)
Australia	0.054	(0.051)	0.052	(0.051)
Austria	0.309***	(0.048)	0.319***	(0.051)
Brazil	0.655***	(0.245)	0.653***	(0.245)
Canada	−0.059	(0.083)	−0.052	(0.083)
Chile	0.160**	(0.065)	0.16**	(0.065)
Colombia	0.282**	(0.131)	0.325**	(0.128)
Czech Republic	0.563*	(0.328)	0.563*	(0.330)
Denmark	0.028	(0.065)	0.027	(0.065)
Egypt	0.077	(0.085)	0.112	(0.093)
Finland	−0.002	(0.037)	0.002	(0.037)
France	0.076	(0.077)	0.084	(0.078)
Germany	0.038	(0.058)	0.041	(0.058)
Hong Kong	0.039	(0.043)	0.008	(0.048)
Indonesia	0.042	(0.046)	0.043	(0.045)
Israel	0.254**	(0.116)	0.252**	(0.116)
Italy	0.323*	(0.193)	0.349*	(0.199)
Japan	−0.032	(0.052)	−0.039	(0.051)
Malaysia	0.090***	(0.033)	0.089***	(0.033)

Private Benefits of Control 565

Table V—*Continued*

Independent Variables	Dependent Variable: Block Premium			
	(1)		(2)	
Mexico	0.348***	(0.129)	0.396***	(0.133)
Netherlands	−0.025	(0.062)	−0.015	(0.062)
New Zeland	0.027	(0.046)	0.028	(0.045)
Norway	0.06	(0.042)	0.061	(0.043)
Peru	0.076	(0.075)	0.08	(0.075)
Phillipines	0.147*	(0.079)	0.148*	(0.080)
Poland	0.045	(0.092)	0.039	(0.092)
Portugal	0.204***	(0.060)	0.207***	(0.059)
Singapore	0.046	(0.064)	0.038	(0.062)
South Africa	−0.014	(0.075)	−0.014	(0.074)
South Korea	0.128	(0.080)	0.137*	(0.081)
Spain	0.058	(0.053)	0.058	(0.052)
Sweden	0.044	(0.057)	0.047	(0.056)
Switzerland	−0.054	(0.073)	−0.051	(0.073)
Taiwan	−0.038	(0.074)	−0.038	(0.073)
Thailand	0.111	(0.080)	0.107	(0.080)
Turkey	0.364	(0.246)	0.363	(0.246)
United Kingdom	0.029	(0.034)	0.02	(0.033)
United States	0.037	(0.038)	0.035	(0.038)
Venezuela	0.234**	(0.107)	0.268**	(0.119)
Number of observations	393		393	
R-squared	0.466		0.470	

*significant at 10% level; **significant at 5% level; ***significant at 1% level.

This finding that the owners' identity (as reflected in the home country of the acquirer) is associated with the extent of private benefits also provides one rationale for the approach in many privatizations of not simply selling to the highest bidder and for the consistent finding in central and eastern Europe (Djankov and Murrell (2000)) of superior returns for firms sold to foreigners (most from countries with higher levels of antidirector rights than in the transition countries) after controlling for possible selection issues.

Cross-listed companies provide another test of whether these estimates reflect the ability to extract private benefits. A subtler prediction of the argument that cross-listing in the United States. acts as a precommitment is that the effect of this cross listing should be a function of the difference between the corporate governance rules in the United States and the rules facing the company in its home market.[16] To test this hypothesis, we measure the superiority in governance as the difference between antidirector rights in the United States and antidirector rights in the target country. In Table V specification 2,

[16] This is the prediction that Doidge (2002) tests using companies with differential voting stock. He finds that the voting premium of companies cross listed in the United States is significantly lower. This is consistent with our findings and an additional confirmation that different methods lead to the same answer: private benefits exist and are important.

we again re-estimate our basic specification (see Table III) and include an inter-action term that is the product of the cross-listing dummy and the measure of the superiority of governance rules. We find a statistically significant negative effect of the superiority of governance rules on the control premia. This means that the reduction in private benefits with cross listing is greater for firms from countries that have weaker investor protections. These results provide direct support for the contention of Coffee (1999), Reese and Weisbach (2001), and Doidge et al. (2001) of a link between cross listing and private benefits.

F.1. Comparing Control Premia Measures

Another check that our estimates measure the value of control comes from comparing them with estimates of the value of control obtained using different methods. Nenova (2001a) provided the largest set of alternative estimates. By using the prices of shares with different voting rights, she estimates the value of control across 18 countries. Table VI (panel A) reports both her numbers and our numbers. The first two columns report the raw measure of private benefits (both Nenova's and ours) and the second two the adjusted measures, after controlling for extraneous factors, which might bias the estimates.

In spite of the different method used, there is a remarkable similarity in findings. Our estimates for countries like Mexico and Germany are identical, and the overall correlation between our measures is 0.59 for the raw mea-sure and 0.62 for the refined measure (statistically different from zero at the 2 percent level).[17] There are, however, notable exceptions. Nenova finds that both Australia and Brazil have a ratio of value of control to value of equity equal to 0.23, while we find only 0.02 for Australia and 0.65 for Brazil. What can explain these differences?

As we discussed, both sets of measures can have pluses and minuses. One possible sample selection story that could account for these differences goes as follows. Companies are more likely to issue dual class shares when private benefits of control are large (Grossman and Hart (1988) and Zingales (1995b)). Hence, a measure of private benefits of control based on the voting premium of companies that issued dual-class shares tends to overestimate the value of con-trol. Most importantly, this upward bias is not homogeneous across countries, but it is more severe the fewer the percentage of dual class companies in the population of traded companies in a country. And this percentage varies widely across countries.

The final column in Table VI reports the percentage of dual-class firms with prices available by Datastream as a percentage of the total population of Data-stream firms in the country in that year. In countries that allow dual-class shares, on average only 14 percent of the firms have two classes of shares traded. There is a wide cross-sectional variation: Brazil has 59 percent of such firms, while Australia and the United Kingdom have only 1 percent.

---

[17] If we exclude Brazil, as we should for reasons to be discussed in Section III.G., the correlation increases to 0.69 using the raw data and 0.86 using the refined data.

Table VI
Comparing Control Premia Measures

Panel A reports Nenova's (2001a) estimates of the value of control based on the price difference between classes of shares with differential voting rights and ours, based on control block transactions. The first column reports Nenova's raw voting premium, defined as total vote value (value of a vote times number of votes) as a share of firm's market value. The second column reproduces our raw block premium (Table III column (1)). The third column reports Nenova's fixed effect estimates of the value of control, where she controls for differences in the dividend rights between the two classes of stock, differences in liquidity, and the presence of a conversion option (Nenova, Table VI, Col. 4). The fourth column reports our fixed effect estimates of the value of control (Table V). The fifth column reports the percentage of firms in Datastream sample that have multiple share classes with available price data, where the number of firms with multiple share classes is taken from Nenova and the number of firms with equity prices in Datastream for 1997 is reported in Appendix Table AII. Panel B reports OLS regressions of the difference between Nenova's control premia and ours. In column 1 there is the difference between the raw estimates, in column 2 a difference between the fixed effect estimates. The explanatory variable is the percentage of firms that have dual-class shares and price data available in each country (column 5 of Panel A). Robust standard errors are in parentheses.

Panel A: Data Comparisons

| | Raw Data | | Estimated Country Fixed Effects | | |
Country	Premia Using Voting/Nonvoting Shares (Nenova, Table V (2000))	Block Premia (Table III, Col 1)	Premia Using Voting/Nonvoting Shares (Nenova, Table V, Col. 4 (2000))	Block Premia (Table V, Col 2)	Percentage of Equities with Dual-Class Shares and Available Price Data
Australia	0.232	0.020	0.185	0.052	0.01
Brazil	0.232	0.650	0.180	0.653	0.59
Canada	0.028	0.013	0.035	−0.052	0.04
Switzerland	0.054	0.063	0.054	−0.051	0.19
Chile	0.231	0.183	0.231	0.16	0.07
Germany	0.095	0.095	0.148	0.041	0.14
Denmark	0.008	0.077	0.009	0.027	0.20
Finland	−0.050	0.025	0.053	0.002	0.24
France	0.281	0.019	0.282	0.084	0.02
United Kingdom	0.096	0.014	0.090	0.02	0.02

Table VI—Continued

Panel A: Data Comparisons

Country	Raw Data		Estimated Country Fixed Effects		Percentage of Equities with Dual-Class Shares and Available Price Data
	Premia Using Voting/Nonvoting Shares (Nenova, Table V (2000))	Block Premia (Table III, Col 1)	Premia Using Voting/Nonvoting Shares (Nenova, Table V, Col. 4 (2000))	Block Premia (Table V, Col 2)	
Hong Kong	−0.029	0.003	−0.029	0.008	0.01
Italy	0.294	0.369	0.345	0.349	0.31
South Korea	0.289	0.157	0.338	0.137	0.11
Mexico	0.364	0.345	0.460	0.396	0.06
Norway	0.058	0.015	0.058	0.061	0.11
Sweden	0.010	0.074	0.010	0.047	0.19
United States	0.020	0.010	0.016	0.035	0.08
South Africa	0.067	0.017	0.063	−0.014	0.07

Panel B: Can Differences between Benefits-Estimates Be Explained by Potential Selection Bias in Voting Rights Approach?

	Dependent Variable			
	Nenova Measure − Our Measure		Refined Nenova Measure − Our Refined Measure	
Percentage of dual-class firms in country	−0.873***	(0.109)	−0.816***	(0.218)
Constant	0.127***	(0.029)	0.144***	(0.032)
Number of observations	18		18	
Adjusted R-squared	0.76		0.63	

*** significant at 1% level.

We test the possible effects of the sample selection described above by regressing the difference between Nenova's estimates and our estimates against the percentage of companies with dual class shares. If there exists a bias, we expect Nenova's estimates to exceed ours in countries with few dual-class stocks like Australia and the United Kingdom (i.e., a negative coefficient in the regression). This is indeed what we find. In countries where dual class shares are more rare Nenova's number significantly exceeds ours. The effect is economically very important. A one standard deviation increase in the percentage of dual class shares leads Nenova's estimates to exceed ours by 22 percentage points.[18] This variable alone explains 76 percent of the difference in raw estimates and 63 percent of the difference in refined estimates.

Overall, these results give confidence that the Barclay and Holderness method to estimate private benefits indeed measures private benefits (and not overpayment) and it does so introducing smaller biases than the alternative method. That the two sets of estimates differ in the way predicted by theory is also a strong indication these estimates are indeed measuring the value of private benefits of control.

F.2. An Analysis of Outliers

Another way to verify that we are indeed measuring private benefits of control is an in-depth analysis of the outliers. In Brazil, we estimate private benefits to be 65 percent of the value of equity. Could private benefits really be this large, or is this finding the result of some problem in the way we infer private benefits? Nenova (2001b), as part of a study of the impact of legal reform on private benefits in Brazil, independently collected information on control sales in Brazil between 1995 and 2000, identifying eight transactions that meet our initial sample selection criteria, including six transactions not in our database.[10] In the sample of eight transactions (Nenova (2001b), Table III) she reports an average value of private benefits of 42 percent, not too dissimilar from our estimate. In addition, we asked a Brazilian investment bank to give us all the privatization data where the Government sold a controlling block of a firm already listed.[20] Their search produced 23 privatization transactions with the requisite data, including 21 transactions that were not

[18] Using differential voting shares to estimate the value of control can induce also another bias. When ownership is highly concentrated, the price of voting shares tends to underestimate the value of votes, because control is securely held in the hands of the largest shareholder. There is some weak evidence this might be the case if we use Nenova's (2001a) raw estimates. Nenova, however, is aware of this problem and in her regressions she controls for ownership concentration. Consistently, her refined measure seems completely unaffected by this bias.

[19] Her approach, albeit very similar, is not strictly comparable with our own, as she uses the price on the date of sale and compares the sale price with the price of voting shares on the exchange.

[20] This sample only includes transaction where sale price is cash. That is, we excluded privatizations where sale price could include so-called "privatization currencies" that included government debt that was trading at a discount.

included in our original data set.[21] The average control premia in this sample is 129 percent.

In sum, independent estimates lead to a very similar conclusion: Private benefits of control in Brazil are extremely high.

F.3. Within-country Variation in Private Benefits

Another check to verify whether our method captures private benefits is to see whether our estimates change when external conditions, which affect the ability to extract private benefits, change. While the fact that we have relatively few transactions from many countries limits our ability to systematically explore time series variation, at least for three events, we have this possibility.

The first event we explore is the passage in Italy of a corporate governance reform in 1998, also known as the Draghi reform. Among other things, this reform made it easier for minority shareholders to sue management appointed by the controlling shareholder. Such reform should limit the ability to extract private benefits. When we segment our data into those observations before and after July 1998, we find that before the reform the average value of private benefits is 47 percent, while after the reform it is only 6 percent.[22]

The second event we explore focuses on Brazil in the 1990s where, as Nenova (2001b) reports, there were two important changes in the legal environment. The first change occurred on May 5, 1997 when Law 9457 was adopted. This law, designed to enhance government revenues from selling State-owned controlling blocks, eliminated several protections of minority investors: the right to be bought out at book value in case of major transactions, such as mergers and spinoffs, the requirement for acquirers to make a mandatory offer to other holders of voting shares at the same price as the control block, etc. The elimination of these protections makes control more valuable. The second change was the passage of Instruction 299 by the Brazilian securities and exchange commission (CVM), reinstating these rights and adding new disclosure requirements.

These legal changes suggest that private benefits will differ depending on which legal regime is in effect, with private benefits expected to be greatest in the period when Law 9457 was in effect, and lower both before and after. This is in fact what we find in our sample of transactions: the premia are highest during the period of law 9457 at 119 percent, with lower levels in the pre-9457 period at 53 percent, and in the postinstruction 299 period of 37 percent. Similar findings are found using our methods in the Nenova sample (27 percent for the pre-9457 period to 61 percent in the 9457 period to 37 percent in the postinstruction 299 period). A similar trend is revealed in our privatization

---

[21] They identified 12 transactions where the stake sold was 19.26 percent, which we excluded because this level was below our selection criteria, but in Brazil accounted for 50.1 percent of the voting shares in the company. In addition, they were able to identify stock market prices for a number of firms that we were not able to collect using Datastream or were not identified by SDC.

[22] The p-value for the equality of the two means is only 21 percent, but this is not surprising given we have only six observations before and two afterward.

sample where we just have data for the first two periods (with values of 109 percent in the pre-9457 period increasing to 131 percent in the 9457 period).

The third event we explore focuses on changes in the economic environment rather than changes in the legal regime to protect investors. It has been suggested that stealing will increase when the expected return on investment declines and that the Asian crisis presents such an event (Johnson et al. (2000)). We test for this, examining whether the levels of private benefits are different for emerging markets in Asia during the Asian crisis, where following Johnson et al. we define the crisis to be 1997 and 1998.[23] Based on a regression of private benefits with country fixed effects we find that the Asian crisis period is indeed associated with higher private benefits (coefficient of 0.068), although this is not significant at conventional significance levels (p-value $= 0.162$).

In sum, in all three instances, our estimates move as theory predicts private benefits should move. Having established some degree of confidence in our estimates, we now move to use them in international comparisons.

III. Effects of Private Benefits on Financial Development

A. *Theoretical Predictions*

We have shown that the magnitude of private benefits of control varies greatly across countries. We have not shown, however, that larger private benefits are necessarily more inefficient. Can we derive any implication on the effects of larger private benefits of control on the development of financial markets that is independent of their characterization as efficient or inefficient?

The answer is yes. In countries where a controlling party can appropriate a larger share of the value of a company, entrepreneurs will be more reluctant to take their companies public. If they sell a minority position, outside investors will be willing to pay less for it than what it is currently worth to the entrepreneur, because they factor in the possibility a new acquirer will dilute the value of the company in the future. As a result, entrepreneurs are reluctant to sell (Zingales (1995b)). At the same time, when control value is high they do not want to sell a majority of votes in the market because they will not receive an adequate compensation for it. Atomistic shareholders will pay for the voting rights they expect to receive in a future tender offer. If, as it is likely to be the case, the market for corporate control is not perfectly competitive, atomistic shareholders will receive less in a tender offer than what a controlling shareholder would have obtained in a private negotiation (Zingales (1995b)). Hence, three implications follow:

(1) Since fewer companies will list in countries with high private benefits of control, the importance of the equity market relative to GDP should be smaller;

---

[23] Specifically, countries included in this test include Hong Kong, Indonesia, Korea, Malaysia, Philippines, Singapore, Taiwan, and Thailand.

(2) Since incumbents are more likely to retain control after they take their company public in countries with high private benefits of control, the percentage of companies widely held should be smaller;

(3) Since it is more profitable to sell control in a private negotiation in countries with high private benefits of control, a revenue maximizing government should prefer to sell control in private transactions rather than in public offerings.

All these predictions are independent of the direct welfare implications of private benefits of control. In fact, they are derived from Zingales (1995b), where private benefits of control have no efficiency consequences, but only distributional ones.

B. Test

In Table VII we test these three predictions using our private benefits measure as an independent variable. We focus on our estimated country fixed effects from Table V. Since our explanatory variable is estimated, OLS estimates are biased and inconsistent. Thus, we also report instrumental variable (IV) estimates, where we use the family of origin of a country's legal system as an instrument for the extent of private benefits. As we show below in Table XI, legal origin is highly correlated with our private benefit measure. All of the reported results are robust to using the raw measure of private benefits from Table II in place of the estimated country fixed effects from Table V.

We begin by focusing on the relation between the size of private benefits and ownership concentration (specification 1). As a measure of ownership concentration that is available for almost all of the countries in our data set we use the percentage of equity controlled by the three largest shareholders in the 10 largest nonfinancial firms where the state is not a shareholder (La Porta et al. (1998)). To control for other possible factors, we insert in all the regressions the log GDP per capita.

As predicted, countries with higher private benefits have more concentrated ownership. A one standard deviation increase in the size of private benefits translates into 11 percent more of the equity held by the largest three shareholders in the instrumental variables specification. This simple specification seems to also have a very high explanatory power (r-squared $= 0.45$).

In specification 2, we test the effect of private benefits on the way firms are privatized. Our dependent variable is the percentage of privatizations that took place as a private asset sale, rather than as a share offering from Megginson et al. (2000). Asset sales almost always involve the sale of a majority (or 100 percent) of the shares to a controlling shareholder or group. Share offerings disperse ownership to a greater extent. To control for other factors, we include not only the per capita GDP, but also the importance of the equity market, on the basis that governments are more likely to sell shares in public offerings if the market is more developed.[24]

---

[24] The results are robust to excluding this variable.

Table VII

Testing the Theoretical Predictions on the Effects of Private Benefits on Financial Market Development

In specification 1 of Panel A the dependent variable is the average concentration of ownership as measured by the combined stakes of the three largest shareholders in the 10 largest nonfinancial, nonforeign corporations where the state is not a shareholder (see La Porta et al. (1997)). In specification 2 the dependent variable is the percentage of privatization transactions that took the form of an asset sale rather than a share offering (Megginson et al. (2000)). In Panel B the dependent variables are: (1) the number of initial public equity offerings in 1995 to 1996; (2) the number of listed domestic firms; (3) the ratio of the stock market capitalization held by minority investors to GNP (all from La Porta et al. (1997)). The explanatory variables are the average log GDP per capita 1970 to 1995 (World Bank) and our fixed effect estimates of the country average level of value of control from Table V. More complete variable descriptions and sources are provided in Table I. The instruments are the families of origin of a country's legal system (English, French, German, Scandinavian, and Soviet). Robust standard errors are in parentheses.

Panel A: Dependent Variables: Ownership Structure

	Dependent Variables			
	(1) Ownership Concentration (3 largest)		(2) Percentage of Privatizations as Asset Sales (not share offerings)	
Independent Variables	OLS	Instrumental Variables	OLS	Instrumental Variables
Country control premia	0.365** (0.124)	0.591** (0.261)	0.999*** (0.240)	2.005** (0.797)
Log per capita income	−0.047*** (0.015)	−0.033 (0.021)	−0.024 (0.057)	0.022 (0.061)
Constant	0.807*** (0.127)	0.559*** (0.207)	0.554 (0.505)	0.037 (0.583)
Number of obs.	36	36	36	36
R-squared	0.445		0.276	

Table VII—*Continued*

Panel B. Dependent Variable: Capital Market Structure Based on Aggregate Data

| | Dependent Variables | | | | | |
| | (1) Initial Public Offerings in 1996/Population | | (2) Number of Listed Domestic Firms/Population | | (3) Equity Market Capitalization/GNP | |
Independent Variables	OLS	Instrumental Variables	OLS	Instrumental Variables	OLS	Instrumental Variables
Country control premia	−2.753** (1.263)	−12.66** (5.609)	−24.03 (26.74)	−199.3* (94.21)	−1.265*** (0.413)	−3.747** (1.307)
Log per capita income	0.451** (0.195)	−0.082 (0.419)	8.643*** (3.079)	−0.327 (5.711)	−0.041 (0.065)	−0.168 (0.103)
Constant	−2.315 (1.543)	3.472 (4.064)	−45.60** (24.69)	51.57 (57.79)	0.943 (0.614)	2.319** (0.988)
Number of obs.	34	34	37	37	37	37
R-squared	0.203		0.168		0.213	

*significant at 10% level; **significant at 5%; ***significant at 1% level.

Private Benefits of Control   575

We find that in countries with large private benefits, governments are more likely to divest companies through private sales. A one standard deviation increase in the size of private benefits translates into 36 percent more firms being privatized through private negotiations in the instrumental variables specification. These results are consistent with evidence from privatizations in specific countries. In Brazil, for example, government interest in receiving the control premia at the time of privatization led them to weaken existing protections for minority investors so that minority holders of voting shares no longer had the right to an equal offer at the same price as the control block. In Mexico, Lopez-de-Silanes (1997) reports that the price per share for sales that did not involve control were just one quarter of the prices for sales of control blocks, helping to explain the fact that 87 percent of all sales in his sample of Mexican firms involved sales of control.

In Table VII, panel B, we test the link between private benefits and capital market development, beginning with the various aggregate indicators of financial development introduced by La Porta et al. (1997): number of IPOs/population, the number of listed firms/population, and the external market capitalization relative to GDP. Private benefits also explain a significant fraction of the cross-sectional variation in these measures. Our measure of private benefits is significant in all regressions with the exception of the OLS specification with the number of listed firms, where the single data point of Israel, with an unusually high level number of firms, reduces our level of significance. All the regressions include log per capita GDP as a regressor, to control for other possible factors.[25] A one standard deviation increase in private benefits translates into a 67 percent decline in the percent of external equity capitalization/GNP.

IV. What Curbs Private Benefits of Control?

A. *Theoretical Predictions*

Since the extent of private benefits of control seems to matter for security market development, the question of what curbs them becomes of central importance for any attempt to foster security market development.

The evidence of systematic differences in legal rules and the correlation between these rules and features of financial development La Porta et al. (1997, 1998, 1999) has focused the attention on the importance of the legal system. To capture the effect of the legal framework, we use three empirical proxies: (1) the formal rights of minority shareholders, (2) the degree of accounting disclosure (which allows minority shareholders to identify abuses), and (3) the quality of legal enforcement.

---

[25] Similar results obtain if we follow La Porta et al. (1997) and include GDP growth to capture future growth prospects and log GDP to capture any economies of scale in financial development.

A.1. Legal Institutions

(i) *The legal environment.* The ability of a controlling shareholder to appropriate some of the value generated is limited by the possibility of being sued. Thus, a greater ability to sue should translate into smaller private benefits of control (Zingales (1995a)). The same reasoning applies to any legal right attributed to noncontrolling shareholders (La Porta et al. (1997)). Accordingly, we examine the explanatory power of legal rights that give minority investors leverage over insiders in firms focusing on the so-called antidirector rights index developed by La Porta et al. (1997) and used by Pistor, Raiser, and Gelfer (2000) for the transition countries. We focus our attention on the level of shareholder rights in the country of the target firm. As seen above, we also examine the impact of shareholder rights in the acquirer's country based on the hypothesis that these might also constrain private benefits (Dyck (2000)).

(ii) *Disclosure standards.* Disclosure standards regulate the information available to noncontrolling shareholders. The more accurate this information is, the more difficult it is for a controlling shareholder to appropriate value without incurring legal penalties or, at least, reputational costs. Thus, measures of quality of disclosure should be negatively correlated with the size of private benefits of control.

(iii) *Enforcement.* The strength of legal protections depends upon the expectations of speedy and predictable enforcement. Thus, we include as one of our contractual variables a measure of the strength of a country's law and order tradition as measured by the country risk rating agency, International Country Risk. This rule of law index is scaled from zero to 10.

A.2. Extra-legal Institutions

The possibility of extracting private benefits is intrinsically related to managerial discretion, a discretion that courts cannot easily restrict. As a result, extra-legal institutions may play an important role in constraining private benefits (Dyck (2000)), both in settings with legal protections as well as in settings where legal protections are nonexistent or not enforced.

The potential constraints imposed by extra-legal institutions have not been prominent in current debates, at least in part because of a lack of empirical examination. We focus our attention on five institutional factors that, at least in theory, have the potential to raise expectations of penalties for activities that produce private benefits for controlling shareholders. Some of these factors that can raise the costs to the controlling shareholder for diverting activities (such as the penalties produced by product market competition and by public opinion pressure) are constraints external to the firm. Other factors (such as the sanctions that can be introduced by moral norms, labor, and the government as tax collector) are more "internal" to the firm.

(iv) *Product market competition.* The degree of product market competition affects the opportunity to appropriate private benefits in two dimensions. First, the more competitive markets are, the more verifiable prices become. When prices are more "objective," it is more difficult for a controlling shareholder to

Private Benefits of Control 577

tunnel out resources through manipulated transfer prices without incurring legal and/or reputational costs. Second, in a competitive market the distortions produced by the extraction of private benefits are more likely to jeopardize the survival of the firm. Hence, competition represents a natural constraint to the extraction of private benefits.

The extent of product market competition is based both on industry and on country characteristics. In our regressions we include controls for industry characteristics, which we constrain to be constant across countries. The extent of product market competition is also influenced by country level characteristics, particularly government policies regarding entry and competition. We use as our proxy for the extent of product market competition at the national level the response to the survey question, "competition laws prevent unfair competition in your country?" as reported by the World Competitiveness Yearbook for 1996. This variable, which is available for all of our countries, captures cross-country differences in the extent to which national policy makers allow for barriers to competition over and above those constraints associated with industry.

(v) *Public opinion pressure.* Controlling shareholders might limit their efforts to divert firm resources not out of fear of legal sanction but rather out of concern for their reputation. As Dyck and Zingales (2002b) argue, reputation to reduce diversion, the information about improper behavior must be publicized. For example, shareholders' activist Robert Monks succeeded in initiating some major changes at Sears, not by means of the norms of the corporate code (his proxy fight failed miserably), but through the pressure of public opinion. He paid for a full-page announcement in the *Wall Street Journal* where he exposed the identities of Sears' directors, labeling them the "non-performing assets" of Sears (Monks and Minnow (1995)). The embarrassment for the directors was so great that they implemented all the changes proposed by Monks. Similarly, recent efforts to stem diversionary practices by the powerful Korean Chaebol have also come not from court cases but through the public identification and dissemination of behavior through the media by shareholder activists. Public humiliation is not only a tool of activists, but is also viewed as an important tool of regulators. In Hong Kong, for example, the main sanction available to securities regulators was not financial penalties but the threat and use of publishing those who violate listing requirements through the press.[26]

Critically, for reputation to work, though, it is necessary to have a "public opinion: that is, a combination of an independent press that publicizes the facts and of a large set of educated investors, who read the newspapers and sanction improper behavior" (Zingales (2000)). We try to capture this idea with an indicator of newspapers' diffusion, measured as the circulation of daily newspapers normalized by population.

(vi) *Internal policing through moral norms.* Regardless of the reputational cost and/or the legal punishment the appropriation of private benefits trigger,

[26] While public opinion pressure is likely to act as a restrain in the extraction of private benefits, it does not necessarily push managers in the direction of shareholders' value maximization. In fact, in Dyck and Zingales (2002b) we show that media pressure also induces companies to be more environmentally conscious even if this does not necessarily benefit shareholders.

a controlling shareholder might choose not to appropriate value for moral considerations. But what constitutes a measure of the strength of such an internal policeman? Coffee (2001) proposes the violent crime rate as a proxy for these moral norms, noting that this at least captures an important difference between Scandinavian and other countries. Stulz and Williamson (2001) focus on culture as an indicator of norms. They use religion as their proxy for cultural norms and hypothesize that certain religious traditions will be more antagonistic to investor rights, such as the historical antagonism Catholics and Muslims had toward the payment of interest. To test for an impact of moral norms we use both proposed measures: (1) the number of violent crimes reported by the World Competitiveness Yearbook based on Interpol data for 1993 and (2) Stulz and Williamson's classification of countries by their primary religious orientation.

(vii) *Labor as monitor.* Additional constraints on controlling shareholders might come from the presence of economic entities with a direct interest in firm decisions that could penalize efforts to extract private benefits directly without having to turn to the courts. From this perspective, it is clear that labor has the potential to monitor controlling shareholders and the ability to penalize diversions without resorting to legal sanctions. Labor is privy to inside information on customers and suppliers and can hold up the controlling shareholder by threatening to withhold services and in some cases, through their position on the board of directors. Stiglitz (1985), for example, suggests that unions have both the potential for low cost monitoring and have a strong incentive to monitor. "Labor is also motivated to take actions that protect the long-term survival of the firm, and particularly where employees are also owners through the investment of their pension funds in company stock, there interests are not narrowly focused on wages," (Stiglitz (1985)). At the same time, it is theoretically ambiguous how labor might act for it does not necessarily have the incentive to constrain private benefits, possibly aligning itself with the controlling shareholder against outside investors and labor's information access might not include critical information that is the source of private benefits. We test for the effect of labor on private benefits using as a cross-country measure of the extent of potential labor power the degree of employee protection. This measure is available for all OECD countries.

(viii) *Government as monitor through tax enforcement.* There is one de facto minority shareholder that is common to all companies: the Government. As for minority shareholders, the Government has an interest in ascertaining the value produced by a company and getting a share of it. Transfer pricing, for instance, is disciplined by the tax code. In the United States, intracorporate transfers should take place at the price the two units would have charged in a competitive market. Hence, how tax authorities enforce their rules on transfer pricing affects the incentives to transfer profits to related companies. The stricter the enforcement, the less controlling shareholders will use transfer prices to siphon out value at the expense of minority shareholders.[27]

---

[27] Tax authorities should be particularly concerned about diversions of revenues from taxed to nontaxed entities, be those entities domestic or foreign.

Unlike noncontrolling shareholders, however, the tax authority does not face any free-rider problem in monitoring and enforcing its right. On the contrary, by aggressively prosecuting a company the Government sets an example that induces all others to behave. Thus, it has an incentive to prosecute cases even when the cost of prosecution is higher than the money recoverable. Furthermore, the Government has the benefit of disciplinary powers that are simply not available to dispersed shareholders. Therefore, better tax enforcement can have an important role in reducing the private benefits of control.

Note that this effect is true only for the quality of the enforcement not for the level of the tax rates. In fact, a higher tax rate increases a company's benefit from hiding income. In so doing, it subsidizes the siphoning out activity of the largest shareholder. For any dollar siphoned out by the majority shareholder, minority shareholders lose only $(1-t)$ dollars, where t is the corporate tax rate. Hence, the higher the t, the lower the incentives of minority shareholders to stop this activity.

For this reason we want a measure of tax compliance, not of tax revenues. To this purpose, we use an index developed by the World Competitiveness Report, which assesses the level of tax compliance. The index goes from zero to six where higher scores indicate higher compliance.

That an effective corporate taxation system might have this positive externality has not been emphasized in the corporate finance literature, or, to our knowledge, in the public finance literature.[28] Any evidence in this direction would be an important element in the debate on the costs and benefits of corporate income taxation, particularly in countries with high private benefits.

B. Test

The large panel data set of 393 transactions from 39 countries provides a unique sample to try and identify the main institutional curbs of private benefits of control discussed above. In what follows, we describe the empirical proxies used and their effect on the private benefits of control. The definition for all these proxies is reported in Table I. Table VIII reports their actual values. In Table IX we test the impact of each institution in isolation and in Table X we try to test them one against the other. For these regressions, we include all of the control variables used in Table V as well as an indicator variable that identifies countries that have any form of tender offer requirement.

We start with the impact of "legal" factors, that is, factors that directly or indirectly rely on the court enforcement of certain rights. Information disclosure is the prerequisite for any legal action. Thus, we start (column 1) with the quality of the accounting standards, as measured by the CIFAR index. Firms in countries with better accounting standards have lower private benefits of control. This effect is both statistically and economically significant.

---

[28] For example, Gresik's (2001) recent review of the literature on rationales for and effects of corporate income taxation in the context of transnationals does not mention any spillovers between government actions and agency costs.

Table VIII
Institutional Variables

This table presents summary statistics of the institutional variables used in Tables IX to XI. Variable definitions and sources can be found in Table I.

Panel A

Country	Legal Origin	Accounting Standards (0–90)	Antidirector Rights (0–6)	Rule of Law at Country Level (1–10)	Competition Laws	Newspaper Circulation/Pop	Serious Crime/100,000 Population	Labor Protection Measure	Tax Compliance (1–6)	Acceptability of Cheating on Taxes (1–10)	Primary Religion
		Legal Institutions					Extra Legal Institutions				
Argentina	French	45	4	5.35	4.85	1.2	8.2		2.41	1.97	Catholic
Australia	English	75	4	10	5.52	3.0	57.5	0.9	4.58	2.16	Protestant
Austria	German	54	2	10	5.29	2.9	57.3	2.2	3.6	1.97	Catholic
Brazil	French	54	3	6.32	4.9	0.4			2.14	3.11	Catholic
Canada	English	74	5	10	5.37	1.6	122.3	0.6	3.77	2.34	Catholic
Chile	French	52	5	7.02	5.4	1.0	53.7		4.2	1.98	Catholic
Colombia	French	50	3	2.08	4.71	0.5	129.1		2.11	1.92	Catholic
Czech Republic	Soviet		2	8.3	4.89	2.5	177.2		2.54		Atheist
Denmark	Scand.	62	2	10	5.16	3.1	46.1		3.7	2.48	Protestant
Egypt	French	24	2	4.17	4.6	0.4			3.57		Muslim
Finland	Scand.	77	3	10	5.26	4.6	47.1	2.0	3.53	2.63	Protestant
France	French	69	3	8.98	5.83	2.2	126.8	3.0	3.86	3.28	Catholic
Germany	German	62	1	9.23	5.91	3.1	74.1	2.5	3.41	2.94	Protestant
Hong Kong	English	69	5	8.22	5.85	8.0	190.8		4.56		Local beliefs
Indonesia	French		2	3.98	4.42	0.2	4.6		2.53		Muslim
Israel	English	64	3	4.82	5.11	2.9	68.9		3.69		Judaism
Italy	French	62	1	8.33	5.14	1.0	61.7	3.3	1.77	2.28	Catholic
Japan	German	65	4	8.98	5.64	5.8	2.7	2.4	4.41	1.49	Buddhist
Malaysia	English	76	4	6.78	4.84	1.6	34.5		4.34		Muslim
Mexico	French	60	1	5.35	4.93	1.0	100.8		2.46	3.35	Catholic
Netherlands	French	64	2	10	5.53	3.1	122.8	2.1	3.4	3.08	Catholic

Private Benefits of Control

Panel A

Country	Legal origin	Accounting Standards (0–90)	Antidirector Rights (0–6)	Rule of Law at Country Level (1–10)	Competition Laws	Newspaper Circulation/Pop	Serious Crime/100,000 Population	Labor Protection Measure	Tax Compliance (1–6)	Acceptability of Cheating on Taxes (1–10)	Religion
New Zealand	English	70	4	10	5.4	2.2	52.3	5	3.10	1.0	Protestant
Norway	Scand.	74	4	10	4.96	5.9	26.9	3.96	2.15	2.6	Protestant
Peru	French	38	3	2.5	5.05	0.8	90.9	2.66	3.00		Catholic
Phillipines	French	65	3	2.73	4.61	0.8	99.6	1.83	2.61		Catholic
Poland	Soviet		3	8.7	5.06	1.1	12.4	2.19	3.82		Catholic
Portugal	French	36	3	8.68	4.81	0.8	45.2	2.18		3.7	Catholic
Singapore	English	78	4	8.57	5.21	3.2	225.2	5.05	2.44		Buddhist
South Africa	English	70	5	4.42	4.89	0.34	8.5	2.4	1.64		Protestant
South Korea	German	62	2	5.35	4.9	3.9	169.6	3.29	2.57		Protestant
Spain	French	64	4	7.8	5.07	1.0	80.1	1.91	2.30	3.1	Catholic
Sweden	Scand.	83	3	10	5.08	4.5	38.3	3.39	2.50	2.2	Protestant
Switzerland	German	68	2	10	5.22	3.3	34	4.49	1.98	1.0	Catholic
Taiwan	German	65	3	8.52	5.56	2.7	70.4	3.25			Buddhist
Thailand	English	64	2	6.25	4.77	0.6	69.2	3.41	1.24		Buddhist
Turkey	French	51	2	5.18	5.14	1.1	96.4	2.07	2.65		Muslim
United Kingdom	English	78	5	8.57	5.74	3.3	272.5	4.67	1.95	0.5	Protestant
United States	English	71	5	10	5.96	2.12	86.5	4.47	1.98	0.2	Protestant
Venezuela	French	40	1	6.37	4.24	2.06		1.56			Catholic

Panel B: Correlation Matrix

	Accounting Standards (0–90)	Antidirector Rights (0–6)	Rule of Law at Country Level (1–10)	Competition Laws	Newspaper Circulation	Serious Crime/100,000 Population	Labor Protection Measure	Tax Compliance (1–6)	Acceptability of Cheating on Taxes (1–10)
Accounting standards	1.00								
Antidirector rights	0.32	1.00							
Rule of law	0.53	0.06	1.00						
Competition laws	0.49	0.26	0.59	1.00					
Newspaper circulation	0.54	−0.01	0.62	−.00	1.00				
Serious crime	0.19	0.33	−0.09	0.35	−0.13	1.00			
Labor protection	−0.57	−0.55	−0.54	0.26	−0.10	−0.35	1.00		
Tax compliance	0.58	0.40	0.65	−0.46	0.65	−0.08	−0.78	1.00	
Cheat	0.08	−0.11	0.17	0.74	−0.11	0.07	0.46	−0.10	1.00

A one standard deviation increase in accounting standards reduces the value of control by 9.0 percentage points. Together with the other control variables, accounting standards explain 21 percent of the variation in private benefits of control (the firm-specific control variables alone explain just 15 percent).

Our second variable (column 2) is the extent of legal protections for minority investors, measured using La Porta et al. (1998) index of antidirector rights. Countries with more antidirector rights have lower private benefits of control. A one standard deviation increase in antidirector rights reduces the value of control by 4.4 percentage points. Together with the firm-specific variables, antidirector rights explain 17 percent of the variation in private benefits of control.

Finally, we use the quality of law enforcement, which we measure using the IBR index of the quality of the law enforcement in a country. Countries with better law enforcement have lower private benefits of control. A one standard deviation increase in our law enforcement measure reduces the value of control by 7.0 percentage points. Together with the firm-specific variables, rule of law explains 20 percent of the variation in private benefits of control.

In sum, we find that legal institutions are strongly associated with lower levels of private benefits. When we combine the two legal variables that are available for our full sample in one regression (Table X, column 1), both are statistically significant and the R-squared is 21 percent.

We also test the explanatory power provided by extra-legal institutions, which are suggested by a functional rather than an institutional perspective. Here we focus on crude country-wide measures of product market competition, scope of reputational penalties, moral norms, employee protections, and diligence of tax authorities.

Table IX, columns 4 to 9, explores the explanatory power of these factors one at a time. In column 4 we test the effect of competition. After having controlled for industry type, we find that countries with more competitive product markets, at least as measured by this survey of the World Competitiveness Report, have lower private benefits of control. A one standard deviation increase in our measure of competition reduces the value of control by 6.0 percentage points. Together with the firm specific variables, competition explains 20 percent of the variation in private benefits of control.

In column 5 of Table IX, we explore the idea that public opinion pressure might curb the amount of private benefits extracted. We measure the importance of this pressure with the diffusion of newspapers (number of copies sold per 100,000 inhabitants). Diffusion captures both the importance of public opinion and the credibility of newspapers (less credible newspapers sell less).[29] Countries where newspapers are more diffused have lower private benefits

---

[29] In Dyck and Zingales (2002b), we study the determinants of newspapers' diffusion. We find that the type of dominant religion and the degree of ethnolinguistic fractionalization explain 41 percent of the variation in press diffusion. When we use these as instruments for press diffusion, the results are unchanged.

Table IX
Institutional Determinants of Private Benefits of Control—Univariate Analysis

The dependent variable is the block premia as a percent of firm equity. The explanatory variables include all of variables introduced in Table V except the country fixed effects, but including a dummy to indicate the presence of a mandatory tender offer law. In place of the country fixed effects, we introduce one at a time several institutional variables: (1) accounting standards index; (2) antidirector rights index; (3) rule of law index; (4) tax compliance index; (5) diffusion of the press as measured by the newspaper circulation/population; (6) an index of the extent of competition laws; (7) incidence of violent crimes; (8) extent of legal protections for labor; (9) a dummy variable if primary religion is Catholicism. More complete descriptions of variables are provided in Table I. Standard errors, which are reported in parentheses, are robust and clustered by country.

				Dependent Variable: Block Premium					
	Legal Institutions				Extra Legal Institutions				
Independent Variables	(1)	(2)	(3)	(4)	(5)	(6)	(7)	(8)	(9)
Accounting standards	−0.007*** (0.002)								
Antidirector rights		−0.036** (0.015)							
Rule of law			−0.023*** (0.011)						
Competition laws				−0.147*** (0.046)					
Newspaper circulation/pop					−0.036** (0.014)				
Violent crime incidence						0.000 (0.000)			
Labor protection							0.038 (0.023)		
Catholic is primary religion								0.118* (0.066)	
Tax compliance									−0.085*** (0.025)

Table IX—*Continued*

Independent Variables	Dependent Variable: Block Premium								
	Legal Institutions			Extra Legal Institutions					
	(1)	(2)	(3)	(4)	(5)	(6)	(7)	(8)	(9)
Variables Controlled for:									
Buyer bargaining power	y	y	y	y	y	y	y	y	y
Ownership variables	y	y	y	y	y	y	y	y	y
Financial distress	y	y	y	y	y	y	y	y	y
Foreign acquirer	y	y	y	y	y	y	y	y	y
Crosslisted in the U.S.	y	y	y	y	y	y	y	y	y
Buyer identity	y	y	y	y	y	y	y	y	y
Seller identity	y	y	y	y	y	y	y	y	y
Industry group	y	y	y	y	y	y	y	y	y
Tangibility of assets	y	y	y	y	y	y	y	y	y
Interaction of relative strength of antidirector rights (home—target nation) and foreign acquiror dummy	y	y	y	y	y	y	y	y	y
Interaction of relative strength of antidirector rights (US—target nation) and crosslisted in the US dummy	y	y	y	y	y	y	y	y	y
Presence of takeover law	y	y	y	y	y	y	y	y	y
Constant	y	y	y	y	y	y	y	y	y
Number of observations	381	393	393	393	393	377	233	393	393
Countries included	36	39	39	39	39	36	18	39	39
R-squared	0.213	0.174	0.203	0.203	0.200	0.175	0.208	0.184	0.230

*significant at 5% level; **significant at 1% level.

Table X

Institutional Determinants of Private Benefits
of Control—Multivariate Analysis

The dependent variable is the block premia as a percent of firm equity. The explanatory variables include all of the variables introduced in Table V except the country fixed effects, but including a dummy to indicate the presence of a mandatory tender offer law. As institutional variables in specification (1), we use antidirector rights index and rule of law index. In specification (2), a dummy variable if primary religion is Catholicism, a tax compliance index, the diffusion of the press as measured by the newspaper circulation/population and the index of the extent of competition laws. The independent variables in specification (3) are antidirector rights index, rule of law index, tax compliance index, diffusion of the press as measured by the newspaper circulation/population. More complete descriptions of variables are provided in Table I. Standard errors, which are reported in parentheses, are robust and clustered by country.

Independent Variables	Dependent Variable: Block Premium		
	(1)	(2)	(3)
Antidirector rights	−0.026** (0.012)		−0.003 (0.019)
Rule of law	−0.026*** (0.010)		−0.006 (0.011)
Catholic		0.019 (0.056)	
Tax compliance		−0.064*** (0.021)	−0.061* (0.033)
Newspaper circulation/ population		−0.020** (0.009)	−0.018* (0.010)
Competition laws		−0.042 (0.036)	
Variables Controlled for:			
Buyer bargaining power	y	y	y
Ownership variables	y	y	y
Financial distress	y	y	y
Buyer characteristics	v	v	v
Seller characteristics	y	y	y
Foreign acquirer	y	y	y
Crosslisted in the U.S.	y	y	y
Industry type	y	y	y
Tangibility of assets	y	y	y
Interaction of relative strength of antidirector rights (home—target nation) and foreign acquirer dummy	y	y	y
Interaction of relative strength of antidirector rights (US—target nation) and cross listed in the US dummy	y	y	y
Presence of takeover law	y	y	y
Constant	y	y	y
Number of observations	393	393	393
Countries included	39	39	39
R-squared	0.213	0.245	0.243

*significant at 10% level; **significant at 5%; ***significant at 1% level.

of control. A one standard deviation increase in newspapers' diffusion reduces the value of control by 6.4 percentage points. Together with the firm-specific variables, newspapers' diffusion explains 20 percent of the variation in private benefits of control. Columns 4 and 5 suggest that institutions external to the firm are associated with private benefits.

In columns 6 and 8, we test the idea that countries with higher moral norms have lower private benefits. Consistent with Coffee's prediction, countries with worse norms as proxied by a higher violent crime rate have higher private benefits of control, but the effect is economically and statistically insignificant. To investigate moral norms, we introduce indicator variables for the four main religions (Buddhist, Catholic, Muslim, and Protestant), which differ in their impact on moral attitudes (Guiso, Sapienza, and Zingales (2003)). As a country religion we use the dominant one (see Stulz and Williamson (2001)). We find that Catholic countries have significantly higher private benefits, and Protestant ones significantly lower (estimate not reported). The effect of the Muslim and Buddhist religion is not significant.

In columns 7 and 9, we test whether the strength of other entities that have a direct economic interest in firm decision making is associated with lower levels of private benefits. In column 7 we examine the impact of labor as a monitor of private benefits. As an index of potential labor strength, we use both an unweighted and a weighted (not reported) index of employee protections based on average indictors on regular contracts and short-term contracts from OECD data compiled in Pagano and Volpin (2000). The restriction to OECD countries unfortunately limits our number of countries and observations, but is perhaps a purer test of the contention that labor can work as monitors, since this literature has focused on organized labor in developed economies. Inconsistent with the hypothesis that labor is an effective monitor, and consistent with Pagano and Volpin's counter contention that entrepreneurs and workers will align themselves against the interests of minority investors, we find that increased labor power is associated with higher private benefits, although this result is not statistically significant (p-value of 0.204 for employee protections, 0.13 for weighted employee protections).

In column 9 we investigate the possibility that a government interested in enforcing tax rules can reduce private benefits. This column shows that those countries with a higher degree of tax compliance, as measured by the World Competitiveness Report, have lower private benefits of control. A one standard deviation increase in our measure of tax compliance reduces the value of control by 8.6 percentage points, a significant amount. Together with the firm specific variables, tax compliance explains 23 percent of the variation in private benefits of control.

Tax compliance is an equilibrium outcome, affected both by tax enforcement and by the attitude of citizens toward cheating on their taxes. To try to identify the impact of tax enforcement in an unreported regression, we include a measure of willingness to cheat on taxes as measured in the World Value Survey.

In this survey people are asked to rate from one to 10 the statement "cheating on taxes if you have a chance is...," where one is never justifiable and 10 is always justifiable. We find this variable to be insignificant, and the coefficient on tax compliance to remain significant, suggesting the effect of tax compliance comes from tax enforcement and not from differences in moral values across countries. We also examine the robustness of this result to the inclusion of the marginal tax rate and our results are unchanged.

In Table X (column 2), we combine the four extra-legal institutions that individually had a statistically significant effect. All four variables retain the predicted sign, but the magnitudes of their coefficients drop and only tax compliance and newspaper diffusion remain statistically significant at the 5 percent level. Together these four variables are able to explain 24 percent of the variation in private benefits.

The evidence, thus far, is consistent with both the legal and the extra-legal institutions playing a role in constraining private benefits. In fact, a crude R-squared test suggests they have roughly the same explanatory power. Can we distinguish which one is more important?

There are two obstacles to doing so. First, many of these institutional variables are highly correlated, as panel B of Table VIII shows. Shareholder's protection, though, is not correlated with newspapers' circulation and has a correlation of only 0.4 with tax compliance. Second, and most important, all these proxies are measured with error. Hence, their statistical significance in a multivariate analysis might be more related to the level of noise in these measures than to their actual importance.

Nevertheless, we think it is interesting to try and put all these variables in one regression. This is what we do in column 3 of Table X. When all the institutional variables we found to be significant in the previous regressions are simultaneously included, only newspapers' diffusion and tax compliance remain significant. The paucity of observations and the high degree of multicollinearity caution us against drawing any strong conclusion from this comparison. We can say, however, that the results are inconsistent with an exclusive focus on legal variables as institutional curbs to private benefits.

C. The Effect of Legal Families

Since LLSV's (1998) seminal paper, the origin of a country's legal system has played an important role in all the institutional explanations of cross-country differences. LLSV claim that legal traditions differ in their respect for property rights and, hence, in their ability to protect minority shareholders. We should have already accounted for this effect by inserting the LLSV index of antidirector rights. Nevertheless, it is possible that the origin of a country's legal system is a better indicator of the degree of protection of outside investors than the antidirector index. For this reason, we repeat some of the previous

estimates substituting the country of origin of the legal system for the antidirector rights variable.

As Table XI, panel A shows, the average level of private benefits differs
substantially across different legal families. Private benefits are highest in
former communist countries (36 percent), then countries with a French code
(21 percent), and countries with a German, English, and Scandinavian code
seem to have the lowest level of private benefits (respectively, 11, 5.5, and 4.8
percent). Panel B, column 1, shows that the levels of private benefits are significantly lower in countries with German, English, and Scandinavian legal
origins than in French legal origin countries. Thus, the distinction is not in
terms of civil law versus common law, but it is more complex.

In Table XI, panel B, we report how these results are changed after we control
for the most significant extra-legal institutions (diffusion of readership and tax
enforcement). Any distinction between English-based legal systems and the
others disappears. If anything, common law countries have *higher* (not lower)
private benefits of control once these extra-legal institutions are taken into
consideration, but this effect is not statistically significant. Only Scandinavian
countries have lower private benefits of control even after controlling for extra-
legal institutions.

Overall, these results confirm the previous ones: Extra-legal institutions are
important and they should be controlled for in any cross-country analysis.

Table XI
Private Benefits of Control and Legal Origin

Panel A presents descriptive statistics of block premia by legal origin, first presenting averages at the country level and second presenting averages based on the full set of 393 transactions. Panel B provides OLS regressions of block premia on legal origin and our other explanatory variables. The independent variables examined are those included in Table IX with
(1) legal origin; (2) tax compliance and newspaper circulation; (3) English origin to capture the
difference between common and civil law origin, tax compliance and newspaper circulation; (4)
all legal origin dummies, tax compliance, and newspaper circulation. More complete descriptions of variables are provided in Table I. Robust standard errors clustered by country are in
parentheses.

| | Panel A: Block Premium by Legal Origin | | | | | |
| | Groups of Legal Origin | | | All Transactions | | |
Law Origin	Mean	Standard Deviation	Number of Countries	Mean	Standard Deviation	Number of Observations
Scandinavian origin	0.048	0.033	4	0.041	0.075	42
English origin	0.055	0.080	11	0.045	0.123	196
German origin	0.109	0.152	6	0.051	0.138	57
French origin	0.212	0.171	16	0.251	0.439	88
Soviet origin	0.356	0.314	2	0.400	0.639	10

Table XI—*Continued*

Independent Variables	Panel B: Investigating Explanatory Power of Legal Origin			
	Dependent Variable: Block Premium			
	(1)	(2)	(3)	(4)
English origin	−0.155**		0.043	−0.024
	(0.067)		(0.044)	(0.062)
Soviet origin	0.128			0.141
	(0.201)			(0.207)
German origin	−0.228**			(−0.121)
	(0.097)			(0.084)
Scandinavian origin	−0.189***			−0.098*
	(0.058)			(0.053)
Tax compliance		−0.070***	−0.087***	−0.066***
		(0.021)	(0.027)	(0.022)
Newspaper circulation		−0.021**	−0.015	−0.003
		(0.010)	(0.011)	(0.008)
Variables controlled for:				
Buyer bargaining power	y	y	y	y
Ownership variables	y	y	y	y
Financial distress	y	y	y	y
Buyer identity	y	y	y	y
Seller identity	y	y	y	y
Industry group	y	y	y	y
Tangibility of assets	y	y	y	y
Foreign acquirer	y	y	y	y
Crosslisted in the U.S.				
Interaction of relative strength of antidirector rights (home—target nation) and foreign acquirer dummy	y	y	y	y
Interaction of relative strength of antidirector rights (US—target nation) and crosslisted in the US dummy	y	y	y	y
Constant	y	y	y	y
Number of observations	393	393	393	393
Number of countries (clusters)	39	39	39	39
R-squared	0.243	0.242	0.244	0.260

*significant at 10% level; **significant at 5%; ***significant at 1% level.

V. Conclusions

In this paper we apply the Barclay and Holderness (1989) approach to measure the magnitude of private benefits of control across countries. That we obtain estimates very consistent with previous studies, using different approaches, indicates that the extraction of private benefits is a very real phenomenon that can be consistently measured.

We then use these estimates to test several theoretical predictions from the corporate finance literature on the negative effects that large private benefits have on financial development. In countries where private benefits of control are large, ownership is more concentrated, privatizations are less likely to take place as public offerings, and capital markets are less developed by several measures. These results vindicate the emphasis that, since Shleifer and Vishny (1997), corporate finance research has put on the importance of protecting outside investors against expropriation by insiders. They also suggest the importance of gaining a better understanding of what are the institutions that help curb private benefits.

We find that many institutional variables, taken in isolation, seem to be associated with a lower level of private benefits of control: better accounting standards, better legal protection of minority shareholders, better law enforcement, more intense product market competition, a high level of diffusion of the press, and a high rate of tax compliance.

The possible role of tax enforcement in reducing private benefits, and thus indirectly enhancing financial development, is probably the most important new fact that emerges from our analysis. Improving the corporate taxation system is well within the range of feasible reforms. If this is indeed a primary mechanism by which private benefits of control can be curbed and financial markets fostered, the benefits of financial development might be within reach for many more countries. Before jumping to any conclusion, though, more research is needed. In particular, it would be useful to show that within a country changes in the level of tax enforcement lead to changes in the size of private benefits.

Our results suggest also other avenues for future research. We find that public opinion pressure helps to curb private benefits of control. A strong pressure from the media on corporate managers, however, will not always increase shareholders value. In fact, in Dyck and Zingales (2002b) we find that strong media also induce corporate managers to bow to environmental pressures, which are not necessarily in the shareholders' interest. The broader question, then, which awaits future research, is how media pressure interacts with social norms in shaping corporate policy. We also do not discuss, in this context, what are the incentives of the media to expose bad corporate practices and how these incentives may vary over the business cycle. We address this in a separate paper (Dyck and Zingales (2003)).

Finally, in this paper we do not try to distinguish between the three potential sources of private benefits: psychic value, perquisites, and dilution. That private benefits are smaller in a country with better protection of investors, better tax enforcement, and more media pressure suggests that not all private benefits are psychic. Further work, however, is needed to establish the importance of dilution and its welfare implications.

Appendix

A.1. Steps to Identify Transactions

We used the following approach to implement the first criterion that a transaction be a control transaction between unrelated parties: (1) The transaction had to be identified in the SDC database and through the transaction the

Private Benefits of Control   591

acquirer had to move from a shareholding position of less than 20 percent to shareholding of more than 20 percent shareholding.[30] (2) The block involved in the transaction had to be 10 percent or greater. (3) The block had to be the largest block in the company. (4) News stories surrounding the transaction had to confirm a transfer of control from the seller to the acquirer, with news stories identified by using the company name and transaction date in Nexis-Lexis and Dow-Jones Interactive search engines, often with the use of both English and foreign language media.

Illustrative of the steps we took to identify control transactions is our exclusion of related party transactions. With related parties it is questionable whether control is transferred and the price of the deal is unlikely to reflect the value of control. Systematically, we excluded transactions where SDC reported that the acquirer involved management, as management already has control rights prior to sale. Using qualitative data we identified further related party transactions excluding transfers of shares between subsidiaries and parents of the same company and other deals that don't transfer control. For example, we excluded the sale of 36 percent of the shares of Shin Corp in Thailand in September 2000. News stories reported that "Telecoms Tycoon turned politician Thaksin Shinawatra and his wife have sold their 35.4 percent stake in their flagship Shin Corporation at a deep discount, in what appears to be an attempt to comply with the laws on ministers' ownership of companies. The stake was sold to their son and relatives at just 10 baht a share, less than 6 percent of the stocks closing price yesterday of 177 baht.... Analysts said the move was purely political and would have no impact on shareholders or on the company."[31]

To implement the second criterion, that a control price be available and reflect the value of control, we restricted our attention to SDC transactions that met three additional criteria:

(1) There had to be data in SDC to identify a control price. In many cases SDC reports a price per share in a separate data field where they value cash offers at face value and offers of shares at the exchange price on the day prior to the announcement of the transaction. In other instances, the price per share is not reported in the data field but can be derived by combining information in available data fields and information from other data sources on the number of shares outstanding. For example, SDC would report the total price paid and the percentage of shares sold and we would construct an estimate of the per share price involved in the offer by collecting information on the number of shares outstanding at the time of the transaction. For many transactions, SDC reported that no

[30] For Australia and Canada we used a 15 percent cutoff due to the presence of takeover rules for stakes exceeding 20 percent.

[31] "Thaksin, wife sell entire stake in flagship," Harish Mehta, Business Times Singapore, September 7, 2000.

terms were disclosed or that the reported price was only one component of the compensation. We are unable to use such transactions.

(2) The form of sale had to involve purchases where assets used to establish a per share sale price include securities that could be priced objectively (we exclude transactions that involve warrants, convertible bonds, notes, liabilities, debt-equity swaps, etc.), and where the terms of sale were not determined by exercising an option or included an option to buy additional shares in addition to the shares purchased.

(3) The synopsis field and news stories had to confirm the price per share and to ensure that the reported price was not misleading. We excluded observations where news stories identified other considerations, and adjusted the price per share from the SDC reported price if two news stories reported a price that deviated from the SDC price.

To implement the third criterion that an exchange price be available we begin by restricting our attention to those transactions where the company whose shares are being acquired is covered by Datastream international, the data provider with the most extensive coverage of international firms.[32] We also are interested in identifying the exchange price after the market is aware of the purchase of shares by the new controlling shareholder. A traditional approach in the finance literature of focusing on the share price on the day of announcement is not warranted with our database. In many cases, the transfer of control leads to a suspension of trading of the company shares either because there is a need for time for the information about the control transfer to be communicated broadly or there are limits to movement of the exchange price per day. While the suspension is of limited duration in established markets like the United States and the United Kingdom, the suspension can last for a day or more in other settings. Consequently, we use as a standard approach the control price two days after announcement. Where news stories indicated a longer delay, we used the first date after restrictions on trading or pricing of securities. This produced modifications in 17 cases where we use a later date for all of our calculations.

A.2. The Special Case of Dispersions of Control Blocks

In 17 transactions we identify through reading news stories that the controlling block is not sold intact but rather sold to a financial intermediary that then sells the block to a variety of institutional investors. We elected to include these deals in our data set. In the Barclay and Holderness (1989) data set such transactions were excluded by construction of their sample, but as they argued, such

---

[32] We attempted to access additional information sources for price information for local stocks not covered during our time period by Datastream through direct contacts with country stock exchanges and through appealing to news reports that often reported share price information for large local companies. These efforts produced 26 additional observations.

Private Benefits of Control   593

transactions should be included if a private benefit measure is to reflect the general benefits and costs of control. Such transactions are only likely if there is a limited benefit to control of enterprises and costs to control. Our data set includes nine transactions from the United Kingdom, three from Germany, and one from Finland, Japan, New Zealand, Norway, and Taiwan. Our results are robust to the exclusion of these transactions, with small increases in our raw measures of private benefits for the United Kingdom (from 1.6 to 2.4 percent), Germany (from 9.5 to 11.8 percent) and New Zealand (2.6 to 3.6 percent).

A.3. The Special Case of Companies with Dual Class Shares

We identify all transactions that involve firms with multiple classes of shares. When this is the case we measure the control premium for the shares with voting power relative to the shares that lack voting power, where Datastream provides price information for both classes. For example, we have 11 observations from Brazil that involve firms with dual class shares and Datastream has price series for both classes for 10 of these 11 observations. In Brazil, the principle difference between the two classes is the voting right with largely equal rights to cash flow. Our data set includes 38 dual class firms altogether, including companies from Canada, Denmark, Finland, Germany, Italy, Mexico, Norway, Sweden, and the United States.

A.4. Biases from Not Reporting Terms of Sale

We made some steps to investigate this bias. When the SDC field reported other considerations we made efforts using stories from local media to see if subsequent to the announcement the other considerations became known. For almost all cases we were unsuccessful. However, for Malaysia, a country with an active business press, we were able to identify additional information. For the years 1995 and 1996, we identified all stories regardless of whether SDC included a transaction price or not. Using this technique we identified nine transactions not identified in our original sample and we were able to identify prices reported in the local press for eight of these transactions. Comparing the estimated private benefits from these transactions and from our reported transactions is revealing. The average control premia is similar between the initial sample used and this new SDC sample with unreported prices with a control premia as a percentage of equity of 6.9 percent for our core sample and 4.5 percent for our sample of "unreported prices."

Table AI

Laws Regarding Control Transactions

Country	Law Requiring Mandatory Purchase of Additional Shares	Voluntary Code Requiring Purchase of Additional Shares	Shareholding that Triggers Mandatory Purchase of Shares	Year of Passage of Dominant Legal Statute	Legal and Regulatory Bases on Takeovers
Argentina	N		—	—	Resolution 227, National Securities Commission
Australia	Y		20	1989	Corporations Law
Austria*	Y		30	1999	Council of Vienna Stock Exchange, State Commissioner
Brazil (1)	Y		50	1976	Law 6404, law 9457, CVM rule #299
Canada	Y		20	1975	Canada Business Corporations Act, Provincial legislation
Chile (2)	N		—	1994	Law 18.045
Colombia	N		—	1979	Act No. 32
Czech Republic	Y		50	1991	Czech Commercial Code
Denmark	Y		50	n/a	Danish Securities Trading Act, Stock Exchange Ethics Rules
Egypt			?		
Finland	Y		67	1989	Securities Market Act
France	Y		33	1992	COB regulations, Stock Exchange Council
Germany* (3)	N	Y	50	1995	Voluntary takeover code (Ubernahmekodex)
Hong Kong	N	Y	35	1975	Hong Kong code on Takeovers and Mergers
Indonesia	Y		20	1995	Decree of Capital Market Supervisory Agency No. 22/PM/1
Israel	N		—		
Italy	Y		30	1998	Law no. 149
Japan	N		—		Securities and Exchange Law Ch. II.2
Kenya	N		—	1985	Company Act, Capital Markets Authority Act
Malaysia	Y		33	1993	Malaysian Code on takeovers and mergers, Companies Act
Mexico	N		—		Corporation Law, Credit Law, other regulatory acts
Netherlands	N		—	1970	Merger Code of the Social Economic Council
New Zealand	N		—	1986	Companies Act 1986
Norway	Y		45	1985	Securities Trading Act
Peru	N		—		Stock Market Law
Phillipines* (4)	Y		—	1998	Revised tender-offer rules, Securities and exchange commission
Poland	Y		33	1991	Act on Public Trading in Securities and Trust Funds

Portugal	Y		50	1986	Securities Act
Singapore	N	Y	25	1985	Singapore Code on Takeovers and Mergers
South Africa	Y		30	1991	Securities Regulation Code on Takeovers and Mergers
South Korea	Y		25	?	Securities and Exchange Law
Spain	Y		25	1991	Law No. 24, Royal Decree 1197
Sweden	N		—	1991	Financial Instruments Trading Act
Switzerland*	Y	Y	33	1998	Federal Act on Stock Exchanges and Securities Trading
Taiwan	N		—	1988	Securities and exchange Law, company law 1983
Thailand	Y		25	1992	Securities and Exchange Act
Turkey*	Y		25	1986	Capital Market Law
United Kingdom	N	Y	30	1968	City code on Takeovers and Mergers
United States	N		—	1934	Securities and Exchange Act
Venezuela	N		—	—	Capital Markets Law

Sources: ISSA All data from ISSA Handbook, 6th and 7th edition.

(1) Prior to 1997, Brazil law 6404 required equal offer to minority investors with voting shares (but not nonvoting preferred shares). This protection eliminated in May 1997 (Law 9457) with reform to enhance privatization proceeds. In 1999, CVM rule #299 reintroduces protections for minorities, now extending to voting and nonvoting class an equal price offer.

(2) In December 2000 (after our observations) Chile has a new law, ley de OPSAS, governing control transactions.

(3) Germany has a voluntary takeover code (Ubernahmekodex) in place since 1995. This code "was deemed a failure in early 2000, when both stock market supervisors and the takeover commission appointed by Mr. Schröder demanded a mandatory law." EIE Country Commerce, section 2.2. 2000.

(4) The Securities and Exchange Commission "issued tender-offer rules in October 1998 outlining the requirements for acquiring majority control in existing companies through open-market purchases or private negotiations. The new rules implement Section 33 of the Revised Securities Code and require bidders for majority control of listed companies to make the same offer of purchase to minority share holders. (EIU March 1999). The SEC generally failed to enforce tender-offer rules in major deals involving mergers and acquisitions from 1998 to 2000 because of loop holes in the old regulations (EIU March 2001).

Securities Regulation Code (RA 8799 effective August 2000, implementing rules January 2001) requires those assembling >15% to make offer.

Note: Canada has both federal and provincial legislation, where Ontario is most important. Rules require mandatory offer if >20% of voting shares, whereby at least a pro-rata offer for % bought although usually either for 2/3 or 90% of voting rights.

Table AII

Number of Firms with Equities Priced in Datastream, by Year

Country Code	1989	1990	1991	1992	1993	1994	1995	1996	1997	1998	1999	2000	1990–2000
AR	12	13	14	23	61	66	70	73	78	80	84	93	655
AU	452	474	487	515	594	697	741	1095	1176	1178	1287	1506	9750
BD	618	700	735	742	777	800	835	893	926	1015	1188	1348	9959
BR		75	143	234	314	371	371	456	481	500	540	557	4042
CB				104	109	133	122	113	108	98	85	72	944
CL	115	127	134	151	164	170	177	196	209	220	219	221	1988
CN	1502	1971	1976	2024	2195	2353	2473	2653	2981	3222	3352	3759	28959
CZ					38	57	91	114	129	128	131	126	814
DK	205	210	249	252	261	267	277	296	295	303	291	304	3005
ES	110	125	133	138	149	152	154	165	184	211	234	264	1909
EY						10	12	65	72	82	101	103	445
FN	58	67	70	71	76	123	128	153	178	198	228	258	1550
FR	508	628	640	663	693	793	859	1084	1143	1287	1229	1416	10435
HK	251	266	322	371	429	494	518	567	676	723	756	1072	6194
ID		107	120	133	150	192	213	225	259	261	292	313	2265
IS	196	202	201	267	475	542	558	567	569	593	667	710	5351
IT	283	309	319	323	325	348	366	388	406	419	443	535	4181
JP	2011	2321	2520	2592	2677	2954	3136	3347	3552	3582	3829	4304	34814

Private Benefits of Control   597

	1	1	43	42	45	48	47	51	52	53	50	47	
KN	604	660	678	685	694	739	796	1017	1135	1140	1299	1569	476
KO	46	52	75	99	132	151	145	152	172	163	170	160	10412
MX	346	404	447	493	544	607	663	757	847	872	738	776	1471
MY	237	260	271	273	277	288	303	326	361	408	437	482	7148
NL	80	97	100	114	128	160	182	217	273	287	269	274	3686
NW	68	74	80	91	111	126	130	145	154	153	157	176	2101
NZ			22	48	76	98	100	105	102	99	104	96	1397
PE													850
PH	64	96	103	114	137	160	187	212	231	229	222	225	1916
PO			6	11	12	22	27	51	103	167	200	221	820
PT	101	110	116	135	140	149	144	148	155	152	143	148	1540
SA	161	458	454	469	483	526	535	606	641	724	770	736	6402
SD	177	197	202	213	232	296	318	362	442	484	532	633	3911
SG	142	172	176	195	222	255	273	293	337	348	409	534	3214
SW	259	295	295	290	309	325	343	375	390	401	426	459	3908
TA	161	178	199	240	271	305	340	451	515	620	738	856	4713
TH	244	291	350	410	441	521	537	576	602	579	546	531	5384
TK	70	100	125	135	152	178	209	236	270	298	302	387	2392
UK	1812	1872	1749	1713	1782	1841	1932	2084	2222	2272	2301	2625	22393
US	274	393	415	419	427	438	462	662	929	1235	2671	4743	12794
VE		10	10	11	14	19	21	22	23	25	29	53	237
Grand Total	11,168	13,315	13,979	14,803	16,116	17,771	18,795	21,298	23,378	24,809	27,469	32,692	224,425

598   *The Journal of Finance*

REFERENCES

Aghion, Philippe, and Patrick Bolton, 1992, An incomplete contract approach to financial contracting, *Review of Economic Studies* 59, 473–494.

Barclay, Michael, and Clifford Holderness, 1989, Private benefits of control of public corporations, *Journal of Financial Economics* 25, 371–395.

Bebchuk, Lucien, 1999, A rent-protection theory of corporate ownership and control, Working paper 7203, NBER.

Bebchuk, Lucien, and Christine Jolls, 1999, Managerial value diversion and shareholder wealth, *Journal of Law, Economics and Organization* 2, 487–502.

Burkart, Mike, Denis Gromb, and Fausto Panunzi, 1998, Why higher takeover premia protect minority shareholders, *Journal of Political Economy* 106, 172–204.

Coffee, John, 1999, The future as history: The prospects for global convergence in corporate governance and its implications, *Northwestern University Law Review* 93, 641–708.

Coffee, John, 2001, Do norms matter? A cross-country examination of private benefits of control, Mimeo, Columbia University Law School.

DeAngelo, Harry, and Linda De Angelo, 1985, Managerial ownership of voting rights, *Journal of Financial Economics* 14, 36–39.

Demsetz, Harold, and Kenneth Lehn, 1985, The structure of corporate ownership: Causes and consequences, *Journal of Political Economy* 93, 1155–1175.

Djankov, Simeon, and Peter Murrell, 2000, The determinants of enterprise restructuring in transition: An assessment of the evidence, Working paper, University of Maryland.

Doidge, Craig, 2002, U.S. cross listings and the private benefits of control: Evidence from dual class firms, Working paper, University of Toronto.

Doidge, Craig, Andrew Karolyi, and Renee Stulz, 2001, Why are foreign firms listed in the U.S. worth more? Working paper, Ohio State University.

Dyck, I.J. Alexander, 2000, Ownership structure, legal protections and corporate governance, in Boris Pleskovic, and Nicholas Stern, eds.: *Annual World Bank Conference on Development Economics*.

Dyck, I.J. Alexander, 2001, Privatization and corporate governance: principles, evidence and future challenges, *World Bank Research Observer* 1, 59–84.

Dyck, I.J. Alexander, and Luigi Zingales, 2002a, Private benefits of control: An international comparison, Working paper 8711, NBER.

Dyck, I.J. Alexander, and Luigi Zingales, 2002b, The corporate governance role of the media, in Roumeen Islam, ed.: *The Right to Tell: The Role of Mass Media in Economic Development*, Chap. 7 (The World Bank, Washington).

Dyck, I.J. Alexander, and Luigi Zingales, 2003, The bubble and the media, in Peter Cornelius, and Bruce Kogut, eds.: *Corporate Governance and Capital Flows in a Global Economy*, Chap. 7 (Oxford University Press, New York).

Glaeser, Edward, Simon Johnson, and Andrei Shleifer, 2001, Coase vs. the Coasians, *Quarterly Journal of Economics* 116, 853–900.

Gresik, Thomas, 2001, The taxing task of taxing transnationals, *Journal of Economic Literature* 39, 800–838.

Grossman, Sanford, and Oliver Hart, 1980, Takeover bids, the free rider problem, and the theory of the corporation, *Bell Journal of Economics* 11, 42–69.

Grossman, Sanford, and Oliver Hart, 1988, One share one vote and the market for corporate control, *Journal of Financial Economics* 20, 175–202.

Guiso, Luigi, Paola Sapienza, and Luigi Zingales, 2003, People's opium? Religion and economic attitudes, *Journal of Monetary Economics* 50, 225–282.

Harris, Milton, and Artur Raviv, 1988, Corporate governance: Voting rights and majority rules, *Journal of Financial Economics* 20, 203–235.

Holthausen, Robert, Richard Leftwich, and David Mayers, 1990, Large-block transactions, the speed of response, and temporary and permanent stock price effects, *Journal of Financial Economics* 26, 71–95.

Private Benefits of Control 599

Jensen, Michael, and William Meckling, 1976, Theory of the firm: Managerial behavior, agency costs and ownership structure, *Journal of Financial Economics* 3, 305–360.

Johnson, Simon, Peter Boone, Alasdair Breach, Eric Friedman, 2000, Corporate governance in the Asian financial crisis, *Journal of Financial Economics* 58, 141–186.

Johnson, Simon, Rafael La Porta, Florencio Lopez-de-Salines, and Andrei Shleifer, 2000, Tunneling, *American Economic Review* 90, 22–27.

La Porta, Rafael, Florencio Lopez-de-Salines, and Andrei Shleifer, 1999, Corporate ownership around the world, *Journal of Finance* 54, 471–517.

La Porta, Rafael, Florencio Lopez-de-Salines, and Andrei Shleifer, 2000, Investor protection and corporate governance, *Journal of Financial Economics* 59, 3–27.

La Porta, Rafael, Florencio Lopez-de-Salines, Andrei Shleifer, and Robert W. Vishny, 1997, Legal determinants of external finance, *Journal of Finance* 1, 1131–1150.

La Porta, Rafael, Florencio Lopez-de-Salines, Andrei Shleifer, and Robert W. Vishny, 1998, Law and finance, *Journal of Political Economy* 6, 1113–1155.

Lease, Ronald C., John J. McConnell, and Wayne H. Mikkelson, 1983, The market value of control in publicly traded corporations, *Journal of Financial Economics* 11, 439–471.

Lease, Ronald C., John J. McConnell, and Wayne H. Mikkelson, 1984, The market value of differential voting rights in closely held corporations, *Journal of Business* 4, 443–467.

Lopez-de-Silanes, Florencio, 1997, Determinants of privatization prices, *The Quarterly Journal of Economics* 4, 965–1025.

Megginson, William L., Robert C. Nash, Jeffrey M. Netter, and Annette B. Poulsen, 2000, The choice between private and public markets: Evidence from privatizations, Working paper, University of Georgia.

Milgrom, Paul, and Robert Weber, 1982, A theory of auctions and competitive bidding, *Econometrica* 50, 1089–1122.

Monks, Robert, and Nell Minnow, 1995, *Watching the Watchers: Corporate Governance for the 21st Century* (Blackwell Publishing, Malden, MA).

Morck, Randall, Bernard Yeung, and Wayne Yu, 2000, The information content of stock markets: Why do emerging markets have synchronous stock price movements? *Journal of Financial Economics* 58, 215–260.

Nenova, Tatiana, 2001a, The value of corporate votes and control benefits: A cross-country analysis, Mimeograph, Harvard University.

Nenova, Tatiana, 2001b, Control values and changes in corporate law in Brazil, Working paper, The World Bank.

Nicodano, Giovanna, and Alessandro Sembenelli, 2001, Private benefits, block transaction premiums, and ownership structure, Working paper, Universita' di Torino.

Pagano, Marco, and Paolo Volpin, 2000, The political economy of corporate governance, Working paper, London Business School.

Pistor, Katherina, Martin Raiser, and Satanislaw Gelfer, 2000, Law and finance in transition economies, *Economics of Transition* 82, 325–368.

Rajan, Rajan, and Luigi Zingales 1998, Financial dependence and growth, *American Economic Review* 88, 559–586.

Reese, William, and Michael Weisbach, 2001, Protection of minority shareholder interests, cross-listings in the United States, and subsequent equity offerings, Working paper, NBER.

Reynolds, Thomas H., and Arturo A. Flores, 1989, *Foreign Law: Current Sources of Codes and Basic Legislation in Jurisdictions of the World* (F.B. Rothman, Littleton, CO).

Rydqvist, Kristian, 1987, Empirical investigation of the voting premium, Working paper No. 35, Northwestern University.

Shleifer, Andrei, and Robert Vishny, 1986, Large shareholders and corporate control, *Journal of Political Economy* 94, 461–488.

Shleifer, Andrei, and Robert Vishny, 1997, A survey of corporate governance, *Journal of Finance* 52, 737–783.

Stiglitz, Joseph, 1985, Credit markets and the control of capital, *Journal of Money, Credit and Banking* 17, 133–152.

Stulz, Renee, and Rohan Williamson, 2001, Culture, openness and finance, Working paper 8222, NBER.

Zingales, Luigi, 1994, The value of the voting right: A study of the Milan stock exchange experience, *Review of Financial Studies* 7, 125–148.

Zingales, Luigi, 1995a, What determines the value of corporate votes? *Quarterly Journal of Economics* 110, 1047–1073.

Zingales, Luigi, 1995b, Insider ownership and the decision to go public, *Review of Economic Studies* 62, 425–448.

Zingales, Luigi, 1998, Why it's worth being in control, in George Bickerstaffe, ed.: *The Complete Finance Companion* (FT Pitman Publishing, London).

Zingales, Luigi, 2000, In search of new foundations, *Journal of Finance* 55, 1623–1653.

FERRETING OUT TUNNELING: AN APPLICATION TO
INDIAN BUSINESS GROUPS*

Marianne Bertrand
Paras Mehta
Sendhil Mullainathan

Owners of business groups are often accused of expropriating minority share-holders by tunneling resources from firms where they have low cash flow rights to firms where they have high cash flow rights. In this paper we propose a general methodology to measure the extent of tunneling activities. The methodology rests on isolating and then testing the distinctive implications of the tunneling hypothesis for the propagation of earnings shocks across firms within a group. When we apply our methodology to data on Indian business groups, we find a significant amount of tunneling, much of it occurring via nonoperating components of profit.

I. Introduction

Weak corporate law and lax enforcement mechanisms raise fears of expropriation for minority shareholders around the world. These fears seem especially warranted in the presence of business groups, a common organizational form in many developed and developing countries. In a business group, a single shareholder (or a family) completely controls several independently traded firms and yet has significant cash flow rights in only a few of them.[1] This discrepancy in cash flow rights between the different firms he controls creates strong incentives to expropriate. The controlling shareholder will want to transfer, or *tunnel*, profits across firms, moving them from firms where he has

* We thank Abhijit Banerjee, Simon Johnson, Tarun Khanna, Jayendra Nayak, Ajay Shah, Susan Thomas, two anonymous referees, the editor (Edward Glaeser), and seminar participants at the MIT Development and Public Finance Lunches, the Harvard/MIT Development Seminar, the NBER-NCAER Conference on Reforms, the Harvard Business School Conference on Emerging Markets, the University of Michigan, the London Business School, the London School of Economics, the University of Chicago Graduate School of Business, and Princeton University for their useful comments. The second author is also grateful for financial support from a National Science Foundation Graduate Fellowship.
1. In many cases, control is maintained through indirect ownership. For example, the ultimate owner may own firm A, which in turn owns firm B, which in turn owns firm C. Such ownership structures, which are quite common according to La Porta, Lopez-d-Silanes, Shleifer, and Vishny [1999], are called pyramids. It is the chain of ownership in pyramids that generates the sharp divergence between control and cash flow rights. Dual class shares are another way to generate such a divergence. In India, the country we study below, dual class shares have not been allowed so far, although recent legislation has attempted to change this.

The Quarterly Journal of Economics, February 2002

low cash flow rights to firms where he has high cash flow rights.[2] Cash can be transferred in many ways: the firms can give each other high (or low) interest rate loans, manipulate transfer prices, or sell assets to each other at above or below market prices, to list just a few. If prevalent, tunneling may have serious consequences. By reducing the returns to being an outside shareholder, it can hinder equity market growth and overall financial development. Illicit profit transfers may also reduce the transparency of the entire economy, clouding the accounting numbers and complicating any inference about firms' health. In fact, several observers argued that tunneling made it hard to assess solvency during the emerging market crises of 1997–1998, and possibly exacerbated the crisis.[3]

Anecdotes of tunneling are easy to find. In India, for example, one group firm, Kalyani Steels, had more than two-thirds of its net worth invested in other companies in its group. Yet these investments yielded less than a 1 percent rate of return, fueling speculation that they were merely a way to tunnel profits out of Kalyani Steels. However, hard evidence of tunneling beyond anecdotes of this kind remains scarce, perhaps because of the illicit nature of this activity. The strongest statistical evidence so far is cross-sectional: group firms where the controlling shareholder has higher cash flow rights have higher q-ratios and greater profitability.[4] While informative, this cross-sectional relationship is not a test of tunneling since it could also result from differences in preexisting efficiency or any number of other unobservable factors.

This paper introduces a general procedure to quantify tunneling. It is based on tracing the propagation of earnings shocks

---

2. Johnson, La Porta, Lopez-de-Silanes, and Shleifer [2000] argue that the expropriation threat is especially big in business groups. Bebchuk, Kraakman, and Triantis [2000], Wolfenzon [1999], and Shleifer and Wolfenzon [2000] provide theoretical models of various forms of tunneling. In the United States something akin to business groups existed historically, although cartelization was the major issue surrounding them. In modern times, expropriation of shareholders in large U. S. firms is thought to occur through poor decision making [Berle and Means 1934; Jensen and Meckling 1976] or high executive compensation [Bertrand and Mullainathan 2000, 2001].

3. Johnson, Boone, Breach, and Friedman [2000] show that countries with better legal protection against tunneling were less affected by the crisis.

4. Examples of papers that have documented such correlations include Bianchi, Bianco, and Enriques [1999], Claessens, Djankov, Fan, and Lang [1999], and Claessens, Djankov, and Lang [2000]. A broader literature has studied groups more generally [Khanna and Palepu 2000; Hoshi, Kashyap, and Scharfstein 1991]. Other papers have documented differences in the price of voting and nonvoting shares [Zingales 1995; Nenova 1999].

FERRETING OUT TUNNELING   **123**

through a business group. Consider a group with two firms: firm H, where the controlling shareholder has high cash flow rights, and firm L, where he has low cash flow rights. Suppose that firm L experiences a shock that would (in the absence of tunneling) cause its profits to rise by 100 dollars. Because some of this increase will be tunneled out of firm L, the actual profits of firm L will rise by less than 100 dollars, with the shortfall measuring the amount of diversion. Since the shortfall is being tunneled to H, we would also expect H to respond to L's shock even though H is not directly affected by it. Moreover, we would not expect this pattern if instead H were to receive the shock: there is no incentive to tunnel from a high- to a low-cash-flow-right firm.[5] We develop a general set of tests based on these observations and use variation in mean industry performance as a source of profit shocks.[6]

As an illustration, we apply this test to a panel of Indian firms. We find evidence for the full set of predictions implied by tunneling. Other results suggest that these findings are not due to mismeasurement of a firm's industry, simple coinsurance within groups or internal capital markets. Moreover, the magnitudes of the effects we find are large: more than 25 percent of the marginal rupee of profits in low-cash-flow-right firms appears to be dissipated.[7]

Our procedure further allows us to examine the mechanics of tunneling. Indian groups appear to tunnel by manipulating nonoperating components of profits (such as miscellaneous and nonrecurring items). In fact, there is no evidence of tunneling on operating profits alone. Rather, nonoperating losses and gains seem to be used to offset real profit shocks or transfer cash from other firms. Finally, we examine whether market prices incorporate tunneling. We find that high market-to-book firms are more

5. This asymmetry is important. Money flows only from low- to high-cash-flow-right firms, not vice versa. As we will see, this is a crucial distinction between tunneling and other theories of why shocks might propagate through a group, most notably risk sharing.

6. Other papers have used shocks in a related way. Blanchard, Lopez-de-Silanes, and Shleifer [1994] examine how U. S. firms respond to windfalls (winning a law suit) to assess agency models. Lamont [1997] uses the oil shock to assess the effects of cash flow on investment. Bertrand and Mullainathan [2001] use several shock measures to assess the effects of luck on CEO pay.

7. It is worth noting that business groups may add social value in other ways that offset the social costs they may impose through tunneling. They might help reduce transaction costs, solve external market failures, or provide reputational capital for their members. We will not, therefore, be attempting to test whether groups are on net bad but merely whether, and if so how much, they tunnel.

sensitive to both their own shock and shocks to the other firms in their group. Firms whose *group* has a high market-to-book are also more sensitive to their own shock, but are not significantly more sensitive to the group's shock. This suggests that the stock market at least partly penalizes tunneling activities.

II. A TEST FOR TUNNELING

We begin by describing the exact implications of tunneling for the propagation of shocks.[8] Let us return to the fictional example of two group firms, high-cash-flow-right firm H and low-cash-flow-right firm L. Consider again a 100-dollar profits shock affecting firm L. Because the controlling shareholder would benefit more if these 100 dollars were in H, he will look for a way to divert them out of L. This gives the first prediction: group firms should on average underrespond to shocks to their own profits.

Of course, since tunneling may be costly (either because of resource dissipation or because of a risk of being caught), the controlling shareholder may transfer only some of the 100 dollars out of firm L. How much he transfers will be a function of his cash flow rights in L. The less his cash flow rights in L, the less he values the extra dollar left in L and the more of the profits he will want to tunnel out of L. This gives the second prediction: the underresponse to shocks to own profits should be larger in low-cash-flow-right firms.

The cash tunneled from firm L eventually ends up in firm H. So H will appear to respond to L's shock even though H is not directly affected by L's shock. This gives the third prediction: group firms will on average be sensitive to shocks affecting other firms in the group.[9]

We know from above that when cash flow rights in firm L are low, more money will be tunneled out of L. But this also implies that more money will be tunneled into H when cash flow rights in L are low. This gives the fourth prediction: group firms will be more sensitive to shocks affecting low-cash-flow-right firms in their group than to shocks affecting high-cash-flow-right firms.

8. Bertrand, Mehta, and Mullainathan [2000] present a model that formalizes these implications.
9. This prediction distinguishes tunneling from a pure mismanagement interpretation of the profits shortfall. The first two predictions could simply reflect a dissipation of resources through inefficient operation rather than a diversion to other group firms.

Finally, suppose that a 100-dollar shock were now to affect firm H instead of firm L. Since the controlling shareholder has more cash flow rights in H than in L, he will have no incentives to tunnel from H to L. This means that H will respond one for one to its own shock, which is just another way to understand the second prediction above. It also means that L will not be sensitive to H's shock. A more general version of this observation gives the fifth prediction: low-cash-flow-right firms will be less sensitive to shocks affecting other firms in their group.

To transform these general predictions into testable implications, we need to isolate specific shocks using available data. Industry shocks provide an ideal candidate since they affect individual firms but are to a large extent beyond the control of individual firms. Some notation will be helpful in defining these mean industry movements. Let $perf_{ktI}$ be a level measure of reported performance for firm k in industry I at time t (in our case profits before depreciation, interest, and taxes). A_{ktI} be a measure of the firm k's assets (in our case, total book value of assets), and $r_{ktI} = perf_{ktI}/A_{ktI}$ be a measure of return on assets for that firm. To isolate the industry shock, we compute the asset-weighted average return for all firms in industry I: $\hat{r}_{It} = \Sigma_k A_{ktI} r_{ktI} / \Sigma_k A_{ktI}$.[10] Given this industry return, we can predict what firm k's performance ought to be in the absence of tunneling by calculating $pred_{ktI} = A_{ktI} * \hat{r}_{It}$.

Our empirical test will then consist of regressing a firm's actual reported performance on its predicted performance and on the predicted performance of other firms in its group.[11] More specifically, we can test the five implications above: (1) group firms should be less sensitive to shocks to their industry than nongroup (stand-alone) firms; (2) low-cash-flow-right group firms will show smaller sensitivities to shocks to their industry than high-cash-flow-right ones; (3) group firms should be sensitive to industry shocks affecting other firms in their group; (4) group firms should be especially sensitive to shocks affecting the low cash-flow-right firms in their group; (5) low-cash-flow-right group

10. A mechanical correlation arises if we include a firm itself in estimating its industry return and then use that industry return to predict the firm's own return. To prevent this, we exclude, for every firm, the firm itself in computing its industry return. In this sense, $\hat{r}_{It}$ should actually be indexed by k, but we drop this subscript for simplicity.

11. Given that this is a predicted *level* of performance, our terminology of shocks may seem inappropriate. But since we include firm fixed effects, we will in fact be identifying the effect of industry *shocks*.

firms should show smaller sensitivities in predictions 3 and 4. These five predictions form a simple test of tunneling, one that requires only firm-level data on earnings, industry, group membership, and ownership structure.[12]

III. AN APPLICATION TO INDIAN BUSINESS GROUPS

We now apply this test to Indian data. As in many other countries, group firms in India are often linked together through the ownership of equity shares. In most cases, the controlling shareholder is a family; among the best-known business families in India are Tata, Bajaj, Birla, Oberoi, and Mahindra.[13]

Nominally, corporate governance laws in India are quite good, consistent with its English colonial past and its common law heritage [Sarkar and Sarkar 1999]. In reality, however, corruption makes these laws difficult to enforce and shareholder expropriation a major concern in India. In recent years the role of corporate governance in financial development has received significant attention from the Indian business press and central government. Business groups have come under particular scrutiny for advancing their private interests at the expense of outside shareholders.[14] Tunneling is also allegedly a problem.[15] Indeed, greater oversight of related party transactions was one of

---

12. A notable feature of these tests is their symmetry. One might have thought that there should be no tunneling for negative groups. This is in fact not clear. For example, suppose that an industry earns a 10 percent natural rate of return and a negative shock reduces it to 5 percent. Since this reduces the amount that can be tunneled out, we will see just as much sensitivity to this shock (for example, among high-cash-flow-right group firms) as to a positive one. Rather than asymmetry in changes, one might expect that below some nominal rate of return, tunneling would cease. A priori, it is unclear where this threshold lies. We tried some thresholds (e.g., zero nominal rate of return) and found standard errors that were too large to reject either linearity or significant nonlinearity. Johnson and Friedman [2000] provide further discussion of asymmetry.

13. Piramal [1996] and Dutta [1997] provide accounts of groups in India.

14. One Financial Times Asia article charges that the "boards of Indian companies, especially the family-owned ones, are prime examples of crony capitalism. They are invariably filled with family members and friends. . . . In such an environment, the promoter can operate to further his own interests even as he takes the other shareholders for a ride."

15. A 1998 Financial Times Asia article reports that "[c]hanneling funds to subsidiaries and group companies in the form of low or nil interest loans or low-yield investments is not new. Such a lockup of costly funds often results in poor financial performance. JCT, Kalyani Steels, Bombay Burmah Trading Company; and DCM Shriram Industries are examples. JCT's average return over the last four years on outstanding loans and advances of Rs. 270 crores is just 4 percent. Similarly Kalyani Steels' 1996–97 investments in group companies was worth Rs. 196.80 crores—more than two-thirds its net worth—while the company earned just 1.45 crores as dividends."

the specific recommendations made by a government committee organized to study corporate governance.[16] Thus, with its weak corporate governance and allegations of impropriety, India provides an ideal location to test for tunneling.

III.A. Data Source

We use Prowess, a publicly available database maintained by the Centre for Monitoring Indian Economy (CMIE). Prowess includes annual report information for companies in India between 1989 and 1999. It provides much of the information needed for this analysis: financial statements, industry information, group affiliation for each firm, and some corporate ownership data. We exclude state-owned and foreign-owned firms from our sample since these may not be comparable to the private sector domestic firms that interest us. Our sample contains about 18,500 firm-year observations, although sample sizes vary because of missing variables for some firms.[17]

We rely on CMIE classification of firms into group and non-group firms, and of group firms into specific group affiliation. CMIE classification is based on a "continuous monitoring of company announcements and a qualitative understanding of the groupwise behavior of individual companies" (Prowess Users' Manual, v.2, p.4). Note also that CMIE assigns each company to a unique ownership group, based on the group most closely associated with that company. Conversations with local experts corroborate these classifications; which group a firm belongs to is widely known.

---

16. The Kumar Mangalam Committee recommended measures to strengthen the board of directors' role in "reduc[ing] potential conflict between the specific interests of management and the wider interests of the company and shareholders including misuse of corporate assets and abuse in related party transactions." These measures included guidelines for strengthening the independence of boards and for the establishment of an audit committee by the board of directors to review, among other things, "[a]ny related party transactions, i.e. transactions of the company of material nature with promoters or the management, their subsidiaries or relatives, etc. that may have potential conflict with the interests of the company at large."

17. Prowess does not use consolidated accounting data, which implies that our findings are not caused by accounting mechanics. In fact, during the sample period under study, Indian accounting standards did not require disclosing consolidated accounts for group firms. Very few firms used consolidated financial statements in practice [Price, Waterhouse & Co. 1999].

III.B. Measurement of Controlling Shareholder's Cash Flow Rights

A key variable in our analysis is the cash flow rights of the controlling shareholder in a particular firm. There are two components to cash flow rights. First are *direct* rights, which are derived from shares that the controlling shareholder (or his family) has in the company. Second are *indirect* rights, which are derived from shares held by another company in which the controlling shareholder has some shares.

Prowess provides two reasonable proxies for direct cash flow rights. Both are derived from data on equity holding patterns, which is available for about 60 percent of firms (all of them publicly traded). For these firms, CMIE reports the shares of equity held by foreigners, directors, various financial institutions, banks, various governmental bodies, the top fifty shareholders, corporate bodies, and others.[18]

As in many countries, Indian families typically control the firms they have financial stakes in by appointing family members or family friends to the board of directors and to top managerial positions. Since the company shares held by these board members benefit the controlling shareholder in some sense, the information on director ownership provides a first proxy for direct cash flow rights.[19]

The equity held by "other shareholders," where others are defined as shareholders that are neither directors, nor banks, nor foreigners, not financial institutions, nor government bodies, nor corporate bodies, nor the top fifty shareholders, provides a second proxy. By measuring the shares held by small, minority share-

---

18. The exact ownership categories reported by CMIE are Foreigners, Insurance Companies, Life Insurance Corporation, General Insurance Corporation, Mutual Funds, Unit Trust of India, Financial Institutions (Industrial Financial Corporation of India, Industrial Development Bank of India, Industrial Credit and Investment Bank of India, Industrial Credit and Investment Corporation, Commercial Banks), Government Companies (Central Government Companies, State Government Companies), State Finance Corporation, Other Government Organizations, Corporate Bodies, Directors, Top Fifty Shareholders, and Others.

19. For example, the Financial Times Asia reports that "the boards of Indian companies . . . are invariably filled with family members and friends, whether or not they are qualified for the position" [Financial Times Asia Intelligence Wire, October 10, 1999]. The article goes on to say: "In such an environment, the promoter can operate to further his own interests even as he takes the other shareholders for a ride." Of course, if some of the directors are not family members or friends, this proxy will overstate the direct cash flow rights.

holders, it captures the amount of cash flow rights the family does *not* own.[20]

Although both variables are good proxies for direct cash flow rights, they do little to capture indirect cash flow rights. Because Prowess only provides information by ownership category, it is impossible to back out of such indirect cash flow rights.[21] Consequently, our ranking of firms (in terms of cash flow rights) within a group is noisy. For example, suppose that the ultimate owner owns 10 percent of firms A and B and firm B owns 40 percent in firm A. The ultimate owner seemingly has a 10 percent direct cash stake in both firms but actually has a 14 percent stake in firm A. If we modify the example so that the direct ownership stake in firm A is actually 9 percent, then adding indirect cash flow rights reverses the ranking.[22]

Three points should be noted about this important measurement issue. First, indirect cash flow rights by their very nature should be smaller than direct rights because they are diminished as they pass through the chain of ownership. In the above example, despite the large indirect ownership of A by B (40 percent), the final difference is only 4 percent since A has only a 10 percent direct stake in B. Moreover, when our ranking of firms was wrong in the second example above, this was because both B and A were very close in terms of direct cash flow rights (10 percent versus 9 percent).[23] Second, to the extent that any significant error is introduced into our rankings of firms, there will be an attenuation bias. This will bias our estimates toward zero, raise standard errors, and make it *more* difficult to find evidence of tunneling. Finally, although these imperfect measures may make the CMIE

20. The two measures, the equity stake of directors and the equity stake held by minority shareholders, correlate negatively. The correlation is imperfect, however, (about $-.35$ for group firms), suggesting that these are not redundant proxies. Besides measuring the absolute level of director and other equity holdings, we also measure their relative levels within each group. Finally, because we use within-group differences in director and other ownership levels to identify the direction and magnitude of money flows across firms in a business group, we exclude from the sample all groups where there is no difference between the maximum and the minimum level of direct ownership or between the maximum and minimum level of other ownership.

21. Indian disclosure laws do not mandate release of this information. We have attempted to gather this information in many other ways, from investment bankers to the groups themselves; our attempts have been fruitless.

22. We are grateful to an anonymous referee for providing variants of these examples.

23. This is not to say that one cannot construct examples where indicted ownership matters, but rather that because of the multiplication by the direct ownership in firms, indirect ownership will have on average a smaller effect on cash flow rights.

data a less than perfect place to apply our test, it is highly representative of the typical data available to implement our test in most countries. Detailed data on ownership between firms are usually hard to get, whereas many countries have readily available categorical ownership data of the kind provided by CMIE.

III.C. Measurement of Performance

The CMIE data were collected with a focus on accounting numbers. Consequently, we cannot use it to compute reliable annual stock return measures for many firms between 1989 and 1999. More specifically, we lack dividend data for many observations, which is especially troubling since dividend payments would be the most direct way for a controlling shareholder to affect final returns.[24] Moreover, comparisons with both aggregate data and data on specific firms from the Bombay Stock Exchange show that the stock prices reported on CMIE are themselves noisy. In several cases, the returns we computed lagged or led true returns.[25] These problems constrain us to use the more reliable "profits before depreciation, interest and tax" as our specific performance measure, $perf_{ktI}$. Our asset measure, $Assets_{ktI}$, is total assets. Each firm's industry comes from CMIE's classification of firms into industries. Our sample contains 134 different "four-digit" industries.[26]

III.D. Summary Statistics

Table I reports summary statistics for the full sample and for group and nongroup firms separately. In this table, and throughout the remainder of the paper, nongroup firms are referred to as "stand-alones." Group firms and stand-alones, respectively, account for about 7,500 and 11,000 of the observations in our full sample. All nominal variables in the sample are deflated using

24. By examining the firms with some, not necessarily reliable dividend data, we see that dividends are a sizable fraction of returns.
25. Despite the noisiness, we did estimate the regressions below using market value as a dependent variable, and the results are quite similar. But, because of ths noisiness of the data, we do not have great faith in these results. They are available as Table B in the unpublished appendix, available from the authors upon request. The average level of market capitalization appears much more reliable, however, and we use it in subsection IV.B. to relate q ratios to the extent of tunneling.
26. They can be found in Table A of the appendix available from the authors upon request. The breakdown is at roughly the level of the four-digit SIC code in the United States.

TABLE I

SUMMARY STATISTICS

Sample:	All	Groups	Stand-alones
Total assets	131.80	252.76	49.69
	(525.91)	(741.6)	(272.66)
Total sales	94.39	188.16	30.73
	(305.66)	(459.77)	(57.84)
Profit before depreciation, interest, and	16.84	32.90	5.94
taxes	(63.84)	(90.99)	(30.48)
Ratio of PBDIT to total assets	.126	.142	.115
	(.128)	(.115)	(.134)
Ratio of operating profit to total assets	.284	.328	.254
	(.285)	(.312)	(.261)
Ratio of nonoperating profit to total assets	−.157	−.186	−1.38
	(.259)	(.288)	(.235)
q ratio	.537	.645	.447
	(.818)	(.916)	(.714)
Year of incorporation	1974.55	1967.51	1979.33
	(20.03)	(22.89)	(16.18)
Director equity	16.70	7.45	22.99
	(18.33)	(13.05)	(18.72)
Other ownership	29.90	27.57	31.48
	(17.39)	(16.06)	(18.07)
Director equity spread	—	15.19	—
		(14.88)	
Other ownership spread		33.31	
		(21.66)	
Sample size	18600	7521	11079

a. *Data Source:* Prowess, Centre for Monitoring Indian Economy (CMIE), for the years 1989–1999. All monetary variables are expressed in 1995 Rs. crore, where crore represents 10 million.

  b. Standard deviations are in parentheses.

  c. "Operating profit" refers to manufacturing sales revenue minus total raw material expenses, energy expenses, and wages and salaries. "q ratio" is the ratio of market valuation to total assets. "Director equity spread" is the difference between the minimum and maximum level of director equity in a group; "Other ownership spread" is the difference between the minimum and maximum level of other ownership in a group. Ownership and ownership spread variables are measured in percentages and so range from 0 to 100.

the Consumer Price Index series from the International Financial Statistics of the International Monetary Fund (1995 = 100).

    The average group firm in the sample belongs to a group with fifteen firms. Many groups in our data, however, consist of two or three firms.[27] Group firms are, on average, twelve years older than nongroup firms: the typical group firm was created in 1967,

    27. Some ownership groups have several smaller companies that are set up for taxation or retail business purposes. It is much more difficult for CMIE to get access to the annual reports of these smaller companies. CMIE also tracks sub-

TABLE II
SENSITIVITY TO OWN SHOCK: GROUP VERSUS STAND-ALONE
DEPENDENT VARIABLE: PROFIT BEFORE DIT

	(1)	(2)	(3)	(4)
Own shock	1.05	.10	−4.58	−5.10
	(.02)	(.05)	(.48)	(.47)
Own shock* group	**−.30**	**−.30**	**−.26**	**−.27**
	(.02)	(.02)	(.02)	(.02)
Ln assets	.16	2.98	−.33	2.47
	(.32)	(.34)	(.33)	(.34)
Own shock* ln assets	—	.10	—	1.0
		(.00)		(.01)
Own shock* year of incorp.	—	—	.003	.003
			(.000)	(.000)
Sample size	18600	18600	18588	18588
Adjusted R^2	.93	.93	.93	.93

a. *Data Source:* Prowess, Centre for Monitoring Indian Economy, for years 1989–1999. All monetary variables are expressed in 1995 Rs. crore, where crore represents 10 million. Sample includes both stand-alone and group firms.
b. All regressions also include year fixed effect and firm fixed effects.
c. Standard errors are in parentheses.

the typical stand-alone firm in 1979. More importantly, group firms tend to be much larger than stand-alones. The average group firm has total assets of Rs. 253 crores, while the average stand-alone has total assets of Rs. 52 crores. Stand-alones also have lower levels of sales and profits. We will control for these size and age differences in our analysis.

The average level of director ownership among group firms is 7.5 percent. The average level of ownership by other shareholders is 27.5 percent. The gap in director ownership between the top and bottom of a group (i.e., the gap between the firm with the highest level of director ownership and the firm with the lowest level of director ownership) is 15 percent on average. The average gap in other ownership is 33 percent.

III.E. Sensitivity to Own Shock

In Table II we test the first prediction of tunneling: group firms should be less sensitive to shocks to their own industry than stand-alones. We estimate

---

sidiary companies with small turnover but does not include them in the database we use in this paper.

$$(1) \quad perf_{kt} = a + b(pred_{kt}) + c(group_k * pred_{kt})$$
$$+ d(controls_{kt}) + Firm_k + Time_t,$$

where $group_k$ is a dummy variable for whether firm k is in a group or not, $controls_{kt}$ are other variables that might affect firm performance (specifically age and log assets), $Firm_k$ are firm fixed effects, and $Time_t$ are time dummies.[28] The coefficient b measures the general sensitivity of firms to industry performance; the interaction term $group_k * pred_{kt}$ captures the differential sensitivity of group firms. If group firms are less sensitive, as tunneling would predict, then c should be negative. Note that because the regression is expressed in performance levels, the magnitude of the effects can easily be interpreted.

Column (1) displays our basic result. A one-rupee shock leads to about a one-rupee (1.05) increase in earnings for a stand-alone firm. For a group firm, it leads to .3 rupee smaller increase, or only a .75 rupee increase.[29] This suggests that 30 percent of all the money placed into a group firm is somehow dissipated.

In Table I we saw that stand-alone firms are smaller and older on average than group firms. This could confound our estimate of the effect of group affiliation if size or age affects a firm's responsiveness to shocks. In column (2) we include an interaction between the logarithm of total assets and the industry shock. In column (3) we do the same for age. In column (4) we include both interactions simultaneously. The direct effects are always included. From these, it is clear that both size and age do affect the responsiveness to shocks. But it is also clear that the difference between group and stand-alone firms remains significant even in the presence of additional controls.[30] In short, the data support the first prediction.

28. The inclusion of firm fixed effects deals with several issues. First, even though we are using level of predicted performance, we are identifying off of changes in predicted performance, hence our use of the term "shocks" throughout the paper. Second, the fixed effects account for any inherent, fixed differences between firms. Third, because firms do not change groups in our sample, the firm fixed effects also account for any fixed differences between groups.

29. We have also estimated this and all regressions below excluding small groups, which we define as groups with less than five firms in the CMIE data. The results were not affected when we restrict ourselves to that subsample.

30. We have also attempted more flexible specifications by allowing for more nonlinear terms for size and age in the interaction. These produced identical results.

The second prediction provides a more stringent test: *within*-group firms, high-cash-flow-right firms should show greater sensitivity to own shocks. We estimate for the set of group firms

$$(2) \quad perf_{kt} = a + b(pred_{kt}) + c(cash_k * pred_{kt})$$
$$+ \, d(controls_{kt}) + Firm_k + Time_t,$$

where $cash_k$ is the cash flow rights of the controlling party in firm k, measured either with director or other ownership. The interaction term, $cash_k * pred_{kt}$, measures differential sensitivity by level of cash flow rights. Under the tunneling hypothesis, we would expect $c > 0$.[31]

Panel A of Table III uses director equity as the proxy for cash flow rights. Column (1) shows that group firms where director equity is higher are more sensitive to their own industry shock. Each one-percentage point increase in director equity increases the sensitivity to a one-rupee industry shock by .03 rupee. Recall that among group firms, the average difference in director ownership between the firm with the greatest and the firm with the lowest director ownership was about 15. Thus, for each rupee of industry shock, the typical firm with the highest director ownership is .45 rupee more sensitive than the typical firm with the lowest director ownership. This suggests that group firms with high controlling party's cash flow rights may be as sensitive to the marginal rupee as stand-alone firms. The magnitude of this effect is striking and suggests that ownership plays a large role in the extent of the sensitivity.

To assess whether the findings in column (1) capture some aspects of director ownership that are unrelated to group membership, we reestimate equation (2) in column (3) on the subsample of stand-alone firms. We find that director ownership also increases the responsiveness to shocks for stand-alone firms. The effect, however, is quantitatively much smaller, only a sixth of the size of the effect for group firms (.004 versus .025 for group firms).

In columns (2) and (4) we allow for the effect of own industry shock to differ by firm size and firm age. These additional controls do not alter the estimated coefficient on "Own shock · director equity" for the sample of group firms (column (2)). They do, however, lead to an increase in the coefficient on "Own shock ·

31. When we use "Other ownership" in the interaction, we expect a negative term since this measure is negatively related to cash flow rights.

TABLE III
SENSITIVITY TO OWN SHOCK BY DIRECTOR AND OTHER OWNERSHIP
DEPENDENT VARIABLE: PROFIT BEFORE DIT

Panel A: Director equity

	Sample:			
	Groups (1)	Groups (2)	Stand-alones (3)	Stand-alones (4)
Own shock	.713	−5.075	1.058	−4.316
	(.009)	(.742)	(.006)	(.518)
Own shock * director equity	**.025**	**.030**	**.004**	**.019**
	(.003)	(.003)	(.001)	(.001)
Ln assets	.052	4.261	−.590	1.568
	(.733)	(.807)	(.176)	(.178)
Own shock * ln assets	—	.118		.201
		(.008)		(.006)
Own shock * year of incorp.	—	.002	—	.002
		(.000)		(.000)
Sample size	7521	7510	11079	11078
Adjusted R²	.92	.93	.95	.96

Panel B: Other ownership

	Sample:			
	Groups (1)	Groups (2)	Stand-alones (3)	Stand-alones (4)
Own shock	.919	−5.764	1.033	−3.983
	(.023)	(.743)	(.052)	(.603)
Own shock * other ownership	**−.007**	**−.007**	**.001**	**.002**
	(.001)	(.001)	(.000)	(.000)
Ln assets	1.616	5.189	−.292	2.049
	(.724)	(.806)	(.166)	(.180)
Own shock * ln assets	—	.103	—	.154
		(.008)		(.006)
Own shock * year of incorp.	—	.003	—	.002
		(.003)		(.000)
Sample size	7521	7510	11079	11078
Adjusted R²	.92	.93	.95	.96

a. *Data Source:* Prowess, Centre for Monitoring Indian Economy, for years 1989–1999. All monetary variables are expressed in 1995 Rs. crore, where crore represents 10 million.

b. All regressions also include year fixed effect and firm fixed effects.

c. Standard errors are in parentheses.

director equity" in the sample of stand-alone firms (.019 instead of .004). Because standard errors are relatively small, we can still reject that the effect of director ownership on industry shock sensitivity is the same between group firms and stand-alone firms. More director equity increases the responsiveness of a firm to its own industry shock, and this effect is significantly larger among group firms.

In Panel B of Table III we use our other proxy for direct cash flow rights, the ownership stake of other small shareholders. As predicted, we find that the sensitivity of a group firm to its own industry shock decreases with its level of other ownership. A one-percentage point increase in other ownership decreases the responsiveness of a group firm to a one-rupee shock by about .01 rupee (column (1)). Given that the average spread between highest and lowest other ownership among group firms is about 33, the implied magnitude of the effect is the same as in Panel A. Among stand-alone firms (column (3)) the effect of other ownership is of the opposite sign and economically small. Finally, note that the coefficient on "Own shock · other ownership" is roughly unaffected by the inclusion of controls for firm age and firm size interacted with own industry shock (columns (2) and (4) for group and stand-alone firms, respectively).

In summary, these results in Table III are consistent with the idea that fewer resources are tunneled out of the group firms where the promoting family has higher equity stakes and where there are fewer minority shareholders to expropriate. In fact, group firms where the controlling party has a large stake show the same sensitivity to their own industry shocks as stand-alone firms.

III.F. Sensitivity to Group Shocks

We now examine whether a firm responds to shocks affecting other firms in its group (prediction 3). We estimate

$$(3) \quad perf_{kt} = a + b(pred_{kt}) + c(opred_{kt}) + d(controls_{kt})$$
$$+ Firm_k + Time_t,$$

where $opred_{kt} = \Sigma_{j \neq k} \, pred_{jt}$, the sum being over all other firms in the same business group (excluding the firm itself). A positive

TABLE IV
SENSITIVITY OF GROUP FIRMS TO GROUP AND SUBGROUP SHOCKS
DEPENDENT VARIABLE: PROFIT BEFORE DIT

	(1)	(2)	(3)	(4)	(5)
Own shock	.730	.732	.732	.732	.732
	(.009)	(.009)	(.009)	(.009)	(.009)
Group shock	.011	—	—	—	—
	(.001)				
Shock below median (director equity)	—	.016	—	—	—
		(.002)			
Shock above median (director equity)	—	−.002	—	—	—
		(.005)			
Shock below 66th pctile (director equity)	—	—	.015	—	—
			(.002)		
Shock above 66th pctile (director equity)	—	—	−.001	—	—
			(.001)		
Shock above median (other ownership)	—	—	—	.014	—
				(.002)	
Shock below median (other ownership)	—	—	—	.007	—
				(.004)	
Shock above 33rd pctile (other ownership)	—	—	—	—	.017
					(.002)
Shock below 33rd pctile (other ownership)	—	—	—	—	−.002
					(.004)
Sample size	7521	7521	7521	7521	7521
Adjusted R²	.93	.92	.92	.92	.92

a. *Data Source:* Prowess, Centre for Monitoring Indian Economy, for years 1989–1999. All monetary variables are expressed in 1995 Rs. crore, where crore represents 10 million.

b. Sample is group firms only

c. "Shock below median (director equity)" is a variable that sums the industry shocks to all the firms in the same group (excluding the firm itself) that have below median level of director ownership in their group. All the other subgroup shocks are defined accordingly.

d. Also included in each regression are the logarithm of total assets, year fixed effects, and firm fixed effects.

e. Standard errors are in parentheses.

coefficient on $opred_{kt}$ suggests that firms within a group are in fact sensitive to each other's shocks.[32]

In column (1) of Table IV we find a moderate response of group firms to each other's shocks. The coefficient on "Group shock" of .011 suggests that for each rupee earned by the group, an *average* firm in the group receives .011 rupee. Since we know that group firms underreact by about $1 - .73 = .27$ rupee to a

32. Note that we control for the firm's own shock, $pred_{kt}$. This control means that we do not confuse an overlap of industry between firms in the same group with a flow of cash within that group.

one-rupee shock and since there are about fifteen firms in each group, this coefficient implies that about 61 percent of the money that is tunneled out reappears elsewhere in the group.[33]

The next prediction of tunneling (prediction 4) is that the source of the shock matters: firms should respond more to groups affecting low-cash-flow-right firms than to groups affecting high-cash-flow-right firms. We study this prediction in columns (2) to (5). We define $Hopred_{kt}$ as the sum of shocks affecting all high cash-flow-right firms in k's group and $Lopred_{kt}$ as the equivalent sum for low-cash-flow-right firms. We then estimate

$$(4) \quad perf_{kt} = a + b(pred_{kt}) + c_L(Lopred_{kt}) + c_H(Hopred_{kt})$$
$$+ \, d(controls_{kt}) + Firm_k + Time_t.$$

If group firms are in fact more sensitive to groups to the firms with low cash flow rights, we should find that $c_L > c_H$.

In column (2) we classify a group's firms as low- or high-cash-flow-right using the median director equity in that group as a threshold. We find that firms show greater sensitivity to shocks affecting the low-cash-flow-right firms in their group. A one-rupee shock to firms below group median in terms of director ownership increases the average group firm's earnings by .02 rupee. By contrast, the average group firm's earnings do not respond to industry shocks to firms in the high-cash-flow-right group. Column (3) instead contrasts shocks to firms below and above the sixty-sixth percentile of director equity in their group. This isolates a smaller group of firms in the high-cash-flow-right group and allows resources to be equally skimmed from a larger number of firms. The results are very similar.

In column (4) we classify a group's firms as low- or high-cash-flow-right using the median other shareholders' equity in that group as a threshold. In this case, we find that the average group firm is equally sensitive to shocks to the two subgroups. In column (5) we isolate a larger set of firms with low cash flow rights by using the thirty-third percentile of other shareholders' equity as the breaking point. The results suggest that few to no resources are transferred from the subgroup of firms with low levels of other equity. In contrast, the coefficient on the shock to firms

---

33. The remaining 39 percent may be a dissipation factor, suggesting real costs of redistribution. Alternatively, it may reflect redistribution to firms that are not in our sample. Most notably, tunneling may occur through nonpublic firms such as holding companies, which are not represented in our data set.

TABLE V
SENSITIVITY TO GROUP SHOCK BY LEVEL OF DIRECTOR OWNERSHIP IN GROUP
DEPENDENT VARIABLE: PROFIT BEFORE DIT

	(1)	(2)	(3)	(4)	(5)	(6)	(7)	(8)
				Below topmost firm		Topmost firm		
Level in group:	Lower ⅔	Top ⅓						
Own shock	.62	.89	.63	.63	.63	1.01	1.01	1.01
	(.01)	(.02)	(.01)	(.01)	(.01)	(.02)	(.02)	(.02)
Group shock	.013	.010	.012	—	—	.020	—	—
	(.002)	(.002)	(.001)			(.008)		
Shock below 66th pctile (director equity)	—	—	—	.015	—	—	.032	—
				(.002)			(.012)	
Shock above 66th pctile (director equity)	—	—	—	.003	—	—	.007	—
				(.006)			(.018)	
Shock below 33rd pctile (other ownership)	—	—	—	—	−.000	—	—	−.013
					(.004)			(.025)
Shock above 33rd pctile (other ownership)	—	—	—	—	.017	—	—	.034
					(.002)			(.011)
Sample size	4905	2616	5780	5780	5780	1741	1741	1741
Adjusted R^2	.90	.95	.90	.97	.97	.97	.97	.97

a. *Data Source:* Prowess, Centre for Monitoring Indian Economy, for years 1989–1999. All monetary variables are expressed in 1995 Rs. crore, where crore represents 10 million.

b. Firms are separated into different "Level in group" based on their within-group level of director equity. For example, "Topmost Firm" are the set of firms that have the highest level of director ownership in their group.

c. Also included in each regression are the logarithm of total assets, year fixed effects, and firm fixed effects.

d. Standard errors are in parentheses.

with high levels of other equity is large (about .02) and statistically significant. These results complement the findings in Table III: not only are more resources "disappearing" from low-cash-flow right firms, these resources are also the ones more likely to "show up" elsewhere in the group.

III.G. Does Money Go to the Top?

In Table V we test the final prediction of tunneling: resources should disproportionately flow toward high-cash-flow-right firms. We rank firms based on their within-group level of director equity and construct four different subsamples: firms with below the sixty-sixth percentile of director equity in their group, firms with above the sixty-sixth percentile of director equity in their group, firms with strictly less than the highest level of director equity in their group, and firms with the highest level of director equity in their group. We compare sensitivity to group shocks and subgroup shocks for firms in the four different samples by reestimating equations (3) and (4) separately for these samples. In addition to the variables reported in the table, each regression includes the logarithm of total assets, year fixed effects, and firm fixed effects. The dependent variable in all regressions is still profit before depreciation, interest, and taxes.

When we contrast firms above and below the sixty-sixth percentile in director equity (columns (1) and (2)), we find no statistically significant differences in their sensitivity to the overall group shock. In fact, the point estimate on "Group shock" is higher for firms with low levels of director ownership (.013 versus .010).[34] In columns (3) to (6), we contrast the sensitivity to the group shock for the firms with the highest level of director ownership in their group compared with that for all other firms in the group. With this split of the data, the theoretically expected patterns emerge. Firms at the very top gain about .02 rupee for every one-rupee shock to their group (column (6)). All the other firms gain only .012 rupee for the same one-rupee shock (column (3)). Because standard errors are rather large in column (6), however, these two estimates are not statistically different.

Interestingly, when we break down the overall group shock into two subshocks, the results become even more suggestive. We find that top firms gain between .032 and .034 rupee for every one-rupee shock to group firms either below the sixty-sixth percentile in terms of director equity or above the thirty-third percentile in terms of other ownership (columns (7) and (8)). All the other firms gain between .015 and .017 rupee on average for the same subshocks (columns (4) and (5)). To summarize, these results give some evidence that the firms with the highest level of director equity in their group seem to benefit most from shocks to the rest of the group. Moreover, these firms benefit the most from shocks to firms with low director equity or higher other shareholders' ownership.

III.H. Alternative Explanations

Although these findings match the predictions of the tunneling hypothesis, other possible explanations need to be considered.[35] First, suppose that group firms are more diversified than

---

34. Similar results follow if we use median cutoffs.
35. A purely mechanical explanation could be that cross-ownership between firms generate dividend payments that look like tunneling. This effect, however,

stand-alones and low-cash-flow-right ones are more diversified than high-cash-flow-right ones. Then the reduced sensitivity to the industry shock could reflect mismeasurement of these firms' industries. We investigate these questions directly by using detailed product data to construct diversification measures. For these measures, we find no difference between group and nongroup firms. Nor do we find any difference between high- and low-cash-flow-right group firms in the extent of their diversification. This suggests that differences in industry mismeasurement do not drive our findings.[36]

Another possibility is that coinsurance between group firms generates both reduced sensitivity to own shock and redistribution between firms. Such coinsurance may be common in countries such as India, where capital markets are still nascent [Khanna and Palepu 2000]. Insurance may also take a financing form in which a rich group firm invests in other firms' products, essentially forming a groupwide internal capital market. A simple coinsurance scheme, however, could not generate all of our results. Specifically, why do high-cash-flow-right firms systematically receive less insurance or financing? More generally, why does cash flow in only one direction, from low- to high-cash-flow-right firms?

For an insurance story to accommodate our findings, high-cash-flow-right firms within a group would have to be better providers of insurance or financing. We test this hypothesis in several ways and find no evidence for it. First, we find no difference in cash richness (a proxy for ease of insurance provision) between high- and low-cash-flow-right group firms. Second, we find that adding an interaction of industry cash richness with the various shock measures does not affect the results. Finally, to examine the possibility that these results reflect internal capital markets, we control for the extent of borrowing between firms in a group. This also does not affect the results. As a whole, we find little support for these alternative explanations.

---

would be too small to explain our results. Moreover, our results do not change when we exclude "earnings from dividends" from our measure of earnings.

36. All the results in this section are described in detail in Bertrand, Mehta, and Mullainathan [2000] as well as in Tables C and D of the unpublished appendix.

TABLE VI
SHOCK SENSITIVITY: AN ACCOUNTING DECOMPOSITION

Panel A: Sensitivity to own shock

Sample:	Groups	Stand-alones
Dep. variable:		
Operating profits	1.22	1.17
	(.018)	(.009)
Nonoperating profits	−.478	−.103
	(.014)	(.006)

Panel B: Sensitivity to own shock by director ownership

Sample:	Groups	Stand-alones
Dep. variable:		
Operating profits	.0123	.0082
	(.0056)	(.0013)
Nonoperating profits	.0131	−0.0038
	(.0043)	(.0008)

Panel C: Sensitivity to group shock by level of director ownership in group

Sample:	Topmost firm	Below topmost firm
Dep. variable:		
Operating profits	.0066	.0114
	(.0128)	(.0026)
Nonoperating profits	.0134	.0006
	(.0078)	(.0020)

a. *Data Source:* Prowess, Centre for Monitoring Indian Economy, for years 1989–1999. All monetary variables are expressed in 1995 Rs. crore, where crore represents 10 million.

b. Each coefficient contains the result of a separate regression in which the dependent variable is either operating profits or nonoperating profits, as indicated. In Panel A the reported coefficient is the coefficient on "Own shock." In Panel B the reported coefficient is the coefficient on "Own shock · director equity." In Panel C, the reported coefficient is the coefficient on "Group Shock." Also indicated in each regression are the logarithm of total assets, year fixed effects, firm fixed effects, and "Own shock" (Panels B and C).

c. In Panel C the subsamples are for group firms only. Topmost firm and below topmost firms are defined using director's equity. For example, "Topmost firm" are the set of firms that have the highest level of director ownership in their group.

d. Standard errors are in parentheses.

IV. OTHER RESULTS

IV.A. An Accounting Decomposition

If business groups in India are indeed tunneling resources, as the evidence so far strongly suggests, how are they doing it? We address this question in Table VI where we replicate the previous analysis but replace our standard profits measure with other balance sheet items. More formally, we decompose profits into two components. *Profits = Operating Profits + Nonoperating Profits*. Operating profits are defined as sales minus total raw material expenses minus energy expenses minus wages and salaries.[37] Nonoperating profits are the "residual." They include such diverse items as write-offs for bad debts, interest income, amortization, extraordinary items, and unspecified items.

Panel A of Table VI compares the sensitivity of group and stand-alone firms to their own shock for these two measures (as in Table II). Each entry in this panel is the coefficient on "Own shock" from a separate regression. We see in the first row that group firms' operating profits are, if anything, *more* sensitive to their own industry shock.[38] It is on nonoperating profits that group firms are far less sensitive to their own shock. More specifically, nonoperating profits seem to fall when there is a positive shock to a firm's industry. Although nonoperating profits decline moderately in stand-alone firms, the fall is much larger for group firms.

In Panel B we examine the differential sensitivity to own industry shock by the controlling party's cash flow rights (as in Table III). Each entry in this panel belongs to a separate regression. For simplicity, we only report in this table the coefficient on "Own shock * director equity." Each regression also includes the logarithm of total assets, firm fixed effects, year fixed effects, and the direct effect of "Own shock." As a benchmark, we report in the second column the equivalent regressions for stand-alone firms. The first row shows that there is little evidence of tunneling in operating profits. While group firms' sensitivity rises with director equity, stand-alone firms show a nearly equivalent rise. The difference is only about .004. In the second row, however, we see a much greater effect on nonoperating profits. The difference between group and stand-alone firms is around .017, or four times the difference on operating profits.

In Panel C we examine how each of the two profit measures respond to the group shock (as in Table V). Each entry represents the coefficient on "Group shock" from a separate regression which includes year and firm fixed effects, the logarithm of total assets,

37. Total raw material expenses include raw material expenses, stores and spares, packaging expenses, and purchase of finished goods for resale.
38. In all regressions in Table VI, the shock measure relates as before to total industry profits (operating and nonoperating). So, the shock measures have not changed, only the dependent variables have.

and own shock. These results complement those of Panels A and B since they tell us about the mechanisms for tunneling money into a firm. We find a pattern very similar to that in Panels A and B. Much of the differential sensitivity of high- and low-cash-flow-right firms to the group shock occurs on nonoperating profits.

Hence, according to the findings in Table VI, the tunneling of money both into and out of firms in India occurs through nonoperating profits.[39] This implies that transfer pricing (which would affect operating profits) is not an important source of tunneling in India. Moreover, it suggests that nonoperating profits may be a force that moves in the opposite direction of operating profits and serves to dampen final earnings. In unreported regressions, we examine this by simply regressing a firm's nonoperating profits on its operating profits, while controlling for size, year dummies, and firm fixed effects. As expected, we find a strong negative coefficient. When we interact operating profits in this regression with a variety of variables, we find results quite similar to our tunneling findings. Group firms show a much more negative relationship between operating and nonoperating profits. Also, among group firms, the ones with low cash flow rights show the most negative relationship. This evidence reinforces the view that manipulation of nonoperating profits is a primary means of removing cash from and placing cash into group firms in India.

IV.B. Market Valuation

Given our findings so far, it is natural to ask whether stock prices reflect the extent of this tunneling. Does the market penalize firms or groups which show more evidence of tunneling? To address this issue, we compute for each firms an average "q" ratio. We do this by first regressing standard firm level market-to-book ratios on log(total assets), year fixed effects, industry fixed effects, and firm fixed effects. The value of the firm fixed effect in this regression is the variable we call "Firm Q." Our q measure is, therefore, the market premium for the firm relative to other firms in its industry, size class, and year. We also compute an average q ratio for each group. To do this, we estimate a similar regression at the firm level but include group fixed effects instead of firm fixed effects. The group fixed effects from these

---

39. We have attempted further decomposition of nonoperating profits and found no consistent pattern. No one subcomponent of nonoperating profits is systematically more important. This may be because different firms tunnel in different ways.

FERRETING OUT TUNNELING **145**

TABLE VII
SENSITIVITY TO OWN AND GROUP SHOCK BY FIRM AND GROUP Q RATIOS
DEPENDENT VARIABLE: PROFIT BEFORE DIT

	(1)	(2)	(3)	(4)
Own shock	−.046	.388	.600	.049
	(.056)	(.027)	(.017)	(.060)
Own shock * firm Q	.178	—	—	.143
	(.013)			(.016)
Own shock * relative Q	—	.143	—	—
		(.011)		
Own shock * group Q	—	—	.414	.171
			(.037)	(.044)
Group shock	−.008	.010	.011	−.008
	(.003)	(.002)	(.003)	(.004)
Group shock * firm Q	.012	—	—	.012
	(.001)			(.001)
Group shock * relative Q	—	.008	—	—
		(.001)		
Group shock * group Q	—	—	.006	−.001
			(.007)	(.006)
Adjusted R^2	.94	.94	.93	.94

a. a. *Data Source:* Prowess, Centre for Monitoring Indian Economy, for years 1989–1999. All monetary variables are expressed in 1995 Rs. crore, where crore represents 10 million.

b. Sample is group firms only.

c. "Firm Q" is a variable that represents the estimated firm fixed effects in a regression of firm-level q ratios (market valuation over total assets) on log(total assets), year fixed effects, industry fixed effects, and firm fixed effects. "Group Q" is a variable that represents the estimated group fixed effects in a regression of firm-level q ratios on log(total assets), year fixed effects, industry fixed effects, and group fixed effects. "Relative Q" is the difference between "Firm Q" and the mean of "Firm Q" within groups.

d. Also included in each regression are the logarithm of total assets, year fixed effects, and firm fixed effects.

e. Standard errors are in parentheses.

regressions define the variable we call "Group Q." Finally, we form a "Relative Q" measure for each firm, which equals its own q minus its group q, and captures a firm's performance relative to the rest of the group.

In Table VII we examine how these new variables influence the sensitivity of a firm to its own shock and to the group shock. In column (1) we show that firms with higher q are *more* sensitive to both their own shock and to the group shock. Under the tunneling interpretation, this suggests that firms that have more money transferred to them and less money taken away from them have higher q ratios. In column (3) we see the same pattern for relative q. In column (3) we see that the groups with the highest q ratios are those with firms that show higher sensitivity to their own shock, and thus have less money taken away from them. The coefficient on group shock interacted with "Group Q" is positive but insignificant. In column (4) we include interactions of the shock measures with both "Firm Q" and "Group Q." The results are qualitatively similar.

The findings in this section suggest that the stock market (at least partly) recognizes tunneling and incorporates it into pricing. Firms that have more resources tunneled to them are valued more by the market. Firms that have less money tunneled away from them are also valued more. Finally, groups that tunnel less money are valued more. These results complement previous empirical findings that market valuations positively correlate with the controlling shareholders' cash flow rights.[40]

V. Conclusion

We have developed a fairly general empirical methodology for quantifying tunneling in business groups. We examined whether shocks propagate between firms in a business group in accord with the controlling shareholder's ownership in each firm. We applied the methodology in Indian data and found significant amounts of tunneling, mostly via nonoperating components of profits. We also found that market prices partly incorporate tunneling.

These results raise some questions. If groups expropriate minority shareholders so much, how do they persist? Why do minority shareholders buy into them in the first place? We feel that there are three broad possibilities. First, groups may grow through acquisitions. If this is the case, and markets are efficient, then the act of takeover would generate a one-time drop in share price amounting to the extent of tunneling. Second, shareholders may not recognize the extent of tunneling that takes place in groups. For example, the lack of detailed ownership information may make it difficult for shareholders to figure out with great reliability which group firms are high- and which are low-cash-flow-right firms. Finally, groups may provide other benefits, which offset the costs imposed by tunneling. To cite one example, they may provide important political contacts, which are quite

40. For example, Bianchi, Bianco, and Enriques [1999], Claessens, Djankov, Fan, and Lang [1999], and Claessens, Djankov, and Lang [2000]). In the Indian data we find that firms with a higher level of other equity within a group have a lower q ratio. We do not, however, find a significant relationship between level of director ownership and q ratio within groups.

valuable in a heavily regulated economy. Given the extent of tunneling found here, assessing the relevance of each of these possibilities appears to be an important direction for future research.

UNIVERSITY OF CHICAGO GRADUATE SCHOOL OF BUSINESS, NATIONAL BUREAU OF ECONOMIC RESEARCH, AND CENTRE FOR ECONOMIC AND POLICY RESEARCH
MASSACHUSETTS INSTITUTE OF TECHNOLOGY
MASSACHUSETTS INSTITUTE OF TECHNOLOGY AND NATIONAL BUREAU OF ECONOMIC RESEARCH

REFERENCES

Bebchuk, Lucian, R. Kraakman, and G. Triantis, "Stock Pyramids, Cross-Ownership, and Dual Class Equity: The Mechanisms and Agency Costs of Separating Control from Cash Flow Rights," in *Concentrated Corporate Ownership*, A National Bureau of Economic Research Conference Report. R. Morck, editor (Chicago, IL: University of Chicago, 2000).

Berle, A., and G. Means, *The Modern Corporation and Private Property* (New York, NY: Macmillan, 1934).

Bertrand, Marianne, and Sendhil Mullainathan, "Agents with and without Principals," *American Economic Review Papers and Proceedings*, XC (2000), 203–208.

Bertrand, Marianne, and Sendhil Mullainathan, "Are CEOs Rewarded for Luck? The Ones without Principals Are," *Quarterly Journal of Economics*, CXVI (2001), 901–932.

Bertrand, Marianne, Paras Mehta, and Sendhil Mullainathan, "Ferreting out Tunneling: An Application to Indian Business Groups," National Bureau of Economic Research Working Paper No. 7952, 2000.

Bianchi, M., M. Bianco, and L. Enriques, "Pyramidal Groups and the Separation between Ownership and Control in Italy," mimeo, Bank of Italy, 1999.

Blanchard, Olivier, Florencio Lopez-de-Silanes, and Andrei Shleifer, "What Do Firms Do with Cash Windfalls," *Journal of Financial Economics*, XXXVI (1994), 337–360.

Claessens, Stijn, Simeon Djankov, and Harry Lang, "The Separation of Ownership and Control in East Asian Countries," mimeo, World Bank, 2000.

Claessens, Stijn, Simeon Djankov, Joseph Fan, and Harry Lang, "Expropriation of Minority Shareholders: Evidence from East Asia," Policy Research Paper No. 2088, World Bank, 1999.

Dutta, Sudipt, *Family Business in India* (New Delhi: Response Books, Sage Publications, 1997).

Hoshi, Takeo, Anil Kashyap, and David Scharfstein, "Corporate Structure, Liquidity, and Investment: Evidence from Japanese Industrial Groups," *Quarterly Journal of Economics*, CVI (1991), 33–60.

Jensen, Michael, and William Meckling, "Theory of the Firm: Managerial Behavior, Agency Costs, and Ownership Structure," *Journal of Financial Economics*, III (1976), 305–360.

Johnson, Simon, P. Boone, A. Breach, and E. Friedman, "Corporate Governance in the Asian Financial Crisis," *Journal of Financial Economics*, LVIII (2000), 141–186.

Johnson, Simon, Rafael La Porta, Florencio Lopez-de-Silanes, and Andrei Shleifer, "Tunneling," *American Economic Review Papers and Proceedings*, XC (2000), 22–27.

Johnson, Simon, and Eric Friedman, "Tunneling and Propping," MIT Working Paper, 2000.

Khanna, Tarun, and Krishna Palepu, "Is Group Membership Profitable in Emerging Markets? An Analysis of Diversified Indian Business Groups," *Journal of Finance*, LV (2000), 867–891.

Lamont, Owen, "Capital Flows and Investment: Evidence from the Internal Capital Markets," *Journal of Finance,* LII (1997), 83–109.

La Porta, Rafael, Florencio Lopez-de-Silanes, Andrei Shleifer, and Robert Vishny, "Corporate Ownership around the World," *Journal of Finance,* LIV (1999), 471–517.

Nenova, Tatiana, "The Value of a Corporate Vote and Private Benefits: Cross-Country Analysis," mimeo, Department of Economics, Harvard University, 1999.

Piramal, G. *Business Maharajas* (Bombay: Viking Press, 1996).

Price, Waterhouse & Co., *Doing Business in India* (New York: Price Waterhouse, 1999).

Sarkar, Jayati, and Subrata Sarkar, "The Governance of Indian Corporates," *India Development Report,* 1999–2000, Kirit S. Parikh, editor (New Delhi: Oxford University Press, 1999).

Shleifer, Andrei, and Daniel Wolfenzon, "Investor Protection and Equity Markets," National Bureau of Economic Research Working Paper No. 7974, 2000.

Wolfenzon, Daniel, "A Theory of Pyramidal Ownership," mimeo, Department of Economics, Harvard University, 1999.

Zingales, Luigi, "What Determines the Value of Corporate Votes," *Quarterly Journal of Economics,* CX (1995), 1047–1073.

[2004]

Available online at www.sciencedirect.com

SCIENCE @ DIRECT*

Journal of Financial Economics 74 (2004) 277–304

JOURNAL OF
Financial
ECONOMICS

www.elsevier.com/locate/econbase

Cross-country determinants of mergers and acquisitions ☆

Stefano Rossi, Paolo F. Volpin*

London Business School, Regent's Park, London NW1 4SA, UK

Received 7 August 2002; accepted 6 October 2003

Available online 13 May 2004

Abstract

We study the determinants of mergers and acquisitions around the world by focusing on differences in laws and regulation across countries. We find that the volume of M&A activity is significantly larger in countries with better accounting standards and stronger shareholder protection. The probability of an all-cash bid decreases with the level of shareholder protection in the acquirer country. In cross-border deals, targets are typically from countries with poorer investor protection than their acquirers' countries, suggesting that cross-border transactions play a governance role by improving the degree of investor protection within target firms.

© 2004 Elsevier B.V. All rights reserved.

JEL classification: G28; G32; G34

Keywords: Mergers and acquisitions; Corporate governance; Investor protection

☆ We thank Richard Brealey, Ian Cooper, Antoine Faure-Grimaud, Julian Franks, Denis Gromb, Ernst Maug, Thomas Noe, Antoinette Schoar, Henri Servaes, Oren Sussman, David Webb, an anonymous referee, and participants at the 2004 AFA meetings in San Diego, at the 2003 EFA meetings in Glasgow and at seminars at Humboldt University, London Business School, London School of Economics, Norwegian School of Economics and Business, Norwegian School of Management, and Tilburg University. Paolo F. Volpin acknowledges support from the JP Morgan Chase Research Fellowship at London Business School.

*Corresponding author. Tel.: +44-20-72625050; fax: +44-20-77243317.

E-mail address: pvolpin@london.edu (P.F. Volpin).

278 *S. Rossi, P.F. Volpin / Journal of Financial Economics 74 (2004) 277–304*

1. Introduction

In a perfect world, corporate assets would be channelled toward their best possible use. Mergers and acquisitions (M&A) help this process by reallocating control over companies. However, frictions such as transaction costs, information asymmetries, and agency conflicts can prevent efficient transfers of control. Recent studies on corporate governance employ measures of the quality of the legal and regulatory environment within a country as proxies for some of these frictions, and show that differences in laws, regulation, and enforcement correlate with the development of capital markets, the ownership structure of firms, and the cost of capital (see, e.g., La Porta et al., 1997, 1998; Bhattacharya and Daouk, 2002).

In this paper we analyze a sample of mergers and acquisitions announced in the 1990s and completed by the end of 2002. Our sample comprises firms in 49 major countries and shows that differences in laws and enforcement explain the intensity and the pattern of mergers and acquisitions around the world. The volume of M&A activity is significantly larger in countries with better accounting standards and stronger shareholder protection. This result holds for several measures of M&A activity, and also when we control for other characteristics of the regulatory environment such as antitrust legislation and takeover laws. Our findings indicate that a more active market for mergers and acquisitions is the outcome of a corporate governance regime with stronger investor protection. We also show that hostile deals are relatively more likely in countries with better shareholder protection. One explanation is that good protection for minority shareholders makes control more contestable by reducing the private benefits of control.

Next, we provide evidence on cross-border mergers and acquisitions. We show that the probability that a given deal is cross-border rather than domestic decreases with the investor protection of the target's country. Even after we control for bilateral trade, relative GNP per capita, and cultural and geographical differences, we find that targets are typically from countries with poorer investor protection compared to their acquirers. This result suggests that cross-border M&A activity is an important channel for effective worldwide convergence in corporate governance standards, as argued by Coffee (1999).

Selling to a foreign firm is a form of contractual convergence similar to the decision to list in countries with better corporate governance and better-developed capital markets. Pagano et al. (2002) and Reese and Weisbach (2002) show that firms from countries with weak legal protection for minority shareholders list abroad more frequently than do firms from other countries. We show that firms in countries with weaker investor protection are often sold to buyers from countries with stronger investor protection.

We also analyze the determinants of the takeover premium and the method of payment in individual transactions. We show that the premium is higher in countries with higher shareholder protection, although this result is driven by deals with US and British targets. We find that the probability of an all-cash bid decreases with the degree of shareholder protection in the acquirer country, indicating that acquisitions paid with stock require an environment with high shareholder protection.

S. Rossi, P.F. Volpin / Journal of Financial Economics 74 (2004) 277–304 279

Our paper belongs to the growing literature exploring cross-country variation in governance structures around the world. Recent studies show that better legal protection of minority shareholders is associated with more developed stock markets (La Porta et al., 1997), higher valuation (La Porta et al., 2002), greater dividend payouts (La Porta et al., 2000b), lower concentration of ownership and control (La Porta et al., 1999), lower private benefits of control (Dyck and Zingales, 2004; Nenova, 2003), lower earnings management (Leuz et al., 2003), lower cash balances (Dittmar et al., 2003), and higher correlation between investment opportunities and actual investments (Wurgler, 2000). Our paper shows that better investor protection is correlated with a more active market for mergers and acquisitions.

We structure the paper as follows. Section 2 describes the data. Section 3 contains the analyses of the determinants of M&A activity. Section 4 discusses the main results. Section 5 concludes.

2. Data

Our sample contains all mergers and acquisitions announced between January 1, 1990 and December 31, 1999, completed as of December 31, 2002, and reported by SDC Platinum, a database from Thomson Financial. Because we wish to study transactions clearly motivated by changes in control, we focus on mergers (business combinations in which the number of companies decreases after the transaction) and acquisitions of majority interests (when the acquirer owns less than 50% of the target company's stock before the deal, and more than 50% after the deal). A second reason for this sample selection is that the coverage of transfers of minority stakes (below 50%) is likely to be severely affected by cross-country differences in disclosure requirements. By selecting only transfers of stakes above 50%, we minimize these disclosure biases. However, in interpreting the results, we note that the availability and quality of the data might be better in some countries (such as the US and UK) because of broader SDC coverage. A related concern is that the coverage of small countries improves over time. To address this concern, we replicate our analysis on the subsample of deals announced in the second half of the 1990s and find similar results.

The availability of empirical measures of investor protection limits our set to 49 countries. The sample from SDC includes 45,686 deals, 22% of which have a traded company as the target. Excluded deals represent about 6% of the original dataset in number and 1% in value.

The appendix describes the variables we use in this paper and indicates their sources. These variables can be classified into three broad categories corresponding to three different levels of analysis. The first set of variables is at the country level. It includes measures of M&A activity from the target's perspective, as well as broad macroeconomic conditions and proxies for the legal and regulatory environment. We use these variables in our cross-country analysis of the determinants of international mergers and acquisitions. Our second category of variables measures the flow of M&A activity and cultural differences and similarities between any ordered pairs of acquirer and target countries (there are 49×48 or 2,352 ordered pairs). The third set of variables is at the individual deal level and includes data on the premium paid, the value of the deal, and the means of payment. We use these data, together with the country-level variables defined above, in our analysis of the determinants of the premium and the means of payment.

2.1. M&A activity

Tables 1 and 2 show the data on M&A activity sorted by target country. We define volume as the percentage of traded firms that are targets of successful mergers or acquisitions. We interpret this variable as a measure of the ability of an economy to reallocate control over corporate assets. We also use other measures of volume, such as the total number of completed deals divided by population, the value of all completed deals divided by GDP, and the value of completed deals among traded companies divided by stock market capitalization. The qualitative results do not change. As is apparent from Table 1, the market for corporate control plays a different role in different countries. For example, volume is very low in Japan (only 6.4% of Japanese traded companies are targets of a completed deal during the 1990s) and very high in the US (65.6% of US traded companies are targets in a completed deal). The table also shows some similarities across countries. For example, volume in France, Italy, and the United Kingdom is similar, although their governance regimes are quite different.

Of all mergers and acquisitions, we focus on hostile deals, since they are likely to play an important governance role. We examine the number of attempted hostile takeovers as a percentage of the total number of traded companies. The intuition is that the disciplinary role of hostile takeovers is related to the threat they represent to incumbent managers. In other words, it is likely that attempted (but failed) hostile takeovers play just as important a role in disciplining management as hostile takeovers that are eventually completed.

In all countries, the frequency of hostile takeovers is very small. According to SDC, they are absent in 21 out of 49 countries, and when present they never exceed the 6.44% observed in the United States. Therefore, according to SDC Platinum, hostile takeovers are rare. However, this conclusion could be unwarranted, because our source might fail to record all unsuccessful takeovers. Moreover, in some countries the corporate governance role of hostile takeovers could be performed by hostile stakes, as Jenkinson and Ljungqvist (2001) show for Germany.

We define the cross-border ratio as the percentage of completed deals in which the acquirer is from a different country than the target. In the case of mergers, we follow our data source to distinguish acquirers from targets. For example, in the merger between Daimler and Chrysler, Thomson codifies Daimler as the acquirer and Chrysler as the target.

The number of cross-border mergers and acquisitions is 11,638, corresponding to 25% of the total. Table 1 shows that different countries play different roles in the cross-border M&A market. For instance, 51% of the acquirers in Mexican deals are foreign, compared to only 9.1% in the United States.

S. Rossi, P.F. Volpin / Journal of Financial Economics 74 (2004) 277–304 281

Table 1

Data on international mergers and acquisitions sorted by target country

Volume is the percentage of traded companies targeted in a completed deal. Hostile takeover is the number of attempted hostile takeovers as a percentage of domestic traded firms. Cross-border ratio is the number of cross-border deals as a percentage of all completed deals.

Country	Volume (%)	Hostile takeover (%)	Cross-border ratio (%)
Argentina	26.80	0.65	53.73
Australia	34.09	4.60	27.16
Austria	38.14	1.03	51.55
Belgium	33.33	0.56	45.14
Brazil	23.08	0.00	52.03
Canada	30.05	2.73	22.66
Chile	10.57	0.42	64.79
Colombia	19.42	0.00	66.67
Denmark	24.03	0.81	38.26
Ecuador	10.53	0.00	68.97
Egypt	1.46	0.00	47.62
Finland	45.45	0.91	22.67
France	56.40	1.68	33.81
Germany	35.51	0.30	26.05
Greece	12.66	0.00	23.13
Hong Kong	33.91	0.41	38.52
India	2.01	0.02	56.02
Indonesia	10.60	0.48	61.03
Ireland	28.90	4.62	52.73
Israel	9.43	0.23	46.94
Italy	56.40	3.04	36.13
Japan	6.43	0.00	13.25
Jordan	0.00	0.00	55.56
Kenya	1.80	0.00	28.57
Malaysia	15.23	0.19	11.27
Mexico	27.51	0.00	51.02
Netherlands	26.49	1.32	43.43
New Zealand	49.82	0.70	46.15
Nigeria	0.61	0.00	58.33
Norway	61.24	5.86	36.76
Pakistan	0.48	0.00	55.56
Peru	12.21	0.00	56.88
Philippines	21.41	0.00	37.97
Portugal	31.37	1.96	40.00
Singapore	34.06	0.40	31.41
South Africa	23.89	0.45	24.65
South Korea	4.81	0.00	53.85
Spain	15.72	0.17	37.55
Sri Lanka	4.83	0.00	42.86
Sweden	62.06	3.74	35.48
Switzerland	38.48	1.43	43.59
Taiwan	0.89	0.00	49.37
Thailand	17.14	0.00	43.24
Turkey	6.12	0.00	45.45
United Kingdom	53.65	4.39	23.46
United States	65.63	6.44	9.07
Uruguay	7.55	0.00	85.00
Venezuela	14.91	0.00	56.60
Zimbabwe	6.35	0.00	46.15
World average	23.54	1.01	42.82

Table 2
Summary statistics on the sample of individual deals sorted by target country
Premium is the bid price as a percentage of the closing price of the target four weeks before the announcement. All-cash bid is a dummy variable that equals one if the acquisition is entirely paid in cash, and zero otherwise.

Country	Premium		All-cash bid		N obs.
	Mean	Std. dev.	Mean	Std. dev.	
Australia	129.5	37.4	0.60	0.49	212
Austria	129.8	25.2	0.83	0.41	6
Belgium	137.2	56.1	0.86	0.38	7
Brazil	110.5	0.0	0.00	0.00	1
Canada	132.9	40.1	0.36	0.48	157
Chile	149.9	24.5	1.00	0.00	3
Denmark	142.2	41.2	0.83	0.41	6
Finland	149.7	53.2	1.00	0.00	7
France	133.4	53.6	0.88	0.32	112
Germany	116.7	35.3	0.77	0.44	13
Greece	165.5	112.8	0.67	0.58	3
Hong Kong	129.8	56.1	0.93	0.25	46
India	178.6	113.2	0.67	0.50	9
Indonesia	222.5	150.1	1.00	0.00	2
Ireland	121.1	22.7	0.78	0.44	9
Israel	220.2	153.2	0.50	0.71	2
Italy	127.7	26.8	0.88	0.33	26
Japan	99.0	41.7	0.36	0.48	73
Malaysia	151.7	76.8	0.91	0.29	23
Mexico	124.5	17.0	1.00	0.00	2
Netherlands	144.7	37.9	0.50	0.52	16
New Zealand	129.2	17.6	0.94	0.25	16
Norway	136.0	37.6	0.76	0.43	37
Philippines	157.7	81.0	0.56	0.53	9
Portugal	149.9	57.1	1.00	0.00	4
Singapore	152.9	79.3	0.85	0.37	39
South Africa	129.5	63.2	0.68	0.48	28
South Korea	145.1	102.7	0.50	0.58	4
Spain	119.8	30.0	0.70	0.48	10
Sweden	141.7	40.6	0.71	0.46	45
Switzerland	111.0	33.3	0.89	0.33	9
Thailand	126.0	79.3	0.92	0.28	13
Turkey	127.5	0.0	1.00	0.00	1
United Kingdom	145.8	41.9	0.64	0.48	614
United States	144.3	42.4	0.37	0.48	2443
Total	141.6	44.7	0.48	0.50	4007

To study the cross-country variations in the premiums and means of payment, we use transaction-level data. The premium is the bid price as a percentage of the closing price four weeks before the announcement. We characterize the means of payment of an individual deal with a dummy variable that equals one if the acquisition is entirely

S. Rossi, P.F. Volpin / Journal of Financial Economics 74 (2004) 277–304   283

paid in cash, and zero otherwise. We compute these variables using data available from SDC Platinum. After excluding deals with incomplete information, we have 4,007 observations from 35 countries.

As shown in Table 2, the data are highly concentrated: the target is a US firm in 60% of the sample and a UK firm in 15% of the sample. The bid price ranges from 99.6% of the pre-announcement price (in Japan) to 227.1% (in Indonesia). In Italy, 88% of the acquisitions of Italian targets are paid entirely in cash. In the US, only 37% of the deals are paid wholly in cash.

2.2. Investor protection

By reshuffling control over companies, mergers and acquisitions help allocate corporate assets to their best possible use. Investor protection can affect the volume of mergers and acquisitions because it affects the magnitude of frictions and inefficiencies in the target country. As proxies for investor protection, we use several indexes developed by La Porta et al. (1998): an index of the quality of the accounting standards, an index of shareholder protection that combines an index of the quality of law enforcement (rule of law) and an index of the rights that shareholders have with respect to management (antidirector rights), and a dummy variable for common-law countries. These indexes are highly correlated (their pair-wise correlations range between 40% and 60%) because they all reflect to some degree the underlying quality of investor protection in a country. However, they measure different institutional characteristics.

Accounting standards measure the quality of the disclosure of accounting information. The accounting standards quality index is created by the Center for International Financial Analysis and Research and rates the 1990 annual reports of at least three firms in every country on their inclusion or omission of 90 items. Thus, each country obtains a score out of 90, with a higher number indicating more disclosure. This variable affects M&A activity because good disclosure is a necessary condition for identifying potential targets. Accounting standards also reflect corporate governance, because they reduce the scope for expropriation by making corporate accounts more transparent.

Our second measure is an index of shareholder protection that ranges between zero and six. It captures the effective rights of minority shareholders with respect to managers and directors and is defined as an antidirector rights index multiplied by a rule of law index and divided by ten. When minority shareholders have fewer rights, they are more likely to be expropriated. As a consequence, the stock market is less developed, and raising external equity, particularly to finance a takeover, is more expensive. At the same time, with low shareholder protection, the private benefits of control are high and the market for corporate control is relatively less effective, because incumbents will try to entrench themselves via ownership concentration and takeover deterrence measures (Bebchuk, 1999).

The common law measure is a dummy variable that equals one if the origin of the company law is the English common law, and zero otherwise. La Porta et al. (1998) argue that legal origin is a broad indicator of investor protection and show that countries with common law as the legal origin better protect minority shareholders than do countries with civil law as the legal origin. Although common law should not directly affect mergers and acquisitions, we include this variable because it is correlated with other proxies of investor protection and is truly exogenous. Hence, it is a good instrument for investor protection.

We note that the number of observations in our empirical analysis varies with the measure of investor protection used, because accounting standards are not available for Ecuador, Indonesia, Ireland, Jordan, Kenya, Pakistan, Sri Lanka, and Zimbabwe.

3. Determinants of M&A activity

We examine five dimensions of mergers and acquisitions: the volume, the incidence of hostile takeovers, the pattern of cross-border deals, the premium, and the method of payment.

3.1. Volume

We start with the relation between the volume of M&A activity and investor protection at the target-country level. Our specification is

$$\text{Volume} = \alpha + \beta X + \gamma \text{ investor protection} + \varepsilon, \tag{1}$$

where the dependent variable, volume, is the percentage of traded firms that are targets of successful mergers or acquisitions. The variables for common law, accounting standards, and shareholder protection are proxies for investor protection. Control factors (X) in all specifications are GDP growth, which proxies for the change in economic conditions, and the logarithm of the 1995 per capita GNP, which proxies for the country's wealth.

Table 3 reports the coefficients of six Tobit models derived from specification (1). We estimate Tobit models because the dependent variable (volume) is bounded between zero and 100 by construction. Column 1 shows that the frequency of mergers among traded companies is 7.5% higher in common-law countries than in civil-law countries. The results in Column 2 show that accounting standards are positively and significant correlated with volume. A 12-point increase in the accounting standards measure (from the quality of accounting standards in Italy to that in Canada) correlates with a 5% increase in the volume of mergers and acquisitions. Column 3 finds a similar result for shareholder protection. A one-point increase in shareholder protection (for instance, the adoption of voting by mail in a country like Belgium) is associated with 4% more volume. Thus, we find that there are more mergers and acquisitions in countries with better investor protection. We note that a one-point increase in the index of antidirector rights (such as the adoption of voting by mail) translates into a one-point increase in shareholder protection only in a country like Belgium, which also scores ten in the index of rule of law. In a country like Italy, which scores 8.33 in the index of rule of law, the same

S. Rossi, P.F. Volpin / Journal of Financial Economics 74 (2004) 277–304   285

Table 3

Determinants of the volume across countries

The table presents the results of six Tobit models estimated by maximum likelihood for the sample of 49 target countries. The dependent variable is volume, the percentage of traded companies targeted in a completed deal. The independent variables are: common law, a dummy variable that equals one if the origin of the company law is the English common law, and zero otherwise; accounting standards, an index of the quality of accounting disclosure; shareholder protection, a measure of the effective rights of minority shareholders; ownership concentration, the average equity stake owned by the three largest shareholders in the ten largest nonfinancial domestic firms in 1994; mandatory bid rule, a dummy variable that equals one if acquirers are forced to make a tender offer to all shareholders when passing a given ownership threshold, and zero otherwise; market return, the average annual stock market return in the 1990s; and market dominance, a survey-based measure of product market concentration. The logarithm of GNP per capita and GDP growth are included in all regressions as control variables. Standard errors are shown in parentheses.

	(1)	(2)	(3)	(4)	(5)	(6)
Log (GNP per capita)	9.00***	5.61***	6.40***	4.49**	4.75**	8.81***
	(1.24)	(1.94)ʻ	(1.48)	(2.04)	(2.02)	(2.05)
GDP growth	−2.42	−2.57*	−2.42**	−3.05**	−3.11**	−2.33
	(1.12)	(1.12)	(1.07)	(1.32)	(1.36)	(1.48)
Common law	7.52*					9.06*
	(3.97)					(5.06)
Accounting standards		0.47**		0.35*	0.43**	
		(0.18)		(0.20)	(0.20)	
Shareholder protection			4.27***	2.96	4.65**	
			(1.69)	(2.01)	(2.32)	
Ownership concentration					0.38*	
					(0.20)	
Mandatory bid rule						−0.58
						(4.10)
Market return						0.21
						(0.15)
Market dominance						−3.40
						(3.57)
Constant	−48.1***	−43.1***	−31.8***	−30.8*	−58.4***	−38.3**
	(12.0)	(16.5)	(12.5)	(18.1)	(22.1)	(17.7)
Pseudo R^2	0.10	0.08	0.10	0.09	0.09	0.09
N observations	49	41	49	41	39	41

***, **, * indicate significance at 1% percent, 5%, and 10% levels, respectively.

change in minority shareholders' rights implies only a 0.833-point increase in shareholder protection.

In Column 4, we estimate a joint regression with accounting standards and shareholder protection and find that only the former is statistically significant. This result suggests that disclosure rules are more relevant for takeovers than are shareholder rights. In Column 5, we add ownership concentration, which is potentially an important explanatory variable. Ownership concentration in a country is the average equity stake owned by the three largest shareholders in the ten largest nonfinancial domestic firms in 1994, from La Porta et al. (1998). We find

286   *S. Rossi, P.F. Volpin / Journal of Financial Economics 74 (2004) 277–304*

that, as in the individual regressions, the coefficients on accounting standards and shareholder protection are positive and significant. The coefficient on ownership concentration is also positive and significant. This finding indicates that, when we control for investor protection, countries with more concentrated ownership have more mergers and acquisitions. This result is consistent with Shleifer and Vishny (1986), who argue that transfers of control are easier in companies with more concentrated ownership structure because they overcome the free-rider problem in takeovers.

The results in Column 5 help explain why shareholder protection is not significant in Column 4. On the one hand, shareholder protection reduces the costs of raising external equity, thereby increasing the volume of mergers. On the other hand, it decreases ownership concentration, which makes friendly transfers of control less likely. By controlling for ownership concentration, we are able to disentangle the two effects.

In Column 6, we evaluate the robustness of the results on investor protection by adding further control variables to capture cross-country differences in the regulatory environment. We show the results only with the common law variable as our proxy for investor protection, although we obtain similar results for accounting standards and shareholder protection. A mandatory bid rule, which we capture with a dummy variable that equals one if acquirers are forced to make a tender offer to all shareholders when passing a given ownership threshold and zero otherwise, might reduce the volume of mergers and acquisitions because it imposes further costs on the potential bidder. The market return, calculated as the average annual stock market return during the 1990s, might affect M&A activity because of valuation waves (Shleifer and Vishny, 2003). However, there are two opposing effects when the stock market is booming. Targets could become too expensive, reducing the volume of deals, but acquirers enjoy low takeover costs because they can pay with more highly valued stock, leading to a high takeover volume. Market dominance, a measure of product market concentration in 1995 from the 1992 Global Competitiveness Report (published by the World Economic Forum), could reduce the volume because of lower availability of targets.

The results in Column 6 show that common law is still significant and its coefficient is virtually unchanged from Column 1. None of the control variables are statistically significant. Note that the number of observations decreases from 49 to 41 because market return is not available for Taiwan and Uruguay and market dominance is not available for Ecuador, Kenya, Nigeria, Pakistan, Sri Lanka, Uruguay, and Zimbabwe.

3.2. Hostile takeovers

Many financial economists argue that hostile takeovers play an important governance role (for instance, see Manne, 1965; Jensen, 1993; and Franks and Mayer, 1996). To analyze cross-country differences in the frequency of hostile takeovers, we estimate

$$\text{Hostile takeover} = \alpha + \beta X + \gamma \text{ investor protection} + \varepsilon, \tag{2}$$

S. Rossi, P.F. Volpin / Journal of Financial Economics 74 (2004) 277–304 287

Table 4
Incidence of hostile takeovers
The table presents the results of six Tobit models estimated by maximum likelihood on the sample of 49 target countries. The dependent variable is hostile takeover, or attempted hostile takeovers as a percentage of traded firms. The independent variables are: common law, a dummy variable that equals one if the origin of the company law is the English common law, and zero otherwise; accounting standards, an index of the quality of accounting disclosure; shareholder protection, a measure of the effective rights of minority shareholders; ownership concentration, the average equity stake owned by the three largest shareholders in the ten largest nonfinancial domestic firms in 1994; cross-border regulation, a dummy variable that equals one if foreign buyers need government approval, and zero otherwise; market return, the average annual stock market return in the 1990s; and mandatory bid rule, a dummy variable that equals one if acquirers are forced to make a tender offer to all shareholders when passing a given ownership threshold, and zero otherwise. The logarithm of GNP per capita and GDP growth are included in all regressions as control variables. Standard errors are shown in parentheses.

	(1)	(2)	(3)	(4)	(5)	(6)
Log (GNP per capita)	1.30***	0.93**	0.75***	0.61*	0.64**	1.08**
	(0.26)	(0.35)	(0.27)	(0.32)	(0.32)	(0.26)
GDP growth	0.08	0.04	0.06	−0.10	−0.05**	0.09
	(0.19)	(0.21)	(0.17)	(0.18)	(0.19)	(0.19)
Common law	1.53**					1.57**
	(0.68)					(0.70)
Accounting standards		0.07**		0.02	0.02	
		(0.03)		(0.03)	(0.03)	
Shareholder protection			0.88***	0.84**	0.73**	
			(0.25)	(0.26)	(0.31)	
Ownership concentration					−0.01	
					(0.03)	
Cross-border regulation						−1.80*
						(0.93)
Market return						0.02
						(0.02)
Mandatory bid rule						−0.04
						(0.59)
Constant	−12.0***	−12.2***	−8.34***	−7.93**	−7.06*	−9.75***
	(2.63)	(3.32)	(2.53)	(3.09)	(3.61)	(2.62)
Pseudo R^2	0.20	0.17	0.24	0.23	0.22	0.23
N observations	49	41	49	41	39	47

***, **, * indicate significance at 1%, 5%, and 10% levels, respectively.

where the hostile takeover variable is the number of attempted hostile takeovers in the 1990s as a percentage of the number of domestic traded companies. Common law, accounting standards, shareholder protection, and ownership concentration are proxies for investor protection, as described in Section 2.2. We include GDP growth and the logarithm of GNP per capita as control factors in all specifications.

The results are presented in Table 4. The first three columns show that common law, accounting standards, and shareholder protection are positively and significantly correlated with hostile takeovers. To interpret these results, note that hostile takeovers require that control be contestable, a feature that is less common in countries with poorer investor protection.

Column 4 shows that shareholder protection dominates accounting standards. A one-point increase in shareholder protection (e.g., the introduction of voting by mail in Belgium) is associated with 0.8 percentage points more hostile takeovers. Shareholder protection makes control more contestable by reducing the private benefits of control.

In Column 5, we add ownership concentration as a control variable. This variable is not significant. It marginally reduces the coefficient on shareholder protection without affecting its statistical significance. This result compares with Table 3, in which ownership concentration is positive and significant. According to Shleifer and Vishny (1986), ownership concentration facilitates only friendly transfers of control, not hostile takeovers. Hence, the insignificant coefficient in Column 5 of Table 4 is not surprising.

To evaluate the robustness of the main result that hostile takeovers are more common in countries with better investor protection, in Column 6 we add some control variables to the specification in Column 1 to capture cross-country differences in the regulatory environment. As in Table 4, we control for mandatory bid rules and market returns. We also incorporate cross-border regulation with a dummy variable that equals one if a foreign buyer needs government approval before acquiring control of a domestic firm, and zero otherwise. Because of cultural differences, deals initiated by foreign bidders are more likely to be hostile. Hence, we expect cross-border regulation to reduce the frequency of hostile takeovers.

The results in Column 6 show that common law is significant and that its coefficient is virtually unchanged from Column 1. The frequency of attempted hostile takeovers among traded companies is 1.6% higher in common-law than in civil-law countries. Cross-border regulation is also significant and negative, as predicted. The requirement of government approval for foreign acquisitions reduces the frequency of attempted hostile takeovers by 1.8%. Market returns and mandatory bid rules are not statistically significant.

3.3. Cross-border mergers and acquisitions

La Porta et al. (2000a, p. 23) write that "When a British firm fully acquires a Swedish firm, the possibilities for legal expropriation of investor diminish. Because the controlling shareholders of the Swedish company are compensated in such a friendly deal for the lost private benefits of control, they are more likely to go along. By replacing the wasteful expropriation with publicly shared profits and dividends, such acquisitions enhance efficiency." This statement implies two testable hypotheses that we address in this section: first, the probability that a deal is cross-border rather than domestic is higher in countries with lower investor protection; and second, the acquirers in cross-border deals will come from countries that have higher investor protection than the targets' countries.

3.3.1. Target-country analysis
As before, we adapt specification (1) by changing the dependent variable

$$\text{Cross-border ratio} = \alpha + \beta X + \gamma \text{ investor protection} + \varepsilon, \tag{3}$$

S. Rossi, P.F. Volpin / Journal of Financial Economics 74 (2004) 277–304 289

where the cross-border ratio is the number of cross-border deals as a percentage of all completed deals by target country. Common law, accounting standards, and shareholder protection are our proxies for investor protection. We expect the cross-border ratio to decrease with investor protection. As before, we control for the logarithm of GNP per capita, as a measure of a country's wealth, and GDP growth as a proxy for the change in macroeconomic conditions.

Table 5 reports the coefficients of six Tobit models derived from specification (3). The results confirm our prediction: the probability that a completed deal is cross-border rather than domestic is higher in countries with lower investor protection. The coefficients on common law, accounting standards, and shareholder protection are all negative and significant at the 1% level. In economic terms, the probability that a completed deal is cross-border is 14.5% higher in civil-law than in common-law countries. Raising the accounting standards measure by 12 points (from Italy's to Canada's accounting standards) decreases cross-border deals by 5%. An increase in shareholder protection by one point (for instance, the adoption of voting by mail in Belgium) decreases the cross-border ratio by 4%. Ownership concentration, which we add in Column 5 as a control variable, is not statistically significant.

To evaluate the robustness of the results, in Column 6 we augment the specification in Column 1 with some control variables. We add cross-border regulation because we expect fewer cross-border deals when there are more regulatory requirements. We control for market returns because we expect fewer cross-border deals when the stock market is booming and the target firms' stocks are (potentially) overvalued. At the same time, this variable will not be significant if the acquirer's stock market is also thriving. We include openness, a measure of the cultural attitude towards cross-border deals (from the 1996 Global Competitiveness Report) because such deals are more likely if the country is friendlier to foreigners.[1] Our results show that common law is still significant and that its coefficient is unaffected. Openness is negative and significant, as predicted. The coefficients on market return and cross-border regulation are not significant.

3.3.2. Ordered-pair analysis

The results in Table 5 indicate that cross-border mergers and acquisitions play a governance role by targeting firms in countries with lower investor protection. To explore this hypothesis, we arrange our dataset to produce a worldwide matrix of (49×48) matched pairs. In these pairs, we define each entry, cross-border deals$_{s,b}$, as the number of deals in which the acquirer comes from country b (for buyer) and the target is in country s (for seller), as a percentage of the total number of deals in country s.

---

[1] Another potential determinant of international mergers and acquisitions is tax competition across countries. For instance, taxes can affect M&A activity if it is easier for domestic firms to take advantage of investment tax credits and accelerated depreciation in the target country than for foreign firms. Moreover, the tax treatment of foreign income differs across countries. However, we do not control for taxes in our study because the complexity of the issue requires a paper on its own.

Table 5

Cross-border versus domestic deals

The table presents the results of six Tobit models estimated by maximum likelihood on the sample of 49 target countries. The dependent variable is cross-border ratio, or cross-border deals as a percentage of all completed deals. The independent variables are: common law, a dummy variable that equals one if the origin of the company law is the English common law, and zero otherwise; accounting standards, an index of the quality of accounting disclosure; shareholder protection, a measure of the effective rights of minority shareholders; ownership concentration, the average equity stake owned by the three largest shareholders in the ten largest nonfinancial domestic firms in 1994; cross-border regulation, a dummy variable that equals one if foreign buyers need government approval, and zero otherwise; market return, the average annual stock market return in the 1990s; and openness, a survey-based measure of the cultural attitude towards cross-border deals. The logarithm of GNP per capita and GDP growth are included in all regressions as control variables. Standard errors are shown in parentheses.

	(1)	(2)	(3)	(4)	(5)	(6)
Log (GNP per capita)	-5.32^{***}	-1.99	-1.47	-0.64	-1.21	-4.77^{***}
	(1.20)	(1.74)	(1.50)	(1.79)	(1.72)	(1.51)
GDP growth	1.75	0.90	1.44	1.48	1.38	3.48^{***}
	(1.08)	(1.17)	(1.08)	(1.15)	(1.16)	(1.19)
Common law	-14.5^{***}					-16.1^{***}
	(3.83)					(4.02)
Accounting standards		-0.67^{***}		-0.53^{***}	-0.41^{**}	
		(0.16)		(0.17)	(0.17)	
Shareholder protection			-6.03^{***}	-3.55^{**}	-4.14^{**}	
			(1.71)	(1.76)	(1.98)	
Ownership concentration					-0.11	
					(0.17)	
Cross-border regulation						5.05
						(4.36)
Market return						-0.15
						(0.13)
Openness						7.77^{***}
						(2.84)
Constant	87.7^{***}	96.5^{***}	62.7^{***}	81.7^{***}	85.0^{***}	38.1^{*}
	(11.7)	(14.8)	(12.7)	(15.9)	(18.8)	(20.0)
Pseudo R^2	0.06	0.07	0.05	0.09	0.08	0.09
N observations	49	41	49	41	39	41

***, **, * indicate significance at 1%, 5%, and 10% levels, respectively.

With the newly arranged dataset, we can study the pattern of cross-border mergers and acquisitions by simultaneously controlling for the characteristics of target and acquirer countries. The specification is

$$\text{Cross-border deals}_{s,b} = \beta X_{s,b} + \gamma \Delta \text{ (investor protection)}_{s,b} + \delta_b + \zeta_s + \varepsilon_{s,b}, \quad (4)$$

where the dependent variable is the number of cross-border deals in which the acquirer comes from country b and the target from country s ($b \neq s$) as a percentage of the total number of deals (cross-border and domestic) in country s. Our hypothesis is that the volume of cross-border M&A activity between country b (the

S. Rossi, P.F. Volpin / Journal of Financial Economics 74 (2004) 277–304 291

acquirer) and country s (the target) correlates positively with the difference in investor protection between the two countries. The proxies for investor protection are accounting standards and shareholder protection.

We note that our specification also includes fixed effects for target and acquirer countries. These fixed effects control for all cultural and institutional characteristics of the two countries, including the level of investor protection in the individual countries. We control for differences in the logarithm of GNP per capita of the acquirer and target countries as a measure of the relative economic development of the two countries. We also include two dummy variables equal to one if the acquirer and target share the same cultural background, that is, if they have the same official language and if they belong to the same geographical area.

Table 6 reports our results. In Columns 1 and 2, we include only one measure of investor protection per regression. We find that the volume of M&A activity between two countries is positively correlated with their difference in investor protection. This result means that acquirers typically come from countries with better accounting standards and stronger shareholder protection than the targets' countries.

In Column 3, we estimate the marginal impact of each variable by estimating a joint regression with the two measures. We find that only the difference in shareholder protection is statistically significant. On average, shareholder protection increases in the target company via the cross-border deal. This finding is consistent with the view that such acquisitions enhance efficiency because the increase in shareholder protection curbs the expropriation of minority shareholders and, therefore, reduces the cost of raising external equity. We also find that richer countries are more likely to be acquirers than targets, and that most cross-border deals happen between countries sharing the same language and geographical area.

In Column 4, we add the difference in market return between acquirer and target countries as a control variable. We would expect more deals when the acquirer's stock market is booming relatively to the target's stock market, but we find no such evidence.

A potentially important missing variable in the analysis is the volume of trade between two countries. In fact, companies that export to a given country might engage in M&A activity in that country for reasons that have nothing to do with governance. To control for this alternative explanation, in Column 5 we add bilateral trade to our regression. We define bilateral trade$_{s,b}$ as imports from country b to country s as a percentage of total imports of country s. Bilateral trade is not available for six countries: Belgium, Brazil, Israel, Nigeria, Switzerland and Zimbabwe. The number of observations in Column 5 changes accordingly. The results for shareholder protection are unchanged. The acquirer typically has stronger shareholder protection than the target. As we expected, bilateral trade is positive and significant, confirming that trade is an important motive for cross-border mergers and acquisitions. Same language and the difference in the logarithm of GNP per capita are no longer significant once bilateral trade is added to the baseline specification.

Table 6

The governance motive in cross-border M&A

The table presents the results of five OLS regressions for the sample of matched country pairs. The dependent variable is cross-border deals$_{s,b}$, or the number of cross-border deals where the target is from country s and the acquirer is from country b ($s \neq b$) as a percentage of the total number of deals in country s. The independent variables are the difference between acquirer and target countries' investor protection as measured alternatively by accounting standards, an index of the quality of accounting disclosure, and by shareholder protection, a measure of the effective rights of minority shareholders. We include as control variables the difference between the acquirer's and the target's logarithm of GNP per capita; same language, a dummy variable that equals one if the target and acquirer come from countries with the same official language, and zero otherwise; and same geographical area, a dummy variable that equals one if the target and acquirer come from the same geographical area. In Column 4, we add the difference between country b and country s in market return, the average annual stock market return in the 1990s. In Column 5, we add bilateral trade$_{s,b}$, the value of imports by country s from country b as a percentage of total imports by country s. The regressions contain fixed effects both for target and acquirer country (not shown). The standard errors shown in parentheses are adjusted for heteroskedasticity using Huber (1967) and White (1980) corrections.

	(1)	(2)	(3)	(4)	(5)
Δ(Accounting standards)$_{b-s}$	0.02***		0.01		
	(0.01)		(0.00)		
Δ(Shareholder protection)$_{b-s}$		1.93***	1.89***	1.89***	1.21***
		(0.19)	(0.21)	(0.20)	(0.23)
Δ(Log(GNP per capita))$_{b-s}$	0.10*	0.97***	0.40***	0.95***	0.06
	(0.05)	(0.10)	(0.05)	(0.10)	(0.04)
Same language	0.86**	0.97***	0.86**	1.02**	0.08
	(0.36)	(0.30)	(0.36)	(0.31)	(0.22)
Same geographical area	1.30***	1.12***	1.30***	1.13***	0.36***
	(0.14)	(0.11)	(0.14)	(0.12)	(0.15)
Δ(Market return)$_{b-s}$				0.00	
				(0.00)	
Bilateral trade$_{s,b}$					0.67***
					(0.10)
Adjusted R^2	0.53	0.50	0.53	0.51	0.67
N observations	1640	2352	1640	2162	1677

***, **, * indicate significance at 1%, 5% and 10% levels, respectively.

3.4. Premium

We use the sample of individual transactions to analyze the cross-country determinants of the takeover premium. We estimate the specification

$$\text{Log (premium)} = \alpha + \beta X + \gamma \text{ shareholder protection} + \varepsilon, \qquad (5)$$

where premium is the bid price as a percentage of the target's closing price four weeks before the announcement of the deal, shareholder protection is measured at the target country level, and X is a set of control factors. Control variables at the deal level are target size, the logarithm of the target's market capitalization four weeks before the announcement, a dummy variable (cross-border) that equals one if the

S. Rossi, P.F. Volpin / Journal of Financial Economics 74 (2004) 277–304 293

deal is cross-border and zero otherwise; a dummy variable (hostile bid) that equals one if the deal is hostile and zero otherwise; a dummy variable (tender offer) that equals one if the deal involves a tender offer and zero otherwise; and a dummy variable (contested bid) that equals one if the number of bidders is larger than one and zero otherwise.

Table 7 shows the results of six regressions based on specification (5). In all regressions, the standard errors shown in parentheses are adjusted for hetero-skedasticity, using the Huber (1967) and White (1980) corrections, and for clustering at the country level following Huber (1967). We correct for clustering because observations within a country are likely to be correlated with each other. We also include year and industry (at one-digit SIC-code level) dummies, but we do not report their coefficients.

In Column 1, we find that shareholder protection is positively correlated with the takeover premium. An increase in the level of shareholder protection by one point (e.g., the introduction of voting by mail in Belgium) is associated with a 0.04 increase in the logarithm of the premium, which translates into an average increase of 6% in the premium. Target size is negative and significant, that is, larger deals are associated with lower premiums.

In Column 2, we add the deal-level dummy variables for cross-border, hostile bid, tender offer, and contested bid. The result on shareholder protection does not change and the new controls are all positive, as expected. All but hostile bids are statistically significant. We interpret the finding on tender offers as evidence of the free rider hypothesis: that is, the bidder in a tender offer needs to pay a higher premium to induce shareholders to tender their shares. This theory would also predict that the premium paid should be higher the more diffuse the target's ownership structure. However, we cannot test this hypothesis directly because we do not have data on ownership structure for individual target companies. Contested bids are associated with a 0.1 increase in the logarithm of the premium, which translates into an average premium increase of 15%, consistent with the view that competition for targets is associated with higher premiums. Cross-border deals are associated with a 0.03 increase in the logarithm of the premium, which translates into an average premium increase of 3%.

Our finding that takeover premiums are higher in countries with higher shareholder protection can be interpreted by noting that the takeover premium measures the gain available to all target shareholders. There are two reasons why the premium might be higher in countries with stronger shareholder protection. First, shareholder protection reduces the cost of capital and therefore increases (potential) competition among bidders and the premium paid by the winning bidder. Second, diffuse ownership is more common in countries with higher shareholder protection. In turn, diffuse ownership exacerbates the free-rider problem in takeovers by forcing bidders to pay a higher takeover premium than otherwise (Grossman and Hart, 1980).

A concern with this interpretation is the possibility that the premium measures the private benefits of control. To explore this issue, in Column 3 we add the difference between the acquirer and target countries' shareholder protection as a further

Table 7
Determinants of the takeover premium

The table presents the results of six OLS regressions for the sample of individual deals. The dependent variable is the natural logarithm of premium, or the bid price as a percentage of the closing price of the target four weeks before the announcement. Independent variables at the country level are shareholder protection, a measure of the effective rights of minority shareholders, and mandatory bid rule, a dummy variable that equals one if in 1995 there was a legal requirement to make a tender offer when shareholdings after the acquisition exceed a given ownership threshold, and zero otherwise. The control variable at the cross-country level is the difference between the acquirer and target countries' shareholder protection. Control variables at the deal level are: target size, the logarithm of the target's market capitalization four weeks before the announcement; cross-border, a dummy variable that equals one if the deal is cross-border, and zero otherwise; hostile bid, a dummy variable that equals one if the deal is hostile, and zero otherwise; tender offer, a dummy variable that equals one if the deal involves a tender offer, and zero otherwise; contested bid, a dummy variable that equals one if the number of bidders is larger than one, and zero otherwise; and bidder M/B, the equity market-to-book ratio of the bidder four weeks before the announcement. In all regressions, we also include year and industry (at one-digit SIC-code level) dummies (not shown). In Column 6 we add two dummy variables that identify deals where the target firm is from the US (US targets) and from the UK (UK targets), respectively. The standard errors (in parentheses) are adjusted for heteroskedasticity using Huber (1967) and White (1980) corrections and for clustering at country level using the Huber (1967) correction.

	(1)	(2)	(3)	(4)	(5)	(6)
Shareholder protection	0.04***	0.05***	0.05***	0.07***	0.04***	−0.01
	(0.01)	(0.01)	(0.01)	(0.02)	(0.01)	(0.02)
Target size	−0.01***	−0.01***	−0.01***	−0.02**	−0.02***	−0.02***
	(0.00)	(0.00)	(0.00)	(0.01)	(0.00)	(0.00)
Cross-border		0.03*	0.03*	0.02	0.03**	0.04**
		(0.02)	(0.02)	(0.03)	(0.01)	(0.02)
Hostile bid		0.04	0.04	0.03	0.04	0.06***
		(0.03)	(0.03)	(0.06)	(0.03)	(0.02)
Tender offer		0.05***	0.05***	0.04	0.07***	0.08***
		(0.01)	(0.01)	(0.02)	(0.01)	(0.01)
Contested bid		0.10**	0.10**	0.05	0.10**	0.11***
		(0.04)	(0.04)	(0.05)	(0.04)	(0.04)
Δ(Shareholder protection)$_{b-s}$			0.00			
			(0.01)			
Bidder M/B				0.01		
				(0.00)		
Mandatory bid rule					−0.06**	−0.01
					(0.02)	(0.04)
US targets						0.16**
						(0.07)
UK targets						0.09***
						(0.03)
R^2	0.03	0.04	0.05	0.08	0.05	0.06
N observations	4007	4007	4007	1005	4007	4007
N countries	35	35	35	27	35	35

***, **, * indicate significance at 1%, 5%, and 10% levels, respectively.

S. Rossi, P.F. Volpin / Journal of Financial Economics 74 (2004) 277–304   295

control variable. If the premium measures the private benefits of control, we expect to find a negative and significant coefficient on this control variable, as in Dyck and Zingales (2004). The reason is that an acquirer coming from a country with lower shareholder protection is better able to extract private benefits of control than an acquirer coming from a country with stricter rules.

In Column 3, we find that the difference between acquirer and target countries' shareholder protection is not statistically significant. This result indicates that premium is not a proxy for the private benefits of control but for the total premium available to all shareholders. This finding also indicates that acquirers from countries with better shareholder protection do not need to pay more than acquirers from countries with weaker shareholder protection in cross-border deals.

According to Rau and Vermaelen (1998), glamour firms (as measured by high market-to-book ratios) will tend to overestimate their ability to create synergies in the target and should therefore be willing to pay more than managers of value firms (as measured by low market-to-book ratios). Therefore, in Column 4, we add the equity market-to-book ratio (M/B) of the bidder four weeks before the announcement. We obtain this information from Datastream. As a result of the matching procedure, the number of observations in Column 4 drops to 1,005. Contrary to the prediction, our results show that the bidder M/B is not correlated with the premium.

Comment and Schwert (1995) show that takeover laws are an important determinant of the takeover premium. Therefore, in Column 5 we control for differences in takeover laws across countries. The mandatory bid rule variable equals one if in 1995 there was a legal requirement to make a tender offer when shareholdings after the acquisition exceed a given ownership threshold, and zero otherwise. For instance, the mandatory bid variable rule equals one in the United Kingdom, where the threshold is 30%, and zero in the United States, where only a few states have a similar provision. We find a negative and significant coefficient for the mandatory bid rule, perhaps because a mandatory bid rule increases the cost of takeovers and therefore reduces competition among bidders. However, a mandatory bid rule might also increase the premium, because only high-premium takeovers that compensate the bidders for the high takeover costs succeed. To distinguish between the two effects, in an unreported regression we add the interactive term of mandatory bid rule multiplied by target size. The coefficient on this interactive term should measure the impact on the premium that is due to reduced competition, because larger deals are more likely to be deterred. The coefficient on the mandatory bid rule should reflect the fact that low-premium takeovers do not go through. We find that the coefficient on the mandatory bid rule is negative and significant, and that the coefficient on the interactive term is not significant. This result suggests that the mandatory bid rule variable captures an institutional difference across countries.

Because 75% of the deals have a US or UK target, in Column 6 we check the robustness of our findings by using two dummy variables that identify deals with US and UK targets, respectively. The results show that higher premiums are a feature of US and UK targets. The logarithm of the premium is 0.16 higher in the US and 0.09 higher in the UK than in the other countries. Note that the mandatory bid rule is no longer significant. This finding suggests that the mandatory bid rule is significant in Column 5 only because it captures the difference between US and UK targets.

3.5. Means of payment

Legal protection of investors may also affect the means of payment used in mergers and acquisitions. In a country with low investor protection, target shareholders are likely to prefer cash over the bidder's equity as the takeover currency, due to the risk of expropriation for being minority shareholders. We therefore expect less equity financing and more cash financing in countries with lower shareholder protection.

We estimate the following regression for the method of payment:

$$\text{Prob (all-cash bid)} = \alpha + \beta X + \gamma \text{ shareholder protection} + \varepsilon. \tag{6}$$

In this regression, which is similar to Eq. (3), our control variables are the same as those in Table 6: target size, cross-border, hostile bid, tender offer, contested bid, bidder M/B, and mandatory bid rule. We expect that larger deals are less likely to be paid entirely with cash. Cross-border deals might more often be paid in cash because shareholders dislike receiving foreign stocks as compensation. To entice shareholders to tender, hostile bids, tender offers, and contested bids are likely to be in cash.

Table 8 reports the results of six regressions based on specification (6). In all regressions, the standard errors shown in parentheses are adjusted for heteroskedasticity using Huber (1967) and White (1980) corrections, and for clustering at the country level following Huber (1967). We also include year and industry dummies (at the one-digit SIC-code level), but we do not report their coefficients.

Across all specifications, we find that shareholder protection is negatively correlated with all-cash bids. We note that a one-point increase in the level of shareholder protection is associated with a reduction of between 13% and 18% in the probability of using only cash as the means of payment. Our interpretation of this result is that stocks are a less popular means of payment in countries with lower shareholder protection because stocks entail a higher risk of expropriation.

Among the control variables, target size is negative and significant, and cross-border, hostile bid, and tender offer are positive and significant, as we expected. Contested bids are not associated with more cash as a method of payment. The probability of using only cash as the method of payment is 17% higher in cross-border deals.

To deepen the analysis of the means of payment in cross-border deals, in Column 3 we add the difference between acquirer and target countries' shareholder protection as a further control variable. We expect that the use of stocks as a method of payment will be positively correlated with the degree of investor protection in the acquirer country, when acquirer and target countries are different. We find evidence in favor of this prediction because the coefficient on the difference between acquirer and target countries' shareholder protection is negative and significant.

S. Rossi, P.F. Volpin / Journal of Financial Economics 74 (2004) 277–304 297

Table 8

Means of payment

The table reports estimates of six Probit models for the sample of individual deals. The dependent variable is all-cash bid, or a dummy variable that equals one if the acquisition is entirely paid in cash, and zero otherwise. Independent variables at the country level are shareholder protection, a measure of the effective rights of minority shareholders, and mandatory bid rule, a dummy variable that equals one if in 1995 there was a legal requirement to make a tender offer when shareholdings after the acquisition exceed a given ownership threshold, and zero otherwise. The control variable at the cross-country level is the difference between the acquirer and target countries' shareholder protection. Control variables at the deal level are: target size, the logarithm of the target's market capitalization four weeks before the announcement; cross-border, a dummy variable that equals one if the deal is cross-border, and zero otherwise; hostile bid, a dummy variable that equals one if the deal is hostile, and zero otherwise; tender offer, a dummy variable that equals one if the deal involves a tender offer, and zero otherwise; contested bid, a dummy variable that equals one if the number of bidders is larger than one, and zero otherwise; and bidder M/B, the equity market-to-book ratio of the bidder four weeks before the announcement. In all regressions, we also include year and industry (at one-digit SIC-code level) dummies (not shown). In Column 6 we add two dummy variables that identify deals where the target firm is from the US (US targets) and from the UK (UK targets), respectively. Displayed coefficients are the change in probability for an infinitesimal change in the independent variables. The standard errors (in parentheses) are adjusted for heteroskedasticity using Huber (1967) and White (1980) corrections and for clustering at country level using the Huber (1967) correction.

	(1)	(2)	(3)	(4)	(5)	(6)
Shareholder protection	−0.18***	−0.13***	−0.14***	−0.08**	−0.15***	−0.16***
	(0.03)	(0.03)	(0.03)	(0.03)	(0.02)	(0.04)
Target size	−0.06***	−0.07***	−0.07***	−0.02	−0.08***	−0.08***
	(0.01)	(0.02)	(0.02)	(0.02)	(0.02)	(0.02)
Cross-border		0.17***	0.14**	0.21***	0.14***	0.14***
		(0.04)	(0.05)	(0.05)	(0.04)	(0.05)
Hostile bid		0.10***	0.09**	0.08	0.10**	0.09**
		(0.04)	(0.04)	(0.08)	(0.04)	(0.04)
Tender offer		0.33***	0.32***	0.36***	0.34***	0.37***
		(0.08)	(0.08)	(0.11)	(0.09)	(0.08)
Contested bid		0.04	0.04	0.12*	0.05	0.04
		(0.04)	(0.04)	(0.07)	(0.04)	(0.04)
Δ(Shareholder protection)$_{b-s}$			−0.06***	−0.01	−0.06***	−0.05***
			(0.01)	(0.03)	(0.01)	(0.02)
Bidder M/B				0.00		
				(0.00)		
Mandatory bid rule					−0.06	
					(0.08)	
US targets						0.04
						(0.10)
UK targets						−0.10
						(0.06)
Pseudo R^2	0.11	0.18	0.19	0.20	0.19	0.19
N observations	4007	4007	4007	1005	4007	4007
N countries	35	35	35	27	35	35

***, **, * indicate significance at 1%, 5%, and 10% levels, respectively.

298   *S. Rossi, P.F. Volpin / Journal of Financial Economics 74 (2004) 277–304*

Bidder *M/B* might be correlated with the use of stocks as means of payment because the bidder could try to take advantage of market booms, as argued by Shleifer and Vishny (2003). In Column 4, we add the bidder *M/B*, but we find that its coefficient is not significantly different from zero.

The mandatory bid rule might require the bidder to make a cash offer or an offer with a cash alternative, as in the UK. If so, mandatory bid rules should be positively correlated with all-cash bids. However, UK bidders often avoid the mandatory tender offer by bidding for 29.9% of the shares, which is just below the 30% threshold for the mandatory tender offer, and then acquiring the remaining shares via a share offer. In this case, mandatory bid rules should not be correlated with all-cash bids. In Column 5, we control for mandatory bid rules, and find that the coefficient is not statistically significant.

In Column 6, we show that our results are not driven by deals involving US and UK firms. The coefficient on shareholder protection is even larger in absolute terms than in Column 1, and equally significant in statistical terms when we include two dummy variables for deals in which the target is a UK or US firm, respectively.

As a further robustness check (not reported), we estimate the specification in Column 2 with weighted least squares, in which the weights are the inverse of the number of observations by country. With this procedure, all countries have the same impact on the final results. The coefficient on shareholder protection is identical to that in Column 2.

One concern is that the control variables used in regressions (5) and (6) (tender offer, hostile bid, and cross-border) are themselves endogenous. As a result, our estimates could be inconsistent. To address this issue, we estimate a recursive system with five equations, one for each endogenous variable: premium, all-cash bid, tender offer, hostile bid, and cross-border. Exogenous variables are target size, bidder *M/B*, shareholder protection, and mandatory bid rule. We do not present the results of these regressions here, because the coefficients on shareholder protection are similar to those in Tables 7 and 8.

4. Discussion

The results presented in Section 3 have implications for the impact of investor protection on M&A activity and the role of cross-border takeovers as a catalyst for convergence in corporate governance regimes. We discuss both implications below.

4.1. M&A activity and investor protection

Overall, the results in Section 3 characterize M&A activity as correlating with investor-friendly legal environments. We interpret these findings along the lines of La Porta et al. (2000b) and argue that a more active market for mergers and acquisitions is the outcome of a corporate governance regime with stronger investor protection.

S. Rossi, P.F. Volpin / Journal of Financial Economics 74 (2004) 277–304 299

With low shareholder protection, there are large private benefits of control (Nenova, 2003; Dyck and Zingales, 2004), and therefore the market for corporate control does not operate freely. Conversely, with high investor protection, there are low private benefits of control, and there is an active market for corporate control. Moreover, better accounting standards increase disclosure, which helps acquirers identify potential targets. Hence, there are more potential targets in countries with better shareholder protection and accounting standards. This view yields two testable predictions: across target countries, both the volume of takeovers and the takeover premium should increase with better shareholder protection and accounting standards.

The results on volume, reported in Table 3, are strongly consistent with this view. The results on the premium, reported in Table 7, are weakly consistent with this view. Table 7 shows that higher shareholder protection in the target company is associated with higher premiums, although US and UK firms drive the results. Our results reject the alternative view that the market for corporate control is a substitute for legal protection of shareholders. According to Manne (1965) and Jensen (1993), if the market for corporate control works efficiently, firms with poor corporate governance become the targets of takeovers from more efficient firms. Extending their argument across countries, the volume of M&A activity and the premium paid should be greater in countries with lower investor protection. These predictions are inconsistent with our findings.

4.2. Convergence in corporate governance

The results in Table 6 relate to the ongoing debate among legal scholars on the possibility of effective worldwide convergence in corporate governance standards. Coffee (1999) argues that differences in corporate governance will persist but with some degree of functional convergence. Hansmann and Kraakman (2001) believe that formal convergence will happen soon. Bebchuk and Roe (1999) question the idea of rapid convergence because political and economic forces will slow down any change. Gilson (2001) argues that convergence will happen through all three channels (formal, contractual, and functional).

Our findings are consistent with the prediction by Coffee (1999) that companies from countries with better protection of investors will end up buying companies from countries with weaker protection. The case for target shareholders to sell out to bidders with higher governance standards is clear. Targets stand to gain from the lower cost of capital associated with higher investor protection. However, it is not obvious why acquirers seek to take over a poorly governed company. The results in Table 7, Column 3, show that acquirers from countries with better investor protection do not pay higher takeover premiums than acquirers from countries with weaker investor protection. Hence, they share part of the surplus created by improving the corporate governance of the target.

One concern is that they might import the poorer governance of their targets (poor accounting and disclosure practices, board structures, and so on). However, anecdotal evidence of cross-border deals with high press coverage suggests that this is not the case. The targets almost always adopt the governance standards of the acquirers, whether good or bad. In Daimler's acquisition of Chrysler, for instance, the resulting company has adopted a two-tier board structure, as required by German law. Thus, if convergence occurs, it is towards the acquirers' governance standards.

A related issue is that a deal could be motivated by the agency and hubris problems of the acquirer rather than by the desire to improve the governance regime in the target company. If so, the deal might not create value. Assessing this issue requires a study of the performance of the target and acquirer after the acquisition, which we cannot do with our large sample. Instead, we indirectly test this issue. If countries with poorer investor protection (in particular, lower governance standards, as measured by lower shareholder protection) have more severe agency problems, the hypothesis predicts more acquisitions by companies in countries with lower shareholder protection. This is not what we observe. If we sort our data by acquirer country, we find rather the opposite (not reported): more acquisitions by companies in countries with higher shareholder protection.

Our analysis also sheds light on the question as to whether cross-border deals might lead to greater international stock market integration and to a reduction of the home bias in equity investment in target countries. If the foreign bidder pays with stock, target shareholders face the problem of disposing of a new investment domiciled abroad. As a result, they might choose to keep the foreign stocks. In aggregate, these individual decisions would imply a reduction of the home bias in equity investment in target countries. We show in Table 8, Column 3, that target shareholders accept the acquirer's shares more often if the investor protection in the acquirer's country is greater than in the target's country. Hence, the reduction of the home bias puzzle goes together with a convergence in corporate governance regime. In this sense, our findings are consistent with Dahlquist et al. (2003).

5. Conclusion

Using a large sample of deals in 49 major countries, announced in the 1990s and completed by the end of 2002, we find that better investor protection is associated with more mergers and acquisitions, more attempted hostile takeovers, and fewer cross-border deals. We also find that better investor protection is associated with the greater use of stock as a method of payment, and with higher takeover premiums. These results indicate that domestic investor protection is an important determinant of the competitiveness and effectiveness of the market for mergers and acquisitions within a country.

In cross-border deals, we find that acquirers on average have higher investor protection than targets, that is, firms opt out of a weak governance regime via cross-border deals. This result indicates that the international market for corporate control helps generate convergence in corporate governance regimes across countries.

S. Rossi, P.F. Volpin / Journal of Financial Economics 74 (2004) 277–304   301

Appendix A. Description of the variables included in our study and their sources

A.1. Country-level variables

Volume	Percentage of domestic traded companies targeted in completed deals in the 1990s. Sources: SDC Platinum, provided by Thomson Financial Securities Data, and the World Development Indicators.
Hostile takeover	Attempted hostile takeovers as a percentage of domestic traded companies. Sources: SDC Platinum and the World Development Indicators.
Cross-border ratio	Number of cross-border deals as target as a percentage of all completed deals. Source: SDC Platinum.
GDP growth	Average annual real growth rate of the gross domestic product in the 1990s. Source: World Development Report.
GNP per capita	Gross national product in 1995 (in US$) divided by the population. Source: World Development Report.
Common law	Equals one if the origin of the company law is the English common law and zero otherwise. Source: La Porta et al. (1998).
Accounting standards	Index created by the Center for International Financial Analysis and Research to rate the quality of 1990 annual reports on their disclosure of accounting information. Source: La Porta et al. (1998).
Rule of law	Assessment of the law and order tradition in the country produced by the risk-rating agency International Country Risk (ICR). Average of the months of April and October of the monthly index between 1982 and 1995. It ranges between zero and ten. Source: La Porta et al. (1998).
Antidirector rights	The index is formed by adding one when (i) the country allows shareholders to mail their proxy vote to the firm, (ii) shareholders are not required to deposit their shares prior to the general shareholders' meeting, (iii) cumulative voting or proportional representation of minorities in the board of directors is allowed, (iv) an oppressed minorities mechanism is in place, (v) the minimum percentage of share capital that entitles a shareholder to call for an extraordinary shareholders' meeting is less than or equal to 10% (the sample median), or (vi) shareholders have preemptive rights that can be waived only by a shareholders' vote. Source: La Porta et al. (1998).

Shareholder protection	Measure of the effective rights of minority shareholders computed as the product of rule of law and antidirector rights divided by ten. It ranges between zero and six.
Ownership concentration	Average equity stake owned by the three largest shareholders in the ten largest nonfinancial domestic firms in 1994. Source: La Porta et al. (1998).
Cross-border regulation	Equals one if in 1995 a foreign buyer needed government approval before acquiring control of a domestic firm and zero otherwise. Source: Economist Intelligence Unit, Country Surveys.
Market return	Average annual stock market return in 1990s adjusted for inflation with the Consumer Price Index. Source: WorldScope.
Market dominance	Response to survey question: "Market dominance by a few enterprises is rare in key industries (1 = strongly disagree, 6 = strongly agree)." Source: The Global Competitiveness Report, 1996.
Mandatory bid rule	Equals one if in 1995 there was a legal requirement to make a tender offer when shareholding after the acquisition exceeds a given ownership threshold and zero otherwise. Source: Economist Intelligence Unit, Country Surveys.
Openness	Response to survey question: "Foreign investors are free to acquire control of a domestic company (1 = strongly disagree, 6 = strongly agree)." Source: The Global Competitiveness Report, 1996.

A.2. Cross-border variables

Cross-border deals$_{s,b}$	Number of deals in which the target is from country s and the acquirer is from country b, shown as a percentage of the total number of deals with target in country s. Source: SDC Platinum.
Same language	Equals one when target and acquirer's countries share the same main language and zero otherwise. Source: World Atlas 1995.
Same geographical area	Equals one when target and acquirer's countries are from the same continent and zero otherwise. We classify all countries into four areas (Africa, America, Asia, and Europe). Source: World Atlas 1995.
Bilateral trade$_{s,b}$	Value of imports by country s from country b as a percentage of total import by country s. Source: World Bank Trade and Production Database.

A.3. Deal-level variables

Premium	Bid price as a percentage of the closing price of the target four weeks before the announcement. Source: SDC Platinum.
All-cash bid	Equals one if the acquisition is entirely paid in cash and zero otherwise. Source: SDC Platinum.
Target size	Logarithm of the market capitalization of the target four weeks before the announcement of the deal in US$ million. Source: SDC Platinum.
Tender offer	Equals one if the acquisition is done through a tender offer and zero otherwise. Source: SDC Platinum.
Cross-border	Equals one if the target country differs from the acquirer country and zero otherwise. Source: SDC Platinum.
Hostile bid	Equals one if the bid is classified as unsolicited and zero otherwise. Source: SDC Platinum.
Contested bid	Equals one if the number of bidders is larger than one and zero otherwise. Source: SDC Platinum.
Bidder M/B	Equity market-to-book ratio of the bidder computed four weeks before the announcement. Source: Datastream.

References

Bebchuk, L., 1999. A rent-protection theory of corporate ownership and control. NBER Working Paper 7203, National Bureau of Economic Research, Cambridge, MA.

Bebchuk, L., Roe, M., 1999. A theory of path dependence in corporate governance and ownership. Stanford Law Review 52, 127–170.

Bhattacharya, U., Daouk, H., 2002. The world price of insider trading. Journal of Finance 57, 75–108.

Coffee, J., 1999. The future as history: the prospects for global convergence in corporate governance and its implications. Northwestern University Law Review 93, 641–708.

Comment, R., Schwert, W., 1995. Poison or placebo? Evidence on the deterrence and wealth effects of modern antitakeover measures. Journal of Financial Economics 39, 3–43.

Dahlquist, M., Pinkowitz, L., Stulz, R., Williamson, R., 2003. Corporate governance and the home bias. Journal of Financial and Quantitative Analysis 38, 87–110.

Dittmar, A., Mahrt-Smith, J., Servaes, H., 2003. International corporate governance and corporate cash holdings. Journal of Financial and Quantitative Analysis 38, 111–133.

Dyck, A., Zingales, L., 2004. Private benefits of control: an international comparison. Journal of Finance 59, 537–600.

Franks, J., Mayer, C., 1996. Hostile takeovers and the correction of managerial failure. Journal of Financial Economics 40, 163–181.

Gilson, R., 2001. Globalizing corporate governance: Convergence of form or function. American Journal of Comparative Law 49, 329–363.

Grossman, S., Hart, O., 1980. Takeover bids, the free-rider problem and the theory of the corporation. Bell Journal of Economics 11, 42–64.

Hansmann, H., Kraakman, R., 2001. The end of history for corporate law. Georgetown Law Journal 89, 439–468.

Huber, P., 1967. The behavior of maximum likelihood estimates under non-standard conditions. In: Proceedings of the Fifth Berkeley Symposium on Mathematical Statistics and Probability, Vol. 1. University of California Press, Berkeley, CA, pp. 221–233.

Jenkinson, T., Ljungqvist, A., 2001. The role of hostile stakes in German corporate governance. Journal of Corporate Finance 7, 397–446.

Jensen, M., 1993. The modern industrial revolution, exit, and the failure of internal control systems. Journal of Finance 48, 831–880.

La Porta, R., Lopez-de-Silanes, F., Shleifer, A., Vishny, R., 1997. Legal determinants of external finance. Journal of Finance 52, 1131–1150.

La Porta, R., Lopez-de-Silanes, F., Shleifer, A., Vishny, R., 1998. Law and finance. Journal of Political Economy 101, 678–709.

La Porta, R., Lopez-de-Silanes, F., Shleifer, A., 1999. Corporate ownership around the world. Journal of Finance 54, 471–517.

La Porta, R., Lopez-de-Silanes, F., Shleifer, A., Vishny, R., 2000a. Investor protection and corporate governance. Journal of Financial Economics 58, 3–27.

La Porta, R., Lopez-de-Silanes, F., Shleifer, A., Vishny, R., 2000b. Agency problems and dividend policies around the world. Journal of Finance 55, 1–33.

La Porta, R., Lopez-de-Silanes, F., Shleifer, A., Vishny, R., 2002. Investor protection and corporate valuation. Journal of Finance 57, 1147–1170.

Leuz, C., Nanda, D., Wysocki, P., 2003. Earnings management and investor protection. Journal of Financial Economics 69, 505–527.

Manne, H., 1965. Mergers and the market for corporate control. Journal of Political Economy 75, 110–126.

Nenova, T., 2003. The value of corporate voting rights and control: a cross-country analysis. Journal of Financial Economics 68, 325–351.

Pagano, M., Roell, A., Zechner, J., 2002. The geography of equity listing: Why do companies list abroad? Journal of Finance 57, 2651–2694.

Rau, R., Vermaelen, T., 1998. Glamour, value and the post-acquisition performance of acquiring firms. Journal of Financial Economics 49, 223–253.

Reese, W., Weisbach, M., 2002. Protection of minority shareholder interests, cross-listing in the United States, and subsequent equity offerings. Journal of Financial Economics 66, 65–104.

Shleifer, A., Vishny, R., 1986. Large shareholders and corporate control. Journal of Political Economy 94, 461–488.

Shleifer, A., Vishny, R., 2003. Stock market driven acquisitions. Journal of Financial Economics 70, 295–311.

White, H., 1980. A heteroskedasticity-consistent covariance matrix estimator and a direct test for heteroskedasticity. Econometrica 48, 817–838.

Wurgler, J., 2000. Financial markets and the allocation of capital. Journal of Financial Economics 58, 187–214.

Available online at www.sciencedirect.com

SCIENCE @ DIRECT®

ELSEVIER   Journal of Financial Economics 72 (2004) 357–384

JOURNAL OF
Financial
ECONOMICS

www.elsevier.com/locate/econbase

The effects of government ownership on bank lending [☆]

Paola Sapienza[a,b,*]

[a] *Kellogg School of Management, Northwestern University, 2001 Sheridan Rd., Evanston, IL 60208, USA*
[b] *CEPR, 90-98 Goswell Road, London EC1V 7RR, UK*

Received 4 February 2002; accepted 25 October 2002

Abstract

This paper uses information on individual loan contracts to study the effects of government ownership on bank lending behavior. State-owned banks charge lower interest rates than do privately owned banks to similar or identical firms, even if firms are able to borrow more from privately owned banks. State-owned banks mostly favor large firms and firms located in depressed areas. The lending behavior of state-owned banks is affected by the electoral results of the party affiliated with the bank: the stronger the political party in the area where the firm is borrowing, the lower the interest rates charged.
© 2003 Elsevier B.V. All rights reserved.

Keywords: Banking; Government; Ownership

JEL classification: G10; H11; L32

[☆] This paper is a revised version of "What do state-owned firms maximize? Evidence from Italian banks." I am indebted to Andrei Shleifer for guidance and encouragement. I also thank Alberto Alesina, Paul Armstrong-Taylor, Richard Caves, Riccardo DeBonis, Xavier Freixas, Anil Kashyap, Randy Kroszner, Janet Mitchell, Patricia Ledesma, Anna Paulson, Luigi Zingales, an anonymous referee, and seminar participants at 1999 European Symposium in Financial Markets, NBER Universities Research Conference on "Macroeconomic Effects of Corporate Finance", American Finance Association, the Federal Reserve of New York, and the CEPR conference on "Will Universal Banking Dominate or Disappear? Consolidation, Restructuring and (Re)Regulation in the Banking Industry" for helpful comments and suggestions. Laura Pisani provided excellent research assistance. All remaining errors are my responsibility.

*Corresponding author. Kellogg School of Management, Northwestern University, 2001 Sheridan Road, Evanston, 22 60208, USA.

E-mail address: paola-sapienza@northwestern.edu (P. Sapienza).

358   *P. Sapienza / Journal of Financial Economics 72 (2004) 357–384*

1. Introduction

La Porta et al. (2002) document that government ownership of banks is pervasive worldwide. In 1995 state ownership in the banking industry around the world averaged about 41.6% percent (38.5% if we exclude former socialist countries). Mayer (1990) shows that bank financing is the main source of outside financing in all countries. Yet despite the prevalence of government-owned banks in many countries, the prominent role of bank financing, and the importance of efficient financial markets for growth, there is very little evidence on how government ownership affects bank lending.

In this paper I use a unique dataset on state-owned banks in Italy, where lending by state-owned banks represents more than half of total lending. Using data on interest rates charged on individual loans, I study the efficiency of the allocation of credit by state-owned banks. Furthermore, I combine data on lending with the political affiliation of the bank and recent election results to study the impact of political power on bank lending behavior.

The debate concerning the role of ownership in banking is framed along the three alternative theories of state ownership: social, political, and agency. The social view (Atkinson and Stiglitz, 1980), which is based on the economic theory of institutions, suggests that state-owned enterprises (SOEs) are created to address market failures whenever the social benefits of SOEs exceed the costs. According to this view, government-owned banks contribute to economic development and improve general welfare (Stiglitz, 1993). In contrast, recent theories on the politics of government ownership (Shleifer and Vishny, 1994) suggest that SOEs are a mechanism for pursuing the individual goals of politicians, such as maximizing employment or financing favored enterprises. The political view is that SOEs are inefficient because of the politicians' deliberate policy of transferring resources to their supporters (Shleifer, 1998).

The agency view shares with the social view the idea that SOEs are created to maximize social welfare but can generate corruption and misallocation (Banerjee, 1997; Hart et al., 1997). Agency costs within government bureaucracy can result in weak managerial incentives in SOEs. According to this view, the ultimate efficiency of SOEs depends on the trade-off between internal and allocative efficiency (Tirole, 1994).

These theories cannot be disentangled by looking at bank profitability: it is not clear whether government-owned banks are less profitable because they maximize broader social objectives, because they have lower incentives, or because they inefficiently cater to politicians' wishes. My empirical strategy addresses these problems. Instead of looking at overall bank performance, where the mix of activities performed by banks might change under government ownership, I focus on the lending relationships of the banks. My data include information on the balance sheets and income statements of over 37,000 Italian firms. The data are collected by Centrale dei Bilanci (CdB), an institution created to provide its members (mainly banks) with economic and financial information for screening Italian companies. For a large subset of the 37,000 companies, CdB members receive a numerical score, which CdB calculates through traditional linear discriminant analysis, to identify the

P. Sapienza / Journal of Financial Economics 72 (2004) 357–384 359

risk profile of the companies (Altman, 1968). I merge this information with data on the credit relationships of the firms surveyed in the CdB database.

The information in this database is available to all the banks prior to lending and has proven to be very accurate in predicting the success or failure of a company (see Altman et al., 1994). Since both privately owned and state-owned banks have access to the same information, I can use this system to check the differences in the credit policies of the various banks.

I look at the individual loan contracts of the two types of banks and compare the interest rate charged to two sets of companies with identical scores that borrow from either state- or privately owned banks, or both. My main result is that, all else equal, state-owned banks charge lower interest rates than do privately owned banks. On average, the difference is about 44 basis points.

I claim that this difference can best be explained by the political view of state-ownership. First, my results show that even companies that are able to access private funds benefit from cheaper loans from state-owned banks. Second, companies located in the south of Italy benefit more by borrowing from state-owned banks than do companies located in the north, consistent with the view that political patronage is more widespread in the south (Ginsborg, 1990). This result holds even after controlling for the presence of credit constraints. Finally, contrary to the social view, state-owned banks are more inclined to favor large enterprises. Overall, my results support the political view of government ownership. However, I note that some of these results could also be consistent with some versions of the social or agency views. For example, one could argue that firms located in the south receive cheaper funds because a socially maximizing government wants to channel funds to depressed areas of the country. My findings that larger firms get cheaper funds could also be consistent with the agency view.

To further distinguish among the different theories, I analyze the relation between interest rates, the political affiliation of the bank, and electoral results. I find that the lending behavior of state-owned banks is affected by the electoral results of the party affiliated with the bank: the stronger the political party in the area where the bank is lending, the lower are the interest rates charged. This result is not driven by omitted bank and firm characteristics, since I show that it is robust to including both bank and firm fixed effects.

Overall, my results support the political view of SOEs and suggest that state-owned banks serve as a mechanism to supply political patronage. These results relate to important policy debates. My findings show that government ownership of banks has distorting effects on the financial allocation of resources. This is consistent with findings that widespread state ownership of banks is correlated with poor financial development (Barth et al., 2000). In turn, a highly politicized allocation of financial resources may have deleterious effects on productivity and growth, as recent research by La Porta et al. (2002) shows.

The paper is organized as follows. The next section outlines the theories of SOEs and their predictions. Section 3 provides a description of the institutional environment. Section 4 describes the data, the sample, and the methodology. Section 5 presents the empirical evidence. Section 6 concludes.

2. Theoretical issues

The three main views of state-owned enterprises—social, agency, and political—have different implications for both the existence and the role of state-owned banks. The social view sees SOEs as institutions created by social welfare maximizing governments to cure market failures. According to this view, private and state-owned enterprises differ because the first maximize profits and the latter maximize broader social objectives. In this literature, the reason for creating public financial institutions is the existence of market failures in financial and credit markets (Stiglitz and Weiss, 1981; Greenwald and Stiglitz, 1986). Thus, state-owned banks or programs of direct credit have often been justified on the grounds that private banks fail to take social returns into account. For example, private banks might not allocate funds to projects with high social returns or to firms located in specific industries (Stiglitz, 1993). Under the social theory, the objective of state-owned banks should be to channel resources to socially profitable projects or to firms that do not have access to other funds.

The agency view shares with the social theory the idea that governments seek to maximize social welfare. Under the agency hypothesis, governments design public financial institutions to cure market failures. However, since SOEs maximize multiple nonmeasurable objectives, managers of SOEs have low-powered incentives (Tirole, 1994). Of course, low powered incentives are not always bad; Laffont and Tirole (1993) show that, under some circumstances, a concern for quality calls for low-powered incentives. But given the incentive problems associated with the control of SOEs, the agency view concludes that decisions on government in-house provision of public goods should depend on the tradeoff between internal and allocative efficiency. Under this hypothesis, state-owned banks channel resources to socially profitable activities, but public managers exert less effort (or divert more resources) than would their private counterparts. The agency view predicts that in general, state-owned banks serve social objectives and allocate resources where private markets fail. However, public managers of state-owned banks exert low effort or divert resources for personal benefits, such as career concerns, with an eye toward future job prospects in the private sector.

According to both the social and agency views, the government role in the economy emerges and evolves to perform the economic functions that markets either cannot handle or cannot perform well. Fundamentally different, the political view is based on the assumption that politicians are self-interested individuals who pursue their own personal, political, and economic objectives rather than maximizing social welfare. The main objective of politicians is to maintain voting support. Hence, SOEs provide jobs for political supporters, and direct resources to friends and supporters (Shleifer and Vishny, 1998). According to this view, politicians create and maintain state-owned banks not to channel funds to economically efficient uses, but rather to maximize their own personal objectives.

Though the agency and the political views make very different assumptions about government objectives, the difference in the empirical implications is not so clearly defined. The merit of the agency view is to show that misgovernance can exist even

P. Sapienza / Journal of Financial Economics 72 (2004) 357–384 361

when the government has the best of intentions (see Banerjee, 1997). Under both views, we would observe some misallocation of resources, but for different reasons. The agency view claims that the misallocation takes place because managers shirk or divert resources for their private use, but under the political view, the misallocation of resources is a political objective, rather than the result of a lack of incentives. State-owned banks will divert resources to areas where there is more political patronage, will finance friends and supporters of politicians, and will maximize political support, e.g., by maximizing employment at the bank level or at other firms.

3. State ownership of banks in Italy

Though there are more privately owned banks than state-owned banks in Italy (864 compared to 117), 58% of total assets in Italy were held by state-owned in 1995, among the highest percentages in the industrialized world.[1] But Italy is not unique in this dimension in most Continental Europe: in Germany, the proportion is 50%, and in France, it is 36%. Latin American countries also show a very high percentage of state ownership.

Data suggest that in general, Italian state-owned banks have a different lending focus from privately owned banks. De Bonis (1998) shows that state-owned banks make more than 11% of their loans to state or local authorities (compared to 1.6% loaned by private banks). The percentage loaned to companies is similar between state- and privately owned banks (55.1% and 57.5%, respectively), but no analysis has investigated the differences within each class of borrowers for the two groups of banks. De Bonis (1998) also finds that state-owned banks are less profitable in making loans than are privately owned banks. In 1995, bad loans represented 57.2% of bank capital for state-owned banks, almost double of that of private institutions (30.2%).

The degree of political influence on state-owned banks is evident in the procedure used to appoint the chairpersons and top executives of state-owned banks. Until 1993, the appointments of the directors and management of the banks was made by a specific Parliamentary commission, specifically the Comitato Interministeriale per il Credito e il Risparmio (CICR), a permanent Parliamentary commission in which the political groups are represented according to their relative strength in Parliament. In 1992, for example, this commission met three times: on October 30th it appointed 72 of chairpersons, vice-chairpersons, and CEO of state-owned banks; on December 1st it appointed other 26; and on December 30th an additional 33.

Over time there could have been differences in the level of political interference. Some authors (e.g., Barca and Trento, 1994; Ginsborg, 1990) claim that close personal ties between party leaders and the managers of SOEs were introduced after the mid-1950s. De Bonis (1998) claims that the management of state-owned banks became independent from the central government after 1993, when the public entities that previously owned the banks were transformed into foundations. Nonetheless, some observers believe that the practice of political appointments of top executives in state-owned banks has survived (e.g., Visentini, 2000).

---

[1] I consider foreign banks operating in Italy as being privately owned.

4. Data and methodology

The two main databases come from the Company Accounts Dataset (CAD) and the Credit Register (CR) compiled by Centrale dei Bilanci (CdB). The CAD reports balance sheets and income statements for more than 50,000 Italian companies. The CR collects information about any individual loan contracts over 80 million lire (about 41,300 Euro) granted by banks to any customer. This information is readily available to the CdB membership, which is mainly composed of banks. Starting in 1991, CdB also developed what it called the Diagnostic System, which was designed to provide banks with a tool for quickly identifying the soundness of the companies included in the database. This system applies traditional linear discriminant analysis based on two samples of businesses of healthy and unsound companies. A numerical score is obtained from two discriminant functions. This score summarizes the "risk profile" of the business. This system has proven to be very successful: it correctly classified in the year immediately prior to distress 87.6% of healthy companies and 92.6% of unsound companies (see Altman et al., 1994). Appendix A provides more details on the numerical score.

For each firm, the CR reports the amount of credit granted by each bank, together with the amount used (outstanding balance). In addition, 90 banks (accounting for over 80% of total bank lending) agreed to file detailed information about the interest rates charged on each loan. These data, collected for monitoring purposes, are highly confidential.

A subset of CR data includes all the companies that were surveyed for at least one year in the CAD. Data on loan contracts are quarterly, but data on balance sheets and income statements are annual. Aggregate information on bank balance sheets and income statements comes from the Bank of Italy's prudential supervision statistical data, where it is reported on a quarterly basis. I constructed the data on bank ownership by using the Bank of Italy legal classification prior to 1990.[2]

Local election results for three national elections, 1989, 1992, and 1994, are from the archives of the Interior Ministry. The local unit is the province (similar to U.S. counties). The archives provide the total valid votes and the votes collected by all the parties running in the elections in each of Italy's 95 provinces.

I collect the data on the political affiliation of the top management of the bank from newspapers. For 36 state-owned banks, I am able to identify the political affiliation of the chairperson. Appendix B provides additional details about these data and the electoral data.

4.1. Private and state-owned banks

The data on loan contracts come from the subset of the CR and CAD datasets previously described. The sample period begins in 1991 and ends in 1995, because

---

[2] Prior to 1990, all state-owned banks had a different legal status from private banks (either corporations and cooperatives). After 1990, all the state-owned banks' charters were modified by law and banks were transformed into corporations.

P. Sapienza / Journal of Financial Economics 72 (2004) 357–384 363

1991 is the first year in which CdB distributed the information on the score to its members. I restrict my attention to privately owned and state-owned banks that file information about interest payments and are members of the CdB. This criterion introduces a potential sample selection, since the banks that file interest rate information are generally larger than the average Italian bank. However, it turns out that the sample of state-owned banks represents more than 90% of state-owned loans. I exclude small state-owned banks from the sample, but they are not the typical state-owned bank. Privately owned banks selected with these criteria are larger than the average privately owned bank, but because I use them as benchmarks for comparisons with the behavior of state-owned banks, it is important that they are similar in size to the state-owned banks.

These selection criteria restrict the total number of banks to 85: 40 have always been privately owned, 43 are state-owned banks, and two were privatized during the period of observation.

Table 1 shows descriptive statistics of the banks in the sample. The median state-owned bank has a ratio of nonperforming loans to total loans of 6.91%, as opposed to 5.25% for privately owned banks. The mean for the two sub samples is statistically different at 1% level of significance. State-owned banks also have a lower return on assets (0.34% for the median state-owned bank, as opposed to 0.51% for the median privately owned bank) and higher operating costs relative to assets (3.05% for the median state-owned bank, as opposed to 2.87% for the median privately owned bank). These differences reflect differences between state-owned and privately owned banks and represent a potential problem in comparing their credit policies of these two subsamples of banks.

4.2. Companies borrowing from privately owned and state-owned banks

Ideally, I would like to compare the entire loan portfolios of state-owned and privately owned banks and, using the balance sheet and income statement information for the companies, compare the credit decisions of these two types of banks. Unfortunately, the information on firm characteristics is available for only a subset of the companies that receive credit from the banks.

To deal with this lack of information, I take a different approach. I compare two matching samples of companies that borrow from state- and privately owned banks, respectively. The advantage of this approach is that I can compare the interest rate charged in the same period to the same company, or to very similar companies, by state- and privately owned banks (many firms have credit ties with both types of banks). Since state- and privately owned banks have access to the same information for evaluating these companies, any difference in the price of the loan is likely to reflect differences in the objectives of the banks, rather than differences in the evaluation skills of the bank's loan officers.

To select the sample of companies in this study, I use the following criteria: from the sample of companies included in CdB, I select a subsample of companies that have a loan with at least one bank in the sample for at least one year and for which there is a numerical score. Because loan characteristics (collateral, etc.)

364 *P. Sapienza / Journal of Financial Economics 72 (2004) 357–384*

Table 1
Summary statistics: the bank sample
Panel A shows summary statistics for the sample of privately owned banks (bank–years). Panel B shows summary statistics for state-owned banks. Return on assets is earnings over total assets. Operating costs include wages and other operating costs.

Variable	Mean	Median	Std dev.	Min	Max	Obs.
Panel A: Privately owned banks						
Total assets (bill. of lire)	11,856	6,318	16,674	186	110,531	192
Total loans (bill. of lire)	4,917	2,570	6,604	80	44,820	192
Percentage of loans over total assets	42.90	43.00	5.14	30.00	56.00	192
Percentage of nonperforming loans to total loans	6.14	5.25	4.02	1.42	23.63	192
Return on assets (%)	0.46	0.51	0.62	−6.47	1.28	192
Operating costs over total assets (%)	3.04	2.87	0.78	1.56	5.96	192
Panel B: State-owned banks						
Total assets (bill. of lire)	27,314	6,070	40,192	547	188,944	199
Total loans (bill. of lire)	12,292	2,586	18,750	218	79,011	199
Percentage of loans over total assets	41.75	42.00	7.59	24.00	70.00	199
Percentage of nonperforming loans to total loans	8.41	6.91	6.23	1.63	39.55	199
Return on assets (%)	0.28	0.34	0.73	−7.19	1.32	199
Operating costs over total assets (%)	3.05	3.05	0.65	1.73	5.65	199

can affect loan rates (Petersen and Rajan, 1994), I focus on homogeneous loan contracts. Specifically, I analyze credit line contracts, the most common loan contract in Italy, in which banks set the amount of the loan and an interest rate. The loans analyzed here exclude long- term, collateralized, and subsidized loans.[3]

From these data I select the subset of companies that have been borrowing from state-owned banks. For each observation in this sample (company–bank–year) I identify a matching company that borrows from a privately owned bank in the same year. Whenever the company borrows in the same year from both state- and privately owned banks, I match the company with itself. If a company borrows only from state-owned banks, I choose a similar firm that borrows from privately owned banks in the same year. In these cases, I identify the matching company as a firm operating in the same industry and in the same geographical area (north, center, and south), with an identical risk profile based on Altman's *z*-score (Altman, 1968, 1993), and similar size (measured by sales). I also require that if the company that receives loans from state-owned banks is itself state owned (privately owned), then the matching company must be state owned (privately owned) as well. These selection

---

[3] There are other characteristics of the relationship between banks and borrowers that I cannot control for. Although the loan contracts included in the sample have homogeneous characteristics, borrowers might have contemporaneous contracts with the bank (deposits, collateralized loans) that might affect the cost of the loan. Also, the quality of service or the probability that the loan is revoked can vary across banks. Unfortunately, I cannot rule out any of these possibilities; therefore my results should be interpreted with these caveats in mind.

P. Sapienza / Journal of Financial Economics 72 (2004) 357–384 365

criteria reduce the sample to a total of 6,968 companies, corresponding to 110,786 company–bank–year observations; 55,393 observations refer to borrowers of state-owned banks and 55,393 to borrowers of privately owned banks.

By construction, the companies that borrow from both state- and privately owned banks have identical scores, operate in identical industries, and are located in the same geographical area. Table 9 in Appendix A shows the scores for the two subsamples of companies.

The summary statistics on the two subsamples of firms (Table 2) also show that the selected companies borrowing from state- and privately owned banks are very similar. None of the differences in the means of the relevant variables are statistically significant. In both subsamples, the median firm has 58 employees, 21 billion lire in sales, 18 billion lire in assets and a coverage ratio (interest expenses divided by EBITDA) of 1.47. The median firm has a leverage ratio of 71%. I define leverage as the book value of short- plus long-term debt divided by sum of the book value of short- plus long-term debt and the book value of equity. Return on sales is slightly below 8%. The majority of the companies are privately held. Seventy are state-owned companies.

Table 2

Summary statistics: the company sample

Summary statistics for the two subsamples of company–bank–years. Panel A shows the summary statistics for the subsample of companies that borrow from privately owned banks (company–bank–year). Panel B shows the summary statistics for the companies that borrow from state-owned banks. Total Assets is beginning-of-year total assets in lire. Sales is beginning-of-year sales in lire. Employees is the number of employees at the beginning of the year. Return on sales is earning before interest, taxes, and depreciation (*EBITDA*) over sales. Age is the number of years since incorporation. Leverage is book value of short- plus long-term debt divided by the sum of book value of short- plus long-term debt and book value of equity. Coverage is interest expense divided by *EBITDA* (I truncate values above 100 at 100 and values below zero at zero).

Variable	Mean	Median	Std dev.	Obs.
Panel A: Companies borrowing from privately owned banks				
Total assets (bill.)	101	18	546	55,393
Sales (bill.)	108	21	654	55,393
Employees	231	58	928	54,782
Return on sales	8.48	7.98	7.25	54,799
Age	25	18	36	55,168
Leverage	68.11	70.69	17.59	54,638
Coverage	1.85	1.47	2.56	55,351
Panel B: Companies borrowing from state-owned banks				
Total assets (bill.)	101	18	547	55,393
Sales (bill.)	108	21	654	55,393
Employees	231	58	928	54,789
Return on sales	8.51	7.95	7.37	54,817
Age	25	18	36	55,173
Leverage	68.12	70.71	17.60	54,646
Coverage	1.86	1.47	2.63	55,349

5. Empirical analysis

5.1. Differences in interest rates

To learn whether state- and privately owned banks behave differently, I examine the interest rate charged to similar companies by these two types of banks. I first compare the average interest rates charged by both types of banks and then present a regression analysis that controls for bank and firm characteristics.

Table 3 reports the average interest rate, minus the prime rate, charged by both types of banks. I define the interest rate as the ratio of the quarterly payments made by the firm to its bank (interest plus fixed fees) to the firm's quarterly loan balance. Of course, this measure of interest rate overestimates the interest rate of a firm with small average balances. For this reason, I eliminate the rates linked to credit lines with less than 50 million lire in average daily balances. The same criterion has been used by Pagano et al. (1998) and Sapienza (2002).

Table 3

Interest rates charged by state-owned and privately owned banks by loan risk category

I define the interest rate paid by the firm to the bank as the ratio of the quarterly payment (interest plus fees) to its quarterly average balance minus the prime rate. The loan risk category is based on the numerical score of the company (see details in Appendix A). Difference is the average difference between the second column (interest rates charged by state-owned banks) and the third column (interest rates charged by privately owned banks). I test the statistical significance of the difference using the t-statistic with reference to a mean of zero. ***, ** indicate statistically significant at the 1% and 5% level, respectively.

Risk category	State-owned banks	Privately owned banks	Difference	Obs.
Panel A: Whole sample				
Highly secure	2.53	2.75	−0.22***	1,420
Secure	2.75	2.97	−0.22***	15,262
Vulnerable	2.84	3.25	−0.41***	409
Highly vulnerable	3.05	3.28	−0.24***	11,743
Uncertainty between vulnerability and risk	3.18	3.43	−0.25***	13,471
Risk of bankruptcy	3.36	3.58	−0.22***	10,472
High risk of bankruptcy	3.69	3.80	−0.11**	2,616
All borrowers	3.07	3.31	−0.23***	55,393
Panel B: Firms borrowing from both state-owned and privately owned banks				
Highly secure	2.52	2.74	−0.22***	1,360
Secure	2.72	2.94	−0.22***	13,373
Vulnerable	2.85	3.26	−0.41***	394
Highly vulnerable	3.02	3.27	−0.24***	10,248
Uncertainty between vulnerability and risk	3.15	3.40	−0.25***	11,899
Risk of bankruptcy	3.33	3.54	−0.21***	9,184
High risk of bankruptcy	3.66	3.79	−0.13**	2,438
All borrowers	3.05	3.27	−0.23***	48,896

Column 3 of Table 3 presents the differences in rates for the two subsets of banks. For the overall sample, these comparisons show that for similar companies, the average interest rate charged by state-owned banks is 23 basis points lower than that charged by private banks. The differences are statistically significant in a *t*-test.

Table 3 also presents the differences in interest rates for various risk profiles of the companies, demonstrating that these differences are not driven by few outliers. Also, to make sure that the differences are not driven by any incorrect matching, Panel B of Table 3 presents the same statistics for the subsample of firms that borrow from both state- and privately owned banks during the same year (the matching firm is itself).

My main finding is that for any risk category, the interest rate charged by state-owned banks is lower than that charged by privately owned banks. The difference in interest rates is statistically significant at the 1% level.

However, the comparisons presented above are not conditioned on other characteristics of the banks, such as differences in the size and riskiness of the portfolio. Table 1 shows that state- and privately owned banks are different in size, profitability, and riskiness. To address this issue, I use a regression model to estimate the difference in interest rates charged by the two types of banks.

I regress r_{ikt}, the relative interest rate charged at time t by bank k to company i (defined as the interest rate minus the prime rate) on a dummy variable, $STATE_{k,t}$, that equals one if at time t bank k is a state-owned bank. The coefficient measures the impact of state ownership on interest rates. A negative (positive) value means that state-owned banks charge a lower (higher) interest rate than do privately owned banks. I also include several regressors to control for firm, market, and bank characteristics. Finally, I include a vector of time fixed effects and a vector of firm fixed effects. By using a firm fixed effect, I compare the interest rate charged by various banks to the same company.

Panel A of Table 4 reports the regression results. Heteroskedasticity-robust standard errors are shown in parentheses. I also adjust the standard errors for within-year clustering. Column 1 reports the estimates of the interest rate regressed on the $STATE_{k,t}$ dummy and time and firm fixed effects. These results are directly comparable to the simple differences in the last row of Table 3: state-owned banks charge interest rates 23 basis points lower than do privately owned banks.

As mentioned before, the coefficients measuring state ownership might capture specific characteristics of state-owned banks and local market structure. To overcome this problem, Columns 2–5 of Table 4 include several other controls. In column 2, I introduce a proxy for the size of the bank, measured by the logarithm of the bank's total assets. Aside for the role size plays in determining market concentration measures, a bank's size should affect prices according to the theoretical literature. For example, in a standard Cournot model with capacity constraints (increasing returns to scale), the bank with lower capacity would supply loans equal to capacity at a lower price than the other bank with higher capacity (see Tirole, 1989). Size could also reflect some implicit characteristics of the loan. Loans from large banks might carry an implicit guarantee of not being revoked, if large banks are perceived to be less likely to fail.

Table 4

Interest rates charged by state-owned and privately owned banks

The dependent variable is the interest rate charged to firm i by bank k at time t minus the prime rate at time t. $STATE_{k,t}$ is a dummy variable equal to one if at time t bank k is a state-owned bank. I measure the size of the bank by logarithm of total assets. The percentage of nonperforming loans is the ratio of nonperforming loans to total loans. I measure market concentration at the province level by the Herfindahl-Hirschman Index (HHI) on total banking lending. The size of the firm is the logarithm of sales. All regressions include year and firm dummies. Heteroskedasticity-robust standard errors are in brackets. The standard errors are corrected for within-year clustering. ***, ** indicate statistically significant at the 1% and 5% level, respectively. The table also reports the p-value of an F-test for the hypothesis that the joint effect of all the variables equals zero. Panel A reports the results for the whole sample. Panels B and C report the results for the subsample of firms that borrow from both state-owned and privately owned banks, respectively.

	(1)	(2)	(3)	(4)	(5)
Panel A					
$State_{k,t}$	−0.2378***	−0.4589***	−0.5019***	−0.4417***	−0.4424***
	(0.0274)	(0.0166)	(0.0180)	(0.0218)	(0.0218)
Size of the bank		0.1936***	0.1730***	0.1723***	0.1728***
		(0.0078)	(0.0037)	(0.0041)	(0.0040)
Percentage of nonperforming loans			0.0337***	0.0338***	0.0336***
			(0.0014)	(0.0014)	(0.0015)
Concentration of loans (HHI)			2.6681***	3.0753***	2.8267***
			(0.4417)	(0.3514)	(0.4197)
Concentration of loans if $State_{k,t} = 1$				−0.8677***	−0.8561***
				(0.3223)	(0.3183)
Size of the firm					−0.2453***
					(0.0051)
Score of the firm					0.0365***
					(0.0081)
Firm fixed effect	Yes	Yes	Yes	Yes	Yes
Time fixed effect	Yes	Yes	Yes	Yes	Yes
Observations	110,786	110,786	110,752	110,752	110,752
Adjusted R-squared	0.407	0.420	0.425	0.425	0.428
p-Value of F-test for total effect equal to zero	0.0000	0.0000	0.0000	0.0000	0.0000
Panel B					
$State_{k,t}$	−0.2293***	−0.4510***	−0.4980***	−0.4374***	−0.4376***
	(0.0261)	(0.0185)	(0.0168)	(0.0221)	(0.0220)
Size of the bank		0.1895***	0.1694***	0.1689***	0.1691***
		(0.0087)	(0.0042)	(0.0046)	(0.0045)
Percentage of nonperforming loans			0.0341***	0.0343***	0.0340***
			(0.0014)	(0.0014)	(0.0014)
Concentration of loans (HHI)			2.8282***	3.2309***	2.9066***
			(0.4835)	(0.4297)	(0.4958)
Concentration of loans if $State_{k,t} = 1$				−0.8756***	−0.8685***
				(0.3341)	(0.3322)
Size of the firm					−0.2648***
					(0.0065)
Score of the firm					0.0335***
					(0.0077)
Firm fixed effect	Yes	Yes	Yes	Yes	Yes

P. Sapienza / *Journal of Financial Economics* 72 (2004) 357–384 369

Table 4. (*Continued*)

	(1)	(2)	(3)	(4)	(5)
Time fixed effect	Yes	Yes	Yes	Yes	Yes
Observations	97,792	97,792	97,760	97,760	97,760
Adjusted R-squared	0.407	0.420	0.425	0.423	0.427
p-Value of F-test for total effect equal to zero	0.0000	0.0000	0.0000	0.0000	0.0000

Panel C

	(1)	(2)	(3)
$State_{k,t}$	−0.4402***	−0.4382***	−0.4373***
	(0.0220)	(0.0225)	(0.0220)
Size of the bank	0.1690***	0.1691***	0.1691***
	(0.0045)	(0.0045)	(0.0045)
Percentage of nonperforming loans	0.0340***	0.0340***	0.0340***
	(0.0014)	(0.0014)	(0.0014)
Concentration of loans (HHI)	2.9151***	2.9104***	2.9071***
	(0.4914)	(0.4976)	(0.4946)
Concentration of loans if the bank is state-owned	−0.8838***	−0.8751***	−0.8672***
	(0.3284)	(0.3258)	(0.3323)
Size of the firm	−0.2646***	−0.2647***	−0.2649***
	(0.0065)	(0.0066)	(0.0064)
Score of the firm	0.0335***	0.0335***	0.0334***
	(0.0076)	(0.0076)	(0.0077)
$State_{k,t} = 1$ if the firm has more than 8% of credit line usage	0.0150		
	(0.0127)		
$State_{k,t} = 1$ if the firm has more than 15% of credit line usage		0.0214	
		(0.0303)	
$State_{k,t} = 1$ if the firm has more than 37% of credit line usage			−0.0364
			(0.0156)
Firm fixed effect	Yes	Yes	Yes
Time fixed effect	Yes	Yes	Yes
Observations	97760	97760	97760
Adjusted R-squared	0.427	0.427	0.427
p-value of F-test for total effect equal to zero	0.0000	0.0000	0.0000

Empirically, Sapienza (2002) finds that bank size has a positive and significant effect on loan rates for a sample of privately owned banks, after controlling for firm characteristics. Column 2 of Table 4 confirms this result. All else equal, a one-standard-deviation increase in the logarithm of bank assets leads to an increase of nearly 14 basis points in the interest rate. Since state-owned banks are generally larger than privately owned banks, the size of the coefficient of $STATE_{k,t}$ increases from 0.23 to 0.46 after I control for bank size, suggesting that the mean differences in Table 3 underestimate the impact of state ownership.

In Column 3 of Table 4, I include two other controls in the regression. First, I include a measure of market concentration—the Herfindahl-Hirschman Index (HHI) on loans—as many studies have identified a positive relation between market concentration and prices (Berger and Hannan, 1989; Hannan, 1991). Another potential problem in my basic regression is that the state-ownership dummy captures the fact that banks with a higher proportion of nonperforming loans charge lower rates. For example, riskier banks might offer loans of inferior quality, with a higher probability of being revoked. For this reason, I include a measure of the riskiness of the bank (the percentage of nonperforming loans).

The HHI has the predicted effect. A one-standard-deviation increase in HHI increases interest rates by seven basis points. Surprisingly, the effect of the percentage of nonperforming loans is positive and significant. A one-standard-deviation increase in the percentage of nonperforming loans causes a 13 basis points increase in interest rates. The regression predicts that, all else equal, a firm would save 50 basis points on loans from state-owned banks.

Consistent with the benign view of government, state-owned banks might forgo exploiting market power when they possess it, while private ones will not. In fact, in Column 4 of Table 4, I consider this possibility and re-estimate the regression, interacting the state-ownership dummy with the HHI. The results show that state-owned banks do in fact exploit market concentration less than otherwise similar private banks. Moving from the area with the lowest HHI to the area with the highest HHI, private banks increase rates by 63 basis points, while state-owned banks increase rates by 44 basis points. This difference in behavior does not explain the systematic difference found between private and state-owned bank rates. First, the results show that state-owned banks exploit market power, but to a lesser extent than private banks. Second, the difference is small; in the province with the median HHI, everything else being equal, state-owned bank rates are lower than private bank rates by six basis points. Finally, the coefficient of the state-ownership dummy remains statistically and economically significant. After controlling for differences in market power exploitation, I find a difference of 44 basis points in rates charged between private- and state-owned banks.

As a further check for robustness, the specification in Column 5 introduces the size of the firm (measured by logarithm of sales) and score. Although both the coefficients of the size of the firm and of the numerical score are statistically significant and have the right sign, the size of the estimated state ownership dummy does not change.[4]

One potential worry is that the results might be attributable to unobservable firm characteristics that are changing over time. If so, the firm fixed effect is not fully controlling for this. To address this point, however, I can use one important feature of my data. I constructed the sample in such a way that a large percentage of companies in the sample receive loans from both state- and privately owned banks during the same year. To ensure that the results presented above hold for the companies that borrow from both types of banks at the same time, I re-estimate the regression model for this subsample of companies only. Panel B of Table 4, presents the results, which show a negative and significant coefficient for the $STATE_{k,t}$

---

[4] I have also estimated some alternative specifications that include, among the regressors, other firms' control variables (i.e., leverage and profitability) but the substantive results (unreported) are unchanged.

P. Sapienza / Journal of Financial Economics 72 (2004) 357–384   371

dummy. All else equal, firms that raise money from both state-owned and private banks pay interest rates to state-owned banks that are lower by 44 basis points, confirming that the results cannot be attributable to unobservable firm characteristics.

5.2. Discussion

Table 4 shows that when I control for firm and bank characteristics, state-owned banks charge interest rates that are 44 basis points lower than those charged by comparable privately owned banks. This result supports many alternative hypotheses. First, consistent with the political view, state-owned banks might be charging lower interest rates to certain firms in accordance with political objectives. For example, firms that are charged lower rates might be political supporters of certain politicians.

Even if politicians maximize social welfare, managers of state-owned banks might lack the ability to screen firms. If bank managers systematically make mistakes in pricing loans, in equilibrium we will observe only public loan contracts with lower interest rates, because the entrepreneurs will choose the contracts with the lowest interest rates. Also, managers of state-owned banks could be diverting bank resources for their own benefit, favoring firms that bribe them or that offer other types of benefits in exchange (e.g., future jobs). These latter two interpretations support the predictions of the agency view.

Are the results in Tables 3 and 4 consistent with the social view? One problem with answering this question is that the social view is vague on the specific social welfare maximizing tasks that a state-owned bank is likely to perform. So, in the remaining paragraphs of this section, I will explore several potential objectives of state-owned banks according to the social view.

One way to explain the difference in interest rates is to claim that state-owned banks are either more efficient than privately owned banks or have lower costs, and thus are able to charge lower interest rates. During the period of observation, regulation and tax laws are identical for both state- and privately owned banks, so the argument that state-owned banks are more efficient in making loans should be based on the fact that state-owned banks are better-managed organizations. The data do not confirm this hypothesis. It is well documented in the literature that state-owned Italian banks are less efficient than their private counterparts (see Martiny and Salleo, 1997). Table 1 confirms this fact for my sample.

The central prediction of the social view is that to cure market failures, benevolent public banks are willing to lend to companies at lower interest rates. According to this view, state-owned banks favor enterprises that find it difficult or too expensive to raise capital from private banks. This argument assumes implicitly that state-owned banks make loans to companies with positive net present value (NPV) projects that are unable to raise capital from other sources. As it turns out, the data contradict this hypothesis.

The results in Table 4, Panel B, show that state-owned banks charge lower interest rates even if the firm is able to raise capital from alternative sources. However, one could argue that these companies are rationed in terms of the funds they obtain from the private banks. To consider this possibility, I look at the ratio of the outstanding balance to the available amount (credit line) offered by privately owned banks. To prove that these companies are rationed, I must show that the outstanding balance is equal to the credit line. In fact, companies that borrow from privately owned banks have a percentage of loan use below 14% on average, suggesting that they could borrow larger amounts from privately owned banks. To further explore this issue, I restrict the sample to companies that borrow from both state-owned and private banks and have unused credit lines with private banks. The estimates (not reported) confirm the previous results. In Table 4, Panel C I also check whether firms that use a bigger fraction of their line of credit from private banks (and thus are more constrained) receive a bigger discount from state-owned banks. In Columns 1, 2, and 3 of Table 4, Panel C, I report the results of the baseline regression where I add a new dummy that is equal to one if the bank is state owned and if the firm has an average percentage of used credit from private banks that exceeds a given threshold. As thresholds, I use 15% (75th percentile), 37% (95th percentile), and 72% (99 percentile). All the reported results show that the new dummy has a positive but insignificant coefficient. These findings suggest that the firms receiving lower rates from state-owned banks are able to raise capital from other private banks.

An alternative scenario consistent with my findings supports the social view. The government might wish to subsidize certain firms (e.g., firms that have difficulty accessing capital) by reducing the firm's average cost of capital. However, to maintain incentives, the government might want the firm to face the market interest rate at the margin. In this case, the government might offer a loan below the market rate for less than the full size of the project. The initial loan granted by the state-owned bank could then trigger more loans by private banks. Unfortunately, I am not able to test this hypothesis with my data because I do not have information on when the loans are initiated.

The results presented in Table 4 are thus consistent with all the three views of SOEs.

5.3. Subsample analysis: geographic location and firm size

To further investigate the behavior of state-owned banks and distinguish among the different theories, I study whether there is some class of borrowers that has a greater advantage in borrowing from state-owned banks. I look at two different dimensions: geographical location and company size. I focus on the subsample of firms that receive loans from both state-owned and private banks. By doing this, I exclude firms that may face difficulties obtaining loans in the private market.

As a first approximation, Table 5 presents the average interest rates charged by state-owned and private banks to the firms that borrow from both types of banks. The first three rows divide the sample according to the geographical location of the companies. The differences between the interest rates charged by private banks and state-owned banks suggest that companies located in the south of Italy benefit more

P. Sapienza / *Journal of Financial Economics* 72 (2004) 357–384   373

Table 5
Differences in interest rates charged by state-owned and privately owned banks by region and borrower size

I define the interest rate as the ratio of the quarterly payment (interest plus fees) paid to the bank by the firm to its quarterly average balance, minus the prime rate. Difference is the average difference between the second column (interest rates charged by state-owned banks) and the third column (interest rates charged by privately owned banks). North includes the following regions: Piedmont, Valle d'Aosta, Lombardy, Trentino, Veneto, Friuli Venezia Giulia, Liguria, and Emilia Romagna. Center includes Tuscany, Umbria, Marche, and Lazio. South includes Abruzzo Molise, Campania, Puglia, Basilicata, Calabria, Sicily, and Sardinia. For the difference, I test statistical significance using the *t*-statistic with reference to a mean of zero. *** indicates statistically significant at the 1% level, ** indicates statistically significant at the 5% level.

Interest rate-prime:	State-owned banks	Privately owned banks	Difference	Obs.
Borrowers classified by geographical location				
North	3.03	3.22	−0.18***	38,786
Center	3.02	3.41	−0.39***	6,292
South	3.20	3.65	−0.45***	3,818
Borrowers classified by size				
First quintile in sales	3.70	3.86	−0.16***	9,780
Second quintile in sales	3.34	3.55	−0.21***	9,778
Third quintile in sales	3.12	3.36	−0.24***	9,780
Fourth quintile in sales	2.84	3.10	−0.25***	9,780
Fifth quintile in sales	2.23	2.51	−0.28***	9,778
All borrowers	3.05	3.27	−0.23***	48,896

than do other companies from borrowing by state-owned banks, even when they have access to private funds.

Table 6 looks at the same issue from within a regression framework. Table 6 includes an interaction between company location and the $STATE_{k,t}$ dummy. For firms located in northern Italy (the omitted indicator), borrowing from state-owned banks saves 44 basis points, all else equal. For firms located in the south, a relationship with the state-owned bank would save 75 basis points. This finding is consistent with Alesina et al. (1999), who find that public employment in Italy is used as a subsidy from the north to the less wealthy south.

It is hard to reconcile this result with the incentive view. There is no particular reason why the managers of state-owned banks should have weaker incentives when they price loans to firms located in the south.

By contrast, both the social and the political views support the fact that state-owned banks apply higher discounts to firms located in the south of the country. The south of Italy is the poorest part of the country with an unemployment rate four times higher than in the center-north. For at least 50 years, the south has been the focus of regional development policy, with massive capital inflows and real income transfers from the government. Lower interest rates to southern firms are consistent

Table 6
Regression results on interest rates charged by state-owned and privately owned banks in different areas
The dependent variable is the interest rate charged to firm i by bank k at time t minus the prime rate at time t. $STATE_{k,t}$ is a dummy variable equal to one if at time t bank k is a state-owned bank. North includes the following regions: Piedmont, Valle d'Aosta, Lombardy, Trentino, Veneto, Friuli Venezia Giulia, Liguria, and Emilia Romagna. Center includes Tuscany, Umbria, Marche, and Lazio. South includes Abruzzo Molise, Campania, Puglia, Basilicata, Calabria, Sicily, and Sardinia. I measure the size of the bank by logarithm of total assets. The percentage of nonperforming loans is the ratio of nonperforming loans to total loans. I measure market concentration at the province level by the Herfindahl-Hirschman Index (HHI) on total banking lending. Size of the firm is the logarithm of sales. All regressions include year and firm dummies. Heteroskedasticity-robust standard errors are in brackets. The standard errors are corrected for within-year clustering. ***, ** indicate statistically significant at the 1% and 5% level, respectively. The table also reports the p-value of an F-test for the hypothesis that the joint effect of all the variables equals zero.

	(1)	(2)	(3)	(4)	(5)
$State_{k,t}$	−0.1806***	−0.4102***	−0.4490***	−0.4562***	−0.4566**
	(0.0231)	(0.0195)	(0.0143)	(0.0203)	(0.0202)
State if firm is located in the South	−0.2709***	−0.2370***	−0.3097***	−0.3132***	−0.3143**
	(0.0401)	(0.0683)	(0.0365)	(0.0370)	(0.0365)
State if firm is located in the North	−0.2137***	−0.1501***	−0.1814***	−0.1818***	−0.1815***
	(0.0112)	(0.0123)	(0.0145)	(0.0154)	(0.0154)
Size of the bank		0.1870***	0.1655***	0.1655***	0.1657***
		(0.0097)	(0.0058)	(0.0057)	(0.0056)
Percentage of nonperforming loans			0.0356***	0.0356***	0.0353***
			(0.0016)	(0.0016)	(0.0016)
Concentration of loans (HHI)			2.7801***	2.7296***	2.4032***
			(0.4705)	(0.4473)	(0.5120)
Concentration of loans if $State_{k,t} = 1$				0.1093	0.1200
				(0.3012)	(0.2977)
Size of the firm					−0.2652***
					(0.0064)
Score of the firm					0.0334***
					(0.0076)
Firm fixed effect	Yes	Yes	Yes	Yes	Yes
Time fixed effect	Yes	Yes	Yes	Yes	Yes
Observations	97,792	97,792	97,760	97,760	97,760
Adjusted R-squared	0.408	0.420	0.426	0.426	0.428
p-Value of F-test for total effect equal to zero	0.0000	0.0000	0.0000	0.0000	0.0000

with a policy of subsidization, aimed at stimulating the southern regions.[5] On the other hand, in the south the practice of political patronage is more widespread than in the north. Southern politics in Italy is largely organized around the distribution of patronage (see Golden, 2001; Ginsborg, 1990). This evidence suggests that there is another reason why firms located in the south are favored by the interest rate policy

[5] The fact that these subsidization policies have systematically failed to close the gap between the center-north and the south raises some doubts about the rationale of the development policy for the south. Nonetheless, perhaps ex ante the government undertook these policies to maximize social welfare.

P. Sapienza / Journal of Financial Economics 72 (2004) 357–384 375

of state-owned banks: such favorable terms may be due to state-owned banks pursuing political objectives.

Table 5 also reports the differences across firm size in the interest rates charged by state- and privately owned banks. The results show that on average, the largest firms have more advantages in borrowing from state-owned banks. The difference between the interest rates charged by privately owned and state-owned banks is higher for the companies in the largest quintile. The relation across quintiles is nearly monotonic, but the differences across quintiles are not statistically significant.

Table 7 looks at the same issue in a regression framework. The results confirm that state-owned banks favor larger enterprises. The reduction in interest rates applied to companies in the largest quintile (the omitted indicator) by central government-owned banks is around 55 basis points. Firms in the smallest quintile that borrow from state-owned banks save about 41 basis points, all else equal.

This result does not support the social view. If market imperfections prevent firms from raising money, then the benevolent state-owned banks should charge relatively lower interest rates to small companies that are more likely to be credit rationed.[6] Instead, the results appear to support both the agency view and the political views. Managers of state-owned banks who lack incentives might be more prone to favor larger enterprises because their personal rewards are likely to be higher (e.g., a career in a larger firm is more valuable than one in a smaller firm). At the same time, state-owned banks might favor large enterprises in order to maximize a larger political consensus.

To sum up, while the social view and the incentive view alone can explain some results, the only interpretation consistent with both results is the political view of SOEs.

5.4. Electoral results, party affiliation, and lending behavior

To clarify the relation between politicians' objectives and the lending behavior of state-owned banks, I collect data on the political affiliations of the top executives of state-owned banks. Ideally, I would like to link the credit policy of the bank to the political affiliation or voting behavior of the beneficiaries of the loans. Unfortunately, this information is not publicly available. Instead, I use the voting record of the province where the borrower is located. Although this is an approximation, it provides new insights on the influence of politics on SOEs.

Because I am interested in the relation between the party affiliation of state-owned banks and their lending behavior, I focus only on the subsample of firms that borrow from state-owned banks. I determine the political affiliation of 36 state-owned banks in my sample (not always for the whole sample period). The final sample is reduced

---

[6] Other evidence against the social view is that state-owned banks do not favor any particular industry. In another (unreported) regression I look at differences in interest-rate discounts across industries. I use the Rajan and Zingales (1998) measure of external financial dependence and check whether firms in industries that are more dependent on outside funds receive cheaper loans from state-owned banks. In contrast to the social view, the results do not support this hypothesis.

376 *P. Sapienza / Journal of Financial Economics 72 (2004) 357–384*

Table 7
Regression results on interest rates charged by state-owned and privately owned banks by firm size
The dependent variable is the interest rate charged to firm i by bank k at time t minus the prime rate at time t. $STATE_{k,t}$ is a dummy variable equal to one if at time t bank k is a state-owned bank. I measure the size of the bank by logarithm of total assets. The percentage of nonperforming loans is the ratio of nonperforming loans to total loans. I measure market concentration at the province level by the Herfindahl-Hirschman Index (HHI) on total banking lending. Size of the firm is the logarithm of sales. All the regressions include year and firm dummies. Heteroskedasticity-robust standard errors are in brackets. The standard errors are corrected for within-year clustering. ***, ** indicate statistically significant at the 1% and 5% level, respectively. The table also reports the p-value of an F-test for the hypothesis that the joint effect of all the variables equals zero.

	(1)	(2)	(3)	(4)	(5)
$State_{k,t}$	−0.2965***	−0.5151***	−0.5703***	−0.4937***	−0.4792***
	(0.0301)	(0.0427)	(0.0324)	(0.0321)	(0.0323)
$State_{k,t}$ if firm in smallest size quintile	0.1906***	0.1868***	0.2006***	0.2113***	0.1582***
	(0.0366)	(0.0338)	(0.0380)	(0.0377)	(0.0391)
$State_{k,t}$ if firm in second size quintile	0.0933**	0.0899**	0.1038**	0.1104**	0.0859**
	(0.0419)	(0.0411)	(0.0443)	(0.0446)	(0.0417)
$State_{k,t}$ if firm in third size quintile	0.0466	0.0396	0.0483	0.0536	0.0359
	(0.0431)	(0.0398)	(0.0412)	(0.0413)	(0.0401)
$State_{k,t}$ if firm in fourth size quintile	0.0287	0.0272	0.0320	0.0356	0.0258
	(0.0253)	(0.0231)	(0.0241)	(0.0242)	(0.0237)
Size of the bank		0.1894***	0.1692***	0.1684***	0.1688***
		(0.0085)	(0.0040)	(0.0044)	(0.0043)
Percentage of nonperforming loans			0.0344***	0.0346***	0.0342***
			(0.0013)	(0.0013)	(0.0013)
Concentration of loans (HHI)			2.8206***	3.3630***	3.0251***
			(0.4919)	(0.4608)	(0.5301)
Concentration of loans if $State_{k,t} = 1$				−1.1806***	−1.0980***
				(0.3375)	(0.3233)
Size of the firm					−0.2476***
					(0.0078)
Score of the firm					0.0334***
					(0.0076)
Firm fixed effect	Yes	Yes	Yes	Yes	Yes
Time fixed effect	Yes	Yes	Yes	Yes	Yes
Observations	97,792	97,792	97,760	97,760	97,760
Adjusted R-squared	0.407	0.420	0.425	0.425	0.427

to 108 state-owned-bank-year observations corresponding to 26,698 company-bank(state-owned)-year observations. I focus on the political affiliation of the chairperson because in Italian state-owned banks, the chairperson has strategic tasks and often acts as the CEO. Overall, in my sample the chairpersons are linked to five different political parties (see Appendix B for details). The political affiliations of the chairpersons of the state-owned banks are relatively stable over time. In only four of the 36 banks does the political affiliation change during the sample period.

I use provincial electoral results from three national elections—1987, 1992, and 1994. For each observation in the dataset, I create a new variable that signifies the local political strength of the party. This variable is equal to the ratio of votes

P. Sapienza / Journal of Financial Economics 72 (2004) 357–384 377

received by the party affiliated to the bank's chairperson in the geographical area in which the firm borrows to the total valid votes in the same geographical area. The geographical areas are the 95 Italian provinces. The electoral results are from the previous national election.[7] For example, the chairman of Banco di Roma in 1991 was affiliated with the Christian Democrats. In 1991, Banco di Roma lent to 771 firms in my dataset. These firms were located in 55 different provinces. For each of these observations, I measure the local political strength of the party as the percentage of votes received by Christian Democrats in the province in which the firms are borrowing.

The variation in my measure of local political strength of the party has two different sources. First, because there are coalition governments, banks are affiliated to five different parties over the sample period. Some banks are affiliated with stronger parties, and others with weaker parties. Second, because there is enough variation in electoral results across provinces (see Appendix B for sample statistics), the local political strength of the party differs across provinces for those banks that lend in several provinces. In the case of Banco di Roma, the average provincial party strength of Christian Democrats (based on 1987 elections) was 33%, with a minimum of 8% and a maximum of 52%.

Table 8 reports how interest rates charged to borrowers of state-owned banks change according to the political strength of the party affiliated to the bank. The dependent variable is the interest rate charged to firm i by bank k at time t minus the prime rate at time t. The regression also includes controls at the bank level (size and percentage of nonperforming loans), the concentration of loans (HHI on loans), firm size, and year and firm dummies. I correct the standard errors for within-year clustering.

The first column of Table 8 reports the results for all state-owned bank–firm–year observations for which I was able to find a political affiliation for the chairperson of the bank. The political strength of the party has a negative and significant effect on the interest rate charged to borrowers. A one-standard-deviation increase in the political strength of the party decreases interest rates by an average of two basis points. The effect is small, but not negligible. For example, the largest party in my sample varies in political strength between 7% (Bolzano) and 52% (Avellino). The results imply that a borrower in Avellino pays nine basis points less than a borrower in Bolzano. All the other variables have the predicted sign.

If political support for the party with which the chairperson is affiliated is stronger in the south regions, it is possible that the coefficient of the local political strength of the party is capturing a "south effect." The fact that I include a firm fixed effect in the specification should partially address the problem (each firm borrows generally only in one area). However, in a separate (non reported) regression I have added a south dummy. The coefficient of the local political strength of a party remains statistically and economically significant.

---

[7] I use 1987 electoral results for loans in year 1991, 1992 electoral results for loans in years 1992 and 1993, and 1994 electoral results for loans in 1994 and 1995.

Table 8
Regression results on interest rates charged by state-owned banks by electoral results, party affiliation and
The dependent variable is the interest rate charged to firm i by bank k at time t minus the prime rate at
time t. I measure the local political strength of the party by the percentage of votes received by the party to
which the chairperson of the state-owned bank is affiliated in the area where the firm is borrowing. I
measure the size of the bank by logarithm of total assets. The percentage of nonperforming loans is the
ratio of nonperforming loans over total loans. I measure market concentration at the province level by the
Herfindahl-Hirschman Index (HHI) on total banking lending. Size of the firm is the logarithm of sales. All
the regressions include year and firm dummies. Heteroskedasticity-robust standard errors are in brackets.
The standard errors are corrected for within-year clustering. ***, ** indicate statistically significant at the
1% and 5% level, respectively. The table also reports the p-value of an F-test for the hypothesis that the
joint effect of all the variables equals zero. The Column 1 sample includes all observations (state-owned-
banks–firm–year) for which the political affiliation of the chairperson of the state-owned bank is available.
Column 2 is the same sample, excluding 1994 and 1995. Columns 3 and 4 include only loans from national
state-owned banks.

	(1)	(2)	(3)	(4)
Local political strength of the party	−0.2001**	−0.2295***	−0.3240***	−0.2837***
	(0.0806)	(0.0844)	(0.1239)	(0.1005)
Size of the bank	0.1702***	0.1641***	0.1282***	
	(0.0065)	(0.0033)	(0.0237)	
Percentage of nonperforming loans	0.0303***	0.0230***	0.0206***	
	(0.0045)	(0.0030)	(0.0061)	
Concentration of loans (HHI)	7.3368***	8.0807***	7.9113***	7.7236***
	(1.2113)	(0.7930)	(0.7298)	(0.7004)
Size of the firm	−0.3744***	−0.3277***	−0.3432***	−0.3435***
	(0.0742)	(0.0690)	(0.0853)	(0.0849)
Score of the firm	0.0321***	0.0328**	0.0258	0.0258
	(0.0087)	(0.0144)	(0.0167)	(0.0167)
Time fixed effect	Yes	Yes	Yes	Yes
Firm fixed effect	Yes	Yes	Yes	Yes
Bank fixed effect	No	No	No	Yes
Observations	26,698	25,049	17,671	17,671
Adjusted R-squared	0.4881	0.4953	0.5088	0.5087

The political affiliation effect could be underestimated for two possible reasons.
First, the chairperson's political affiliations in years 1994 and 1995 might be
measured with noise due to political scandals and changes in the practice
of appointing top executives in state-owned banks. Second, the national electoral
results are not a good measure of party strength for local government-owned
banks.

In Column 2 of Table 8, I restrict the sample to the period 1991–93. After 1993,
major political parties were beset by scandals. They underwent far-reaching changes,
which resulted in the wholesale turnover of the existing political class and the
dissolution of the major political parties. During the same period, a campaign by the
judiciary made significant inroads in uncovering major financial scandals involving
several state-owned banks. In fact, eight of the state-owned banks in my sample were
involved in fraud or bribery scandals, resulting in the resignation of several of the
top executives and board members.

P. Sapienza / Journal of Financial Economics 72 (2004) 357–384   379

These changes affect my regressions in two ways. First, for the year 1994 and after, I was not able to determine more than a very few political affiliations in the banks. Most of the previously appointed chairpersons remained in charge, even though their party disappeared. Some chairpersons were convicted and temporarily replaced by the vice-chairperson, who was often affiliated with a party that had also disappeared. In general, the active parties made very few new appointments after 1993. This fact explains the relatively small size of my sample for the years 1994 and 1995.

Second, because of the turmoil of the political parties, some authors (e.g., De Bonis, 1998) claim that the management of the banks became slowly more independent from politics or had no clear guidance from politicians in making decisions. For example, Piazza (2000) analyzes nonvoluntary turnover in Italian state-owned banks over the period 1994–1999. He finds that there is a weak link between electoral dates and chairperson turnover between 1994–96, but not in the subsequent period. For both reasons, in Column 2 of Table 8, I check whether the results change if I drop the observations for year 1994 and beyond. I find that the results are substantially the same.

I measure the political strength of the party using national election data. However, my sample contains two types of state-owned banks: national government-owned banks and local government-owned banks. In national banks, the appointments of the top executives are influenced by the party leaders of the ruling coalition. By contrast, the appointment of the management of local banks is decided by local bureaucracies, such as the local branch of the party, the mayor of the largest city, and other local politicians (see De Bonis, 1998). If such is the case, local government banks could be affected by local elections and the national electoral results might not be a good measure of the strength of the local political class.

To address this issue, in Column 3 of Table 8 I re-estimate the regression for only the subsample of firms (17,671 observations) that borrow from national state-owned banks and find that the local strength of the political party to which the bank is affiliated has a stronger negative effect. A one standard-deviation increase in political strength decreases the interest rate by 3.5 basis points. The effect is statistically significant at the 1% level. The fact that the coefficient is larger than in Columns 1 and 2, as predicted, suggests that my measure of party strength is doing a good job of measuring the degree of influence of political parties on state-owned banks.

National banks lend in different provinces. Therefore, when I restrict the sample to national banks, I can introduce a dummy at the bank level. By using a bank fixed effect, I can use a bank that lends in a given province as a control for itself in a different province. Thus, I can compare the interest rate charged by the same bank in two different provinces, and how it changes according the political strength of the party to which the bank is affiliated. I do this in Column 4 of Table 8. The coefficient of the local political strength of the party measures how interest rates change according to the electoral results of the party that appointed the chairman of the bank. For example, when I compare a bank affiliated with the Christian Democrats I find that interest rates are reduced by 12.5 basis points in Avellino compared to Bolzano, all else equal. This result suggests that the effect measured in Table 8 is not driven by some omitted bank characteristics in the regression.

380 *P. Sapienza / Journal of Financial Economics 72 (2004) 357–384*

The results of this section provide strong evidence for the political view of SOEs and suggest that state-owned banks are a mechanism for supplying political patronage. In areas in which the political party that runs the state-owned banks is stronger, borrowers get a higher discount than in other areas. The effect is statistically significant and robust across all regressions.

6. Conclusions

This paper shows that state-owned banks charge systematically lower interest rates to similar or identical firms than do privately owned banks. This finding is strong and statistically significant. Firms that borrow from state-owned banks pay an average of 44 basis points less than do firms that borrow from private banks. This finding is robust to various specifications. It holds even if the firms are able to borrow from, and have unused credit lines with, private banks.

This initial finding can be explained by both the agency and political views of SOEs. To test whether the evidence supports the social view, one has to articulate potential hypotheses from this theory. One hypothesis is that state-owned banks are able to charge lower rates because they either are more efficient or have lower costs. The data do not confirm this hypothesis. An alternative prediction from the social view is that state-owned banks lend to firms for which raising capital from private banks is either difficult or too expensive. Restricting the sample to firms that borrow from both state-owned banks and private banks still results in a significant interest rate differential of 44 basis points. This result holds even after controlling for the percentage of the credit lines used in private banks, thus ruling out the possibility that state-owned banks lend to credit-constrained enterprises. Thus, the data do not seem to support the social view unless one posits that state-owned banks attempt to reduce the average cost of capital of certain firms, while still allowing firms to face market interest rates at the margin.

The next step in distinguishing among the three hypotheses was to examine interest rate differentials across regions and firm sizes. Both the social and political views would support the fact that state-owned banks apply higher discounts in southern Italy, which is poorer and characterized by widespread political patronage. The agency theory cannot readily account for this. As for firm size, interest rates charged by state-owned banks are lower the larger the firm, which counters the social view, but would be consistent with the political and agency views.

Finally, I examine the relation between the party affiliation of the top management of state-owned banks, electoral results of the party, and lending behavior. I use data on the political appointments of the chairpersons of state-owned banks to compare interest rates across state-owned banks. I find that the party affiliation of state-owned banks' chairpersons has a positive impact on the interest rate discount given by state-owned banks in the provinces where the associated party is stronger. This result provides evidence that state-owned banks are a mechanism for supplying political patronage. In sum, while the agency and social views explain some of the evidence, these theories cannot account for all the results. The political view is the only interpretation consistent with all the results.

The obvious question is how generalizable these results are to other borrowers outside the sample. Because of the limited sample that I use in this paper, some caution is required. Since I do not observe the banks' entire loan portfolios, I cannot rule out the possibility that state-owned banks are also addressing other objectives. My results do not imply that incentives and social goals never matter, only that the political view can explain some of the behaviors of state-owned banks.

In a broader context, it could be argued that these results provide an explanation of the observed negative correlations between government ownership of banks and financial development (Barth et al., 2000), and between economic growth and productivity (La Porta et al., 2002). Furthermore, since political patronage could be even more prevalent in the developing world than in Italy, the case for state ownership of banks is significantly weakened.

Appendix A. Diagnostic system

The company data contain a numerical score for the firms in the sample that describes the risk profile of the firm following Altman (1968, 1993). Both state- and privately owned banks had access to the numerical score at the time when they lent to the firms. The score was obtained by CB using two discriminant functions. This score express the "risk profile" of the business. A detailed description of the methodology used by CB to calculate the numerical score is in Altman et al. (1994). I use the score to classify the companies into seven zones: highly secure, secure, vulnerable, highly vulnerable, uncertainty between vulnerability and risk, risk of bankruptcy, and high risk of bankruptcy. Table 9 below describe the risk profile of the companies contained in my sample borrowing from state- and privately owned banks. By construction, the risk profile is identical in the two subsamples, thus only one table is included.

Appendix B. Electoral results and party affiliation in banks

Historically, the Italian political system has been a multi-party system. Until 1994, both chambers (The Senate of the Republic and the Chamber of Deputies) were

Table 9

Score	Frequency	Percent	Cumulative Frequency
High secure	1,420	2.6	1,420
Secure	15,262	27.6	16,682
Vulnerable	409	0.7	17,091
Highly vulnerable	11,743	21.2	28,834
Uncertainty between vulnerability and risk	13,471	24.3	42,305
Risk of bankruptcy	10,472	18.9	52,777
High risk of bankruptcy	2,616	4.7	55,393

elected on a proportional basis. Voters cast ballots both for parties and for candidates within those parties. Seats were divided up according to the proportion of the total vote each party received. Parties would allocate their seats to candidates based on how many votes each received in his or her district. Since no single party could ever count on winning a straight majority of seats in Parliament, majority rule has depended on party alliances and coalitions. After 1994, the electoral system of the Senate was changed to a mixed system with a simple majority vote for 75% of the seats and a proportional representation (d'Hondt method) on the basis of regional voting results for remaining 25%.

For each party affiliated with the state-owned banks, I have collected electoral results for the Chamber of Deputies from three national elections: 1987, 1992, and 1994. I use the Chamber of Deputies electoral results because the electoral system did not change over the sample period. During those years, no single party controlled a majority of seats in either chamber of the Italian Parliament. I collect the data at the provincial level.

I collect appointments of the chairpersons of state-owned banks from newspapers. Overall, in my sample the affiliation of chairpersons is to one of five different parties. The main one, the Christian Democrats, made appointments to 29 banks in the sample. The second most influential party, the Italian Socialist Party, made appointments to nine banks in the sample; both the Italian Liberal Party and the Social Democratic Party made appointments to two banks, while and National Alliance made appointments to only one bank.

Table 10 shows the electoral results for these five parties in the provinces where they lent money to the firms in the sample. Panel A presents results for 1987 elections, Panel B for 1992 elections, and Panel C for 1994 elections. For example, banks affiliated with the socialist party lent money in 1992 and 1993 (Panel B) to firms located in 91 provinces.

Table 10

	Mean	Std. dev.	Min	Max	Number of provinces
Panel A: 1987 election					
Christian Democrats	0.34565932	0.08607512	0.08375919	0.52429986	80
Socialist Party	0.13883011	0.028753	0.06012196	0.20933744	89
Italian Liberal Party	0.02274278	0.01556027	0.00539812	0.09755591	52
Social Democratic Party	0.02849019	0.01601734	0.00475035	0.09887846	71
Panel B: 1992 election					
Christian Democrats	0.30600768	0.09383184	0.07377624	0.51638401	89
Socialist Party	0.13649238	0.03488646	0.04451371	0.26654419	91
Italian Liberal Party	0.02806362	0.01906862	0.01006228	0.13501064	70
Social Democratic Party	0.02611314	0.01770669	0.00560963	0.07984234	76
Panel C: 1994 election					
Socialist Party	0.0183175	0.0066557	0.0094487	0.0324773	33
National Alliance	0.1293044	0.0635202	0.0404381	0.2955712	66

References

Alesina, A., Danninger, S., Rostagno, M.V., 1999. Redistribution through public employment: the Case of Italy. NBER WP 6746.

Altman, E.I., 1968. Financial ratios, discriminant analysis and the prediction of corporate bankruptcy. Journal of Finance 23, 589–609.

Altman, E.I., 1993. Corporate Financial Distress and Bankruptcy. Wiley, New York.

Altman, E.I., Giancarlo, M., Franco, V., 1994. Corporate distress diagnosis: comparisons using linear discriminant analysis and neural networks (the Italian experience). Journal of Banking and Finance 18, 505–529.

Atkinson, A.B., Stiglitz, J.E., 1980. Lectures on Public Economics. London, McGraw Hill.

Banerjee, A., 1997. A theory of misgovernance. Quarterly Journal of Economics 112, 1289–1332.

Barca, F., Trento, S., 1994. State-ownership and the evolution of Italian corporate governance. Unpublished working paper, Bank of Italy.

Barth, J.R., Caprio, Jr., G., Levine, R., 2000. Banking systems around the globe: do regulation and ownership affect performance and stability? Working Paper 2325, World Bank.

Berger, A.N., Hannan, T.H., 1989. The price-concentration relationship in banking. Review of Economics and Statistics 71, 291–299.

De Bonis, R., 1998. Public sector banks in Italy: past and present. Bank of Italy, unpublished manuscript.

Ginsborg, P., 1990. A History of Contemporary Italy: Society and Politics, 1943–1988. Penguin Books, London.

Golden, M., 2001. The effects of the personal vote on political patronage, bureaucracy and legislation in postwar Italy. Unpublished working paper, Department of Political Science, UCLA.

Greenwald, B., Stiglitz, J.E., 1986. Externalities in economies with imperfect information and incomplete markets. Quarterly Journal of Economics 101, 229–264.

Hannan, T.H., 1991. Bank commercial loan market and the role of market structure: Evidence from surveys of commercial lending. Journal of Banking and Finance 15, 133–149.

Hart, O., Shleifer, A., Vishny, R., 1997. The proper scope of government: theory and an application to prisons. Quarterly Journal of Economics 112, 1127–1162.

La Porta, R., Lopez-de-Silanes, F., Shleifer, A., 2002. Government ownership of banks. Journal of Finance 57 (1), 256–301.

Laffont, J.-J., Tirole, J., 1993. A Theory of Incentives in Regulation and Procurement. MIT Press, Cambridge, MA.

Martiny, M., Salleo, C., 1997. The efficiency of Italian banks: some empirical evidence. Unpublished working paper, Bank of Italy.

Mayer, C., 1990. Financial systems, corporate finance, and economic development. In: Hubbard, R.G. (Ed.), Asymmetric Information, Corporate Finance and Investment. University of Chicago Press, Chicago, pp. 307–332.

Pagano, M., Panetta, F., Zingales, L., 1998. Why do companies go public? an empirical analysis. Journal of Finance 53, 27–64.

Petersen, M., Rajan, R., 1994. The benefits of lending relationships: evidence from small business data. Journal of Finance 49 (1), 3–37.

Piazza, M., 2000. What drives top management turnover in Italian banks? Bank of Italy, unpublished manuscript.

Rajan, R., Zingales, L., 1998. Financial dependence and growth. American Economic Review 88 (3), 559–586.

Sapienza, P., 2002. The effect of banking mergers on loan contracts. Journal of Finance 57 (1), 329–368.

Shleifer, A., 1998. State versus private ownership. Journal of Economic Perspectives 12, 133–150.

Shleifer, A., Vishny, R.W., 1994. Politicians and firms. Quarterly Journal of Economics 109, 995–1025.

Shleifer, A., Vishny, R.W., 1998. The Grabbing Hand: Government Pathologies and Their Cures. Harvard University Press, Cambridge, MA.

Stiglitz, J.E., 1993. The role of the state in financial markets. Proceedings of the World Bank Annual Conference on Economic Development, Washington DC, International Bank for Reconstruction and Development/World Bank, pp. 19–56.

Stiglitz, J.E., Weiss, A., 1981. Credit rationing in markets with imperfect information. American Economic Review 71, 393–410.

Tirole, J., 1989. The Theory of Industrial Organization. The MIT Press, Cambridge, MA.

Tirole, J., 1994. The internal organization of governments. Oxford Economic Papers 46, 1–29.

Visentini, G., 2000. Mixed and market oriented economies: the Italian situation. Universita' Luiss Guido Carli, Rome, Italy, unpublished manuscript.

RELATED LENDING*

Rafael La Porta
Florencio López-de-Silanes
Guillermo Zamarripa

In many countries, banks lend to firms controlled by the bank's owners. We examine the benefits of related lending using a newly assembled data set for Mexico. Related lending is prevalent (20 percent of commercial loans) and takes place on better terms than arm's-length lending (annual interest rates are 4 percentage points lower). Related loans are 33 percent more likely to default and, when they do, have lower recovery rates (30 percent less) than unrelated ones. The evidence for Mexico in the 1990s supports the view that in some important settings related lending is a manifestation of looting.

I. Introduction

In many countries, banks are controlled by persons or entities with substantial interests in nonfinancial firms. Quite often, a significant fraction of bank lending is directed toward these related parties, which include shareholders of the bank, their associates and family, and the firms they control. Proponents of related lending argue that close ties between banks and borrowers may be efficient. For example, Lamoreaux [1994, page 79] writes of post-Revolution New England that " . . . given the generally poor quality of information, the monitoring of insiders by insiders may actually have been less risky than extending credit to outsiders." Critics of related lending claim that it allows insiders to divert resources from investors.

The view that close ties between banks and borrowers are valuable is related to Gerschenkron's [1962] analysis of long-term bank lending in Germany, to the optimistic assessments of bank lending inside the keiretsu groups in Japan [Aoki, Patrick, and

* The views expressed here are those of the authors and not of the institutions they represent. We thank two anonymous referees, David Baron, John Campbell, Simeon Djankov, Daniel Kessler, Michael Kremer, Kenneth R. French, Peter C. Mayer, Stewart Myers, Paul Romer, Raghuram Rajan, David Scharfstein, Andrei Shleifer, Jeremy Stein, Tuomo Vuolteenaho, Luigi Zingales, and seminar participants at Harvard University, the Haas School of Business at the University of California (Berkeley), University of Michigan Business School, Massachusetts Institute of Technology Sloan School of Management, Stanford Business School, Texas A&M at College Park, and the Yale School of Management for helpful comments and to Lucila Aguilera, Juan Carlos Botero, Jamal Brathwaite, Jose Caballero, Claudia Cuenca, Mario Gamboa-Cavazos, Soledad Flores, Martha Navarrete, Alejandro Ponce, and Ekaterina Trizlova for excellent arm's-length research assistance.

The Quarterly Journal of Economics, February 2003

Sheard 1994; Hoshi, Kashyap, and Scharfstein 1991], and to theoretical work on credit rationing [Stiglitz and Weiss 1981]. Related lending may improve credit efficiency in several ways. Bankers know more about related borrowers than unrelated ones because they are represented on the borrower's Board of directors and share in the day-to-day management of the borrower. They may be able to use such information to assess the ex ante risk characteristics of investment projects or to force borrowers to abandon bad investment projects early [Rajan 1992]. In addition, both holdup problems and incentives for pursuing policies that benefit one class of investors at the expense of others may be reduced when banks and firms own equity in each other. Thus, *related lending* may be better for both the borrower and the lender because more information is shared and incentives are improved. We call this optimistic assessment of related lending the *information view*.

The alternative view is that close ties between banks and borrowers allow insiders to divert resources from depositors or minority shareholders to themselves. This view is related to the idea of looting [Akerlof and Romer 1993] and tunneling [Johnson et al. 2000] as well as the revisionist view of the benefits of keiretsu groups in Japan [Morck and Nakamura 1999; Kang and Stulz 1997]. Looting can take several forms. If the banking system is protected by deposit insurance, the controllers of a bank can take excessive risk or make loans to their own companies on nonmarket terms, fully recognizing that the government bears the costs of such diversion. Even without deposit insurance, the controllers of a bank have a strong incentive to divert funds to companies they control, as long as their share of profits in their own companies is greater than their share of profits in the bank. The basic implication is that related lending is very attractive to the borrower, but may bankrupt the lender. We call this pessimistic assessment of related lending the *looting view*. Admittedly, elements of both the information and looting view are likely to be simultaneously present in the data. Ultimately it is an empirical question whether related lending is, on balance, positive or negative.

We study related lending in Mexico using a newly assembled database of individual loans. In Mexico, banks are typically controlled by stockholders who also own or control nonfinancial firms. This is in direct contrast to previous studies of ownership structures in Germany and Japan where banks exert control over

RELATED LENDING 233

"group" firms but not vice versa. Nevertheless, the Mexican banking structure is common in many developing countries.[1] Banks that are controlled by persons or entities with substantial nonfinancial interests are prominent in Bangladesh, Bolivia, Bulgaria, Brazil, Chile, Colombia, Ecuador, Estonia, Guatemala, Hong Kong, Indonesia, Kazakstan, Kenya, Korea, Latvia, Paraguay, Peru, Philippines, Russia, South Africa, Taiwan, Thailand, Turkey, and Venezuela.[2] Faccio, Lang, and Young [2000] report that the ultimate controlling shareholder of 60 percent of the publicly traded firms in Asia also controls a bank. Even in Europe, this figure is as high as 28 percent. In fact, the Mexican banking setup is similar not only to that of many developing countries, but can also be seen in the early stages of development in England, Japan, and the United States [Cameron 1967; Patrick 1967; Lamoreaux 1994].

Using all banks in Mexico, we first examine the identity of each bank's top 300 borrowers by total loan size. For each bank, we then collect information on the borrowing terms of a random sample of 90 loans from the top 300 loans outstanding at the end of 1995 and track their performance through December 1999. We find that 20 percent of loans outstanding at the end of 1995 were to related parties and that banks sharply increase the level of related lending when they are in financial distress. Related parties borrow at lower rates and are less likely to post collateral. However, after controlling for borrower and loan characteristics, related borrowers are 33–35 percent more likely to default than unrelated ones. We also find that the default rate on loans made

1. This structure is partially the result of the privatization policies implemented during the last two decades [La Porta, Lopez-de-Silanes, and Shleifer 2002]. Barth, Caprio, and Levine [2001] document that while the ownership of banks by nonfinancial firms is unrestricted in 38 countries (including Austria, Germany, Switzerland, and the United Kingdom, as well as Bolivia, Brazil, Indonesia, Russia, and Turkey), the ownership of banks by nonfinancial firms is prohibited in only four countries (British Virgin Islands, China, Guernsey, and Maldives).

2. Three general sources on the links between banks and nonfinancial firms are AmericaEconomia [Annual Edition, 1995–1996, pages 116–128], Backman [1999] and Lindgren, Garcia, and Saal [1996]. Country-specific sources include Edwards and Edwards [1991] for Chile, Revista Dinero [http://www.dinero.com/old/pydmar97/portada/top/topmenu.htm] for Colombia, Standard & Poor's [Sovereign Ratings Service, November 2000, page 9] for Ecuador, African Business [May 1999] for Kenya, Garcia-Herrero [1997] for Paraguay, Koike [1993] and *The Economist* [8/5/2000, pages 70–71] for Philippines, Nagel [1999] and Laeven [2001] for Russia, The Financial Mail [12/6/1996] for South Africa, Euromoney [December 1997] for Thailand, and Verbrugge and Yantac [1999] for Turkey. Finally, Beim and Calomiris [2001] discuss the importance of related lending in financial crises.

to related persons and to privately held companies related to the bank is 77.4 percent. The equivalent rate for unrelated parties is 32.1 percent. Moreover, recovery rates are $0.30 per dollar lower for related borrowers than for unrelated ones. Finally, to the extent that we can measure it, related borrowers emerge from the crisis relatively unscathed—bank owners lose control over their banks but not their industrial assets.

Overall, the results for Mexico are consistent with the *looting view* and challenge the *information view*. The sheer magnitude of the gap in default rates between related and unrelated loans makes it difficult to argue that it is optimal to lend to related parties on better terms than to unrelated ones. Nevertheless, our results may be consistent with some versions of the *information view*. Naturally, related lending may be advantageous in other settings (e.g., contemporary Germany or Japan) albeit prone to subversion in countries with institutional setups similar to Mexico's in the 1990s.

The paper proceeds as follows. In Section II we present the hypotheses and develop a simple model of looting. Section III presents the sample and basic empirical methodology. Section IV describes the incentives for related lending in Mexico and documents its prevalence. Section V contrasts the lending terms of related and unrelated loans and studies their performance in the aftermath of the financial crisis of 1994. Section VI concludes.

II. A Simple Model of Looting and Alternative Hypotheses

The banking literature stresses the incentives for excessive risk-taking when banks are financially distressed. Here we draw attention to other forms of looting that have received considerably less attention.[3] Specifically, we focus on the incentives for insiders to divert cash for their own benefit. Our key assumption is that insiders structure self-dealing transactions to minimize recovery on related-party loans when these default.[4] Specifically, we assume that related parties can avoid repaying their loans at

---

3. Akerlof and Romer [1993] is one notable exception. Their model is deterministic: looting takes place when the value of the bank's capital falls below a threshold. Instead, we emphasize the option-like nature of default as insiders may default on their bank loans at the cost of forgoing their equity in the bank. Also see Laeven [2001].

4. Consistent with this assumption, the auditor commissioned by the Mexican Congress found that some related loans " . . . were granted without any appropriate reference to the capacity of the debtors to repay" and that loan officers

the cost of forgoing their equity in the bank.[5] As a result, related parties repay their bank loans when the value of their equity in the bank is high but default otherwise.

We assume that each bank is controlled by a single shareholder who owns a fraction α of the cash flows of the bank and a larger fraction β ($>\alpha$) of the cash flows of an industrial firm (i.e., the "related party") which she also controls. We also assume that the controlling shareholder has effective control over lending decisions. She can direct the bank to lend to related parties on nonmarket terms but needs to engage in costly transactions to avoid repayment in the bad state. As a result, when a controlling shareholder directs the bank to lend L to a related party, the controlling party only receives $\phi(L)$ and $L - \phi(L)$ is wasted [Burkart, Gromb, and Panunzi 1998; Johnson et al. 2000; La Porta et al. 2002]. We assume that $\phi_L > 0$ and $\phi_{LL} < 0$.

The model has two periods. In the first, a fraction of the assets of the bank must be financed by deposits (D) and the rest by shareholders' equity (E). Investors are risk-neutral, and there is no deposit insurance.[6] For simplicity, we assume that the risk-free rate is zero while the promised (gross) interest on deposits is r. In the first period, the bank lends L to the related party and $E + D - L$ to unrelated parties. Both borrowers promise to pay R per dollar borrowed. Loans are due in the second period, and time ends. The world may be in either a "good" or "bad" state in the second period, with probabilities q and $(1 - q)$, respectively. In the good state, loans are repaid in full. In the bad state, the bank recovers a fraction $\gamma(<R)$ per dollar of unrelated loans. However, the bank recovers nothing when the insider defaults on her loan. In expectation, loans are unprofitable when made to related parties ($R_R = q * R < 1$) and profitable when

---

had accepted " . . . collateral from the borrower that they knew was false or of no value to the bank" [Mackey 1999].

5. Default is not tightly linked to bankruptcy in Mexico. In our sample, fourteen related party borrowers who defaulted were publicly traded firms, and it is easy to follow them in the post-1995 period. Only one publicly traded nonfinancial firm went bankrupt (Fiasa). Courts finally sanctioned Fiasa's bankruptcy because it did not have a known address, which suggests that creditors may have faced similar difficulties locating the firm's assets [*El Economista* 9/11/2000].

6. Deposit insurance creates further incentives to engage in related lending. Without deposit insurance, the extent of related lending is limited by the need to allow outside financiers to break even on their investment. Because deposit insurance pays for the losses of depositors in the bad state, it increases the level of related lending that is compatible with outside investors recouping their investment.

made to unrelated ones ($R_U = q * R + (1 - q) * \gamma > 1$). Finally, to make our results interesting, we assume that the bank goes bankrupt if the insider defaults ($\gamma * (E + D - L) < r * D$).

We consider the equilibrium in which the insider does not default in the good state (otherwise, outside shareholders cannot break even). In the good state, the insider willingly pays back her loan if her share of the payment owed to the bank ($\beta * R * L$) falls short of the value of her equity in the bank were related loans to be paid; i.e., when

$$(1) \qquad \alpha * (R * (E + D) - r * D) \geq \beta * R * L.$$

Consider next the bad state. The insider defaults if her share of the payment owed to the bank exceeds the value of her equity in the bank were related loans to be reimbursed, i.e., when

$$(2) \qquad \alpha * (\gamma * (E + D - L) + R * L - r * D) < \beta * R * L.$$

In the bad state, the insider always defaults. This occurs because $\beta > \alpha$ and repayments on unrelated loans are insufficient to reimburse depositors in the bad state. As a result, banks are very fragile: related parties optimally default on their loans from the bank precisely when outside borrowers are in financial distress.

Depositors are indifferent between investing in the riskless asset or in the bank. They are paid in full in the good state and receive the value of the bank's equity in the bad state. As a result, the value of deposits D is given by

$$(3) \qquad D = q * (r * D) + (1 - q) * (\gamma * (E + D - L)).$$

The insider receives profits from looting ($= \beta * \phi(L)$) and, in the good state, from her equity holdings. In the good state, the insider receives her pro-rata share of the profits of the bank ($= \alpha * (R * (E + D) - r * D)$) and bears a fraction β of the cost of repaying the loan ($= R * L$). In the bad state, related loans default, and the insider forgoes her equity in the bank. Accordingly, the expected profits of the insider are given by

(4)

$$E(\pi) = \beta * \phi(L) + q * (\alpha * (R * (E + D) - r * D) - \beta * R * L).$$

Using equation (3) in equation (4), the expected profits of the insider can be rewritten as follows:

(5) $E(\pi) = \beta * (\phi(L) - R_R * L) + \alpha$

$$* (R_U * (E + D - L) + R_R * L - D),$$

where $R_U (= q * R + (1 - q) * \gamma)$ and $R_R (= q * R)$ denote the expected rates of return on loans to unrelated and related parties, respectively. The first term captures the "private benefits" that the insider does not share with other shareholders, and the second term represents the insider's pro-rata share in the expected profits of the bank. We have so far assumed that the insider controls a single related party. A straightforward generalization of (5) to the case when the insider controls multiple related parties predicts that the insider will direct the bank to offer better borrowing terms (e.g., lower interest rates and less demanding collateral requirements) to high-β entities than to low-β ones.

The insider picks the level of related lending to maximize her expected profits. The first-order condition for this problem can be written as

(6) $$\beta * \phi_L = \alpha * (R_U - R_R) + \beta * R_R.$$

This says that at the margin, the cost from engaging in related lending must exactly offset its benefit. Consider shifting \$1 in loans from unrelated parties to related ones. The insider is a shareholder in the related party and receives $\beta * \phi_L$ when a dollar is diverted from the bank. On the other hand, as a shareholder in the bank, the insider bears a fraction α of the reduction in expected profits ($= R_U - R_R$) resulting from the change. In addition, as a shareholder in the related party, the insider pays a fraction β of the marginal payment owed to the bank (R_R). According to equation (6), related lending is restrained by the insider's equity stake in the bank (α) and by the presence of attractive opportunities to lend to outsiders. Related lending increases with the insider's equity stake in the related party (β) and when expected returns on related loans are low (for example, because of bad corporate governance).

In our empirical work, we focus on five questions. First, what is the extent of related lending? Second, do banks lend to related parties at different and possibly more favorable terms? Third, which related parties get the most beneficial terms? Fourth, how do related and unrelated loans perform in the "bad" state of the world? Fifth, when does related lending increase?

Equations (5) and (6) are helpful to answer these questions for Mexico. Before the crisis, the bad state had occurred in Mexico with certain regularity. In addition, rules on related lending allowed insiders to default with relative impunity while inadequate investor protection made recovery on nonperforming loans to unrelated parties very difficult. As a result, expected returns on both related and unrelated loans may have been low during the sample period. Equation (6) predicts that related lending should be high in Mexico if R_U and R_R are low. Moreover, the *looting view* predicts that related parties borrow at below-market terms and that high-β entities should receive the most beneficial borrowing terms. As a result, loans to related parties (and, in particular, to high-β entities) should perform very poorly in the bad state because such loans are backed by collateral of very dubious quality, if any. Low levels of collateral contribute to the bad performance of related loans by increasing the insider's incentive to default and by lowering the bank's recovery rate when default does occur. Finally, equation (6) predicts that related lending increases when the bad state becomes more likely.

Evidence on the size and terms of related lending is insufficient to distinguish between the *looting* and *information views*. Most plausible versions of the *information view* predict that related lending should be large in Mexico as it mitigates moral hazard and asymmetric information problems, both likely to be high in Mexico [La Porta et al. 1997, 1998]. The *information view* is also consistent with lending at advantageous terms to related parties as banks minimize costs by lending to borrowers they know well or to firms whose investment policies they control and pass some of these efficiency gains to borrowers.[7]

Different versions of the *information view* make opposing predictions regarding the performance of related-party loans during a severe recession. A standard version of the *information view* holds that advantageous lending terms for related parties are justified by low expected default rates and high expected recovery rates. In this view, related lending facilitates the optimal allocation of capital by removing informational barriers to selecting good projects or empowering banks to curtail excessive risk-tak-

---

7. The information view is also consistent with related parties borrowing on less advantageous terms than unrelated ones (for example, low-quality debtors may be monitored by banks while high-quality debtors borrow against collateral). The opposite is true in our data, and thus, we focus on related lending that takes place on beneficial terms.

ing by borrowers. In sum, related lending may improve loan performance.[8] It is possible, however, to construct versions of the *information view* that make the opposite prediction regarding the performance of related-party loans in a downturn. For example, a model could include three states (good, bad, and awful) and not just two. In the good state of the world, both related and unrelated loans pay as promised. In contrast, unrelated loans default more often than related ones in the bad state of the world. Finally, in the awful state of the world, related parties default more often than unrelated ones.[9] If the awful state of the world is infrequent enough, it may be fair to grant beneficial terms (e.g., low interest rates and collateral requirements) to related parties. Note, that an implication of the *three-state-information view* is that loans made in the awful state break even. In contrast, the *looting view* predicts that such loans lose money on average.

III. DATA AND METHODOLOGY

III.A. *Data*

This paper is based on a new database describing the terms and performance of a sample of loans made by seventeen Mexican banks circa 1995. We are interested in comparing the terms offered to related and unrelated borrowers as well as the ex post performance of those loans. We follow standard legal practice and define related debtors as those who are (1) shareholders, directors, or officers of the bank; (2) family members of shareholders, directors, or officers of the bank; (3) firms where the previous two categories of individuals are officers or directors; or (4) firms where the bank itself owns shares.[10]

---

8. In fact, related borrowers may (inefficiently) take too few risks. For example, critics of German banks argue that banks veto worthwhile investment projects because, as creditors, they do not internalize the benefits that accrue to shareholders when risky projects are successful [Wenger and Kaserer 1998].

9. One way to motivate the awful state of the world is to argue that related borrowers are negatively affected by the loss of banking relationships (perhaps because relationship banks have specialized human capital that other banks cannot easily substitute). Both Bernanke [1983] and Diamond and Rajan [2000] emphasize the losses that result from severing the ties between bankers and their related borrowers during financial crises.

10. We checked the accuracy of the reported classification of related and unrelated borrowers using a list of all the officers and directors of all banks, publicly traded firms (and their subsidiaries), and the top-500 firms (and their subsidiaries) in 1995. With rare exceptions, all the borrowers with links to the banks as officers and directors had been appropriately classified as "related" by our primary sources. In addition, we examined whether unrelated loans are

Banks were required to submit to the banking supervisor a list of the 300 hundred largest loans together with their size and the names of each of the borrowers. Starting in December 1995, banks were also required to disclose the affiliation of these debtors, which allows us to classify borrowers as related and unrelated ones. We use the sample of top-300 loans from each bank for two very different purposes: to get a snapshot of the aggregate magnitude of related and unrelated lending in Mexico, and to select a random sample of loans for further analysis of their terms and ex post performance.[11] Specifically, for each bank that existed when privatization was concluded in 1992, we draw a random sample of approximately 90 different borrowers from the 300 largest loans in December 1995 or, when unavailable, in March 1996. Note that our random sample of loans may be biased toward the "cleaner" forms of self-dealing as it is drawn from loans that were scrutinized by regulators. Then, we collect data on the terms of each of the loans in the random sample and follow their evolution through time until December 1999 as they are repaid, renewed, and restructured. Our random sample includes loans from all but two banks that existed when privatization was concluded in 1992. The two missing banks (Bancrecer and Banoro) are under state administration at the time of writing, and their management feared that disclosing information on related lending might create obstacles to finding buyers for the banks. Three new banks entered the market in 1994 and are not part of our random sample as they may not have had sufficient time to

---

reclassified as related ones six months after a forced change in control. The implicit assumption is that most knowable cases of fraud and misreporting are likely, by that period, to be identified by the new management of the bank. We found very few mistakes (two to three per bank) in the initial classification of a debtor as related or unrelated. In contrast, it is rather common that performing loans be reclassified as nonperforming.

Our definition of related party leaves out two potentially important modes of self-dealing. First, associates of Bank X may have systematically borrowed from Bank Y whereas associates of Bank Y may have systematically borrowed from Bank X. In fact, audits of some of the bankrupt banks revealed that related lending sometimes took exactly that form. As a robustness check, we have expanded the definition of related lending to include borrowers associated with other banks (eight borrowers). The results are qualitatively similar, and we do not report them in the text. Second, some bankers may have avoided related-lending regulations by lending to firms controlled by front men [Mackey 1999]. Unfortunately, we have no way of addressing outright fraud in our database. Fraud, however, biases the results against our findings.

11. Section IV presents time-series statistics on the evolution over time of the proportion of the largest 300 loans that were given to related parties. For the period before December 1995, we manually classified loans as related or unrelated using secondary sources.

reach "steady state." Our random sample represents 93 percent of the assets of the banking system at the end of 1994.

Whenever possible, we sample 45 related and 45 unrelated loans for each bank.[12] The National Banking and Securities Commission sent an official request to gather information on the loans in our random sample. Although the information was supplied by the banks, the credit files were made available to the regulator to verify their accuracy. Each bank was required to extract and supply the following information: (1) characteristics of the debtor (assets, total liabilities, liabilities with the bank, sales, and profits); (2) characteristics of the credit (interest rates, maturity, collateral, and guarantees); (3) performance of the credit (date of default, percentage recovered, terms of any renewals, restructures or loan forgiveness); (4) amount of the yearly payments made by the borrower between 1993 and 1999; and (5) analogous information about other credits that the debtor had, or obtained within four years of the date of the loan, with the same bank.

The total number of loans in the sample is over 1500. Some borrowers had more than one loan outstanding with the same bank. In such cases, we report the weighted average of the terms (e.g., interest rates) of all loans by the same borrower and compute total promised payments and total actual payments by borrower.

An important characteristic of our sample is that banks were in varying degrees of financial distress at the time we took the snapshot of their loan portfolio. The first bank failures (Cremi, Union, and Oriente) took place in the second half of 1994, and the last one (Serfin) in 1999 (see the first column in Table I). At the onset of the financial crisis, the government took over financially distressed banks with the goal of restructuring them and finding a buyer for them in better times. The government took over three banks in this fashion in 1994 (Cremi, Union, and Oriente). Three years later, the government sold the branches of those three banks but retained most of their (nonperforming) loans. Later, the government focused on finding buyers for the failing banks (eleven banks) and skipped the restructuring process. As a result, the related party that made the loan in our random sample is typically not the agent that tries to recover from a nonperforming

---

12. In some cases banks did not have 45 related loans among the largest 300 loans and we had to settle for less. Those cases are Banpais (40), Cremi (38), and Citibank which did not have any related loans.

borrower. We believe that this is an advantage as related parties may have procrastinated before pulling the plug on loans to their associates.[13]

III.B. Methodology

In this subsection we discuss how we compute interest rates and recovery rates. We introduce the remaining variables as we discuss them in the text (see the Appendix for definitions of the variables). Loans vary on the date on which they were granted and on their maturity. This complicates direct comparisons across loans since interest rates were highly volatile over the sample period. To partially address this difficulty, we report realized real interest rates over the maturity of the loan. To illustrate, consider a loan that, in period t, pays a spread of s over the reference rate i and has a maturity of T months.[14] Letting the inflation rate be π, we compute the average real rate for this loan as follows:

$$(7) \qquad \frac{1}{T} \sum_{t=1}^{T} \frac{1 + i_t + s}{1 + \pi_t}.$$

In addition to real interest rates, we also compute the average difference between the interest rate paid by the loan and the "risk-free" rate as measured by the one-month rate on government bonds. Continuing with the previous example and letting r^f be the currency- and maturity-matched rate on government bonds (i.e., depending on the currency of the loan, the U. S. or Mexican government bond rate), our measure of spread over government rates is computed as follows:

$$(8) \qquad \frac{1}{T} \sum_{t=1}^{T} (1 + s - r_t^f).$$

We keep floating and fixed interest rates separate as they present different risk characteristics. For the same reason, we also keep domestic and foreign interest rates separate and deflate using the Mexican or U. S. wholesale price index as appropriate.

---

13. We include bank-fixed effects in the regressions to capture the fact that banks faced different incentives to loot. We also include in the regressions a dummy for whether the bank is under government or private management.
14. For data availability reasons, we are only able to follow loans through December 1999. For fixed loans, s is zero, and i is the promised coupon rate.

As a result, we group loans in four categories: (1) domestic/fixed; (2) domestic/floating; (3) dollar/fixed; and (4) dollar/floating.

One of the goals of the paper is to assess the number of loans that paid less than initially contracted ("bad loans"). To examine the performance of the loans in our random sample, we track them from the formation period (i.e., December 1995 or, when not available, March 1996) through 1999 as they are either (1) paid at maturity; (2) paid in advance; (3) renewed; (4) restructured; (5) transferred to FOBAPROA; (6) settled in court; or (7) in default and not yet settled. We aggregate all these outcomes into a single performance measure ("recovery ratio") by keeping track of the net cash flows paid to the bank by the borrower after the loan enters the sample. Keeping track of loan performance over time is important as problems with related loans may take time to show up if banks renew related loans without paying attention to their credit quality or restructure loans without assessing the repayment ability of the borrower.[15]

Our calculations are designed to avoid these problems. Specifically, we define the recovery ratio as follows:

$$(9) \qquad \frac{1}{capital_0} * \sum_{t=1}^{T} \frac{payment_t - renew_t}{1 + r_t},$$

where $capital_0$ is the face value of the loan when it was first made; $payment_t$ includes coupon and amortization payments received, amounts recovered in court, and collateral repossessed; $renew_t$ is the face value of loan renewals; r_t is the contracted interest rate; and T is the maturity of the loan extended, if necessary, by renewals, restructurings, or court awards.

Identifying bad loans involves some judgment calls. The most obvious bad loans are those that defaulted. For regulatory purposes, loans were classified in default after 90 days of missing a payment, or in the case of a one-payment loan, after 30 days of missing the payment. Forced restructurings of performing loans are more difficult to capture. Most loans were typically restructured because the borrower was financially distressed. However, it is possible that some loans were restructured at no loss to the bank. We err on the conservative side by classifying restructured

---

15. At least some of that may have taken place. "Interest accruing on these loans [referring to loan to directors] was frequently capitalized rather than paid. In some cases, additional loans were issued to borrowers for the purpose of paying interest on the initial loans" [Mackey 1999, page 216].

loans as bad loans only when the bank simultaneously takes an accounting loss. Thus, our proxy for bad loans underestimates the true level of noncompliance by not capturing, for example, a bank that grants additional time without interest to pay back a debt.[16]

IV. FACTS ABOUT RELATED LENDING IN MEXICO

IV.A. Banking in Mexico

Many of the ownership and control features of the banks in our sample can be traced back to privatization that returned commercial banks to the private sector by 1992, ten years after all commercial banks had been nationalized.[17] Privatization took place gradually through the placement of minority stakes in the stock market in 1987. By 1992, government ownership of commercial banks was fully eliminated.

In privatization, control of banks was auctioned off to the highest cash bidder. However, important ownership restrictions were put in place at the time to prevent banks from becoming controlled by either nonfinancial corporations or by foreigners [Lopez-de-Silanes 1997]. Specifically, at least 51 percent of the votes of a bank had to be held by a Mexican group, and control over banks by corporations was ruled out. Instead, banks had to be controlled by a dispersed group of individuals. Each of the members of the controlling group could own up to 5 percent of the equity of a bank without question, or up to 10 percent with the express consent of the Ministry of Finance. Foreign entities could own up to 30 percent of a bank's equity in low-voting shares under similar ownership-dispersion requirements as those that applied to individuals.

These ownership restrictions, coupled with the low level of development of financial markets, severely limited competition in the privatization auctions by restricting potential bidders to do-

16. Twenty-nine of the loans in our random sample were sold to FOBAPROA although they were not technically in default. On average, FOBAPROA paid 88.7 percent of the face value of the loans but has recovered only 15–20 percent of their face value so far. Because banks had incentives to sell to FOBAPROA, those loans with the worst repayment expectations, we classify all loans sold to FOBAPROA as bad loans even if they had not technically defaulted at the time when they were transferred to the government. We compute recovery rates for loans transferred to the government in the same manner as for all other loans in the sample. Specifically, we ignore payments from FOBAPROA and keep track of all coupon and amortization payments made by the borrower.

17. See La Porta and Lopez-de-Silanes [1999] for a general account of privatization in Mexico.

mestic investors with cash to bid. Nevertheless, the average (median) control premium paid for banks at the time of their privatization was 51.8 percent (50.0 percent) [López-de-Silanes and Zamarripa 1995].[18] These data are consistent with the view that controlling shareholders of banks perceived private benefits of control to be high.

Just as corporations were not allowed to control banks, banks were not allowed to own more than 5 percent of the capital of nonfinancial corporations.[19] Beyond these ownership restrictions, few rules addressed potential conflicts of interest. Related loans could not exceed 20 percent of a banks' loan portfolio, and no special approval was required on loans to related parties as long as *each* loan was smaller than 0.2 percent and 1 percent of the bank's net capital for loans to individuals and firms, respectively.[20] When those limits where exceeded, loans to related parties had to be approved by a majority of the members of the Board of Directors. No rules limited the participation of interested directors in such decisions.

Key to the interpretation of the results in the paper is that, in practice, ownership dispersion requirements and rules separating banks and industrial firms were insufficient to avoid potential conflicts of interest. To illustrate this point, consider the case of Banco Serfin (the third largest bank) which is representative of the other banks in the sample. Adrián Sada González was the Chairman of the Board and owned 8 percent of the capital and 10.1 percent of the votes in Serfin. Although his stake in Serfin met the letter of the law regarding ownership dispersion requirements, it seriously underestimates Sada González's control over the Board of Serfin. Other directors and officers of the bank owned 33.6 percent of the capital and 42.7 percent of the votes in Serfin. Two sons of Adrián Sada González sat on the Board, and eleven of the forty-four members of the Board of Serfin were related to each other by blood or marriage. Because reporting requirements do not allow us to know the ownership of each director and officer, we cannot pin down the fraction of the votes

18. The number of nonfinancial firms with publicly traded equity at the time of privatization is too small to compute the value of control for those firms.
19. Higher percentages were possible with the authorization of the Ministry of Finance.
20. In February 1995 restrictions on related lending were changed. The new rules allowed banks to lend to related parties up to their net capital.

effectively controlled by Adrián Sada González, but it clear that he exercised effective control over Serfin.

Serfin had close ties with many of the largest corporations in Mexico. Adrián Sada González was also the largest shareholder and Chairman of the Board of Vitro—a publicly traded maker of glass products.[21] In fact, the Board of Serfin included the controlling shareholders of fourteen other publicly traded firms. To put this figure in perspective, only 185 firms were publicly traded in 1995. Furthermore, many of the publicly traded firms controlled by Serfin's directors and officers were among its largest borrowers. For example, eight of the top twenty loans to firms in the private sector were given to publicly traded firms controlled by members of Serfin's board. Another three of the largest twenty private-sector loans went to privately held firms owned by Serfin's directors and officers. Finally, the son of a member of the Board was among the top twenty private sector borrowers. All in all, related parties obtained twelve of the largest twenty loans outstanding to the private sector in 1995. The example of Serfin suggests that the separation between the control of industrial and financial firms may have been more apparent than real. It also suggests that the agency problems in Mexican banking were different from those in, for example, Japan where both banks and industrial firms are typically widely held and run by professional managers.[22]

Lending policies were also shaped by other features of the banking regulation. At the time of privatization, Mexico created a deposit insurance system ("FOBAPROA") similar to the FDIC in the United States. FOBAPROA guaranteed all deposits equally, regardless of the creditworthiness of the bank. At the same time, minimum capitalization requirements were independent of the riskiness of a bank's loan portfolio. Banks were allowed to set interest rates and to allocate credit freely. Bank supervision was lax partly because regulators were overwhelmed by the rapid growth of credit that followed privatization and partly because prudential regulation was inappropriate [Gil-Díaz and Carstens 1997; López-de-Silanes and Zamarripa 1995].

---

21. Officers and directors of Vitro (including Adrián Sada González) owned 23.2 percent of the capital and 38.64 percent of the votes in Vitro.

22. The only bank in our sample that is clearly different from Serfin is Citibank. From a regulatory standpoint there was no difference between Citibank Mexico and domestic banks. However, Citibank operated in Mexico as a wholly owned subsidiary of the United States parent, and most large loans made by Citibank's Mexican subsidiary had to be approved by its parent company.

RELATED LENDING   247

In summary, banks were acquired by local families that already controlled industrial groups and had the financial resources required to bid in the privatization auction. Furthermore, during the sample period, related lending was largely unregulated and poorly supervised while banks operated under a generous deposit insurance system. We turn next to measuring the extent of related lending.

IV.B. The Size of Related Lending

Table I presents basic data on related lending for each of the banks in the sample. We group banks into two categories. The first group of thirteen banks ("*bankrupt banks*") includes those that were either taken over by the government or acquired by other banks to avoid a government takeover. The remaining five banks ("*survivor banks*") did not experience changes in control during the sample period. Although some of the members of the group of *survivor banks* experienced considerable financial distress during the sample period, we separate both groups of banks since they may have faced different incentives. We are particularly interested in the level of related lending when *bankrupt banks* change control (the *event period*) since incentives for self-dealing increase as the value of the bank's equity falls. For comparison purposes, we define September 1997 as the *event period* for *survivor banks* (roughly, the median date of change in control for *bankrupt banks*).[23] We present snapshots of the percentage of the top-300 loans made to related parties at three points in time: (1) December 1993 (i.e., before the devaluation), (2) one-year before the *event period,* and (3) during the *event period.*

Table I shows that the mean (median) bank in the sample had 13 percent (14 percent) of the top-300 outstanding loans with related parties in 1993. Related lending in 1993 is moderately higher for *bankrupt banks* than for *survivor banks* (14 percent versus 10 percent, respectively, for both the means and medians). The difference in the fraction of loans to related parties for *bankrupt* and *survivor banks* increases sharply as bankruptcy looms closer. Consistent with the *looting view,* the mean (median) fraction of related lending increases by 13 (13) percentage points for

---

23. The level of related lending by *survivor banks* between December 1994 and December 2000 is fairly stable at around 13 percent, and the choice of *event period* for *survivor banks* does not qualitatively affect the results.

TABLE I
THE SIZE OF RELATED LENDING

| | | Related Loans/private sector loans | | | | Nonperforming loans/Private sector loans |
	Event period	December 1993	Twelve months before the Event	At the date of the Event	Related loans/ Value paid in privatization (%)	Six months after the Event
Panel A: Bankrupt banks taken over						
Cremi	6-1994	0.28	0.25	0.43	5.47	0.47
Union	6-1994	0.17	0.13	0.37	7.05	0.49
Oriente	12-1995	0.15	0.09	0.22	1.42	0.14
Banpais	3-1995	0.21	0.17	0.30	1.67	0.62
Probursa	6-1995	0.05	0.04	0.21	0.59	0.20
Centro	6-1995	0.14	0.20	0.31	1.33	0.36
Inverlat	6-1995	0.22	0.24	0.37	1.17	0.28
Mexicano	12-1996	0.04	0.06	0.07	0.56	0.06
Banoro	1-1997	0.05	0.10	0.13	0.39	0.11
Confia	5-1997	0.15	0.17	0.24	1.35	0.27
Atlantico	12-1997	0.14	0.21	0.26	0.41	0.52
Bancrecer	12-1997	0.14	0.12	0.21	2.72	0.35
Promex	12-1997	0.15	0.19	0.27	0.54	0.29
Serfin	6-1999	0.11	0.18	0.35	0.72	0.26
Mean		**0.14**	**0.15**	**0.27**	**1.81**	**0.32**
Median		**0.14**	**0.17**	**0.27**	**1.25**	**0.29**
Panel B: Survivor banks						
Bancomer	6-1997	0.10	0.20	0.17	0.46	0.10
Banamex	6-1997	0.16	0.20	0.18	0.31	0.25
Citibank	6-1997	0.00	0.00	0.00	—	0.00
Bital	6-1997	0.10	0.15	0.20	0.71	0.08
Banorte	6-1997	0.15	0.13	0.10	0.19	0.06
Mean		**0.10**	**0.14**	**0.13**	**0.42**	**0.10**
Median		**0.10**	**0.15**	**0.17**	**0.38**	**0.08**
Panel C: All banks						
Mean all banks		**0.13**	**0.15**	**0.23**	**1.50**	**0.26**
Median all banks		**0.14**	**0.17**	**0.22**	**0.72**	**0.26**
Panel D: Tests of difference in means (t-stats) and medians (z-stats)						
Bankrupt versus survivor means		**−1.18**	**−0.49**	**−2.79**[b]	**1.35**	**2.81**[b]
Bankrupt versus survivor medians		**−0.98**	**−0.23**	**−2.59**[a]	**2.23**[b]	**2.69**[b]

a = significant at 1 percent; b = significant at 5 percent; c = significant at 10 percent.

The table presents summary statistics on related loans in Mexico, including (1) the ratio of related loans outstanding to total private sector loans (computed in December 1993, one year before the *event period,* and at the *event period*); (2) related loans outstanding at the *event period* scaled by the price paid for the bank's control in the privatization auction; (3) the ratio of nonperforming loans to all private sector loans outstanding, computed six months before the *event period*. We group banks into two categories. The first group of thirteen banks ("*bankrupt banks*") includes those that were either taken over by the government or acquired by other banks to avoid a government takeover. The remaining five banks ("*survivor banks*") did not experience changes in control during the sample period. The *event period* is the date when *bankrupt banks* change control and June 1997 for *survivor banks.* Panel A presents summary statistics for *bankrupt banks* while Panel B presents summary statistics for *survivor banks.* Panel C shows the sample mean and median of each variable for all banks. Panel D, reports tests of differences in means (*t*-statistics) and medians (*z*-statistics) for *bankrupt* and *survivor banks.* The exact definition of related loans can be found in the Appendix.

bankrupt banks between December 1993 and the *event period.* Furthermore, most of this increase in related lending by *bankrupt banks* is concentrated in the year preceding the *event period* when the mean (median) fraction of related lending jumps by 12 (10) percentage points.[24] In contrast, the mean (median) fraction of related lending increases by 3 (7) percentage points for *survivor banks* between December 1993 and the *event period.* In sum, related lending by *bankrupt* and *survivor banks* is comparable in 1993 but markedly diverges as banks plunge into financial distress.

Observable differences in corporate governance (e.g., ownership structures, board composition, etc.) do not explain the increase in related lending. Recall that all banks (except Citicorp) have similar corporate governance structures and are publicly traded entities controlled by a small number of individuals. Similarly, all banks were privatized in the same manner. One version of the *three-state information view* that may explain the increase in the fraction of related loans is that such borrowers required additional loans in the post-devaluation period to keep attractive projects viable. Contrary to these predictions, related lending by survivor banks in the six months that follow the devaluation is roughly constant at 13 percent (not reported).[25] In the *looting view,* increases in related lending are tied to reductions in the profitability of loans to unrelated parties and in the value of the insiders' equity in the bank. As a crude proxy for the shock that hit banks, we compute the change in nonperforming unrelated loans between December 1993 and the bankruptcy date as a fraction of the bank's capital in December 1993.[26] The correlation between this variable and the change in related lending in the same period is 0.63. This result is consistent with the *looting view,* although the number of observations (14) is too small to achieve statistical significance.

To assess the economic significance of the *looting view,* Table I compares the volume of related lending relative to the price that

24. The level of related lending in bankrupt banks peaks at the time of the change in control and drops quickly afterwards (which suggests that concealment of related lending is not a very important problem in the sample of large loans).

25. Furthermore, Section V presents evidence that loans made by *bankrupt banks* after the big devaluation were highly unprofitable.

26. As an alternative measure of the size of the shock to a bank's capital, we examined the ratio of accumulated losses in the two years that precede the bank's bankruptcy to the level of capital at the beginning of that period. The results are qualitatively similar to those reported in the paper.

bidders paid to gain control of the banks. The results show that the mean (median) bidder obtained $1.50 ($0.72) in (top-300) loans for each dollar that she paid at the privatization auction. These figures likely underestimate the magnitude of related lending if the controllers of banks were able to camouflage some self-dealing transactions.

Finally, Table I also reports the fraction of nonperforming loans made to borrowers in the private sector. We compute nonperforming loans based on the loans to the private sector in the sample of top-300 loans for each bank six months after the *event period*. We examine nonperforming loans six months after *bankrupt banks* experience a change in control as auditors are, by that time, typically able to identify most of the inappropriate practices followed by the previous management. At the same time, six months is probably not long enough for new management to turn around the bank, alter its lending policies, and deal aggressively with nonperforming loans. Naturally, nonperforming loans are significantly higher for distressed banks than for healthier ones (32 percent versus 10 percent). More interestingly, consistent with the predictions of the looting view, the correlation between nonperforming loans and related lending is very high (0.815). However, more micro-level data are needed to examine this issue in detail, and we postpone such analysis until Section V.

To review the results thus far, consistent with both views of related lending, banks make large loans to related parties. Banks step up the intensity of related lending as a forced change in control looms closer. Related loans are strongly correlated with the fraction of nonperforming loans. Although the last two findings require further examination, which we undertake in the next three sections, they are consistent with the *looting view* and difficult to reconcile with the *information view*.

V. LENDING TERMS AND EX POST PERFORMANCE

V.A. *Lending Terms*

The *information view* maintains that related borrowers may obtain preferential terms (e.g., lower interest rates) because they are easier to screen and monitor. Under the *looting view,* better terms for related borrowers reflect self-dealing by bank insiders. Table II describes the borrowing terms for related and unrelated borrowers with the following five categories of variables: (1) in-

TABLE II

TERMS OF THE LOANS FOR THE SAMPLE OF UNRELATED AND RELATED LOANS

Variable	N	Unrelated loans Mean Median	N	Related loans Mean Median	Difference	*t*-statistic *z*-statistic
Panel A: Real interest rates						
Flexible rate & domestic	381	0.0956	264	0.0675	0.0281	5.28[a]
currency		0.0987		0.0736	0.0251	7.67[a]
Flexible rate & U. S.	185	0.1247	173	0.1022	0.0225	6.44[a]
dollars		0.1294		0.0981	0.0313	8.59[a]
Fixed rate & domestic	181	0.0438	123	−0.0250	0.0688	4.83[a]
currency		0.0744		−0.0367	0.1111	5.87[a]
Fixed rate & U. S.	111	0.1200	119	0.0792	0.0408	6.36[a]
dollars		0.1197		0.0732	0.0465	6.69[a]
Panel B: Interest rate spreads						
Flexible rate & domestic	381	0.0654	264	0.0344	0.0310	6.42[a]
currency		0.0700		0.0400	0.0300	12.36[a]
Flexible rate & U. S.	185	0.0687	173	0.0412	0.0275	10.75[a]
dollars		0.0700		0.0388	0.0312	10.55[a]
Fixed rate & domestic	181	0.0461	123	−0.0865	0.1326	10.40[a]
currency		0.0518		−0.1032	0.1550	9.39[a]
Fixed rate & U. S.	111	0.0691	119	0.0217	0.0474	7.67[a]
dollars		0.0609		0.0145	0.0464	7.77[a]
Panel C: Collateral						
Collateral dummy	858	0.8380	679	0.5272	0.3108	14.02[a]
		1.0000		1.0000	0.0000	13.21[a]
Collateral value/loan	847	2.8950	671	1.1878	1.7072	10.09[a]
		1.8399		0.5209	1.3190	14.51[a]
Panel D: Guarantees						
Personal guarantees	858	0.6632	679	0.4772	0.1860	7.47[a]
dummy		1.0000		0.0000	1.0000	7.34[a]
Panel E: Maturity						
Maturity (months)	858	45.6241	679	48.7284	−3.1043	−1.27
		36.0000		36.0000	0.0000	0.98
Panel F: Grace period						
Grace period (months)	858	4.8077	679	12.1845	−7.3768	−10.83[a]
		0.0000		6.0000	−6.0000	−11.89[a]

a = significant at 1 percent; b = significant at 5 percent; c = significant at 10 percent.

The table presents raw results for the random sample of unrelated and related loans. For each empirical proxy, the table reports the number of usable observations, the mean, and the median values for unrelated and related loans. For each variable, the table reports *t*-statistics and *z*-statistics for differences in means and medians, respectively. Definitions for each variable can be found in the Appendix.

252   *QUARTERLY JOURNAL OF ECONOMICS*

terest rates; (2) collateral; (3) guarantees; (4) original maturity; and (5) grace period. The results in this section, and in the remainder of the paper, are based on the random sample of loans.

Panel A in Table II shows the results for real interest rates. Interest rates on related loans are consistently lower for related parties than for unrelated ones. To illustrate, consider the case of flexible rate loans in domestic currency (the most frequent type of loan in our sample). The mean (median) real interest rate on these loans is 9.56 percent (9.87 percent) for unrelated loans but only 6.75 percent (7.36 percent) for related ones. Spreads over government bonds tell a very similar story (Panel B). Continuing with the case of flexible rate loans in domestic currency, the mean (median) spread is 6.54 percent (7.00 percent) for unrelated loans but only 3.44 percent (4.00 percent) for related ones.

Panel C reports the incidence of collateral and guarantees as well as their value as a fraction of the loan's principal at the time it was granted. Although related parties borrow at lower rates, their loans are less likely to be backed by collateral. Whereas 84 percent of the unrelated loans are collateralized with assets, only 53 percent of related loans are backed by collateral. Furthermore, the mean (median) collateral-to-face-value ratio is 1.19 (0.52) for loans to related parties compared with 2.89 (1.84) for loans to unrelated parties (differences in means and medians are both significant at 1 percent). Parallel results hold for the frequency of guarantees (see Panel D). Related loans are less likely to have personal guarantees (47.7 percent versus 66.3 percent). The evidence on interest rates and collateral requirements is consistent with the *looting view,* but can be reconciled with the *information view* if, for example, related parties are high-quality borrowers.

Panel E shows that unrelated loans have slightly shorter maturities than related ones (although the difference is not statistically significant). The mean (median) maturity is 45.6 (36) months for unrelated loans and 48.7 (36) months for related ones. Similarly, unrelated parties have shorter grace periods than related ones (7.4 months shorter for means and 6 months shorter for medians) before banks have the right to pull the plug on them (Panel F). One interpretation of these findings is that banks shorten the maturity of loans to unrelated parties to facilitate monitoring and gain bargaining power over low-quality borrowers. The alternative interpretation is that banks are soft on related parties.

Since differences in the ex ante financial risk characteristics of the two types of borrowers may account for the observed divergence in borrowing terms, we examine whether our results on borrowing terms survive in regressions that control for size, profitability, and leverage. The independent variables include fixed-year and bank effects and dummies for fixed-rate and foreign currency loans. The dependent variables are (1) real interest rates; (2) interest rate spread over the risk-free rate; (3) a dummy that takes a value equal to 1 if the loan has collateral; (4) the collateral-to-face-value ratio; (5) the guarantee-to-face-value ratio; (6) the maturity period; and (7) the grace period.

Table III presents the results.[27] In the regressions using real interest rates as the dependent variable, size and leverage have the expected signs, but only size is significant. Fixed-rate loans and domestic-currency loans pay lower real rates (probably because of the surprise devaluation of 1994 and the inflation that ensued). The key finding in the interest-rate regression is that related loans pay 4.15 percentage points less than unrelated ones, and this difference is significant at the 1 percent level. Results using interest rate spreads as the dependent variable are very similar and imply that related loans pay 5.15 percentage points less than unrelated ones (also significant at the 1 percent level).

The results on collateral are also interesting. Large firms post collateral less frequently and, when they do, in smaller amounts. Similarly, highly leveraged firms post larger amounts of collateral. Related loans are 30 percent less likely to have collateral, and the predicted collateral-to-loan ratio is roughly 2.9 units lower for related parties than for unrelated ones. To put this figure in perspective, note that the mean collateral-to-loan ratio is 2.14 with a standard deviation of 3.38. The results on guarantees, maturity, and grace period also confirm our findings on Table II: loans to related parties are less likely to be backed by personal guarantees, have longer maturities, and longer grace periods than loans to unrelated parties.

To summarize, related parties borrow at lower interest rates and for longer maturities than unrelated ones. They also post less collateral against their loans and offer fewer personal guarantees

27. In this section we report results based on pooling corporate and noncorporate borrowers. To check the robustness of the results, we rerun all regressions using the subsample of corporate borrowers and including the log of sales as a measure of size, the debt-to-asset ratio as a proxy for financial risk, and the income-to-sales ratio as a measure of profitability. The results are qualitatively similar, and we do not report them.

TABLE III
Loan Terms Regressions

Independent variables:	Interest rates		Collateral			Maturity in months (Tobit)	Grace period in months (Tobit)
	Real interest rates	Interest rate spreads	Collateral dummy (Probit)	Collateral value/loan (Tobit)	Personal guarantees (Probit)		
Related dummy	−0.0415[a]	−0.0515[a]	−0.2992[a]	−2.9842[a]	−0.2286[a]	6.0365[b]	20.2374[a]
	(0.0036)	(0.0037)	(0.0250)	(0.2477)	(0.0277)	(2.3681)	(1.6612)
Log of assets	−0.0061[a]	−0.0040[a]	−0.0358[a]	−0.2372[a]	−0.0280[a]	−1.3380[c]	−1.0094[b]
	(0.0012)	(0.0011)	(0.0084)	(0.0754)	(0.0089)	(0.7214)	(0.5033)
Total debt/ total assets	0.0015	0.0100	0.0158	1.7421[a]	0.0413	−13.5593[a]	−6.4817[c]
	(0.0090)	(0.0085)	(0.0568)	(0.5262)	(0.0620)	(5.1138)	(3.4959)
Domestic currency dummy	−0.0564[a]	−0.0309[a]	−0.0612[b]	−0.3994	−0.0638[b]	2.7273	−0.0459
	(0.0041)	(0.0038)	(0.0278)	(0.2599)	(0.0299)	(2.5095)	(1.7268)
Fixed interest rate dummy	−0.0422[a]	−0.0385[a]	−0.2318[a]	−1.3471[a]	0.0416	−27.9162[a]	−16.4636[a]
	(0.0048)	(0.0052)	(0.0299)	(0.2795)	(0.0317)	(2.6349)	(1.9197)
Individual dummy	0.0042	0.0065	−0.0798[c]	−0.6483[c]	−0.3719[a]	−7.7577[b]	−9.6037[a]
	(0.0052)	(0.0054)	(0.0429)	(0.3816)	(0.0399)	(3.7026)	(2.5244)
Constant	0.2035[a]	0.1166[a]		5.6623[a]		58.4428[a]	−2.6504
	(0.0283)	(0.0304)		(1.7884)		(17.6659)	(11.6765)
Bank dummies	Yes	Yes	Yes	Yes	Yes	Yes	Yes
Loan year dummies	Yes	Yes	Yes	Yes	Yes	Yes	Yes
Industry dummies	Yes	Yes	Yes	Yes	Yes	Yes	Yes
Number of observations	1470	1470	1418	1418	1470	1470	1470
Adjusted R^2/ Pseudo R^2	0.29	0.25	0.20	0.05	0.13	0.02	0.05
Log-likelihood			−707.40	−3145.93	−870.20	−7608.91	−3121.96

a = significant at 1 percent; b = significant at 5 percent; c = significant at 10 percent.

The table presents OLS and Probit regressions for the cross section of loans. OLS regressions have robust standard errors. In the case of the continuous regressors, probit derivatives are calculated based on the average of the scale factor. In the case of binomial regressors, probit derivatives are computed as the average of the difference in the cumulative normal distributions evaluated with and without the dummy variable. Standard errors are shown in parentheses. Definitions for each variable can be found in the Appendix.

than unrelated creditors. The preferential treatment received by related parties does not appear to be tied to differences in size, profitability, or leverage. These results are consistent with the view that related lending is a manifestation of self-dealing. An alternative interpretation is that related loans are safer than arm's-length ones in ways that are not picked up by our controls. We compare these two interpretations in the next section.

V.B. Ex Post Performance

The devaluation in December 1994 started a severe and prolonged downturn in the Mexican economy, during which many borrowers defaulted on their bank loans. In this section we compare the default and recovery rates of related and unrelated loans in our sample. Under the simple version of the *information view,* related parties borrow on beneficial terms because screening and monitoring reduce their default rates and enhance their recovery rates. In contrast, the *looting view* predicts that related lending takes place on advantageous terms although related borrowers have higher default rates and lower recovery rates than unrelated ones. Similarly, the *three-state information view* also predicts that unrelated loans perform better than related ones in a severe financial crisis.

Panel A in Table IV shows the incidence of bad loans in our sample. Consistent with both the *looting* and *three-state information views,* the default rate is 37 percent for unrelated borrowers and 66 percent for related ones (the difference is statistically significant at 1 percent). The number of performing loans restructured with forgiveness ("other bad loans") is very small. As a result, the fraction of all bad loans is 39 percent for unrelated borrowers and 70 percent for related ones.[28] One can interpret these findings in two ways. One interpretation is that related borrowers were hit disproportionately hard by the crisis. A more cynical interpretation is that related borrowers found it easier to default. Recall that related loans are less likely to be collateralized, raising the incentive to default. In addition, as pointed out by the FOBAPROA officer in charge of recovering bad loans, " . . . proper procedure was not followed when [related] loans were granted, they lacked some of the required legal documentation, collateral was not duly registered in the Public Register of Property, there was no follow up of how borrowed funds were used or of how loans performed . . . " [*Jornada* 8/2/99]. Plenty of anecdotal evidence is consistent with this view including loans backed by buildings that were never built or by planes that could not fly.

---

28. One possible concern is that related loans may disproportionately mature in 1995 when defaults may have been more likely. However, unrelated loans are *less* likely to mature in 1995 than unrelated ones (51.5 percent versus 58.5 percent).

TABLE IV
PANEL A: LOAN PERFORMANCE FOR THE SAMPLE OF UNRELATED
AND RELATED LOANS

	Unrelated loans		Related loans			
	N	Frequency	N	Frequency	Difference	t-statistic
Performance of the loans						
Loans that defaulted	317	0.3695	451	0.6642	−0.2947	−11.99[a]
Other bad loans	15	0.0175	24	0.0353	−0.0178	−2.21[b]
All bad loans	332	0.3869	475	0.6996	−0.3127	−12.81[a]
Breakup of bad loans by outcome						
Restructured	44	0.1325	59	0.1242	0.0083	0.35
Sold to FOBAPROA	10	0.0301	19	0.0400	−0.0099	−0.74
Sent to court	205	0.6175	256	0.5389	0.0786	2.22[b]
Sent to collection department	35	0.1054	72	0.1516	−0.0462	−1.03
Other loan outcomes	38	0.1145	69	0.1453	−0.0308	−1.27

PANEL B: RECOVERY RATES FOR THE SAMPLE OF UNRELATED AND
RELATED BAD LOANS

	Unrelated loans		Related loans			t-statistic
	N	Mean Median	N	Mean Median	Difference	z-statistic
All bad loans						
All bad loans	332	0.4624	475	0.2721	0.1903	7.62[a]
		0.4475		0.1500	0.2975	6.49[a]
All bad loans & no collateral	53	0.4206	204	0.2580	0.1626	3.08[a]
		0.4299		0.1000	0.3299	2.14[b]
All bad loans & collateral < median	95	0.3705	315	0.2694	0.1011	2.52[b]
		0.1800		0.1200	0.0600	1.56
All loans						
All loans	858	0.7920	679	0.4908	0.3012	15.07[a]
		1.0000		0.4000	0.6000	13.94[a]

a = significant at 1 percent; b = significant at 5 percent; c = significant at 10 percent.
The table presents data on the incidence and recovery rates of nonperforming loans in the random sample of loans. "Other loan outcomes" include (1) bad loans that were later fully or partially liquidated without requiring court intervention or internal collection; (2) loans for which the required reserve was applied and the bank assumed a complete loss; and (3) loans for which negotiations between the bank and the borrower are still undergoing at the time of writing. N is the number of loans in each category. The table reports t-statistics and z-statistics for differences in means and medians, respectively. Definitions for each variable can be found in the Appendix.

Panel A also shows the collection procedures followed by banks. One may wonder how aggressive were collection efforts, particularly when the government took over banks. Collection efforts were fairly aggressive as most bad loans were sent to court (461 loans out of 807). Only 13.3 percent of bad loans to unrelated parties and 12.4 percent of bad loans to related parties were restructured but not sent to court. Finally, a few loans (3–4 percent) were sold to FOBAPROA.

Panel B of Table IV presents data on the recovery rate of bad loans. As predicted by both the *looting* and *three-state information views,* the mean (median) recovery rate for bad loans was 46.2 percent (44.8 percent) for unrelated borrowers and 27.2 percent (15.0 percent) for related ones (the differences are statistically significant at 1 percent). Some of the large differences in recovery rates may stem from the fact that unrelated credits are backed by more collateral than related ones. But even when the loan is not backed by collateral, collection is substantially higher for unrelated parties. The mean (median) recovery rate for an uncollateralized unrelated bad loan is 42.1 percent (43 percent), while a similar related loan yields only 25.8 percent (10 percent). We obtain similar results if we compare the recovery rates of bad loans backed by less collateral than the median loan in the sample.

Finally, the last section of Panel B shows recovery rates for all loans. We shift the focus of the analysis from bad loans to all loans to aggregate the effects of default rates and recovery rates into a single number. Related loans are doubly hit: higher default probabilities and lower recovery rates in default than unrelated ones. As a result, the mean (median) gap in the recovery rate of all loans widens to 30 percent (60 percent) from 19 percent (30 percent) for all bad loans. The recovery rate for the median related loan in our sample is a paltry 40 percent.

For robustness, we check whether our results survive in regressions that control for size, profitability, and leverage, as well as bank, year-of-loan, and industry effects. Table V shows that borrowers that are bigger, more profitable, and less leveraged when the loan was made are less likely to default and have higher recovery rates when they do. Controlling for everything else, related borrowers are 33–35 percent more likely to default (depending on whether we use the sample of all borrowers or of only corporate ones). The results on recovery rates also show an economically large effect of related lending: the recovery rate

TABLE V
LOAN PERFORMANCE REGRESSIONS

| | *Dependent variables:* | | | | | |
| | Default | | Recovery rates | | | |
Independent variables:	All loans (Probits)		All bad loans (Tobits)		All loans (Tobits)	
Related dummy	0.3303[a]	0.3509[a]	−0.2768[a]	−0.2840[a]	−0.6991[a]	−0.7796[a]
	(0.0315)	(0.0287)	(0.0461)	(0.0429)	(0.0664)	(0.0635)
Log of sales	−0.0572[a]		0.0170		0.0919[a]	
	(0.0096)		(0.0132)		(0.0176)	
Log of assets		−0.0466[a]		0.0263[c]		0.0874[a]
		(0.0100)		(0.0155)		(0.0199)
Net income/sales	−0.6273[a]		0.1403		1.0442[a]	
	(0.0933)		(0.1154)		(0.1594)	
Total debt/total assets	0.1833[b]	0.2884[a]	−0.0484	−0.0227	−0.2301[c]	−0.4537[a]
	(0.0732)	(0.0678)	(0.0994)	(0.0932)	(0.1380)	(0.1327)
Domestic currency dummy	0.0788[b]	0.0482	0.1691[a]	0.1229[a]	0.0048	−0.0167
	(0.0360)	(0.0331)	(0.0503)	(0.0462)	(0.0685)	(0.0645)
Fixed interest rate dummy	0.0434	0.0445[b]	−0.0329	−0.0443	−0.0883	−0.1075
	(0.0379)	(0.0345)	(0.0515)	(0.0472)	(0.0703)	(0.0662)
Individual dummy		0.1328[a]		−0.1058[c]		−0.2742[a]
		(0.0470)		(0.0579)		(0.0878)
Constant			0.4317[b]	0.3817[c]	0.6188[b]	0.9430[a]
			(0.2075)	(0.2331)	(0.2883)	(0.3146)
Bank dummies	Yes	Yes	Yes	Yes	Yes	Yes
Year of loan dummies	Yes	Yes	Yes	Yes	Yes	Yes
Industry dummies	Yes	Yes	Yes	Yes	Yes	Yes
Number of observations	1307	1470	665	791	1307	1470
Log-likelihood	−629.10	−730.70	−523.07	−620.48	−993.69	−1174.78
Adjusted R^2/Pseudo R^2	0.31	0.28	0.16	0.15	0.23	0.22

a = significant at 1 percent; b = significant at 5 percent; c = significant at 10 percent.
The table presents probit and tobit regressions of the cross section of loans. In the case of the continuous regressors, probit derivatives are calculated based on the average of the scale factor. In the case of binomial regressors, probit derivatives are computed as the average of the difference in the cumulative normal distributions evaluated with and without the dummy variable. Standard errors are shown in parentheses. Definitions for each variable can be found in the Appendix.

drops by 0.28 for a bad loan made to a related borrower, and by 0.70–0.78 for all related loans. The related dummy is significant at 1 percent in all regressions. In sum, all the univariate results survive in the regressions.

The above results fit well with the *looting view* of related lending as they show that, controlling for observable measures of risk, related parties borrow on advantageous terms. However, these also fit the *three-state information view*. Whereas there can be little disagreement that 1995 was a very bad year, it is less clear that the devaluation of that year was a rare event. In fact, the country experienced six devaluations during the period 1970 – 1995 of 20 percent or more in real terms (in 1976, 1982, 1985, 1986, 1994, and 1995). Note also that for the *three-state information view* to explain why banks step up their lending to related parties as the crisis sets (Table I), it is necessary to further assume that related parties, although unable to repay their pre-crisis loans, enjoyed attractive investment opportunities going forward. To examine the nature of the investment opportunities available to related parties in the post-1994 period, we distinguish between "old" and "new" borrowers depending on whether the first loan to a borrower was made before or after December 1994, respectively. The pre-1994 loans should, ceteris paribus, perform significantly worse than the post-1994 ones as the devaluation that took place in 1994 adversely impacted credit quality. In fact, default rates for loans made before and after December 1994 are not statistically different (78.9 percent versus 74.5 percent, respectively), and neither are recovery rates (39.8 percent versus 38.4 percent, respectively). The next section further suggests that the *three-state* model would need additional refinements to fit the data.

V.C. Further Results

A straightforward prediction of the *looting view* is that the returns that the bank earns on related loans should be lowest for loans to parties in which the insider has a large equity stake. Data on ownership are simply not available except for rare exceptions (e.g., companies with ADRs in the United States). As a proxy for ownership, we use a dummy that takes a value equal to 1 if the borrower is a publicly traded firm and 0 otherwise. We test the prediction of the looting view that related privately held firms borrow on very attractive terms despite a high incidence of default with a low recovery rate. In contrast, a plausible version of the *information view* would hold that banks will charge higher interest rates on loans to closely held firms than to publicly traded ones because the former are more opaque.

Table VI shows the results of regressions that explain the borrowing terms and the performance of the loans using the same control variables of the previous regressions but adding the interaction term between related party and publicly traded firm. Publicly traded firms pay lower interest rates than nonpublicly traded firms or individuals. However, among related borrowers,

TABLE VI
PUBLICLY TRADED DEBTOR REGRESSIONS

	Dependent variables:					
	Interest rates		Collateral		Default	Performance
Independent variables:	Real interest rates	Interest rate spreads	Collateral dummy (Probit)	Collateral/ loan (Tobit)	All bad loans (Probit)	Recovery rate (Tobit)
Related dummy	−0.0450[a]	−0.0547[a]	−0.3295[a]	−3.1174[a]	0.4064[a]	−0.8442[a]
	(0.0039)	(0.0040)	(0.0268)	(0.2653)	(0.0301)	(0.0656)
Publicly traded	−0.0339[a]	−0.0198[b]	−0.3069[a]	−1.6776[a]	−0.0955	0.2570
	(0.0098)	(0.0089)	(0.0671)	(0.5277)	(0.0710)	(0.1731)
Publicly traded	0.0302[a]	0.0248[a]	0.1838[a]	1.4215[b]	−0.2943[a]	0.5209[b]
and related	(0.0118)	(0.0105)	(0.0425)	(0.7051)	(0.0808)	(0.2072)
Individual dummy	0.0031	0.0004	−0.0895[b]	−0.7141[c]	0.1131[b]	−0.2177[a]
	(0.0052)	(0.0054)	(0.0436)	(0.3818)	(0.0484)	(0.0861)
Log of assets	−0.0048[a]	−0.0034[a]	−0.0237[a]	−0.1738[b]	−0.0361[a]	0.0634[a]
	(0.0013)	(0.0012)	(0.0087)	(0.0779)	(0.0102)	(0.0200)
Total debt/total	−0.0037	−0.0087	−0.0017	−1.6537[a]	0.2994[a]	−0.4528[b]
assets	(0.0089)	(0.0084)	(0.0570)	(0.5255)	(0.0683)	(0.1295)
Domestic currency	−0.0574[a]	−0.0314[a]	−0.0713[b]	−0.4517[c]	0.0429	0.0322
dummy	(0.0041)	(0.0038)	(0.0278)	(0.2298)	(0.0337)	(0.0632)
Fixed interest rate	−0.0417[a]	−0.0381[a]	−0.2289[a]	−1.3169[a]	0.0392	−0.0971[a]
dummy	(0.0048)	(0.0051)	(0.0301)	(0.2791)	(0.0352)	(0.0648)
Constant	0.1933[a]	0.1103[a]		5.1223[a]		1.0783[a]
	(0.0281)	(0.0301)		(1.7938)		(0.3096)
Bank dummies	Yes	Yes	Yes	Yes	Yes	Yes
Year of loan dummies	Yes	Yes	Yes	Yes	Yes	Yes
Industry dummies	Yes	Yes	Yes	Yes	Yes	Yes
Number of observations	1470	1470	1418	1418	1470	1470
Adjusted R^2/Pseudo R^2	0.30	0.25	0.21	0.05	0.30	0.23
Log-likelihood			−697.08	−3140.80	−708.75	−1152.98

a = significant at 1 percent; b = significant at 5 percent; c = significant at 10 percent.
The table presents OLS, probit and tobit regressions of the cross section of loans. OLS regressions have robust standard errors. In the case of the continuous regressors, probit derivatives are calculated based on the average of the scale factor. In the case of binomial regressors, probit derivatives are computed as the average of the difference in the cumulative normal distributions evaluated with and without the dummy variable. Definitions for each variable can be found in the Appendix.

banks offer worse terms to publicly traded firms! Related publicly traded firms face higher real interest rates and have higher collateral requirements than related individuals and privately held firms. Nonetheless, loans to related parties are 29.4 percentage points less likely to be bad when made to publicly traded firms than to individuals and privately held firms. Similarly, among related parties, the recovery rate on loans to publicly traded firms is 52.1 percentage points higher than on loans to individuals and privately held firms. In contrast, borrowing terms and ex post performance line up much better for unrelated parties. Among the unrelated parties, publicly traded firms pay lower interest rates and post less collateral than individuals and privately held firms, although the two groups have similar recovery rates.

In summary, among related parties, banks offer better terms to individuals and privately held firms than to publicly traded ones. However, loans to individuals and privately held companies are substantially more risky than loans to publicly traded firms. Thus, consistent with the *looting view,* the closeness of the relationship between the controllers of the bank and the borrower matters for the terms on which related parties borrow. These results place constraints on the structure of a successful *three-state information* model. Specifically, the version of the *information view* that fits these data is one in which non-publicly traded firms with close ties to the bank are the best performers in the intermediate state of the world and unrelated parties are the worst performers. Furthermore, the *information view* would also need to justify on efficiency grounds the sharp increase in related lending that takes place once banks are in financial distress.

VI. CONCLUSION

Banking crises are common. There is widespread agreement among economists that the fragility of the banking system is related to moral hazard problems. There is less agreement on the precise nature of the moral hazard problem that makes banks so fragile. One view is that banking crises result from bad management. Another view is that deposit insurance may create incentives for banks to take excessive risk. Yet another view is that financial crises result from soft budget constraints created by reputational problems. Here we draw attention to related lending as another manifestation of moral hazard problems. Close ties between lender and borrower may enhance the allocation of credit. However, bank insiders may use their control over lending policies to loot the bank at the expense of minority shareholders or the deposit insurance system or both. Looting makes banks inherently fragile since related parties default on their loans to the bank when the economy fails and the continuation value of their equity in the bank is low. The case of Mexico in the 1990s suggests that the risk that related lending may lead to looting is great when banks are controlled by industrial firms, outside lending has relatively low rates of return, and corporate governance is weak.

Our results shed light on five issues. First, related lending was a large fraction of the banking business in Mexico in 1995. Second, when the economy slipped into a recession, the fraction of related lending almost doubled for the banks that subsequently went bankrupt and increased only slightly for the banks that survived. Third, the borrowing terms offered to related parties were substantially better than those available to unrelated ones, even after controlling for observable financial characteristics. Fourth, related loans had much higher default rates and lower recovery rates than unrelated ones. Fifth, the worst-performing loans were those made to persons and companies closest to the controllers of banks. In fact, in most cases, a dollar lent to a related person or a related privately held company turned out to be a dollar lost. All five findings are consistent with the *looting view* and speak to the relevance of related lending as a potential source of bank fragility for countries with institutional setups similar to that of Mexico in the 1990s.

The results in this paper may have profound implications for the regulatory design of banking institutions. The Basel rules primarily address the incentives of banks to take excessive risks. The results in this paper show the importance of looting as a key determinant of banking stability. The best way to reduce the fragility of financial systems may be to reduce the importance of related lending. This may be achieved by explicit regulation of related lending as well as by enhanced reporting requirements, better investor protection (such as more scrutiny of self-dealing transactions and directors' liability in bankruptcy), and closer supervision.

APPENDIX: DESCRIPTION OF THE VARIABLES

This appendix describes the variables collected for the terms and performance of a random sample of loans made by seventeen Mexican banks circa 1995. The first column gives the name of the variable, and the second column describes it. Sources: SAM-300 database (largest 300 loans of each bank together with their size and the names of the borrowers behind each of them), SENICREB

RELATED LENDING 263

database (complete list of loans made by each of the privatized banks), and each bank's database as reported at the request of the Mexican Banking Commission.

Variable	Description
Related loans	Article 73 of the Mexican Code of Mercantile Institutions stipulates that a related loan is a loan for which the borrower is either (1) a shareholder with 1 percent or more of the voting rights of the bank; (2) a person who has family ties—by marriage or blood up to the second degree—with a shareholder of 1 percent or more of the voting rights of the bank; (3) a director, officer, or employee of a company or trust fund that holds 1 percent or more of the voting rights of the bank or a director, officer, or employee of the bank itself with the power to engage into contracts or transactions under the name bank; or (4) a person holding 10 percent or more of the voting rights of a company that holds 1 percent or more of the shares in the bank.
Unrelated loan	A loan given to a borrower which is not related.
Real interest rate	The average real interest rate paid during the duration of the loan. The average real interest rate is computed as $$\frac{1}{T}\sum_{t=1}^{T}\frac{(1 + i_t + s)}{(1 + \pi_t)},$$ where i is the reference interest rate assigned to the loan, s is the spread above the interest rate and π the inflation rate. For loans in Mexican pesos the inflation rate was calculated using the Producer Price Index (INPP) excluding oil products. For loans in U. S. dollars the inflation rate was calculated using the U. S. Producer Price Index (PPI) of finished products.
Interest rate spread	The average interest rate spread of the loan above the benchmark risk-free security rate. The average interest rate spread is computed as $$\frac{1}{T}\sum_{t=1}^{T}(i_t + s - r^f),$$ where r^f is the risk-free security rate and s is the spread agreed to in the contract between the bank and the borrower above the loan reference rate i. For loans in Mexican pesos the risk-free security is the 28-day Treasury bills (CETES) rate. For loans in U. S. dollars, the risk-free security rate is the one-month LIBOR rate.

Variable	Description
Collateral dummy	Dummy that takes a value equal to 1 if the loan is backed up by collateral; the variable is 0 otherwise. Definitions for collateral include physical tangible assets, financial documents (e.g., title documents, securities, etc.), intangibles, and business proceeds pledged by the borrower to ensure repayment on his loan. Collateral does not include personal guarantees such as obligations backed only by the signature of the borrower or the submission of wealth statements from guarantors to the bank—a standard practice in Mexico.
Collateral value/loan	The ratio of collateral value to loan value when the loan was first granted.
Personal guarantees dummy	Dummy that takes a value equal to 1 if the loan is secured by a personal guarantee; the variable is 0 otherwise. A personal guarantee is defined as the obligation to repayment by a letter of compromise. Usually, the debtor must submit wealth statements from a guarantor who is willing to back her loan.
Maturity	The number of months to maturity of the loan starting from the moment in which the loan is given.
Grace period	The number of months beyond maturity given to a debtor in order for her to repay her due balance with the bank. A grace period is granted to a debtor on an individual basis.
Related dummy	Dummy that takes value of 1 if the loan is related; the variable is 0 otherwise.
Log of assets	The natural logarithm of total assets in millions of U. S. dollars deflated to December 1995. Total assets are equal to the total value of current assets, long-term receivables, investment in unconsolidated subsidiaries, other investments, net property plant and equipment, and other assets. Total assets figures are from 1989–1998 (the first available) and are deflated to December 1995 using Mexico's Producer Price Index and then converted to U. S. dollars using the average 1995 exchange rate.
Total debt/total assets	The ratio of total debt to total assets. Total debt is equal to the sum of all interest-bearing obligations of the debtor plus all other liabilities. Total debt and total assets figures are from 1989–1998 (the first pair available) in millions of Mexican pesos that were deflated to December 1995 using Mexico's Producer Price Index and then converted to U. S. dollars using the average 1995 exchange rate.

Domestic currency dummy	Dummy variable that takes a value equal to 1 if the currency is domestic, that is, Mexican pesos or the inflation-adjusted currency units UDIs (*Unidad de Inversión*); the variable is 0 otherwise.
Fixed interest-rate dummy	Dummy variable that takes a value equal to 1 if the loan pays a fixed interest rate; the variable takes a value equal to 0 otherwise. A fixed interest rate loan pays an annual percentage rate on a fixed basis without being updated during the duration of the loan.
Individual dummy	Dummy variable that takes a value equal to 1 if the debtor is an individual—not a firm; the variable is 0 otherwise.
Bank dummies	Seventeen bank-fixed effects dummy variables.
Loan year dummies	Six fixed-year effect dummy variables. We generated a year of origination dummy variable for the years of 1990, 1991, 1992, 1993, 1994, 1995, and 1996. The year of loan dummy takes a value equal to 1 if the loan was originated in that year; the variable is 0 otherwise. The year of origination of the loan is the year when the loan was contracted and granted.
Industry dummies	Twelve industry dummy variables. We classified every debtor in one of twelve broad sectors of the economy. The following are the industries captured: (1) agriculture, fishery, and forestry; (2) mining; (3) manufacture of food, beverages, and tobacco; (4) construction; (5) electricity, gas, and water; (6) commerce, hotels, and restaurants; (7) transportation; (8) financial services; (9) community services; (10) civil and mercantile associations; (11) government, defense, public security; and (12) foreign and international organizations.
Loans that defaulted	Loan that has stopped payment on principal and interest and has defaulted on the original terms of the borrower's loan agreement, as of the moment we drew the sample of random loans. In Mexico, the general rule for the classification of a loan as nonperforming is after 90 days of missing a payment, or in the case of a one-payment loan, after 30 days of missing the payment.
Other bad loans	Performing loans that were either sent to Fobaproa or restructured with forgiveness.
All bad loans	Sum of other bad loans and nonperforming loans. Total bad loans are the loans that (1) were nonperforming; or (2) were sold to Fobaproa; or (3) had recovery rates of less than 100 percent.

Variable	Description
Restructured loans	Loan for which the original terms have been altered due to the deterioration of the debtor's financial condition. A restructure is generally undertaken in order to avoid complete default or uncollectibility from the debtor. In most cases, a restructure involves the extension of the maturity of the loan, a change of the interest rate terms, or the rescheduling of interest payments.
Loans sold to FOBAPROA	Nonperforming loan sold to the deposit insurance agency Fobaproa (Fondo de Protección al Ahorro Bancario).
Loans sent to court	Nonperforming loan for which the bank initiated a judicial proceeding (generally civil lawsuit) against the debtor in a Mexican court of law in order to recover the debtor's due balance with the bank, either by taking over the assets put forward as guarantee or by achieving a court injunction favorable to the bank.
Loans sent to collection department	Nonperforming loan for which the bank filed an internal payment collection procedure. The procedure works on a borrower-by-borrower basis and is intended to make the borrower resume payments on her defaulted loan, either by negotiating a restructure, a forgiveness of her debt, or both. This procedure functions as a warning for the borrower with due payments and is less stringent than a court procedure. Generally, if administrative collection fails, the bank will then file a lawsuit against the debtor in a Mexican court of law.
Other loan outcomes	Other loan outcomes include (1) bad loans that were later fully or partially liquidated without requiring court or internal collection; (2) loans for which required reserve was applied and the bank assumed a complete loss; and (3) loans for which negotiations between the bank and the borrower are still undergoing.
Log of sales	The natural logarithm of sales in millions of U. S. dollars deflated to December 1995. Sales are equal to the total value of products and services sold, minus sales returns and discounts. Sales figures are from 1989–1998 (the first available) and are deflated to December 1995 using Mexico's Producer Price Index and then converted to U. S. dollars using the average 1995 exchange rate.

Net income/sales	The ratio of net income to sales. Net income is equal to operating income minus interest expenses and net taxes paid, as well as the cost of any extraordinary items. Net income and sales figures are from 1989–1998 (the first pair available) in millions of Mexican pesos and are deflated to December 1995 using Mexico's Producer Price Index and then converted to U. S. dollars using the average 1995 exchange rate.
Publicly traded	Dummy variable that takes a value equal to 1 if the borrowing company was listed and publicly traded on the Mexican Stock Exchange during the year of 1995; the variable is 0 otherwise.
Publicly traded and related	Dummy variable that takes a value equal to 1 if the borrowing company was both publicly traded and related; the variable is 0 otherwise.

DEPARTMENT OF ECONOMICS, HARVARD UNIVERSITY
SCHOOL OF MANAGEMENT, YALE UNIVERSITY
NATIONAL BANKING AND SECURITIES COMMISSION (MEXICO)

REFERENCES

Akerlof, George A., and Paul Romer, "Looting: The Economic Underworld of Bankruptcy for Profit," *Brookings Papers on Economic Activity*, Microeconomics No. 2 (1993), 1–73.

Aoki, Masahiko, Hugh Patrick, and Paul Sheard, "The Japanese Main Banking System: An Introductory Overview," in Masahiko Aoki and Hugh Patrick, eds., *The Japanese Main Banking System* (Oxford, UK: Oxford University Press, 1994), pp. 3–50.

Backman, Michael, *Asian Eclipse: Exposing the Dark Side of Business in Asia* (Singapore: John Wiley & Sons Asia Pte Ltd, 1999).

Barth, James R., Gerard Caprio, Jr., and Ross Levine, "The Regulation and Supervision of Banks around the World. A New Database," World Bank, 2001.

Bernanke, Benjamin, "Nonmonetary Effects of the Financial Crisis in the Propagation of the Great Depression," *American Economic Review*, LXXIII (1983), 257–276.

Beim, David O., and Charles W. Calomiris, *Emerging Financial Markets* (New York, NY: McGraw-Hill Irvin, 2001).

Burkart, Mike, Denis Gromb, and Fausto Panunzi, "Why Higher Takeover Premia Protect Minority Shareholders," *Journal of Political Economy*, CVI (1998), 172–204.

Cameron, Rondo, *Banking in the Early Stages of Industrialization. A Comparative Study* (New York, NY: Oxford University Press, 1967).

Diamond, Douglas, and Raghuram Rajan, "Banks, Short-Term Debt, and Financial Crises: Theory, Policy Implications and Applications," NBER Working Paper No. 7764, 2000.

Edwards, Sebastian, and Alejandra Cox Edwards, *Monetarism and Liberalization: The Chilean Experiment* (Chicago, IL: The University of Chicago Press, 1991).

Faccio, Mara, Larry H. P. Lang, and Leslie Young, "Debt, Agency Costs and Institutions," 2000.

Garcia-Herrero, Alicia, "Banking Crises in Latin America in the 1990s: Lessons from Argentina, Paraguay, and Venezuela," IMF working paper No. WP/97/140, 1997.

Gerschenkron, Alexander, *Economic Backwardness in Historical Perspective, A Book of Essays* (Cambridge, MA: Harvard University Press, 1962).

Gil-Díaz, Francisco, and Augustín Carstens, "Pride and Prejudice: The Economics Profession and Mexico's Financial Crisis," in Sebastian Edwards and Moisés Naím, eds., *Mexico 1994: Anatomy of an Emerging Market Crash* (Washington, DC: Carnegie Endowment for International Peace, 1997).

Hoshi, Takeo, Anil Kashyap, and David Scharfstein, "Corporate Structure, Liquidity, and Investment: Evidence from Japanese Industrial Groups," *Quarterly Journal of Economics,* CVI (1991), 33–60.

Johnson, Simon, Rafael La Porta, Florencio López-de-Silanes, and Andrei Shleifer, "Tunneling," *American Economic Review Papers and Proceedings,* XC (2000), 22–27.

Kang, Jun-Koo, and René Stulz, "Is Bank-Centered Corporate Governance Worth it: A Cross-Sectional Analysis of the Performance of Japanese Firms During the Asset Price Deflation," NBER Working Paper No. 6328, 1997.

Koike, Kenji, The Ayala Group During the Acquino Period: Diversification Along with a Changing Ownership and Management Structure," *The Developing Economies,* XXXI (1993), 442–464.

Lamoreaux, Naomi R., *Insider Lending. Banks, Personal Connections, and Economic Development in Industrial New England* (New York, NY: Cambridge University Press, 1994).

Laeven, Luc, "Insider Lending and Bank Ownership: The Case of Russia," *Journal of Comparative Economics,* XXIX (2001), 207–229.

La Porta, Rafael, and Florencio López-de-Silanes, "The Benefits of Privatization: Evidence from México," *Quarterly Journal of Economics,* CXIV (1999), 1193–1242.

La Porta, Rafael, Florencio López-de-Silanes, and Andrei Shleifer, "Government Ownership of Banks," *Journal of Finance,* LIII (2002), 265–302.

La Porta, Rafael, Florencio López-de-Silanes, Andrei Shleifer, and Robert Vishny, "Legal Determinants of External Finance," *Journal of Finance,* LII (1997), 1131–1150.

La Porta, Rafael, Florencio López-de-Silanes, Andrei Shleifer, and Robert Vishny, "Law and Finance," *Journal of Political Economy,* CVI (1998), 1113–1155.

La Porta, Rafael, Florencio López-de-Silanes, Andrei Shleifer, and Robert Vishny, "Investor Protection and Corporate Valuation," *Journal of Finance,* LIII (June 2002), forthcoming.

Lindgren, Carl-Johan, Gillian Garcia, and Mathew Saal, "Bank Soundness and Macroeconomic Policy," International Monetary Fund, 1996.

López-de-Silanes, Florencio, "Determinants of Privatization Prices," *Quarterly Journal of Economics,* CXII (1997), 966–1028.

López-de-Silanes, Florencio, and Guillermo Zamarripa, "Deregulation and Privatization of Commercial Banking," *Revista de Análisis Económico,* X (1995), 113–164.

Mackey, Michael W., "Report of Michael W. Mackey on the Comprehensive Evaluation of the Operations and Functions of the Fund for the Protection of Bank Savings 'FOBAPROA' and Quality of Supervision of the FOBAPROA Program 1995–1999," 1999.

Morck, Randall, and Masao Nakamura, "Banks and Corporate Control in Japan," *Journal of Finance,* LIV (1999), 319–339.

Nagel, Mark Steven, "Supplicants, Robber Barons, and Pocket Banks," Harvard University, Ph.D. Thesis in Political Science, 1999.

Patrick, Hugh T., "Japan, 1968–1914," in Rondo Cameron, *Banking in the Early Stages of Industrialization. A Comparative Study* (New York, NY: Oxford University Press, 1967).

Rajan, Raghuram, "Insiders and Outsiders: The Choice between Informed and Arm's-Length Debt," *Journal of Finance,* XLVII (1992), 1367–1400.

Stiglitz, Joseph, and Andrew Weiss, "Credit Rationing in Markets with Imperfect Information," *American Economic Review,* LXXI (1981), 393–410.

Verbrugge, James A., and Cavit Yantac, "Bank Privatization in Turkey," University of Georgia, 1999.

Wenger, E., and C. Kaserer, "The German Model of Corporate Governance: A Model That Should Not Be Imitated," in S. W. Black and M. Moersch, eds., *Competition and Convergence in Financial Markets* (Amsterdam: Elsevier, 1998), pp. 41–78.

ELSEVIER   Journal of Financial Economics 64 (2002) 181–214

www.elsevier.com/locate/econbase

The value of durable bank relationships: evidence from Korean banking shocks ☆

Kee-Hong Bae[a,b], Jun-Koo Kang[c,*], Chan-Woo Lim[d]

[a] *College of Business Administration, Korea University, Seoul, South Korea*
[b] *Hong Kong University of Science and Technology, Hong Kong*
[c] *The Eli Broad College of Business, Michigan State University, East Lansing, MI 48824, USA*
[d] *College of Business Administration, Korea University, Seoul, South Korea*

Received 16 November 1999; received in revised form 4 May 2001

Abstract

Using a large sample of exogenous events that negatively affected Korean banks during the 1997–98 period, we examine the value of durable bank relationships in Korea. We show that adverse shocks to banks have a negative effect not only on the value of the banks themselves but also on the value of their client firms, and that this adverse effect on firm value is a decreasing function of the financial health of both the banks and their client firms. Our results are concentrated in the second half of the sample period when Korean banks experienced severe difficulties. © 2002 Elsevier Science B.V. All rights reserved.

JEL classification: G21; G3

Keywords: Bank durability; Main bank; Korean banking crisis; Bank relationship; Client firm value

1. Introduction

In the banking literature, "relationship banking" is portrayed as being valuable to both banks and their client firms (Ramakrishnan and Thakor, 1984; Fama, 1985;

☆ We are grateful for comments from Dong-Hyun Ahn, Ted Fee, Mark Flannery (the referee), Charles Hadlock, Inmoo Lee, Philsang Lee, Naveen Khanna, Kyung Suh Park, William Schwert (the editor), and seminar participants at the Korea University. This work was supported by a Korea Research Foundation Grant (KRF-1999-C00291).

*Corresponding author. Tel.: +517-353-3065; fax: +517-432-1080.

E-mail address: kangju@pilot.msu.edu (J.-K. Kang).

Sharpe, 1990; Diamond, 1991). A bank provides the firm with loans and diverse financial services on the basis of a continuing relationship. It continuously acquires information about the firm and can thus intervene quickly and informally. Since the continuity of the relationship allows the bank to have a competitive advantage in collecting information and monitoring the borrowing firm, it reduces informational asymmetries and the costs of financial distress for the client firm.

The advantages of relationship banking are known to be much greater in bank-centered financial systems, such as those in Germany and Japan, than in the capital-market-centered systems of Anglo-Saxon countries (Aoki, 1990; Hoshi et al., 1991; Kaplan, 1994; Kaplan and Minton, 1994; Kang and Shivdasani, 1995). In a bank-centered financial system, firms obtain most of their external financing from their main banks, although they maintain banking relationships with several banks. The main bank is particularly knowledgeable about the firm's prospects. The main bank sometimes acts like a management consultant, providing advice to management and sending directors to the firm's board in periods of financial distress to help the firm improve its performance.

However, relationship banking has a cost. As Rajan (1992) argues, because bank financing makes the bank well informed about the firm, it tends to make the firm hostage to the bank and hence enables the bank to extract rents. Further, an unexpected deterioration in bank durability imposes costs on client firms (Slovin et al., 1993; Gibson, 1995; Kang and Stulz, 2000). When a bank does poorly and suffers from a decreased ability to lend to a borrower, the client firm is adversely affected, since the firm loses the benefits of the durable bank relationship for the future. For example, Slovin et al. (1993) examine the effect on client firm value of the near-failure of the Continental Illinois Bank and its subsequent rescue by the Federal Deposit Insurance Corporation (FDIC). They find that the bank's impending insolvency and the subsequent FDIC rescue had negative and positive effects, respectively, on client firm share prices. These results imply that an unanticipated reduction in bank durability imposes significant costs on borrowers. On a macro-economy level, Bernanke (1983) examines the effects of the U.S. financial crisis during the period of the Great Depression on the real costs of credit intermediation. He shows that the failures of banks and other lenders reduced the efficiency of the financial sector in performing its intermediary functions and adversely affected the real economy. He argues that the difficulties of the banks during the Great Depression increased the costs of intermediation, making credit from the bank expensive and difficult to obtain. He also shows that bank failures are not caused by anticipations of future changes in aggregate output and refutes the opposite direction of causality.

In this paper, we provide direct evidence on the value of durable main bank relationships, using a large sample of exogenous events that negatively affect bank credit availability. Our evidence is from Korea during 1997–98, a period during which banks experienced substantial difficulties that forced them to contract credit. Our objective is to provide some systematic evidence on the extent to which firm value is related to the degree of financial health of both the main bank and the client firm.

K.-H. Bae et al. / Journal of Financial Economics 64 (2002) 181–214 183

For a sample of 113 bank-specific events that affected Korean banks adversely during the 1997–98 period, we find that the bank and a portfolio of client firms experience average three-day announcement returns of -2.49% and -1.26%, respectively, both of which are significant at the 0.01 level. The results from our cross-sectional analysis show that client firms of banks with high nonperforming loan ratios and/or poor stock market performance suffer a greater loss in their share values, and that client firms perform worse on days when their banks' stock price performance deteriorates.

We also find that the costs of bank distress are higher for bank-dependent firms and financially weak firms. Firms that borrow more from banks and are highly levered experience a larger drop in the value of their equity. In contrast, firms with alternative means of external financing and firms with more liquid assets experience a smaller drop in share value.

However, the subperiod analysis indicates that the results are mainly driven by the banking crisis period, during which banks were saddled with huge amounts of bad loans that forced them to pull back sharply on lending. This result is consistent with that of Slovin et al. (1993) and suggests that bank difficulties impose costs on borrowers and that the financial health of banks is an important factor for the continuity of the bank–firm relationship.

Overall, our findings provide strong support for the argument that a bank-centered financial system imposes costs on borrowers when their bank is in financial distress, and that bank distress is more costly for financially constrained firms and/or firms that are in weak financial health. They also suggest that the combination of bank and firm conditions determines the impact of bad news about a bank on its customers.

Our paper is related to two recent studies on the costs of the bank-centered financial system in Japan. Gibson (1995) uses a sample of 1,355 Japanese firms from 1991 to 1992 to examine whether the health of the main bank influences the investment of client firms. He shows that a firm with a low-rated main bank (AA−) invests 30% less than a firm with a high-rated main bank (AA+). However, his results indicate that two banks rated AA – have significant effects on firm investment with equal magnitude but opposite signs, which suggests that the investment effect he documents does not seem to be tightly associated with the financial health of the main bank.

Kang and Stulz (2000) examine the costs of a bank-centered financial system using a sample of 1,380 Japanese firms for the period 1986–93. Unlike Gibson, Kang and Stulz take the view that the whole banking sector in Japan was experiencing difficulties during the 1990–93 period, so that high bank dependence is costly for a firm irrespective of the identity of its main bank. They show that firms that borrow more from banks suffer larger drops in stock prices and cut investments back more substantially during the 1990–93 period.

We extend this literature by providing evidence for an explicit link between firm value and the financial health of banks. Unlike Gibson, we focus on the effect of bank difficulties on the market value of client firms, not on their investment behavior. Our approach is also different from that of Kang and Stulz in that we

184   *K.-H. Bae et al. / Journal of Financial Economics 64 (2002) 181–214*

focus on the explicit link between the financial heath of the main banks and their client firms. We extensively utilize variables that capture the financial health of each main bank and each client firm, and examine the importance of the financial health of both the main bank and the client firm in relationship banking.

In addition, while previous research uses data from Japan to examine the importance of bank-firm ties, our paper uses data from Korea where banks have also played a key role in corporate financing. Therefore, the results in this paper can provide complementary evidence on the costs of a bank-centered financial system and help us better understand the value of durable bank relationships.

Finally, the Gibson (1995) and Kang and Stulz (2000) studies may suffer from a potential causality problem. Firms in severe financial distress can adversely affect banks since borrowers become less creditworthy and bank loans lose value. In other words, poor firm performance affects main bank performance and the causality could run from the firm to the bank, which makes the results for bank–firm relationships difficult to interpret. To avoid this problem and to investigate bank–firm relationships in an unambiguous way, we adopt an event-study approach and focus on the exogenous shocks that affect Korean banks adversely. In this respect, our approach is similar to Slovin et al. (1993). However, their experiment focuses on only one bank in near-bankruptcy, while our paper uses a dataset of various main banks and client firms that differ in their financial characteristics. This dataset allows us to explore the cross-sectional variation of the valuation effect of bank–firm relationships in a more informative way. James (1987), Lummer and McConnell (1989), and Billett et al. (1995) also use the event-study approach, but they focus on the positive side of bank loans in bank–firm relationships. They find that the announcements of new bank loans and loan renewal agreements have a positive effect on firm value.

Our paper is also related to several recent studies that examine the value of durable bank relationships. Ongena et al. (2000) measure the impact of bank distress announcements on the stock prices of firms maintaining a relationship with a distressed bank, using the near-collapse of the Norwegian banking system during the 1988–91 period. They find that the aggregate impact of bank distress on listed firms is small and statistically insignificant, and attribute this finding to the ease of alternative financing from equity markets when banks are in distress. Djankov et al. (2000) examine the valuation effect of a bank's insolvency on client firms, using a sample of 31 insolvent banks in Indonesia, Korea, and Thailand during the period 1998–99. They find that for the entire sample, the announcement of a bank closure leads to negative abnormal performance of related firms, while the announcement of a nationalization is associated with positive abnormal performance. Their findings suggest that the continuity of the banking relationship adds value to a firm. However, their regression results using all firms do not seem to be entirely consistent with those using a subsample of firms in each country. For instance, they find that announcements of a bank closure are significantly negatively related to the abnormal returns for client firms in Indonesia, but there is an insignificant positive relation for client firms in Thailand. They also find that announcements of a nationalization lead to significantly positive returns for client firms in Korea, but such announcements do

K.-H. Bae et al. / Journal of Financial Economics 64 (2002) 181–214   185

not have any discernable effects on returns for client firms in Indonesia and Thailand. Finally, Karceski et al. (2000) analyze the share price responses of Norwegian borrowers to bank merger announcements during the period 1983–96 by separating borrowers according to whether they are affiliated with the acquiring, target, or rival banks. They find that small borrowers of target banks lose about 3% in equity value when their bank is announced as a merger target and these borrowers are pushed out of the banking relationships after a bank merger.

The paper proceeds as follows. Section 2 presents a brief discussion of some important characteristics of bank financing in Korea. Section 3 describes our sample selection process and the data. Section 4 provides the estimates of abnormal announcement returns for main banks and portfolios of client firms and reports results from cross-sectional regressions. Section 5 summarizes and concludes the paper.

2. Characteristics of bank financing in Korea

There are important characteristics of bank financing in Korea that make the country particularly well suited to our investigation, the first being that the Korean market is predominantly bank-centered. Although the importance of bank financing in Korea has recently decreased due to financial deregulation and capital market liberalization, Korean firms still rely strongly on bank financing and maintain close financial ties with their main banks.

Fig. 1, which uses flow of funds data compiled by the Bank of Korea, shows the composition of financing sources for the corporate sector in Korea since 1990. During the 1990–98 period, loans, stocks, and bonds represent 62.4%, 17.1% and 20.5%, respectively, of external funds raised by Korean firms.[1] Fig. 1 indicates that indirect financing from financial institutions dominates direct financing from the capital market.

Second, the Korean banking industry experienced severe external shocks in late 1997 and 1998. Fig. 2 shows net funds flows to the corporate sector from 1991 to 1998. During the 1991–97 period, the average annual net increases in loans, stocks, and bonds were 40 trillion won, 8 trillion won, and 16 trillion won, respectively. In contrast, the figures for 1998 are strikingly different. The net increases in 1998 were −37 trillion won, 10 trillion won, and 32 trillion won for loans, stocks, and bonds, respectively. Fig. 2 shows very clearly that during 1998, banks experienced a severe credit crunch and were forced to curtail lending to the corporate sector. Consequently, their borrowers had to turn to alternative sources of external finance, notably corporate bonds.

---

[1] According to Bank of Korea, loans include bank loans, loans from other financial institutions, and commercial paper. These loans account for 26.5%, 27.0%, and 8.9% of total corporate financing, respectively. The Bank of Korea classifies loans made from the trust account of deposit banks as loans from other financial institutions, which leads to an understatement in the proportion of loans from banks. Other financial institutions are classified into five categories according to their business activities: development, savings, investment, insurance, and other institutions.

186 *K.-H. Bae et al. / Journal of Financial Economics 64 (2002) 181–214*

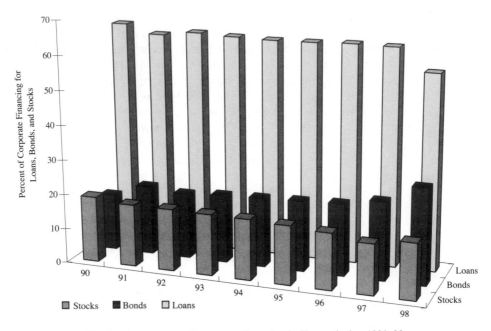

Fig. 1. Composition of corporate financing in Korea during 1990–98.

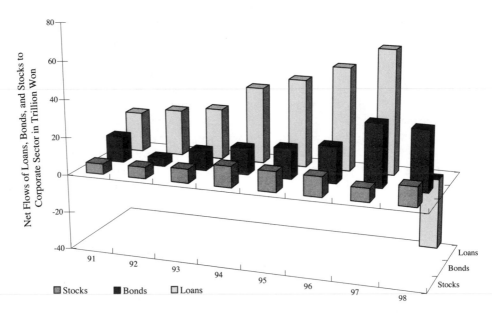

Fig. 2. Net funds flows to corporate sector in Korea during 1990–98.

Finally, the data on bank–firm relationships are readily available for Korea. The data on the identity of main banks and their client firms are compiled by the Korean Listed Companies Association and are publicly available.

K.-H. Bae et al. / Journal of Financial Economics 64 (2002) 181–214 187

3. Sample selection and data

Our sample consists of exogenous events that negatively affected Korean banks from January 1997 to December 1998. As of the end of 1997, there were 15 nationwide commercial banks and ten regional banks in Korea. After deleting banks with no listed client firms (mostly regional banks) or with no events reported during our sample period, we are left with 15 banks in our sample.

Negative news announcements for the banks include bankruptcy of a client firm, credit downgrading of a bank, deterioration of the Bank for International Settlements (BIS) ratio, and other occurrences, such as failure of a scheduled foreign borrowing or a claims suit.

We identify the initial public announcement date of the event from two daily newspapers, *Daily Economics* and *Korean Economics*, publications that are essentially the Korean equivalents of the *Wall Street Journal*. We use as the announcement date the date that a news announcement first appears in either of these two publications. To avoid having results confounded by multiple events that cluster during a short time period, we eliminate events that occur within five calendar days after the first event. Our restrictions result in a final sample of 113 events for the sample of 15 banks.

We obtain the list of client firms for each main bank from the *Annual Statistics* published by the Korean Listed Companies Association. The Korean Listed Companies Association compiles and publishes this list of the main banks of all listed companies in Korea annually. Although a firm can borrow from several banks, the *Annual Statistics* lists only one bank as the main bank that provides the major financing to the firm.

We search the *Annual Statistics* for 1996 and 1997 and match each listed firm with our sample banks. Although bankruptcy of a client firm is an important type of negative news announcement for a bank and is used in the analysis of the announcement returns for the bank, we do not use bankrupt client firms per se when we examine the abnormal returns for client firms. We eliminate bankrupt firms because our objective is to examine the effect of bank difficulties on client firm value. Given that the bankruptcy announcement of a client firm leads to a significant drop in the value of the firm's equity, the inclusion of bankrupt firms in the sample would result in the contamination of the announcement returns for client firms by this bankruptcy effect. This selection criterion results in a final sample of 573 client firms.

We obtain the stock price data from the daily return file of the Korea Investors Service-Stock Market Analysis Tool (KIS-SMAT), which includes all firms listed on both the First and Second Sections of the Korean Stock Exchange (KSE).

Panel A of Table 1 presents the frequency distribution of events according to the identity of the main banks and the type of news announcement. The first column of the table lists the names of the main banks and the second column lists the number of client firms affiliated with each main bank. Among the 15 banks, Commercial Bank, Cho Hung Bank, Korea First Bank, and Hanil Bank have the largest numbers of client firms. Taken together, these four banks have relationships with 60.5% (347) of all sample client firms.

Table 1
Frequency distribution of negative news events experienced by Korean banks

The sample includes negative news announcements associated with Korean banks from January 1997 to December 1998. Negative news announcements concern bankruptcy of a client firm, downgrading of the main bank's credit rating, decreases in the BIS capital ratio, and "other" announcements, including the failure of a scheduled foreign borrowing and a claims suit. The initial public announcement dates of the negative news are obtained from two daily newspapers, Daily Economics and Korean Economics, which are the Korean equivalents to the Wall Street Journal. The date that a news announcement first appears either of these two publications is used as the announcement date. To avoid having results confounded by multiple events that cluster during a short time period, events that occur within five calendar days after the first event are eliminated. These restrictions result in a final sample of 113 events for the sample of 15 banks. The identities of client firms for each main bank are obtained from the Annual Statistics published by the Korean Listed Companies Association. The client firms are restricted to those listed on the Korean Stock Exchange during the sample period. Bankrupt client firms are excluded from the sample of client firms. Bad and nonperforming loan ratios are obtained from the Monthly Financial Statistics Bulletin published by the Financial Supervisory Service. Nonperforming loans include (1) substandard or partially recoverable loans (the amount expected to be collected by collateral liquidation from customers who have loans that are overdue at least three months), (2) doubtful loans (the portion of credit in excess of the partially recoverable loans that are expected to be a loss but have not yet been realized as such), and (3) estimated losses (the portion of credit in excess of the partially recoverable loans that must be accounted as a loss because collection is not possible in a foreseeable period). Bad loans are computed by excluding the partially recoverable loans from nonperforming loans.

Panel A: Distribution of events by main banks and by type of event

Main bank	Number of client firms	Type of events				Total
		Bankruptcy	Credit downgrade	BIS deterioration	Others	
Commercial	94	8	3	0	1	12
Cho Hung	88	9	4	0	1	14
Korea First	75	12	3	0	2	17
Hanil	90	4	6	0	0	10
Seoul	59	5	3	0	0	8
KorAm	13	0	2	2	1	5
Shinhan	21	2	4	0	0	6
Hana	3	0	2	0	0	2
Korea Exchange	63	3	4	0	0	7
Kookmin	2	0	2	0	0	2
Daegu	10	1	2	0	0	3
Pusan	13	3	4	1	0	8
LTCB	4	1	5	0	0	6
KDB	8	2	3	0	0	5
Industrial	30	6	2	0	0	8
Total	573	56	49	3	5	113

K.-H. Bae et al. / Journal of Financial Economics 64 (2002) 181–214

189

Panel B: Distribution of events before and during the banking crisis period

	Before the crisis (January 97–November 21, 97)	During the crisis (November 22, 97–December 98)	Total
Bankruptcy of client firms	18	38	56
Credit downgrading of banks	24	25	49
BIS deterioration	3	0	3
Others	3	2	5
Total	48	65	113

Panel C: Bad and nonperforming loan ratios of main banks as of the end of 1996 and 1997

	Bad loans/total loans			Nonperforming loans/total loans			Nonperforming loans/net equity		
	1996 (percent)	1997 (percent)	Difference (percentage points)	1996 (percent)	1997 (percent)	Difference (percentage points)	1996 (percent)	1997 (percent)	Difference (percentage points)
Commercial	0.42	1.43	1.01	4.37	4.85	0.48	65.19	103.77	38.58
Cho Hung	0.64	2.40	1.76	4.62	6.99	2.37	74.07	166.55	92.48
Korea First	1.23	5.55	4.32	6.69	11.39	4.70	100.90	1,305.94	1,205.04
Hanil	0.66	1.68	1.02	2.39	3.63	1.24	36.68	85.97	49.29
Seoul	2.39	6.10	3.71	9.33	10.35	1.02	169.34	342.74	173.40
KorAm	0.64	1.78	1.14	1.75	3.36	1.61	26.46	71.40	44.94
Shinhan	0.80	1.64	0.84	2.75	4.05	1.30	33.68	60.17	26.49
Hana	0.10	0.94	0.84	0.79	2.37	1.58	11.37	35.96	24.59
Korea Exchange	0.72	1.43	0.71	4.04	5.74	1.70	62.00	126.39	64.39
Kookmin	0.37	1.06	0.69	2.45	3.25	0.80	37.87	46.22	8.35
Daegu	0.84	3.19	2.35	4.23	8.44	4.21	48.44	91.85	43.41
Pusan	0.63	3.49	2.86	4.05	8.44	4.39	58.18	134.23	76.05
LTCB	0.40	1.10	0.70	1.90	6.70	4.80	63.54	167.92	104.38
KDB	0.01	0.10	0.09	1.80	7.30	5.50	29.65	99.55	69.90
Industrial	1.40	1.40	0.00	4.40	7.30	2.90	141.02	255.26	114.24
Mean	0.75	2.22	1.47	3.70	6.28	2.57	63.89	206.26	142.37
Median	0.64	1.64	1.01	4.04	6.70	1.70	58.18	103.77	64.39
Standard Deviation	0.58	1.69	1.28	2.18	2.70	1.69	43.49	314.93	296.97

The last column of Table 1 shows the number of news events associated with each bank. Korea First Bank and Cho Hung Bank have the most frequent negative news events, with 17 and 14 cases, respectively. A breakdown of news announcements by type of events shows that the most frequent types of negative announcements are bankruptcies of client firms (56 cases), followed by credit downgrades of banks (49 cases). BIS deterioration accounts for three cases, and five cases are related to the failure of scheduled foreign borrowings and claims suits.

Panel B of Table 1 shows the frequency distribution of events by two subperiods, before and during the Korean financial crisis. We set November 22, 1997 as a cutoff date. November 22 is the day on which Korea sought a rescue package from the IMF to control the financial crisis that had started with a sharp decline of the Korean won against the U.S. dollar in the middle of November 1997. The numbers of events before and during the banking crisis are 48 and 65, respectively.

One notable feature in Panel B of Table 1 is that the frequency of bankruptcies among client firms during the crisis period (38) is more than twice the number before the crisis period (18), indicating that more client firms ran into financial trouble during the crisis period. The credit-downgrading events of the banks are evenly distributed across the two sample periods, with 24 and 25 cases, respectively.

Panel C of Table 1 presents bad loan and nonperforming loan ratios for our sample banks as of the end of 1996 and 1997. We obtain data for bad loan and nonperforming loan ratios from the *Monthly Financial Statistics Bulletin* published by the Financial Supervisory Service. According to the *Monthly Financial Statistics Bulletin*, nonperforming loans include (1) substandard or partially recoverable loans (the amount expected to be collected by collateral liquidation from customers who have loans that are overdue at least three months); (2) doubtful loans (the portion of credit in excess of the partially recoverable loans that are expected to be a loss but have not yet been realized as such); and (3) estimated losses (the portion of credit in excess of the partially recoverable loans that must be accounted as a loss because collection is not possible in a foreseeable period). Bad loans are computed by excluding the partially recoverable loans from nonperforming loans.

The average ratio of bad loans to total loans tripled, from 0.75% at the end of 1996 to 2.22% at the end of 1997. The largest increase in the bad loan ratio from 1996 to 1997 comes from Korea First Bank, followed by Seoul Bank. These two banks served as the main bank for several large corporations that went bankrupt after 1995. One of these bankruptcies was the Hanbo Group, the eleventh largest business group in Korea. The average ratio of nonperforming loans to total loans also significantly increased, from 3.70% at the end of 1996 to 6.28% at the end of 1997. By comparison, the average nonperforming loan ratio for Japanese banks as of March 31, 1993 as reported in Gibson (1995) is 3.39%.

One way to understand the magnitude of this deterioration in ratios is as follows. The average total loans outstanding for our sample banks were 19.85 trillion won in 1996 and 24.03 trillion won in 1997. Multiplying the average nonperforming loan ratios by these values implies a nonperforming loan amount of 0.73 trillion won at the end of 1996 and 1.51 trillion won at the end of 1997. These numbers translate into 58.4% and 139.8% of the average net equity values of our sample banks in 1996

K.-H. Bae et al. / Journal of Financial Economics 64 (2002) 181–214   191

and 1997, respectively. In other words, as of the end of 1997, nonperforming loans for our sample banks averaged 1.4 times their net equity, which implies that the average bank is de facto insolvent if we assume that all nonperforming loans are written off. The last column of Panel C of Table 1 shows the ratio of nonperforming loans to bank net equity for each individual bank. The mean and median increases in the ratio from 1996 to 1997 are 142.37 and 64.39 percentage points, respectively, with a standard deviation of 296.97. A large part of the change is due to the Korea First Bank, which experienced an increase of 1,205.04 percentage points. The second highest change is from Seoul Bank, with an increase of 173.40 percentage points.

Although the whole of the banking sector in Korea experienced difficulties during the crisis period, it should be noted that there is a large cross-sectional variation in the nonperforming loan ratios for our sample banks. The average and median increase in the ratio of nonperforming loans to total loans from 1996 to 1997 are 2.57 and 1.70 percentage points, respectively, with a standard deviation of 1.69. The highest change in the ratio of nonperforming loans to total loans is also from the Korea First Bank, which experienced an increase of 4.70 percentage points. In contrast, the Commercial Bank realized the smallest increase (0.48 percentage point).

To put things in perspective, consider a bank with an increase in the nonperforming loan ratio one standard deviation lower and another bank with an increase one standard deviation higher than the average value. The increase in the nonperforming loan ratio is 0.88 of a percentage point for a bank at one standard deviation lower and as much as 4.26 percentage points for a bank at one standard deviation higher. The equivalent figures for the bad loan ratio are 0.19 and 2.75 percentage points, respectively.

In Table 2, we present the summary statistics of a sample of 486 client firms for which we are able to find financial data from several sources. We obtain bank loan data from the firms' annual audit reports and other financial data from the Listed Company Database of Korean Listed Companies Association and the firms' annual reports. Our statistics are the average values of variables at the end of fiscal years 1996 and 1997. The table reports the descriptive statistics including the mean, the standard deviation, the median, and the first and third quartile values.

The average and median sizes of our sample firms measured by total assets are 688 billion won and 167 billion won, respectively. Assuming an exchange rate of 1,200 won to a U.S. dollar, these figures amount to $57 million and $14 million, respectively. Investment securities account for an average of 8.15% of total assets. We define bank debt as the sum of bank loans and corporate bonds guaranteed by the bank. It is a common practice in Korea for main banks to guarantee the corporate bonds issued by their client firms, making corporate bonds de facto bank loans. During our sample period, among our 486 sample firms, only 145 firms issued bonds that were not guaranteed by a bank. The average bank debt represents 28.65% of total assets. Nonbank debt, as measured by total debt minus bank debt, accounts for 39.03%. The medians show a similar pattern. For the sample firms, the main bank borrowing averages 5.71% of total assets and ranges from zero to 59.81%.

192   *K.-H. Bae et al. / Journal of Financial Economics 64 (2002) 181–214*

Table 2
Summary statistics of client firms of main banks
The sample includes 486 Korean client firms whose main banks experience negative shocks from January 1997 to December 1998 and for which financial data are available from several sources. Bank loan data are obtained from a firm's annual audit report and other financial data are from the Listed Company Database of the Korean Listed Companies Association. The summary statistics are the average values of variables at the end of fiscal years 1996 and 1997. Bank debt is the sum of bank loans and corporate bonds guaranteed by the bank. Main bank debt is the sum of loans from the main bank and corporate bonds guaranteed by the main bank. Nonbank debt is total debt minus bank debt. The no guaranteed bond issue dummy takes the value of one if a firm's debt includes public bonds that are not guaranteed by the bank. Cash flow is computed as the sum of operating income and depreciation. Liquid assets are cash plus marketable securities. The foreign bank dummy takes the value of one if the firm borrows from foreign banks.

	Mean	Standard deviation	$Q1$	Median	$Q3$
Total assets (in billion won)	687.69	1,767.84	79.05	166.84	500.44
Investment securities/total assets (percent)	8.15	6.89	3.14	6.42	11.37
Main bank equity ownership held by client firms (percent)	0.03	0.24	0.00	0.00	0.00
Total debt/total assets (percent)	67.67	15.45	57.40	68.54	79.18
Bank debt/total assets (percent)	28.65	12.38	19.33	27.58	37.05
Main bank debt/total assets (percent)	5.71	7.37	0.69	2.98	8.41
Non-bank debt/total assets (percent)	39.03	13.36	29.54	39.04	47.84
Cash flow/total assets (percent)	8.65	5.77	5.57	8.19	11.58
Liquid assets/total assets (percent)	9.87	7.40	4.40	7.95	13.19
No guaranteed bond issue dummy	0.30	0.46	0.00	0.00	1.00
Foreign bank dummy	0.24	0.43	0.00	0.00	0.00
Number of banks from which a firm borrows	6.02	2.95	4.00	5.50	7.50

In comparison, Kang and Stulz (2000) report that for a sample of Japanese firms listed on the Tokyo Stock Exchange as of fiscal year-end 1989, the mean and median ratios of bank loans to total assets are 21% and 16%, respectively. For a sample of Japanese firms from 1977 to 1993, Kang et al. (2000) show that the average fraction of a firm's total borrowings from its main bank to the sum of the book value of debt and the market value of equity is 3.6%, with a minimum of zero and a maximum of 14.6%. These results suggest that Korean firms tend to borrow more from banks than do their Japanese counterparts and that bank loans are an important source of financing in Korea.

As a measure of liquidity, we examine the ratio of cash flow to total assets and the ratio of liquid assets to total assets. We compute cash flow as the sum of operating income and depreciation. Liquid assets are cash plus marketable securities. The means for these variables are 8.65% and 9.87%, respectively.

The last two rows of Table 2 present the summary statistics on the frequency of foreign bank borrowing by our sample firms and the number of banks from which they borrow. The foreign bank dummy takes a value of one if the firm borrows from

K.-H. Bae et al. / Journal of Financial Economics 64 (2002) 181–214 193

a foreign bank and zero otherwise. We find that this variable has a mean of 0.24. That is, 116 firms borrow from foreign banks. Our sample firms on average borrow from six different banks, with a median of 5.5 banks, suggesting that many firms in our sample maintain multiple bank relationships.

4. Empirical results

4.1. Announcement returns for main banks and portfolios of client firms

In this section, we examine the abnormal returns for the main banks and their client firms around the time of the announcement of negative news impacting the main banks. We compute abnormal returns by using a standard event-study methodology following Brown and Warner (1985). We estimate market model parameters by using days -220 to -20 relative to the news announcement. The daily abnormal return is accumulated to obtain the cumulative abnormal return (CAR) from day $-t$ before the news announcement date to day $+t$ after the announcement date. We use t-statistics to test the hypothesis that the average CARs are equal to zero and sign-rank test statistics to test the hypothesis that the CARs are distributed symmetrically around zero.

One concern in the estimation of the abnormal returns is the impact of overlapping estimation periods on the independence of the computed returns. Since we use the market-model approach to estimate abnormal returns for the events and the estimation periods (day -220 to day -20) of different events overlap in many cases, it is likely that t-statistics in the analyses of the abnormal returns are biased upwards. To see whether the overlapping estimation period affects our results in a significant way, we repeat all analyses below using the market-adjusted-return method and obtain results that are qualitatively similar to those reported in the paper. We also experiment with the constant-mean-return model for which the benchmark return is estimated by averaging the returns from day -30 to day -11 and find that our results do not change when we use this approach. Therefore, our results do not seem to be affected by overlapping estimation periods, although we cannot entirely rule out the possibility of such an effect in our abnormal returns.

Table 3 presents the CARs $(-1, 1)$ for main banks and for portfolios of client firms. In tests not reported here, we also experiment with CARs $(-1, 0)$ and CARs $(-2, 2)$ and obtain results similar to those reported here.

Panel A of Table 3 shows the announcement returns for the main banks. The numbers in parentheses are t-statistics and those in brackets are median returns. The first number in braces is the number of events with positive CARs and the second number is the total number of events. The average and median CARs during the 1997–98 period are -2.49% and -1.61%, respectively, both of which are significant at the 0.01 level. Although our sample consists of 113 news events, we estimate the CARs for main banks with 100 events since the Korean Development Bank (KDB) and the Industrial Bank were not listed during our sample period. Only 39 out of 100 news events show positive CARs.

Table 3
Three-day cumulative abnormal returns (CARs) for the main bank and the portfolio of client firms around the announcement of negative news to the main bank

The sample includes negative news announcements associated with Korean banks from January 1997 to December 1998. The CARs for the main bank from day -1 to day $+1$ are computed as the difference between realized returns and estimated returns, using the market model over the pre-event period of day -220 to day -21. To obtain the CARs for the portfolio of client firms, client firms of each bank are combined into a single equally weighted portfolio and the announcement returns corresponding to each event are computed. A sample of 113 events is used for client firms. A sample of 100 events is used for main banks, since the Korea Development Bank (KDB) and the Industrial Bank were not listed on the Korean Stock Exchange during the sample period. The t-statistics appear in parentheses and median returns in brackets. The first number in braces is the number of events with positive CARs and the second number is the total number of events. Figures in parentheses of the last column are t-statistics for the test of equality of means and those in brackets are p-values of the Wilcoxon Z-test for equality of medians; ***, **, and * denote the significance of the parameter estimates at the 0.01, 0.05 and 0.10 levels, respectively.

Panel A: CARs for main banks News events	Full period (January 97– December 98)	Before the crisis (January 97– November 21, 97)	During the crisis (November 22, 97– December 98)	Test of difference
Total sample	-2.49***	-0.67	-3.92***	
	(-3.30)	(-0.72)	(-3.55)	(2.26)**
	$[-1.61]$***	$[0.29]$	$[-4.38]$***	$[0.01]$**
	{39/100}	{22/44}	{17/56}	
Bankruptcy of client firms	-2.81**	-1.18	-3.63**	
	(-2.15)	(-0.54)	(-2.22)	(0.89)
	$[-3.22]$**	$[1.76]$	$[-4.61]$**	$[0.22]$
	{20/48}	{10/16}	{10/32 }	
Credit downgrade of banks	-2.65**	-0.92	-4.38***	
	(-2.94)	(-1.13)	(-2.84)	(1.98)*
	$[-1.32]$**	$[-0.90]$	$[-5.08]$**	$[0.12]$
	{16/44}	{9/22}	{7/22}	
BIS deterioration	-0.87	-0.87	—	
	(-0.28)	(-0.28)	—	—
	$[-1.96]$	$[-1.96]$	—	—
	{1/3}	{1/3}	—	
Others (failure of scheduled foreign borrowing and claims suit)	1.00	4.15	-3.72	
	(0.40)	(1.69)	(-1.50)	(2.26)
	$[-0.47]$	$[5.05]$	$[-3.72]$	$[0.14]$
	{2/5}	{2/3}	{0/2}	
Panel B: CARs for portfolios of client firms News events	Full period (January 97– December 98)	Before the crisis (January 97– November 21, 97)	During the crisis (November 22, 97– December 98)	Test of difference
Total sample	-1.26***	-0.26	-2.00***	
	(-2.86)	(-1.07)	(-2.72)	(2.23)**
	$[-0.46]$***	$[-0.00]$	$[-1.30]$***	$[0.03]$**
	{47/113}	{24/48}	{23/65}	
Bankruptcy of client firms	-1.01**	-0.99*	-1.02*	
	(-2.31)	(-1.91)	(-1.70)	(0.03)
	$[-0.86]$**	$[-0.71]$*	$[-0.98]$*	$[0.86]$
	{21/56}	{7/18}	{14/38}	

K.-H. Bae et al. / Journal of Financial Economics 64 (2002) 181–214   195

Table 3 (*continued*)

Panel B: CARs for portfolios of client firms

News events	Full period (January 97– December 98)	Before the crisis (January 97– November 21, 97)	During the crisis (November 22, 97– December 98)	Test of difference
Credit downgrade of banks	−1.74*	0.32	−3.72**	
	(−1.97)	(1.29)	(−2.28)	(2.45)**
	[−0.09]	[0.48]	[−3.90]**	[0.02]**
	{23/49}	{15/24}	{8/25}	
BIS deterioration	0.08	0.08	—	
	(0.34)	(0.34)	—	—
	[0.04]	[0.04]	—	—
	{2/3}	{2/3}	—	
Others (failure of	−0.16	−0.99	1.09	
scheduled foreign	(−0.18)	(−1.39)	(0.60)	(−1.07)
borrowing and	[−0.29]	[−0.29]	[1.09]	[0.77]
claims suit)	{1/5}	{0/3}	{1/2}	

Panel C: CARs for portfolios of client firms by government-owned vs. nongovernment-owned banks

News events	Wholly government- owned bank (KDB)	Nongovernment- owned banks	Test of difference
Total sample	−3.01	−1.18***	
	(−1.84)	(−2.60)	(1.07)
	[−2.66]	[−0.42]***	[0.31]
	{1/5}	{46/108}	
Bankruptcy of client firms	−0.75	−1.03**	
	(−0.39)	(−2.27)	(0.75)
	[−0.75]	[−0.86]***	[0.88]
	{1/2}	{20/54}	
Credit downgrade of banks	−4.51	−1.56*	
	(−2.04)	(−1.68)	(1.23)
	[−6.55]	[−0.38]	[0.23]
	{0/3}	{23/46}	

The breakdown of the sample by type of news announcement shows a similar pattern. The average and median CARs for the subsamples of bankruptcy and credit downgrade are all significantly negative at the 0.05 level.

Panel A of Table 3 also presents the CARs for Korean banks in the two subperiods, before and during the crisis. The banks realize significant mean and median CARs of −3.92% and −4.38% during the crisis period. In contrast, the mean (median) CAR before the crisis is −0.67% (0.29%) and is not significant. Furthermore, only 17 out of 56 events show positive CARs during the crisis period, but 22 of 44 events show positive CARs before the crisis. Tests of differences in mean and median CARs across the two subperiods reject the null hypothesis that they are equal. These results suggest that negative announcement returns for the full sample period are mostly attributable to the crisis period, when banks faced substantial problems that limited their ability to renew old loans and extend new loans to firms.

Panel B of Table 3 reports the effect of banking shocks on client firm value. Since the events that affect client firms of the same main bank are perfectly clustered in calendar time, we combine the client firms of each main bank into a single equally weighted portfolio and compute the announcement returns. (In tests not reported here, we also experiment with value-weighted portfolio returns and obtain results that are qualitatively similar.)

During the full sample period, the average and median CARs $(-1, 1)$ for the portfolios of client firms are -1.26% and -0.46%, respectively, both of which are significant at the 0.01 level. Out of 113 events, 66 (58%) show negative reactions. Consistent with the results for the banks, our subperiod analysis indicates that client firms realize negative returns only during the crisis period. The tests of differences in mean and median returns across the two subperiods reject the null hypothesis of equal announcement returns.

The classification by type of news announcement indicates that client firms experience a mean CAR of -1.01% in the case of bankruptcy announcements and -1.74% in the case of credit downgrade announcements. These announcement returns are significant at the 0.05 and 0.10 levels, respectively. The median returns, however, are significant only for bankruptcy announcements.

The fact that the announcement returns for both main banks and portfolios of client firms are negative only during the crisis period suggests that the financial health of the main banks is an important factor for the continuity of the bank-firm relationship. When banks are financially healthy, their ability to lend to client firms is less likely to be distorted by negative shocks, since they have enough capital to buffer themselves against those shocks. However, when the financial health of the main banks is extremely poor, as it was during the crisis period, the banks become vulnerable to even small negative shocks. As the bank tightens credit to its client firms and bank durability significantly deteriorates so that the termination of bank-firm relationships becomes a real possibility, client firms must turn to more expensive sources of external finance and firm value is thus adversely affected.

There is one issue to be addressed in interpreting our announcement returns for the portfolio of client firms. As noted earlier, the KDB and the Industrial Bank were not listed during our sample period and the Korean government wholly owns the KDB. This means that the KDB cannot really fail, but Panel B of Table 3 includes not only client firms that belong to the KDB but also client firms for which failure might actually be an issue. To see whether our results are significantly different between firms associated with the KDB and those associated with other banks, we examine the portfolio CARs $(-1, 1)$ for these two types of firms separately. The results presented in Panel C of Table 3 show that the mean and median CARs $(-1, 1)$ for the portfolio of client firms associated with the KDB are insignificantly negative and those for the portfolio of client firms associated with non-government-owned banks are significantly negative at the 0.01 levels. The evidence, therefore, indicates that our results in Panel B of Table 3 are not affected by including firms that have relationships with a government-owned bank. Nevertheless, we repeat all analyses below excluding firms affiliated with the KDB and find the qualitative

K.-H. Bae et al. / Journal of Financial Economics 64 (2002) 181–214   197

results unchanged. Excluding both the KDB and the Industrial Bank also leaves the results unchanged.

4.2. Announcement returns and the quality of main banks

The previous section investigates the hypothesis that under a bank-centered system, banking shocks cause the bank-firm relationship to be costly for borrowing firms and that a deterioration in bank durability has a negative effect on client–firm value. In this section, we further show that firm value is an increasing function of the degree of financial health of the main bank, and that client firms affiliated with poorly performing banks suffer more from banking shocks.

There are several ways to measure the financial health of a bank. One readily available measure is the ratio of nonperforming loans to total loans. There is a large cross-sectional variation in this ratio across the banks during our sample period, which suggests that this ratio captures the variation of bank quality better than other measures. We also use the ratio of bad loans to total loans, rather than the nonperforming loan ratio, as a proxy for the financial health of banks. We find that our results are not affected. As the ratio of nonperforming or bad loans to total loans could be differentially important for banks with different ratios of loans to total assets, we repeat the analysis using the ratio of nonperforming or bad loans to net equity. We find that the results are very similar to those using the ratio of nonperforming or bad loans to total loans. We could also use a bank's credit rating as a measure of bank health. In fact, credit ratings are likely to be more informative than accounting measures of bank health since, as Gibson (1995) points out, accounting measures are backward-looking, while credit ratings are forward-looking. However, it turns out that there is little variation in credit ratings among our sample banks, since the whole banking sector was experiencing difficulties during our sample period. In fact, during the crisis period, there are only three classes of credit ratings for our sample banks: A3 for three banks, B1 for four banks, and BAA2 for eight banks. In tests not reported here, we find that credit ratings have little power to explain the cross-sectional variation in the returns of client firms.

Alternatively, market-based measures of bank health might reflect bank quality more fully and more accurately than accounting measures of bank health. We use two market-based measures of bank condition. First, we estimate the cumulative bank-industry adjusted excess return from day -110 to day -11 before the event date. Second, we compute the ratio of the quasi-market value of the bank (debt plus market value of equity) to total assets to proxy for Tobin's q. In computing the market value of bank equity, we use the closing stock price five days before the announcement date.

Table 4 shows the extent to which the CARs for client firms differ depending on these measures of bank condition. We compare the CARs for client firms associated with bad-quality banks to those associated with good-quality banks. We partition our sample banks into "bad" and "good" by the medians of nonperforming loans to total loans (panel A), bank-industry adjusted cumulative excess returns (panel B), and Tobin's q (panel C). For events before the crisis, we use the median ratios as of

Table 4
Three-day cumulative abnormal returns (CARs) for the portfolio of client firms classified by subperiod and measures of main bank quality

The sample includes Korean client firms whose main banks experience negative shocks from January 1997 to December 1998. The client firms of each main bank are combined into a single equally weighted portfolio and the abnormal announcement returns corresponding to each event are computed as the difference between realized returns and estimated returns, using the market model over the pre-event period of day −220 to day −21. For events before the crisis period, the median ratio of nonperforming loans to total loans (industry-adjusted cumulative excess returns from day −110 to day −11 and Tobin's q) as of the end of 1996 is used to split the total sample into "bad" banks and "good" banks. For the events during the crisis period, the median ratio of nonperforming loans to total loans (industry-adjusted cumulative excess returns from day −110 to day −11 and Tobin's q) as of the end of 1997 is used. Tobin's q is measured by the ratio of the sum of the market value of equity and the book value of debt to total assets, where the market value of equity is measured five days before the event dates. Figures in parentheses (brackets) are t-statistics (p-values) to test for the null hypothesis of zero means (medians). Figures in braces are the number of events with positive CARs and the total number of events, respectively. Figures in parentheses and brackets in the last two columns are t-statistics for the test of equality of means and p-values of the Wilcoxon Z-test for equality of medians, respectively; ***, **, and * denote the significance of the parameter estimates at the 0.01, 0.05 and 0.10 levels, respectively.

Quality of main bank	Before the crisis (January 97–November 21, 97)		During the crisis (November 22, 97–December 98)		Test of difference	
	Mean	Median	Mean	Median	t-test	Wilcoxon Z-test
Panel A: CAR by subperiod and the ratio of nonperforming loans to total loans						
Bad	−0.40	0.11	−2.43**	−1.25**	(2.03)**	[0.15]
	(−0.10)	[0.53]	(−2.62)	[0.02]		
		{15/29}		{15/40}		
Good	−0.06	−0.04	−1.30	−1.41	(1.00)	[0.11]
	(−0.20)	[0.85]	(−1.08)	[0.26]		
		{9/19}		{8/25}		
Test of difference	(−0.71)	[0.78]	(−0.73)	[0.84]		
Panel B: CAR by subperiod and industry-adjusted cumulative excess returns						
Bad	−0.24	−0.39	−2.97***	−1.36***	(2.58)**	[0.04]**
	(−0.82)	[0.43]	(−2.93)	[0.00]		
		{9/22}		{8/28}		
Good	0.10	0.16	−0.47	−0.46	(0.43)	[0.81]
	(0.31)	[0.38]	(−0.37)	[0.84]		
		{14/22}		{13/28}		
Test of difference	(−0.78)	[0.24]	(−1.52)	[0.14]		
Panel C: CAR by subperiod and Tobin's q						
Bad	0.23	0.76	−2.72*	−2.04**	(2.00)**	[0.03]**
	(0.63)	[0.29]	(−1.91)	[0.05]		
		{14/22}		{9/28}		
Good	−0.37	−0.24	−0.72	−0.47	(0.40)	[0.91]
	(−1.67)	[0.19]	(−0.87)	[0.56]		
		{9/22}		{12/28}		
Test of difference	(1.41)	[0.06]	(−1.20)	[0.22]		

K.-H. Bae et al. / Journal of Financial Economics 64 (2002) 181–214   199

the end of 1996. For the events during the crisis period, we use the median ratios as of the end of 1997.

Panel A of Table 4 shows that the CARs for the portfolio of client firms before the crisis are small and are not significant when bank quality is measured by the nonperforming loan ratio. The CARs for the portfolio of client firms associated with good-quality banks during the crisis period are also not statistically significant. However, the CARs for the portfolio of client firms associated with bad-quality banks during the crisis period are significantly negative. The mean and median CARs are -2.43% and -1.25%, respectively, and they are significant at the 0.05 level. The t-test rejects the equality of the mean CARs between bad-quality banks before and during the crisis period. Panels B and C of Table 4 show remarkably similar results. The mean and median CARs are significantly negative only for banks with poor stock market performance and with low Tobin's q during the crisis period, and they are significantly different from those for good-quality banks before the crisis. To further examine the importance of bank condition to abnormal returns for client firms, in unreported tests we also experiment with a stricter measure of bank health, dividing our sample into four groups according to two measures of bank health: low nonperforming loan/high Tobin's q, low nonperforming loan/low Tobin's q, high nonperforming loan/high Tobin's q, and high nonperforming loan/low Tobin's q. We find that only client firms associated with bad-quality (high nonperforming loans/low Tobin's q) banks suffer a significant loss in market value. We obtain similar results when we replace Tobin's q with industry-adjusted cumulative excess returns.

To clarify the relation between main-bank health and its effect on the market value of client firms, we use multivariate regression analysis. All regressions are estimated using ordinary least squares (OLS) and White's (1980) adjustment for heteroskedasticity. The regression results are presented in Table 5. In the first regression, we regress the CAR for the portfolio of client firms on (1) the nonperforming loan ratio of the main bank, (2) a dummy variable that takes the value of one if the type of news event is the bankruptcy of the client firm, and (3) a dummy variable that takes the value of one if the type of news event is the credit downgrade of the bank. The estimate on the coefficient of the nonperforming loan ratio is significantly negative at the 0.10 level. When we use the ratio of nonperforming loans to net equity in place of the ratio of nonperforming loans to total loans, the coefficient estimate is -0.0080 with a t-statistic of -1.94. These results indicate that client firms of poor banks suffer a bigger loss in their share values than do client firms of healthy banks. There is no evidence that a particular type of news event has a bigger impact on client-firm value.

Although not reported here, we also estimate the regression with the CAR for the main bank as the dependent variable, and the nonperforming loan ratio and dummy variables for the type of news events as independent variables. The coefficient estimate on the nonperforming loan ratio is -0.0054 with a t-statistic of -1.91. This result suggests that poor-quality banks suffer more from negative shocks. The dummy variables for the type of news events are not significant.

Table 5
OLS regression of the three-day cumulative abnormal returns (CARs) for the portfolio of client firms on measures of main bank quality

The sample includes Korean client firms whose banks experienced negative shocks from January 1997 to December 1998. For the portfolio of client firms, the dependent variable is the CAR from day −1 to day +1. The client firms of each main bank are combined into a single equally weighted portfolio and the abnormal announcement returns corresponding to each event are computed as the difference between realized returns and estimated returns, using the market model over the pre-event period of day −220 to day −21. Nonperforming loans include (1) substandard or partially recoverable loans (the amount expected to be collected by collateral liquidation from customers who have loans that are overdue at least three months), (2) doubtful loans (the portion of credit in excess of the partially recoverable loans that are expected to be a loss but have not yet been realized as such), and (3) estimated losses (the portion of credit in excess of the partially recoverable loans that must be accounted as a loss because collection is not possible in a foreseeable period). Tobin's q is measured by the ratio of the sum of the market value of equity and the book value of debt to total assets, where the market value of equity is measured five days before the event dates. White's (1980) heteroskedastic-consistent t-statistics are in parentheses; ***, **, and * denote the significance of the parameter estimates at the 0.01, 0.05 and 0.10 levels, respectively.

Independent variables	CAR for the portfolio of all client firms				CAR for the portfolio of client firms that do not hold equity of their main banks	CAR for the portfolio of client firms that hold equity of their main banks
	(1)	(2)	(3)	(4)	(5)	(6)
Intercept	0.0145 (1.44)	−0.0010 (−0.17)	0.0114 (1.09)	−0.8814* (−1.82)	−0.8703* (−1.79)	0.8525 (−1.52)
Nonperforming loans/ total loans of main bank	−0.0031* (−1.85)			−0.0020 (−1.00)	−0.0013 (−0.62)	−0.0039 (−1.62)
CARs (−1, 1) for main bank		0.1282* (1.82)	0.1106* (1.65)	0.1189* (1.79)	0.1104* (1.69)	0.1476* (1.88)
Industry-adjusted cumulative excess returns (−110, −11)				0.0405* (1.78)	0.0421* (1.72)	0.0386* (1.66)
Tobin's q				0.9035* (1.83)	0.8847* (1.78)	0.9015 (1.57)
Dummy variable for bankruptcy of client firm		−0.0023 (−0.27)	0.0026 (0.24)	0.0124 (0.93)	0.0155 (1.23)	−0.0007 (−0.03)
Dummy variable for credit downgrades of bank		−0.0103 (−0.97)	−0.0104 (−0.86)	0.0056 (0.37)	0.0071 (0.49)	−0.0080 (−0.38)
Number of observations	113	100	100	100	100	88
F-statistic	1.58	1.69	1.79	2.16**	1.83*	2.71**
Adjusted R^2	0.0152	0.0203	0.0309	0.0658	0.0479	0.1055

K.-H. Bae et al. / Journal of Financial Economics 64 (2002) 181–214 201

In the second regression, we drop the nonperforming loan ratio and replace it with the CAR for the main bank. The question we ask here is whether client firm value is more negatively affected on days that the bank performs worse. If the magnitude of the stock price effect for main banks reflects ability to withstand exogenous shocks, we would expect a positive relation between the CAR for the portfolio of client firms and the CAR for the main bank. The CAR for the main bank has a coefficient of 0.1282 with a t-statistic of 1.82. Evaluating the estimated coefficient at the mean indicates that all else being constant, a 10% decrease in the CARs for the main bank results in about a 1.3% decrease in the CARs for the portfolios of client firms. Therefore, the effect of banking shocks on firm value seems to be both statistically and economically significant.

In the third regression, we include both the nonperforming loan ratio and the CAR for the main bank as explanatory variables. It turns out that only the coefficient on the CAR for the main bank is significantly positive. The coefficient on the nonperforming loan ratio has the predicted sign, but is not statistically significant. We attribute the insignificance of the coefficient on the nonperforming loan ratio to its negative correlation with the CAR for the main bank. The correlation between the two variables is -0.1943 with a p-value of 0.05. Alternatively, the CAR for the main bank might represent not only nonperforming loans that the bank accumulated in the past, but also the effect of a shock on the bank's future cash flows. Thus, the CAR might serve as a better proxy for bank health.

The next regression further confirms that market-based measures of bank condition are more important than accounting-based measures of bank condition in explaining the CAR for the portfolio of client firms. In this regression, we include two additional variables that are expected to capture the market's assessment of the bank's relative performance: the industry-adjusted cumulative excess return and Tobin's q. The coefficients on these two variables are significantly positive, again indicating that client firms of well-performing banks suffer less. Overall, the regression results support the notion that bank distress is costly to borrowers and borrowers suffer more when their banks are in a weak financial position.

The results of these regressions, indicating that the CAR for the main bank is positively related to the CAR for its borrowing firms, raise the possibility that these results are caused by bank equity ownership held by client firms, not by the banking relationship. If client firms hold shares of their main bank and the stock price of the main bank drops due to banking shocks, we would expect a reduction of the stock price of client firms even if the bank–firm relationship has no value. In order to address this possibility, we collect data on main bank equity ownership by each client firm at the end of fiscal years 1996 and 1997. We are able to obtain data on bank equity ownership for all firms in the sample. The mean (median) is 0.03% (0.00%) with a standard deviation of 0.22%. The low holding of main bank equity by client firms is largely attributable to a legal constraint that prevents industrial firms from owning more than 4% and 15% of the stocks of any single nationwide commercial bank and regional bank, respectively. There are 387 firms (79.6%) that do not hold any equity in their main banks. We then re-estimate the full regression separately for the portfolio of client firms that do not hold equity of their main banks and for the portfolio of client firms that hold equity of their main banks. An implication of the bank-ownership effect is that the positive relation between the CAR for the main bank and the CAR for client firms should be more pronounced for firms that hold equity in their main banks than for firms that hold no equity in their main banks. If the bank-firm relationship has no value and only the bank-ownership effect exists, we would also expect that the positive relation does not hold for firms with no main bank equity ownership. However, we find that the coefficients on the CAR for the main bank are significantly positive in both regressions, suggesting that the bank-firm relationship we document is not driven by the bank-ownership effect. Although the coefficient on the CAR for the main bank is larger when firms hold equity in their main banks than when firms do not, they are not significantly different from one another ($F = 0.13$ with a p-value of 0.71). This finding further suggests that the positive coefficients on the CAR for the main bank are not due to ownership of bank equity by client firms.

In Table 6, we present the distribution of client firms according to industry and main banks. We also show the distribution of client firms by membership in the top 30 chaebols and by main banks. A chaebol is a business group in Korea in which member firms are bound together by a nexus of explicit and implicit contracts, maintain substantial business ties with other firms in the group, and cross-guarantee the debt of the other member firms. Our objective here is to show that the results of the CAR for the portfolio of client firms are not driven by either the industry effect or the chaebol effect. For example, if the main bank's borrowers are grouped in similar lines of business or if all firms within one chaebol borrow from the same bank, the returns for client firms within a main bank will tend to move together and thus simply reflect common industries (chaebols) and not the banking relationship per se.

The results show that out of 486 client firms, 106 firms belong to the top 30 chaebols. We find that all but three firms that belong to the top 30 chaebols maintain a banking relationship with more than one bank and that they tend to be evenly distributed across different main banks. There are 14 different industries in the sample. The machinery and equipment industry has the largest number of client firms (129) followed by the chemical industry (91), while the electricity and gas industry has the smallest number of client firms (3). Table 6 clearly shows that the main bank maintains a relationship with various types of firms that operate in different lines of business. Further, while not reported for the sake of brevity, we are not able to find any evidence that a particular chaebol focuses on a certain industry.

4.3. Announcement returns and financial characteristics of client firms

We focus now on how the financial characteristics of client firms are related to their stock return performance during announcement days. When main banks experience large shocks, their borrowers could turn to external capital markets, utilize internally generated cash flows, or curtail new investments. For example, highly levered firms tend to have more difficulties obtaining external financing

K.-H. Bae et al. / Journal of Financial Economics 64 (2002) 181–214 203

Table 6

Distribution of client firms by chaebol affiliation and main-bank affiliation and by industry and main-bank affiliation

The sample includes 486 Korean client firms whose main banks experience negative shocks from January 1997 to December 1998 and for which financial data are available from several sources. A chaebol is a business group in Korea in which member firms are bound together by a nexus of explicit and implicit contracts, maintain substantial business ties with other firms in the group, and cross-guarantee the debt of the other member firms. Top 30 chaebols are the 30 largest business groups as ranked by the Korea Fair Trade Commission in the order of the aggregate assets of all affiliated firms within each group.

	Commercial	Cho Hung	Korea First	Hanil	Seoul	KorAm	Shinhan	Hana	Korea Exchange	Daegu	Pusan	LTCB	KDB	Industrial	Total
No. of client firms	86	72	58	76	47	12	17	3	54	9	12	3	8	29	486
No. of non-chaebol firms	66	58	45	50	36	11	17	3	38	9	10	2	6	29	380
No. of top 30 chaebol firms	20	14	13	26	11	1	0	0	16	0	2	1	2	0	106
No. of top 30 chaebols	12	8	7	11	8	1	0	0	5	0	1	2	2	0	—
Industry															
Fishery	1				1				1						4
Foods & beverages	11	3	2	5	4	2			2		1			4	30
Textiles	13	10	11	9	3		3		3	1					57
Wood & paper products	3	4	3	4	5	1			2			1		4	28
Chemical	20	15	10	18	10	2	3		5	3			1	4	91
Nonmetallic mineral	2	2	2	4	1		2		2				2	1	19
Basic metal	5	7	1	3	7		1		5	1	2		2	1	34
Machinery & equipment	15	16	16	11	11	4	6	2	20	5	5	1	2	15	129
Other manufacture	1	2	2	1					1						5
Construction	10	3	5	7	3		6		6	1	1				37
Wholesale & retail	3	6	5	7	2	1	2	1	3	1	1				29
Transport & storage	1	3	1	5	2	2			2		1				15
Electricity & gas	1								1			1			3
Hotels & restaurants		2		2					1						5
Total	86	72	58	76	47	12	17	3	54	9	12	3	8	29	486

204   *K.-H. Bae et al. / Journal of Financial Economics 64 (2002) 181–214*

during a banking crisis. These firms would therefore suffer more during this period. In contrast, if borrowers have pre-established relationships with other banks or have alternative sources of financing, they can turn to those sources for funding. Financially less-constrained firms or firms with alternative sources of financing would therefore suffer less from bank distress. In this section, we explore the hypothesis that the financial health and constraints of client firms are important for overcoming banking shocks.

4.3.1. Fixed effects regression of CARs on firm characteristics

A straightforward approach to investigate the hypothesis that a more financially constrained firm suffers more from bank distress is to estimate cross-sectional regressions of the announcement returns for the portfolio of client firms measured in Section 4.1 on explanatory variables that are proxies for the financial constraints of client firms.

One way to obtain the measure of the financial constraints of client firms within a portfolio is to use the average values for client firms, such as the average leverage ratio, the average liquidity ratio, etc. However, this approach poses an immediate problem: the average value will be from a mixture of firms with different financial characteristics. To the extent that client firms with various financial characteristics are evenly distributed within each main bank, the average firm characteristics of client firms within a portfolio will converge to the mean value and will hence show little variation across different main banks. This in turn will give us little statistical power to determine the relation between firm characteristics and announcement returns.

To avoid this problem, we use a fixed effects regression. For a sample of 486 client firms for which financial data are available, we compute the cumulative abnormal returns from day −1 to day +1 for each news event and for each client firm. We use the CAR (−1, 1) as the dependent variable and the variables in Table 2 as independent variables. For the analysis of the full sample period, we calculate independent variables as the average values of variables at the end of fiscal years 1996 and 1997. For the analysis of the period before (during) the crisis, we use the values at the end of fiscal year 1996 (1997).

We also include a dummy variable that takes the value of one if the firm belongs to one of the top 30 chaebols and 134 industry dummy variables to control for a possible industry effect in all regressions. The results are similar if industry effects are not controlled. Finally, we add a dummy variable for each event, so that any common movement in a bank's borrowers' CARs would be captured by the fixed effect. We would then have a testable hypothesis that common movements across firms on the same announcement day are statistically significant, by testing the joint hypothesis that all event dummies have zero coefficients.[2]

Panel A of Table 7 shows the results for the full sample period. To conserve space, the table does not report coefficients on the industry dummies and the event dummies. In the first regression, we include firm size, a top-30 chaebol dummy, the

---

[2] We thank the referee for suggesting this approach.

Table 7
Fixed effect regression of the three-day cumulative announcement returns (CARs) on firm characteristics
The sample includes Korean client firms whose main banks experience negative shocks from January 1997
to December 1998. Only client firms for which financial data are available are used. The dependent variable
is the three-day cumulative abnormal return for the client firm. Independent variables used in the full
sample period are calculated as the average values of variables at the end of fiscal years 1996 and 1997.
Those in the period before (during) the crisis are the values at the end of fiscal year 1996 (1997). Bank loan
data are obtained from a firm's annual audit report and other financial data from the Listed Company
Database of the Korean Listed Companies Association. The top 30 chaebol dummy takes the value of one
if the firm belongs to one of the 30 largest business groups in Korea. Bank debt is the sum of bank loans
and corporate bonds guaranteed by the bank. Main bank debt is the sum of loans from the main bank and
corporate bonds guaranteed by the main bank. Nonbank debt is total debt minus bank debt. Cash flow is
computed as the sum of operating income and depreciation. Liquid assets are cash plus marketable
securities. The no guaranteed bond issue dummy takes the value of one if a firm's debt includes public
bonds that are not guaranteed by the bank. The foreign bank dummy takes the value of one if the firm
borrows from foreign banks. The depositary receipt dummy takes the value of one if the firm's stock is
listed abroad. All regressions include 13 industry dummy variables to control for industry effects and a
dummy variable for each event. White's (1980) heteroskedastic-consistent t-statistics are in parentheses; ***,
**, and * denote the significance of the parameter estimates at the 0.01, 0.05 and 0.10 levels, respectively.

Panel A: Full period (January 97–December 98)				
Independent variables	(1)	(2)	(3)	(4)
Intercept	−0.0081	−0.0246	−0.0211	−0.0238
	(−0.33)	(−0.98)	(−0.84)	(−0.85)
Log (total assets)	0.0008	0.0005	−0.0003	−0.0003
	(0.76)	(0.44)	(−0.26)	(−0.24)
Top 30 chaebol dummy	0.0013	0.0022	0.0011	0.0014
	(0.38)	(0.63)	(0.31)	(0.40)
Investment securities/total assets	0.0035	0.0092	0.0107	0.0093
	(0.22)	(0.56)	(0.65)	(0.56)
Main bank holdings of client firm	−0.2325	0.0974	0.2348	0.1719
	(−0.32)	(0.13)	(0.32)	(0.17)
Total debt/total assets	−0.0375***			
	(−4.78)			
Bank debt/total assets		−0.0296***		
		(−3.13)		
Main bank debt/total assets			−0.0336**	−0.0288**
			(−2.30)	(−1.95)
Non-bank debt/total assets		−0.0176*	−0.0077	−0.0159*
		(−1.82)	(−0.88)	(−1.75)
Cash flow/total assets		0.0636***	0.0707***	0.0747***
		(3.71)	(4.17)	(4.23)
Liquid assets/total assets		0.0706***	0.0779***	0.0746***
		(4.51)	(5.08)	(4.79)
No guaranteed bond issue dummy				0.0072***
				(2.85)
Foreign bank dummy				0.0017
				(0.49)
Depositary receipt dummy				0.0049
				(0.63)
Number of banks from which a firm borrows				−0.0002
				(−0.39)
Number of observations	5,108	5,108	5,108	5,012
F-statistic	13.14***	13.16***	13.11***	12.64***
Adjusted R^2	0.2147	0.2194	0.2186	0.2208

Table 7 (*continued*)

Panel B: Subperiod

Independent variables	Before the crisis (January 97– November 21, 97)		During the crisis (November 22, 97– December 98)	
	(1)	(2)	(4)	(5)
Intercept	−0.0299	−0.0148	−0.0654*	−0.1018**
	(−1.21)	(−0.53)	(−1.78)	(−2.33)
Log (total assets)	−0.0032***	−0.0041***	0.0019	0.0036
	(−2.60)	(−2.87)	(1.07)	(1.59)
Top 30 chaebol dummy	−0.0014	−0.0021	0.0032	0.0039
	(−0.38)	(−0.56)	(0.56)	(0.66)
Investment securities/total assets	0.0149	0.0110	0.0134	0.0173
	(0.79)	(0.59)	(0.53)	(0.68)
Main bank holdings of client firm	1.5781	1.5503	−0.3083	−0.6899
	(1.52)	(1.47)	(−0.30)	(−0.42)
Total debt/total assets				
Main bank debt/total assets	−0.0240*	−0.0227	−0.0184	−0.0272*
	(−1.65)	(−1.56)	(−1.29)	(−1.83)
Nonbank debt/total assets	0.0132	0.0112	−0.0117	−0.0051
	(1.51)	(1.24)	(−0.52)	(−0.22)
Cash flow/total assets	0.0886***	0.0751***	0.0607***	0.0608***
	(3.97)	(3.29)	(2.51)	(2.32)
Liquid assets/total assets	0.0230	0.0224	0.1226***	0.1006***
	(1.34)	(1.29)	(5.10)	(3.95)
No guaranteed bond issue dummy		0.0056**		0.0137***
		(2.05)		(3.34)
Foreign borrowing dummy		0.0021		−0.0007
		(0.59)		(−0.11)
Depositary receipt dummy		0.0113		0.0001
		(1.43)		(0.01)
Number of banks from which a firm borrows		0.0003		−0.0002
		(0.58)		(−0.27)
Number of observations	2,373	2,373	2,735	2,639
F-statistic	5.21***	5.00***	14.12***	13.32***
Adjusted R^2	0.0890	0.0905	0.2514	0.2568

ratio of investment securities to total assets, main bank shareholdings by the client firm, and the leverage ratio. Since highly levered firms would have more difficulty obtaining external financing during a banking crisis, we expect such firms to experience a larger drop in the value of their equity. We would expect larger firms to be more established and that they might suffer less from adverse shocks. Therefore, we expect the coefficient on firm size to be positive. Finally, we expect investment securities to affect equity returns adversely, since the value of investment securities drops significantly during our sample period.

Most of explanatory variables have the expected signs, although not all of them are significant. Firm size and membership in a chaebol seem to have little effect on announcement returns for client firms, although they have the expected sign. The

K.-H. Bae et al. / Journal of Financial Economics 64 (2002) 181–214 207

coefficients on the ratio of investment securities to total assets and main bank holdings are not significant. The only significant variable in the regression is the leverage ratio. The coefficient has an estimate of -0.0375 and is significant at the 0.01 level, which indicates that firms that carry a larger debt burden realize more negative announcement returns.

To investigate the impact of debt composition on announcement returns, we show a second regression in which we partition total debt into bank debt and nonbank debt. We expect that the leverage effect is more pronounced if the firm has a higher fraction of bank debt in its capital structure, because in a bank-centered financial system, firms that are more bank dependent usually have not developed alternative financing channels and thus will have more difficulty obtaining external funds during a crisis period. We also add the ratios of cash flow to total assets and liquid assets to total assets. We expect less of a drop in value for firms with more cash flow and more liquid assets, since these firms are likely to have less demand for external financing. The coefficients on both the bank debt and nonbank debt ratios are significantly negative. However, both the magnitude of the estimate and the significance level are larger for bank debt than for nonbank debt, indicating that bank debt is a more important variable than nonbank debt in explaining the announcement returns for client firms. Consistent with our hypothesis, the coefficients on the ratio of cash flow to total assets and the ratio of liquid assets to total assets are significantly positive with t-statistics of 3.71 and 4.51, respectively.

In the third regression, we further investigate the results on the bank loan ratio by including the fraction of debt from the firm's main bank to total assets. We find that CARs are negatively and significantly related to a firm's borrowings from its main bank, but that the coefficient on the nonbank debt ratio is statistically indistinguishable from zero. The negative relation between the CAR and the main bank loan ratio is consistent with the view that a firm's bank dependence negatively affects its performance when the main bank experiences difficulties. The coefficient on the main bank loan ratio is statistically different from the coefficient on the nonbank debt ratio ($F = 2.87$ with a p-value of 0.09).

To examine more closely the effect on firm performance of a firm's financial ability to overcome banking shocks, we include a dummy variable that takes the value of one if a firm's debt includes public bonds that are not guaranteed by the bank. We also add three additional variables to further capture the possible substitution effect of main bank financing: a dummy variable that takes the value of one if the firm has borrowed from a foreign bank, a dummy variable that takes the value of one if the firm is listed on a foreign stock exchange, and the number of banks from which the firm borrows. Among our sample, only 14 firms are listed on the New York Stock Exchange, the London Stock Exchange, or the Luxembourg Stock Exchange. We expect less of a drop in the value of equity for firms that are able to issue public bonds for which the bank does not guarantee payment, since these firms tend to have better access to capital markets. Along the same line, we expect less of a drop for firms that are able to borrow from foreign banks, are listed on a foreign stock exchange, or have multiple bank relationships. These firms are more likely to have access to alternative sources of bank financing when their main banks are in financial distress. It turns out that the dummy variable for public bond issue is significantly positive at the 0.01 level. This result suggests that firms that can obtain financing through other sources and need not rely on banks experience lower losses in the market value of their equity during the period of banking shocks. The other three variables that are expected to capture the substitution effect are not significant. While not reported, we find that the joint hypothesis that the coefficient estimates on all event dummies are zero is strongly rejected at the 0.001 level. In another regression not reported here, we replace the number of banks from which a firm borrows with a dummy variable for a multiple bank relationship. The coefficient on this dummy variable is again not significant.

In Panel B of Table 7, we report the regression estimates for subperiods. In both subperiods, the ratio of cash flow to total assets and the dummy variable for public bonds are significantly positive, and the ratio of main bank debt to total assets is significantly negative. However, the adjusted R^2 of the regressions in the period of the banking shocks are about three times larger than those in period before the banking shocks (25% vs. 9%). These results suggest that the regression model in the second subperiod fits the data better than that in the first subperiod. To the extent that main bank debt captures the extent of bank dependence, our finding that the main bank debt ratio is negative in both periods implies that firms that are more bank dependent realize more-negative announcement returns even during the period before the banking crisis. The ratio of liquid assets to total assets is significantly positive only in the second subperiod.

Overall, the regression analysis in Table 7 indicates that firms that depend more on bank financing experience a larger drop in equity value when their main banks experience difficulties. In contrast, firms with alternative means of financing and firms with more liquidity experience a lower drop. These results are consistent with the view that bank relationships are less valuable when banks perform poorly, and that financially constrained client firms are more sensitive to adverse shocks to banks.

4.3.2. An alternative specification

One limitation with the fixed effects regression is that it does not allow us to examine how the financial health of the bank and the combination of bank and firm conditions will determine the impact of bad news about a bank on its customers. This is because the event dummies used in the fixed effects regression are perfectly correlated with the variable for bank health, such as the nonperforming loan ratio of the main bank. To gain further insight into this issue, we compute the average announcement returns for each client firm across different events and relate these returns to the main bank health and the financial characteristics of each client firm. We compute the average announcement returns for each client firm across news events as follows. First, we select the sample of 486 client firms for which financial data are available. For each negative news event and for each client firm, we compute the cumulative abnormal returns from day -1 to day $+1$, using a market model. We then average the cumulative abnormal returns for the client firm across news events.

K.-H. Bae et al. / Journal of Financial Economics 64 (2002) 181–214 209

For example, the Korea Exchange Bank has 54 client firms for which financial data are available. There are seven news events during the sample period, resulting in seven cumulative abnormal returns for each of the 54 client firms. We average the cumulative abnormal returns across the seven news events for each client firm, resulting in 54 average cumulative abnormal returns. We call this average announcement return for the client firm across news events the "ARC." We apply the same procedures to client firms of other main banks, resulting in 486 ARCs. We then examine the relation between the ARCs and main bank and firm characteristics using OLS regressions.

While not reported, we find that the results using ARCs are similar to those using CARs in Panel B of Table 3. The average ARC for the sample of 486 client firms during the full sample period is −1.04% and is significant at the 0.01 level. The median ARC is −0.81% and is also significant at the 0.01 level. The results also show that the average ARC before the crisis is not statistically different from zero, but it is significantly negative during the crisis period. The mean and median differences in ARCs before and during the crisis period are statistically significant, rejecting our null hypothesis of equal returns across the two subperiods. Breaking down the ARCs by type of news event indicates that the most negative ARC is in the subsample of credit downgrades during the crisis period. Overall, the results indicate that our new metric preserves the general messages delivered by the previous results using portfolio returns. A potential problem with the ARCs is that the assumption of the cross-sectional independence in the OLS regression to estimate the market model might not be justified, since the events we consider are perfectly clustered among client firms of the same main bank. However, to the extent that the main banks maintain lending relationships with many firms in various industries as shown in Table 6, inferences based on residuals from the market model would probably not be affected by this concern. Further, given that this bias applies to periods both before and during the crisis, it is less likely that any results favoring our hypothesis are due to the problem of cross-sectional dependence.

For the cross-sectional analysis, we use the ARC(−1, 1) as the dependent variable and use variables from Table 7 and the nonperforming loan ratio as independent variables. Panel A of Table 8 presents the results for the full sample period. We find that the results of regressions (1) through (4) are similar to those in the fixed effects regression model. The firms that have larger debt, low cash flow, and low liquidity realize a larger drop in the value of their equity. We also find that the coefficients on the nonperforming loan ratio are negative and significant at the 0.10 level, which indicates that client firms of financially weak banks experience a bigger loss.

To examine the interaction effect between bank and borrower conditions, we add two additional variables in the fifth regression: (1) an interaction between a dummy variable for bad-quality banks and a dummy variable for highly leveraged firms and (2) an interaction between a dummy variable for bad-quality banks and a dummy variable for low cash flow/low liquidity firms. A dummy variable for bad-quality banks takes the value of one if both the nonperforming loan ratio for the bank is above the sample median and the Tobin's q for the bank is below the sample median. A dummy variable for high-leverage firms takes the value of one if the ratio of total

Table 8

OLS regression of the three-day average announcement returns for client firms across news events (ARCs) on the nonperforming loan ratio of the main bank and firm characteristics

The sample includes Korean client firms whose main banks experience negative shocks from January 1997 to December 1998. Only client firms for which financial data are available are used, resulting in 486 sample firms. The dependent variable is the three-day cumulative abnormal return for the client firm across news events (ARC). Independent variables used in the full sample period are calculated as the average values of variables at the end of fiscal years 1996 and 1997. Those in the period before (during) the crisis are the values at the end of fiscal year 1996 (1997). Nonperforming loan ratios are obtained from the *Monthly Financial Statistics Bulletin* published by Financial Supervisory Service. Bank loan data are obtained from a firm's annual audit report and other financial data from the Listed Company Database of the Korean Listed Companies Association. The top 30 chaebol dummy takes the value of one if the firm belongs to one of the 30 largest business groups in Korea. Nonperforming loans include (1) substandard or partially recoverable loans (the amount expected to be collected by collateral liquidation from customers who have loans that are overdue at least three months), (2) doubtful loans (the portion of credit in excess of the partially recoverable loans that are expected to be a loss but have not yet been realized as such), and (3) estimated losses (the portion of credit in excess of the partially recoverable loans that must be accounted as a loss because collection is not possible in a foreseeable period). Bank debt is the sum of bank loans and corporate bonds guaranteed by the bank. Main bank debt is total debt minus bank debt. Cash flow is computed as the sum of operating income and depreciation. Liquid assets are cash plus marketable securities. The no guaranteed bond issue dummy takes the value of one if a firm's debt includes public bonds that are not guaranteed by the bank. The foreign bank dummy takes the value of one if the firm borrows from foreign banks. The depository receipt dummy takes the value of one if the firm's stock is listed abroad. The bad-quality bank dummy takes the value of one if the nonperforming loan ratio for the bank is above the sample median and the Tobin's q is below the sample median. The highly leveraged firm dummy takes the value of one if the ratio of total debt to total assets for the client firm is above the sample median. The low cash flow/low liquidity firm dummy takes the value of one if both the ratio of cash flow to total assets and the ratio of liquid assets to total assets for the client firm are below the sample medians. All regressions include 13 industry dummy variables to control for industry effects. White's (1980) heteroskedastic-consistent t-statistics are in parentheses; ***, **, and * denote the significance of the parameter estimates at the 0.01, 0.05 and 0.10 levels, respectively.

Panel A: Full period (January 97–December 98)

Independent variables	(1)	(2)	(3)	(4)	(5)
Intercept	0.0221	0.0292	0.0057	−0.0010	0.0107
	(0.79)	(0.09)	(0.19)	(−0.03)	(0.31)
Nonperforming loan/total loan of main bank	−0.0011*	−0.0011*	−0.0012*	−0.0010	−0.0008
	(−1.67)	(−1.67)	(−1.85)	(−1.44)	(−1.26)
Log (total assets)	0.0022*	0.0019	0.0008	0.0010	0.0010
	(1.69)	(1.40)	(0.59)	(0.56)	(0.59)
Top 30 chaebol dummy	0.0045	0.0052	0.0035	0.0039	0.0039
	(1.13)	(1.32)	(0.88)	(0.99)	(0.92)
Investment securities/total assets	−0.0174	−0.0117	−0.0055	−0.0092	−0.0162
	(−0.76)	(−0.50)	(−0.24)	(−0.40)	(−0.71)
Main bank holdings of client firm	0.2743	0.4285	0.7807	0.7908	0.6577
	(0.98)	(0.48)	(0.86)	(0.86)	(0.76)

Panel B: Subperiod

Independent variables	Before the crisis (January 97–November 21, 97)			During the crisis (November 22, 97–December 98)		
	(1)	(2)	(3)	(4)	(5)	(6)
Intercept	0.0459 (1.51)	0.0622* (1.77)	0.0578 (1.61)	-0.0321 (-0.67)	-0.0497 (-0.90)	-0.0520 (-0.93)
Nonperforming loan/total loan of main bank	-0.0004 (-0.74)	-0.0003 (-0.54)	-0.0004 (-0.77)	-0.0018** (-2.07)	-0.0015* (-1.82)	-0.0012 (-1.36)
Log (total assets)	-0.0026* (-1.77)	-0.0037** (-2.06)	-0.0029* (-1.64)	0.0042* (1.80)	0.0052* (1.76)	0.0054* (1.85)
Top 30 chaebol dummy	-0.0003 (-0.08)	-0.0013 (-0.40)	-0.0015 (-0.37)	-0.0004 (-0.06)	0.0012 (0.16)	0.0014 (0.18)
Total debt/total assets	-0.0527*** (-4.26)					-0.0367*** (-2.86)
Bank debt/total assets		-0.0483*** (-3.27)				
Main bank debt/total assets				-0.0383* (-1.77)	-0.0352* (-1.71)	
Nonbank debt/total assets			-0.0354*** (-2.39)	-0.0195 (-1.44)	-0.0257* (-1.88)	
Cash flow/total assets			0.0591** (2.09)	0.0716** (2.47)	0.0682** (2.06)	0.0642** (2.25)
Liquid assets/total assets			0.0511** (2.12)	0.0644*** (2.69)	0.0654*** (2.66)	0.0522** (2.13)
No guaranteed bond issue dummy					0.0091*** (2.71)	0.0075*** (2.30)
Foreign bank dummy					0.0008 (0.21)	0.0023 (0.60)
Depositary receipt dummy					0.0031 (0.44)	0.0022 (0.35)
Number of banks from which a firm borrows					-0.0001 (-0.15)	0.0002 (0.29)
Bad-quality bank dummy * highly leveraged firm dummy						-0.0332* (-1.72)
Bad-quality bank dummy * low cash flow/low liquidity firm dummy						0.0080 (0.27)
Number of observations	486	486	486	486	482	482
F-statistic	2.20***	2.32***		1.90***	1.91***	2.48***
Adjusted R^2	0.0449	0.0563		0.0394	0.0470	0.0769

Table 8 (continued)

Panel B: Subperiod

	Before the crisis (January 97–November 21, 97)			During the crisis (November 22, 97–December 98)		
Investment securities/total assets	−0.0007 (−0.03)	−0.0017 (−0.06)	−0.0031 (−0.12)	−0.0282 (−0.82)	−0.0379 (−1.09)	−0.039 (−1.20)
Main bank holdings of client firm	0.8799 (1.09)	0.8500 (1.00)	0.7526 (0.85)	−0.9915 (−1.37)	−0.9897 (−1.44)	−0.7604 (−1.14)
Total debt/total assets			−0.0178 (−1.28)			−0.0337* (−1.83)
Main bank debt/total assets	−0.0378* (−1.72)	−0.0352 (−1.58)		−0.0531* (−1.76)	−0.0532* (−1.79)	
Non-bank debt/total assets	−0.0010 (−0.08)	−0.0033 (−0.25)		−0.0218 (−1.05)	−0.0349* (−1.64)	
Cash flow/total assets	0.1014*** (3.21)	0.0946*** (2.88)	0.0947*** (2.84)	0.0146 (0.40)	0.0240 (0.67)	0.0198 (0.56)
Liquid assets/total assets	0.0081 (0.37)	0.0118 (0.58)	0.0094 (0.41)	0.0856*** (2.57)	0.0822** (2.43)	0.0742** (2.23)
No guaranteed bond issue dummy		0.0028 (0.81)	0.0029 (0.85)		0.0136** (2.38)	0.0126** (2.32)
Foreign borrowing dummy		0.0029 (0.83)	0.0027 (0.73)		0.0023 (0.29)	0.0046 (0.59)
Depositary receipt dummy		0.0054 (0.89)	0.0048 (0.74)		−0.0001 (−0.01)	−0.0027 (−0.26)
Number of banks from which a firm borrows		0.0008 (1.13)	0.0010 (1.33)		−0.0015 (−1.06)	−0.0011 (−0.77)
Bad-quality bank dummy * highly leveraged firm dummy			0.0023 (0.35)			−0.0714*** (−2.70)
Bad-quality bank dummy * low cash flow/low liquidity			0.0068 (0.94)			0.0122 (0.44)
Number of observations	482	478	478	486	482	482
F-statistic	1.65**	1.42*	1.42*	1.60**	1.67**	2.15***
Adjusted R^2	0.0290	0.0226	0.0230	0.0266	0.0351	0.0605

debt to total assets for the client firm is above the sample median. A dummy variable for low cash flow/low liquidity firms takes the value of one if both the ratio of cash flow to total assets and the ratio of liquid assets to total assets for the client firm are below the sample medians. The coefficients on the interaction variables thus measure the marginal impact of a client firm with high total debt or with low cash flow/low liquidity when it borrows from the bad bank.

The results show that the coefficient on the first interaction variable is negative and significant at the 0.10 level. This result suggests that the combination of bank and firm conditions is important in determining the value of durable bank relationships. The coefficient on the second interaction variable, however, is not significant.

In Panel B of Table 8, we report the regression estimates for subperiods. The results indicate that our findings for the full sample period mirror those for the period during the banking shocks. In contrast, most of the variables in the period before the banking shocks are insignificant except for the main bank debt ratio.

5. Summary and conclusion

In this paper, using a large sample of exogenous events that negatively affect Korean banks, we examine the value of durable bank relationships. We present systematic evidence on the extent to which firm value is related to the degree of financial health of its main bank during a period of banking shocks. We also show that the costs of bank distress are higher for financially constrained and unhealthy firms. Firms that are tied to banks with larger bad loans and firms that have few alternative means of external financing suffer more from adverse shocks to banks. Firms with high leverage (bank loans) and less liquidity experience a larger drop in the value of their equity. Overall, the results in this paper indicate that the financial health of both banks and client firms matters in maintaining the benefits of relationship banking during a banking crisis period.

Our results suggest that there are benefits to a firm from diversifying its financing sources or from cultivating alternative financing channels. Since the capital market is relatively undeveloped in countries that adopt a bank-centered financial system, our results also suggest that these nations would benefit from diversifying their financial systems. In a well-diversified financial system, firms can easily access other means of financing offered by capital markets, which can help to buffer them against the adverse effect of banking shocks.

References

Aoki, M., 1990. Toward an economic model of the Japanese firm. Journal of Economic Literature 28, 1–27.

Bernanke, B.S., 1983. Nonmonetary effects of the financial crisis in the propagation of the Great Depression. American Economic Review 73, 257–276.

Billett, M., Flannery, M., Garfinkel, J., 1995. The effect of bank identity on a borrowing firm's equity return. Journal of Finance 50, 699–718.

Brown, S.J., Warner, J.B., 1985. Using daily stock returns: the case of event studies. Journal of Financial Economics 15, 3–31.

Diamond, D., 1991. Monitoring and reputation: the choice between bank loans and directly placed debt. Journal of Political Economy 99, 689–721.

Djankov, S., Jindra, J., Klapper, L., 2000. Corporate valuation and the resolution of bank insolvency in East Asia. Working paper, World Bank.

Fama, E., 1985. What's different about the bank? Journal of Monetary Economics 15, 29–40.

Gibson, M.S., 1995. Can bank health affect investment? Evidence from Japan. Journal of Business 68, 281–308.

Hoshi, T., Kashyap, A., Scharfstein, D., 1991. Corporate structure, liquidity and investment: evidence from Japanese industrial groups. Quarterly Journal of Economics 106, 33–60.

James, C., 1987. Some evidence on the uniqueness of bank loans. Journal of Financial Economics 19, 217–235.

Kang, J.-K., Shivdasani, A., 1995. Firm performance, corporate governance, and top executive turnover in Japan. Journal of Financial Economics 38, 29–58.

Kang, J.-K., Shivdasani, A., Yamada, A., 2000. The effect of bank relations on investment decisions: an investigation of Japanese takeover bids. Journal of Finance 55, 2197–2218.

Kang, J.-K., Stulz, R.M., 2000. Do banking shocks affect borrowing firm performance? An analysis of the Japanese experience. Journal of Business 73, 1–23.

Kaplan, S.N., 1994. Top executives, turnover, and firm performance in Germany. Journal of Law, Economics, and Organization 10, 142–159.

Kaplan, S.N., Minton, B.A., 1994. Appointments of outsiders to Japanese boards: determinants and implications for managers. Journal of Financial Economics 36, 225–258.

Karceski, J., Ongena, S., Smith, D.C., 2000. The impact of bank consolidation on commercial borrower welfare. Working paper, University of Florida, Gainesville.

Lummer, S., McConnell, J., 1989. Further evidence on the bank lending process and the capital market response on bank loan agreements. Journal of Financial Economics 25, 99–122.

Ongena, R., Smith, D.C., Michalsen, D., 2000. Firms and their distressed banks: lessons from the Norwegian banking crisis (1988–1991). Working paper, Tilburg University, Tilburg.

Rajan, R., 1992. Insiders and outsiders: the choice between relationship and arm's length debt. Journal of Finance 47, 1367–1400.

Ramakrishnan, R., Thakor, A., 1984. Information reliability and a theory of financial intermediation. Review of Economic Studies 52, 415–432.

Sharpe, S.A., 1990. Asymmetric information, bank lending, and implicit contracts: a stylized model of customer relationships. Journal of Finance 45, 1069–1087.

Slovin, M.B., Sushka, M.F., Polonchek, J.A., 1993. The value of bank durability: borrowers and bank stakeholders. Journal of Finance 48, 247–266.

White, H., 1980. A heteroskedasticity-consistent covariance matrix estimator and a direct test for heteroskedasticity. Econometrica 48, 817–838.

[2001] Argentina
Chile
Mexico

G21
G28
O16

359-81

Chapter Eleven

359

THE JOURNAL OF FINANCE • VOL. LVI, NO. 3 • JUNE 2001

Do Depositors Punish Banks for Bad Behavior? Market Discipline, Deposit Insurance, and Banking Crises

MARIA SOLEDAD MARTINEZ PERIA and SERGIO L. SCHMUKLER*

ABSTRACT

This paper empirically investigates two issues largely unexplored by the literature on market discipline. We evaluate the interaction between market discipline and deposit insurance and the impact of banking crises on market discipline. We focus on the experiences of Argentina, Chile, and Mexico during the 1980s and 1990s. We find that depositors discipline banks by withdrawing deposits and by requiring higher interest rates. Deposit insurance does not appear to diminish the extent of market discipline. Aggregate shocks affect deposits and interest rates during crises, regardless of bank fundamentals, and investors' responsiveness to bank risk taking increases in the aftermath of crises.

OVER THE LAST TWO DECADES, both developed and developing countries have endured severe banking crises. The U.S. savings and loans (S&Ls) debacle in the 1980s, the Chilean banking crisis in the 1980s, the Argentine and Mexican crises in the mid-1980s and 1990s, as well as the recent financial turmoil in Asia and Russia are only a few examples. At all times and, particularly, to avoid banking crises, regulators need to find ways to promote prudent behavior by banks. The standard recommendation is for countries to tighten supervision and prudential regulation. Alternatively, rather than depending exclusively on regulatory action, banking authorities can also increase their reliance on market discipline to oversee banks.

* Martinez Peria and Schmukler are with the World Bank. We are grateful to René Stulz and an anonymous referee, who helped us to substantially improve the paper. We thank Allen Berger, Jerry Caprio, Asli Demirguc-Kunt, Barry Eichengreen, Eduardo Fernandez-Arias, Aart Kraay, Andy Levin, Maury Obstfeld, George Pennacchi, Andrew Powell, Jim Powell, and Luis Servén for very helpful suggestions. We are highly indebted to Carlos Arteta, Cicilia Harun, José Pineda, Bernadette Ryan, Marco Sorge, Jon Tong, Matias Zvetelman, and, particularly, Miana Plesca for excellent research assistance at different stages of the project. We received helpful comments from participants at presentations held at the Central Bank of Chile, the Conference on Deposit Insurance–World Bank, the European Econometric Society Meetings, the Federal Reserve Board, the Latin American and Caribbean Economic Association, and the World Bank. The findings, interpretations, and conclusions expressed in this paper are entirely those of the authors and do not necessarily represent the views of the World Bank, its Executive Directors, or the countries they represent. The Latin American and Caribbean Regional Studies Program, the Research Committee of the World Bank, and the Central Bank of Argentina kindly provided financial support for the project.

Market discipline in the banking sector can be described as a situation in which private sector agents (stockholders, depositors, or creditors at large) face costs that increase as banks undertake risks, and take action on the basis of these costs (Berger (1991)). For example, uninsured depositors, who are exposed to bank risk taking, may penalize riskier banks by requiring higher interest rates or by withdrawing their deposits.

Market discipline can be beneficial in several ways. This type of discipline may reduce the moral hazard incentives, which government guarantees create for banks to undertake excessive risks. Also, market discipline may improve the efficiency of banks by pressuring some of the relatively inefficient banks to become more efficient or to exit the industry. Moreover, the social cost of supervising banks may be lowered if regulators cede greater control to market forces that can distinguish between good and bad banks.

The existing literature on market discipline primarily focuses on whether market discipline exists in a particular country during a given period. Most of the papers focus on the U.S. commercial banking industry, supporting the hypothesis that market discipline is at work.[1] Baer and Brewer (1986), Hannan and Hanweck (1988), Ellis and Flannery (1992), and Cook and Spellman (1994), among others, analyze how yields on deposits respond to bank risk taking, as captured by balance sheets and by market measures of risk. Goldberg and Hudgins (1996) and Calomiris and Wilson (1998) examine this question by concentrating on the level or change of deposits. Park (1995) and Park and Peristiani (1998) combine both approaches mentioned above.[2] Calomiris and Mason (1997) study whether bank failures are related to bank risk characteristics. Whereas the literature on market discipline is quite vast for the United States, there are only a few papers on this subject regarding developing countries. Valdés and Lomakin (1988) examine interest rate changes associated with bank riskiness in Chile in the mid-1980s. Schumacher (1996), D'Amato, Grubisic, and Powell (1997), and Calomiris and Powell (2000) analyze whether market discipline exists in the case of Argentina during the 1990s.

The present paper empirically examines two issues largely unexplored by the literature on market discipline. First, the paper studies the interaction between deposit insurance and market discipline.[3] Second, the paper investigates the impact of banking crises on market discipline. To study these two issues, we focus on the experiences of the Argentine, Chilean, and Mexican banking sectors over the last two decades. The developments in these countries and the unique bank level data we put together enable us to shed new light on the links between market discipline, deposit insurance, and banking crises.

---

[1] Flannery (1998) provides an excellent survey of this literature.

[2] Other studies, like Avery, Belton, and Goldberg (1988), Gorton and Santomero (1990), and Flannery and Sorescu (1996), look at the existence of risk premia on subordinated notes and debentures, rather than deposits.

[3] Demirguc-Kunt and Huizinga (2000) analyze how different design features of deposit insurance schemes affect deposit interest rates and market discipline.

The deposit insurance scheme in place in a country may affect the extent of market discipline. Deposit insurance systems are designed to protect small depositors and to avoid systemic crises. If depositors know that their funds are safe and liquid, they will not have an incentive to withdraw their deposits from their bank when they see other banks fail. Consequently, deposit insurance can lower the probability of systemic bank runs. At the same time, a credible deposit insurance system reduces the incentives of depositors to monitor banks, diminishing the degree of market discipline. However, if the deposit guarantee is not credible or if there are costs associated with the recovery of deposits following a bank failure, insured depositors will be compelled to monitor banks.

Because our dataset discriminates between insured and uninsured depositors, we are able to examine the link between market discipline and deposit insurance. In particular, we can test whether both insured and uninsured depositors discipline banks. Furthermore, because in some cases, the deposit insurance scheme was introduced or modified during our sample of study, we can examine the extent of market discipline before and after a change in the deposit insurance coverage. Comparing the response of insured and uninsured depositors to changes in bank risk taking is interesting because we are dealing with three countries, each with different deposit insurance schemes.

Banking crises are a unique time to study market discipline. First, during crises, banks tend to be weak and the probability of bank failures rises. Thus, to avoid losing their funds, depositors might increase market discipline during these periods. On the other hand, banking crises tend to be associated with large macroeconomic effects and bank runs (which affect all banks regardless of their fundamentals) and with bank interventions (which, in many cases, temporarily freeze deposits and interest rates). Consequently, during crises, we might observe an increase in the relative importance of the aggregate factors. Second, traumatic episodes may act as wake-up calls for depositors, increasing depositors' awareness of the risk of their deposits. Also, deposit insurance funds might be depleted during a crisis, diminishing the ability of insurance schemes to guarantee deposits.[4] As a consequence, after crises, we might see a rise in market discipline. In this paper, we assess the link between crises and market discipline by studying banking crises in three countries. In particular, we compare the responsiveness of depositors to bank risk taking before, during, and after crises.

The remainder of this paper is organized as follows. Section I describes the empirical methodology. Section II discusses the data and variables. Section III presents the empirical results. Section IV concludes.

I. Methodology

We estimate two sets of models to study market discipline, one for deposits and one for interest rates. In each model, we test whether bank risk

---

[4] We thank René Stulz for raising this point.

characteristics significantly explain the behavior of deposits and interest rates. We measure the reaction of deposits to bank risk taking with the following reduced form equation for each country:

$$\Delta Deposits_{i,t} = \mu_i + d_t + \beta'\ Bank\ Fundamentals_{i,t-1} + \varepsilon_{i,t}, \qquad (1)$$

such that $i = 1,\ldots,N$ and $t = 1,\ldots,T$. N is the number of banks in each country. The panel is unbalanced, so T, the number of observations per bank, varies across institutions.

The left-hand side variable, $\Delta Deposits_{i,t}$, represents the first difference of the log of time deposits held by bank i at time t. The vector of bank risk characteristics, *Bank Fundamentals*$_{i,t-1}$, is described in the next section. This vector is included with a lag, to account for the fact that balance sheet information is available to the public with a certain delay. The time specific effect is represented by d_t, included to control for macroeconomic and banking sector developments, common across banks, and μ_i stands for bank specific or fixed effects.

A common test of market discipline is whether the estimates of β are individually or jointly different from zero. If there is no market discipline, deposit growth should be uncorrelated with bank risk characteristics, and we should fail to reject $\beta = 0$. However, the finding that deposits respond to bank risk is not enough to conclude that market discipline is at work. Depositors can discipline banks by withdrawing their funds or by requiring higher interest rates on their deposits. If market discipline is present, we should observe that risky banks are forced to pay high interest rates or, at least, that those risky banks do not pay lower interest rates (when, at the same time, they face deposit withdrawals).

Even though most of the literature studies market discipline by analyzing either deposits or interest rates, an examination of both variables provides a more complete test of market discipline. The analysis of interest rates can help distinguish between market discipline and other alternative hypotheses, such as regulatory discipline. For example, banks may respond to regulatory pressure to comply with capital standards by reducing their assets, and consequently their liabilities. Thus, risky banks might lower their interest rates to decrease deposits. As a result, under regulatory discipline, interest rates should be negatively correlated with bank risk. On the other hand, a positive correlation between interest rates and risk is a sign of market discipline.

To analyze whether depositors discipline bank risk taking by requiring higher interest rates, we estimate the following equation for each country:

$$Interest\ Rates_{i,t} = \mu_i + d_t + \beta'\ Bank\ Fundamentals_{i,t-1} + \omega_{i,t}. \qquad (2)$$

The left-hand-side variable, *Interest Rates*$_{it}$, is the implicit interest rate paid by bank i on its deposits at time t. We assume that the error terms $\varepsilon_{i,t}$ and $\omega_{i,t}$ are independently distributed with mean zero and variance $\sigma_{i,t}^2$.

Do Depositors Punish Banks for Bad Behavior? 1033

We report between and within or pooled estimators of equations (1) and (2). Between estimators are obtained by regressing the mean of deposits of each bank on mean values of the explanatory variables, excluding time effects. Within or fixed effects estimators highlight the variation of deposits over time, using deviations from each bank's mean. Based on specification tests, we report pooled estimations, which exclude banks' fixed effects, when these effects are jointly insignificant. We only calculate between estimators for the case of Argentina, for which there is a large number of banks.[5] In all the estimations, we conduct and report two additional diagnosis tests. First, we present F-tests to evaluate the joint significance of bank fundamentals. Second, we test the joint significance of time effects to determine whether systemic shocks—common across banks—are important in explaining the behavior of deposits and interest rates.

We estimate various versions of equations (1) and (2) for each country. First, we distinguish between insured and uninsured deposits. As discussed before, this distinction is important because, a priori, we expect to find differences in the degree of market discipline across these two types of depositors. Among uninsured deposits, we distinguish between medium and large time deposits, to study whether there are different patterns of behavior across deposit size.

Second, using equations (1) and (2), we divide the sample period to test for the presence of market discipline before, during, and after banking crises. As an additional way to evaluate the effects of deposit insurance and banking crises on market discipline, we study the relative importance of bank fundamentals before, during, and after crises, and among insured and uninsured deposits. We calculate the proportion of the variance explained by these variables by estimating equations (1) and (2) with time-specific effects, after removing bank-specific effects. Then, we reestimate these equations, including bank fundamentals. We assign any correlation among the independent variables to the time specific effects. Namely, to be on the safe side, we potentially bias the results against the bank risk characteristics. For each estimated equation, we report the proportion of the adjusted R-squared captured by bank risk characteristics.

II. Data and Variables

One important contribution of this paper is the novel dataset we put together and analyze. In particular, we work with bank-level data for Argentina, Chile, and Mexico to examine different aspects of market discipline. Some bank-level data have become more easily available in the last few

---

[5] Alternative specifications are displayed in the full working paper version of this paper, which can be downloaded from http://www.worldbank.org/research. The paper displays estimates that use the level of deposits, as other papers have computed. To check whether the results are robust to potential endogeneity, we use generalized method of moments (GMM) estimates, combining variables in levels and first differences. The lessons from the alternative estimates are the same as the ones put forth in this paper.

years and a number of financial services have started to report cross-country data. However, detailed, comprehensive, and reliable panel datasets are still not available. Moreover, existing data do not contain the level of disaggregation necessary to evaluate the behavior of insured and uninsured deposits separately. Also, available datasets do not account for the large number of bank mergers, acquisitions, and privatizations that took place in the second half of the 1990s. If not handled appropriately, bank panels would distort the evolution of balance sheet information over time.

We collected bank-specific data in close consultation with the financial supervisors and regulators of the countries in our sample. In particular, we put together our dataset with the help of the Central Bank of Argentina, the Superintendency of Banking (Argentina), the Central Bank of Chile, the Superintendency of Banking and Financial Institutions (Chile), and the National Banking and Securities Commission (Mexico).[6] These agencies oversee banks in each country. All banks are required to disclose their financial statements to the banking authorities on a regular basis. Bank-specific balance sheet information is collected periodically, but published and available to the public with a lag of around two months. Most bank-specific data are available at a quarterly frequency, although some variables exist on a monthly basis.

For each country, we gathered historical data. We constructed consistent variables over time and we built panels for each country. We also controlled for those cases when banks merged, were acquired, or were privatized. Typically, these processes cause a sudden change in the bank accounts. For those cases when a bank merged or was acquired or privatized, we treat the resulting larger bank as a new bank in the sample. For Argentina, the dataset covers the period 1993 to 1997. In the case of Chile, we use monthly data for the period 1981 to 1986, which includes the banking crisis that occurred during the 1980s. For the period 1991 to 1996, we work with quarterly data. Finally, in the case of Mexico, the data is quarterly and covers the sample 1991 to 1996.[7]

Bank-level variables used in this paper include individual bank time deposits, interest rates paid on deposits, and a group of bank risk characteristics. For Argentina and Chile in the 1990s, we have data on time deposits by size. Consequently, we can study the behavior of insured, uninsured, medium, and large time deposits. In the case of Argentina, we use data on both peso and U.S. dollar deposits, given that around half of the deposits are in dollars. Also, comparing the behavior of deposits denominated in different currencies is interesting because, in addition to the bank default risk and aggregate factors that affect dollar deposits, peso deposits are also subject to currency risk. For Chile in the 1980s and for Mexico, we only have informa-

---

[6] We are grateful to Alejandra Anastasi, Tamara Burdisso, Laura D'Amato, Gina Casar, Claudio Chamorro, Leonardo Hernandez, Víctor Manuel López, Klaus Schmidt-Hebbel, and Agustín Villar for comments and help in understanding the data.

[7] In March 1997, the accounting system changed, making it difficult to consolidate data from before and after that date.

tion on total time deposits. Local currency deposits are expressed in real terms (adjusted by the consumer price index), to control for the potential growth in nominal figures that can be due to inflation. With respect to the interest rates paid on deposits, we use an implicit measure, as marginal rates are not available. This implicit rate is calculated by dividing the total interest rate expenses by the total interest-bearing deposits. Contrary to the data on deposit flows, we have no information on interest rate expenses by amount of deposits. Therefore, we can only examine the behavior of the interest paid on all deposits.

The measures of risk we calculate are akin to those used in the CAMEL rating system of banks. CAMEL stands for capital adequacy, asset quality, management, earnings, and liquidity. Deteriorating CAMEL indicators would signal an increase in the risk profile of banks.

Capital adequacy is measured by the capital to assets ratio. We expect the capital adequacy variable to have a positive effect on bank deposits. On the other hand, higher capitalization ratios should, in principle, allow banks to pay lower interest rates on their deposits.

A number of indicators are used as measures of asset quality. A clear signal of asset quality is the ratio of nonperforming to total loans. This ratio measures the percentage of loans a bank might have to write off as losses. We expect this variable to have a negative impact on deposits and a positive effect on interest rates.

The concentration of loan portfolios also captures the quality of the assets held by banks. In general, a large exposure to a vulnerable sector, like real estate, raises bank risk. On the other hand, because most real estate loans are mortgage loans (i.e., loans for which the assets in question serve as collateral), it is possible that these loans can be considered relatively safe. Thus, it is a priori unclear what impact the proportion of real estate loans should have on deposits and interest rates. We face a similar uncertainty when analyzing personal or consumption loans, which are typically granted without collateral. However, personal loans may be easier to recall than other loans (like mortgage loans), given that they are usually smaller and have a shorter maturity. Consequently, one can expect a rise in this type of lending to indicate either an increase or a decrease in the risk exposure of banks.

We measure bank profitability by the return on assets ratio. Assuming we are adequately controlling for risk, we expect this variable to have a positive effect on deposits. On the other hand, we expect higher profitability to enable banks to offer lower interest rates.

The efficiency of banks is measured by the ratio of noninterest expenditures to total assets. Less efficient banks are expected to have higher expenditures. However, it is also the case that banks that offer better services to customers might have higher expenditures to total assets. If we could control for the quality of service, we would expect an increase in noninterest expenditures to have a negative effect on deposits and a positive impact on interest rates. In our case, given that we cannot control for the quality of bank services, the effect of this variable is indeterminate.

The cash-to-assets ratio is included as an indicator of banks' liquidity and risk. In general, banks with a large volume of liquid assets are perceived to be safer, because these assets would allow a bank to meet unexpected withdrawals. In this sense, controlling for other factors, we expect more liquid banks to suffer fewer deposit withdrawals and to be able to pay lower interest rates. To the extent that the ratios of bonds to assets and (financial) investments to assets can be considered as measures of liquidity, we would expect them to have a positive effect on bank deposits and a negative impact on interest rates. However, the recent history in emerging markets shows that bonds can sometimes become illiquid, and their prices suffer large fluctuations. Thus, a priori, it is difficult to predict the effect of this variable.

III. Results

We report the results under three headings. First, to assess the impact of deposit insurance and banking crises on market discipline, we examine whether deposits and interest rates are indeed affected by bank risk characteristics. Second, we study the link between market discipline and deposit insurance. To do so, we compare the extent of market discipline among insured and uninsured deposits, and among deposits in periods with and without deposit insurance. Finally, we evaluate the relation between market discipline and banking crises. In particular, we contrast the response of deposits and interest rates before, during, and after episodes of stress in the banking sector. To minimize the number of tables and to avoid referring to different specifications throughout the paper, we work with a particular partition of the data that enables us to jointly shed light on the three questions of interest. Thus, the next three sections refer to the same tables, although particular specifications may sometimes provide more detail than needed.

A. *Responsiveness of Deposits and Interest Rates to Bank Risk Taking*

This section evaluates whether there is evidence of market discipline, that is, whether depositors respond to bank risk taking by withdrawing their deposits and/or by requiring higher interest rates on deposits. Here, we do not focus our analysis on particular specifications, but we do so in the following sections. The estimations of equations (1) and (2) are displayed in Tables I to V. Fixed effects and time effects are not reported to save space.

Tables I to III present the results for Argentina. These tables show estimations for peso and dollar deposits and for interest rates over the following periods: June 1993 to September 1994, June 1993 to March 1995, and June 1995 to March 1997. Our dataset begins in June 1993, when bank-level data were made available systematically to the public on a quarterly basis. The Mexican crisis, which triggered a banking crisis in Argentina, started in December 1994. Therefore, our first estimation covers the precrisis period, June 1993 to September 1994. Our second estimation, for the period June 1993 to March 1995, includes the so-called tequila crisis. For the period

Table I

Argentina—Response of Growth of Peso Deposits to Bank Risk Characteristics

The table reports regression results of the growth of peso deposits on bank risk characteristics. Between and within (fixed effects) or pooled results are reported. When the fixed effects are not jointly significant at 10 percent, pooled OLS results are reported. Estimators for time dummies, fixed effects, and the constant term are not reported in the table, even though they are included in the regressions. t-Statistics are in parentheses. Robust standard errors with the White correction for heteroskedasticity are obtained. The sign $ denotes both Argentine pesos and U.S. dollars. F-tests for fixed effects, time effects, and bank fundamentals (risk characteristics) test the null hypothesis that the corresponding group of variables is equal to zero.

| | June 1993–September 1994 Precrisis Period | | June 1993–March 1995 Crisis Period | | June 1995–March 1997, by Size of Deposits Postcrisis Period | | | | | | | |
| | | | | | <$10,000 Insured Deposits | | >$20,000 Uninsured Deposits | | >$20,000 & <$100,000 Medium Deposits | | >$100,000 Large Deposits | |
Explanatory Variables	Between Estimates	Within Estimates	Between Estimates	Within Estimates	Between Estimates	Within Estimates	Between Estimates	Within Estimates	Between Estimates	Within Estimates	Between Estimates	Within Estimates
Lag(capital/assets)	-0.067 (-0.470)	-0.018 (-0.098)	0.218* (1.679)	0.243 (1.493)	-0.284 (-1.061)	2.749** (2.384)	-0.410 (-1.325)	6.376*** (4.061)	-0.261 (-0.943)	3.216*** (2.714)	-0.411 (-0.892)	5.348** (2.378)
Lag(nonperforming loans/total loans)	-0.101 (-1.188)	-0.131 (-1.212)	0.104 (1.295)	0.115 (1.253)	0.070 (0.425)	-0.642** (-2.003)	-0.039 (-0.217)	-0.502 (-0.807)	0.208 (1.353)	-0.721 (-1.413)	-0.084 (-0.251)	-3.521** (-2.212)
Lag(real estate loans/total loans)	-0.005 (-0.043)	0.006 (0.034)	0.272*** (2.685)	0.236* (1.835)	0.065 (0.365)	-0.614 (-1.370)	-0.280 (-1.555)	-0.101 (-0.150)	0.023 (0.148)	-0.287 (-0.580)	-0.262 (-0.941)	-0.455 (-0.699)
Lag(personal loans/total loans)	0.044 (0.734)	0.013 (0.174)	0.043 (0.796)	0.039 (0.717)	0.098 (0.782)	-0.328 (-0.948)	-0.036 (-0.277)	-0.781* (-1.826)	-0.024 (-0.211)	-0.265 (-0.595)	0.092 (0.484)	-0.800 (-0.921)
Lag(return/assets)	1.839** (2.179)	0.404 (0.838)	1.154 (1.419)	0.534 (1.419)	6.100** (2.082)	6.160 (1.374)	17.799*** (5.104)	7.944 (1.457)	9.228*** (3.149)	4.623 (1.127)	15.005** (2.35)	-7.268 (-1.585)
Lag(cash/assets)	-0.259 (-1.413)	-0.251 (-1.114)	0.165 (0.910)	0.078 (0.451)	0.612 (0.935)	0.473 (0.700)	-0.440 (-0.587)	0.201 (0.228)	0.357 (0.523)	0.711 (1.032)	0.196 (0.212)	-1.230 (-1.055)
Lag(bonds/assets)	0.581* (1.959)	-0.161 (-0.493)	0.419 (1.467)	0.479* (1.610)	-0.020 (-0.042)	0.189 (0.38)	0.109 (0.228)	0.538 (0.786)	-0.128 (-0.301)	-0.425 (-0.842)	-0.070 (-0.100)	2.338** (2.410)
Lag(expenditure/assets)	0.032 (0.031)	-0.715 (-0.576)	-0.852 (-0.857)	-0.249 (-0.253)	-4.628 (-1.511)	-7.287* (-1.952)	-1.266 (-0.378)	-6.720* (-1.788)	-1.575 (-0.551)	-6.934* (-1.702)	-2.528 (-0.477)	-3.560 (-0.305)
Adjusted R-squared	0.047	0.009	0.053	0.320	0.054	0.264	0.272	0.262	0.073	0.244	0.166	0.166
F-test fixed effects		0.467		0.618		1.771***		1.522***		1.455**		1.441*
F-test time effects		2.975**		66.424***		8.245***		5.887***		12.060***		4.562***
F-test bank fundamentals		0.679		1.681*		12.000***		11.458***		8.692***		5.777***
Number of banks	152		155		83		75		82		57	
Number of observations	152	747	155	1045	83	462	75	377	82	453	57	293

* = 10% level of significance; ** = 5% level of significance; *** = 1% level of significance

Table II
Argentina—Response of Growth of Dollar Deposits to Bank Risk Characteristics

The table reports regression results of the growth of U.S. dollar deposits on bank risk characteristics. Between and within (fixed effects) or pooled results are reported. When the fixed effects are not jointly significant at 10 percent, pooled OLS results are reported. Estimators for time dummies, fixed effects, and the constant term are not reported in the table, even though they are included in the regressions. *t*-Statistics are in parentheses. Robust standard errors with the White correction for heteroskedasticity are obtained. The sign $ denotes both Argentine pesos and U.S. dollars. *F*-tests for fixed effects, time effects, and bank fundamentals (risk characteristics) test the null hypothesis that the corresponding group of variables is equal to zero.

| | June 1993–September 1994 Precrisis Period | | June 1993–March 1995 Crisis Period | | June 1995–March 1997, by Size of Deposits Postcrisis Period | | | | | | | |
| | | | | | <$10,000 Insured Deposits | | >$20,000 Uninsured Deposits | | >$20,000 & <$100,000 Medium Deposits | | >$100,000 Large Deposits | |
Explanatory Variables	Between Estimates	Within Estimates	Between Estimates	Within Estimates	Between Estimates	Within Estimates	Between Estimates	Within Estimates	Between Estimates	Within Estimates	Between Estimates	Within Estimates
Lag(capital/assets)	0.021 (0.201)	0.102 (0.760)	0.046 (0.563)	0.155 (1.523)	−0.287 (1.223)	1.866* (1.857)	−0.177 (−0.657)	1.709 (1.094)	−0.141 (0.494)	2.622*** (2.955)	−0.023 (−0.072)	−0.101 (−0.247)
Lag(nonperforming loans/total loans)	−0.197*** (−3.161)	−0.232 (−1.029)	−0.114** (−2.238)	−0.139* (−1.710)	−0.087 (−0.612)	−0.736** (−2.191)	−0.101 (−0.641)	−0.465* (−1.659)	−0.020 (−0.127)	−0.328 (−0.926)	−0.180 (−0.795)	−0.319 (−0.870)
Lag(real estate loans/total loans)	0.026 (0.306)	0.034 (0.421)	0.055 (0.863)	0.031 (0.485)	0.034 (0.229)	−0.075 (−0.224)	0.059 (0.374)	0.673 (1.155)	0.040 (0.248)	0.124 (0.378)	0.102 (0.537)	0.187 (0.931)
Lag(personal loans/total loans)	0.054 (1.245)	0.033 (0.866)	0.060* (1.739)	0.052 (1.509)	0.039 (0.358)	0.458 (1.097)	−0.092 (−0.812)	−0.801 (−1.101)	−0.073 (−0.619)	0.099 (0.22)	−0.075 (−0.584)	−0.124 (−1.021)
Lag(return/assets)	0.105 (0.171)	−0.042 (−0.075)	−0.145 (−0.283)	−0.528 (−1.399)	5.254** (2.052)	4.894 (1.257)	7.249** (2.383)	8.333** (1.817)	6.602** (2.195)	4.247 (1.115)	2.537 (0.583)	4.094** (1.978)
Lag(cash/assets)	−0.036 (−0.272)	0.116 (0.796)	0.025 (0.215)	0.164 (1.410)	0.096 (0.178)	0.436 (0.900)	−0.144 (−0.220)	−0.749 (−0.566)	−0.107 (−0.153)	0.987** (2.044)	−0.320 (−0.506)	0.031 (0.054)
Lag(bonds/assets)	−0.349 (−1.614)	−0.367 (−0.660)	−0.078 (−0.435)	0.070 (0.411)	0.269 (0.645)	0.238 (0.682)	0.411 (0.981)	−1.683** (−2.191)	0.444 (1.014)	−0.279 (−0.774)	0.127 (0.267)	−0.982* (−1.890)
Lag(expenditure/assets)	0.466 (0.623)	0.692 (0.859)	0.216 (0.344)	0.693 (1.247)	−0.231 (−0.086)	−7.422* (−1.785)	2.994 (1.025)	−9.270*** (−3.263)	2.697 (0.919)	−13.761*** (−3.926)	4.219 (1.167)	4.614 (1.283)
Adjusted R-squared	0.079	0.028	0.024	0.289	0.114	0.285	0.040	0.155	0.108	0.317	0.001	0.006
F-test fixed effects		0.721		0.914		2.185***		1.358**		2.577***		0.855
F-test time effects		2.669**		53.561***		4.380***		1.900*		6.045***		1.084
F-test bank fundamentals		2.539***		2.899***		14.502***		9.006***		12.623***		1.416
Number of banks	152		155		83		75		82		57	
Number of observations	152	747	155	1045	83	462	75	377	82	453	57	293

* = 10% level of significance; ** = 5% level of significance; *** = 1% level of significance.

Table III
Argentina—Response of Interest Rates Paid on Deposits to Bank Risk Characteristics

The table reports regression results of the interest rates paid on deposits on bank risk characteristics. Between and within (fixed effects) or pooled results are reported. When the fixed effects are not jointly significant at 10 percent, pooled OLS results are reported. Estimators for time dummies, fixed effects, and the constant term are not reported in the table, even though they are included in the regressions. t-Statistics are in parentheses. Robust standard errors with the White correction for heteroskedasticity are obtained. F-tests for fixed effects, time effects, and bank fundamentals (risk characteristics) test the null hypothesis that the corresponding group of variables is equal to zero.

Explanatory Variables	June 1993–September 1994 Precrisis Period		June 1993–March 1995 Crisis Period		June 1995–March 1997 Postcrisis Period	
	Between Estimates	Within Estimates	Between Estimates	Within Estimates	Between Estimates	Within Estimates
Lag(capital/assets)	−0.008 (−0.607)	−0.090*** (−3.214)	0.003 (0.281)	−0.048*** (−2.575)	0.017 (1.093)	0.019 (1.344)
Lag(nonperforming loans/total loans)	0.052*** (5.343)	−0.004 (−0.362)	0.019*** (2.638)	−0.012* (−1.659)	−0.009 (−0.970)	−0.008 (−1.028)
Lag(real estate loans/total loans)	−0.001 (−0.112)	−0.009 (−0.899)	−0.012 (−1.572)	−0.007 (−0.793)	0.000 (−0.045)	−0.017 (−1.268)
Lag(personal loans/total loans)	0.019** (2.458)	0.014 (1.456)	0.007 (1.235)	0.005 (0.610)	0.005 (0.545)	−0.043** (−2.479)
Lag(return/assets)	−0.020 (−0.803)	−0.001 (−0.242)	−0.024 (−0.897)	0.000 (0.114)	−0.178 (−1.207)	−0.002 (−0.091)
Lag(cash/assets)	−0.085*** (−4.873)	−0.003 (−0.224)	−0.110*** (−7.673)	−0.009 (−1.297)	−0.134*** (−3.208)	−0.064*** (−3.735)
Lag(bonds/assets)	−0.002 (−0.073)	0.011 (1.161)	−0.033 (−1.550)	−0.011 (−1.130)	−0.116*** (−3.654)	−0.005 (−0.560)
Lag(expenditure/assets)	0.007 (0.068)	0.026 (0.288)	0.086 (1.042)	−0.131 (−1.572)	−0.117 (−0.745)	0.013 (0.153)
Adjusted R-squared	0.334	0.822	0.368	0.745	0.332	0.728
F-test fixed effects		16.073***		11.857***		10.727***
F-test time effects		9.554***		32.310***		28.413***
F-test bank fundamentals		8.190***		6.621***		6.603***
Number of banks	102	102	114	114	79	79
Number of observations		501		750		570

* = 10% level of significance; ** = 5% level of significance; *** = 1% level of significance.

Table IV
Chile—Response of Growth of Peso Deposits and Interest Rates Paid on Deposits to Bank Risk Characteristics

The table reports regression results of the growth of peso deposits and of interest rates on bank risk characteristics. Between and within (fixed effects) or pooled results are reported. When the fixed effects are not jointly significant at 10 percent, pooled OLS results are reported. Estimators for time dummies, fixed effects, and the constant term are not reported in the table, even though they are included in the regressions. Robust standard errors with the White correction for heteroskedasticity are obtained. The label UF stands for unidades de fomento, a Chilean unit of account. F-tests for fixed effects, time effects, and bank fundamentals (risk characteristics) test the null hypothesis that the corresponding group of variables is equal to zero. The crisis period is divided into two subperiods, which include separately the first and second round of bank interventions.

Explanatory Variables	June 1981–November 1986 Growth of Deposits			February 1991–November 1996 Growth of Deposits, by Size of Deposits				
	1981–1982 Crisis Period First Phase	1983–1984 Crisis Period Second Phase	1985–1986 Postcrisis Period	<120 UF Insured Deposits	>120 UF Uninsured Deposits	>120 UF & <1,500 UF Medium Deposits	>1,500 UF Large Deposits	Interest Rates
Lag(capital/assets)	0.199	0.117	0.272*	−0.011	−0.070	−0.178	−0.123	−0.047*
	(1.004)	(0.868)	(1.796)	(−0.059)	(−0.450)	(−1.350)	(−0.590)	(−1.953)
Lag(nonperforming loans/total loans)	−0.004	−0.039	−0.647***	−1.375***	−0.572	−0.206	−0.802	0.037
	(−0.060)	(−0.378)	(−2.583)	(−2.619)	(−0.695)	(−0.513)	(−0.839)	(0.476)
Lag(return/assets)	2.467	0.539	0.149	−0.056	4.920**	3.365*	5.182**	−0.558**
	(1.194)	(0.457)	(0.045)	(−0.034)	(2.175)	(1.797)	(1.947)	(−2.320)
Lag(cash/assets)	−0.439	−0.383	−0.058	−0.091	0.323*	0.190**	0.370*	0.014
	(−1.433)	(−1.556)	(−0.338)	(−0.660)	(1.927)	(2.340)	(1.850)	(1.251)
Lag(investments/assets)	0.093	0.017	0.067	−0.159	−0.121	−0.001	−0.186	0.012
	(0.609)	(0.235)	(0.424)	(−1.566)	(−1.195)	(−0.011)	(−1.381)	(1.296)
Lag(expenditure/assets)	−1.987*	1.400	1.347	0.557	−0.399	−0.345	−0.229	−0.046
	(−1.833)	(1.305)	(1.021)	(1.441)	(−1.061)	(−1.182)	(−0.513)	(−0.725)
Adjusted R-squared	0.054	0.049	0.064	0.357	0.023	0.226	0.018	0.625
F-test fixed effects	1.310	0.692	1.637**	1.987***	0.659	0.976	0.498	12.643***
F-test time effects	1.763**	2.690***	1.419	14.571***	1.513*	7.764***	1.401	21.2344***
F-test bank fundamentals	1.667	1.122	4.017***	2.977***	2.883***	2.842***	2.598**	4.264***
Number of banks	21	37	37	34	37	32	37	30
Number of observations	304	808	721	547	619	527	619	506

* = 10% level of significance; ** = 5% level of significance; *** = 1% level of significance.

Table V
Mexico—Response of Growth of Peso Deposits and Interest Rates Paid on Deposits to Bank Risk Characteristics

The table reports regression results of the growth of peso deposits and of interest rates paid on bank risk characteristics. Between and within (fixed effects) or pooled results are reported. When the fixed effects are not jointly significant at 10 percent, pooled OLS results are reported. Estimators for time dummies, fixed effects, and the constant term are not reported in the table, even though they are included in the regressions. t-Statistics are in parentheses. Robust standard errors with the White correction for heteroskedasticity are obtained. F-tests for fixed effects, time effects, and bank fundamentals (risk characteristics) test the null hypothesis that the corresponding group of variables is equal to zero. The last two columns display pooled estimates due to the small number of observations per bank, because many institutions enter the sample during this period. Data for up to 12 banks are available before 1996. For comparison, the same banks are used in one of the estimations for the period December 1995 to December 1996.

Explanatory Variables	March 1991–September 1994 Precrisis Period 12 Banks		March 1991–September 1995 Crisis Period 12 Banks		December 1995–December 1996 Postcrisis Period 12 Banks		All Banks	
	Growth of Deposits	Interest Rates	Growth of Deposits	Interest Rates	Growth of Deposits	Interest Rates	Growth of Deposits	Interest Rates
Lag(capital/assets)	−0.843 (−1.351)	0.166 (0.762)	−0.756 (−1.500)	0.068 (0.428)	0.015 (0.019)	−0.597*** (−3.028)	3.171*** (3.358)	−0.384** (−2.270)
Lag(nonperforming loans/total loans)	0.117 (0.182)	0.319* (1.864)	−0.190 (−0.495)	0.257** (1.973)	−0.229 (−0.367)	0.082 (0.508)	0.507 (0.351)	−0.104 (−0.470)
Lag(real estate loans/total loans)	0.368 (1.250)	−0.156** (−2.404)	0.166 (0.941)	−0.195*** (−3.004)	−0.108 (−0.427)	−0.242*** (−3.870)	0.985 (1.465)	−0.126* (−1.807)
Lag(personal loans/total loans)	−0.813* (−1.687)	0.085 (0.542)	−0.257 (−0.812)	0.014 (0.114)	2.476* (1.865)	−0.064 (−0.216)	0.357 (0.113)	−0.823*** (−3.739)
Lag(return over assets)	6.892 (1.540)	−0.046 (−0.032)	4.088 (1.274)	−1.776** (−2.106)	4.277* (1.805)	0.265 (0.431)	3.435 (0.855)	0.959 (1.332)
Lag(cash/assets)	0.510 (0.673)	−0.371*** (−3.025)	−0.137 (−0.249)	−0.187 (−1.304)	0.595 (0.884)	−0.193* (−1.785)	−1.799 (−1.331)	0.123 (0.628)
Lag(expenditure/assets)	6.145 (1.393)	1.874 (1.313)	6.714* (1.891)	1.364 (1.442)	−4.917 (−1.108)	−0.556 (−0.648)	−2.841 (−0.314)	3.049** (2.065)
Adjusted R-squared	0.072	0.644	0.073	0.808	0.1994	0.816	0.398	0.176
F-test fixed effects	0.705	10.664***	1.519	6.801***	1.301	2.258*	2.096***	8.150***
F-test time effects	1.773*	6.619***	1.727**	38.088***	1.872	21.454***	2.867**	1.853
F-test bank fundamentals	1.539	4.782***	1.213	3.464***	2.227**	13.302***	4.388***	1.959*
Number of banks	12	10	12	10	12		34	31
Number of observations	158	99	195	139	55	44	111	103

* = 10% level of significance; ** = 5% level of significance; *** = 1% level of significance.

starting in June 1995, our dataset enables us to analyze the behavior of time deposits by size. We conduct separate estimations for insured (those below 10,000 pesos or dollars) and uninsured deposits (those above 20,000 pesos or dollars). To analyze the degree of market discipline exercised by medium size and large depositors, we distinguish between deposits in the 20,000–100,000 peso/dollar range and those larger than 100,000 pesos or dollars.

The results in Tables I and II support the finding that deposits respond to bank risk taking. In particular, the ratio of nonperforming loans has a significant negative effect on both peso and dollar deposits. Also, in several specifications, we find that a rise in the capital-to-assets ratio fosters deposit growth. An increase in the expenditures-to-asset ratio is associated with a fall in deposits. Meanwhile, profitable banks attract more deposits. Medium size dollar deposits increase as banks' cash-to-assets ratio rises. The ratio of real estate loans to total loans has a positive effect during the crisis period.

Table III presents between and within estimates of the interest rate paid by Argentine banks on deposits. We find that across sample periods, there is evidence of market discipline. As expected, the significant coefficients take the opposite sign to the ones in the regressions using deposits. We find that banks with higher capital-to-assets and cash-to-assets ratios pay lower interest rates. Also banks with a larger share of nonperforming loans pay higher interest rates. Finally, Tables I to III show that bank risk characteristics are jointly significant, even after controlling for fixed effects and time effects.

The results for Chile, including those for deposits during the 1980s, for peso (or UF) time deposits during the 1990s, and for interest rates, are displayed in Table IV.[8] There is no information on deposits by size in the 1980s and for interest rates. Because Chile suffered a banking crisis in the 1980s, we divide the sample into three periods to capture the different phases of the crisis. For the period 1991 to 1996, we estimate a number of specifications. Given that we have information on the size of deposits, we present estimates for small, medium, and large time deposits. Small or insured deposits are those smaller than 120 UFs. Medium deposits are defined as those between 120 and 1,500 UFs. Large deposits are those above 1,500 UFs. We also estimate an equation for uninsured deposits, namely, all deposits above 120 UFs.[9]

Overall, we find that deposits respond to bank risk taking in the period following the 1980s banking crisis. We find that a rise in bank capitalization and in the cash-to-assets ratio lead to an increase in the growth rate of deposits. On the other hand, a surge in the ratio of nonperforming loans to assets has a negative impact on deposits. Return over assets has a positive effect in the growth rate of deposits during the 1990s. In the case of interest

---

[8] UFs are unidades de fomento or units of account, equal to around 4,000 dollars in 1997.

[9] Dollar deposits in Chile account for only a small fraction of total deposits in Chile (around two to three percent). So, those results are only reported in the working paper version of this paper.

rates, the results indicate that Chilean depositors require higher interest rates as bank risk taking increases. In particular, as the bank capitalization ratio and the return over assets increase, interest rates drop. These signs, as expected, are opposite to the ones obtained in the regressions in which deposit growth is the dependent variable. The F-tests show that risk characteristics are jointly significant in most equations for peso deposits and interest rates.

Table V displays estimates of the percent change of peso time deposits and interest rates in Mexico. We estimate four sets of regressions. For the period March 1991 through September 1995, we only have information for the 12 most important Mexican banks, which held 80 to 90 percent of total deposits. Approximately 18 banks were in business at the beginning of the sample period. We study the behavior of deposits during the precrisis period, March 1991 through September 1994. To test for the effect of the Mexican crisis, we expand the sample to include data through September 1995. For the postcrisis period, December 1995 to December 1996, we estimate two sets of regressions. First, we use the 12 banks for which we have data for the whole sample to compare precrisis, crisis, and postcrisis results. The other set of regressions includes all banks in the sample. The greater number of banks in the postcrisis period is largely the outcome of the deregulation of the Mexican banking sector and the lifting of restrictions on foreign entry after 1995.

The regressions for Mexico provide some evidence that deposits respond to bank risk, particularly in the postcrisis period. During this period, banks with higher returns on assets, higher capital over assets, and a higher proportion of personal loans attract more deposits. Bank risk characteristics are not significant in the precrisis and crisis periods. On the other hand, the evidence suggests that interest rates do respond to bank risk taking throughout the three periods. A higher proportion of nonperforming loans raises the interest rates paid by banks. A rise in the cash-to-assets ratio and the capital-to-assets ratio reduce the interest rates charged to banks. Banks that increase the return on assets and the proportion of personal loans and real estate loans pay lower interest rates. The F-tests indicate that bank fundamentals are generally jointly significant.

In the three countries, the F-tests for bank fundamentals show that bank risk characteristics jointly affect the behavior of deposits and interest rates in most specifications; this is a sign of market discipline. However, the coefficients on various bank risk characteristics are individually not different from zero. This can be due to two factors. Because bank risk characteristics are highly collinear, the individual significance of certain indicators is not captured in the estimations. Alternatively, the results could suggest that depositors only monitor banks by following a few variables. Future research might help to disentangle the relative importance of individual bank risk indicators.

Summarizing, the results discussed in this section indicate that there is evidence of market discipline across the three countries. We find support for the notion that deposit growth falls as bank risk taking increases. Moreover, the evidence suggests that depositors require higher interest rates when banks undertake more risk. The finding that depositors charge higher interest rates to riskier banks suggests that the behavior of deposits is not just the consequence of regulatory pressures on risky banks. We proceed, in the next two sections, to investigate whether the differences across specifications are related to the existence of deposit insurance and to the occurrence of banking crises.

B. Market Discipline and Deposit Insurance

Having found evidence of market discipline, we now concentrate on the effects of deposit insurance on market discipline by comparing the behavior of insured and uninsured deposits. To study the relationship between market discipline and deposit insurance, we refer again to Tables I to V, but we complement those results by calculating the proportion of the variance explained by bank fundamentals across different periods and types of deposits.

As mentioned before, all three countries in our sample have different insurance schemes, which varied over time. Argentina had no deposit insurance whatsoever before the Mexican crisis of 1994 to 1995. Then, for the estimations using data up to March 1995, we concentrate on total time deposits, which is equivalent to studying the behavior of uninsured deposits. After that, we separate insured from uninsured deposits. In April 1995, following the tequila crisis, Argentina introduced a partial deposit insurance scheme that covers deposits up to 20,000 pesos or dollars, depending on their maturity.[10] Deposits with a maturity of more than 90 days are protected up to 20,000 dollars or pesos. For deposits with a shorter maturity, the guarantee covers them up to 10,000 pesos or dollars. Because we do not have data on the maturity of deposits, there is no clear way to separate insured from uninsured deposits with full certainty. To reduce the probability of including uninsured deposits in the insured group, we work with a conservative cut off point of 10,000 pesos or dollars.

In the case of Chile, in the 1980s, a limited insurance scheme was in place; however most deposits were de facto protected. Thus, the distinction between insured and uninsured deposits in the 1980s is not very clear. Prior to November 1986, Chile had, in principle, a limited deposit insurance scheme. This deposit insurance, first introduced in January 1977 and expanded in December 1981, protected deposits up to 3,500 dollars. However, throughout this period, several banks were taken over and most deposits were de facto fully insured. In 1986, a new banking law redefined the deposit insurance scheme. According to the current legislation, only deposits of up to 120 UFs are covered in the Chilean system. In the 1990s, the clear rule about the insurance coverage permits us to study the behavior of insured and uninsured deposits separately.

---

[10] In September 1998, the insurance coverage was extended to deposits up to 30,000 pesos or dollars.

Do Depositors Punish Banks for Bad Behavior? 1045

During the period under study, Mexico had no formal system of deposit insurance. The Credit Institutions Law of 1990 established FOBAPROA, a trust administered by the central bank, created for preventive support to commercial banks and to protect savings. The law did not obligate FOBAPROA to explicitly guarantee or insure any obligations of commercial banks. Nevertheless, each December, FOBAPROA used to announce the maximum amount of the obligations it intended to protect. In general, FOBAPROA expressed an intention to protect all deposits, even though FOBAPROA was not an explicit deposit insurance scheme and was not liable in the event of an uncovered default. For the period we analyze, FOBAPROA implicitly protected 100 percent of deposits. The dataset for Mexico does not provide information regarding the size or the currency denomination of deposits, but the legislation on deposit insurance does not distinguish between small and large deposits. Due to legal restrictions, almost 100 percent of deposits are held in local currency.

The results from Table I to V yield some lessons regarding the effects of deposit insurance on market discipline. Insured and uninsured depositors discipline banks in Argentina and Chile. There are no significant differences in the response of deposits to bank risk characteristics across type of deposits. In the case of Mexico, we find evidence of market discipline, despite the government's promise to protect all deposits. Therefore, the results suggest that the deposit insurance is not fully credible in any of the three countries, because even insured depositors exercise market discipline.

Another way of studying the effect of deposit insurance on market discipline is to consider the results displayed in Table VI. The table shows the proportion of the R-squared explained by bank risk characteristics and an adjusted R-squared (in brackets) of the regression, which reflects the proportion of the total variance only explained by the time-varying variables. The variance explained by bank fundamentals, relative to the variance explained by all time varying dummies, is the product of these two numbers. The results for Argentina indicate that the proportion of the variance of deposits explained by bank fundamentals increases substantially after the deposit insurance system is established. This increase occurs even for insured deposits. The proportion of the variance explained by bank fundamentals in the estimations for insured deposits is at least as large as the one obtained using the equations for uninsured deposits. The evidence for Chile is more mixed. We find that the proportion of the variance explained by bank fundamentals among uninsured deposits is larger than the one explained by these variables in the regression for insured deposits. However, the adjusted R-squared values tend to be lower for uninsured deposits than for insured deposits.

The finding that even insured depositors discipline banks may be due to a number of reasons. Previous confiscation of deposits (as in Argentina during the 1980s) or instances when the government did not keep its promise could be fresh in depositors' minds. Deposit protection can be uncertain when the insurance schemes are underfunded and the fiscal costs of repaying deposits

Table VI

Percentage of Variance Explained by Bank Risk Characteristics

The figures indicate the percentage of the adjusted R-squared explained by bank risk characteristics, as a proportion of all the time varying variables. Adjusted R-squared are in brackets. To make the results comparable, we report the figures from the same type of estimates for each country. We choose the most frequently used estimator. For Argentina, the results correspond to the within estimates, whereas in Chile and Mexico, the results correspond to the pooled estimates. The breakdown corresponds to the estimations displayed in the previous tables. The sign $ denotes both Argentine pesos and U.S. dollars. The label UF stands for unidades de fomento, a Chilean unit of account. In the case of Chile during the 1980s, the crisis period is divided into two subperiods, which include separately the first and second round of bank interventions. In Mexico, data for up to 12 banks are available before 1996. For comparison, the same banks are used in one of the estimations for the period December 1995 to December 1996.

Panel A: Argentina

| | June 1993–September 1994 Precrisis Period | June 1993–March 1995 Crisis Period | June 1995–March 1997, by Size of Deposits Postcrisis Period | | | |
| | | | <$10,000 Insured Deposits | >$20,000 Uninsured Deposits | >$20,000 & <$100,000 Medium Deposits | >$100,000 Large Deposits |
Specification						
Growth of peso deposits	35% [0.02]	2% [0.33]	63% [0.23]	72% [0.24]	41% [0.25]	58% [0.19]
Growth of dollar deposits	68% [0.05]	9% [0.33]	84% [0.22]	93% [0.16]	74% [0.22]	100% [0.06]
			All Deposits			
Interest rates	80% [0.12]	10% [0.38]	10% [0.44]			

Do Depositors Punish Banks for Bad Behavior? 1047

Panel B: Chile

Specification	Total Deposits			February 1991–November 1996 Peso Deposits (UF), by Size of Deposits			
	1981–1982 Crisis Period First Phase	1983–1984 Crisis Period Second Phase	1985–1986 Postcrisis Period	<120 Insured Deposits	>120 Uninsured Deposits	>120 & <1,500 Medium Deposits	>1,500 Large Deposits
Growth of deposits	24% [0.05]	2% [0.05]	70% [0.04]	3% [0.32]	82% [0.02]	8% [0.23]	100% [0.02]

Panel C: Mexico

Specification	March 1991–September 1994 Precrisis Period	March 1991–September 1995 Crisis Period	December 1995–December 1996 Postcrisis Period	December 1995–December 1996 Postcrisis Period
	12 Banks			All Banks
Growth of deposits	34% [0.07]	11% [0.07]	69% [0.20]	77% [0.18]
Interest rates	36% [0.27]	5% [0.72]	50% [0.82]	83% [0.08]

are large. Finally, it is possible that we observe discipline by insured depositors because, even if the insurance is credible, depositors may want to avoid any costs they might face (typically in the form of delays) when banks fail. Repayments through the insurance fund usually take time, imposing liquidity costs on depositors. Moreover, when a bank fails, there are efforts to sell the failing bank to other institutions, to minimize the cost for the insurance fund. One of the major incentives for a healthy bank to buy a failing bank is to acquire the failed bank's deposits. Therefore, if deposits are returned through the deposit insurance, the value of the failing bank decreases. As a consequence, both insured and uninsured deposits are typically paid once the acquisition process is completed.

C. Market Discipline and Banking Crises

As mentioned in the introduction, banking crises are unique episodes to examine market discipline. First, during crises, there are large aggregate shocks to the economy and to the banking sector. Also, bank interventions, typical of crises, temporarily immobilize deposits and interest rates. Second, the risks of bank failures and of losing deposits, temporarily or permanently, become more evident and are magnified during these events. Moreover, the ability of the deposit insurance system to continue guaranteeing deposits can be questioned and jeopardized. We refer once more to Tables I to VI to analyze whether the responsiveness of depositors to bank risk taking is affected by banking crises.

The results for Argentina suggest that the extent of market discipline diminishes during the crisis and increases sharply afterwards. The within estimates show that bank fundamentals are mostly nonsignificant up to March 1995, but become significant after June 1995, that is, after the tequila crisis. Moreover, Table VI illustrates that the proportion of the variance explained by bank fundamentals increases substantially in the postcrisis period. This occurs for the models estimated with equations (1) and (2) for peso and dollar deposits. During the crisis, the proportion explained by bank fundamentals decreases notably, probably due to large systemic shocks. Time effects become particularly relevant during this period. The estimations regarding the behavior of interest rates do not signal such large differences between the period covering the crisis and the following period.

Table VI shows that time effects explain a higher proportion of the variance for peso deposits than for dollar deposits. This result is interesting because peso and dollar deposits are affected by different risks. Both peso and dollar deposits are subject to banks' default risk. However, peso deposits are also affected by currency risk. For a given level of bank fundamentals, aggregate shocks that only increase currency risk should prompt depositors to withdraw their peso deposits, but not their dollar deposits. Thus, changes in currency risk, partially captured by aggregate effects, might explain why time effects are relatively more important among peso deposits than among dollar deposits for all specifications.

For Chile, it is more difficult to compare the crisis and noncrisis periods. The 1980s crisis was less defined in time. However, there were two rounds of bank interventions. In 1981 and 1982, the central bank took over and liquidated a series of financial institutions. By 1983, the crisis had expanded, which prompted the government to take further action. The central bank liquidated a new set of institutions and took over weak banks, including the two largest private banks. These interventions revealed the government's concern with the health of the banking system. The crisis was over in 1985.

The results for Chile suggest that deposits become more responsive to bank fundamentals after bank interventions. No variable is statistically significant in the first two subperiods of the 1980s, whereas capital over assets and the proportion of nonperforming loans become significant afterwards. Other variables are significant in the 1990s. As in the case of Argentina, Table VI shows that the variance explained by bank fundamentals decreases in the midst of the crisis and increases afterwards.

The case of Mexico also offers very similar evidence. Bank fundamentals only become significant in the regressions using deposits in the aftermath of the crisis. As in the previous cases, the proportion of the variance explained by bank risk characteristics decreases substantially during the crisis and increases afterwards to levels above the precrisis ones. In the case of Mexico, this effect can be observed both in the models using deposits and interest rates.

In sum, the results suggest two conclusions. First, bank fundamentals explain relatively less before and during crises. In crisis times, systemic effects tend to become more relevant, implying that deposits and interest rates are correlated across banks, regardless of their fundamentals. Second, the extent to which depositors shift their funds in and out of banks becomes more evident following banking crises, when the intensity of aggregate shocks diminishes and bank interventions cease. The evidence for Argentina and Mexico, where the crisis was clearly defined in time, is very suggestive. The degree of market discipline via deposit withdrawals rises substantially. Following crises, high interest might not fully compensate depositors for the risks they undertake. Depositors realize that their funds can be lost, so the degree to which they discipline banks via deposit withdrawals increases relative to precrisis periods.

IV. Conclusions

This paper concentrates on two issues largely unexplored by the existing literature on market discipline. In the first place, we empirically analyze the relationship between market discipline and deposit insurance. Second, we investigate the impact of banking crises on market discipline. The developments in Argentina, Chile, and Mexico, together with the detailed bank-level dataset we gather, provide a unique opportunity to study these issues.

The results presented in this paper show that depositors in Argentina, Chile, and Mexico punish banks for risky behavior, both by withdrawing their deposits and by requiring higher interest rates. The use of deposits and interest rate data enable us to distinguish market discipline from alternative hypotheses, like regulatory discipline. Also, we compare the behavior of large and small deposits. Ex ante, one could argue that large depositors, with a significant value at risk, would be the primary monitors of banks. However, deposits tend to represent a larger proportion of a small depositor's wealth, so even this type of depositor might discipline banks. The evidence shows no significant difference across depositors: Both large and small depositors discipline banks.

Regarding the relationship between market discipline and deposit insurance, we find that deposit insurance does not necessarily decrease market discipline. We could reject the null hypothesis that insured and uninsured depositors do not respond to bank risk taking. This result suggests that none of the deposit insurance schemes is fully credible. Insured depositors would not need to respond to bank risk taking if they perceived that their deposits were safe and liquid. Nevertheless, depositors are prompted to exercise market discipline when there is uncertainty about the future availability of their deposits, insured or uninsured.

With respect to market discipline and banking crises, the results show that large systemic effects take place during crises, affecting deposits and interest rates across banks, regardless of bank fundamentals. Also, the relative importance of market discipline rises after banking crises for all types of deposits. Before and during crises, the extent of market discipline tends to be more limited, particularly when compared with aggregate effects. These results suggest that, following bank interventions and failures, depositors become more aware of the risk of losing deposits; thus, they start exercising a stricter market discipline. In sum, crises seem to be wake-up calls for depositors.

There exists another potential rationale for the increase in market discipline after crises. If the deposit insurance funds were depleted during a crisis, insured depositors would have an incentive to start monitoring banks more closely. Although this might be the case in some crises, the insurance funds were not depleted in the episodes we analyze. Whenever a bank was in difficulties, governments tried to find buyers or took over the failing bank. Even though the deposit insurance funds were not exhausted, it became obvious during these events that the existing schemes were underfunded, indicating the limits of the deposit insurance coverage.

The cases analyzed suggest that traumatic events teach depositors that they should be concerned about the safety of their deposits at all times. The case of Argentina shows that the responsiveness of depositors to bank risk characteristics increased after the crisis, although at that time the authorities introduced an insurance to guarantee deposits. This implies that the crisis had a greater impact on depositors than the introduction of the deposit insurance system. In the case of Chile and Mexico, depositors were de facto covered during crises, yet their responsiveness increased following central bank interventions.

To conclude, the literature has argued that the existence of deposit insurance might diminish the extent of market discipline. However, the fact that we find market discipline among insured depositors suggests that deposit insurance schemes are not always fully credible. There are important rea-

Do Depositors Punish Banks for Bad Behavior? 1051

sons for this lack of credibility. Many governments have reneged on their promises in the past, the deposit insurance schemes tend to be undercapitalized, and depositors are concerned about the cost of repayment (typically in the form of delays) through the deposit insurance fund. As an example, following the tequila crisis, while the Argentine central bank and the deposit insurance administrators tried to find a buyer for every failing bank, deposits were indefinitely frozen to conserve the bank's franchise value. This type of experience seems to remind depositors that, despite the presence of deposit insurance, it might still be justified to monitor banks for bad behavior.

REFERENCES

Avery, Robert, Terrence Belton, and Michael Goldberg, 1988, Market discipline in regulating bank risk: New evidence from the capital markets, *Journal of Money, Credit, and Banking* 20, 597–610.

Baer, Herbert, and Elijah Brewer, 1986, Uninsured deposit as a source of market discipline: Some new evidence, *Economic Perspectives*, Federal Reserve Bank of Chicago, 23–31.

Berger, Allen, 1991, Market discipline in banking, *Proceedings of a Conference on Bank Structure and Competition*, Federal Reserve Bank of Chicago, 419–437.

Calomiris, Charles, and Joseph Mason, 1997, Contagion and bank failures during the great depression: The June 1932 Chicago banking panic, *American Economic Review* 87, 863–883.

Calomiris, Charles, and Andrew Powell, 2000, Can emerging market bank regulators establish credible discipline? The case of Argentina, mimeo, Banco Central de la Republica Argentina.

Calomiris, Charles, and Berry Wilson, 1998, Bank capital and portfolio management: The 1930s capital crunch and scramble to shed risk, Working paper no. 6649, NBER.

Cook, Douglas, and Lewis Spellman, 1994, Repudiation risk and restitution costs: Toward understanding premiums on insured deposits, *Journal of Money, Credit, and Banking* 26, 439–459.

D'Amato, Laura, Elena Grubisic, and Andrew Powell, 1997, Contagion, bank fundamentals or macroeconomic shock? An empirical analysis of the Argentine 1995 banking problems, mimeo, Banco Central de la Republica Argentina.

Demirguc-Kunt, Asli, and Harry Huizinga, 2000, Market discipline and financial safety net design, mimeo, The World Bank.

Ellis, David, and Mark Flannery, 1992, Does the debt market assess large banks' risk? Time series evidence from money center CDS, *Journal of Monetary Economics* 30, 481–502.

Flannery, Mark, 1998, Using market information in prudential bank supervision: A review of the U.S. empirical evidence, *Journal of Money, Credit, and Banking* 30, 273–305.

Flannery, Mark, and Sorin Sorescu, 1996, Evidence of bank market discipline in subordinated debenture yields: 1983–1991, *Journal of Finance* 4, 1347–1377.

Goldberg, Lawrence, and Sylvia Hudgins, 1986, Response of uninsured depositors to impeding S&L failures: Evidence of depositor discipline, *Quarterly Review of Economics and Finance* 36, 311–325.

Gorton, Gary, and Anthony Santomero, 1990, Market discipline and bank subordinated debt, *Journal of Money, Credit, and Banking* 22, 119–128.

Hannan, Timothy, and Gerarld Hanweck, 1988, Bank insolvency risk and the market for large certificates of deposit, *Journal of Money, Credit, and Banking* 20, 203–211.

Park, Sangkyun, 1995, Market discipline by depositors evidence from reduced form equations, *Quarterly Review of Economics and Finance* 35, 497–514.

Park, Sangkyun, and Stavros Peristiani, 1998, Market discipline by thrift depositors, *Journal of Money, Credit, and Banking* 30, 347–364.

Schumacher, Liliana, 1996, Bubble or depositor's discipline? A study of the Argentine banking panic (December 1994/May 1995), Ph.D. Dissertation, University of Chicago.

Valdés, Salvador, and Alexandra Lomakin, 1988, Percepción sobre la garantía estatal a los depósitos durante 1987 en Chile, *Cuadernos de Economía* 75, 229–245.

Index

Page numbers in *italics* appear in Volume I; those in **bold** appear in Volume II.

Page numbers in *italics* appear in Volume I; those in **bold** appear in Volume II.

Page numbers in *italics* appear in Volume I; those in **bold** appear in Volume II.

Page numbers in *italics* appear in Volume I; those in **bold** appear in Volume II.

Page numbers in *italics* appear in Volume I; those in **bold** appear in Volume II.

Page numbers in *italics* appear in Volume I; those in **bold** appear in Volume II.